Contemporary
Newsmakers

ISSN 0883-1564

Contemporary Newsmakers

A Biographical Guide to People in the News in
Business, Education, Technology, Social Issues,
Politics, Law, Economics, International Affairs,
Religion, Entertainment, Labor, Sports, Design,
Psychology, Medicine, Astronautics, Ecology,
and Other Fields

Ann Evory and Peter M. Gareffa
Editors

1985
Cumulation

GALE RESEARCH COMPANY • BOOK TOWER • DETROIT, MICHIGAN 48226

STAFF

Ann Evory and Peter M. Gareffa, *Editors*

Michael L. LaBlanc, *Senior Assistant Editor*

Mary Sullivan and Denise Wiloch, *Assistant Editors*

Joseph A. Kuskowski, *Editorial Assistant*

Mary Rose Bonk, Christine Joan May, Mary Alice Rattenbury,
Michael Ruffner, and Shirley Seip, *Research Assistants*

Amy C. Bodwin, Peter M. Gareffa, Gary Hoffman, and Michael L. LaBlanc, *Interviewers*

Anne M.G. Adamus, Stephen Advokat, Amy C. Bodwin, Ingeborg Boyens, Michelle Brown, John Castine,
Victoria France Charabati, Barbara A. Cicchetti, Lori R. Clemens, Candace Cloutier, Dean David Dauphinais,
William C. Drollinger, William C. Drollinger, Jr., Steven C. Drollinger, Diane L. Dupuis, Sandra Giraud,
Marian Walters Gonsior, Gary Graff, John E. Haynes, Gary Hoffman, Tom Hundley, Debra G. Hunter,
Tim Kiska, Mark Kram, Joe LaPointe, Jeanne M. Lesinski, James G. Lesniak, Anita Pyzik Lienert, Paul Lienert,
Glen Macnow, Joan E. Marecki, Greg Mazurkiewicz, Bill McGraw, Bill Mitchell, Patricia Montemurri,
Louise Mooney, Joshua Muravchik, Joanne M. Peters, Nancy E. Rampson, Bryan Ryan, Jon Saari,
Barbara Welch Skaggs, Mary Solomon Smyka, Susan Stefani, Deborah A. Straub, Warren Strugatch,
Susan M. Trosky, Polly A. Vedder, David Versical, and Thomas Wiloch, *Contributing Editors*

Jeanne Gough, *Permissions Supervisor*
Patricia A. Seefelt, *Permissions Coordinator, Illustrations*
Margaret A. Chamberlain, *Senior Permissions Assistant*
Colleen M. Crane, *Permissions Assistant*

Mary Beth Trimper, *Production Supervisor*
Dorothy Kalleberg, *Senior Production Associate*
Arthur Chartow, *Art Director*

Frederick G. Ruffner, *Publisher*
Dedria Bryfonski, *Editorial Director*
Christine Nasso, *Director, Literature Division*

Copyright © 1986 by Gale Research Company

ISBN 0-8103-2201-3
ISSN 0883-1564

Computerized photocomposition by
AMTEC Information Services, Inc.
Lakewood, California

Contents

Preface   xi

Preface

"There is properly no history, only biography."
—Ralph Waldo Emerson, *History*

Since history is written through the actions of men and women, biography is an important tool to help us understand our present and our past. Unfortunately, comprehensive biographical information on people currently in the news is often difficult to find. With the publication of *Contemporary Newsmakers (CN)*, Gale Research Company has taken a step toward remedying that situation.

Since 1962, Gale has published *Contemporary Authors (CA)*, a comprehensive source of information on current writers that is notably easy to use because of its unique format. Librarians have often pointed out to Gale editors the need for a series that covers reference-worthy "nonwriters" in the same depth as *CA* covers major writers. *CN* is designed to do this.

For those people currently in the news, *CN* provides personal and career data in an easy-to-use format that presents facts in captioned paragraphs. Narrative accounts of subjects' views and achievements are presented in informative sidelights written in a clear, readable style, quoting evaluations and comments from the listees' peers, friends, and critics. Most entries contain portraits of the newsmakers, and some include additional photographs specially selected to complement sidelights material. Finally, for some subjects an exclusive interview is provided.

From students writing papers on topical issues to general readers interested in current events and the people behind them, *CN* is designed to assist a variety of users. Teachers preparing assignments, researchers seeking facts, and librarians fielding questions can all turn to *CN* for detailed entries on the people making today's news. Just as *CA* meets the need for information on writers, *CN* serves an equally broad range of users who need information on nonwriters. Normally, no overlap between *CA* and *CN* will occur.

Scope and Frequency

CN is a comprehensive biographical guide to people in the news in such fields as business, education, technology, social issues, politics, law, economics, international affairs, religion, entertainment, labor, sports, design, psychology, medicine, astronautics, and ecology. *CN* provides biographical material on newsmakers in two broad categories—individuals who are quite well known and about whom information is widely available in newspapers and magazines but not in reference books, and people who are less well known but who, because of the importance or interesting nature of their activities, are currently in the news and are deserving of wider coverage.

The emphasis of *CN* is on those people involved in topical issues; for example, included in this cumulation are entries on Lebanese Shiite Muslim leader Nabih Berri, National Abortion Rights Action League director Nanette Falkenberg, Band Aid and Live Aid organizer Bob Geldof, artificial heart inventor Robert K. Jarvik, Northern Irish politician Martin McGuinness, and Palestinian U.N. observer Zehdi Labib Terzi.

CN entries are first published in paperbound quarterly issues identified by a year and issue number. Each issue is about 125 pages in length and covers approximately 50 newsmakers. All of the entries in each year's quarterly issues are then interalphabetized and published in an annual clothbound cumulation. If significant new information becomes available on the newsmakers following the publication of their entries in the quarterly issues, their listings are updated prior to inclusion in the annual cumulation. Over 14 percent of the nearly 200 entries in the 1985 Cumulation contain such updated information.

CN Differs from Existing Biographical Sources

The editors believe *CN* satisfies a need unmet by existing reference tools. Although *Current Biography* does an admirable job of providing biographical information on some important people of the day, there are far more newsworthy individuals than can be covered by a single source. *CN* profiles approximately 200 newsmakers per year. It is the intention of the editors not to include in *CN* full sketches on those people who have up-to-date entries in *Current Biography*.

Other biographical sources, such as Newsbank's *Names in the News,* cover an impressive number of people but contain only reprinted material that does not necessarily highlight or include important career and personal data. Indexes such as *Biography Index* and Gale's own *Biography Almanac* are valuable reference tools but serve a different function than a biographical source such as *CN.* The *Who's Who* publications provide important information, but it is not in their scope to supply the kind of sidelights that many students and researchers need. In addition to presenting rich sidelights material, *CN* differs from the *Who's Who* publications in its greater frequency and in its scope, which concentrates on the innovators who help shape our culture and society—such as Nautilus exercise equipment inventor Arthur A. Jones, pop singers Cyndi Lauper and Madonna, and Federal Express Corporation founder Frederick W. Smith—rather than established or establishment figures. In short, *CN* fills a gap on reference shelves.

Compilation Methods

As is the case with *CA,* the information contained within *CN* is secured directly from the subjects whenever possible. Through questionnaires, personal correspondence, and telephone calls, the editors make every effort to contact the biographees slated for an upcoming issue. For example, contributing editor Joshua Muravchik, whose work has also appeared in *Commentary, New Republic,* and the *New York Times,* was able to speak with Nicaraguan politician Arturo Cruz in between Cruz's many trips to and from the United States. During their conversation, Cruz provided some of the information that appears in his *CN* sketch and verified the accuracy of the entry.

If persons of special interest to *CN* users fail to reply to requests for information, the editors gather data from other reliable sources, including published interviews, feature stories, news articles, etc., and verify this information later with the subjects if possible.

The editors recognize that entries on particularly active newsmakers may eventually become outdated. To insure *CN's* timeliness, future issues will provide revisions of selected sketches when they require significant change.

Format

The format of *CN* is similar to that of *CA,* with one important addition—*CN* includes portraits of the subjects, when available. In selected entries, additional illustrations of people and events important to the listees' careers also enliven the text.

So that a reader needing specific information can quickly focus on the pertinent portion of an entry, typical *CN* sketches are clearly divided into the following sections:

> **Entry heading**—Cites the form of the name by which the listee is best known, followed by the birth date, when available.

> **Personal**—Provides the newsmaker's full name if different from the entry heading, date and place of birth, family data, and information about the subject's education, politics, and religion.

> **Addresses**—Notes home and office addresses, when available.

> **Occupation**—Identifies the listee's primary fields of activity.

> **Career**—Indicates past and present career positions, with inclusive dates, as well as civic activities and military service.

Member—Highlights memberships in various professional and civic associations and official posts held.

Awards, honors—Lists awards and honors received.

Sidelights—Provides a personal dimension to the entry and fills in the details that make for interesting biography. Subjects are encouraged to supply comments on their work and interests. Whether these remarks are long or short, serious or humorous, they are incorporated into sidelights with minimal editing, in the belief that they make possible a better understanding of the biographee. For example *CN* contributing editor Joe LaPointe learned from sportscaster Brent Musburger that Musburger had been unable to get either cable television or a satellite dish antenna installed at his Connecticut home. Having been assigned to cover the 1985 NCAA basketball tournament, he was forced "to go to a saloon [equipped for cable reception] to do my homework."

In addition to the subjects' own comments, sidelights explain why these people are in the news and detail their rise to prominence. For instance, in this cumulation, contributing editor Diane L. Dupuis traces Bobby Ray Inman's career from his commission as an ensign in the U.S. Navy, through his work with Naval Intelligence, the National Security Agency, and the Central Intelligence Agency, to his present position as head of Microelectronics and Computer Technologies Corporation, a Texas-based computer research and development firm.

Sources—Lists magazine and newspaper articles and books containing additional information on the biographees.

When applicable, *CN* sketches include "Discography" sections that provide information on songs or albums recorded by the biographees. To provide a complete record of newsmakers' accomplishments, a few *CN* sketches necessarily contain "Writings" sections that list books and articles, often of a specialized nature, written by the listees. Potential *CN* subjects known primarily as writers, however, fall outside the scope of *CN;* their entries would appear instead in *CA.*

Exclusive Interviews

In addition to the information noted above, selected *CN* sketches also include exclusive interviews with the newsmakers. Prepared specifically for *CN,* the never-before-published conversations presented in the section of the entry headed *"CN* Interview" give readers an opportunity to learn the subjects' thoughts, in depth, about their careers and interests. This cumulation features interviews with feminist attorney Gloria Allred, priest and civil rights activist George Clements, Parents' Music Resource Center co-founder Tipper Gore, veterinarian Patrick Redig, and anti-nuclear power activist Mary Sinclair.

Brief Entries and Obituary Notices Make *CN* Timely and Comprehensive

The editors feel that having some information, however brief, on individuals very recently in the news is preferable to waiting until full-length sketches can be prepared. Some abbreviated listings for such persons are included in *CN.* These short profiles, identified by the heading "Brief Entry," highlight the subjects' careers, provide sources where additional information can be found, and include portraits, when available.

Brief entries are not intended to replace sketches. Instead, brief entries maintain *CN*'s currency and comprehensiveness by covering people just coming into the news—as exemplified by the brief entry in this cumulation on Trevor Ferrell, the young Philadelphia man who initiated a campaign to aid street people—and providing basic data about newsworthy individuals on whom little information is currently available—such as actor Jim Varney who portrays the popular Ernest P. Worrell character in numerous television commercials.

CN also publishes obituary notices on deceased newsmakers within the scope of the series. These notices provide dates and places of birth and death, highlight the subjects' careers, and list other sources where information can be found. Photographs are also included, when available. The heading "Obituary Notice" distinguishes obituaries from full-length sketches.

Obituary coverage is not limited to people with previous *CN* entries but includes a wide variety of recently deceased newsmakers. As a result of our efforts to provide obituary information on key figures in the news, *CN* may occasionally duplicate obituaries in other biographical sources.

Indexes

To best serve the needs of a wide variety of users by providing access to entries in a number of ways, *CN* contains cumulative nationality, occupation, and subject indexes. Each of these indexes will be cumulated in future quarterly issues and the annual hardcover cumulations.

> **Cumulative Nationality Index**—Listee names are arranged alphabetically under their respective nationalities and are followed by the *CN* year and issue number in which their entries were originally included. The Cumulative Nationality Index reflects the diversity of newsmakers covered in *CN;* this cumulation, for example, contains listings on Argentine, British, Canadian, Irish, Israeli, Lebanese, Nicaraguan, Palestinian, South African, and Soviet figures, among others, who have recently been in the news.

> **Cumulative Occupation Index**—All newsmakers' names, with references to the *CN* year and issue number originally containing their entries, are listed alphabetically under broad occupational categories or fields of primary activity. Readers interested in surveying recent developments in business, for example, will find entries on People Express Airlines founder Donald Calvin Burr, E.F. Hutton president Robert M. Fomon, Playboy Enterprises president Christie Hefner, Inacomp Computer Centers founder Rick Inatome, Ford Motor Company president Donald Eugene Petersen, Cincinnati Reds owner Marge Schott, and Toyota Motor Corporation chairman Eiji Toyoda, among others, in this cumulation.

> **Cumulative Subject Index**—This index includes citations to key subjects, topical issues, company names, products, organizations, awards, etc., that are discussed in *CN*. Under each subject citation are listed newsmakers associated with that topic and the year and issue number in which their entries first appeared.

The Cumulative Subject Index is designed to allow access to the facts in *CN*, even when readers are unfamiliar with the names of individuals associated with a particular topic. A student interested in writing a paper on the broadcast industry, for example, will be directed to information on this topic through the citation for "Broadcasting" in the Cumulative Subject Index, which will refer the student to the entries on sportscaster Brent Musburger, ABC Television executive Frederick S. Pierce, and NBC Entertainment president Brandon Tartikoff.

Including citations ranging from "Atari" to "Women's rights," the Cumulative Subject Index not only leads to answers to specific questions but also invites browsing, allowing *CN* users to discover topics they may wish to explore further.

A cumulative index to listees appears in all *CN* quarterly issues and will be included in future annual cumulations.

Suggestions Are Welcome

The editors welcome comments and suggestions from users to enhance the usefulness of this series. If readers would like to suggest newsmakers to be covered in the future, they are encouraged to send these names to the editors.

Contemporary
Newsmakers

Gloria Allred

1941-

PERSONAL: Full name, Gloria Rachel Allred; born July 3, 1941, in Philadelphia, Pa.; daughter of Morris Bloom (in sales) and Stella Davidson; married, 1960 (divorced); married Raymond Allred (an aircraft parts dealer), 1968; children: Lisa (first marriage). *Education*: University of Pennsylvania, B.A. (with honors in English), 1963; New York University, M.A., 1966; Loyola University, J.D. (with honors), 1974.

ADDRESSES: Office—6380 Wilshire Blvd., Suite 1404, Los Angeles, Calif. 90048.

OCCUPATION: Attorney.

CAREER: High-school English teacher in Philadelphia, Pa., for two years, and Los Angeles, Calif., for four years; labor organizer for Los Angeles Teachers' Association for one year; Allred, Maroko, Goldberg & Ribakoff (law firm), Los Angeles, founder and partner, 1975—. Lecturer, University of Southern California, 1976—. Advance person for Brown for Governor Campaign, 1974; bureau coordinator for Carter Campaign, 1976.

MEMBER: National Organization for Women (coordinator, Los Angeles chapter, 1977—), Save Equal Rights Amendment (chairperson), Delta Theta Phi.

AWARDS, HONORS: Outstanding Citizen Award, Southgate Business and Professional Women's Club, 1976; certificate of appreciation, American Women in Radio and Television.

WRITINGS: Contributor of articles to periodicals.

SIDELIGHTS: To her opponents, Gloria Allred is a feisty, feminist lawyer, more interested in furthering pet causes than in practicing law. To her admirers, she is a rebel in the tradition of the civil rights activists of the 1960s or the muckrakers of the Teddy Roosevelt era. Her controversial cases have made her a force to be reckoned with in California politics, and her influence has spread across the United States. She has represented a homosexual seeking the right to adopt a child, has sought child custody rights for the father of an illegitimate child, and has made headlines by prompting groundbreaking family-rights legislation.

CN INTERVIEW

CN interviewed Gloria Allred by telephone at her office in Los Angeles, Calif., in June, 1985.

CN: What category fits you best? Is feminist a fair description?

ALLRED: Sure, I'm a feminist. I'm a feminist attorney. How's that?

AP/Wide World Photos

CN: How does this square with your representing LeVar Burton in his lawsuit to gain joint custody of his illegitimate child?

ALLRED: How about, "consistently"? Absolutely consistently.

CN: How's that?

ALLRED: Well, he was a father who wished to play a major role in his son's life even though he had not been married to the mother of the child and wasn't going to be married to the mother of the child. He still felt that he would like to have joint legal custody of the child and take an active role in his life. And I think it's important that he and other single fathers play that role, because children need the love and support of both parents. So I was very happy to support him in that, and I am always encouraging fathers to take an active role. But it turns out that a lot of fathers who've never been married to the mothers decide not to take any part in the child's life.

CN: And so you were removing a potential legal obstacle to his having a normal relationship with his child?

1

ALLRED: Well, I succeeded in supporting his wishes that he be able to take an active role in the child's life. And he did get joint custody of the child and the visitation rights that he wanted. He was a role model for other fathers, to encourage them to become active in their children's lives.

CN: How do you describe the cases that you and your firm specialize in?

ALLRED: Well, we're a civil litigation firm, we have thirteen attorneys, and we do all kinds of civil litigation. I suppose we're best known for family law cases and for civil rights cases.

CN: But you don't do that exclusively?

ALLRED: No, we also do business litigation and personal injuries, as well as family law and civil rights.

CN: So, your practice is probably far more general than has often been described?

ALLRED: Absolutely. In fact, we're the cover story on the *American Bar Association Journal* this month. It looks at the practice and how we handle different cases. Most people don't know that we are very diversified as civil litigators.

CN: Is the activist role, in both your personal ideology and your law practice, filling a void among law firms? Are you filling a need that isn't satisfied elsewhere?

ALLRED: In terms of what?

CN: Would you expect that the representation, say, of a woman raped in a shopping mall is better handled by a firm like yours than the typical firm? Or one where the majority of people are male?

ALLRED: Well, I feel that men are not the enemy, and women are not the enemy, ignorance is the enemy. And I always think it's better for anyone to be represented by a feminist than to be represented by a non-feminist.

CN: On any sort of case?

ALLRED: Whether it's a feminist male or a feminist female. I consider the difference to be between feminist and non-feminist, rather than male and female, because men can be feminists. In fact, a requirement of working in this firm is that any attorney here must be a feminist.

CN: Now how do you. . . ?

ALLRED: I ask them.

CN: You ask them?

ALLRED: We discuss it. Yeah.

CN: What if you meet someone who doesn't describe himself as a feminist but is an altogether honorable and fair person? What if he just doesn't happen to use that term to describe himself?

ALLRED: Well, we discuss what the term means. The dictionary defines it as a person who believes in legal, social, political, and economic equality for women with men. So I think it is very important for me to have people who believe in legal, political, social, and economic equality for women with men working here in the law firm. And anyone who doesn't believe in that kind of equality is either a male chauvinist or a racist, or both. That type of person, will need to look for work elsewhere, because they're not going to be here.

CN: What percent of your cases are civil rights cases?

ALLRED: Well, those, I guess, are the ones we're the most visible on, but actually they are a small percent of the actual law practice. We do a lot of day-to-day divorce cases. They are not issues of public interest or importance to other people and so, therefore, are not on the news. In fact, they are confidential, and should be confidential between the parties. But these cases that we do that are civil rights court cases *are* of public interest and importance and do have an impact on many people. And they are the ones most in the news, even though they are a smaller percent of our cases, in fact, than family law cases, for example.

CN: Was the LeVar Burton representation atypical? Do you represent a lot of celebrities?

ALLRED: I wouldn't say a lot of celebrities. We've represented some celebrities. We've represented, for example, Lynn Redgrave, the actress, in her case against Universal. We were suing them because we alleged that she was terminated from the hit series "House Calls" because she wanted to breast-feed her baby during a break in the filming. So that's a sex-discrimination civil-rights type of case. I've represented McKenzie Phillips, another actress ("One Day at a Time"), on a spousal support issue she had with her ex-husband. He was seeking alimony from her. So we have represented some celebrities and still do, but I would say that a large part of our practice is the typical person who has been wronged or is in need of protection and representation. Vigorous representation. Assertive representation. We handle a lot of those cases, and we do also have a lot of precedent-setting cases and cases that will be called "cases of first impression," unusual cases making new law. Probably much more of those cases than most law firms ever have.

CN: And that's because you're on the cutting edge of some social issues?

ALLRED: I guess. Well, a lot of people, when they have unusual issues, interesting issues, important issues, they come to us. A lot of times they have gone to other attorneys, and the other attorneys don't even *see* the issue. Or they see it, and they don't want to get involved with it. Then we listen to it, and if we think it's important—and if we have the resources at that time, if we can make the time commitment and so forth—we tend to assist these.

CN: Has the much publicized increasing conservative inclination of the country had an effect on doing battle on legal grounds? Has it made it more important for people to have access to the courts?

ALLRED: I think it's always important for people to have access to the courts. Particularly women, and minorities, too, in the past have not had access. Now we have, in the last twenty years begun to have new rights, and we need to educate people about those rights and help them to vindicate those rights by providing access to the courts. Otherwise it is meaningless to have rights.

CN: *Would the actual seeking the exercising of these rights in court be more important as society becomes, perhaps, more conservative?*

ALLRED: I think it is always important. But yes, I do think so. I do think that change is accomplished when those who would prevent the change know that we are serious about having our rights. One of the ways they know we're serious about it is when we go to court to protect ourselves. And that's what we do when the matter cannot be resolved in an alternative way.

CN: *You had a much publicized—I guess a feud might be the way to characterize it—with John Schmitz, a California state senator.*

ALLRED: Yeah. It's still in litigation. We're waiting for a trial date. It's what you call "at issue."

CN: *At one point you presented him with a chastity belt?*

ALLRED: I presented it to him. It was at a hearing he was holding in Los Angeles when he was a state senator. He was proposing an amendment to our state constitution which would have eliminated the right to choose abortion and which would have eliminated many modern forms of birth control. And I presented the chastity belt to him after I testified.

CN: *Did you get any criticisms from the legal community for this action?*

ALLRED: Well, not particularily.

CN: *It seems a bit flamboyant.*

ALLRED: Yes. Well, you know I'm an activist.

CN: *Are you an activist more than a lawyer?*

ALLRED: No. I'm an activist lawyer. I believe in seeking change and winning rights through the legal process and also through the political process. And both of those go hand in hand. Sometimes the legal remedies are inadequate, and, therefore, we must utilize the political process by influencing public opinion, working to support new laws, and helping to educate our legislators about what we want to protect our rights. All of those things were involved in my presentation of the chastity belt. I wanted to draw the attention of the public to the fact that he was trying to eliminate the right to choose abortion and modern forms of birth control. And we didn't want him to go through all this without the public even knowing what was happening. A lot of times these hearings don't get covered, don't get noticed, and people lose their rights before they even know what happened to them.

CN: *To what do you attribute the development of your particular brand of activism?*

ALLRED: I would say I attribute it to life experience as a woman growing up in the United States of America. To give you more specifics, for example: being married as a teenager, giving birth to a child, getting divorced, not receiving child

support, basically having to raise a child by myself, getting paid less than a man in my first job for what I consider to be equal work and equal experience, having been raped, having to have an abortion when abortion was illegal and unsafe, almost dying from it. These are just a few of the things.

CN: *Were you in favor of the availability of abortion even before your rape?*

ALLRED: I have always been pro-choice.

CN: *Even back when it was illegal?*

ALLRED: Well, it wasn't illegal to *have* an abortion, it was illegal for a doctor to give it, which is an important distinction. I wasn't breaking any law. The law said that doctors couldn't perform abortions, and, therefore, young women like myself had to resort to being into the hands of butchers and quacks and almost dying; and some did, in fact, die. So, I have always been in favor of safe and legal abortions and the right to choose that, in support of women's rights. And certainly almost dying from an unsafe one, an illegal one, awoke me to the need to have safe and legal abortions and caused me to commit myself to forever fight for the right to have safe and legal abortions. I certainly would never want my daughter to be in the position that I was in and be in danger of dying from an illegal and unsafe abortion if it were necessary for her to have one.

CN: *Do you get hate mail for your stands?*

ALLRED: I get lots of thanks, and appreciation, and praise; and I also get some hate mail; I get some threats. I'm a lightning rod for change. A lot of people love me. Some people hate me. Generally, there's not too much in the way of middle ground. People come up to me in elevators, and parking lots, and street corners, and in court houses, in department stores, in restaurants and ask me for legal advice and help in solving their problems. And I am very happy that people feel that they have access to me and would like to have advice as to how to protect themselves. I would say, generally, most of it is positive because I am involved in very current issues, and by the definition of what I do, seeking rights for women is controversial, and, of course, there are going to be a lot of people who disagree with me—bigots—and those people will certainly express themselves most vociferously, as they always do.

CN: *A caption in a* Time *magazine article about you said, "Her tactics include turkeys, frogs, and chastity belts." How representative are those tactics of your work?*

ALLRED: Well, I'd say most of my battles are won in court. But sometimes a battle has to be waged in a different way. And so I do whatever I need to do in order to win the battle, as long as it's legal, and peaceful, and helps to win change. Sometimes that will include giving a chastity belt to a congressperson, or—one time—hanging diapers in the governor's office.

CN: *You did that?*

ALLRED: Yes. It was Jerry Brown, Jr., because he was set to veto a child-support bill that we had worked very hard to win; it was for a payroll deduction for child support to be taken out of the father's wages if he didn't pay. And his staff had written a letter saying that Brown was going to veto it.

So we ran down with mothers and children, and we hung diapers in there and held a press conference. And he tore up his veto message and signed the bill. So I'm saying, if it helps, I will do it. And in some cases it has helped, but I would say that ordinarily, ninety-nine percent of what I do, I do in a very traditional, conventional, yet assertive way. But sometimes it is necessary to be dramatic to make a point. We live in a media age and sometimes it is necessary to do that and I will continue to do that where it is helpful.

SOURCES:

PERIODICALS

Los Angeles, August, 1982.
Los Angeles Times, December 29, 1983, July 9, 1984, July 22, 1984, August 31, 1984.
Money, March, 1981.
Ms., November, 1985.
New York Times, October 1, 1981, January 10, 1983.
Time, December 3, 1984.

—Interview by Gary Hoffman

Hobie Alter
1934-

BRIEF ENTRY: Born 1934, in California. American sailboat designer; inventor. Best known as the designer of the popular Hobie Cat sailing catamaran, Hobie Alter has established a reputation as a creative thinker whose strength lies in looking at existing designs and finding ways to improve them.

In the 1950s, when surfers were using traditional—but heavy and unwieldy—redwood surfboards, Alter pioneered the light, easy-to-handle, balsa-wood board. He sold the first one he made and went on to improve the design further by experimenting with revolutionary plastics and fiberglass. Alter soon became the first manufacturer of mass-produced urethane-foam surfboards.

Alter used the same kind of logic in designing his Hobie Cat that he had applied to surfboards: make it lighter, stronger, faster, and as maintenance-free as possible. A sixteen-foot Hobie Cat—the most popular model—consists of twin fiberglass pontoons joined by an aluminum frame, covered with a canvas "trampoline" on which the boat's occupants sit; an aluminum mast sprouts from the frame and attached to this are the brightly-colored sails that have become a Hobie trademark. The entire package weighs approximately two hundred pounds, easily towed behind even the smallest compact car. Wrote Geoffrey Norman in *Esquire,* "The essential and enduring nature of Hobie Alter's contribution to sailing [is that] he made the sport accessible." Concludes Norman, "It is no exaggeration to say that the Hobie Cat has worked a small but important revolution in American sport."

AP/Wide World Photos

SOURCES:

PERIODICALS

California Magazine, December, 1983.
Esquire, July, 1981.
Motor Boating & Sailing, November, 1982.
Sail, January, 1980.
Time, August 3, 1981.
Town and Country, July, 1983.

Robert Anastas

BRIEF ENTRY: American teacher, counselor, social activist. Robert Anastas is the founder of Students Against Drunken Driving (SADD), a nationwide organization dedicated to informing teenagers of the dangers of drinking and driving. SADD employs a number of methods to get across its message, but the heart of the group's strategy is its "Drinking-Driver Contract." In this agreement, signed by both parents and teenagers, students promise to call their parents "for advice or transportation" in the event that "I have been drinking or a friend or date who is driving me has been drinking." In return, parents pledge to provide transportation "with no questions asked and no argument at that time." Parents also agree to "seek safe, sober transportation home" if they or whomever is driving "has had too much to drink."

Anastas, a high school teacher and substance abuse counselor, founded SADD in 1981 at Massachusetts's Wayland High School after two of his students died in alcohol-related accidents. Currently, there are SADD chapters in over 7,000 high schools throughout the country. The group has also launched programs aimed at college and elementary-school students. At all levels, SADD holds seminars and presents lectures and films that warn of the risks of driving while intoxicated. These measures notwithstanding, Anastas stresses the importance of the lifetime contract between parent and child. "All parents ought to sign the agreement—because they can't lecture their kids about booze or drugs after a fatal crash," he told Michael J. Weiss of the *Ladies Home Journal.* "Either pick them up now or get the hearse later." Address: SADD, Box 800, Marlboro, Mass. 01752.

SOURCES:

PERIODICALS

Glamour, February, 1985.
Ladies Home Journal, February, 1985.

Moshe Arens

1925-

PERSONAL: Born December 7, 1925, in Kaunas, Lithuania (now U.S.S.R.); came to United States in 1939; immigrated to Palestine (now Israel) in 1947; married Murial Eisenberg. *Education*: Massachusetts Institute of Technology, degree in mechanical engineering, 1947; California Institute of Technology, degree in aeronautical engineering.

ADDRESSES: Home—49 Hagderat, Savyon, Israel.

OCCUPATION: Israeli politician.

CAREER: Worked on a *kibbutz* (communal farm) in Israel, 1948-51; worked as an engineer in the U.S. aircraft industry, until 1957; associate professor at Technicon (Israel Institute of Technology), Haifa; vice-president of engineering and deputy director, Israel Aircraft Industries (A.I.A.; state-operated engineering and manufacturing firm), Lod; government of Israel, member of Knesset (parliament), beginning 1973, member of Finance Committee, 1973, chairman of Defense and Foreign Relations Committee, beginning 1977, ambassador to the United States, 1982-83, minister of defense, 1983-84, minister without portfolio, 1984—. *Military service*: Served in U.S. Army.

MEMBER: Aerospace Industries Association of America (associate fellow).

AWARDS, HONORS: Israel Defense Prize, 1971.

WRITINGS: Author of several technical publications on propulsion and flight mechanics.

SIDELIGHTS: As Israel's ambassador to the United States from 1982 to 1983, Moshe Arens was frequently described in Washington diplomatic circles as a square peg in a round hole. Trained not as a diplomat, but as an aeronautical engineer, Arens comes across as low key, organized, analytical and articulate. He shares the hardline views of his political mentor, Menachem Begin, but eschews the rhetorical fireworks of the former prime minister. Describing himself as a "dilettante talking about a profession he's brand new at," Arens once told the *Washington Post*, "I never expected to be a diplomat. This was thrust upon me. I've been an engineer all my life."

Arens became familiar to a wide American audience during the Israeli invasion of Lebanon when he was a frequent guest on ABC's "Nightline" and other news programs. Throughout the controversy surrounding the invasion, Arens was always blunt and cool in his defense of Israel's policies. Said "Nightline" moderator Ted Koppel, "He is very straightforward, very tough and never beats around the bush."

Arens's effective performance in Washington helped boost his political stock back in Israel. In 1983, he was recalled to

Jerusalem to succeed Ariel Sharon as defense minister and was subsequently appointed minister without portfolio in the National Unity government formed after the deadlock 1984 elections. Though he is given no more than an outside chance of rising to the top leadership position in the Likud party, most observers expect that he will remain a strong candidate for key cabinet posts if his party can regain the upper hand in the next government.

The second of three children (he has a younger sister who lives in the United States; his older brother died in 1984) Moshe Arens was born in Kaunas, Lithuania, in 1925. His early childhood was spent in the Latvian city of Riga until 1939 when his family fled to New York to escape Nazi onslaught. "Riga probably had the highest percentage of Jews exterminated of any community in Europe, more than 95 percent. So you can imagine that that made some impression on me," Arens once said in an interview.

Although he describes his family as "not particularly" Zionist, Arens said he made up his mind as a child that he would someday go to Palestine. As a teenager in New York, he joined the local chapter of Betar, the youth movement of

Vladimir Jabotinsky's militant Zionist Revisionist Party, which in 1948 evolved into Begin's Herut Party. His late brother, Richard Arens, once said that Moshe never viewed the United States as anything more than a "way station" on the road to Palestine.

In 1943, Arens enrolled in the engineering program at the Massachusetts Institute of Technology, but withdrew a year later to serve in the U.S. Army. The war ended before Arens ever saw combat, and he returned to M.I.T. and graduated in 1947 with a degree in mechanical engineering.

At this time, the Zionist struggle for statehood in Palestine was approaching its climax. Although his family protested, Arens left the United States to join the struggle. He enlisted in the Irgun, the Revisionist Party's underground terrorist organization. The leader of the Irgun was Menachem Begin, and Arens today admits to being "in some awe" of the firebrand leader.

After Israel achieved statehood in 1948, Arens settled on a kibbutz; but in 1951, he and his wife, the former Murial Eisenberg, returned to the United States so that Arens could continue his engineering studies at the California Institute of Technology. He obtained a degree in aeronautical engineering and worked in the U.S. aviation industry for a few years before going back to Israel in 1957.

For a time, Arens taught at the Technicon in Haifa, but he soon moved to a position with Israel Aircraft Industry, one of Israel's largest and most successful state-owned enterprises. A.I.A. was first established to service the military aircraft that Israel had purchased from foreign manufacturers, but it gradually expanded into the manufacture of jet fighters, small cargo and passenger aircraft, missiles, radar, light ships and other weapon systems—all of which helped reduce Israel's dependence on foreign military suppliers. Arens, as vice-president in charge of engineering, played a key role in the development of the Lavie and Kfir jet fighter systems, two of A.I.A.'s most successful projects.

All the while, Arens maintained his interest in politics. In 1973, he won a seat in the Knesset, Israel's parliament, running as a candidate on the Likud list. At the time, it appeared that the Likud bloc—the right-wing electoral merger of Begin's Herut, the liberal party and two other smaller parties—was destined to remain a perennial opposition party. However, the Labor Party's domination of Israeli politics, which predated statehood, began to slip after the 1973 Middle East War. Lingering doubts about the Labor government's preparedness for the war created a favorable climate for Begin's hard-line approach. Begin also capitalized on the mounting discontent of Israel's large, economically depressed population of Sephardic or Oriental Jews, which had largely been ignored by the Labor Party.

Moshe Arens (in sweater) tours the harbor of Sidon, Lebanon, with Israeli Army officers in June 1984. AP/Wide World Photos.

In the 1977 elections, Begin scored a stunning upset, becoming Israel's first prime minister from a party other than Labor. Arens, riding the coattails of his party's victory, became chairman of the Knesset's Defense and Foreign Relations Committee.

Although Begin had been Arens's political mentor for nearly two decades, the two did not always see eye-to-eye. Often, it was Arens who appeared the more hawkish. For instance, he voted against the historic Camp David accords that brought peace between Israel and Egypt in 1978. Arens felt that Begin had been too compromising in his negotiations with the Egyptians. Despite the differences, though, Begin and Arens are said to share a close relationship. "It's easier for him to communicate with me because we know each other very well," Arens told the *Washington Post* in 1982 shortly after he was confirmed as U.S. ambassador. "That's one of my advantages, and it stems from the fact that I am not a professional diplomat. I come out of the body politic in Israel, out of Begin's party. I guess he feels communication with me is easy because he understands what I have to say, and he can trust me with what he has to say."

When it became known in Washington that Arens would be the next ambassador, it was taken as a signal that the Begin Administration intended to make a more aggressive case for its interests and resist U.S. pressures for a more flexible posture on Arab-Israeli issues. While Arens repeatedly emphasized that Israeli and U.S. interests were parallel and sought to improve communications between Washington and Jerusalem, the *Washington Post* reported in 1982 that "most observers feel that he usually had the opposite effect." According to the *Post*'s John Goshko, "He is regarded to have put a belligerent, highly politicized stamp on the embassy to the point where it currently is not regarded as a major channel in the dialogue between the two governments, or an especially reliable interpreter of American attitudes to Jerusalem."

Early on in his tenure, Arens warned that the Israeli invasion of Lebanon was imminent. "I would almost say it's a matter of time," he told reporters. Post-mortem analyses of the 1982 invasion, in which Israel tried to destroy the Palestine Liberation Organization (P.L.O.) and install a friendly government in Lebanon, suggest that Arens was instrumental in conveying to Jerusalem the impression that, as far as the United States was concerned, Israel had the "green light" to proceed with it plans. The Reagan administration denies that a green light was ever given.

The invasion was a military triumph, but a political disaster. As casualties mounted, public opinion in Israel soured. Ironically, when Defense Minister Ariel Sharon, the architect of the invasion, was forced to resign following a determination that he was indirectly responsible for the massacre of hundreds of Palestinians in the Sabra and Shatila refugee camps of Beirut, U.S. officials were pleased that Arens was chosen as his successor, Arens being viewed as more moderate that Sharon.

As defense minister, Arens tried to cut Israel's losses and salvage the modest goal of the original invasion plan: a secure northern border. He also endured the criticism of the man he replaced. Sharon, who had managed to retain his cabinet rank despite his forced resignation as minister of defense, blamed Arens for failing to cash in on Israel's military success.

After the 1984 election, the Likud bloc had to yield the defense ministry to Labor. Arens, however, retained a key spot in the cabinet as minister without portfolio. As such he seems virtually assured of a continuing role as a prominent figure in the Likud party and on the Israeli political scene.

SOURCES:

BOOKS

Frankel, William, *Israel Observed: Anatomy of a State*, Thames & Hudson, 1980.

Meyer, Lawrence, *Israel Now: Portrait of a Troubled Land*, Delacorte, 1982.

Schiff, Ze'ev, and Ehud Ya'ari, *Israel's Lebanon War*, Simon & Schuster, 1984.

Silver, Eric, *Begin: The Haunted Prophet*, Random House, 1984.

PERIODICALS

New York Times, February 24, 1983, February 28, 1984, May 31, 1984.

Washington Post, September 27, 1982, February 12, 1983, June 9, 1983, September 13, 1983, November 21, 1983, March 22, 1984.

—Sidelights by Tom Hundley

Rosanna Arquette

1959-

PERSONAL: Born 1959, in New York; daughter of Lewis (a writer and director) and Mardi (a poet and playwright) Arquette.

ADDRESSES: Office—c/o Orion Pictures Co., 4000 Warner Blvd., Burbank, Calif. 91505.

OCCUPATION: Actress.

CAREER: Actress in television films, beginning 1978, including "Having Babies II," "Dark Secret of Harvest Home," "Zuma Beach," and "The Executioner's Song," and in motion pictures, beginning 1981, including "S.O.B.," "Baby It's You," "Desperately Seeking Susan," "After Hours," "Silverado," and "The Aviator."

SIDELIGHTS: In less than a decade Rosanna Arquette has gone from playing bit parts in forgettable made-for-television movies to star in such critically acclaimed feature films as *Desperately Seeking Susan.* Hailed as one of the freshest new faces in Hollywood, Arquette's stardom is unusual because her exposure as an actress has not been in commercial blockbusters but in low-budget art films. Arquette explained to *Moviegoer* interviewer Dale Pollock that she avoids doing roles simply for the sake of her career. Rather, she told him, "I do a movie for the character—what I'm going to put into the character or what I'm going to get out of the character. *That's* why I do a film."

Arquette was born into a theatrical family in New York in 1959. Her grandfather was Cliff Arquette who played Charley Weaver on *The Jack Parr Show* and *Hollywood Squares.* Arquette's father, Lewis, a writer and director, was formerly head of Chicago's improvisational comedy troupe, The Committee. In fact, Arquette made her acting debut at the age of eight in a production directed by her father. Her mother, Mardi, is a writer and activist in the peace movement. Arquette was raised in the heady atmosphere of 1960s-style political activism. She recalled her childhood experiences for *Rolling Stone*: "I was raised at love-ins, my mother painting STOP THE WAR on my body and us marching with Martin Luther King. Waking up in Woodstock and dancing naked." Arquette's upbringing is reflected today in her agreement with the anti-nuclear movement and her admiration for performer/activists Jane Fonda and Paul Newman.

In her early teens, Arquette lived with her parents and four younger siblings in an actors' and musicians' commune in Virginia guided by an Eastern spiritual philosophy. She left the commune at the age of thirteen when she could no longer abide the racist attitudes of her small-town high school classmates and moved by herself to New Jersey where she lived with family friends. From there, Arquette took off hitchhiking across the country. She arrived in Los Angeles

at the age of seventeen and began landing parts in such television movies as "Having Babies II," "Dark Secret of Harvest Home," and "Zuma Beach." Of her early experiences in television, Arquette told *Moviegoer*, that she played "every pregnant teenage runaway hooker drug addict that was ever on the planet."

Ironically, in 1982, television also provided Arquette with the role that first brought her to the attention of critics and a larger audience. She beat out well-known actresses Mariel Hemingway, Tatum O'Neal and Diane Lane for the role of Nicole Baker in the television film "The Executioner's Song." The four-hour dramatization of the life and death of convicted murderer Gary Gilmore was adapted by Norman Mailer from his Pulitzer Prize-winning book of the same title. Actor Tommy Lee Jones starred opposite Arquette as Gilmore.

The relationship between Gilmore and Baker was the focus of the story. Described by the *New York Times* as "a spacey 20-year-old with two little children, a gallery of past husbands and boyfriends and no firm grip on anything but the pills she pops," the real life Baker met with Arquette during the filming. Arquette found it easy to identify with Baker. "When I did Nicole," Arquette told *Rolling Stone*, "I don't know how to explain it—that was the closest I ever got, I think, to actually losing it. It was so heavy being there. I love her." *People* called Arquette "stunningly right" as Baker, and Baker agreed. As Arquette told *People*: "After she saw the film she told me she loved it. 'Rosanna,' she said, 'you did me! You did me!' "

In 1983, Arquette appeared in her first starring role in a motion picture, "Baby It's You." The low-budget ($3 million) film was written and directed by independent filmmaker John Sayles. Set in Trenton, New Jersey, in 1967, the film follows its heroine, Jill Rosen, a smart, pretty, ambitious high school senior, to college at Sarah Lawrence. Along the way Jill falls for Sheik, who couldn't be a more inappropriate match for her. As Janet Maslin described the character played by Arquette, "Jill is poised, popular, a little aloof and hoping to be a star performer some day; in line with this, she stars triumphantly in a high school play and practices singing 'Stop! In the Name of Love' in front of the mirror in her bedroom." In contrast to Jill's All-American wholesomeness, Sheik, who is nicknamed for the brand of contraceptive he favors, sports slicked-back hair and shark-skin suits. He idolizes Frank Sinatra and tells Jill early in their affair that the only three people who matter are "Jesus Christ, Frank Sinatra and me."

When he cast Arquette for the role, director Sayles told *Rolling Stone*, "I knew she was the only person who could play the innocent in the first half of the movie and bring out the emotional depth for the second part." Despite the mixed reviews the film received, critics singled out Arquette's performance for praise. According to Maslin, she played the role of Jill "crisply and confidently." *People* lauded Arquette by reporting that she "shades her performance with wonderful touches of surprise and puzzlement." In David Ansen's opinion, Arquette "makes this movie live. This seductive 23-year-old actress . . . always finds the fresh note. Like Sissy Spacek or Debra Winger, she's a presence you can't keep your eyes off, for fear of missing crucial information."

With the release of "Desperately Seeking Susan" in 1985, Arquette was included in the front ranks of young Hollywood actresses. The movie was made for $5 million, low-budgeted by Hollywood standards, and was directed by Susan Seidelman, whose previous film was the widely acclaimed "Smithereens." Described by the *Detroit Free Press* as "a stylish punk-rock version of those old '30s screwball comedies," the film features Arquette as Roberta Glass, a bored housewife in Fort Lee, New Jersey. In search of vicarious thrills, Roberta scours newspaper personal ads and becomes intrigued by a series of ads placed under the heading "Desperately Seeking Susan." Roberta begins to spy on the assignations of punk-rock star Susan and the man who places the ads. Through a number of mishaps the two women exchange identities, and Roberta gets the chance to live out her fantasy life through Susan's persona.

Real-life rock-star Madonna played the role of Susan. Although Arquette and Madonna appeared cheek-to-cheek in publicity shots and publicly professed affection and admiration for each other, press reports surfaced regarding tension between the two performers and between Arquette and Seidelman. The director attributed much of the problem to the fact that Madonna, who was just beginning her ascent to stardom when she was hired for the part, eclipsed Arquette by the time the movie was released. "It's no secret that Rosanna and I knocked heads a lot," Seidelman told Lindsey Gruson in the *New York Times*. "She was hired to be the star. But her participation was clouded by Madonna's fast-rising star. It took the edge off her performance. People would come up to the set and say 'Madonna, Madonna, is this "The Madonna Movie?"' Even the strongest actress would be shaken by that." For her part, Arquette told *Moviegoer* that the film was the most difficult she had ever done: "The tension on the set was unbelievable, and I hate working that way. It was a complete nightmare."

Arquette became publicly critical about the Madonna hype surrounding the release of the movie. Indeed, Orion, the distributor of the film, accelerated the release date to capitalize on Madonna's fame as a singer. Arquette also resented the fact that a video clip featuring an unreleased Madonna song, "In the Groove," was gratuitously inserted into the movie. Ultimately, Orion's ploy proved successful: The film grossed $20 million in the first three days of release, drawing a crowd largely comprised of under-21-year-old Madonna fans. Arquette told the *Detroit Free Press* somewhat ruefully, "It would be great to have Madonna fans come see it, but it would be great to have adults come see it, too."

Nor was Madonna entirely happy with the studio's strategy. She told an interviewer in *Rolling Stone*, "I have a big audience of kids for my music, and you know how they use soundtracks to push movies—I think they're using me in the same way, and it's really a drag, because I'm trying to establish myself as an actress, not as a singer making movies. But I'll be happy if it becomes a commercial success, simply because it's a different kind of movie than most of what's out now."

Arquette's experience in making her next film, the black comedy "After Hours," was much more positive. In contrast to director Seidelman's need for total control over her actors, Martin Scorsese, the director of "After Hours," was "never negative," Arquette told *Rolling Stone*. "In one situation he came up to me and said, 'Do you think you should laugh in this scene?' and I said, 'Oh no, Marty. I can't see where she'd laugh in this scene.' He said, 'Oh, yeah. You're right. You're right. Forget I ever said anything.' And he walks away. That's what he does, very subtly. It's like he planted the seed, watered it and split. And as I was doing the scene, I don't know where it came from, but I just started laughing."

The actress also enjoyed working with director Lawrence Kasdan (who had directed "The Big Chill") in the western "Silverado." The movie is set in the 1880s, and Arquette plays a pioneer woman who crosses the continent by covered wagon. Among Arquette's other recent projects are a public television play entitled "Survival Guide" and a movie, "The Aviator," that "At the Movies" reviewer Roger Ebert called "transcendentally bad."

Arquette's personal life, once featured in the tabloids, has stabilized recently. In late 1983, Arquette took a trip to Italy and made some major decisions about the direction of her life. While her personal life was once more important to her than her career, Arquette decided to put renewed emphasis on acting. She ended her two-and-one-half year romantic relationship with Steve Porcaro, keyboardist with the rock band Toto, though they remain friends. (Arquette, as most rock fans know, was *the* Rosanna in Toto's hit song of the same name). And she entered a drug rehabilitation program. Arquette now avoids the Hollywood scene by living high above it in a rustic cabin—complete with mice, she says—in Topanga Canyon, California.

Arquette has several projects pending. She would like to do theater and is considering taking up directing. Still, her primary goal at this point in her career is to grow as an actress. To that end, she is studying with drama coach Sondra Seacat, who also coaches actress Jessica Lange. As Arquette told interviewer Dale Pollock: "I just want to work. I want to keep growing, as a human being and as an actress. *Richer* and *deeper* are definitely the words for my life right now. I'm opening doors to a lot of areas that I haven't been able to explore. I've worked from instinct a lot, now it's time to polish my technique. As an actress, I'm just a baby. I have a lot to learn."

SOURCES:

PERIODICALS

Commonweal, May 20, 1983.
Detroit Free Press, March 29, 1985.
Maclean's, November 29, 1982, October 14, 1985.
Moviegoer, April, 1985.
New York, November 8, 1982.
New York Times, March 25, 1982, October 19, 1982, November 28, 1982, June 5, 1983, April 14, 1985.
Newsweek, April 11, 1983.
People, November 29, 1982.
Rolling Stone, June 9, 1983, May 9, 1985.
Time, April 18, 1983, September 23, 1985.
Variety, February 24, 1982.
Vogue, March, 1985.
Washington Post, April 29, 1983.

—*Sidelights by Barbara Welch Skaggs*

Count Basie

1904(?)-1984

OBITUARY NOTICE: Full name, William James Basie; born August 21, 1904 (one source says 1906), in Red Bank, N. J.; died of pancreatic cancer, April 26, 1984, in Hollywood, Fla.; ashes interred at Pine Lawn Cemetery, Farmingdale, N.Y. Musician and bandleader. One of the foremost big bands of the 1930s and 1940s, Count Basie's band is generally credited with having perfected and epitomized the jazz style known as swing. The first of the Basie bands was formed in Kansas City in 1935 after Basie, former student of famed "stride" piano stylist Thomas "Fats" Waller, had served as pianist with various vaudeville acts, in theatres, and in other bands, including one under the leadership of Bennie Moten. During one of the Basie band's regular radio broadcasts from Kansas City's Reno Club in 1936, a radio announcer dubbed the leader "Count," in the manner of Basie's popular fellow bandleaders Duke Ellington and Earl Hines, and the nickname remained with Basie throughout his career. The radio broadcasts also served to attract the attention of influential jazz critic and record producer John Hammond, who eventually arranged to bring Basie's band to New York City. By 1937 the band had released several popular recordings, including Basie's theme, "One O'Clock Jump," and was performing to enthusiastic audiences in New York clubs and ballrooms. After Carnegie Hall appearances in 1938 and 1939 the band's reputation was firmly established, and throughout the 1940s Basie led his band in most of the major ballrooms and theatres across the United States. With its so-called All-American rhythm section consisting of Walter Page on bass, Freddie Green on guitar, Jo Jones on drums, and Basie as a spare, cadenced presence on piano, the Basie band offered an intense, flowing beat that, according to *New Yorker* critic Whitney Balliett, "changed the course of jazz."

Basie and his band, beginning in the 1950s, embarked on tours to Europe, Asia, and South America, performed in 1961 at the inaugural ball for U.S. President John F. Kennedy, and in 1966 became the first U.S. band to play a command performance for Britain's reigning monarch, Queen Elizabeth. They appeared at jazz festivals, on television, and in films, including 1960's "Cinderfella" and 1974's "Blazing Saddles." Recipient of numerous awards, in 1981 Basie was honored by Washington's Kennedy Center for his achievement in the performing arts. Tunes popularized by the Basie band's many recordings include "Jumpin' at the Woodside," "April in Paris," "L'il Darlin'," and "Lester Leaps In." Deemed by the *New Republic* "probably the most exciting band that ever played jazz," Basie's band featured or performed with, at various times, such highly acclaimed musicians as vocalists Billie Holiday, Jimmy Rushing, Ella Fitzgerald, Joe Williams, Helen Humes, and Frank Sinatra, saxophonists Lester Young, Illinois Jacquet, Herschel Evans, and Eddie "Lockjaw" Davis, trombonists Dickie Wells, Vic Dickenson, and J. J. Johnson, drummer Buddy Rich, arranger Neal Hefti, and trumpeters Buck Clayton, Clark Terry, and Thad Jones. Jones, also a composer, arranger,

and former co-leader of the Thad Jones–Mel Lewis big band, was chosen in 1985 to take charge of the band that Basie led until his death.

SOURCES:

BOOKS

Current Biography, Wilson, 1942, June, 1984.
The International Who's Who, 47th edition, Europa, 1983.
Who's Who in America, 42nd edition, Marquis, 1982.
Who's Who Among Black Americans, 3rd edition, Who's Who Among Black Americans, 1981.
Who's Who of Jazz: Storyville to Swing Street, Chilton, 1972.

PERIODICALS

Ebony, January, 1984.
Maclean's, May 7, 1984.
New Republic, May 21, 1984.
Newsweek, May 7, 1984.
New Yorker, May 21, 1984.
New York Times, April 27, 1984, May 1, 1984.
People, May 14, 1984.
Time, May 7, 1984.

Owen Beattie

BRIEF ENTRY: Canadian anthropologist. The head of a team of University of Alberta researchers, Owen Beattie captured the attention of historians, scientists, and laymen in 1984 when he disinterred three bodies preserved for 138 years in the permafrost on Canada's Beechey Island. The bodies were those of Petty Officer John Torrington, Able Seaman John Hartnell, and Royal Marine William Braine, all members of an ill-fated British expedition led by Sir John Franklin in search of the fabled Northwest Passage to China.

Franklin's expedition—the worst tragedy in the quest to find the Northwest Passage—left England with two ships and 138 men in 1845 but mysteriously disappeared. After the three sailors died and were buried on Beechey Island, the remaining explorers sailed southwest until their ships became trapped in ice near King William Island. The 105 survivors abandoned the ships the following spring, struggled to endure life on the frozen tundra, but eventually perished.

Beattie was able to account for seven of the men on King William Island, concluding in *Newsweek* that because the bones were scattered on the surface of the island, "the men literally dropped as they walked." His close examination of the bones suggested evidence of lead poisoning, scurvy, and even cannibalism. Since the three corpses unearthed on Beechey Island were in flawless condition, Beattie believes analysis of their tissue and internal organs will help determine whether it was scurvy, toxins in the food, or merely despair that killed the remaining crew. *Address:* Department of Anthropology, University of Alberta, Edmonton, Alberta, Canada.

SOURCES:

PERIODICALS

Newsweek, October 8, 1984.
Time, October 8, 1984.

Photograph by Lynda Beattie. Courtesy of Owen Beattie

Boris Becker

1967-

BRIEF ENTRY: Born November 22, 1967, in Liemen, West Germany. German professional tennis player. Boris Becker won the 1985 men's singles championship at Wimbledon, England, becoming the youngest player, and the first German, ever to do so. His victory also made him the first unseeded champion in Wimbledon history.

Becker started playing competitive tennis as an eight year old in Leimen, West Germany, and began his association with his coach, Gunther Bosch, a year later. Schooled at the West German Tennis Federation, Becker was playing in the adult divisions of an area tennis league by the time he was eleven. In late 1984, world renowned coach Ion Tiriac began working with Becker, at the request of Bosch. "He always had the good forehand and backhand," Bosch said of Becker in the *Washington Post*. "The potential was always there. The head needed work." With the help of Tiriac, who had coached such outstanding players as Guillermo Vilas and Ilie Nastase in the past, Becker started playing up to his potential. He won his first Grand Prix championship, the Queen's Club grass court tournament, in June of 1985, just three weeks before his Wimbledon triumph.

At Wimbledon Becker became a crowd favorite with his aggressive style of play: diving after shots, thrusting his clenched fists into the air after winning big points, and yelling at himself when he made mistakes. He used his strength and speed to defeat Hank Pfister, Joakim Nystrom, Tim Mayotte, Henri LeConte, and Anders Jarryd before overpowering Kevin Curren in the four-set final. After his Wimbledon win, Becker told the *New York Times*, "I'm the first German [Wimbledon champion], and I think this will change tennis in Germany. They never had an idol, and now maybe they have one."

AP/Wide World Photos

SOURCES:

PERIODICALS

Los Angeles Times, July 8, 1985, July 28, 1985.
Maclean's, July 22, 1985.
Newsweek, July 15, 1985, September 9, 1985.
New York Times, July 8, 1985, August 25, 1985.
People, July 22, 1985.
Sporting News, July 15, 1985.
Sports Illustrated, July 15, 1985, July 22, 1985, August 12, 1985.
Time, July 22, 1985.
Washington Post, July 8, 1985.
World Tennis, March, 1984, April, 1985.

Ricky Bell

1955-1984

OBITUARY NOTICE: Full name, Ricky Lynn Bell; born April 8, 1955, in Houston, Tex.; died of cardiac arrest, November 28, 1984, in Inglewood, Calif. American professional football player. An outstanding running back for the University of Southern California and professional football's Tampa Bay Buccaneers and San Diego Chargers, Bell was the number one pick in the 1977 National Football League (NFL) draft. During his junior year in college, the young athlete led the nation in rushing with 1,875 yards, and in his senior year, he finished second to the University of Pittsburgh's Tony Dorsett in the balloting for the prestigious Heisman Trophy. After leaving Southern Cal, Bell joined the Tampa Bay team and proceeded to set several club records during the next five years, including rushing for a total of 3,057 yards.

Beginning in 1981, however, Bell began suffering a series of minor injuries that significantly reduced his playing time. At his request, he was traded to the San Diego Chargers in the spring of 1982, but continuing weight loss, muscle aches, and severe skin problems forced him to retire from football altogether before the end of the 1983 season. Doctors attributed Bell's death a year later to cardiac arrest brought on by dermatomyositis and polymyositis, two rare, chronic diseases that affect the skin, muscles, and various connective tissues in the body. The injuries he sustained while playing for the Buccaneers are now thought to be early symptoms of the illnesses that led to his death.

SOURCES:

BOOKS

Who's Who Among Black Americans, 3rd edition, Who's Who Among Black Americans, 1981.

PERIODICALS

Los Angeles Times, November 29, 1984, November 30, 1984, December 4, 1984.
Newsweek, December 10, 1984.
New York Times, November 29, 1984, December 4, 1984.

AP/Wide World Photos

Richard Belzer

1944-

PERSONAL: Born August 4, 1944, in Bridgeport, Conn.; son of Charles (a candy and tobacco retailer) and Francis Belzer; married Gail Susan Ross (divorced); married Dalia Danoch (divorced); married Harlee McBride (an actress). *Education*: Attended Dean Junior College, Franklin, Mass., for one year.

ADDRESSES: Home—New York, N.Y.; and Los Angeles, Calif. *Office*—"Hot Properties," Lifetime Network, 1211 Avenue of the Americas, New York, N.Y. 10036.

OCCUPATION: Comedian, television show host, and actor.

CAREER: Worked at a variety of jobs, including census taker, unlicensed schoolteacher, tobacco retailer, and reporter for the Bridgeport (Conn.) *Post*; disc jockey for radio station WNBC in New York City; actor in a number of films, including "Fame," "Author! Author!," "The Groove Tube," "Night Shift," and "Scarface"; stand-up comedian appearing at a variety of clubs, mostly in New York City and Los Angeles, Calif., including Catch a Rising Star and The Comedy Store; regular performer on cable television show "Thicke of the Night"; currently host of cable television talk show "Hot Properties."

SIDELIGHTS: He calls himself "a charmingly acerbic New York comedian." Others call Richard Belzer vicious, vulgar, self-destructive—a man whose unhappy upbringing forged his mastery of the scatological putdown, "Sometimes, I'm stunned at how vicious he can be," comedian and friend Robin Williams told *Rolling Stone.* "The way he comes back at people is truly amazing. He's out there juggling a razor, a hand grenade and a cobra—and being funny at the same time." Added David Brenner, another comedian and producer who, like Williams, has achieved the stardom that so far has eluded Belzer, "I think Richie wants to be the hippest, funniest, brightest cult-followed comedian in New York City, East Side and some West."

Yet despite more than a dozen years of ruling the spotlight at the Catch a Rising Star Manhattan bistro, a successful stint as a disc jockey at one of New York City's top radio stations, and a spate of small movie roles (Robert De Niro even patterned his manic, half-crazed stand-up comic character in "The King of Comedy" after Richard Belzer), "The Belz" remains perched on the periphery of commercial success. "I feel there's no one in the history of show business who's been as ready for stardom as me," Belzer told *Rolling Stone.* But there has been an almost self-destructive aspect to Belzer that has seemed to pull him back from the brink of success. "I realized I had a black side, like Lenny [Bruce]," he continued. "And I knew I had to overcome it."

Richard Belzer has had to overcome that and a lot more: the death of his mother, his father's suicide, two failed marriages, the death of his good friend Freddie Prinze, cancer. Perhaps that, in part, explains his comedy style: a rapid fire, shoot-all-prisoners approach that can be hilarious one instant while vulgar and insulting the next. Menachem Begin on acid, Mick Jagger as a rooster, an insect making love to its mate before it eats it are all part of Belzer's schtick. For a moment he is Jack Benny, arm folded under his chin, that baleful stare, and "Rochester, roll me a joint and turn on the stereo." Next instant, he is attacking the audience. "You part of the act? Then get your f——ing feet off the stage."

There is a nervous unpredictability about Belzer. It is almost as if even he cannot control the staccato flow of barbs and taunts that freely flit from satire to lampoon to mean-spirited invective. It is as fascinating to watch, say many observers, as it is often off-putting and self destructive. For example, the time Jack Rollins, whom Woody Allen, Robert Klein, Dick Cavett, and David Letterman all credit with launching their careers, caught Belzer's act. "Nice tie, Sparky," Belzer shot at Rollins from Catch A Rising Star's stage one night. "Couldn't guess your weight, huh? Now find your f——ing seat and sit in it." *Rolling Stone* reported that Rollins laughed but still hasn't signed Belzer.

"You know," Belzer told the magazine shortly after the Rollins incident, "I would rather starve than be an asshole on a sitcom for $5,000 a week. Now, if that's self-destructive, then I have to argue the definition. For whatever reasons it's taken me this long to make it, it's not self-destructiveness or fear of success. This is my destiny. . . . Look, if I was in it just for the fame and the money, I could have made it already. I can't see where I'm doing anything wrong. I think I'm being true to myself, and that's very important to me."

Indeed, Belzer's heroes are Jagger, De Niro, Bruce Springsteen, Richard Pryor, and Marlon Brando; people he calls "authentic." He told *Crawdaddy* magazine: "The great ones—Pryor, Lenny, Jackie Mason—all started out as something they weren't. "And they were all eventually accepted as great by being their own self."

Perhaps that is why Richard Belzer is as likely to offend as he is to entertain; as likely to make an audience gasp as guffaw; as prone to make them cry as he is to fill their eyes with tears of laughter. His own childhood was forged in sadness and rejection, and acceptance as an adult can only come on Belzer's terms. "I carry a lot of sadness around with me that is just part of my whole history and life," he told *Rolling Stone.* Indeed, for Belzer comedy was always his shield against a world he found harsh and cruel.

As a child growing up in Bridgeport, Connecticut, he was beaten often—usually by his mother—with straps and sticks and hangers and almost anything lying about the house. There was also laughter, mostly with his brother Leonard, who is three years older and now is one of Belzer's main comedy writers.

Most of Belzer's animosity was directed at his mother, whom he considered vile and evil. His father, Belzer thought, was simply a weak man who tried to accommodate his overbearing and vicious wife, sometimes by hitting the boys. He would often lie awake at night, Belzer told *Rolling Stone,* and only partly in jest tell his brother, "Let's kill her." Sometimes he would even dream about her dying.

Once, when she was about to thrash him again, Belzer made her laugh by impersonating Jerry Lewis, whom he resembled a little, and she left him alone. Comedy wouldn't always work as the antidote for her rejection, Belzer discovered, but it did sometimes. He told *Rolling Stone* that when his mother died of cancer in 1963, his father told him, "Mommy has expired." And Belzer recalled thinking, "Expired? What is she, a . . . magazine? She's dead."

In high school during the early 1960s, Belzer was the class clown. Later he enrolled in Dean Junior College in Franklin, Massachusetts; after a little more than a year there, he was thrown out for spearheading a demonstration promoting later curfews in the women's dorms. His father talked him into joining the army, but Belzer quickly realized he had made a mistake and tried faking a back injury and feigning suicide to get discharged. Finally he was sent to see an army psychiatrist. While he failed to convince the doctor that he was a bedwetter, that he caught VD during his first romantic tryst, or that he was overcome with hatred for the military, he did convince the psychiatrist that perhaps the military would be better off without Richard Belzer. He was discharged on July 22, 1964, and went to work for his father's candy and tobacco business. During this period, he married Gail Susan Ross; the marriage lasted six years. In 1967—just four years after his mother died—Belzer's father committed suicide.

Belzer was at a low point. His marriage was falling apart, and he drifted aimlessly from job to job, teaching school, selling furniture, reporting. During this nadir he bought and sold drugs and sometimes tried heroin himself. For reasons even Belzer isn't sure of, he passed through this phase and later answered an ad in the *Village Voice* for an audition for a video show called "The Groove Tube." He got the job and played ten separate roles in the production.

The show opened November 9, 1971, to rave reviews, and Belzer also starred later in the film version. Ken Shapiro—director, producer, writer, and one of the stars of the film—went on to become a millionaire, according to *Rolling Stone.* Belzer made about $20,000.

Still, "The Groove Tube" led to an offer to perform at the Escape Hatch, a small club in New Jersey. Belzer pulled together material from his high school days and floored the audience. That job led to a stint at Catch A Rising Star in 1973, where he started experimenting with his confrontational style of humor. By 1974 he was a regular.

The next year he met Lorne Michaels, who would later launch the innovative television show "Saturday Night Live." Michaels considers Belzer a friend. "Richard was very kind to me," Michaels told *Rolling Stone.* "He let me hang out with him at Catch." But Belzer said Michaels promised him a spot on "Saturday Night Live," which catapulted the careers of such comedians as Chevy Chase, John Belushi, Dan Akroyd and Eddie Murphy. "He said I would be in the cast and then he said I was too funny," Belzer commented. "I was devastated."

Another blow came shortly after, when his friend Freddie Prinze, who at twenty-two was thrust into stardom through the television series "Chico and the Man," shot himself in the head. "I think Freddie's death affected Richard more than he lets on," Belzer's friend and manager, Rick Newman, told *Rolling Stone.* "It opened his eyes to another part of the business, how they can take a piece of you. I think it made him more aware he had to protect himself."

While performing regularly at the Catch, Belzer met and married Dalia Danoch. The marriage lasted four years, and during this time Belzer landed his most lucrative job and one that appeared ideal for his career. He was hired to boost WNBC Radio's audience by teaming up with Scotty Brink, for a program on which the two jousted with their call-in audience and their own advertisers, pushing such items as nuclear powered panty hose and "Schtick: the razor that treats your face like a joke." Belzer was the renegade to Brink as straight man. The show came across as a "Saturday Night Live" for the AM-radio set, an impression aided by guest appearances from such stars as Gilda Radner, Laraine

Newman and Bill Murray. Belzer was making $1,400 a week, and the station's ratings started to climb. He seemed poised for the big break. "Here I am," Belzer told *New York* magazine, "saying to all those people who wouldn't give me a sitcom, 'Okay, I'm too hip, huh? Well, tune into AM.' "

But the radio success was short lived. Belzer refused to give up his late-night stand-up appearances, and his doctor told him his body could not withstand the 'round-the-clock pressure of early morning and late-night performances. Something had to go, and Belzer left the radio program. He listed about, getting bit parts in the movies, including "Fame," "Night Shift," "Author! Author!" and "Scarface," mostly playing stand-up comics. He juggled that with his stand-up stints at Catch in New York and The Comedy Store in Los Angeles. But despite this exposure, Belzer remained on the periphery of commercial success.

That is starting to change, largely because cable television has "discovered" Richard Belzer and partly because Belzer has tempered his own frenetic pace. The abrupt change came when, in 1984, he learned he had cancer. "I found out about it on a Friday and went into the hospital on Saturday," Belzer told *People* magazine. "I was operated on and had 16 radiation treatments and I'm totally cured." Belzer doesn't like to discuss the cancer operation. But it has clearly affected both his personal life and his professional one. The edge is still there in his humor, but more often he is the brunt of the joke rather than the audience.

The "new" Belzer meditates, doesn't drink, doesn't stay up late, gets plenty of rest. He recently married California actress Harlee McBride, who appeared in the movie "The Adventures of Young Lady Chatterly," and of his new life Belzer told *People*, "My vision of life has improved. I'm very happy."

He has appeared as a regular on the cable TV show "Thicke of the Night," has a contract for six specials on the Cinemax cable network, and is a regular talk-show host on "Hot Properties," the Lifetime cable television call-in program. "A lot of people think that I'm a star now, that I've made it—which flatters me," he told *Cable Guide.* "But it's very hard for me to think in those terms. I'm certainly doing better now." Indeed, there is talk of Belzer producing his own comedy album, syndicating a national radio show, and even some discussion of a movie based on his life.

"The one thing I've learned about show biz is there's nothing logical to it," Belzer told Associated Press reporter Andy Beck, according to the *Los Angeles Times.* "If I pine away about people who have made it before me, I'd be in a mental institution. Talent is not a criteria [for success], though I believe in the long run talent will win out."

SOURCES:

PERIODICALS

Cable Guide, May, 1985.
CableVision, December 17, 1984.
Crawdaddy, December, 1978.
Detroit Free Press, March 29, 1985.
Los Angeles Times, October 25, 1984.
Newsday, March 29, 1985.
New York, July 2, 1979.
New York Daily News, March 3, 1985, March 29, 1985.
New York Post, April 1, 1985.
New York Times, November 19, 1984.
On Cable, April, 1985.
People, November 12, 1984.
Rolling Stone, November 12, 1981.

—Sketch by Stephen Advokat

Nabih Berri

1939(?)-

PERSONAL: Born c. 1939, in Freetown, Sierra Leone; son of a merchant; married wife Lila (divorced); married wife Randa; children: six (first marriage); one daughter (second marriage). *Education*: Attended Lebanese University, Beirut; graduated from Beirut Law School, 1963; also studied in France for one year.

ADDRESSES: Barbour St., Al-Nazarah, Beirut, Lebanon.

OCCUPATION: Lebanese political and religious leader.

CAREER: Worked as a merchant in family business in Sierra Leone; practiced law in Beirut, Lebanon; joined Amal political movement in Lebanon, 1974, leader of movement, 1978—; Lebanese minister of justice, 1984—. Generally recognized as leading spokesman for Lebanon's Shiite Muslims.

SIDELIGHTS: Nabih Berri is a non-traditional leader in Lebanon, a country where traditional enmities are honed and nurtured through the generations, and politicians gain ascendency by exploiting the fears of their particular religious or ethnic faction. Berri is the head of the Amal movement and leading spokesman for Lebanon's one million Shiite Muslims, the largest and most impoverished of the country's religious factions. But unlike the traditional warlords who have ruled Lebanon since World War I, Berri has tried to keep his followers on a strictly nationalistic course rather than a religious one.

"Lebanon is a country for all the Lebanese people. We are only the principle minority," he told *El Pais*, a Madrid newspaper, in 1984. In another interview, Berri told *Der Spiegel*: "Shiites demand that the existing religious system in Lebanon be abandoned. Qualifications alone, not the prayer book, should decide who becomes president of Lebanon." Another departure from the leadership of the past is Berri's disdain for any sort of personality cult. There are few posters of him to be found in West Beirut. His approach to politics is low-key and pragmatic.

Nor does Berri belong to one of Lebanon's traditional ruling families, like the Gemayels, the Jumblatts, or the Franjiehs. He is a self-made man from a middle-class background. He lives with his second wife Randa and their daughter in a modest West Beirut flat that is often described as cluttered. A favorite pastime, according to a Beirut newspaper, is watching American westerns on television. Berri was born in Freetown, Sierra Leone, where his father was a merchant; but his roots are in the south Lebanon village of Tibnin, a few miles north of the Israeli border.

He also has strong links to the United States. His first wife, Lila, lives in Dearborn, Michigan, where she works for the police department. Their six children were raised in the area.

According to a *New York Times* profile, Berri lived in Dearborn for brief periods during the 1970s and polished his English by reading the Detroit newspapers in the Dearborn Public Library. Berri still visits his children in Dearborn and holds a U.S. government "green card," which permits him to live permanently in the United States and will eventually make him eligible for citizenship.

Berri first became involved in politics as a student at the Lebanese University in Beirut, where he was president of the student association and a member of the Baath Party, a popular pan-Arab nationalist movement of the 1960s, whose rival factions still rule in Iraq and Syria. After graduating from Beirut Law School in 1963 and studying for a year in France, Berri worked briefly with his father in Sierra Leone before returning to Beirut to practice law.

With the outbreak of the Lebanese Civil War in 1975, Berri became involved in the Amal movement, which was founded in 1974 by Shiite cleric Imam Musa Sadr as the "movement of the disinherited," an attempt to politicize Lebanon's largely passive Shiite population. When Imam Sadr disappeared during a trip to Libya in 1978—a case that has never been resolved—Berri quietly took the reins of Amal.

Lebanon's Shiites, who live primarily in and around West Beirut and in the towns and small villages of the Bekaa Valley and south Lebanon, account for about one million of the country's 3.5 million people. They are by far the largest of Lebanon's religious sects, but historically they have lagged far behind the Christian Maronites and Sunni Muslims for a fair share of Lebanon's political spoils.

Historically the Shiites broke from the orthodox Sunni Muslims during the first century of Islam in a dispute over the proper succession to the Prophet Muhammad. Over the centuries, the Shiites developed a religious outlook that is more mystical, rigid, and passionate than the Sunni. Though Sunnis predominate throughout most of the Arab world, Shiites outnumber Sunnis in Lebanon and Iraq, and significant Shiite communities live in Saudi Arabia and other Persian Gulf states. Iran (which is not an Arab state) is almost entirely Shiite.

In Lebanon, the Maronites and Sunnis profited as merchants and traders in the urban centers while the Shiites scratched a meagre existence out of the rural land in the south. But in the 1960s and 1970s, according to the *Wall Street Journal*, an economic boom in Beirut drew many Shiites to the capital, and "there they clustered in slums and seethed as they looked at their richer neighbors. Raw and illiterate, the Shiites found they didn't have access to civil service or private-sector jobs."

While it was Imam Sadr who first provided the Shiites of Lebanon with an ideological framework, it was Berri, the cool, low-key lawyer, who shaped the Amal movement into an effective political organization and maneuvered into a position where it contends for power with Maronites and Sunnis.

The turning point for Amal (which means "hope" in Arabic) came after the 1982 Israeli invasion of Lebanon. The Shiites at first welcomed the Israelis, grateful that the Palestine Liberation Organization's grip on south Lebanon had been loosened. But that gratitude was short-lived; the Shiites decided their new occupiers were no better than the old ones. Amal and a number of Shiite fundamentalist splinter groups waged an intense guerilla war, and Israel's casualties mounted steadily until it finally withdrew in June, 1985.

The more extreme of the fundamentalist groups also opposed U.S. support of the Israeli invasion as well as U.S. support of the government of Amin Gemayel, a Maronite who has been slow to make reforms. These groups took credit for the suicide car bombers that twice struck U.S. Embassy installations, a truck bomb that killed 241 U.S. Marines at their headquarters near the Beirut airport, the kidnappings of nearly a dozen American civilians since 1983, and the 1985 hijacking of a TWA jetliner.

Berri's own politics and tactics have been far more moderate. After the Israeli invasion, Berri tried to cooperate with the newly-installed Gemayel government and his American sponsors. While pressing Gemayel for reforms, he kept a tight rein on his 6,000- to 8,000-man militia until February,

1984, when Gemayel permitted the Lebanese Army to shell Beirut's predominantly Shiite southern suburbs. Berri ordered Muslim members of the Army to lay down their weapons, and within days Amal had seized effective control of West Beirut. Though this established him as the leading power in Lebanon—with even more authority than President Gemayel—few Americans had heard of Berri until June of 1985, when he emerged as a negotiator in the TWA hijacking crisis.

Despite his differences with Gemayel, Berri prefers to work for the restoration of Lebanon within a legitimate constitutional framework rather than join in the wholesale destruction of the country. He joined the government as justice minister in May, 1984, and continued to push his agenda of secular reforms. "He [Berri] is not a revolutionary by any means," a European diplomat told *The Christian Science Monitor* in 1984. "His commitment is fully to the cause of the underprivileged, which in his country means the Shiites."

When asked by *El Pais* to describe the Shiite community's goals, Berri said: "To be Lebanese on an equal footing with other Lebanese. To cease to be second-class and even third- and fourth-class citizens. And to achieve this there is only one solution: To eliminate confessionalism and secularize the country by granting posts and responsibilities on the criteria of competence and education and not religion. Note that the abolition of the confessional sharing power will continue to benefit the Christians, because the greatest number of university graduates, who will continue to hold key posts, belong to their community. But we are prepared to accept it. It is the essential condition for creating a real nation."

By early 1985, it was apparent that the real test of Berri's political acuity would come not from his rival religious factions, but from within the Shiite ranks. A number of the more militant fundamentalist groups who admire the Islamic revolution in Iran reject Berri's moderate approach. The split between Amal and fundamentalist groups such as "Islamic Amal" in the Bekaa Valley bordered on open warfare in 1985. Berri, who has tried to keep Lebanon's fundamentalists at arm's length, told *The Christian Science Monitor*: "We support the Islamic revolution in Iran, but not on sectarian grounds, and we do not want an Islamic revolution in Lebanon. Our special relations with the Iranian revolution are based more on principles than on sectarian compatibility."

Patience and moderation have never been Lebanon's strong suit. If Berri's approach does not pay dividends soon, many observers believe he may be forced to become more like the militant fundamentalists—or risk losing his following.

SOURCES:

PERIODICALS

Christian Science Monitor, February 16, 1984.
Der Spiegel (Hamburg), February 13, 1984.
Detroit Free Press, June 18, 1985.
Economist, February 11, 1984.
El Pais (Madrid), February 16, 1984.
Financial Times, February 11, 1984.
Le Monde (Paris), February 16, 1984.

London Times, February 21, 1984.
Middle East International (London), February 24, 1984.
New York Times, June 18, 1985.
Wall Street Journal, February 16, 1984, June 25, 1985.

—Sidelights by Tom Hundley

Molly Blackburn

1931(?)-1985

OBITUARY NOTICE: Born c. 1931; died in an automobile accident, December 28, 1985, near Port Elizabeth, South Africa. South African civil rights activist. Considered one of South Africa's leading white anti-apartheid advocates, Molly Blackburn was one of the first whites arrested following President Pieter W. Botha's 1985 crackdown on dissidents. Botha declared a state of emergency on July 20, allowing the country's security forces "almost unlimited powers of search, seizure, and arrest," notes *Maclean's*. Blackburn, who lived in Port Elizabeth, was picked up by Eastern Cape police the next week and charged with attending an illegal meeting—a memorial service for Matthew Goniwe, a black civic leader and an active member of the anti-apartheid movement. Some 15,000 mourners attended the service, according to Blackburn, but only she was arrested.

She called her arrest "pure harassment," reported Larry Olmstead of the *Detroit Free Press*. She was taken into custody shortly before she was to have met with officials of a Ford Foundation fact-finding committee that included former U.S. Secretary of State Cyrus Vance and former Secretary of Defense Robert McNamara. Under emergency regulations, Blackburn could have been "detained indefinitely, without access to family or legal counsel," indicated *Maclean's*; Blackburn was, however, later released on fifty-dollars bond.

Blackburn had been a social and political activist since 1960, when she joined the Black Sash, a women's civil rights group that provides legal and economic aid to blacks and their organizations. In 1975 she became a member of the Cape Provincial Council. She belonged to South Africa's official opposition party, the Progressive Federals.

Through the years she had been arrested several times for attending illegal gatherings, as well as for entering black townships without the necessarry permit. She was instrumental in arranging medical and legal assistance for victims of South Africa's violent unrest. "I feel more comfortable in the black community," she told Olmstead shortly after her 1985 arrest. "Blacks are talking about real issues."

Blackburn and Brian Bishop, a civil rights attorney, were killed when their car collided head-on with another vehicle as they returned to Port Elizabeth from Humansdorp, a black township, where they had been interviewing blacks arrested by security police. The driver of the second car also died in the accident; Blackburn's sister and Bishop's wife were injured in the crash. At Blackburn's funeral, stated an Associated Press report quoted by the *Detroit Free Press*,

David Turnley, Detroit Free Press/Black Star

"Middle-class whites cried and blacks saluted the silver-haired woman who was a constant opponent of white domination in South Africa." Said the Reverend Allan Boesak, president of the World Alliance of Reformed Churches: "There are precious few white people in this country who have been able to do what Molly Blackburn has done. . . . [She] brings us together and anticipates what this country can and should be. She was a true daughter of Africa."

SOURCES:

PERIODICALS

Detroit Free Press, July 28, 1985, December 30, 1985, January 3, 1986.
Maclean's, August 5, 1985.
Time, January 13, 1986.

Hector Boiardi

1897-1985

OBITUARY NOTICE: Born 1897 in Piacenza, Italy; came to the United States in 1917; died June 21, 1985, in a nursing home in Parma, Ohio. Founder and president of Chef Boy-ar-dee, one of the first packaged Italian food businesses in the United States, whose products include Beefaroni, Spaghetti and Meat Balls, ABCs and 123s, and Pac-Man Pasta. Boiardi started in the food business at the age of eleven as a cooking apprentice in an Italian hotel. At seventeen, he came to the United States and with the help of his brother, a maitre d' in the Persian Room of New York's Plaza hotel, established himself as chef at the Plaza. He also worked as a chef in Greenbrier, West Virginia, where he organized the reception for the second marriage of U.S. President Woodrow Wilson.

Later, Boiardi moved to Cleveland, Ohio, and opened Il Giardino D'Italia, which became famous in the area for serving inexpensive Italian foods and sauces. The restaurant quickly became popular, and in response to his customers' demands, he began selling take-home jars of sauces, dry pasta, and grated cheese along with instructions for preparing the food. In 1928, Boiardi opened a small plant in Cleveland and named his company Chef Boy-ar-dee, the phonetic spelling of his last name, because customers and sales people had a difficult time with his real name.

Boiardi's company went national within ten years of its inception. As a result of this expansion, Boiardi found himself in need of large quantities of a particular kind of tomato, on which his sauce was based. In 1938, he went into the depression-ravaged town of Milton, Pennsylvania, and asked the local farmers if they could grow these tomatoes for him. They agreed and set up a new production plant in a closed hosiery mill. Under Boiardi's direction, the company grew until he sold it to American Home Products in 1946 for $6 million. The chairman of American Home Products, John W. Culligan, expressed to the *Chicago Times* the opinion that Boiardi "founded a food business which was among the first in terms of providing a quality product at a reasonable cost in a convenient form."

AP/Wide World Photos

SOURCES:

BOOKS

Fucini, Joseph and Suzy Fucini, *Entrepreneurs*, G. K. Hall, 1985.

PERIODICALS

Chicago Times, June 23, 1985.
Detroit Free Press, June 23, 1985.
Spin, September, 1985.

Sultan Muda Hassanal Bolkiah

1946-

PERSONAL: Full name, Sultan Sir Muda Hassanal Bolkiah Mu'izzadin Waddaulah; born July 15, 1946; son of Sultan Omar Ali Saifuddin (sultan of Brunei); married Rajah Isteri Anak Saleha and Pengiran Isteri Hajjah Mariam; children: (with first wife) one son, five daughters; (with second wife) one son. *Education:* Attended Victoria Institute, Kuala Lumpur, Malaysia, and Royal Military Academy, Sandhurst, England.

ADDRESSES: Home—Istana Darul Hana, Brunei; and The Aviary, Osterley, England.

OCCUPATION: Sultan of Brunei.

CAREER: Crown prince and heir apparent, 1961-67, sultan of Brunei, 1967—, prime minister, minister of finance, and minister of home affairs, 1984—. Sovereign and chief of royal orders instituted by sultans of Brunei. *Military service:* British Army, Coldstream Guards, honorary captain.

SIDELIGHTS: The sultan of Brunei, Sultan Muda Hassanal Bolkiah, is one of the wealthiest human beings on earth. When the 1984 British edition of the *Guinness Book of World Records* touted him as being the "world's richest man," the sultan was furious, reports Anthony Sampson in *Parade* magazine. The ruler made it clear that the approximately $4 billion annual income generated from Brunei's oil and natural gas sales belongs to the people of Brunei rather than to his majesty alone. Still, as Sampson points out, if Sultan Muda claimed just 10 percent of the sultanate's yearly revenues, he'd "net more than a quarter of a billion dollars" per annum.

In September of 1959, the ruler of Brunei at the time, Sultan Omar Ali Saifuddin (Sultan Muda's father), made an agreement with England for the British to handle foreign relations and defense for Brunei. England had actually extended its protective umbrella over Brunei since 1888, not including the sultanate's period of occupation by Japan from 1941 to 1945. British influence was so welcome in Brunei that the country celebrates Queen Elizabeth's birthday as a national holiday, and a museum was built in honor of Winston Churchill. Such actions prompted a *New York Times* reporter to call Brunei "as British as an Islamic country can be." In fact, the royal family was so pleased at being a protectorate of England, says Jared Mitchell in *Maclean's* magazine, that in 1979 it asked to remain in that position for two more decades.

But in early 1984, Brunei opted for official independence from British influence. About 50,000 of the 220,000 population helped celebrate the occasion in the new nation's capital, Bandar Seri Begawan. To demonstrate the still-friendly relationship between the two countries, Prince Charles took part in the ceremony, representing the queen of

England. And the sultan has kept the queen's Sixth Gurkha Rifles unit of the British Army on his payroll to protect the royal family. As a result, observes a reporter in the *New York Times*, he's giving England "one of the best training sites for jungle warfare available in the region."

In *Maclean's*, Mitchell describes Brunei as "a unique amalgam of Islamic monarchy and one of the world's most generous welfare systems." For about four centuries, Sultan Muda's family has reigned over the sultanate, which is located on the northern coast of the island of Borneo in the South China Sea. The island is shared by the much larger countries of Malaysia and Indonesia. (Brunei is about the size of the state of Delaware in the United States, or the province of Prince Edward Island in Canada.) The present sultan's father abdicated the throne on October 5, 1967. Sir Muda was crowned sultan of Brunei at the age of twenty-two.

As a new nation, Brunei is still ruled by the sultan. His majesty serves as prime minister, finance minister, and minister of the interior. Other major governmental posts are held by family members. One of Sultan Muda's brothers, for instance, was appointed minister of culture, youth, and sports, as well as deputy minister of defense. A second brother received the position of minister of external affairs. Sultan Muda's father is defense minister.

The typical Bruneian lifestyle does not seem to be hampered by the autocratic rule of the country. The per capita annual income is approximately $22,000.00—among the highest in the world. (Brunei Shell handles the lucrative oil business for the government, which is why Brunei has been jokingly called a "Shell-fare state.") There is no income tax, and citizens are able to borrow money for homes and cars with little interest (almost half of the work force is on the government's payroll). Public housing includes a village built on stilts in the Brunei River. The homes, designed in the indigenous style of longhouses, are modern and comfortable. Each is equipped with television sets and air conditioning, the latter especially important in the tropical climate of equatorial coastal plains and rain forest.

The sultan used a portion of Brunei's oil and gas proceeds to construct what *House & Garden* calls "unquestionably the largest and costliest royal residence ever built" in time for the independence ceremonies. Named Istana Narul Iman, the palace was built on a hill, south of Bandar Seri Begawan. The structure is comprised of four three-story buildings, which are connected to one another. They are topped with two huge domes, plated with twenty-two-carat gold. The complex takes up fifty acres and looks out on a 300-acre landscaped garden and the Brunei River. Robert Trumbull of the *New York Times* points out that this area would cover more than a third of Central Park in New York City. Moreover, with its 1,788 rooms, the Istana is larger than the 1,400-room Vatican in Rome. And the Vatican sits on just thirteen acres. The price of building the palace has been estimated between $300 million and $500 million. The lower end of the estimate is "twice as much as it cost to build Madison Square Garden," remarks Trumbull.

The Istana was designed by Philippine architect Leandro Locsin, the man responsible for designing public buildings for the Marcos regime. Locsin mixed traditional arabesque styles with modern forms and technology. He also borrowed peak roofs from the longhouses that are native to Brunei. His goal was to symbolize the different dimensions of the new nation.

The throne building is divided into three main sections: the central reception hall, which serves as the entrance way; the royal banquet hall to the south, capable of serving 4,500 guests, 450 in optimum comfort; and, to the north, the throne hall, which seats 2,000. In the latter room, "the lighting is frankly stagy," notes a *House & Garden* writer, "but superb in creating just the right effects, especially when the sultan and his diamond-studded queen are ensconced on their thrones and bathed in a positively supernal aura." There are also a number of less-important rooms, such as the sitting hall, with additional thrones, and a titled persons room. But the *House & Garden* writer expresses the opinion that "Certainly the most pleasing of the interiors at the Istana is the Surao, or prayer room, a domed circular sanctuary that is as visually refreshing for the infidel as it is spiritually restorative for the faithful." Included in the room's decor are calligraphied verses from the Muslim holy book, the Koran, which appear around the room. The

Islamic spiritual leader, the grand mufti, was responsible for their proper design and placement. Each character was painstakingly cut from brass sheets in England, after the verses were proofread in Saudi Arabia.

Besides serving as a public palace, the Istana is also a private residence for the royal family. Islamic law allows for four wives, with the stipulation that each wife receive identical treatment from the husband. The sultan has so far wed two women and is betrothed to a third. The queen, Rajah Isteri Anak Saleha, resides in the palace with her one son and five daughters. The sultan's second wife, Pengiran Isteri Hajjah Mariam, also lives there with her one son. The sultan is currently planning to build what has been called a "mini-Istana," for his second spouse, and he will probably construct similar homes for subsequent wives. Other family members also live at the Istana, including the sultan's brothers and their families and Sultan Muda's father. Eight duplex suites are ready to be finished when the sultan's own children come of age. In fact, his majesty has said that the palace was built with them and their progeny in mind.

Pools and fountains bubble in open courtyards outside of the palace walls. Sultan Muda has also built a rooftop heliport to accommodate the helicopters that he himself enjoys piloting. The underground garage supplies parking space for 800 cars, including the monarch's various Rolls Royces, his Bentley with the twenty-two-carat gold-plated grill, and the remainder of his forty-plus sports car collection.

In September of 1984, Brunei became a member of the United Nations. During his first speech before the General Assembly, Sultan Muda underlined the fact that his nation remains loyal to the West. At the same time, he called for recognition of the Palestinian Liberation Organization (PLO). The sultan's philanthropic side was revealed in New York City during this period when he donated $500,000 to the city's elderly. He handed an additional million dollars over to the UNICEF fund.

What is a million dollars or so to the leader of a country that holds $14 billion in international investments (two thirds of what the United States owns abroad)? The sultan has private investments throughout the world as well. Beginning at home, he and members of his family own the newspaper the *Borneo Bulletin*. In the West, Brunei's potentate privately purchased the Holiday Inn hotel in Singapore and changed its name to the more apt Royal Holiday Inn, even though it is still managed by Holiday Inns International. At the same time, Sultan Muda bought a shopping center next to the hotel from the Goodwood Hotels Corporation. Since then, the sultan has added London's Dorchester Hotel to his holdings; the price tag on that purchase was $50 million. Other financial moves made by his majesty include transferring $5 billion from British banks to New York City financial institutions, and $2 billion from Asia to Switzerland. The sultan has also become active as an investor in China and Hong Kong since Brunei's independence.

It was suggested by reporters in *Newsweek* magazine that, at least in one instance, roles may have changed between Britain and Brunei, with England looking for assistance from a monarch whom it used to help. In late January 1985 the British pound needed a boost. Prime Minister of England Margaret Thatcher met with Sultan Muda and

Mohamed al Fayed, an Egyptian businessman who specializes in acting as a liaison between leaders or power brokers of the East and West. After the meeting, "the sultan began shifting a substantial amount of money—as much as several billion dollars—from dollars into sterling, a move that may have helped the pound," reports *Newsweek*.

As is often the case with personalities living in the world's limelight, the sultan was indirectly involved in a controversy related to the purchase of England's House of Fraser. It was al Fayed who bid, and won, the House of Fraser, a huge retail operation that owns the renowned Harrod's department store. The British conglomerate Lonrho, headed by Chief Executive Officer Roland (Tiny) Rowland, was unable to make a counter bid because of a government inquiry. Nonetheless, Rowland accused al Fayed of acting on behalf of the sultan in the deal, pointing out that that's exactly what happened in the Dorchester Hotel sale. But both Sultan Muda and al Fayed deny Rowland's accusations. Presumably because of unflattering press coverage of the matter, the sultan has since sought other means of gaining financial advice than relying heavily on al Fayed. The two men still conduct some business together and apparently remain friends. Sultan Muda is making plans to train his own officials in money management. And, says *Newsweek*, "the national investment portfolios are now managed by the official Brunei Investment Agency, which is advised by professionals, including Morgan Guaranty and Citibank."

The sultan has also invested in defense for Brunei. Exocet missiles and Scorpion armored cars have been purchased as part of the country's $250 million annual expenditures on defense. That's almost one third of Brunei's budget, points out Jared Mitchell in *Maclean's*. The army, the Royal Brunei Malay Regiment, numbers 3,650 men. Sultan Muda also continues to maintain 750 members of the British Gurkha battalion. Another protective measure made by the sultan has been to become the sixth member of the Association of Southeast Asian Nations, whose other members are Malaysia, Singapore, the Philipines, Thailand, and Indonesia. Despite the unquestionable desirability of Brunei's natural gas and oil resources, the sultanate appears to be well-protected. It seems that the sultan of Brunei is determined to have his country live up to its official title: Abode of Peace.

SOURCES:

PERIODICALS

Christian Science Monitor, May 16, 1983.
House & Garden, October, 1984.
Maclean's, January 16, 1984.
Newsweek, October 21, 1985.
New York Times, September 16, 1980, February 18, 1981, January 1, 1984, January 2, 1984, January 11, 1985.
Parade, July 7, 1985.
Wall Street Journal, August 3, 1983.
Washington Post, January 9, 1984.

—Sidelights by Victoria France Charabati

Mary Boone
1951-

PERSONAL: Born October 29, 1951, in Erie, Pa.; daughter of an engineer. *Education:* Attended Michigan State University, Rhode Island School of Design, and Hunter College of the City University of New York.

ADDRESSES: Home—New York, N.Y. *Office*—417 West Broadway, New York, N.Y. 10019.

OCCUPATION: Art dealer.

CAREER: Former artist; Bykert Gallery, New York City, member of staff, 1970-76; Mary Boone Gallery, New York City, owner and operator, 1976—.

SIDELIGHTS: Art dealer Mary Boone is one of the central figures in a dramatic revitalization of the modern art scene. Since the opening of her gallery in New York City in 1977, Boone has aggressively promoted the work of a group of young painters whose emotional, energetic canvases have stimulated controversy, interest, and financial activity in an art market that had been stagnant for several years. "After a decade or so of no-frills, reductive art, stripped entirely of imagery and totally flat in texture," writes Grace Glueck in the *New York Times,* "contemporary dealers are rejoicing in an explosion of new young artists hipped on tactile surfaces, flashy, fanciful imagery and the forceful application of paint to canvas." Mary Boone is "just about the most influential dealer of [this] new talent around," states Theodore F. Wolff in *Christian Science Monitor.* "She has the power to give instant recognition to almost anyone she chooses, and the knack of doing it with such authority that criticism of her choices ends up seeming petty, ignorant, or vindictive—if not downright reactionary."

Boone arrived in Manhattan when she was nineteen years old, ready to begin a career as an artist. In order to support herself, she took a job at the small, highly-respected Bykert Gallery, a showcase for minimalist art. Even then, Boone's business style was quite unlike the typical art dealer's. An art collector who did business with Boone at the time told *New York's* Anthony Haden-Guest: "I had bought a drawing [from the Bykert Gallery]. . . . I hadn't paid. You know how it is, you pay your dealer last, even after your tailor. And Mary Boone telephoned me. I've never had a call from a dealer like it! It was more or less 'Pay up or we're going to come and rip it off your wall.' " Boone was as energetic in her search for new talent as she was in collecting unpaid bills, according to one of her friends, who recalled to Haden-Guest that "while the rest of us were sitting on our rears, Mary was out there. . . . She was looking at what young artists were up to." When the Bykert Gallery closed in 1976, Boone decided to abandon her painting to concentrate solely on art dealing. Discussing that choice with Lisbet Nelson in *Metropolitan Home,* Boone remarked, "It became very clear that art dealing was what I wanted. . . . I wouldn't miss painting as much." The inherent difficulties

of establishing a career as an independent art dealer did not faze Boone, she explained to Gluek, "because of those early training years at Bykert. I had confidence in what I was doing. By the time I opened my own gallery, I had met a number of artists and developed a group of collectors who trusted what I had to say." She sold paintings from her loft in Soho until she was able to organize a seven-member syndicate which supplied the funds she need to open her own gallery.

Boone's new establishment consisted of just two tiny rooms, but its address was one of the most prestigious in the art world—420 West Broadway. Her gallery was directly beneath Leo Castelli's, who is generally considered the most influential dealer in modern art. Boone opened with two artists: Gary Stephan, an established abstractionist, and Julian Schnabel, a confident beginner. According to Carey Lovelace in *Harper's,* Schnabel met Boone in 1976, in a Greenwich Village restaurant where he was working, and soon convinced her to visit his studio. Born in Brooklyn and raised in Texas, Schnabel had returned to New York City in the mid-seventies. He took jobs as a cook, while telling friends, "I'm going to be the greatest artist in the world." Lovelace describes his "heroically-sized canvases—featuring crude, meaty brushstrokes and encrusted with antlers, wooden beams, and shattered plates" as "brooding and bold in their imagery." They were unlike anything that Boone had ever seen. She described her first reaction to Haden-Guest: "I was struck by the incredible physicality of the paint. . . . It was lush. Holes were dug out of it. I was a bit nonplussed—both attracted and repelled. It wasn't what people were doing then. But I told him we would do something together."

With the dynamism that was becoming her trademark, Boone began promoting Schnabel. First, she brought many collectors to his studio to view his work. No sales were made, but his name began to circulate. Next, she staged a small show at her gallery. "By the time of his first exhibition, he'd already made two of the infamous plate paintings, which I had sold in 1978 for $4,500 apiece," she told Glueck. "But he was trained as a painter and I didn't want him to be seen as some kind of fetish object-maker. So at the first show, we had only oils on canvas." Unfortunately, the sheer size of Schnabel's work made it difficult to show it to advantage in Boone's tiny gallery. Therefore, after one more show there and one at the Dan Weinberg Gallery in San Francisco, Boone approached the venerable Leo Castelli about using his roomy gallery to stage a Schnabel exhibition.

Boone felt that Julian Schnabel merited Castelli's attention. The representative of almost every American artist of the 1960s, including Frank Stella, Robert Rauschenberg, Ellsworth Kelly and Andy Warhol, Castelli had found no new talent worthy of his backing during the 1970s. "Leo wanted new energy," Boone told Glueck, "and I frankly thought of my artists as the kind of people he's handled, young Stellas, young Rauschenbergs and so forth, with the potential of being truly great artists. I wanted them to be seen in the context of Leo's gallery." After seeing Schnabel's work, Castelli agreed to cooperate with the exhibition. It was a tremendous success, a complete sell-out before it opened. Getting Castelli's support for Schnabel's work was "a brilliant move" on Boone's part, art dealer Monique Knowlton told Nilson. "It's always tricky out there for a young, new gallery owner. But with Castelli behind an artist, its almost like a *Good Housekeeping* seal of approval."

With Castelli's cooperation and Schnabel's solid success, Boone's career was firmly established. She was able to open a second, larger gallery at 417 West Broadway, directly opposite her first, and she now represents twelve artists, including Matt Mullican, Ross Bleckner, David Salle, and Troy Brautuch. Roughly all her contemporaries, they represent the vanguard of the new artistic movement that is sometimes called "neo-expressionism" or "maximalism." Nilson states: "Boone's artists tend to share a brash, explicitly human energy whose underpinnings are as emotional and mysterious as they are intellectual and grounded in art history." "It is work that is as considered as it is intuitive," Boone told Nilson.

Boone's style as an art dealer is as unconventional as her painters' work. According to Lovelace, "The Old World-style dealer tries to create an ambience of silent prestige, and lets the forces of the marketplace work on their own to create an artist's reputation and price range." Boone, on the other hand, deliberately structured Schnabel's image—engineering sales to taste-setting art collectors to assure his reputation, listing the names of prestigious buyers at his first show, and spreading rumors that his work was scarce. Lovelace observes that Boone's approach is part of a trend: "A new generation of American artists has rejected the modernist notion of art as a 'spiritualism project' (in the words of Susan Sontag). Abandoning the elitist alienation that was the hallmark of their predecessors, they have thrown themselves wholeheartedly into the art market, a world increasingly embracing salesmanship and public relations. They are now consciously trying to create works that people will both enjoy and buy."

Boone's active salesmanship has certainly produced tangible results: at Schnabel's first show, his paintings were priced at $2,500; his work is now selling for as much as $75,000. But some critics attribute these high prices to Boone's talent for hype rather than Schnabel's artistry. According to Lovelace, New Museum director Martha Tucker said, "It's astonishing to me that the public is treating a thirty-one-year-old like he was an old master." And in a *New York Times* article, Hilton Kramer denounces Schnabel's work as "the pictorial equivalent of a junk-food binge." But such criticism does not ruffle Boone. "We *like* controversy," she told Haden-Guest, adding, "Even the most skeptical and disbelieving person I've brought [to Julian Schnabel's studio] has been changed. . . . The authenticity [of his paintings] is remarkable. They're gritty and passionate and completely committed. People who say they're invented are absurd." Nor is she disturbed by those who disapprove of her style as an art dealer. Her self-confidence is evident in her discussion with Nilson. "Every now and then," she remarked, "somebody will ask me, 'Aren't you glad that you're so successful?' I tell them I'm just beginning to hit my stride. I haven't come that far, compared to what I have to do." She detailed her ambitions to Haden-Guest: "I hope that in the next twenty-five years I will have shown as many great painters as Leo [Castelli]. . . . Pivotal figures! The best. I like heroic art."

"Whatever time may decide about her artists, and the way she has brought them to dramatic public attention, there is simply no denying the fact that she has enlivened the art scene, and brought a bit of true controversy back to it," concludes Wolff. "I'm very certain that Mary Boone will be around for a long, long time."

SOURCES:

PERIODICALS

Christian Science Monitor, May 19, 1983.
Harper's, July, 1983.
Life, May, 1982.
Metropolitan Home, June, 1982.
New York, April 19, 1982.
New York Times, October 18, 1981.
People, September 20, 1982.
Saturday Review, May, 1982.
Savvy, July, 1982.
Washington Post, May 20, 1983.

—*Sidelights by Joan E. Marecki*

Leon Botstein

1946-

PERSONAL: Born December 14, 1946, in Zurich, Switzerland; son of Charles (a physician) and Anne (a physician; maiden name, Wyszewianski) Botstein; married Jill Lundquist, 1970; married second wife, Barbara Haskell, 1982; children: (first marriage) Sarah, Abigail. *Education:* University of Chicago, B.A. (with honors), 1967; Harvard University, A.M., 1968, Ph.D., 1985.

ADDRESSES: Office—Bard College, Annandale-on-Hudson, N.Y. 12504.

OCCUPATION: College president.

CAREER: Harvard University, Cambridge, Mass., tutor in general education, 1968-69; Boston University, Boston, Mass., lecturer in history, 1969; New York City Board of Education, New York, N.Y., special assistant to the president, 1969-70; Franconia College, Franconia, N.H., president, 1970-75; Bard College, Annandale-on-Hudson, N.Y., president, 1975—, Simon's Rock of Bard College, Great Barrington, Mass., president, 1979—.

Adjunct professor, Union Graduate School, Yellow Springs, Ohio, 1973-75; member of Commission on Independent Colleges and Universities, 1979—; member of board of directors, Franklin Delano Roosevelt Four Freedoms Foundation, Arts Coalition of the Empire State, and Albert Schweitzer Center; consultant, National Endowment for the Humanities. Director of Interferon Sciences, Inc. Violinist; principal conductor, White Mountain Music and Art Festival, 1973-75; guest conductor, Hudson Valley Philharmonic, 1981—; conductor or guest conductor of many other orchestras, including Chamber Orchestra of the University of Chicago, Harvard-Radcliffe Orchestra, Boston Medical Orchestra, and London Philharmonic.

MEMBER: Association of Episcopal Colleges (chairman, 1982—), *Harper's* Magazine Foundation (chairman of board, 1983—), New York Institute for the Humanities (former chairman).

AWARDS, HONORS: Annual award, National Conference of Christians and Jews, 1975; Rockefeller fellow, Aspen Institute for Humanistic Studies, 1978; D.H.L., Cedar Crest College, 1980; Professional Achievement Citation, University of Chicago Alumni Association, 1984.

WRITINGS: Music and Its Public: Habits of Listening and the Crisis of Musical Modernism in Vienna, 1870-1914, a book, as yet unpublished. Contributor of articles to numerous newspapers, magazines, and professional journals, including *New York Times, Harper's, New Republic, Partisan Review, Journal of Modern History, Chronicle of Higher Education, Salmagundi*, and *Musical Quarterly*.

SIDELIGHTS: Leon Botstein holds the distinction of having been appointed a college president at the age of twenty-three when, in 1970, Franconia College, in Franconia, New Hampshire, selected him to become its fourth president in seven years. The choice of Botstein, the youngest college president to serve in that capacity at the time of his appointment—and perhaps the youngest ever in the history of American higher education—symbolized an unprecedented move at a period of turmoil in undergraduate education.

The rise of student power, manifested in the demands for curricular relevance and protest against the Vietnam War, had unnerved administrators nationwide and upset the American public. As new students with new ideas arrived on the nation's campuses in the 1960s, the tranquility of the 1950s had given way to a generation nurtured on the dreams of President John F. Kennedy's New Frontier, the Peace Corps, the civil rights movement, the liberating influence of rock and roll, the ideal of a counterculture free of adult repression, the belief in mass demonstration and confrontation as a means of political action, and the inevitable disillusionment brought on by political assassination and a prolonged unpopular war. It was within this cultural climate of upheaval and social disarray that the small New England private college took the radical step of making Leon Botstein its president. "Botstein is an experiment, perhaps the most interesting of this decade," a Franconia alumnus told *Newsweek.*

Born in Zurich, Switzerland, on December 14, 1946, the son of physicians, Botstein is the product of the European Jewish intellectual tradition transplanted to the United States. He is a graduate of New York City's High School of Music and Art and holds a bachelor of arts degree in history with special honors from the University of Chicago. He received his graduate education in history at Harvard University, where he earned a master of arts and Ph.D.

Social historian, violinist, and conductor, Botstein has the rare ability to be intellectually proficient in two distinct disciplines—history and music. In describing his intellectual state of mind as a teenager and how it was positively reshaped at the University of Chicago, Botstein told Noah benShea in a *Center* magazine interview: "When I emerged from high school in New York, I was a highly verbal, oversophisticated, undereducated, arrogant individual. When I went to the University of Chicago I was confronted—supportively—with the pretense of my own intellectuality. . . . Under the influence of several faculty members I developed a genuine interest in broad historical, political, social, and intellectual issues on a theoretical level."

Special assistant to Joseph Monserrat, head of the New York City Board of Education, when he was appointed president of Franconia, Botstein, with little administrative experience, inherited a situation that would have distressed the most seasoned academic administrator. (His father-in-law, a member of the Franconia board of trustees, tried to persuade him not to take the job.) Botstein was picked for the promise of his academic and intellectual leadership and his impressively high energy level. The overriding theme of both his presidencies has been to bring "a common and coherent educational program" to the institutions he has led, something that he sees as "rare among college presidents." He believes the task of most college presidents is "a managerial and preservative function."

Botstein has emerged as the leading spokesman of his generation in interpreting the most difficult educational issues facing America, and he has done it with an acute sensitivity to the complexity and contradictions in contemporary values and beliefs. He is a perceptive interpreter of the liberal educational and cultural experiments of the 1960s, and has, on occasion, set the record straight against attacks from the political right. His obvious strength as a college president is the intellectual leadership he has brought to the job at hand. The style, substance, and spirit of his thinking is modernist and free of the educational jargon that beclouds the ideas of many college presidents. He frequently has his articles appear in popular and liberal journals, among them the *New Republic, Harper's, Change, Partisan Review,* and the *New York Times Magazine.* Botstein has functioned as much as an astute and adept cultural critic as an educational theorist.

For conservative critics, Franconia was a convenient example of the excesses of higher education in the 1960s. It began as a junior college in 1963 before evolving into a four-year

school in 1965 and had granted only twenty-five bachelor's degrees when Botstein took over. Located in the ski country of northern New Hampshire and housed in a former resort hotel, Franconia College, with its unstructured academic programs and upper-middle-class students (many of whom had failed at traditional institutions) troubled the 500 local residents, whose worst fears were confirmed by a state police drug raid in 1968. Adding fuel to the fire was the subsequent series of exposes by the archconservative Manchester *Union Leader,* published by the late William Loeb. The newspaper stories were disastrous for Franconia; the college's creditors panicked, and the school was forced to file for voluntary bankruptcy.

Botstein faced a college in debt, a depleted student body, low faculty morale, and an unaccredited academic program. A Franconia trustee described the college this way in a *New Yorker* profile: "The place was a shambles at the time. The outgoing administration had left almost an impenetrable mess." Another trustee, a resident of Franconia, summed up in a *New Yorker* interview the impact of the college on the lives of the townspeople as one of culture shock: "The college has brought to the town the first long hair, the first miniskirts, the first of everything like that in these parts. . . . We were too damned experimental." A *Time* report called the atmosphere "somewhere between *Alice's Restaurant* and *Alice in Wonderland.*"

Surprisingly, one of Botstein's first acts was to banish dogs from the campus. "Fifty unkempt dogs running around was just too much, so I got rid of them all," he told a *Time* reporter. In the spirit of playfulness and self-mockery, the students wrote a cheer for their few intercollegiate soccer and rugby games: "Franconia College is our school! No dogs, no cats our only rule!" On a more serious side, Botstein recruited new faculty members, implemented fiscal austerity to pay the overdue bills, and secured Federal grants to build three dormitories, a student union, an auditorium, and a new library. Enrollment increased as Franconia's reputation improved, and Botstein even managed to repair the damage between the college and the townspeople. Most importantly, he preserved Franconia's spirit of experimentation and student participation in the life of the college while improving its academic rigor. Reported *Time:* "Students must [now] demonstrate competence in their fields to a faculty committee in order to receive a degree." The *Time* article went on to say that Botstein "had little administrative experience when he acquired the distinction of being perhaps the youngest president in American higher education, but improbably enough, he has turned out to be a smashing success."

A representative of a generation that came to prominence as college students in the 1960s, Botstein, who was born early in the baby boom, has been in a unique position to interpret his generation. In a 1972 viewpoint article in *Change,* he discussed the then recent vogue in experimentation and innovation, saying that it reflected "a widespread dissatisfaction with existing goals, structures and practices in higher education." Botstein argued that four causal factors accounted for the need for educational reform: the discontent of students, the formulation of "new social and ethical values," higher education's desire to "keep pace with modernity," and the rise of new student populations—

especially adults and minorities—with different needs from the traditional student age group.

In his *Change* article, Botstein captured the campus mood between 1967 and 1972 and the inevitable conflict that accounted for student unrest and demands for change: "Over the past five years a sizeable portion of the traditionally college bound population has lost the momentum which carried previous generations of students through traditional structures toward established educational and vocational goals. Most of the students and potential students who constitute this group are from the middle and upper middle class. They have become cynical about the intrinsic value and utility of intellectual pursuits as represented by the university and college. Furthermore, the bleak economic and political situation has all but obliterated the financial incentives and promises of societal usefulness which have in the past rendered attractive the classic vocations into which college graduates enter. . . . Evident among individuals in this group of students is loss of motivation, rejection of bourgeois social conventions, an eventual separation from the institutions of contemporary society (the city, the family), alienation and the resultant turn inward, often into other worldly pseudomystical pursuits."

Eight years later, writing in the *New Republic*, Botstein noted that the "Weimar analogy," popular in the 1960s, had been replaced with a "Vienna analogy." American society had reversed its assumptions about itself: "Weimar like radicalism itself, is absent from the campus culture. Our futurist, often optimistic, enthusiasms of the 1960s have lapsed into apathy. Even the tame heir of 1960s political activism, the post-Watergate vigilance against political corruption, has dissipated into political withdrawal and *ennui* in 1980. The styles of modern culture in art, dress, and architecture of the 1960s have become transmuted into varieties of nostalgia."

Botstein was selected the fourteenth president of Bard College in 1975 at the age of twenty-eight. (Franconia College closed in 1978.) Founded in 1860 as St. Stephen's College and located on a 600-acre campus in Annandale-on-Hudson, New York, Bard College had a reputation in the 1960s and early 1970s as a place for drug use and one of a select number of alternative schools responsive to student pressures for more freedom. Historically, Bard was founded to send men to the Episcopal Church's General Theological Seminary in New York to prepare for the priesthood. In 1919 Bard's new president, Dr. Bernard Iddings Bell, initiated an era of progressive educational reforms; in 1928,

Leon Botstein walks the Bard College campus with the college's former vice-president, David Wagner. UPI/Bettmann Newsphotos.

Bard became affiliated with Columbia University and six years later officially changed its name to Bard College after John Bard, whose estate was the site of St. Stephens. "Then, in the nineteen-thirties," Botstein told interviewer benShea, "Columbia Teachers College sent a man named Donald Tewksbury, and Bard became a kind of Deweyite progressive institution with several important features. One was an absence of a common curriculum. Another was a high premium on individuality, with each student fashioning his own curriculum." Bard broke with Columbia in 1944 over the issue of admitting women.

During his tenure at Bard, Botstein has emerged as a leading advocate for the reform of the undergraduate curriculum. He has written effectively and persuasively in the national media on what he calls the "crisis of literacy": the woeful inadequacy of the American student in writing, speaking, reading, and thinking skills. A dramatic shift had taken place in a very short time. "The problem is not that students, like their predecessors of ten years ago, crave relevance; the problem is that they are no longer able to recognize relevance," Botstein opined in a 1979 *Harper's* article. When faculties of select Eastern universities were debating curricular reform, Botstein, in a 1976 *Change* article, advanced the idea that past successful models were inappropriate, given the fundamental change in the world and students. The content of any new program must be one "that reflects a contemporary ideal of an educated individual." New models of liberal learning, argued Botstein, must cover science and technology, history, and the arts. "The play element, as entertainment and as high culture," said Botstein, "requires universal and serious consideration. The aesthetic dimension in life and the arts themselves has yet to find its proper place in schemes of liberal education." These changes would incorporate the traditional humanities curriculum: "English, literature, languages, the study of high culture—all of these facets could be added and woven into the historical and artistic portion of the curriculum."

Bard has received a great deal of attention for its emphasis on writing skills. First-year Bard students report three weeks early to attend the Workshop in Language and Thinking as a preparatory step for their undergraduate career. In 1982, with $520,000 of funding from the Ford Foundation and the Booth Ferris Foundation, Bard established the Institute for Writing and Thinking, which holds workshops and conferences for high-school teachers on how to teach writing. First-year students are also required to enroll in a year-long seminar that examines distinct historical periods such as Athens of the fifth century B.C. and Europe from 1750 to 1850. (Botstein himself teaches in the seminar program.)

In 1979, Bard acquired Simon's Rock in Great Barrington, Massachusetts, an early admission's college that enrolls approximately 300 students who have completed the tenth or eleventh grades. At Simon's Rock, students complete a two-year associate degree program and then have the option of earning a bachelor's degree at Simon's Rock or Bard, or enrolling in any baccalaureate degree college of their choice. The combining of high school and college in a general education course of study has its roots in Robert Hutchins' *The Higher Learning in America* (1936), a book Botstein favorably reevaluated in a 1978 *Center* magazine article. Early completion of high school and college admission was one of nine proposals to improve American public education

that Botstein advanced in a 1983 *New York Times Magazine* piece. Among his suggestions were higher salaries for teachers, teacher recertification programs, respect for teachers as professionals, recruiting the talents of retired professionals, and reforming the teaching of English and social studies. Botstein concluded: "It is only a nationwide reschooling of America, led by all political parties and all Americans, and financed by all sectors, particularly the Federal Government, that can dispel the specter of the nation drifting toward mediocrity, uniformity and passivity."

Botstein has established himself as an authoritative voice in debating and criticizing contemporary cultural issues. Not only has he written provocatively on reassessing David Reisman's *The Lonely Crowd* and the thinking of Hannah Arendt, whom he greatly admires, but he has produced a series of essays on music that has a depth and range equal to his views on education. In a number of articles published in the *New Republic* and *Harper's*, Botstein examined the future of the piano in light of the deaths of Artur Rubinstein and Glenn Gould, the lack of new music programming by major symphonic orchestras, and the career of Leonard Bernstein. These essays are illustrative of the liberally educated mind in action, erudite in cultural references and conclusions.

Despite an obviously busy schedule, Botstein finds time to perform and conduct music. He is guest conductor of the Hudson Valley Philharmonic and co-conductor of its chamber orchestra series, concentrating on twentieth-century American music. While at Franconia, he founded and was principal conductor of the White Mountain Festival of the Arts. Botstein is scheduled to conduct the London Philharmonic during the 1986-87 season, a major accomplishment for someone who is not a regular member of the international conducting circuit. He also regularly performs with the music faculties of Vassar and Bard colleges on their chamber music programs.

Education remains a volatile issue in the decade of the 1980s as it was in the 1960s, and a number of reports by leading authorities have been written to refocus the debate on the problems affecting American education. One such report, *To Reclaim a Legacy*, by William J. Bennett, former head of the National Endowment for the Humanities and now Secretary of Education, was critiqued by Botstein in a 1985 *New Republic* article. Botstein pinpointed the heart of the conflict between liberal and conservative educators in the battle over curricular reform: "The faculties of American universities are too smart not to recognize that the intent beneath the explicit desire to 'civilize' today's students is the attempt to teach the superiority and the absolute value of particular ideas and notions of political and social conduct in the aftermath of the 1960s. But the teaching of the humanities, if the tradition has any meaning at all, is about criticism and critical inquiry, not mere civility. It is about empowering a new generation to question, to change, to argue, to dispute, and even to be thoroughly disagreeable." He continued: "Education is by its essence conservative, for we can only transmit seriously what we value and know. The central questions—unlike their solutions—rarely change. We must correct the political drift of the Bennett report and build on its basic intent. Students deserve the chance to engage great issues, minds, and texts."

The headline for a 1985 *New York Times* article proclaimed "Bard and Botstein: A College Success," much like the *Time* conclusion twelve years earlier. Among Botstein's numerous achievements, the article listed his "$47.5 million fund-raising campaign that has already produced $16 million." Overall, said one Bard alumnus, now a professor at the school, "he's done everything we could ever have hoped he would do for this college." Through the years, Botstein has evolved from a twenty-three year-old college president— regarded as something of an oddity or, at best, a social experiment—into one of the most highly respected educators and educational theorists in the country. And, in a moment of self-reflection, he told *New York Times* interviewer Gene I. Maeroff, "As I lose the peculiarity of being extremely young, I don't engender either the curiosity or envy which had interfered with my relations with people."

SOURCES:

PERIODICALS

Center, April-May, 1977.

Change, April, 1972, December, 1976, May, 1978.

Christian Science Monitor, November 30, 1984.

Education Digest, March, 1984.

Esquire, December, 1984.

Harper's, September, 1979, June, 1981, May, 1983.

New Republic, December 20, 1980, November 4, 1981, May 21, 1984.

Newsweek, August 3, 1970, September 14, 1981.

New Yorker, May 29, 1972.

New York Times, June 11, 1985.

New York Times Magazine, June 5, 1983.

Partisan Review, July, 1981.

Time, July 13, 1970, April 23, 1973.

U.S. News and World Report, July 5, 1982.

—Sidelights by Jon Saari

Herbert Wayne Boyer

1936-

PERSONAL: Born July 10, 1936, in southwestern Pennsylvania; married, 1959; wife's name, Grace; children: two sons. *Education:* St. Vincent College, Latrobe, Pa., B.A., 1958; University of Pittsburgh, Ph.D., 1963.

ADDRESSES: *Office*—Department of Biochemistry and Biophysics, HSE 1504, University of California, San Francisco, Calif. 94143.

OCCUPATION: Biochemist; entrepreneur.

CAREER: University of California, San Francisco, 1966—, began as assistant professor, professor of biochemistry 1976—. Investigator at Howard Hughes Medical Institute, 1976—. Co-founder of Genentech, Inc., San Francisco, Calif., 1976, vice-president and director, beginning 1976, consultant, 1980—.

MEMBER: American Academy of Arts and Sciences (fellow), American Society of Microbiology.

AWARDS, HONORS: USPHS postdoctoral fellowship at Yale University, 1963-66; V. D. Mattai Award from Roche Institute, 1977; Albert and Mary Lasker Award for basic medical research, 1980; D.Sc. from St. Vincent College, 1981.

WRITINGS: Former member of editorial board, *Biochemistry.*

AP/Wide World Photos

SIDELIGHTS: In December, 1980, University of California, San Francisco, professor Herbert Wayne Boyer and his colleague, Stanley N. Cohen of Stanford University, obtained the first patent in the field of recombinant dioxyribonucleic acid (DNA), the molecule that controls the mechanism of biological inheritance. The patent, entitled "Process for Producing Biologically Functioning Molecular Chimeras," covers a technique developed by the two scientists during the 1970s by which genetic material is transmitted to bacterial organisms via a plasmid (an adhering loop of DNA extracted from a severed DNA molecule). This procedure is commonly known as gene splicing.

Boyer and a handful of other recombinant DNA researchers developed the capabilities of this procedure in stages. Initially, their efforts focused on inserting insulin genes that had been spliced to plasmids into a bacterial strain called E. coli. Once attached to the bacteria, the genes reproduced themselves along with the E. coli. Then, in 1973, Boyer and a research partner, Robert Helling, (concurrently with, yet independently of, Stanley N. Cohen and Annie Chang of Stanford), succeeded in composing DNA chimeras—that is, DNA formed from genes taken from two different organisms. These chimeras not only reproduced themselves in E.

coli but expressed traits controlled by the genes from each source.

A further advance occurred during the mid-1970s, when researchers, including the team that Boyer headed in San Francisco, transmitted an artificial genetic message to bacterial cells. Using plasmids spliced with a synthesized section of DNA called a lactose operator, they were able to trigger lactose production by the bacteria. The lactose operator is not a gene and does not produce new molecules as genes do. Rather, as Harold M. Schmeck, Jr., explained in his *New York Times* report of this development, the lactose operator acts as a signal for letting the previously existing bacterial gene for beta galactosidase production be turned on. "Success of the experiments," concluded Schmeck, "was demonstrated when the cells began to produce beta galactosidase." Quoted in the *New York Times,* Boyer responded to this success, and to similar developments in genetic synthesis following closely upon it by predicting in August, 1976: "The whole technology of synthesizing genes is going to blossom quite rapidly now." And two months later he stated in a university release cited in the *New York Times:* "We've gone out of the area of basic science into the area of practical application," and, according to Schmeck, Boyer "could foresee, within a few years, development of bacterial 'factories' for the production of substances like insulin and pituitary hormone.''

In addition to scientific developments, 1976 heralded the beginning of Boyer's commercial venture, Genentech. Early in the year, Boyer was approached by a young financier named Robert Swanson, who worked for the San Francisco venture-capitalist firm Kleiner and Perkins. Swanson proposed that he and Boyer form a company for manufacturing and marketing commercial quantities of substances produced through gene splicing. Boyer agreed, interested, according to *Time* magazine, "in getting the new technology out of the lab and using it to do some good.'' So the two each invested five hundred dollars in their new firm, Genentech, whose name stands for "genetic-engineering technology.'' Swanson became Genentech's president, while Boyer assumed the posts of vice-president and director. As such, according to *Time,* he "pinpointed promising areas of exploitation and, in his words, 'made sure that the scientists [on Genentech's staff] were being taken care of and their particular value recognized.' '' Boyer also continued to perform research at the University of California, San Francisco.

The year after Genentech's formation brought still another advance in Boyer's recombinant DNA research. Prior to this time, Boyer and his fellow scientists had been able to implant a substance's genes in bacteria, where the genes would replicate themselves. By 1977 they could insert genetic information into the bacterial culture that would instruct the bacteria to reproduce an actual substance, somatostatin, which is normally produced in animal and human brains and helps control the body's production of insulin and human growth hormone.

Remarking that one of "the principal leaders in the work'' on somatostatin was Boyer, "whose team earlier incorporated the gene for making insulin into bacteria,'' Schmeck stressed the significance of the induced production of somatostatin by distinguishing it from the gene-splicing feats that preceded it. While "the insulin gene was reproduced in the bacteria,'' explained Schmeck, in the *New York Times,* "it did not actually make the bacteria produce insulin. In the somatostatin research the scientists did achieve production of the substance by the bacteria.''

The production of somatostatin by bacteria was a turning point in recombinant DNA research, signalling the arrival of the day that Boyer had forecast, according to Boyce Rensberger in a 1976 article for the *New York Times,* when "scientists will be able to synthesize genes that produce medically useful substances, such as hormones,. . . and produce harvestable quantities of the substance.'' And on December 1, 1977, Genentech announced that it expected "to use bacteria to manufacture a human brain hormone called somatostatin by the middle of next year, and human insulin within a year,'' reported Victor K. McElheny in the *New York Times.* At the time of this announcement, insulin had already been used for years in treating diabetes, and somatostatin, which had only recently been linked to the bodily production of insulin and human growth hormone,

had been singled out by medical researchers for its potential use as a treatment for diabetes or growth problems.

During the next few years, Genentech, its research, and its projected goals for manufacturing "medically useful substances'' attracted a great deal of public attention. Shortly after the company's inception, financiers such as Swanson's employer, Kleiner and Perkins, invested large amounts of money in Genentech. And when Genentech offered shares of stock for public purchase in October, 1980, it became a stock market sensation. According to Joel Gurin and Nancy E. Pfund, reporting for the *Nation* magazine, the sale of Genentech stock "was greeted on Wall Street, in the words of one newspaper, as 'the most spectacular new stock offering in at least a decade.' The stock began at $35 a share and soared as high as $88 on the first day of trading.'' Gurin and Pfund further noted that "the company had not put a single product on the market; the excitement was based solely on its imagined future promise.'' And as it turned out, the public's enthusiasm for gene-splicing potentials was not unfounded. Genentech's "prototype bacterial factories have been extremely busy,'' reported *Time* in January, 1981. "They have already produced half a dozen different substances, including insulin, human growth hormone and interferon, the antiviral agent being investigated as a cancer cure.''

In contrast to the warm reception of Genentech by investors was the disapproval expressed by many of Boyer's fellow scientists and educators, who felt that Boyer had sullied his reputation as a "pure scientist'' by using the results of his academic research at the University of California to gain profits through Genentech. Boyer, whose stock in Genentech was by 1981 worth some forty million dollars, discounts this censure, stating, as quoted in *Time*: "If you have a strong conviction that what you're doing is right, then you can stand up against a lot of criticism.'' He maintains, reported *People* magazine: "I violated no rules or laws, and if someone wants to take a moral stand about how pure science should be,. . . I'd like him to define what is science and what is pure science.'' Moreover, as a *Time* article explained, Boyer argues that "the full benefits of genetic engineering—say, the curing of diseases—can never come out of a university setting alone. 'Business is more efficient, ' he says. 'It will bring benefits to the public much faster.' '' As for this 1980 patent, which he shares with Stanley N. Cohen and for which he has also come under fire as a profiteer, both Boyer and Cohen have signed their patent royalties over to the University of California, San Francisco and Stanford University, respectively.

SOURCES:

PERIODICALS

Nation, November 22, 1980.
New York Times, August 29, 1976, October 28, 1976, November 3, 1977, December 2, 1977, December 7, 1977, June 18, 1980, November 20, 1980, December 6, 1980.
People, December 29, 1980.
Time, January 5, 1981, March 9, 1981.

—Sketch by Lori R. Clemens

Willie L. Brown

1934-

PERSONAL: Full name, Willie Lewis Brown, Jr.; born March 20, 1934, in Mineola, Tex.; son of Willie Lewis (a Pullman porter) and Minnie Collins (a domestic housecleaner; maiden name, Boyd) Brown; married Blanche Vitero, 1957 (separated); children: Susan Elizabeth, Robin Elaine, Michael Elliott. *Education:* San Francisco State College (now University), B.A., 1955; Hastings College of Law, J.D., 1958. *Politics:* Democrat. *Religion:* Protestant.

ADDRESSES: Home—515 Van Ness Ave., San Francisco, Calif. 94102. *Office*—Office of the Speaker, California Assembly, State Capitol, Sacramento, Calif. 95714.

OCCUPATION: Attorney; politician.

CAREER: Admitted to the Bar of the State of California and, in 1964, to the Bar of the U.S. Supreme Court. As a youth, picked berries, peanuts, potatoes, and cotton; while in college, worked as a janitor and shoe salesman; Brown, Dearman & Smith (law firm), San Francisco, Calif., partner, 1959—; former college law instructor; California State Assembly, Sacramento, assemblyman, 1964-80, speaker of the assembly, 1980—.

Chairman of California Assembly Committee on Ways and Means, 1971-74, and of Joint Committee on Siting of Teaching Hospitals, 1973-74; vice-chairman of Select Committee on Health Manpower; member of Committee on Efficiency and Cost Control, Committee on Elections and Reapportionment, Committee on Government Administration, Governor's Committee on Aging, Joint Committee on Master Plan for Higher Education, and Select Committee on Deepwater Ports. California representative to Credentials Committee, National Democratic Convention, 1968; co-chairperson of California delegation to National Democratic Convention, 1972, and of California delegation to National Black Political Convention, 1972; delegate to Democratic National Mid-Term Conference, 1974; member of Democratic National Committee, 1977—. *Military service*: Served in U.S. National Guard.

MEMBER: National Association for the Advancement of Colored People, League of Women Voters, National Planned Parenthood Association, Chinese for Affirmative Action, San Francisco Planning and Urban Renewal Association, San Francisco Aid Retarded Children, Sunset Parkside Education and Action Committee, Fillmore Merchants and Improvement Association, Planning Association for Richmond, Haight Ashbury Neighborhood Council, Phi Alpha Delta, Alpha Phi Alpha.

AWARDS, HONORS: Outstanding Freshman Legislator Press Award, 1965; Children's Lobby Award for outstanding legislative efforts, 1974; named Leader of the Future by *Time* magazine, 1974.

UPI/Bettmann Newsphotos

SIDELIGHTS: The self-proclaimed "Ayatollah" of California government, Willie L. Brown rose from a childhood of poverty in Texas to become the first black speaker of the California Assembly and the most powerful Democrat in that state's politics in the middle eighties.

A flamboyant, eloquent, and savvy politician, Brown makes no secret of his quest for power and fame on a regional—and national—basis. As he explained to a San Francisco high school class, as quoted in the *New York Times* in 1984, "The speaker is the judge, jury and executioner in the Assembly." Brown told the *Times* that his power stems from "the ability to put numbers together, to put the appropriate number of votes together on any issue."

But others say Brown's style, as much as his legislative expertise, was instrumental in bringing him power. "Willie has great oratorical skills," fellow Democratic Assemblyman Mike Roos told *Ebony* magazine in 1984. "There's Willie, then there's everybody else. He's playing the game at a higher level than the rest."

Brown garnered national attention during the 1984 Democratic National Convention, which was held in his home town, San Francisco. He hosted a $300,000 party for 15,000 party VIPs and guests on a pier that was larger than the convention hall itself. The bash, entitled "Oh What a Night," was claimed to be the largest party in the party-loving city's history and featured ten stages for entertainers, 400 cases of California wine, and replicas of the city's most famous tourist attractions. It also solidified Brown's position as unchallenged star of California's Democratic Party. "I wanted to show people that no town can throw a party like San Francisco," Brown told the Associated Press. "And I wanted to show them that no man can throw a party like Willie Brown."

Brown is a man given to collecting $1,800 Brioni suits (his closet holds 40 of them), expensive Porsche sports cars, and saddle horses. He hobnobs with Hollywood celebrities and regularly appears in local gossip columns as an escort for attractive woman, including actress Margot Kidder. In 1984, he made *Ms.* magazine's list of the ten sexiest men in America. "If you can't wear it, drive it or make love to it," he told *Newsweek* in 1984, "I don't want it."

That same year he told *Ebony* that his opulent lifestyle enhances his image with reporters and constituents. "The media love it," he said, "I make good copy. You see, politicians are supposed to drive Fords or Chevys or Plymouths. You're expected to have a dog, three kids and a wife. You're supposed to wear white shirts and white shirts only, and wing-tip shoes. I enjoy my lifestyle and was never going to accept any of those rules. It turned out to be an incredible plus with the constituents. Most people who vote for you really don't want you to be anything but yourself. They want you to perform well and represent them well, but they do not require that you look like them or anybody else."

His rise to power did not come easily, Brown was raised in poverty in Mineola, Tex., a town of about 4,000 people outside Dallas. His father, a Pullman porter, abandoned the family when Willie was four. He and his four brothers and sisters were raised by their grandmother while their mother worked as a domestic cleaner. "I can remember using cardboard for the bottom of my shoes," he told *Ebony.* "I can remember the days of being the fourth person on the list for water for the No. 3 washtub. I remember the outdoor toilets, having to raise half of what I ate, and having meat only once a week. There's no reason why anyone should be subjected to that."

At eight, Brown worked the fields picking berries, cotton, peanuts, and potatoes. He also studied hard, he recalls, and had a vague notion of being a mathematics teacher because, he told *Ebony.* "The only groovy people I ever met or admired were math professors."

The day he graduated from Mineola Colored High School, Brown moved to San Francisco to live with an uncle, who was a gambler. Brown worked as a janitor and shoe salesman to support his way through San Francisco State College, where he first became interested in politics. In 1952, he worked on Adlai Stevenson's presidential campaign. He also joined the Young Democrats and became an officer in the local NAACP.

He calls his decision to go to law school "a total fluke." When a friend enrolled at the Hastings College of Law, Brown tagged along, wound up enrolling, and graduated as president of the class of 1958.

Brown then built a lucrative legal practice largely based on defending prostitutes and pimps. His street clientele later would be among the first contributors to his political campaigns. He told *Newsweek* that he decided to enter politics at twenty-eight when he was discriminated against while trying to buy a home in a fashionable San Francisco neighborhood. In 1962, he ran for the State Assembly against a twenty-three-year veteran and lost by 600 votes. Two years later he ran for the same seat and won.

Over the next sixteen years, Brown sponsored more than 140 bills that became California law. Among them were measures calling for tax and other financial benefits for the elderly, consumer auto insurance protection, new birth certificates for transsexuals, renter protection, improved safety for highway patrolmen, and state recognition of Martin Luther King's birthday as a legal holiday. In 1975, after seven years of trying, he convinced fellow lawmakers to pass a bill legalizing any sexual activities between consenting adults.

In 1980, on his second try, Brown was elected speaker. As presiding officer of the Assembly, he appoints all committee heads and members, allots staff and office space, has frequent and direct contact with the governor's office, controls a $40 million budget, and serves on all legislative committees. He won by forging a coalition of twenty-eight Republicans and twenty-three Democrats—ten more votes than were needed to win.

Soon after being elected, however, Republicans attacked him as overly partisan. "Willie Brown was supposed to be the reform measure," Assembly Republican leader Robert Naylor told *Newsweek.* "Obviously that didn't work." In 1984, Naylor and his GOP colleagues pushed a state ballot measure to restructure the Legislature and curtail the speaker's power. Voters approved the proposition by a fifty-three to forty-seven percent margin. But a state court knocked down the measure after Brown and other Democratic leaders filed suit, charging the changes invaded the Legislature's prerogative to set its own rules. "The streets are littered with the bleached bones of Republicans who have tried to beat Willie Brown," he boasted to the *New York Times.*

He also maintained that the ballot move—as well as other attacks on him—were basically racist in nature. "There is an unspoken conspiracy in this country to destroy blacks who move into positions of power," he told *Ebony.* "The standards for me are much higher than those for any other person who has held my spot—twice as high."

Brown claims he tries to head off such attacks by overpaying his taxes, refusing use of a state car, and sending a few hundred dollars a year to the state for use of its credit cards. Still, critics accuse him of using his legislative power for personal gain. Brown maintains a lucrative law practice, and his clients have included Neiman Marcus, Joseph E. Seagram & Sons, Southern Pacific, a Federal Reserve Bank, and major real estate developers. He told the *New York Times* that questions of conflict of interest are fair, but that "Persons I represent and the matters they ask me to support for them clearly have to be respectable. . . . My standard for myself allows me to be investigated by any authority whatsoever and walk away without a glove having been laid on Willie Brown."

In 1984, a complaint about Brown's corporate connections spurred efforts by the state's Fair Political Practices Commission to tighten up California's ethics code for lawyer-legislators. "The speaker is very effective at operating within the loopholes," FPPC Chairman Dan Stanford told *Newsweek.*

Brown continues to support controversial legislative issues. He wants to legalize the growing of up to three marijuana plants, saying it would help take the profit out of the drug trade. He would like to see casino gambling legalized in California, and in 1976 he briefly served as a hired advocate for Resorts International, the casino hotel firm.

Brown also endorses public financing of political campaigns, even though California's current system grants him great power over fundraising. Under the state's long-time policy, the speaker receives donations from individuals and groups interested in legislation and then divides the money among his supporters in the Legislature. The system allows Brown to dole out several million dollars a year, making him easily the biggest single contributor and fundraiser for state legislative candidates.

The system was designed by former Assembly Speaker Jess Unruh, the godfather of California Democrats and current state treasurer. Brown came to Sacramento in 1965 and voted against Unruh's certain re-election as speaker, thus starting his legislative career in the doghouse. But now Unruh speaks highly of Brown. "Willie's an incredibly gifted, able guy," Unruh told *Newsweek*. "Under that surface of flamboyance is a pretty good human being."

Brown gets no exercise beyond riding his horses and sleeps just three or four hours a night. His schedule is so tight, according to *Ebony*, that it is planned up to three months in advance. He has been rumored as a potential candidate for San Francisco mayor, should that job open up. He terms the post "a glamour job," comparable only to the mayoralty of New York City, but told the San Francisco *Enquirer* that he has no intention of challenging incumbent Dianne Feinstein.

Rather, he told *Ebony*, he intends to stay on as speaker: "It's important that I perform well in this position so that successive racial minorities, whether they be black, Hispanic or whatever, will be judged and treated on merit alone and nothing will be taken away from or required of them that is not required of any other person holding this office. I'm trying to break the barrier, the assumptions and the stereotypes by performing well. The system ought to be designed to create a level playing field for all of us. That's my goal."

SOURCES:

PERIODICALS

Detroit Free Press, July 16, 1984.
Ebony, April, 1981, August, 1984.
Los Angeles Times, May 27, 1984.
Ms., September, 1984.
New Republic, October 3, 1983.
New York Times, June 16, 1984, December 2, 1984.
Newsweek, August 1, 1983, June 11, 1984.
Politics Today, July 1979.
San Francisco Chronicle, July 16, 1984.
Time, December 28, 1981.
Washington Monthly, February, 1985.

—Sidelights by Glen Macnow

Yul Brynner

1920(?)-1985

OBITUARY NOTICE: Original name, Taidje Khan; born July 11, 1920 (some sources say 1915 or 1917), on Sakhalin Island, U.S.S.R.; died of complications of lung cancer, October 10, 1985, in New York Hospital-Cornell Medical Center, New York, N.Y. American actor, director, photographer, musician, author, acrobat, radio broadcaster, and political activist. Yul Brynner was most widely recognized for his role as the King of Siam in the Rodgers and Hammerstein musical "The King and I," in which he gave 4,625 performances during his career. The portrayal won him an Antoinette Perry (Tony) Award in 1952, an Academy Award in 1957, and a special Tony in 1985. His performing career began in France when he left school at the age of thirteen and became a circus trapeze acrobat. After a serious accident grounded him, he supported himself as a singer and guitarist and eventually turned to acting. A role in Shakespeare's "Twelfth Night" brought him to America in 1941.

World War II work as a radio announcer and commentator for the U.S. Government Office of War Information interrupted Brynner's performing career, but he returned to the theatre after the war and made his Broadway debut in "Lute Song" in early 1946. He won a Donaldson Award for best debut performance for what critic Howard Barnes called "an extraordinarily honest and restrained characterization" of an Oriental prince. He toured the United States with the show for a year, appeared in the London musical "Dark Eyes," and returned to America in 1948 to direct television shows, reportedly becoming one of television's highest paid directors. In 1951 he accepted the part of the king in "The King and I," on his way to becoming a theatre legend.

An avid photographer, Brynner took hundreds of pictures of the cast and settings of "The King and I" when it was being filmed, some of which later appeared in *Life* magazine. He was also active with the U.S. High Commission for Refugees, making documentary films for the organization and publishing a book, *Bring Forth the Children*, in 1960. In the words of actor Robert Vaughn, Brynner was "a unique and extraordinary personality."

SOURCES:

BOOKS

Current Biography, H.W. Wilson, 1956, November, 1985.
International Motion Picture Almanac, Quigley, 1985.

AP/Wide World Photos

Who's Who in America, 43rd edition, Marquis, 1984.
Who's Who in Hollywood, 1900-1976, Arlington House, 1976.
Who's Who in the Theatre: A Biographical Record of the Contemporary Stage, 17th edition, Gale, 1981.

PERIODICALS

Chicago Tribune, October 13, 1985.
Detroit Free Press, October 10, 1985, October 11, 1985.
Detroit News, October 10, 1985.
Hollywood Studio, June, 1984.
Maclean's, October 21, 1985.
Newsweek, May 16, 1977, October 21, 1985.
New York Times, October 11, 1985.
Time, October 21, 1985.

Donald Calvin Burr

1941-

PERSONAL: Born May 8, 1941, in Hartford, Conn.; son of an electrical engineer and an assistant postmaster; married Brigita Rupner, 1961; children: Cameron, Whitney, Kelsey, Andrew. *Education*: Stanford University, B.A., 1963; Harvard University, M.B.A., 1965.

ADDRESSES: Office—People Express Airlines, 146 Haynes Ave., Newark, N.J. 07114.

OCCUPATION: Airline executive.

CAREER: National Aviation Corp., New York, N.Y., 1965-73, president, 1971-73; Texas International Airlines, Inc., Houston, Tex., 1973-80, began as executive vice-president, became president and chief operating officer; People Express Airlines, Newark, N.J., founder, chairman, president, and chief executive officer, 1981—. Director of Jet Capital Corp.

SIDELIGHTS: When Congress voted to deregulate the airline industry in 1978, it created a new age in aviation. Airlines, now able to adjust their flight schedules and fares, were suddenly thrust into an uncontrolled, newly competitive market. One of the first to take advantage of this new environment was Donald Calvin Burr. With messianic energy and an innovative management philosophy, Burr created People Express, an airline that offers rock-bottom fares and no-frills, pay-only-for-what-you-want service. With fares as low as nineteen dollars from Newark, New Jersey, to Washington, D.C., customers flocked to People Express in such numbers that the company, Burr declared, "outgrew Bell's ability to provide new lines" to receive calls for reservations. At one point, the airline was adding an average of three new planes to its fleet every two months. During this hectic period, it was Burr's energetic leadership as chief executive officer that kept the company's growth under control. Burr himself has admitted that People Express is "very much a Don Burr place." If so, he deserves the credit for earning People Express's distinction as the fastest growing company in aviation history.

Burr opened People Express for business on April 30, 1981, with 250 employees and three second-hand, twin-engine Boeing 737s bought from the German airline Lufthansa. He established Newark as the company's hub city, with the nearly deserted North Terminal of the Newark International Airport, about thirteen miles outside of New York City, as its headquarters. In its first year of operation, People lost $1.7 million, but it has been gaining ever since. Today, People employs four thousand full-time workers and operates sixty-eight planes. In 1984 the company earned a profit of more than $20 million. It is now the largest airline operating out of the three airports in the New York City area and the tenth busiest airline in the United States. The North Terminal, which had only one scheduled flight daily when People began utilizing it, now accommodates about 190 departures each day.

When People first began operating, it scheduled short-run flights between Newark and only four other cities. These routes had become unprofitable for the larger airlines with their rising fuel and labor costs. Soon, flying became attainable to people who had never flown before. With air fares no more expensive than train or bus fares, People Express broke into the "sofa trade," as William Lowther described it in *Maclean's*. People who normally stayed at home or who traveled long distances in the family car soon realized that at People's prices it was worth flying. Burr remarked in *Time*: "We're getting people who wouldn't have traveled to New York to see a show, or buy clothes. If they did, they would have driven or taken a train."

But in order to take advantage of the low fares People's customers must be flexible and patient. They endure the New Jersey airport's uncomfortable North Terminal, which was previously used to handle freight. *Time*'s John S. DeMott revealed that the terminal's "cinder-block loading gates . . . often reach stifling temperatures in summer. Passengers have fainted while waiting for their planes in nearby packed and narrow hallways."

Still, the inconveniences do not discourage customers. In the discount airline business, volume is the key to profit, and People has it. The airline averages an 80 percent occupancy rate on its flights. Burr has noted that "the power of our product" keeps the passengers coming. "Why do you think we have such high load factors? . . . [It is] because the value of the product is so high."

People Express has come to serve a large market that was previously untapped by the larger airlines. Since deregulation, a new division in the industry has emerged. The upstart airlines, like People—and the failed Laker, Braniff, and Air Florida—supply no-frills, low-cost travel, while the more established airlines, DeMott explained, "offer something for everyone while concentrating on travelers who want reasonable comfort and firm reservations." The scheduling of flights is also following this division. Burr told *Forbes,* "The trend is that, where airlines have a choice, instead of putting planes against us, they are switching to where we are not strong."

Part of People Express's success is attributable to Burr's ability to keep operating costs down—and thus maintain low fares. Costs are kept down by offering air travel without the usual amenities. All passengers must carry their luggage on board with them or else pay three dollars for each bag checked. People also does not transfer baggage between flight connections. If passengers want to eat on the planes, they can either bring their own lunches or buy the snacks the airline offers: coffee and soda pop are fifty cents each and a sandwich plate costs six dollars. No hot food is served. Tickets are purchased on the plane; People Express has no ticket offices at which tickets can be purchased before flights. In addition, on most of People's flights there are no assigned seats.

Another of Burr's cost-cutting measures is to buy only second-hand aircraft. Most airlines avoid this practice and buy the newest, most fuel-efficient airplanes. Used planes, however, are relatively inexpensive when compared to brand-new models. When Burr expanded his start-up fleet of three second-hand Boeing 737s, he bought seventeen more Boeing 737s from Lufthansa for only $3.7 million each. New, these aircraft would cost almost three times this amount. People Express has also purchased used Boeing 727s from the bankrupt Braniff Airways and from Alitalia. Since People serves no hot food on its flights, it does not need the galleys these planes are equipped with. So the galleys are removed, and the space is filled with more seats. Seats in the first class sections are also torn out and replaced with seats that require less space. (The only People flight that offers first-class seating is the one to London.) In this way, the airline can increase its passenger-carrying capacity by ten to thirty-five seats per plane, depending on the model. These methods have worked: People Express's costs, according to *Time* magazine, are a little over 5 cents per seat per mile flown, while the industry average is 8.5 cents.

People Express also maintains some of the lowest labor costs in the industry. Burr hires non-union labor and pays wages much lower than the rest of the industry. The average annual salary of People's employees, according to DeMott, is just over $20,000, less than half of the industry average. This pay difference is even more dramatic for People's pilots. Sara Rimer noted in the *New York Times Magazine* that their starting salaries can be as low as $22,000 and can rise to about $56,000. In comparison, pilots with the larger airlines earn an average of more than $100,000 per year.

People Express, however, offers employees something most other airlines do not: part ownership in the company. Each new People employee is required to buy one hundred shares of the company's stock—at a 70 percent discount. If the new employee does not have the money to buy the stock outright, it can be purchased through a payroll deduction plan. Employees also have the option of buying as much stock as they desire. "Now the average employee owns $60,000 worth," disclosed Francine Keifer of the *Christian Science Monitor.* As Burr has remarked, this policy gives employees "a sense that they have a significant stake in the entity, a piece of the rock." People chief financial officer, Robert McAdoo, echoes this sentiment: "We're all in this together."

This spirit of togetherness or "family" is an important element in People's success. The company is egalitarian, endeavoring to treat all employees with the same respect and importance. Thus, Burr hires only managers. Flight attendants at other airlines are called customer service managers at People. Pilots are called flight managers. In the beginning, Burr went so far in his democratic zeal, wrote Rimer, as to outlaw the wearing of "the traditional wings and stripes" on the uniforms of the flight managers. This caused problems among the pilots, who balked at the new anonymity, and the rule was eventually rescinded. People's top officers (including Burr), accountants, flight managers, and customer service managers all take turns answering telephones and taking reservations, loading baggage, and selling snacks on the planes. Customer service managers, noted Rimer, are "expected to work in one or more other areas such as accounting or aircraft scheduling, wherever their curiosity takes them."

This system of "self-management," as Burr has dubbed it, offers employees a unique chance to learn the entire business and to make important decisions affecting the company's future. Self-management encourages high employee productivity and morale. Employees find themselves putting in longer hours and feeling good about it. An employee, quoted by Rimer, asserted that People Express is "definitely a work-ethic company. . . . I'm here all the time. It's because I want to be." The Harvard University Graduate School of Business Administration has begun to present People's "horizontal" corporate structure as a case study in innovative management techniques. Harvard professor D. Daryl Wyckoff, a specialist in transportation, exclaimed that "anyone who isn't studying People Express and the way they're managing people is out of their minds." But Burr has soberly observed that the company "is not a social experiment. It's a hard-driving capitalist business."

He would know. A product of the Harvard business school himself, Burr held a number of positions that eminently qualified him to create and run People. He worked eight years with the Wall Street firm National Aviation Corporation, becoming its president at the age of thirty. He then moved to the unprofitable Texas International Airlines and helped turn the company around. It began to make money again, but Burr was not happy. He declared: "It was grind, grind, grind, with no better purpose than to grind out some profits. It had no vision, no excitement." So Burr left and not long afterward started People Express, attracting to the new venture several of his colleagues from Texas International. Ironically, the man who hired Burr at Texas International now heads the holding company that runs two of People's rivals, Continental Airlines and New York Air.

People Express, however, need not worry about its competition yet. It is clearly the leader of the discount airlines and continues to grow at an amazing rate. In November 1985 Burr purchased Frontier Holdings, the parent company of Frontier Airlines, for $300 million. Frontier, a traditional airline, has service routes in the western United States and is to be operated independently of People and will keep its first-class service and its unionized employees. Industry observers carefully watching People are cautious about its future. Airline analyst Robert J. Joedicke at Lehman Brothers Kuhn Loeb is skeptical: "The bigger you get and the more complex you become the more you compound your costs, lower efficiency and hurt productivity."

Many think People Express will follow Laker, Braniff, and Air Florida into bankruptcy, that the company is expanding too quickly. Burr scoffs at such predictions, asserting in the *New York Times* that it is "unfair to compare our growth . . . to Braniff's because, unlike them, we are not over-extending ourselves in terms of our debt." Industry insiders, though, are not as confident. One, quoted by Lowther, observed, "Everyone admires Burr and his airline. He has done exceptionally well. . . . But over the years we have seen these cut-price people come and go. Eventually, People Express will go."

Despite such gloomy predictions, Burr and People Express are rectifying the problems that arose during the company's expansion and are planning for the future. People has enlarged its telephone reservations system, hoping to prevent the frustrating experience of customers not being able to get through to make reservations. It is also improving its poor record for flight delays. In the past, only 55 percent of People's flights were on time. Recently, this has been increased to about 85 percent. In the great expansion, too, many employees lost touch with the company, and Burr detected the beginnings of a morale problem. To correct this, he devised an elaborate communications network to keep employees informed about the company. A fifteen-minute daily news program, which is internally produced, is aired on television screens scattered throughout People's offices. Burr and the company's officers also regularly hold question-and-answer sessions with employees.

The airline is currently in the process of renovating Terminal C at the Newark International Airport to become its new headquarters in 1987. This terminal will have almost double the capacity of the North Terminal. Burr is also expecting delivery of eleven more planes in 1986, which will make People's fleet almost eighty strong. Clearly, Burr thinks that People Express is here to stay.

AVOCATIONAL INTERESTS: Running, skiing.

SOURCES:

PERIODICALS

Business Week, November 25, 1985.
Christian Science Monitor, December 19, 1983.
Forbes, April 25, 1983.
Fortune, November 11, 1985.
Maclean's, August 8, 1983.
Newsweek, April 4, 1983.
New York Times, June 5, 1983, November 2, 1983, September 9, 1984.
New York Times Magazine, December 23, 1984.
Sales & Marketing Management, January 17, 1983.
Time, February 21, 1983, October 8, 1984, January 7, 1985.
U.S. News and World Report, November 5, 1984.

—Sidelights by Anne M.G. Adamus

Nolan Bushnell
1943-

PERSONAL: Full name, Nolan Kay Bushnell; born February 5, 1943, in Ogden, Utah; son of Clarence H. (a cement contractor) and Delma (Nelson) Bushnell; married twice; second wife's name, Nancy; children: six. *Education:* University of Utah, B.S. (electrical engineering), 1968.

ADDRESSES: *Home*—San Francisco, Calif., Aspen, Colo., Washington, D.C., and Paris, France. *Office*—Catalyst Technologies, 1287 Lawrence Station Rd., Sunnyvale, Calif. 94086.

OCCUPATION: Electronics and business entrepreneur.

CAREER: Repaired radios, television sets, and washing machines as a child; ran a games arcade at an amusement park while attending college; Lagoon Corp., Salt Lake City, Utah, games manager, 1968-70; Ampex Corp., Redwood City, Calif., engineer in Advanced Technology Section, 1970-72; Nutting Associates, Mountain View, Calif., chief engineer, beginning 1972; founder and chairman at various times, Atari, Inc., Sunnyvale, Calif., 1972-79, Pizza Time Theatres, Inc., Sunnyvale, 1977-85, Catalyst Technologies, Sunnyvale, 1981—, Sente Technology, Inc., 1983-84, and Axlon, Inc., 1984—. Founder of numerous other companies, most as a part of his Catalyst Technologies holding company. Owner, Lion & Compass (restaurant), Sunnyvale.

SIDELIGHTS: Dubbed "King Pong" in honor of the electronic ping-pong game he invented in 1972, Nolan Bushnell is one of the most remarkably successful entrepreneurs of the century. According to *Esquire*'s David Owen, Bushnell's simple game, Pong, which combined a black and white television screen, a few hand controls, and a relatively basic computer program to direct the back and forth motion, is regarded as "the great-granddaddy of them all"—all the full-color, action-packed, blipping and beeping Centipedes and Trons and Dragon's Lairs that have revolutionized the entertainment industry in arcades and homes across America.

Bushnell's fascination with electronic forms of diversion began during his college years, when he played games on a school computer during his free time and worked at an amusement park arcade during vacations. His first attempt to market an electronic game, Computer Space, failed when it was introduced in 1971. "It was a great game," the inventor recalled in a *New York Times Magazine* article. "All my friends loved it. But all my friends were engineers. The beer drinkers in the bars were baffled by it. I decided what was needed was a simpler game."

Bushnell then set out to perfect Pong, financing most of his research by leasing pinball machines from other manufacturers and doing some consultant work. Unable to sell a single amusement company on the idea of building his game,

Bushnell and a partner founded their own manufacturing firm in 1972 with an initial investment of $500. They called their company Atari from a Japanese word meaning, "prepare to be attacked!" The choice of name turned out to be somewhat prophetic; Pong took the country by storm, racking up sales of more than 100,000 units by the end of 1974, only about a tenth of which were actually manufactured by Atari. Unable to satisfy demand for the immensely popular game, the new company saw competitors and counterfeiters cash in on the Pong phenomenon. Nevertheless, Atari posted sales of $11 million by the end of 1973, its first full year of operation. The video revolution had begun.

The next few years were rocky ones financially for the young company, which often found itself cash-poor and a bit too vulnerable to the whim of consumers. Pong sales began to drop in 1974, and Bushnell found himself in the position of having to rely on a new race car game, Gran Trak 10, to boost Atari's sagging profits. But manufacturing difficulties held up production of Gran Trak 10 long enough for the company to lose $500,000—the same amount it had made the year before. When the game finally caught on with the public, Bushnell's troubles were still not over as growth surged out of control. "We thought we were making money hand over fist," he says in *Time,* "but the machine was selling for $995 and costing $1,100 to build. We were shipping a $100 bill out the door with every unit."

Bushnell realized that for Atari to survive and be consistently profitable, he would have to diversify and locate new sources of capital so that he would never again be unable to meet demand. In seeking ways to diversify, Bushnell considered both electronic pinball machines for arcade use and video games for home use; "the latter," he reports in *Business Week,* "turned out to be ready first." As a result, Atari plunged into the home video games market, backed by loans Bushnell had managed to secure from a variety of sources, including Time, Inc. When demand continued to outstrip almost everyone's expectations, however, even this additional capital was not enough to guarantee Atari's share of the market. In early 1976, as he faced the upcoming Christmas manufacturing season, Bushnell decided that a merger with another company was the best long-term solution to his cash problems.

Of the several companies Bushnell approached, only Warner Communications indicated more than a passing interest. Negotiations between the two firms were conducted during the summer of 1976, and by fall an agreement had been reached: Warner would buy Atari for $28 million ($15 million of which was Bushnell's in the form of cash and debentures) and Bushnell would stay on in a top position.

In 1977, Atari engineers came up with a major innovation in video technology, a "programmable" video computer system that works like a cassette tape recorder, enabling one to change games merely by inserting a different cartridge. By this time, however, Bushnell had seemingly lost interest in running Atari. Explains Peter W. Bernstein in *Fortune:* "A conceptualist with a disdain for detail and a *bon vivant,* Bushnell never intended to oversee Atari's operations after the sale to Warner. . . . 'I'm not a very good chief operating officer,' he concedes. 'I like to develop the strategy, not to work it.'"

After a bitter dispute with Warner over managing the company in general and marketing the new video computer system in particular, Bushnell left Atari to pursue other business ventures. His first major move was to develop the Pizza Time Theatre concept, an enterprise Bernstein describes as "a zany combination of fast food and electronics."

To while away the time as they await their food, Pizza Time Theatre patrons have a choice of entertainment, including watching movies, playing video games in an arcade adjoining the dining room, or staying at their tables to take in a stage show—a show performed entirely by three-dimensional, computerized, pneumatically-powered robots. In this electronic extravaganza, which replays every eight minutes, a large mouse named Chuck E. Cheese comes out on stage, does a brief stand-up comic routine, and then begins introducing the acts to follow. "Depending on the restaurant," notes Bernstein, "these could be Madame Oink, a French pig who swoons and croons about Gay Paree; Harmony Howlette, a country-and-western coyote who sings like Loretta Lynn; or thirteen others. A few minutes later, as tape-recorded applause breaks out from the rafters and mechanical flags flutter, [the show] is over. Nearby, in another dining room with a quieter atmosphere, Dolli

Dimples, a piano-playing hippopotamus, sings oldies for twenty-cent tokens."

Bushnell came up with the idea for Pizza Time Theatre while he was still with Atari and actively seeking ways to diversify. At an industry show he attended in 1974, he purchased an $800 animal costume and then instructed company engineers to make it sing and talk. Explains Bushnell to Bernstein: "Live entertainers are expensive. You don't have to pay robots." But by the time the first Chuck E. Cheese emerged from Atari's lab some $2.5 million worth of research and development later, the company had been sold to Warner. The new management was less than enthusiastic about Bushnell's project and only allowed one Pizza Time Theatre to open. In 1978, Bushnell, convinced that his idea was indeed a marketable one, bought all assets and rights from Warner for $500,000 and set up his own company.

Seeking to build his concept into an operation to rival McDonald's and Disneyland, Bushnell set out on a course of rapid expansion, often purchasing inexpensive sites at older shopping centers and offering some of the outlets to franchisers in order to keep company costs to a minimum. In its first few years of existence, Pizza Time Theatres posted steady and impressive increases in earnings, from $347,000 in 1978 to $99.2 million in 1982. The wizard of Silicon Valley seemed to have hit it big once again.

As 1982 gave way to 1983, however, Chuck E. Cheese's magic began to fade. Business at the outlets dropped as the video game market collapsed. Compounding the problem was the fact that Pizza Time Theatres had developed a reputation for offering poor quality food and service at high prices. In an attempt to improve customer traffic, the company changed its pizza recipe, expanded the menu, cut the prices in some locations, and revamped the robot-provided entertainment to appeal more to adults. But nothing could stop the relentless downward slide, and in March, 1984, a month after its founder resigned as chairman and chief executive, Pizza Time Theatres filed for reorganization under Chapter 11 of the federal bankruptcy laws.

In retrospect, Bushnell accepts most of the blame for Pizza Time Theatres' troubles, explaining in *Newsweek* that "it turned out to be a little more of a restaurant than I intended." As he told Steve Coll of *Inc.:* "I was not planning to spend a significant amount of time [running] Pizza Time. I thought it was pretty much on automatic pilot. Then right after the middle of [1983], it was very obvious that things were wildly wrong." Despite the apparent setback (Bushnell even had to sell his fledgling video game company, Sente Technologies, Inc., to raise money to help save Pizza Time Theatres), the inventor/entrepreneur refused to give up on any of his ambitious plans for the future. "I am not a person that sits around wringing his hands," he continued in his remarks to Coll. "The Pizza Time situation, being my first what I'd call 'failure,' was a real disappointment. But I'm pretty resilient."

In 1981 Bushnell created one of his more innovative ventures, Catalyst Technologies, a holding company through which Bushnell subsidized groups of inventors in need of support services such as office space, copy machines, secretaries, and accountants. A February *Business Week* article noted that "most of Catalyst's companies have disappeared, along with several millions of Bushnell's money. The strongest survivor, Etak, Inc., makes computerized maps for cars. . . . Bushnell is now disillusioned with . . . venture capital." One of the newer companies spawned by Catalyst is Axlon Inc., which produces a line of soft robotic toys that feature A.G. Bear, a teddy that talks through the use of microchips rather than prerecorded tapes, and Party Animals, whose mouths move in sync with the sounds they produce.

Among the other projects Catalyst Technologies has launched are Androbot, a firm that is developing robots for home use (an idea Bushnell finds particularly fascinating); Zapp's, a singles-oriented bar and grill that features video games as well as traditional games such as shuffleboard and backgammon; TimberTech computer camps, educational facilities designed for children who display a talent for or an interest in working with computers; and I'Ro, a company that produces electronic devices to perform color analyses of human skin and hair and then recommends appropriate makeup and wardrobe colors. In short, remarks Bushnell in *Newsweek,* "we're working on things that are always on the edge of new technologies and new markets. We're always going to be searching for something that isn't there."

The driving force behind these innovations, who estimates his personal worth in the tens of millions of dollars, insists that there is nothing all that unusual about his success in the highly competitive world of California's Silicon Valley. Though he admits that his knowledge of engineering and video syntheses as well as his college work experience in an amusement park have blessed him with a rather "obscure combination" of skills, Nolan Bushnell once told *Forbes*'s John Merwin that "the critical ingredient is getting off your ass and doing something. It's as simple as that. A lot of people have ideas, but there are few who decide to do something about them now. Not tomorrow. Not next week. But today. They start working on that idea today."

SOURCES:

BOOKS

Cohen, Scott, *ZAP!: The Rise and Fall of Atari,* McGraw, 1984.

PERIODICALS

Business Week, November 15, 1976, February 28, 1983, February 17, 1986.
Christian Science Monitor, December 4, 1979.
Esquire, February, 1981.
Forbes, August 3, 1981, October 1, 1984, October 8, 1984.
Fortune, July 27, 1981, July 26, 1982.
Inc., July, 1984, October, 1984.
Los Angeles Times, December 24, 1982.
Newsweek, November 15, 1982, January 23, 1984.
New York Times, January 7, 1984, February 2, 1984, March 17, 1984, March 24, 1984, March 28, 1984, March 29, 1984.
New York Times Magazine, October 25, 1981.
Rolling Stone, September 29, 1983.
Time, June 13, 1977, August 10, 1981, February 15, 1982, March 7, 1983, January 14, 1985.
Wall Street Journal, August 20, 1982.
Washington Post, July 9, 1981, September 27, 1982, October 24, 1982, November 2, 1982.

—Sketch by Deborah A. Straub

Ed Cantrell
1928(?)-

BRIEF ENTRY: Born c. 1928 in Bloomington, Ind. American lawman and hired cattle rustling enforcer. In order to help struggling ranchers, who sometimes suffer grave losses from modern-day rustlers, Ed Cantrell hires himself out to keep guard over threatened cattle. "Rustling is more of a problem today than it was in 1875," said rancher Don King in *Life.* Stan Jolley indicated to the *Detroit News* that what is needed to stop the problem is "some rustlers' bones left lying in the desert." In desperation, Jolley turned to Cantrell, who can draw his gun in .2 seconds and has been target shooting for thirty-five years. Since Cantrell started to exercise his Wyatt Earp style of frontier justice, ranchers have experienced half as many rustling losses. "Don't make me out a hero 'cause I'm not," insisted Cantrell to the *Detroit News.* "I'm just doing a job because I don't know anything else."

In 1978 Cantrell was doing something else. He encountered controversy in that year when he was the Public Safety Director of Rock Springs, Wyoming. The sheriff of Rock Springs thought Cantrell's independent style of law enforcement would help eradicate the gambling, prostitution, and drug trade that had escalated after an oil strike caused an influx of population into the town. One night Cantrell had a fight with Mike Rosa, a problematic narcotics officer on the verge of revealing important evidence; Cantrell shot and killed him. He claims the shooting was in self-defense, but there were no reliable witnesses. After a jury deliberated Cantrell's first-degree murder case, he was acquitted, but his reputation was tarnished. His wife left him, and he was unable to find a job elsewhere as a policeman.

After this episode, Cantrell went to work on the range, where his preference for "frontier justice [instead of] the creaky machinery of modern jurisprudence is fine with his clients," writes a *Time* reporter. How he actually deals with rustlers is a mystery that Cantrell is not clarifying. "Part of my reputation," he told the *Detroit News,* "is built on myth, part fact, so I just don't say much." Cantrell told *Time* that he enjoys his new work thoroughly: "You can come back here when I'm 85, but you'll have to look for me [in the mountains]. . . . I expect I'll still be camping out, avoiding people, and looking for the damned rustlers."

AP/Wide World Photos

SOURCES:

PERIODICALS

Detroit News, May 5, 1985.
Life, December, 1983.
Newsweek, August 7, 1978.
New York Times, July 27, 1978, July 28, 1978, December 1, 1979.

Marc Chagall

1887-1985

OBITUARY NOTICE: Born July 7, 1887, in Vitebsk, Russia (now U.S.S.R.); died March 28, 1985, in St. Paul de Vence, France. Russian-born Jewish artist who lived in France for almost sixty years. Chagall, whose work was characterized by vibrant colors and fanciful, dreamlike imagery, was one of the best-known and most popular artists of the twentieth century. Strongly reflective of childhood memories and religious mysticism, his paintings of floating lovers, flying animals, joyous acrobats, and vibrant flowers prompted his contemporary, Pablo Picasso, to comment that "Chagall must have an angel in his head." A *Newsweek* critic remarked at the time of Chagall's death, "If the ultimate goal of an artist is to create powerful images that permanently alter the consciousness of viewers, then no artist in this century was more successful than Chagall."

His work combined elements of a variety of artistic styles, including surrealism, impressionism, and fauvism, with the primitive qualities of his native folk art, to produce what one art critic described as a "Jewish Disneyland." In addition to his oil and watercolor paintings, which are exhibited in museums throughout the world, Chagall's *oeuvre* encompassed etchings, sculpture, lithographs, engravings, and textiles. He designed stained-glass windows depicting the twelve tribes of Israel for the Hadassah-Hebrew University Medical Center near Jerusalem, the ceiling of the Paris Opera house, murals for New York's Metropolitan Opera and Lincoln Center, and stage sets for Mozart's opera "The Magic Flute." Among Chagall's most famous paintings were *I and the Village, The Rabbi of Vitebsk,* and *The Death Man.*

On the artist's eighty-sixth birthday, the French government honored Chagall with the inauguration of a museum in Nice to house his cycle of sixty-two paintings entitled "The Biblical Message." Chagall claimed that his art relied more on inspiration than formal education and that work was his reason for living. At the age of eighty-two he said: "Work isn't to make money. You work to justify life. Those are small actions and simple truths." Several years later, Chagall explained the secret of his success: "You have to be simply honest and filled with love. When you have love, all the other qualities come by themselves."

AP/Wide World Photos

SOURCES:

BOOKS

Alexander, Sidney, *Marc Chagall,* Cassell, 1979.
Bucci, Mario, *Chagall,* Hamlyn, 1971.
The International Who's Who, 47th edition, Europa, 1983.

PERIODICALS

Chicago Tribune, March 30, 1985, April 3, 1985.
Detroit News, March 29, 1985, March 30, 1985.
Los Angeles Times, March 29, 1985.
Newsweek, April 8, 1985.
New York Times, March 29, 1985.
Time, April 8, 1985.
Washington Post, March 29, 1985.

Konstantin Chernenko

1911-1985

OBITUARY NOTICE: Full name, Konstantin Ustinovich Chernenko; born September 24, 1911, in Bolshaya Tes, Novoselovo, Russia (now U.S.S.R.); died March 10, 1985, of heart failure complicated by emphysema and a liver ailment; buried in Red Square, Moscow, U.S.S.R. General secretary of the Soviet Communist Party. Chernenko, the son of Siberian peasants, became head of the Soviet Union in February, 1984, following the death of party leader Yuri Andropov. The oldest man ever to be elevated to the position, he was chosen by the Politburo as a transitional figure, a compromise between those younger officials who hoped to continue his predecessor's economic reforms and hard-line approach to fighting corruption and those still-influential senior members who feared the repercussions of such actions.

Chernenko, who received virtually no formal schooling, joined the Communist Party at the age of eighteen and served for more than a decade as a propagandist and agitator on various local committees. (During the 1930s, he also spent three years as a border guard in Central Asia.) He left his native region in 1943 to attend a party school in Moscow then was made a propagandist in the Soviet republic of Moldavia, near the Romanian border. It was there that he met and became a close friend of Leonid Brezhnev, at that time a party official working his way up the ranks. Chernenko accompanied Brezhnev to Moscow when the latter was promoted to a position as national party secretary and remained with him throughout the rest of the 1950s and into the 1960s. After Nikita Khrushchev's ouster in 1964 and Brezhnev's subsequent elevation to party leader, Chernenko functioned as his mentor's chief aide and confidant and was soon rewarded with a powerful position as head of the government department that controls party personnel files and determines many important high-level appointments. In 1978, he became a member of the ruling Politburo. Because of his closeness to Brezhnev, many observers regarded him as heir apparent; thus when he was passed over in favor of Andropov following Brezhnev's death in November, 1982, it was assumed that his political career was at an end. But the need to choose yet another party leader after Andropov's death a mere fifteen months later found the Politburo still reluctant to turn over the reins of power to one of the younger members, and, more or less by default, Chernenko succeeded Andropov in the party leader's role.

Chernenko's thirteen months in office were characterized as a period of collective leadership, with the already-ailing chief usually deferring to a fellow member of the old guard, Andrei Gromyko, on foreign policy decisions and to Mikhail Gorbachev (Andropov's right-hand man) on matters involving economics and agriculture. Aside from agreeing to

AP/Wide World Photos

restart arms negotiations with the United States after a four-year hiatus and boycotting the 1984 summer Olympic games in Los Angeles, Chernenko initiated no new major foreign or domestic policies. His long and frequent absences from public view during his brief tenure were cause for much speculation in the West, and his eventual death came as no surprise. He was succeeded by the fifty-four-year-old Gorbachev.

SOURCES:

BOOKS

Who's Who in the Soviet Union, K. G. Saur Verlag, 1984.
Who's Who in the World, 7th edition, Marquis, 1984.

PERIODICALS

Chicago Tribune, March 12, 1985.
Detroit Free Press, March 12, 1985, March 13, 1985.
New York Times, March 12, 1985.
Washington Post, March 12, 1985.

Stanley Clarke
1951-

PERSONAL: Full name, Stanley Marvin Clarke; born June 31, 1951, in Philadelphia, Pa.; son of Marvin and Blanche (Bundy) Clarke; married Carolyn Helene Reese, November 29, 1974; children: Christopher Ivanhoe. *Education:* Attended Philadelphia Music Academy. *Religion:* Scientology.

ADDRESSES: Office—8817 Rangely Ave., Los Angeles, Calif. 90048.

OCCUPATION: Jazz bassist.

CAREER: Musician; composer; record producer. Member of Horace Silver Band, 1970, Joe Henderson Band, 1971, Stan Getz Band 1971-72, and Return to Forever, 1972-76; leader of Stanley Clarke Group, 1976—; member of Clarke/Duke Project, 1980—.

MEMBER: National Academy of Recording Arts and Sciences, American Federation of Television and Radio Artists, Screen Actors Guild, Musicians Local 802.

AWARDS, HONORS: down beat International Critics' Poll, Bassist of the Year award, 1973, Acoustic Bassist of the Year award, 1974, Electric Bassist of the Year award, 1974, 1975; Grammy Award nominations, 1976, 1978, and 1981; Electric Bassist of the Year award, *down beat* International Readers' Poll, 1976; Bassist of the Year award, *Playboy* Readers' Poll, 1976, 1977, 1978, 1979, 1980; Jazz Artist of the Year award, *Rolling Stone* Music Critics' Poll, 1977; named to *Guitar Player* Gallery of Greats, 1980.

DISCOGRAPHY:

RECORD ALBUMS; PRODUCED BY EPIC/CBS RECORDS

Stanley Clarke, 1974.
Journey to Love, 1975.
School Days, 1976.
Modern Man, 1978.
I Wanna Play for You, 1979.
Rock, Pebbles and Sand, 1980.
Let Me Know You, 1982.
Time Exposure, 1984.
Find Out, 1985.

WITH CHICK COREA AND GROUP RETURN TO FOREVER; PRODUCED BY POLYDOR, EXCEPT AS INDICATED

Return to Forever, ECM, 1972.
Hymn to the 7th Galaxy, 1973.
Light as a Feather, 1973.
Where Have I Known You Before?, 1974.
Children of Forever, 1974.
No Mystery, 1975.
Romantic Warrior, Columbia, 1976.
Music Magic, Columbia, 1977.
The Best of Return to Forever, Columbia, 1980.
Midnight Magic, Columbia.

AP/Wide World Photos

OTHER

The Clarke/Duke Project (with George Duke), Epic/CBS Records, 1981
The Clarke/Duke Project II, (with Duke), Epic/CBS Records, 1983.

Also has played on record albums by a number of other artists, including Carlos Santana, Aretha Franklin, Quincy Jones, Paul McCartney, Sonny Rollins, and Chaka Khan.

SIDELIGHTS: "I don't feel I should have to make music to satisfy anyone," said Stanley Clarke in an interview with *Rolling Stone.* "But I do feel that one of an artist's fundamental duties is to create work other people can relate to. I'd be a fool to do something nobody else was going to understand." Thus Jazz bassist Clarke creates music that a wide variety of record-buyers and concert-goers are able to relate to and appreciate.

Born in Philadelphia in 1951, Clarke began his study of music at age ten on the accordion. He played the violin next, then cello, but soon settled on the bass. "The bass was tall and I was tall; it was similar to a violin and a cello, which was the direction I was taking anyway, so I started playing the bass," Clarke said in an interview for *Jazz-Rock Fusion: The People, the Music* by Julie Coryell and Laura Friedman. Clarke's early training was in classical music. He studied music formally at the Philadelphia Musical Academy.

He began his jazz career in 1970 with the Horace Silver Band. In 1971, he joined Joe Henderson and later worked with the Stan Getz Band. While with Getz, Clarke met pianist Chick Corea, who also was a member of the band. In 1972, Corea formed his own group, taking Clarke along with him. The acoustic jazz group called Return to Forever "was a very energetic band," says Mark Gridley in *Jazz Styles*, "whose flashy technical feats impressed musician and non-musician alike." Corea then formed an electric Return to Forever, retaining Clarke, who switched to electric bass, and adding guitarist Al Di Meola and drummer Lenny White. The group was influenced by rock and was one of the forerunners of what was dubbed "jazz-rock fusion" music, combining the melodies and intricacies of jazz with the drive and power of rock. The band became increasingly popular until it broke up in 1976 and each member moved on to solo and other projects.

Clarke had begun releasing solo albums while still with Return to Forever, and in 1976 he formed his own group. The Stanley Clarke Group has had various members over the years and continues to tour and record in between Clarke's other activities. In his solo efforts and with his own band, Clarke has explored and combined many diverse musical influences. As he told *down beat*, his music "has a lot of elements in it—rock and roll, jazz, r&b, funk, classical, Latin, African."

In sessions outside his group, Clarke has worked with rock musicians as well as other jazz musicians. In 1979 he toured with Rolling Stones members Keith Richards and Ron Wood in what was called the New Barbarians tour. In 1980 Clarke teamed with jazz pianist George Duke as The Clarke/Duke Project and had a hit with the song "Sweet Baby." And in 1981 he played on Paul McCartney's album *Tug of War.*

Clarke's talents are not limited to bass playing. He has composed a number of songs and has sung on records by Return to Forever and his own group. He has also worked as a producer. In addition to his own records, he has produced albums for other artists, including guitarist Roy Buchanan and singers Dee Dee Bridgewater and Flora Purim. He wrote a magazine column on bass playing for a while, and he has plans to write a multiple-volume work on the bass. Clarke told *down beat*, "I'm writing a book on acoustic bass, maybe three or four volumes. It's going to be the full thing—everything that anyone would want to know about the acoustic bass."

Clarke had already earned a reputation as an accomplished jazz bassist even before joining Return to Forever. But "during his tenure as bassist for Return to Forever, Clarke established himself as one of the most prodigious instrumentalists in modern music: an exceptionally nimble, resourceful electric and acoustic bassist," says Mikal Gilmore of *Rolling Stone.* Joachim Berendt in *The Jazz Book: From New Orleans to Rock and Free Jazz* describes Clarke's talents by comparing him to two other noted bassists: "Stanley Clarke combines [Miroslav] Vitous' fluidity with Oscar Pettiford's 'soul.'"

Clarke's distinctive style of play rejects the usual background rhythm role of bass players and moves the bass right to the forefront of his music. Says Clarke in the book *Jazz-Rock Fusion,* "Years ago there was a fixed idea that bass players played background, and bass players have this particular theme—kind of subdued, numb, almost looking numb, and just to make a long story short, I wasn't going for any of that." Clarke's trademark on electric bass is a metallic sound. He also imparts some twist on the strings, what Chuck Carman of *down beat* describes as putting "English" on them. Clarke concurs: "I found from plucking the strings in various ways that just the slightest movement can change your whole sound . . . English is a great word. I just use English of various types on the strings."

His solos are known for some very fast runs. Regarding his approach to soloing, he told *Guitar Player* magazine: "On electric bass, I use any finger, even my thumbs—anything! . . . I pluck mainly with three fingers. I have certain patterns that I can only play with four fingers. Sometimes when I get to those real fast runs that just fly, they'll be a fourth finger in there to help play it." It was one of Clarke's influences on bass who helped contribute to his energetic style. According to Mark Gridley in *Jazz Styles*, Scott LaFaro, bassist for Bill Evans, created a modern style that made the bass not just a timekeeper but a melodic instrument. Those young jazz bassists like Clarke influenced by him "interacted with pianists and drummers in an imaginative and highly active manner." Clarke himself told *Rolling Stone*: "I've always been more drawn to melodic than rhythmic playing . . . I had all these melodies running around in my head, all this knowledge of classical music I was trying to apply to R&B and jazz, and I decided it would be a loss in personal integrity just to be a timekeeper in the background, going *plunk plunk, thwack thwack.*"

Although Clarke has a reputation as a very fine musician, his move from pure jazz to jazz-rock fusion upset some jazz critics. His later projects with rock musicians, such as the New Barbarians tour, and the introduction of pop and rock themes to his music, have served to tarnish his image among some jazz purists. Mikal Gilmore says that in recent years "Clarke has seemed to temper his talent, opting instead to play fairly prosaic, overbusy variations of rhythm & blues and even heavy-metal music." Gilmore is especially critical of Clarke's collaboration with George Duke. He states that the music of the Clarke/Duke Project is "pointedly devoid of the sort of compositional or improvisatory prowess that earned either musician his standing in the first place." Some other critics echo Gilmore's sentiments. In a review of a Sonny Rollins album on which both Clarke and Duke played, Chris Albertson of *Stereo Review* says, "Pianist George Duke and bassist Stanley Clarke, men of great jazz potential who were bitten by the chart bug before they could show us more than the tip of their talent, here prove that they have spent too much time in fusionland." In a review of an acoustic jazz recording, *The Griffith Park Collection,* which includes Clarke's former Return to Forever colleagues Lenny White and Corea, Don Heckman of *High Fidelity* says, "One wonders . . . whether White and Clarke have wandered too far down the electronic path to return to the discipline of this kind of music."

The charges of commercialism or "going Hollywood" have been especially biting. Heckman, in a review of a Clarke-produced Maynard Ferguson album called *Hollywood*, quips: "Well, the title certainly tells you what to expect. But if there are any doubts, note that the album was 'produced and directed' by Stanley Clarke . . . . Jazz? Forget it." Clarke acknowledges the criticism he has received but is determined not to let it change him. Asked in *down beat* whether he knows any musicians who changed because of press criticism, Clarke responded: "I've seen guys do that, and I've seen them go right down the drain, too. That's one thing that an artist can't do—if any creative person starts listening to other people, he goes down." His penchant for exploring a number of different musical paths, he realizes, has led to much of the criticism. But as Clarke told *down beat:* "It would get boring for me if I just did one thing and played just one type of music for the rest of my life. I don't think I could take it." And to *Rolling Stone* he said, "I know it upsets some people, but I could never be a conservative jazz musician."

At least one critic, however, has revised his opinion of Clarke. In a *Stereo Review* article, Chris Albertson remarked: "I used to think of Stanley Clarke as one of the defectors, a jazz man drawn away from his art by the waving of the green. Now I am inclined to think that I did Clarke an injustice."

Clarke presents himself, both off and on the stage, in an engaging manner. Says Carman: "Stanley Clarke struck me as a person who nobody could help but like. His expression was either a friendly smile or a more intent look as he listened to questions. Several times during the course of the interview he shied away from 'naming names,' when it might conceivably reflect adversely upon someone." In reviewing a 1983 reunion tour of Return to Forever, Bill Milkowski of *down beat* said, "Clarke remains the same crowdpleaser he always was, an engaging presence with a flashing smile, playing up the rock theatrics during his explosive solos."

Clarke believes in making an emotional impact with his music, to touch his audience. To *down beat* he said, "I have an intention, regardless of what anyone thinks, to have my music reach out to someone. . . . I'm trying to get across good feelings." All in all, Clarke says that his goal is not to bore anyone. As he told Chuck Carman, "It's a nice goal to have. It keeps you busy."

SOURCES:

BOOKS

Berendt, Joachim, *The Jazz Book: From New Orleans to Rock and Free Jazz*, translation by Dan Morgenstern, Barbara Bredigkeit, and Helmut Bredigkeit, Lawrence Hill & Co., 1975.
Coryell, Julie, and Laura Friedman, *Jazz-Rock Fusion: The People, The Music*, Dell, 1978.
Gridley, Mark C., *Jazz Styles*, Prentice-Hall, 1978.
The Rolling Stone Encyclopedia of Rock & Roll, Rolling Stone Press, 1983.

PERIODICALS

down beat, March 24, 1977, July 13, 1978, July, 1983.
Guitar Player, August, 1981.
High Fidelity, July, 1982.
People, December 1, 1975.
Rolling Stone, June 11, 1981.
Stereo Review, April, 1981, May, 1982, December, 1982, January, 1983.

—Sidelights by Greg Mazurkiewicz

George Clements

1932-

PERSONAL: Full name, George Harold Clements; born January 26, 1932, in Chicago, Ill.; son of Samuel George (a Chicago city auditor) and Aldonia (Peters) Clements; children: Joey, Friday, Stewart (all adopted). *Education:* Graduated from Quigley Seminary in 1945; received B.A., M.A., S.T.B., and S.T.L. from St. Mary of of the Lake Seminary.

ADDRESSES: Home—Chicago, Ill. *Office*—Holy Angels Church, 607 Oakwood Blvd., Chicago, Ill. 60653.

OCCUPATION: Clergyman; civil rights activist; educator.

CAREER: Ordained Roman Catholic priest, May 3, 1957; served as associate pastor at St. Ambrose and St. Dorothy churches in Chicago, Ill.; Holy Angels Church, Chicago, pastor, 1969—. Founder and executive director of the National Black Catholic Clergy Caucus; chaplain of Chicago's Afro-American Patrolmen's League, Afro-American Firemen's League, and Afro-American Postal Workers' League; affiliated with the Black Panther Party. Has served on the board of directors of organizations such as the Better Boys Foundation, the National Association for the Advancement of Colored People, the Urban League, Malcolm X College, SCLC's Operation Breadbasket, the Black United Fund, and Paul Hall Boys Club.

AWARDS, HONORS: Named Priest of the Year, 1977, by the Association of Chicago Priests.

WRITINGS:
(Editor) *Black Catholic Men of God,* National Black Catholic Clergy Caucus, c. 1975.

SIDELIGHTS: An activist devoted to improving the social, educational, and political conditions of blacks, both in the United States and in other parts of the world, George Clements participated in civil rights marches during the 1960s, has organized and taken part in a number of groups dedicated to promoting career opportunities and social support systems among blacks, and has become the pastor of Holy Angels Church, a predominantly black Catholic parish of some four thousand members located on Chicago's South Side. And as head of Holy Angels School, the largest black Catholic school in the United States, he has gained a nationwide reputation for policies of strict discipline and rigorous academic training. Clements explains his approach to education, according to Linda Witt in *People* magazine, stating, "We bear down hard on our students at Holy Angels School. . . because we have to give them the best preparation to deal with the white world."

In 1980 Clements took up another cause. Appalled by the number of black children put up for adoption and never given a new home, the priest decided to adopt a son. A spokesman for Clements, quoted in the *New York Times* in

UPI/Bettmann Newsphotos

November, 1980, explained this decision: "He believes a dramatic move has to be made to bring the tragic situation to the front. . . . He hopes this unprecedented move—a father becoming a father—will encourage black people to seriously consider opening their homes to black children out of state institutions." When Clements first announced his intention to adopt a child, the Chicago archdiocese expressed reservations concerning the idea. "It's the church's understanding that it's not the role of the priest to adopt a child. They just don't do that," a spokesman for the archdiocese was quoted as saying in the *New York Times.* "It's just inappropriate to raise a child in a rectory." But church officials could find no specific prohibition in canon law against a priest's adopting a child and, therefore, did not forbid Clements to adopt, much to the priest's satisfaction. As the *New York Times* reported, Clements remarked in July, 1981, when the adoption of his son Joey became final: "If the church had blocked me, I would not have defied them. . . . But they didn't. Thank God they didn't."

Clements, with the cooperation of the Illinois Department of Children and Family Services, began the One Church/One Child adoption program in 1981 in an attempt to find homes for the more than 100,000 black children in foster care across the country. The plan called for each black church in the United States to adopt one black child. Commenting on the Program's success, Lynn Norment observed in *Ebony*, "When the program began in 1981, there were 750 Black children awaiting adoption in Illinois. By the end of 1985, that number was down to 60, which is exceptionally low for a state with such a large Black population." Fifteen other states had initiated the program by early 1986 and efforts to launch a national program were begun.

CN INTERVIEW

CN interviewed George Clements by telephone, February 11, 1985, at Holy Angels Church in Chicago, Ill.

CN: You have established quite a reputation as a social activist, and if I may I'd like to begin with that area of your life. During the 1960s you took part in a number of civil rights marches and demonstrations, and you were also at one time—according to some sources—a director of the Chicago Black Panther Party. How have these activities affected your present role as a parish priest?

CLEMENTS: Well, I was not the director of the Black Panther Party, but I was certainly involved with them. My parish activities, I think, are much more fruitful as a result of my social activities in the sixties, because I feel that I'm a lot more sensitive to the things that go on today. For example, there is a lot of furor at the present time concerning apartheid in South Africa. I don't feel that I would have gone around doing the things I'm doing today in respect to South Africa had it not been for the sensitivity that was built up during the sixties.

CN: So you feel these activities have made you more sensitive to the needs of your parishioners and also to people around the world?

CLEMENTS: I think more so people around the world. I think most priests are certainly sensitive about their own parishioners, but I don't think that I would have had the global view that I have today regarding injustice anywhere in the world had it not been for the involvement in the injustice that was right under my nose right here in this country.

CN: With the arrival of Pope John Paul II and a trend toward conservatism among the Catholic hierarchy, there has been renewed discussion lately about the part the church should play in social activism. . . .

CLEMENTS: I don't see it as a trend toward conservatism. I see it as a trend toward orthodoxy, which I felt we had been getting away from with some of the aberrations that developed from the interpretations that many people put on Vatican II. I feel that there was a need for the pendulum to swing back to what I consider sanity, and so I am just delighted that we have gotten a pontiff who is very concerned about that. I think that social activism can certainly take place without there being utter and complete chaos, which is, to my mind, some of the things that seem to be advocated by some of the more bizarre groups that you find today.

CN: How do you respond to people who think the Church should stay out of politics and other temporal areas completely?

CLEMENTS: Well, I think that depends on what they mean by politics. If they mean by politics that churchmen—people who have official positions in the church, such as priests, religious brothers or nuns, and so forth—that they should not be running for elected office, I certainly would agree. But if they mean that we are to keep silent about any issue that might have political overtones, well then I think that that is foolish.

CN: I'm a little curious about your Black Panther affiliation. In exactly what capacity did you serve?

CLEMENTS: Well, when Fred Hampton was running the Black Panther Party here, he came to me at the time that we were having a lot of upheaval at St. Dorothy's, and he told me that he was definitely not a Catholic but that he was very much in favor of black people being in charge of their own institutions and that he felt that I needed some people who would be agitating on my behalf in a way that my more serene parishioners were not about to; and I told him that, if that's what he felt, to do what he thought he should do. That's what he did. He went down, and he demonstrated at the Chancery office and he created a huge commotion until they decided that they would much prefer to deal with me than with Hampton and the Panthers. As a result of that, I came to Holy Angels. I, upon my arrival here, made this place available for their meetings, for their breakfast program, and for their clothing giveaways, and I certainly did counsel many of them. And to this day I still have contact with some of them, although many of them have their own families, and they're much more mature and so forth. Yes, I was involved with those young black people and I am very proud of my involvement.

CN: After Martin Luther King's assassination you removed a statue of St. Anthony from your church and replaced it with an altar honoring Dr. King. Obviously he was a great hero of yours, but didn't you find his pacifist philosophy antithetical to the sometimes violent nature of the Panthers?

CLEMENTS: No, because I feel this way: that just because I am counseling and also certainly trying to facilitate the movements of people that are in various organizations, that doesn't mean that I am swallowing whole hog everything that they advocate. For example, I have been very much involved with Minister Farrakhan and the Muslims, but I certainly am very far from being a Muslim. So I don't feel any incompatability whatsoever with what I did with the Panthers and what I have been doing with the philosophy of Dr. King. I believe that Dr. King himself would never have turned his back on the Panthers. I think that he believed that all of us that have good will should try and work together for a common goal, which is, of course, social justice.

CN: More recently you've participated in the Afro-American Patrolmen's League, the Afro-American Firemen's League, and the Afro-American Postal Workers' League. What part do you play in these organizations, and what are they trying to do for the black community?

CLEMENTS: Well, the Afro-American Postal Workers' League is now defunct because the black postal workers have won most of the goals that they set out to achieve, which, of course, included parity in the entire postal department. The Firefighters' League also has pretty much dwindled now because we do have blacks that are in policy-making positions in the fire department, which was one of their biggest things, and there has been integration throughout the department now. So, again, their reason for existence is no longer as pronounced. The fact is that they have become somewhat of a different social movement now.

The Afro-American Patrolmen's League is a different story. They were certainly needed seriously because there was so much fear in the black community concerning police brutality, plus the fact that black policemen have not been given a fair shake throughout the department in promotions or in hiring. Now, once again, with the advent of Mayor Washington, we have a black police chief, Superintendent Rice, and there are blacks who are in policy-making positions. The Afro-American Patrolmen's League still exists, but it operates on a minimal level now. That's kind of where I am with them now.

CN: You are also founder and executive director of the National Black Catholic Clergy Caucus. How many members does this group have, and what what are some of its goals?

CLEMENTS: Theoretically, all of the black priests in the country are in it, and when I say "all," that is no astronomical number, because we only have about 300; and that's out of about 60,000 white priests. So our numbers are very miniscule. This organization still is extremely active and very strong. I did help to found the group, because I felt very lonely and felt like I was really kind of lost in a sea of whiteness in the midst of all the furor that was taking place in the civil rights movement, and it was a beautiful thing to find kindred souls around the country that felt the same way as I. Our focus has certainly changed considerably now, because we do not have the kind of outright discrimination that was practiced in some circles in this church some twenty years ago. Our focus now has been more on supporting each other and giving each other a sense of well being within the church. We've turned, more or less, in on ourselves rather than fighting issues within the church.

CN: I'd like to talk about Holy Angels for a moment. Under your direction, the parish school has become widely known for its strict rules and discipline. Do you think the public education system in this country has failed, and how has your alternative system affected the students and parents in your parish?

CLEMENTS: Well, I don't think the public school system has failed *whites.* I think that they are still very much served by this system. I think that the basic flaw in dealing with the public school system is the contention that all students are to be dealt with on an equal level, because all students don't come from equal backgrounds. I feel that what the public school really needs are people who are concerned about discipline and high standards—academic excellence—and who are not nearly so concerned about expensive pay checks. I feel that we have capitulated to teachers' unions throughout this country, and too many of our schools are now centered around the ease of the teacher rather than around the achievement of the student. And I think that we have to get back to a sense of mission among our teachers before we can really do anything about the school system. As long as the teachers are in there because they are trying

to get as powerful salaries as they possibly can, then I don't think we are ever going to have the kind of education we need to have, because there just isn't that much money available in most of the townships and villages and hamlets in this country. And I think we are approaching it from the wrong view.

CN: Before being admitted to Holy Angels, students and their parents sign a contract. Would you like to talk about that a little bit?

CLEMENTS: I think it's very, very important that when people make a commitment they live up to it. The commitment that is made here in September is that they are going to follow all of the rules and regulations of our school. Now, if we detect any reluctance on their part to make this commitment, then we beg them not to make it, because we are definitely going to keep our end of the bargain, and we expect them to keep their end. This is a purely voluntary association; we don't want people to come in unless they are eager and interested and want to take advantage of our rules and regulations so that we can bring about a solid educational foundation for their children and—more importantly—bring about a moral regeneration within their families. And we make it very, very clear that we are using the school here as a tool for our real goal, which is, of course, the moral uplifting of the people who come here through their involvement with the Catholic Church. And we say that the tail does not wag the dog: The school is not the reason that the institution is here; the *church* is the reason we are here on Oakwood Boulevard. The school is something adjunct to that, and we have to continually remind people of that, because they tend to forget that from time to time.

CN: Not too long ago, approximately two hundred kids were suspended from Holy Angels at the same time. Would you like to discuss some of the reasons for these suspensions, and under what circumstances were the students allowed back into the school?

CLEMENTS: These were people who did not live up to their contract. This is nothing new. It happens every year when we enforce our regulations in September. When they enroll, we have them read the contract out loud, and then we tell them if there is any reluctance please don't sign this contract. Once they have signed it, one of the stipulations is that they and their children will attend Mass on Sunday. Now the first Sunday in September, what we do is send a note home by the children to those parents who missed. The second Sunday, we send a much stronger note telling them that sanctions are going to be invoked if they continue. The third Sunday, we have a telephone call that we make to those who have missed, and we tell them that the next Sunday they are going to be suspended. The fourth Sunday is when the suspensions come out, and that's when the two hundred were suspended. Now, suspension means that your child cannot come back to school until you have come up here and have talked to one of the priests and explained why you have missed and make a firm promise that you are going to amend your ways. And that is exactly what happened.

CN: Some of the other points covered in this contract include participation in school activities, fund-raising events, and so on.

CLEMENTS: Correct. And this is not something that is optional. What we do is we have a very low tuition rate. It's only thirty dollars a month. But along with that is an understanding that there will be some sixty dollars a month in compulsory fund raising. That means that when we have events, these people are going to take part in these events and sell the tickets, and if they don't do it, they have to buy them themselves. So that's all understood before they come in, because we are determined that we are going to be self-sufficient, and we do not go out and beg for subsidies from the archdiocese. We are making it on our own.

CN: There are also academic points covered in the contract; limited television viewing time, for instance.

CLEMENTS: Correct. I guess the most outstanding one is the fact that we go twelve months a year. We have no summer vacation whatsoever, which gives us more time to concentrate on the academics. We also expect youngsters to come on Saturdays if they are below grade level. We have a long school day: from eight in the morning until four in the afternoon. No child is ever allowed to leave the grounds. We have silence in the corridors, hallways, classrooms, the cafeteria, and so forth. We *do* have very strict discipline here, which we feel facilitates our academic thrust.

CN: You appeared on the Phil Donahue show recently with the mother of one of the suspended students. At first the studio audience seemed hostile toward you, but after you had presented your point of view—explained the contract—the tone seemed to change, and the audience appeared to decide that a little more discipline might be a positive step for education. Do you find this same attitude in your parish and the surrounding community, too?

CLEMENTS: Our parish is totally behind us. I think that it is very dangerous for us to gauge our success or failure by the applause of people who are not conversive with what we are doing. Certainly, I would like to have the people behind us, but whether they are behind us or not, we feel what we are doing is right, and we will continue doing it. . . . We feel that the extremely important nature of what we are doing, which is to hone students who are to compete in our society, that that takes precedence over whether people agree with us or not. We are not out to achieve popularity here, but we *are* out to achieve a high degree of academic excellence.

CN: Another educator in Chicago, Marva Collins, has achieved a great deal of success with strict classroom discipline and tough, demanding teaching methods. But she also runs a school that, like Holy Angels, is a private school, and some people maintain that her methods—and yours, I assume—would be out of place in public education. Do you think it would be possible to implement some of your methods in a public school?

CLEMENTS: Oh, I definitely think that it's not only *possible,* but it's *necessary.* I think that's a cop-out when people say that you can't do it. The only reason it's not done is because there are not enough people around who have the drive to go ahead and do it. They feel somewhat intimidated by this public school system. For example, when students are behind in their work I don't see any public school system anywhere that would demand that parents and teachers be allowed to deal with those students on Saturday. These buildings are put up by our tax money, and they are empty on weekends. I don't see how they can possibly justify that. If enough parents and enough teachers really demanded it, they would have to open the schools on Saturday.

There are many other things that we do. For example, report cards. We insist that the parents must come up to get the report cards when the children are to receive them. Well, they can do that in the public schools, too. They can insist on parents coming up, and that would be one way of getting parental involvement with the youngsters. I think there are any number of things that we do that they could be doing, but there are just so many people who are intimidated by these teachers' unions.

CN: So you feel the responsibility rests with parents, who are not demanding enough of the school system?

CLEMENTS: Oh, definitely. I definitely do. I think the administration would cave in immediately if there were enough parents that were demonstrating on behalf of excellence in public schools.

CN: You have been in the papers quite a bit for your philosophy on adoption. In fact, you have adopted children yourself. At the time you adopted your first son, Joey, you said that you hoped your example would prompt more people to adopt black children. The adoption got a lot of press attention, and adoptions of black children did increase. Has this trend continued, or are we still experiencing in this country a serious problem in trying to place black kids with adoptive parents?

CLEMENTS: What we are experiencing is a serious problem of family chaos among blacks, and that's resulting in more and more children being available for adoption. But insofar as the adoption process itself, yes, there has been an incredible increase. The National Black Child Development Institute has indicated that there has been a 500 percent increase in black adoptions since we started our campaign. And our campaign revolves primarily around churches. We call it "One Church, One Child," and we are asking that every church in the black community try to persuade at least one family in that church to adopt a child. And, as I say, that's met with astronomical success. The problem is that there are so many youngsters out there. And the comparison is usually made between blacks and whites, and they say that blacks simply don't want to adopt. The fact is that when you get a proportion to our population, blacks, according to the federal government, are adopting eighteen out of every thousand, whereas whites only five out of every thousand. Its just that, of course, there are so many fewer white children available for the white population to select.

CN: That brings up the subject of interracial adoption. Some people feel that it is detrimental to a black child to be placed with white parents. Do you think it's better for the child to be placed with black parents, and are white parents at least a better alternative than the institutional route: orphanages or the foster care system?

CLEMENTS: I think that every child should be placed with a family whose racial background is consonant with his own if that is at all possible. I feel, however, that at times that isn't possible given the geography, and social conditions, and so forth. . . . I certainly go along very much with the idea of getting children into homes, regardless of what the racial background is, if it means the child is not going to have a home otherwise.

Now, I do feel that the responsibility for black children rests with black families, and I think that the hallmark of this is the fact that white families have taken the responsibility for taking in white children. And also I have never heard it stated that it's the responsibility of blacks to take in white children, so why would it be the responsibility of whites to take in black children? I think that all of us have the responsibility to do what we can to find homes for children regardless of their racial background but that a child is certainly going to—all other things being equal—be much more comfortable in a home where the parents' racial background is similar to his own.

CN: People are fascinated with the idea of a priest adopting children. How do you describe, overall, your experiences as a parent?

CLEMENTS: Overall, . . . let's say that it has opened my horizons considerably, because I really didn't realize how narrow-minded I had become as a celibate bachelor. I have my own little world, and I pretty much stayed in it, although I certainly tried to be available to other people. Still, over the years, being a bachelor, you just develop certain behavior patterns, and it kind of precludes other people coming in and disrupting them. And I have found that my entire privacy has been absolutely shattered by these youngsters and that in many ways this has been a good thing for me. This isn't something I would have opted for, but now that I do have it, I understand it, and I think it's made me a better person. I'm certainly a lot less selfish than I was, and I have just been very startled when I go in my drawer to get a pair of socks and discover one of those guys has gone and gotten in ahead of me. I kind of react to that instinctively. I get frustrated, because that's not what I have been accustomed to. Again, it's something I have to learn to live with as parents have all learned to live with the kind of sacrifices you have to make when you have children.

Another thing that has happened, of course, is that I travel a lot, and I find that they are constantly on my mind. Whenever I'm somewhere, I know that the first question that I'm going to be asked when I return home is, "What did you bring me back?" And I have never had to worry about something like that before. And they are always in the forefront of my mind. I'm very concerned about their safety, because this is a dangerous neighborhood. This morning, when my son left for school, I thought he wasn't dressed properly, and we had a big argument about that. He said the kids all laugh at him if he puts on a scarf and earmuffs and all that. And I said, "I don't give a damn what they're laughing about, I'm not going to have you sick." We got into a big thing about all that, but that's just part of the whole struggle.

CN: Sounds like a typical father-son discussion.

CLEMENTS: Yeah, I guess in many ways it is just a typical kind of thing, but in a sense it's sort of necessary, because they certainly are kind of reckless like most teenagers. I have to constantly bring them back to what I think is reality.

CN: I assume there are other priests at Holy Angels.

CLEMENTS: Yes. There are five of us here.

CN: How have your fellow priests and your parishioners reacted to your fatherhood?

CLEMENTS: I think that it's been a total acceptance. At the very beginning there was a lot of skepticism, because people weren't sure what this meant—whether I was going to be leaving the priesthood, or getting married, or whatever. All kinds of rumors circulated. But now that it's been going on, going into my sixth year, people have just accepted it. We don't get nearly the kind of consternation we did get at one time.

SOURCES:

PERIODICALS

Ebony, March, 1986.
New York Times, November 21, 1980, July 8, 1981, November 24, 1981, March 28, 1982.
People, December 22, 1980.

—Sketch by Lori R. Clemens
—Interview by Peter M. Gareffa

Paul Coffey

1961-

PERSONAL: Born June 1, 1961, in Weston, Ontario, Canada; son of Jack (an assistant superintendent for McDonnell-Douglas aircraft manufacturing corporation) and Betty Coffey.

ADDRESSES: Home—Edmonton, Alberta, Canada; and Mississauga, Ontario, Canada (summer). *Office*—Edmonton Oilers, Northlands Coliseum, Edmonton, Alberta, Canada T5B 4M9.

OCCUPATION: Professional hockey player.

CAREER: Member of Edmonton Oilers hockey team, 1980—. As an amateur, played in Ontario Hockey Association for Sault Ste. Marie, Ontario, 1978-79, 1979-80, and for Kitchener, Ontario, 1979-80. Works for drug abuse program of the Royal Canadian Mounted Police; honorary chairman of Canadian Mental Health Association.

AWARDS, HONORS: Named to National Hockey League's second all-star team, 1982, 1983, 1984, and to first all-star team, 1985; James Norris Memorial Trophy, awarded to best defenseman in the National Hockey League, 1985.

SIDELIGHTS: Like several stars on the Edmonton Oilers, Paul Coffey had himself quite a year from May 1984 to May 1985: two National Hockey League (NHL) Stanley Cup championships with the Oilers and, in between, a victory with the Canadian national team that beat the U.S.S.R. and then Sweden for the Canada Cup tournament title in September. But the culmination of an amazing year for Coffey came when he won the James Norris Memorial Trophy, a personal recognition that he felt he deserved in 1984, if not 1983.

Almost from the day he began playing in the NHL, Coffey has been the center of controversy regarding the two styles of defensive play in hockey. From the early days of the game until the mid-1960s defensemen played passively, waiting back in their own zone to break up the offensive plays of opponents. The new style of defense, credited to retired Boston Bruins great Bobby Orr, is one where a defenseman possessing great skating speed makes forays into the opponents' zone and, in effect, quarterbacks the offense. It's a style that Coffey has imitated and perfected to such a degree that he's often compared to Orr, a member of the NHL Hall of Fame. "If you're going to be compared to anybody, you might as well be compared to the best," Coffey told the *Detroit Free Press.* "Bobby Orr, in my mind, was the best. And still is the best. It's nice to hear your name mentioned in the same breath as his."

But Orr, in twelve seasons, won eight consecutive Norris Trophies, from 1968 to 1975; Coffey, in six seasons, has won it only once. And that recognition, from the Professional

Photograph by Bob Mummery

Hockey Writers Association, whose members vote and award the trophy, was a long time coming. Before the 1985 season Coffey wondered what it would take to convince the hockey writers, many of whom criticized him for sacrificing defense to score goals. "People tell me that even though [Orr] won the [Norris] trophy, he still got criticized a lot for being up ice," Coffey said to the *Detroit Free Press.* "If I got the puck or one of my other defensemen have the puck, that means the other teams can't score."

In his two previous seasons, Coffey had produced incredible offensive statistics. In 1983 he scored 29 goals and assisted on 67 goals for a total of 96 offensive points. He followed that in 1984 with 40 goals and 86 assists for 126 points, the third highest total for a defenseman in one season in NHL history. Only Orr's 139 points in the 1970-71 season and 135 points in 1974-75 are better. But in the 1983 and 1984 seasons Rod Langway of the Washington Capitals was voted the Norris Trophy winner. Langway only produced three goals and 29 assists, and nine goals and 24 assists, in those seasons. But Langway's ability to play the classic style of defense—standing up and knocking down onrushing opponents—was a determining factor in the voting, a frustrating experience for Coffey and his boosters. Coffey's teammate,

Wayne Gretzky, currently the top offensive player in the game, lobbied for Coffey in the 1985 season. "If he doesn't win the Norris Trophy this year," Gretzky told the *Sporting News*, "maybe they better come up with a new trophy. Call it the Bobby Orr Trophy for defensemen who get a lot of points. Keep the Norris for the defensive defensemen."

An ironic twist surrounding Coffey's still-young career is that when he played junior hockey he wasn't considered a strong offensive player. In fact, Coffey told the *Edmonton Journal* that his coach at Kitchener, Ontario, Rod Seiling, told him that he "couldn't skate, shoot or pass the puck well enough,. . . but I was good defensively. Here's a guy [Seiling] who played, what, 15 years in the NHL. I was just a kid. I just listened. I let it go in one ear and out the other." "What can you do?," Coffey told the *Edmonton Sun* regarding Seiling's comments. "I guess instead of working on my defensive play when I turned pro, I worked on my skating, shooting and passing."

Twenty years ago Jack and Betty Coffey didn't realize the heights their son would reach playing Canada's national game. They started Paul in organized hockey at age four in Weston, Ontario. Betty Coffey said he took to the game immediately. "We hear all the terrible stories about pressur-ing kids into the game," she told the *Edmonton Sun*. "But there was never a time he didn't want to go. He dedicated himself to hockey even at a young age." Coffey also took up baseball, soccer, and lacrosse. "In baseball and soccer, he was always on all-star teams, but finally had to give them up," Mrs. Coffey said. Scouts began to take notice of Coffey's hockey talent when he was fifteen and then playing for the Toronto Young Nationals. He was named most valuable player in a post-season tournament that year. Said his mother: "That's probably when he began to make a name for himself."

Two years later Coffey was playing in Sault Ste. Marie, an eight-hour drive from his home. In the 1979-80 season he played for Sault Ste. Marie and Kitchener, after being traded. His totals that season of 29 goals and 73 assists, for 102 points, were an indication of his offensive potential. He turned pro after the Oilers selected him in the first round of the 1980 NHL amateur draft, the sixth player taken overall. In his rookie year he played 74 games and scored a meager nine goals and 23 assists. Coffey took great strides towards stardom in his second year, 1981-82, nearly tripling his offensive output with 29 goals and 60 assists on an Edmonton team that would became famous for its goal production. Coffey's offensive style of defense blended in

Paul Coffey keeps a close eye on the puck in a game against the New York Rangers at Madison Square Garden. AP/ Wide World Photos.

well with the Oilers' potent attack, helping the team score more than 400 goals a season over the next four years, a feat never accomplished by any NHL team since the league began in 1917.

On a team with as much talent as Edmonton it is harder for Coffey to be singled out as often as he would if he played for a weaker team. And when you play on the same team as Wayne Gretzky, it makes recognition matters even worse. Gretzky, chosen as the NHL's most valuable player for the last six consecutive seasons, certainly dominates the Oilers' publicity. But that hasn't bothered Coffey as much as his battle to be recognized as the game's best defenseman. "It's never really bothered any of us," Coffey told the *Detroit Free Press.* "Any ink Wayne gets he deserves."

But Coffey has begun to get his share of the limelight. In fact, may observers were shocked when Oilers general manager and coach Glen Sather revealed in May 1984 that the Oiler most often asked about by other teams for trade was Coffey, not Gretzky. That still wasn't enough to influence voters to name Coffey the league's best defenseman in 1984. And all the time that was gnawing at Coffey. He was runner-up to Langway, but that just made it worse when in June he had to attend the NHL awards banquet, which was televised nationally in Canada. He seriously considered not attending the affair. "I had a gut feeling that I wasn't going to win it," Coffey told the *Edmonton Journal.* "I said to myself, 'You go there and the award is announced and they say the winner is Rod Langway.' And there's more people staring at me than at Rod Langway, just to see what my reaction is. As much as you're a winner because you're the second-best defenseman, you feel like a loser."

While Coffey admitted the pain of losing the trophy, he tried to turn the incident into something positive. "I took it the right way," he told the *Edmonton Journal.* "The same thing as when I got cut from Team Canada three years ago. I took it the right way. I worked harder and then made the team. This time I'm just going to work harder to win the Norris." So in August 1984, Coffey trained for Team Canada and easily made the team. He then went on to surprise many observers with his defensive play in the tournament. The *Edmonton Journal* noted that Coffey's performance in the Canada Cup made many writers start to take notice of his defensive work—"specifically one shift in the semifinal against the Soviet Union." The play came in overtime with the score tied at two goals each. Coffey was the lone defenseman back when two Russian forwards broke into the Canadian zone. He broke up the play, took the puck away from one Russian player and skated up the ice. Then Coffey fired a shot that Mike Bossy, of the New York Islanders, deflected in for the winning goal.

That play set the stage for Coffey's 1984-85 regular season, one in which he consciously wanted to win votes for the Norris Trophy. He began to change his game early in the season. He was still playing the Bobby Orr style of defense, skating from one end of the ice to the other with the puck, but less often. By the season's end, though, Coffey's offensive statistics were still startling for a defenseman: 37 goals and 84 assists, for 121 points. So Coffey added more defense to his game but at the same time did not give up his offense. Another factor often overlooked about Coffey is his durability. But that, too, came to the forefront in 1985. At 6

feet, 203 pounds, the left-handed shooting defenseman went through his fourth consecutive season without missing a game due to injury. At the end of the season he had set an Oilers record for most consecutive games played, 378.

When the 1985 Stanley Cup playoffs began, Coffey could no longer influence the Norris Trophy voting since all ballots were cast immediately after regular season play. But he played as if still trying to prove he was the NHL's best defenseman. By the time the Oilers defeated the Philadelphia Flyers in the finals, four games to one, Coffey broke or tied five NHL playoff records, two of which had belonged to Orr: most goals by a defenseman in a playoff year (12) and most assists in a playoff year by a defenseman (25). His 37 total points broke the record set by New York Islander Denis Potvin. Coffey's performance made it difficult not to award him the Conn Smythe Trophy as the most valuable player in the playoffs. Even Gretzky, the Conn Smythe winner, told the *Detroit Free Press:* "From my heart I wish I could put Paul's name beside mine. As I told him, it could have been either him or I."

After the playoffs it was revealed that Coffey had played while battered and bruised. "I had to have the [left] hip frozen before every game of this series," Coffey told the *Edmonton Journal.* "I hurt it in the Chicago series [semifinals], and I was having trouble pushing off on the leg. So I put the needle in—or rather Doc [team doctor Gordon] Cameron did—before each game, and after that it felt all right. But the foot is cracked and the back . . . well, it's just as sore as hell, and getting hit by Brian Propp [of Philadelphia] didn't help any." Propp, in the final game at Edmonton on May 30, ran Coffey into one of the goalposts with a check. Coffey left the ice briefly for medical attention, but came back to score two key goals, including the winner late in the first period of the 8-3 Stanley Cup clinching victory.

Two weeks after the playoffs Coffey was one of the two finalists for the Norris Trophy, but Langway was not, finishing a distant third in the voting with 89 points. This time Coffey's main competitor was Ray Bourque of Boston, who, like Coffey, is better known for his offensive skills. Bourque finished the regular season campaign with 20 goals and 66 assists for 86 points. After the regular season, Oilers coach Sather praised Coffey's play in 1984-85. "I hate comparisons, but [Bobby] Orr never played that good," Sather told the *Sporting News.* "Paul was absolutely awesome. If he doesn't win the Norris Trophy this season, there's something wrong."

Sather's speech wasn't needed. On June 12 the results revealed that the voters were sold on Coffey. He received 223 points in the voting over Bourque's 136. In an analysis of defensive styles of play in *Goal* magazine, Frank Orr, hockey writer of the *Toronto Daily Star,* said: "Coffey and Bourque represent the epitome of the defenseman's evolution. They are among the very best skaters in the NHL and their skills match those of the best forwards, where they very likely would have played in an earlier era." And only the future will tell how Coffey ranks with Orr, who retired at age 31 in 1979. If Coffey continues the pace of the first six years, he will surpass Orr's career totals (270 goals and 645 assists in 657 regular season games) after 10 seasons. And Coffey has no plans of changing his style; Orr never did.

SOURCES:

BOOKS

Halligan, John, senior editor, *National Hockey League Official Guide and Record Book, 1985-86*, National Hockey League, 1985.
Tuele, Bill, editor, *Official Edmonton Oilers 1985-1986 Guide*, Edmonton Oilers, 1985.

PERIODICALS

Detroit Free Press, May 16, 1984, May 19, 1984, May 16, 1985, May 31, 1985.
Detroit News, February 11, 1986.
Edmonton Journal, October 29, 1984, May 31, 1985.
Edmonton Sun, May 30, 1985, May 31, 1985.
Goal, Volume XIII, Issue 3, 1985.
Hockey News, October 18, 1985.
Sporting News, April 15, 1985, April 29, 1985, June 10, 1985, October 14, 1985.
Sports Illustrated, February 15, 1982, May 14, 1984, October 14, 1985.

—Sketch by John Castine

Nicholas Colasanto

1923(?)-1985

OBITUARY NOTICE: Born c. 1923, in Providence, R.I.; died following a heart attack, February 12, 1985, in Los Angeles, Calif. Accountant, actor, and director. Colasanto was best known for his portrayal of Coach Ernie Pantusso, the endearingly befuddled bartender on the popular television series "Cheers." According to the *Chicago Tribune,* Colasanto regarded his "Cheers" character as "innocent and sweet, not dumb." His performance on that show won him two Emmy Award nominations for best supporting actor in a comedy. Prior to becoming an actor, Colasanto, then an accountant, was preparing to work for an oil company in Saudi Arabia, but when he saw a performance by Charles Boyer and Henry Fonda, he decided that he wanted to act. He pursued an acting career in New York City and subsequently appeared in dozens of television shows and in motion pictures, including "Fat City," "The Raging Bull," and Alfred Hitchcock's "Family Plot." In addition, Colasanto acted in various Broadway productions, winning a Tony Award nomination for his performance in "Across the Board Tomorrow Morning."

With the help of his friend and fellow actor, Ben Gazzara, Colasanto got his first break as a director, working on an episode of Gazzara's dramatic television series "Run for your Life." From there he went on to direct about 100 episodes of such television programs as "Bonanza," "Columbo," "Name of the Game," and "Hawaii Five-O." He had been a member of the cast of "Cheers" since its first episode in 1982. The executive producer of the show, Les Charles, told reporters: "We won't try to have another 'Coach' or anything like that character. He's irreplaceable."

AP/Wide World Photos

SOURCES:

PERIODICALS

Chicago Tribune, February 14, 1985.
Los Angeles Times, February 13, 1985.
Newsweek, February 25, 1985.
New York Times, February 14, 1985.
Time, February 25, 1985.
Washington Post, February 17, 1985.

William K. Coors

1916-

BRIEF ENTRY: Born in 1916, in Golden, Colo. American brewery executive. William K. Coors has been head of the family-controlled Adolph Coors Co. since 1946 and is currently its chairman of the board and chief executive officer. Under his direction, the company founded in 1873 by his grandfather has developed from a strictly regional operation based in Golden, Colo., into the sixth-largest brewer in America. Without the benefit of much advertising or promotion, Coors Beer became a national fad in the mid-1970s, when it was the most popular brand in the Rocky Mountain states and had a strong market share in the West but was largely unavailable in the East. Contributing to the Coors mystique was the fact that the beer is brewed unpasteurized in a single brewery and must be refrigerated during shipment.

While expanding its markets into the East and Southeast, Coors has also been trying to polish up its image. According to Kathleen Teltsch in the *New York Times,* the company has a long history of disputes with unions and minorities—a situation aggravated by racist remarks attributed to William Coors in a speech he delivered at a minority business conference in Denver on February 23, 1984. Hailing America as the land of opportunity, Coors reportedly said that if blacks visited Africa they would realize one of the best things slave traders did was "to drag your ancestors here in chains." Though regarded by a number of people at the meeting as inoffensive, the remarks prompted a boycott of Coors Beer by over 500 California liquor stores, and repercussions were felt nationally.

Coors, who maintains he was misquoted and his comments distorted, filed a $150 million libel suit against the source of the report, the *Rocky Mountain News.* To demonstrate a commitment to black communities, Adolph Coors Co. increased the number of its minority vendors and made a $20,000 donation to the United Negro College Fund. Moreover, the company pledged to establish aggressive hiring programs, place blacks in senior-level positions, and use black financial institutions for financing distributorships. *Addresses—Home:* Route 5, Box 763, Golden, Colo. 80401. *Office:* Adolph Coors Co., Golden, Colo. 80401.

SOURCES:

PERIODICALS

Black Enterprise, August, 1984.
Denver Post, November 9, 1984.
Forbes, July 19, 1982, October 24, 1983.
New York Times, April 26, 1984.
Rocky Mountain News, May 16, 1976, May 10, 1977, June 17, 1978, August 8, 1983, December 5, 1984, February 24, 1984, February 25, 1984.

Courtesy of Adolph Coors Company

Richard Joseph Cox
1929-

BRIEF ENTRY: Born August 21, 1929, in Brooklyn, N.Y. American broadcasting executive. The president of CBS's Cable Division since 1981, Richard Joseph Cox has become well known in broadcast circles as an innovator and creative thinker. He was instrumental in the production of the first syndicated soap opera. In 1970 he co-produced "Orlando Purioso," an Off-Broadway play whose cast of sixty actors— all of them Italians who spoke no English—performed their parts among the audience, wheeling about furiously on small platforms; Cox received a special Obie Award for the production. And he was responsible for bringing the Tony Award show to national television for the first time.

Prior to his arrival at CBS Cable, Cox held positions as a vice-president at Young & Rubicam advertising and Doyle, Dane, Bernbach, president of Y & R Ventures, Inc., a broadcast distribution and consulting firm, and owner-president of DCA Productions, Inc., a radio and television production company. Under his direction, CBS Cable has grown tremendously and has received rave reviews from television critics.

Cox sees the function of cable television as "narrowcasting"—broadcasting to a narrower audience—and he believes in presenting the kind of cultural programming that would not appeal to the mass audience that watches network television. Cox insists that, economically, cable television doesn't have to cater to the tastes of fifty million people to be successful, and he intends to keep the CBS Cable Division aimed at the relatively small segment of the population that is hungry for cultural television programming. *Address:* CBS Cable Division, 51 West 52nd St., New York, N.Y. 10019.

SOURCES:

PERIODICALS

Broadcasting, January 4, 1982.

Courtesy of Richard Cox

Tom Cruise

1962(?)-

PERSONAL: Born c. 1962 in Syracuse, N.Y.; son of an electrical engineer and a teacher of dyslexic and hyperkinetic children. *Education:* Graduated from high school in Glen Ridge, N.J.

ADDRESSES: Agent—Andrea Jaffe, PMK, 8642 Melrose Ave., Los Angeles, Calif. 90069.

OCCUPATION: Actor.

CAREER: Worked at a variety of odd jobs in New York City for a short time; actor, 1980—, appearing in a number of feature films, including "Endless Love" and "Taps," 1981, "Losin' It," "The Outsiders," "Risky Business," and "All the Right Moves," 1983, "Top Gun" and "Legends," 1986, and "The Color of Money."

SIDELIGHTS: One of the hottest young actors working in films today is Tom Cruise, who, since 1980, has had roles in six major motion pictures and has received star billing for three of them, including the 1983 hit "Risky Business." Since deciding on an acting career in his late teens, Cruise has pursued his profession with a seriousness that seems to contradict his youthful appearance, "I work very hard," Cruise told *People* magazine. "My craft is the most important thing in my life." Critics such as David Ansen of *Newsweek* have analyzed Cruise's screen appeal, which, paired with a distinct versatility, includes "a straight-ahead, clean-cut sexiness, a presence both modest and strong."

According to Cruise, the decision to become an actor came by accident in his senior year of high school. In order to lose weight for an upcoming wrestling tournament, he was running up and down stairs in his home when he slipped on some homework papers one of his sisters had left behind. He fell, pulled several muscles, and was sidelined for the season. "It was a mess," Cruise told *Seventeen* magazine. "I had to be on crutches, and I was crushed because I couldn't wrestle that season. To cheer me up, a teacher suggested, 'Look, go out for *Guys and Dolls*, the school musical.' That's when I discovered acting." Cruise sensed immediately that performing could satisfy a long unarticulated need for self-expression. "It just felt right," he told *People* of his first experience on the stage. "It felt like I had a way to express myself." He also told *Cosmopolitan* magazine, "I just remember feeling so at home on stage, so relaxed." Wrestling and the many other sports in which Cruise excelled were forgotten as he embarked on a more satisfying undertaking.

The only son in a family of four, Cruise was born in Syracuse, New York. His father was an electrical engineer, whose work necessitated moving frequently. Before he was eleven, Cruise had lived in Kentucky, Missouri, Ohio, Canada, New Jersey, and New York. Cruise told *Seventeen* that the constant mobility caused him to feel "kind of

scattered" growing up. He tried to insure popularity by excelling in athletics, explaining in *People:* "I would pick up a new sport as a way to make friends. I'd go up and say, 'Do you play tennis? Do you want to play sometime?' "

Cruise's childhood was further complicated by dyslexia, a disability he shares with his mother and sisters. He first became aware of the problem, he told *Seventeen*, when he was in kindergarten. "I didn't know whether letters like 'C' or 'D' curved to the right or left. That affects everything you do." That difficulty compounded his struggle for acceptance at each new school. "I was put in remedial reading classes," he recalled to *People*. "When you're a new kid, all you want to do is blend in with everything and make friends. It was a drag. It separated you and singled you out." Patient tutoring by his mother, however, helped him to surmount the problem, and his achievement has helped him to form a philosophy that has carried over into his acting career. He told *Seventeen:* "Right now my dyslexia no longer affects me, but it did influence my life, because growing up, I've always had to overcome something. It's as if God has given you this great mind and then holds you back, saying, 'Ah, but you're going to have to work for this.' I'm a very driven person in that I set goals for myself—goals to prevent myself from quitting."

Cruise's parents divorced when he was eleven, but the family continued to move frequently until he was in high school. Finally settling in Glen Ridge, New Jersey, Cruise completed his schooling there and began to learn not to stereotype himself and others. "I was a jock, and I sang in the chorus," he told *Seventeen.* "Jocks don't do that, so I always felt challenged. I always tried not to fall into the mold, not to judge people by where they came from or what they were."

After graduating, Cruise had no desire to go to college. Instead, he moved to New York and supported himself by doing odd jobs—including busing tables and loading trucks—while attending open calls for stage and film roles. His first part was a small one, a few lines in the movie "Endless Love," starring Brooke Shields and Martin Hewitt. The scene took one day to film, but Cruise made an impression on director Franco Zeffirelli, leading to three years of virtual nonstop work.

The next role Cruise received was more substantial. He was cast as an unstable cadet in the film "Taps," starring Timothy Hutton. The movie concerns a group of students at a military academy who decide to "defend" their school when it is scheduled to be razed in favor of a condominium development. The cadets commandeer weapons and produce a dangerous standoff with the real military troops just beyond the academy walls. As part of his preparation for the role, Cruise gained fifteen pounds by swigging milkshakes. "The character had to make a visual impact," he explained in *Seventeen,* "because he wasn't in that many scenes." Though still a neophyte in the acting business, Cruise was able to persuade director Harold Becker to add a scene that showed his gung-ho character lifting weights. Though small, the role Cruise created was intense and memorable, and offers for more films followed.

Afraid of being typecast as a "crazy," Cruise took a starring role in the comedy "Losin' It." The film described in *Seventeen* as "tasteless," was a box-office failure. The story concerns a group of California teenagers who journey to the Mexican border for an evening of sexual revelry. En route to Tijuana, the boys pick up a hitchhiker (played by Shelley Long) who eventually forms a romantic liaison with Cruise's character. "Losin' It" has run numerous times on cable television, to Cruise's embarrassment. Filming the comedy, he recalled in *Seventeen,* was "the most depressing experience of my life. I won't take any more films like that. But it was an eye-opener. It made me understand how you really have to be careful about what you do. You may feel you can make a script into something good, but you've got to examine all the elements of a project. Who's directing? Who's producing? I've learned to evaluate what everyone has to say before making up my own mind."

Cruise next signed for a supporting role in the "The Outsiders," an artful film based on an S.E. Hinton novel of the same title. Once again determined to sculpt himself properly for the part, Cruise had a cap removed from one of his front teeth and refused to shower for most of the nine weeks of shooting. Cruise, who has few lines in the "The Outsiders," appears in the film as one of a gang of "greasers" who inhabit an Oklahoma town where class lines

are drawn with violent force. The combined effect of this gang is described by Richard Corliss in a review for *Time* magazine: "The greasers, with their sleek muscles and androgynous faces, display a leonine athleticism as they move through dusty lots or do a graceful, two-handed vault over a chain-link fence. Their camaraderie is familial, embracing, unself-consciously homoerotic." Cruise recalled the experience of filming "The Outsiders" in *Seventeen:* "I was nineteen and had an opportunity to work with [director] Francis Ford Coppola, and to act with guys like Matt Dillon and Rob Lowe and Emilio Estevez and have a good time." As with previous films, the friendships Cruise established on the set have continued, in this case with Estevez, whom Cruise describes in *People* as a "close buddy."

Following "The Outsiders" was the 1983 summer release, "Risky Business," starring Cruise and Rebecca De Mornay. Called "this summer's one genuine sleeper" by *Newsweek's* David Ansen, the film was an immediate success, earning $56 million in its first eleven weeks. "Risky Business" catapulted both Cruise and De Mornay into stardom and earned Cruise his first serious critical attention. "Here he is, Superman in miniature," praised Richard Corliss of *Time,* comparing Cruise to "Superman" star Christopher Reeve: "the hooded eyes, the sculpted body, the offbeat comic timing, the self-deprecating manner, the winning smile, Cruise [is] a surprise package of 1983."

"Risky Business" charts the adventures of a high school senior (Cruise) who literally capitalizes on his parents' absence by turning their home into a one-night brothel for his friends. With the help of a shrewd prostitute, Lana (De Mornay), Joel, the young "Future Enterpriser," pairs his friends with those of the prostitute for fun and profit. A *National Review* critic describes the upshot of the action in the film: "It's a triumph for free enterprise: Joel makes a bundle (which he later loses to Lana's pimp), makes Lana (with whom he forms a lasting partnership), and makes Princeton. With Lana and Princeton for mentors, he will end up worldly, wealthy and wise."

Critics have viewed Cruise's performance in "Risky Business" with mixed reactions. In her *New Yorker* review, Pauline Kael notes: "Imagining himself a rock star dancing, [Cruise] is a charmingly clunky dynamo. (At times, he's like a shorter Christopher Reeve, and the film seems to be raising the question 'Can nice boys be sexy?'). . . . [But later in the film] Joel becomes an Example, and he loses whatever likability he had as a goofball kid; Cruise isn't allowed enough emotions to sustain the performance." The *National Review* critic says simply, "Tom Cruise is unremarkable as Joel." On the other hand, praise for Cruise's portrayal comes from Lawrence O'Toole in *Macleans:* "As the gullible, slightly dopey Joel, Tom Cruise gives a sunny performance, beaming with good nature." David Ansen echoes that sentiment in *Newsweek,* writing "Joel, smartly and attractively played by Cruise, is very much a success-obsessed child of the '80s." And Paul Brickman, the director of "Risky Business," describes his satisfaction with Cruise's performance in *Seventeen:* "Tom had a good instinct for the truth of the character. To a certain extent, Tom is a spokesman for his generation."

If Cruise indeed served as a "spokesman for his generation" in a film that satirized wealth and get-rich-quick ideals, he must also have served as a spokesman for another segment of modern youth in "All the Right Moves," his second starring role in 1983. In "All the Right Moves," the principal character, Stef Djordjevic (Cruise) strives for a football scholarship that will allow him to escape the hopeless future in a Pennsylvania steel town. Stef's dreams appear about to be thwarted when he alienates his high school coach, who then tells recruiters Stef has a "bad attitude." Lawrence O'Toole praises the film in *Macleans* as "a decent, modest movie, . . . one of the first films to take a long, hard look at North America's current economic malaise."

While "All the Right Moves" did not achieve the box office success of "Risky Business," it was a modest hit that has accorded Cruise more critical acclaim than had any of his prior roles. Frank Deford comments in *Sports Illustrated:* "As for Cruise, he may be a brooding heartthrob type for the teenagers, but, as he showed in 'Risky Business,' he's also a young actor of consequence. . . . Stef is tough as nails but gentle with his lovely girl friend, loyal to his pals and a stalwart of good humor and inner strength." Says Lawrence Eisenberg in *Cosmopolitan*, "Tom has a quality of self-mockery just below the surface and a chameleonlike way of becoming the disparate characters he plays." Edwin Miller ascribes similar qualities to Cruise in *Seventeen:* "When you see his recent movies, . . . you sense Tom's independence, his cool know-how, his unassuming strength . . . and his vulnerability."

Offscreen, Cruise lives quietly, tending to take short leases on apartments near the sites where his films are being shot. "Everything I have fits into two suitcases," he told *People*. His best friends are, for the most part, fellow actors, including Estevez, Sean Penn and Timothy Hutton, de-scribed by Cruise in *Seventeen* as "really nice guys who don't let you down. All . . . of us care about our work."

Cruise continues to concentrate on his career in films and, perhaps, the stage. "I work at keeping myself in check," he told *Cosmopolitan*, reflecting on his sudden fame. "I'm only human, but I'm trying to keep all this in focus." In *Seventeen*, director Brickman observes: "Tom is very ambitious. He's young in a very tough world, and he's fighting for a career on his own terms. I don't think he'll take the cheap or easy way out. He's very rigorous about the kind of material he wants and the kind of people he wants to work with." As Cruise himself told *People:* "I enjoy the pressure of making a movie. It's like getting psyched up for a wrestling match—but with higher stakes. I thrive on it."

SOURCES:

PERIODICALS:

Cosmopolitan, January, 1984.
Maclean's, August 15, 1983, November 7, 1983.
Mademoiselle, April, 1985.
Moviegoer, December, 1985.
National Review, October 14, 1983.
New Republic, September 19-26, 1983.
Newsweek, August 15, 1983, November 7, 1983.
New Yorker, September 5, 1983.
People, September 5, 1983, March 5, 1984.
Seventeen, February, 1984, April, 1985.
Sports Illustrated, November 14, 1983.
Teen, November, 1982, December, 1983.
Time, December 14, 1981, April 4, 1983, November 7, 1983.

—Sidelights by Mark Kram

Arturo Cruz

1923-

PERSONAL: Full name, Arturo Jose Cruz Porras; born December 18, 1923, in Jinotepe, Nicaragua; son of Arturo Cruz Sanchez and Juanita Porras; married Consuelo Sequeira, August 31, 1952; children: Arturo Jose, Consuelo, Nydia, Fernando, Alvaro, Olga, Roberto. *Education:* Military Academy of Nicaragua, graduate, 1944; Georgetown University, B.S. in foreign service, 1947, M.S., 1972. *Religion:* Roman Catholic.

ADDRESSES: Home—5603 Jordan Rd., Bethesda, Md. 20816.

OCCUPATION: Nicaraguan politician, economist, business executive.

CAREER: Clerk, International Monetary Fund, 1947; member of staff, J. Dreyfus & Co., 1948-56; Banco Nicaraguense, Managua, Nicaragua, deputy general manager, 1957-61; Central Bank for Economic Integration, Tegucigalpa, Honduras, operations manager, 1962-66; Aceitera Corona, Managua, general manager, 1966-69; Inter-American Development Bank, associate treasurer and chief of Capital and Finance Operations Division, 1969-79, 1982-84; president, Central Bank of Nicaragua, 1979-80; member of Nicaragua's ruling junta, 1980-81; Nicaraguan ambassador to the United States, 1981. Member of board of directors, Chamber of Industry of Nicaragua. Lecturer, School of Educational Sciences, Autonomous University of Nicaragua.

WRITINGS: Contributor of articles to journals, including *Foreign Affairs* and *Strategic Review.*

SIDELIGHTS: Arturo Cruz has spent most of his life working as an economist, a business executive, and an international civil servant. But his greatest prominence has come in the years leading up to and following the Nicaraguan revolution of 1979, during which he has emerged as the leading spokesman for Nicaraguans who have been forced to battle first against a dictatorship of the right and then against a dictatorship of the left.

Although he graduated from Nicaragua's military academy, he never served in the military. Instead, he went on from the academy to take a bachelor's degree in the United States. Toward the end of his college years, he joined a Nicaraguan reform movement called Union Nacional de Accion Popular (UNAP), which was led by Pedro Joaquin Chamorro Cardenal and which opposed the dictatorial rule of the elder Anastasio Somoza, the first of three members of the Somoza family who ruled Nicaragua from the mid-1930s until 1979. (The assassination in 1978 of Chamorro—editor of the opposition newspaper, *La Prensa*—proved to be the catalytic event in the overthrow of the Somoza dynasty in Nicaragua.)

UPI/Bettmann Newsphotos

Because of his political activities against Somoza, Cruz was jailed in 1947 for four months. This did little to deter him, though, and in 1954 he joined with other UNAP members in an unsuccessful effort to depose Somoza. This earned Cruz a second prison term of a year's duration and resulted in the dissolution of UNAP. Looking back, Cruz believes that the destruction of UNAP, whose anti-Somoza program was moderate and reformist, was one of the early steps down the path that led in the 1970s to the emergence of the radical Frente Sandinista de Liberacion Nacional (FSLN, or Sandinista National Liberation Front) as the leading force in the movement against Somoza.

Upon the dissolution of UNAP, Cruz joined the Conservative Party, the officially recognized opposition to Somoza's Liberal Party, and he has remained a member of the Conservative Party ever since. (The "Liberal" and "Conservative" parties of Nicaragua were formed along lines of regional and other divisions, and their names bear little relationship to the content of their political programs.)

In 1977, Cruz was approached by representatives of the FSLN and asked to join a small group of prominent

Nicaraguans that would work in alliance with the Sandinistas and serve to give the revolutionary guerrilla movement greater legitimacy in the eyes of Nicaraguans and of the outside world. Cruz joined eagerly, he told *CN*, "because I felt it was worthwhile supporting the Sandinistas who were launching a big, heroic struggle against Somoza, and I expected them to be a 'democratic vanguard' as they promised." Cruz says that he felt some misgivings about the FSLN, but set these aside, "because we democrats were so fed up with Somoza and so convinced that he was an evil, that we rejected the notion that we could not take chances." Only his position as an officer of an international institution (the Inter-American Development Bank) prevented Cruz from being as active a member as he would have wished.

The group, which became known simply as "Los Doce" (The Twelve), was made up of academics, professionals, and businessmen. It was described repeatedly in the U.S. press and elsewhere as "non-Marxist," and it served to inspire the belief that a victory by the FSLN in its war to topple Anastasio Somoza Debayle (the last dictator in the Somoza dynasty) would not necessarily lead to the imposition of a Marxist government. It has been revealed since the FSLN took power that, while Cruz and most of the other members of The Twelve were acting in good faith, some of the group—Cruz believes that the number is four—were secret members of the FSLN all along.

When the Sandinista-led revolution drove Somoza from office in July, 1979, a five-member junta, named by the Sandinistas but including two members who did not share the Sandinista ideology, formally took power. (In a practical sense, much power still rested in the hands of the Sandinista commanders on the ground.) The revolutionary government named Cruz president of the Central Bank of Nicaragua.

The country had been ravaged by civil war, and Cruz saw his primary goal as being "to get the economic system working again, no matter how." That pragmatism brought Cruz into his first conflict with the Sandinista rulers. For ideological reasons, they decreed a complete nationalization of the banking industry, a step that Cruz opposed. Cruz told *CN*: "I was in favor of either an intervention by the government or, if you wish, a partial nationalization, but not one hundred percent nationalization. But in the enthusiasm of the revolution, the radicals had the upper hand and their views prevailed."

The nationalization of the banks, says Cruz, was only part of a larger issue over which he was at odds with the Sandinistas. The Sandinistas insisted that they wanted to preserve the role of the private sector in the Nicaraguan economy, but Cruz felt that their actions worked to undermine the confidence on which economic activity by the private sector depends. He says he told the Sandinistas: "Don't swallow so much. If we don't create confidence among producers and investors we will never get this economy running again. We are losing the best economists. We are losing the best business administrators. We are losing the best producers. Everyone is leaving. People do not want to invest; they just want to get by. Everyone is taking a wait-and-see attitude." But Cruz says that his appeals to the rulers were time and again followed by the announcement of new arbitrary expropriations.

A second step in his disillusionment with the Sandinistas came as he labored to work out a system of priorities for allocation of Nicaragua's scarce currency reserves, which faced a huge backlog of routine claims that had gone unprocessed during the previous six months of civil war. Nicaraguans receiving medical care abroad needed doctors' fees transmitted. Those studying abroad needed their tuition transmitted. The country urgently needed to replace buses destroyed in the fighting with imported ones in order to restore public transportation. Cruz had to persuade other citizens with less urgent needs—those waiting to import cars or luxury items—that their transactions had to wait. But, says Cruz, "I was all the time undermined by the government, which was the first one violating those guidelines because they wanted to import Volvos, speedy vehicles and whatnot for the Commandantes and members of the junta."

After eight months at the Central Bank, a frustrated Cruz submitted his resignation. At just about the same time, the two non-Sandinista members of the governing junta—businessman Alfonso Robelo and Violetta Chamorro, widow of the slain editor of *La Prensa*—also resigned. All of these resignations cast a pall over the image that the Sandinista government projected abroad, and the worried Sandinistas asked Cruz to take one of the vacant seats in the junta. He says that he told the Sandinistas of his disquiet with the direction they were taking and that they replied: "That is precisely why we need you. We want to make a change." And so, after what he describes as "a painful process of soul-searching," Cruz joined the junta and remained a member for almost a year.

"During that period," he has written, "I observed a push for the 'Sandinisation' of almost everything in the land." Above all, he says, what drove him from the junta was the Sandinistas' attitude toward their political opponents, "their continuing reluctance to see their political adversaries as a compliment to their legitimacy." "It was quite clear to me," he adds, "that the 'broad alliance' had been a total hoax, that, in the eyes of the FSLN, the non-Marxist-Leninist elements in that alliance were their tactical allies, but their strategic enemies."

Nonetheless, when he resigned from the junta, Cruz was still willing to serve the revolutionary government in one further capacity—as its ambassador to the United States, a post which he says he accepted "with enthusiasm." Despite his unhappiness with the government, Cruz hoped he could achieve a reconciliation between Washington and Managua, which would have been beneficial to Nicaragua and would have eliminated the specter of U.S. hostility as a rationale for repressive actions by the Sandinista government.

But after seven months, Cruz, for the third and last time, resigned from an office in the Nicaraguan government. He wrote about that decision: "the frequent shutdowns of *La Prensa* and the imprisonment of business leaders for criticizing the government undermined me personally. At such a delicate time, when a head-on collision with the United States was imminent, I realized that, in view of the fact that I dissented from my government regarding its domestic policies and disagreed with its foreign policy, I could not continue being an effective envoy. I therefore left the government permanently."

Cruz took up residence in Washington, accepted an offer to return to work for the Inter-American Development Bank, and began to take an initially low-profile role in the movement of political opposition to the Nicaraguan government. He served, he has written, as "moderator at the meeting where ARDE's creation was decided." ARDE is the acronym for the Alianza Revolucionaria Democratica, a group initially led by Eden Pastora, once the most famous of the Sandinista military commanders, and Alfonso Robelo, a prominent business leader who had worked in alliance with the FSLN in the struggle to overthrow Somoza, both of whom had resigned from the revolutionary government.

In 1984, the Sandinistas announced that national elections would be held. Seeing this as perhaps a last opportunity to arrest the slide toward totalitarian rule, Nicaragua's disparate democratic elements joined together in a rare display of unity. Three centrist political parties, two national labor federations, and the organization comprising the country's professional and business associations formed the Coordinadora Democratica Nicaraguense. They determined to face the elections together, provided that the government would supply the minimum guarantees to make the elections truly meaningful. These guarantees included such things as international oversight of the election, an end to press censorship, an unimpeded opportunity to campaign, and access to the air waves.

The Coordinadora chose Cruz as its candidate for president. Cruz returned to Nicaragua, where he "tested the waters" by holding a couple of campaign rallies. These brought out large and enthusiastic crowds but also government-organized mobs that assaulted Cruz and members of his audience while the police refused to intervene. Ultimately, after some fruitless negotiations between the Coordinadora and the government, mediated by other Latin American statesmen, the government refused to provide the kinds of guarantees that the Coordinadora was seeking. The Coordinadora then announced its refusal to take part in the elections and was joined in this stance by virtually every one of the other, smaller, democratic parties.

Although his candidacy was aborted, his nomination by the Coordinadora left Cruz as the acknowledged main spokesman for Nicaraguan democrats. Their aim, he insists, "is not counterrevolutionary. We are not against the revolution. We want the revolution to return to the three principles on which it was predicated—non-alignment, mixed economy, and pluralism. We want the democratization of the revolution."

SOURCES:

BOOKS

Nolan, David, *The Ideology of the Sandinistas and the Nicaraguan Revolution*, Institute of Interamerican Studies, University of Miami, 1984.

PERIODICALS

Foreign Affairs, summer, 1983.
New Republic, October 8, 1984.
New York Times, October 27, 1978, November 3, 1978, June 10, 1979, July 1, 1979.
New York Times Magazine, July 30, 1978.
Strategic Review, spring, 1984.
Washington Post, September 28, 1984.

—*Sketch by Joshua Muravchik*

Billy Crystal
1947-

PERSONAL: Full name, William Crystal; born March 14, 1947, in Long Beach, N.Y.; son of Jack (a record store owner, record company executive, and producer of jazz concerts) and Helen Crystal; married, 1970; wife's name, Janice; children: Jennifer, Lindsay. *Education:* Attended Marshall University and Nassau Community College; New York University, bachelor's degree in television and film directing, 1970.

ADDRESSES: Office—c/o Press Department, National Broadcasting Co., Inc., 30 Rockefeller Plaza, New York, N.Y. 10112.

OCCUPATION: Comedian and actor.

CAREER: Worked for a short time as a substitute teacher; house manager for play "You're a Good Man, Charlie Brown," New York, N.Y., 1971; member of touring comedy group 3's Company, 1971-75; solo stand-up comedian, 1975—; member of cast of television series "Soap," 1977-81; host of television program "The Billy Crystal Comedy Hour," 1982; member of cast of television series "Saturday Night Live," 1984-1985; other television appearances include "The Tonight Show," "Dinah," "That Was the Year That Was," "All in the Family," and "Love Boat"; appeared in made-for-television movies "Death Flight," "Enola Gay: The Men, the Mission, the Atomic Bomb," and "Breaking Up Is Hard to Do," and in motion pictures "Rabbit Test," 1978, and "Running Scared," 1986.

AWARDS, HONORS: Emmy Award nomination, Academy of Television Arts and Sciences, 1985, for "Saturday Night Live"; Grammy Award nomination, 1985, for *Mahvelous.*

DISCOGRAPHY:

Mahvelous (comedy album), A & M Records, 1985.

SIDELIGHTS: The ability to improvise and play a wide array of unlikely characters has made Billy Crystal one of America's most popular comedic actors. Crystal, who always said he would rather play shortstop than Shakespeare, built a loyal following as the star of two network shows: ABC's "Soap," from 1977 to 1981, and NBC's "Saturday Night Live," which he joined in 1984. He has also consistently been one of the most popular comics on the national campus circuit. It was on "SNL" that Crystal gained widespread acclaim as a versatile mimic. His cast of characters included Sammy Davis, Jr., Herve Villechaize, and Fernando Lamas (whose oft-repeated line, "You look maaaaaavelous" has become an American catch-phrase).

AP/Wide World Photos

Crystal was born into a show business family in 1947. His father, Jack Crystal, managed the famous Commodore Record Store on 42nd Street in New York City and started the Commodore jazz record label. By the time Billy was five years old, he knew some of the nation's top jazz artists, whom he described to *Playboy* as "great characters and funny. . . . I loved the fact that they made people feel good. I would run up on stage and tap dance with them. That's when I started performing." One of his friends was singer Billie Holiday, who frequently babysat for the young boy. "But it's not like my folks said, 'Billie, it's $3 an hour, there's food in the fridge and stay off the phone,'" he told *Sunday's People* magazine. "It's more like I hung out with her sometimes." Holiday and other musicians nicknamed the young boy "Face." Three decades later, Crystal's nightclub act would feature an aging trumpet player talking wistfully to a young boy named "Face."

From the start, Crystal was fascinated with show business. Growing up on Long Island, he recalls, he would watch the Jack Paar show, pulling his chair next to the television to play the sixth guest. His two boyhood heroes were comedian Ernie Kovacs and New York Yankee second baseman Bobby Richardson. Crystal's father died when he was fifteen. "That got me angry," he told *Playboy*. "It still does. You come to a point in life when you want to say, 'I'm doing good.'. . . I miss being able to say that to my dad."

Crystal was captain of his high school baseball team and attended Marshall University on a baseball scholarship. He told *People* magazine that after one year at the school he decided "Huntington, West Virginia was a little too-off Broadway," so he transferred to Nassau (Long Island) Community College. The transfer also marked the end of his dream of playing shortstop for a major league ball club. Crystal says his diminutive size—five-foot-six—rather than a lack of skills prevented him from going further in the game. One year later, Crystal switched to New York University, where he studied directing with Martin Scorsese. He graduated in 1970 with a degree in television and film direction. That same year he married his wife, Janice, whom he had met at school. Her income as a guidance counselor, along with the small amount he brought in as a substitute teacher, kept the couple going as Crystal pursued an acting career. "I never made more than $4,200 a year back then," he later told *People*.

Crystal was house manager of an Off-Broadway theater and then toured with an improvisational group, 3's Company.

After several unsuccessful years, he met talent manager Jack Rollins, who convinced Crystal to try working on his own. "With 3's Company I was hiding from being by myself," he told the *New York Times*. "I wanted to be out there by myself. But I was frightened." Later, Crystal was performing solo at Los Angeles's Comedy Store nightclub in front of television producer Norman Lear and several ABC executives. It was "one of those strange Hollywood nights when everything clicked," Crystal told *People*. Lear hired him to appear on several episodes of the hit series, "All in the Family," and ABC gave him a guest spot on Howard Cosell's short-lived variety show.

In 1977, Lear chose Crystal to star in the comedy "Soap" as Jodie Dallas, the first openly homosexual character in the history of television. The role was assailed both by conservatives and the National Gay Task Force, which put Crystal on its enemies list, saying he advanced gay stereotypes. Eventually the character was toned down, and the homosexual organization called him "the one sane, sensitive person on the whole show." "Soap" and Crystal proved extremely popular. The actor received "very graphic letters from fans. Women find Jodie very sexy. They think they could cure him in one night," he told *People*.

Billy Crystal (center, in Fernando Lamas makeup) with "Saturday Night Live" guests Alex Karras and Tina Turner. AP/Wide World Photos.

Crystal appreciated his new-found fame but considered his role limited and confining. "One character. Boring," he later told the *Detroit Free Press*. Among those watching "Soap" was comedienne Joan Rivers, who like what she saw. Rivers cast Crystal in her film "Rabbit Test," about the first man to become pregnant. The film was neither a critical nor financial success. On the first day of filming for "Rabbit Test," Crystal's wife's own pregnancy test proved positive. The day of the film's screening, she delivered a baby. The couple now has two daughters, Jennifer and Lindsay.

In the early 1980s, Crystal starred briefly in his own comedy hour for NBC, made several cable television specials and appeared as a guest on situation comedies, such as "Love Boat." He also appeared in several television dramas, including NBC's critically acclaimed "Enola Gay: The Men, the Mission, the Atomic Bomb." At that point, Crystal later told the *Columbus Dispatch*, he "felt the need to get back to live comedy before live audiences." He started touring nightclubs and college campuses, a practice he continues to enjoy.

One of Crystal's tours had him opening for Sammy Davis, Jr. "I used to talk with him and I would relate to people, things that Sammy said," he told the *Detroit Free Press*. Unconsciously, Crystal began to take on Davis's characteristics and the imitation became a popular part of his act. But his most famous imitation is of the late actor Fernando Lamas. "The whole thing got started when I was watching 'The Tonight Show,' and Fernando Lamas was on," Crystal told *Playboy*. "I used to love him because he would say, 'You look marveious, John.'. . . He would just say it and that seemed to be the thrust of his in-depth conversation. And then one night. . . Fernando said, 'I'd rather look good than feel good.' I got hysterical. I was running for a pad." Crystal's imitation of Lamas became part of this nightclub act. The character would star in a make-believe talk show, "Fernando's Hideaway," where he pandered over guests as Crystal improvised. "Making it up as we go along is the key to its success," he told the *Washington Post*. "You can't put those things in a script. Improvisation is what makes it work."

Crystal and his characters joined the cast of NBC's long-running "Saturday Night Live" in 1984. In 1976, Crystal was to have been part of the show's original cast. But his only skit got bumped from the first show, and his role became limited to a few guest appearances. He decided to pursue other opportunities. Seven years later, Crystal guest-hosted an episode of "Saturday Night Live" that proved to be the most popular one of the season. Producer Dick Ebersol asked him to join the cast of "SNL" for the 1984-85 season. Crystal agreed, which proved to be a wise career move. Writing "99 percent of my own material," as he told the *Albany Capital Dispatch*, he emerged as the most popular performer on the show. His impersonations became regular skits, as did his portrayals of other zany characters: Willie, a masochist who frets about the pain of "stapling balogna to my face"; Rabbit, an octogenarian veteran of the Negro Baseball League; and an unnamed elderly, punch-drunk boxer, who once boasted of breaking his nose seventy-seven times in one fight.

Doing "Saturday Night Live," "helped eliminate ghosts in my own mind and of how people perceived me. It has taken the anvil of 'Soap' off my chest," Crystal told the *Columbus Dispatch*. And, he said, the show gave him the opportunity to display his versatility. "This show for me has relieved great frustrations that I felt in that I've never had, week in and week out, the place to show people everything I can do. . . . It's been a wonderful year in many ways," he told the *Detroit Free Press*. But the show proved to be a grind. "Every show I go 15 rounds," he said to the *Detroit Free Press*. "It's 18-hour days." And, he told *Sunday's People* magazine, "It's 3 in the morning and I'm writing jokes. . . . No one else in the whole country is up doing this but us." In August, 1985, Crystal was nominated for an Emmy Award for "best individual performance in a variety or music program" for his work on "Saturday Night Live."

When he is not performing, Crystal likes to play tennis and baseball, cook Japanese food, and "collect miniature furniture. It gives me a great feeling of height," he told *People*. He is a frequent guest on television game shows. "I am the world's champion '$20,000 Pyramid' player. I hold the fastest time," he told *Playboy*. "I did it in 26 seconds. I have a cassette of it that I look at now and then. It was ridiculous."

Crystal's character comedy is often compared to that of Lily Tomlin or Richard Pryor, two of his favorite performers. Said the *Los Angeles Times*, "Crystal, perhaps only like Tomlin and Pryor, can comedically move an audience." *Washington Post* critic Joe Sasfy said of a Crystal performance, "He impressively employed a range of surreal vocal effects, as well as some superb physical mimicry,. . . an entertaining and fast-paced blend of topical humor, character sketches and ethnic impressions." Crystal considers his own work "Bittersweet. Nobody else will take a chance on doing anything with poignancy," he told *People*. "I'm not that concerned with getting laughs. If I can move the audience, that's more important to me." His comedic model is Bill Cosby. "Like Cosby, I try to be honest out there," he told the *Albany Capital Dispatch*. "I just rap, just talk. It's real stuff. The jokes are there, but they don't scream 'joke, joke, here comes a joke.' "

In August, 1985, Crystal announced plans to leave the "Saturday Night Live" cast. MGM chose him to co-star with Gregory Hines in the movie "Running Scared," a comedy about a pair of undercover Chicago policemen. He also plans to continue touring nightclubs. And what advice would he offer others? "Mel Brooks once said to me, 'Hang in there. I didn't make it until I was 52 years old,' " Crystal told *Playboy*. "And you've got to do what you believe in."

SOURCES:

PERIODICALS

Albany Capital Dispatch, May 9, 1985.
Christian Science Monitor, April 2, 1985.
Columbus Dispatch, July 8, 1985.
Detroit Free Press, April 26, 1985, June 26, 1985, August 2, 1985.
Los Angeles Times, August 11, 1985.
New York Times, August 1, 1976, September 5, 1979, February 5, 1982, April 7, 1985, June 9, 1985, August 6, 1985.
People, April 8, 1978, October 15, 1979, September 30, 1985.
Playboy, September, 1985.

Rolling Stone, July 18, 1985, October 10, 1985, October 24, 1985.
Sunday's People, June 30, 1985.
TV Guide, November 15, 1980, March 9, 1985.
Washington Post, October 8, 1984, June 18, 1985, June 24, 1985.

—Sidelights by Glen Macnow

Frederick De Cordova

1910-

AP/Wide World Photos

PERSONAL: Full name, Frederick Timmins De Cordova; born October 27, 1910, in New York, N.Y.; son of George (in the theatre business) and Margaret (Timmins) De Cordova; married Janet Thomas, November 27, 1963. *Education:* Northwestern University, B.S., 1931; attended Harvard Law School.

ADDRESSES: Home—1875 Carla Ridge, Beverly Hills, Calif. 90210. *Office*—"The Tonight Show," National Broadcasting Co., Inc., 3000 West Alameda Ave., Burbank, Calif. 91505.

OCCUPATION: Stage, motion picture, and television producer and director.

CAREER: Shubert Enterprises, New York City, assistant to John Shubert, 1932, general stage manager, director, and producer, 1932-41; Alfred Bloomingdale Productions, New York City, general stage director, 1942; Louisville Amphitheatre, Louisville, Ky., producer, 1943; motion picture producer and director under contract to Warner Brothers, Inc., Hollywood, Calif., 1943-48, and Universal International Pictures, Hollywood, 1948-53; television producer and director, Columbia Broadcasting System (CBS), and National Broadcasting Co. (NBC), 1953—, executive producer of "The Tonight Show," NBC, 1970—.

Motion pictures produced or directed include "Too Young to Know," 1945, "That Way With Women," 1947, "Illegal Entry," 1949, "Peggy," 1950, "Bedtime for Bonzo," 1951, "Here Come the Nelsons," 1952, "Bonzo Goes to College," 1952, "I'll Take Sweden," 1965, and "Frankie and Johnny," 1966. Television series produced or directed include "December Bride," 1954-55, "The Burns and Allen Show," 1955-56, "The George Gobel Show," "The Jack Benny Program," 1960-63, "The Smothers Brothers Comedy Hour," 1965-66, and "My Three Sons."

MEMBER: Bel Air Country Club.

AWARDS, HONORS: Emmy Awards, Academy of Television Arts and Sciences, 1963, 1968, 1976, 1977, 1978, and 1979; recipient of five additional Emmy Award nominations.

SIDELIGHTS: Television producer Frederick De Cordova is a major creative force behind NBC's "The Tonight Show." While host Johnny Carson is the program's public face, De Cordova is "Tonight's" gatekeeper. With an audience of some fifteen million, an appearance on "The Tonight Show" is considered a major coup for someone with a book to sell or a movie to promote. But a would-be guest does not come near Carson without De Cordova's blessing. Once a guest is scheduled to appear, De Cordova okays the topic of conversation. And, once the show begins, he decides

how long a guest chats with Carson. De Cordova also supervises the show's writing staff, monitors "Tonight's" song and dance rehearsals, and acts as Carson's majordomo. "I'm chief traffic cop, talent scout, No. 1 fan and critic all rolled into one," is how De Cordova described his job to *People* magazine. Being the chief traffic cop of "The Tonight Show," which is responsible for no less than seventeen percent of NBC's total profits, carries no small amount of clout.

When De Cordova began his stint as executive producer of "Tonight" in New York City on October 19, 1970, he was at an age when most men are planning their retirement. He celebrated his sixtieth birthday only eight days after hiring on. Until De Cordova took over, a "Tonight" executive producer had about the same longevity as a tail gunner on a World War II bomber plane. The show had seen four executive producers in eight years. But De Cordova was a show business veteran with a long resume. He had twenty-three films and some 500 television shows to his credit. In addition, he had some thirty-seven years of total entertainment business experience and was considered one of Hollywood's social lions. Fifteen years after joining the show, he still occupies the executive producer's seat.

The top five "Tonight Show" staff members (left to right): bandleader Doc Severinsen, director Bobby Quinn, host Johnny Carson, Frederick De Cordova, and second banana Ed McMahon. AP/Wide World Photos.

A native of New York City, De Cordova got his show business start as a gofer in a summer stock production in the early 1930s. De Cordova graduated from Northwestern University and made it through Harvard Law School before classmate John Shubert persuaded him to work for the Shubert entertainment empire. He spent the next ten years directing shows in Memphis, Louisville, Nashville, and New York. His last show before moving to Hollywood in 1943 was "Ziegfeld Follies," which featured Milton Berle and Arthur Treacher.

De Cordova went to Hollywood with the thought of becoming an actor but quickly abandoned the plan. As he said in an NBC press department release, "Reading some of my notices led me to become a director and producer." It wasn't until almost four decades later, when he appeared in Martin Scorcese's 1981 film "King of Comedy," that De Cordova tried acting again. After abandoning his fledgling acting career, he worked as a dialogue director in three films, "San Antonio," "Janie," and "Between Two Worlds." He made his solo directorial debut with "Too Young to Know," a 1945 effort about a career woman who was torn between a husband and a job.

De Cordova's movie career spans two periods: 1945-1953, when he directed 21 films; and 1965-1966, when he returned to film after a thirteen-year hiatus in television. Ronald Reagan,

Elvis Presley, Rock Hudson, Errol Flynn, Tony Curtis, and Humphrey Bogart all appeared in De Cordova films.

The 1945-1953 period was a prolific one for De Cordova, though most of his films are known as "B" movies. He directed four films in 1951 and three movies per year in 1947, 1948, 1950, and 1952. The best-known De Cordova film, "Bedtime for Bonzo," is a 1951 comedy about a college professor who experiments with treating a chimpanzee as a child. The college professor was played by Ronald Reagan, who later was elected governor of California and then president of the United States. The movie enjoyed a revival when Reagan's political fortunes began to rise in the late 1960s. As recently as 1980, Reagan still had a sense of humor about the "Bonzo" film. In the midst of the 1980 presidential campaign, the future president autographed a reprinted studio picture of the chimp and himself in bed. The autograph read, "I'm the one with the watch." The success of the movie prompted a sequel, "Bonzo Goes to College." De Cordova directed, but Reagan did not appear. Other movies directed by De Cordova include "Little Egypt" and "Here Come the Nelsons," which featured the popular Ozzie Nelson family.

Eventually, he left the film directing business, proclaiming that he would never be another William Wyler. But he took another shot at movies in the 1960s with "I'll Take Sweden," a 1965 film that featured Bob Hope, Frankie Avalon, Tuesday Weld, and Dina Merrill. His last film was "Frankie and Johnny," which featured Elvis Presley singing saloon songs in a riverboat setting.

After abandoning his film career, De Cordova went into the infant medium of television. Among the shows he produced and directed in that period were "December Bride," "The Burns and Allen Show," "The Jack Benny Program," "The Smothers Brothers Show," and "My Three Sons." All were considered comedy classics, and he won Emmy Awards for producing "The Jack Benny Program" and for directing "The Burns and Allen Show."

"The Tonight Show," where De Cordova has worked for the last decade and a half, is a peculiar kind of American bulletin board. Host Johnny Carson engages in political satire but generally stops before he offends. As De Cordova told an Associated Press reporter, "Nothing is taboo if you do it in good taste and fun, . . . [but] when Nixon was down and out, Johnny felt that wasn't the time to zing him." The show has featured any number of writers and scientists but is not considered highbrow. It brings on movie stars and starlets regularly but isn't considered exceptionally light. As De Cordova told the Associated Press: "I try for an amalgam of guests. I don't want to see it become too Las Vegas showbizzy, or too pretentious and intellectual, either."

Other networks have tried to grab "Tonight's" audience but without much success. ABC is a good example. It used comedian Joey Bishop on late night television from 1967 until 1969. It didn't work. "The Dick Cavett Show," which ran from 1969 until 1972, was an attempt to lure an audience with a slightly more intellectual bent. That didn't work, either. ABC's news division began its "Nightline" show in 1980, but it has still not overtaken Carson.

De Cordova monitors the flow of guests through the use of a set of three-by-five cards, which are tacked on a large corkboard behind his desk. The board tells De Cordova which guests will appear in the next 90 days. Throughout the day, De Cordova will meet with writers, consult with the show's musical director, and chat with Carson by telephone. Just before the show begins, De Cordova will assume a seat next to a camera which is only a few feet away from the host. "I like to be eyeball to eyeball with Johnny," he says. During the show's commercial breaks, he will talk with Carson about the pace of the show, the remaining guests, and the audience's reaction. Once taping is completed, he will retreat to the host's dressing room for a drink. At night, he can often be found on the Hollywood party circuit with his wife of more than twenty years, Janet. De Cordova does not often socialize with Carson, who avoids the Los Angeles party circuit.

At age 75, De Cordova shows no signs of slowing down. He is a regular on the celebrity golf circuit, and he says his vacations give him plenty of time to rest.

SOURCES:

BOOKS

Cannon, Lou, *Reagan*, Putnam, 1982.

PERIODICALS

American Film, April, 1981.
Associated Press Wire Service, July 29, 1982.
Los Angeles, August, 1981.
People, October 8, 1984.
TV Guide, January 31, 1981.

—Sidelights by Tim Kiska

Selma Diamond

1921(?)-1985

OBITUARY NOTICE: Born c. 1921, in London, Ontario, Canada; died of lung cancer, May 13, 1985, in Los Angeles, Calif. Actress and comedy writer. Diamond, who most recently appeared as Selma Hacker, the sardonic court matron on the NBC television series "Night Court," was easily recognized by her two trademarks, a gravel voice and a dangling cigarette. In addition to her acting, Diamond had been one of the few women writers during the Golden Age of Television. Beginning as a contributor to the NBC radio program "The Big Show," she became a top television writer for Perry Como, Milton Berle, and Sid Caesar. Often, she worked as part of a five-person team headed by one of the best-known comedy writers of the 1950's, Goodman Ace. Describing her experience as the only female member of that team, Diamond once said that it was "like Red China—I'm there, they just don't recognize me."

Diamond had also been the model for "The Dick Van Dyke Show" character Sally Rogers, a comedy writer played by actress Rose Marie, according to the show's creator, Carl Reiner. Reiner, who had worked with Diamond during the mid-1950's, when both were writing for "Caesar's Hour," described her comedic style as "very terse. . . . She would just walk in and drop a few plums." Diamond had been a frequent guest on television talk shows and acted in several motion pictures, including "It's a Mad, Mad, Mad, Mad World," "My Favorite Year," "Lovesick," "Twilight Zone—The Movie," and "All of Me."

SOURCES:

PERIODICALS

Chicago Tribune, May 15, 1985.
Detroit Free Press, May 14, 1985.
Newsweek, May 27, 1985.
New York Times, May 14, 1985.
Time, May 27, 1985.

AP/Wide World Photos

Terry Dolan

1950-

PERSONAL: Full name, John Terrance Dolan; born December 20, 1950, in Norwalk, Conn.; son of Joseph William and Margaret (Kelly) Dolan. *Education*: Georgetown University, B.A., 1972, LL.B., 1979. *Politics*: Conservative. *Religion*: Roman Catholic.

ADDRESSES: Home—3129 South 14th St., Arlington, Va. 22204. *Office*—1500 Wilson Blvd., Suite 513. Arlington, Va. 22204.

OCCUPATION: Political organization executive; attorney.

CAREER: Political consultant, 1972-75; National Conservative Political Action Committee (NCPAC), Arlington, Va., executive director, 1975-78, chairman, 1978—. Admitted to the bar of Washington, D.C., 1979. Chairman of Washington Legal Foundation, 1977—, and of National Conservative Foundation, 1979—; member of board of directors of Conservative National Committee and Conservatives Against Liberal Legislation.

MEMBER: American Association of Political Consultants, Americans for Nuclear Energy (treasurer), American Bar Association, Washington, D.C., Bar Association.

SIDELIGHTS: In 1980 voters were introduced to what Steven V. Roberts of the *New York Times* called "a new and highly controversial style in American politics"—the negative-image campaign, an aggressive and expensive media drive devised by New Right conservatives and aimed at liberal, primarily Democratic, candidates. Under the directorship of Terry Dolan, the National Conservative Political Action Committee (NCPAC) became one of the first and most successful organizations to employ this tactic. It targeted six key senate Democrats, depicting them as radical and out of touch with their constituents; only two of the senators won reelection. "What makes the negative campaign unusual," wrote Bernard Weinraub in the *New York Times*, "is that it seeks the defeat of the . . . incumbents without openly promoting any challengers."

NCPAC derives its strategy from a Supreme Court decision that in effect allows a political action committee (PAC) to spend unlimited amounts for or against a political cause, as long as it remains independent of any particular candidate or campaign. "The law itself was designed by liberals and labor for their own benefit," Peter Goldman and Howard Fineman of *Newsweek* explained. "But it was Dolan who married it with devastating effect to the arts of the TV spot and the direct-mail begging letter—and to his own instinct for politics as demolition derby."

Dolan entered politics in 1972 as a volunteer in Richard Nixon's reelection campaign. He joined Virginia-based NCPAC in 1975, after three years as a political consultant to

UPI/Bettmann Newsphotos

conservatives and in 1978 was promoted to chairman. Initially, NCPAC confined its efforts to raising funds "in behalf of candidates who are opposed to insane taxing policies of state and Federal Government," Dolan stated in the *New York Times*. NCPAC shifted from the role of conservative support group to that of anti-liberal crusader when Dolan and others realized that a 1976 Supreme Court decision had created a loophole in the federal election law. In 1974 the Court had restricted PACs to direct contributions of $5,000 to an individual candidate. Two years later it ruled that constitutional guarantees of freedom of speech prohibit imposing any such restriction on independent groups that do not declare support for a specific candidate. As a result, "a PAC can spend all the money it can lay hands on so long as it campaigns against a candidate without supporting his opponent," noted L. J. Davis of *Harper's*. The Court's judgment led to a proliferation of independent expenditure committees, including NCPAC.

NCPAC is considered among the most effective, ambitious, and well-organized of the independent expenditure groups, and much of its success is credited to Dolan. He first came to national attention during the 1980 senate races, when NCPAC launched a $1.2 million campaign to unseat six prominent liberal Democrats: John Culver of Iowa, Thomas Eagleton of Missouri, Frank Church of Idaho, George McGovern of South Dakota, Alan Cranston of California, and Birch Bayh of Indiana. In television, radio, and newspaper advertisements and through an extensive direct-mail campaign, the senators were attacked for their views and voting records on such issues as abortion, gun control, deficit spending, and the Equal Rights Amendment.

In Indiana, for example, voters were told that Bayh had supported $46 billion in deficit spending. Showing a large sausage in the background, the NCPAC commercial charged that "one very big piece of baloney is Birch Bayh telling us he's fighting inflation." Another television spot, viewed by South Dakotans, featured a basketball player dribbling a ball while an announcer stated, "Globetrotter is a great name for a basketball team, but it's a terrible name for a senator." The voice-over continued: "While the energy crisis was brewing, George McGovern was touring Cuba with Fidel Castro. He also took a one-month junket to Africa. All at the taxpayer's expense. No wonder he lost touch with South Dakota. With so many problems at home, we need a senator and not a globetrotter." After the elections only Cranston and Eagleton retained their senate seats. Most political analysts agree that NCPAC efforts greatly contributed to the defeat of the other four.

In 1982 Dolan and NCPAC met with far less success. There were fewer big-name Democrats up for reelection, and those who were—Edward Kennedy of Massachusetts, Patrick Moynihan of New York, and Paul Sarbanes of Maryland—represented traditionally liberal constituencies. In addition, Roberts observed that "the current power of conservatives has forced some liberals to drift rightward, and their shift has defused some of [NCPAC's] arsenal."

While the political climate favored conservative candidates, economic conditions did not. The country was in the midst of a recession, which many Americans blamed on the policies of Republicans, especially Ronald Reagan. Dolan himself attributed the conservatives' setback to the president, but for a different reason. He contends that Reagan has been influenced by White House moderates and liberals and has abandoned the conservative agenda. "We're on the defensive largely because of the initiatives of the Reagan Administration," Dolan told David Shribman of the *New York Times*. "Everything played into our hands in 1980. Not any more. We have a President who talks about arms freezes, we have a President who prepares $100 billion budget deficits. We have a President backing away from much of the coalition that elected him."

Roberts, however, believes that NCPAC "has been hampered by its own success." He explains that "potential victims are now forewarned, and forearmed, the element of surprise has been lost." Several senators targeted by NCPAC in 1982, for instance, embarked early on their campaigns. And according to Goldman and Fineman, NCPAC's previous triumphs "inspired an alphabet soup of new liberal PACs to plagiarize its hit-and-run tactics and turn them on NCPAC and its conservative friends, quite literally with a vengeance." Meanwhile, Republicans worried that Dolan's negative approach could backfire. "The Massachusetts Republican leadership invited them to stay away, for fear that a NCPAC attack would only martyr

Teddy [Kennedy]—not defeat him," Goldman and Fineman maintained. "Even GOP National Chairman Richard Richards, a handpicked Reagan man, accused NCPAC of making 'all kinds of mischief.' The charge stung the committee, seeming as it did to signal the President's own displeasure."

The rift between Dolan and the Republican party continues. Dolan views NCPAC as the "conscience, the cutting edge" of the conservative effort, he told Roberts. "We've never been in the mold of respectable, establishment Republicans, and we don't want to be." In 1983 Dolan again accused the president of deserting the conservative program. John Dillin of the *Christian Science Monitor* wrote: "[Dolan] says that Reagan was elected on 'the most conservative platform in modern history' and then 'surrendered' everything after getting into office. Why? It's all the product of 'savvy White House pragmatists'—who are 'the same people Reagan defeated in 1980.' " Dillin noted that many Reagan policies, such as tax and spending cuts, a strong defense, and business deregulation, "reflect essentially traditional Republicanism." What angers Dolan and other conservatives is Reagan's failure to "harness the American voters' 'moral outrage' " on several issues, among them forced busing, abortion, Soviet troops in Afghanistan, and the Soviet Union's alleged use of chemical warfare. "Conservatives call this a mistake," stated Dillin. "Such issues . . . could be a powerful force turning middle-class Americans toward conservative (Republican) candidates."

Dolan's disillusionment with the GOP seemingly reached its peak in the summer of 1984, when he announced that he would resign as chairman of NCPAC to help organize the Conservative Populist party. Shortly thereafter, he addressed an unauthorized, pre-convention platform hearing called by liberal Republicans, who feared that the party's official platform would be unduly influenced by the New Right and would cost the president votes. Dolan told the assemblage that it could "help the Republican party by leaving it," the *New York Times* reported. He termed the meeting "a cheap media stunt" and added: "Since I am myself not adverse to cheap media stunts, I want to congratulate you for coming up with one of the cheapest of all, a bunch of senators largely ignored by their party because they act as if they are members of the other party giving advice on how their party should conduct itself. If the media buys this, they will buy anything."

Dolan's critics agree that he is "not adverse to cheap media stunts," and worse. As head of NCPAC Dolan has been branded an extremist and a liar; his methods have been denounced as unfair, exploitative, and a threat to democracy. Many observers maintain that there is some truth to these charges. "In Idaho, Church was criticized for his strong attacks on the CIA, which was fair enough," commented *Time*'s Edwin Warner, "but he was also falsely accused of disclosing the names of CIA agents and thereby putting their lives in danger." A television commercial, also against Church, "showed an abandoned missile silo, making the point that he had voted against military programs," Warner continued. "In fact, the Air Force had removed the missile because it was outdated, and Church had voted in favor of the weapon's replacement."

NCPAC's sometimes slanted advertisements are not all that disturb its critics. They argue that the organization evades campaign finance laws by claiming independence. "The key to Dolan's continued success lies in his remaining 'independent' of the candidate whose cause he is aiding," asserted *New York*'s Michael Kramer. "Prove Dolan isn't independent and you destroy his effectiveness. But, as Dolan gleefully pointed out, 'no one can rationally define independence—it's a ridiculous concept.' "

During the 1982 New York senate race between incumbent Democrat Patrick Moynihan and Republican challenger Bruce Caputo, for example, NCPAC ran a series of commercials attacking the former while disavowing any direct ties to the latter. However, "Moynihan boosters point to strong overlaps between [NCPAC] and the Caputo campaign," the *New York Times* reported. "Both employ the same political consultant. [NCPAC] has already provided $4,400 to Mr. Caputo, apart from the much larger sums its anti-Moynihan advertising will require." Moynihan's response, said Kramer, was that Dolan is "manifestly violating the law's intent. The connection between Dolan and Caputo is clear. To believe otherwise requires a degree of innocence unattainable in our time."

According to Kramer, Dolan has called the election statute "a stupid law." Moreover, he has acknowledged that "groups like ours are potentially very dangerous to the political process." Dolan further explained: "Ten independent expenditure groups, for example, could amass this great amount of money and defeat the point of accountability in politics. We could say anything we want about an opponent of Senator Smith, and the senator wouldn't have to say anything. . . . A group like ours could lie through its teeth, and the candidate it helps stays clean."

Dolan made these remarks, Goldman and Fineman pointed out, in an argument for election law reform. They noted that "even as he defends his work, [Dolan] laments the anomalies in the election-finance law that make 'independent' political commandos like NCPAC possible." In fact, a number of suits seeking to block the efforts of NCPAC and other independent expenditure committees have been filed. The Federal Elections Commission and the Federal Communications Commission have heard similar complaints. So far, rulings have been in favor of the independent organizations.

Dolan concedes that NCPAC's activities take advantage of a legal loophole, but he insists that, with few exceptions, the group's advertisements are accurate and carefully researched. He freely admits that NCPAC's negative image strategy is perceived as less than estimable. According to Weinraub, Dolan admits that "there's no question about it—we are a negative organization. . . . We're interested in ideology. We're not interested in respectability. We're going to . . . send a shiver down the spine of every . . . liberal Senator and Congressman." Dolan further stated: "Images are important, not issues. . . . Start with an image like George McGovern doesn't represent South Dakota. Keep hitting away. That's more effective than George McGovern did or didn't do X, Y or Z for South Dakota." Michael Malbin, a political scientist with the American Enterprise Institute, told the *Newsweek* reporters that "in some ways" negative campaign advertising is "an improvement on what was popular in the 1970's—all those ads showing a guy walking on a beach with a coat over his shoulder."

Dolan and others contend that the anger directed at NCPAC stems from ideological rather than ethical concerns. The *National Review*'s William F. Buckley, Jr., stated that Dolan is "both philosophical and shrewd. He says simply that, if the voters are informed, but want in any event to go with a particular candidate, why let them do so. Shrewd, too, in divining that the general furor results less from the circulation of information by [NCPAC] than by its ideological predisposition. How many people have denounced the labor unions' political action committees, or those representing civil rights, or ecology, or the interests of education, or of the aged?" In examining the 1980 elections, Warner found that NCPAC was most concerned with familiarizing voters with their representatives' performances. "N.C.P.A.C.'s main object was to expose the incumbent's voting record for the citizens back home," he wrote. "The Senators tended to vote to the left of their constituents while playing down this fact in their campaigns." Conservative activist Richard Viguerie's summation, according to Warner, is that "N.C.P.A.C. went up to the doorstep and left the dead cats."

SOURCES:

PERIODICALS

Christian Science Monitor, May 23, 1983, December 22, 1983.
Harper's, October, 1980.
National Review, May 15, 1981.
Newsweek, June 1, 1981.
New York, December 14, 1981.
New York Times, November 2, 1975, October 28, 1976, August 17, 1979, March 24, 1980, October 5, 1980, November 18, 1981, January 14, 1982, July 27, 1982, August 17, 1982, August 30, 1982, September 6, 1982, June 4, 1984, July 31, 1984.
Time, December 8, 1980.

—Sketch by Denise Wiloch

Angelo R. Donghia

1935-1985

OBITUARY NOTICE: Born March 7, 1935, in Vandergrift, Pa.; died of pneumonia, April 10, 1985, in New York, N.Y. Interior designer and businessman. Considered one of America's most influential interior designers, Angelo R. Donghia was noted for his bold, contemporary approach to home and commercial furnishings. Some of his style innovations—gray flannel upholstery on over-stuffed furniture, shiny lacquered walls, and bleached wood floors—have become contemporary design standards. In addition to homes, Donghia decorated restaurants, hotels, corporate offices, and clubs. His clients and commissions included Mary Tyler Moore, Neil Simon, Halston, PepsiCo, Miami's Omni International Hotel, and the Metropolitan Opera Club.

Donghia decided to become a designer as a child, and he subsequently attended Parsons School of Design. Upon graduation in 1959, he joined New York's prestigious Yale Burge Interiors. He became the firm's vice-president in 1963 and a partner in 1966. In 1968 Donghia founded & Vice Versa, a trend-setting fabric and wall-covering company. His first showroom opened in Los Angeles in 1976. Two years later he established Donghia Furniture. Donghia was one of the first decorators to successfully mass-market designer products, and through Donghia Companies he promoted his own line of glassware, china, sheets, fabrics, wallpaper, and furniture.

SOURCES:

PERIODICALS

Chicago Tribune, April 14, 1985.
Newsweek, April 22, 1985.
New York Times, April 12, 1985.
Time, April 22, 1985.

Fred R. Conrad/NYT Pictures

Jean Dubuffet

1901-1985

OBITUARY NOTICE: Born July 31, 1901, in Le Havre, France; died of emphysema, May 12, 1985, in Paris, France. French artist. Jean Dubuffet was a proponent of "l'art brut" or "art in the raw." He believed that the primitive and untaught artist should be the most highly esteemed and, in accordance with this view, deliberately cultivated a spontaneous, naive approach to art, creating highly original work in a number of artistic media. The values of conventional art were worthless, Dubuffet argued. Writing in *Newsweek*, John Ashbery quotes Dubuffet as saying, "Banality is what interests me most." He has influenced artists throughout the world to abandon traditional materials and make art from discarded items, rubbish, sand, rocks, and similar materials. Dubuffet, John Russell writes in the *New York Times*, was "widely regarded as the most important artist to emerge from France at the end of World War II."

After studying art as a young man, and abandoning it because he found his work imitative, Dubuffet spent many years in his family's wine business. For a time he ran his own wholesale wine business and worked, too, as a technical draftsman in Brazil. It wasn't until 1942 that Dubuffet returned to his artistic endeavors and begin to paint seriously. In his first one-man show, held in Paris in late 1944, Dubuffet shocked the art community. His crudely-rendered figures moved critics to compare his work to that of mental patients, young children, and subway graffitists. In his second show in 1946 Dubuffet again stunned the critics, this time by altering the surface of his canvas by adding plaster, concrete, putty, and asphalt into which he embedded pebbles and sticks of wood. Over this textured surface he again painted naive scribbled figures. Although altered painting surfaces had been used by earlier artists, Dubuffet used this technique to create a vari-textured surface resembling an aged cave wall—a deliberately primitive approach. Over the years to follow, during which he had over 60 other one-man shows, Dubuffet worked in a variety of styles and media, experimenting with painting, printmaking, sculpture, and assemblage. This constant change was essential to him. "Unless one says goodbye to what one loves," Russell quotes Dubuffet, "and unless one travels to completely new territories, one can expect merely a long wearing-away of oneself and an eventual extinction."

Despite his mercurial style changes and his rejection of conventional standards, Dubuffet's work is included in the collections of many prominent art museums in Europe and the United States, including the Musee des Arts Decoratifs in Paris, the Museum of Modern Art and the Guggenheim Museum in New York, and the Art Institute of Chicago. Two major examples of his sculpture are also found in the

AP/Wide World Photos

United States: "Monument with Standing Beast," a 10-ton fiberglass structure, at the State of Illinois Center in Chicago and "Group of Four Trees," a 43-foot tall work, at the Chase Manhattan Plaza in New York. At the time of the artist's death, Robert Hughes asserts in *Time*, Dubuffet "was the most honored senior painter in France—indeed the most important French visual artist of any kind to emerge since World War II."

SOURCES:

PERIODICALS

Chicago Tribune, May 16, 1985.
Los Angeles Times, May 16, 1985.
Newsweek, May 27, 1985.
New York Times, May 15, 1985.
Time, May 27, 1985.
Times (London), May 16, 1985.
Washington Post, May 16, 1985.

Amy Eilberg

1955(?)-

AP/Wide World Photos

BRIEF ENTRY: Born c. 1955, in Philadelphia, Pa. American rabbi. In May of 1985 the dream that Amy Eilberg harbored for many years came true: she was ordained the first female rabbi in the century-long history of Judaism's Conservative branch. The more liberal Reform wing of Judaism began ordaining women rabbis in 1972, but the Conservatives, the largest Jewish denomination in America, had delayed making a similar break with tradition until, in 1983, the faculty of the Jewish Theological Seminary voted to train and ordain women as well as men. Then, in February of 1985, in a move that drew Conservative Jews closer to the liberal Reform Jews and further distanced them from the more conservative Orthodox branch, the Rabbinical Assembly passed a measure that admitted anyone, male or female, ordained by its seminary to membership in the Conservative rabbinate.

Eilberg was raised in Philadelphia, Pennsylvania, in a household active in Jewish communal affairs but not rigidly attentive to matters of ritual—at least not until fourteen-year-old Amy took part in a summer program of the United Synagogue Youth, the national youth organization of the Conservative movement. Six weeks of daily practice of traditional Judaism prompted her, upon returning home, to convince her parents to create a kosher home, in which all food would be prepared according to strict Jewish dietary laws. By the time Amy graduated from high school, she knew that she wanted to follow the example of her father, Joshua Eilberg, a former congressman from Pennsylvania, and her mother, Gladys, a social worker, in pursuing a career in public service. Her bent, however, was toward a profession that would enable her to serve the Jewish community. During her undergraduate days at Brandeis University, moreover, that desire took very definite shape: she wanted to be a rabbi.

The Jewish Theological Seminary, the only school that could provide her with the training she needed, excluded women applicants from the one program she sought—rabbinical ordination—although it admitted them to all others. Undaunted, Amy invented her own time schedule, confident that the day would come when she could indeed qualify for the rabbinical doctorate. Consequently, she enrolled at the seminary anyway, in a program of Judaic studies, and obtained a master's degree in Talmud, the collection of writings that comprise Jewish law, in 1978. After spending another year teaching in the seminary's branch in Israel she undertook the course work required for her Talmud doctorate, interrupting her studies in order to obtain a second master's, in social work, from Smith College in 1984. She was still a student at Smith when the seminary faculty took its historic vote, and the goal she had set ten years earlier was finally within reach. In September, 1984, Eilberg returned to the Jewish Theological Seminary and completed her requirements for ordination, becoming the first of the eighteen women who enrolled that year to finish. "The long vigil is over," commented Amy, "and the wait was fully justified." After her ordination Eilberg assumed the duties of chaplain at Methodist Hospital in Indianapolis, Indiana, and of community rabbi for the Jewish Welfare Federation. She and her husband, Howard Schwartz, live in Bloomington, Indiana, where Schwartz teaches religious studies at Indiana University.

SOURCES:

PERIODICALS

Detroit Free Press, May 13, 1985.
Ms., December, 1985.
New York Times, February 17, 1985.
People, April 29, 1985.
Time, February 25, 1985.

Elmer W. Engstrom

1901-1984

OBITUARY NOTICE: Born August 25, 1901, in Minneapolis, Minn.; died October 30, 1984, in Hightstown, N.J. American electronics executive. Engstrom worked for the RCA Corporation for 41 years, serving as president between 1961 and 1965. He played a major role in RCA's development of the world's first color television tube. Other products developed under Engstrom's supervision include equipment for sound motion pictures and broadcasting receivers.

After graduating from the University of Minnesota in 1923, Engstrom joined the Radio Engineering Department of the General Electric Company. When GE's radio and engineering activities were transferred to RCA in 1930, Engstrom became a division engineer. For the next 25 years, he served in various research capacities at RCA. He directed the company's television research and development efforts for several years and eventually headed RCA's development of the first color television system. When, in 1942, RCA consolidated all of its research efforts in Princeton, N.J., Engstrom was named director of general research. From that position he graduated to vice-president, executive vice-president, senior executive vice-president, and finally, in 1961, to president. When he was presented with the Founders Award of the Institute of Electrical and Electronics Engineers in 1966, Engstrom was cited for "his foresighted application of systems engineering concepts in bringing television to the public." Engstrom retired from RCA in 1971.

SOURCES:

BOOKS

The International Who's Who, 1980-81, Europa, 1980.

PERIODICALS

New York Times, November 2, 1984.

AP/Wide World Photos

Sam Ervin

1896-1985

OBITUARY NOTICE: Full name, Samuel J. Ervin, Jr.; born September 27, 1896, in Morganton, N.C.; died of respiratory and kidney failure, April 23, 1985, in Winston-Salem, N.C. Politician, lawyer, judge, lecturer, and author. A United States senator for twenty years, Sam Ervin is best remembered for his role in the 1973 Watergate hearings. As Democratic chairman of the Senate Select Committee on Presidential Campaign Activities, Ervin presided over the investigation that eventually led to Richard Nixon's resignation. Ervin, who described himself as "just an ol' country lawyer," became the hero of Watergate, an event he considered "the greatest tragedy this country has ever suffered." Throughout the widely televised hearings, Ervin displayed indignation, persistence, down-home common sense, and humor. His approach "helped reassure Americans that there were still people in Washington with moral bearings solidly fixed," recalled Kurt Andersen of *Time*.

The son of a lawyer, Ervin attended the University of North Carolina then served eighteen months in France during World War I. He was twice wounded and twice cited for gallantry in battle. After the war he earned a degree from Harvard Law School. He returned to North Carolina to practice law and to pursue a political career. In 1925 Ervin was elected to the North Carolina General Assembly. He became a county judge ten years later and a superior court judge in 1937, and he was named to the North Carolina Supreme Court in 1948. Ervin joined the U.S. Senate in 1954.

Although he championed a number of liberal causes, such as the censuring of Senator Joseph McCarthy and the fight to block a government-proposed citizen surveillance system, Ervin was considered a staunchly conservative southern Democrat. He opposed most civil rights legislation and the Equal Rights Amendment; he was against giving eighteen-year-olds the right to vote. He strongly supported the Vietnam War, and he generally favored business over labor in legislative disputes. A states' rights advocate, Ervin revered the U.S. Constitution, which, he said, "should be taken like mountain whiskey—undiluted and untaxed," *Newsweek* reported. His colleagues regarded him as the Senate's foremost authority on the document. Ervin retired from the Senate in 1974, shortly after the Watergate

UPI/Bettmann Newsphotos

investigation. He spent his later years practicing law in his home state, lecturing, and writing. Ervin's account of the Watergate hearings, *The Whole Truth*, was published by Random House in 1981.

SOURCES:

PERIODICALS

Detroit Free Press, April 24 1985.
Newsweek, May 6, 1985.
Time, May 6, 1985.

Emilio Estevez

1962-

PERSONAL: Born 1962 in New York, N.Y.; son of Martin (an actor; professional name, Sheen) and Janet Estevez. *Education*: Graduated from high school in Santa Monica, Calif.

ADDRESSES: Home—Malibu, Calif. *Agent*—Creative Artists, 1888 Century Park E., Los Angeles, Calif. 90067.

OCCUPATION: Actor.

CAREER: Began acting at a very young age in neighborhood productions and school plays; appeared in television productions "Seventeen Going on Nowhere," "To Climb a Mountain," "Making the Grade," and "In the Custody of Strangers"; feature films include "Tex," 1982, "The Outsiders," 1983, "Repo Man," 1984, "The Breakfast Club," 1985, "St. Elmo's Fire," 1985, "That Was Then. . . This Is Now," 1985, and "Overdrive," 1986. Has also appeared on stage, including a role in "Mister Roberts" at the Burt Reynolds Dinner Theatre.

WRITINGS: Author of screenplay "That Was Then. . . This Is Now" (adapted from the S.E. Hinton novel of the same title), Paramount, 1985; also author of three original screenplays, including "Wisdom" and "Clear Intent," as yet unproduced, and a play, "Echoes of an Era," produced at Estevez's high school.

SIDELIGHTS: Among the group of young film stars who have become known as Hollywood's "whiz kids" or "brat pack" is Emilio Estevez, the ambitious young actor who has appeared in such movies as "Repo Man," "The Breakfast Club," and "St. Elmo's Fire." Estevez, whose involvement in the various aspects of filmmaking has expanded to include screenwriting and directing, is probably the busiest member of the group, which is comprised of such other actors as Timothy Hutton, Sean Penn, and Rob Lowe. "Starmakers have their eyes and their money on Emilio Estevez, who at 23 is one of the most productive young actors in Hollywood," declared the *Chicago Tribune*'s Robert Blau. "His promise as an actor, his glaring intensity and his slicked-back hair recall [James] Dean and [Marlon] Brando, whose careers were launched by the kind of teen-age road-and-romance movies that Estevez has been starring in for the last five years."

"I knew I had an ability to perform from an early age," Estevez told *Teen* magazine. Although he didn't begin acting professionally until after high school, Estevez grew up performing in neighborhood dramatic productions and in school plays. He also began writing at an early age. One effort was a science-fiction story he wrote as a second grader and submitted to the producers of television's "Night Gallery" series. The story was rejected, but Estevez continued to write, turning out, for example, a play about Vietnam War veterans entitled "Echoes of an Era." Under the

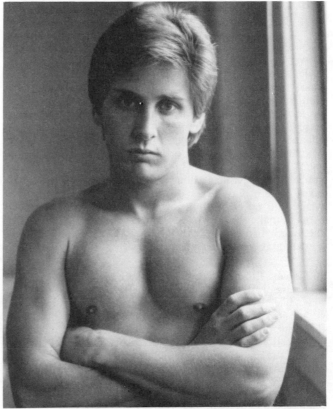

direction of his boyhood friend Sean Penn, Estevez starred in his high school's production of that play. He landed his first professional acting job—a part in an after-school television special entitled "Seventeen Going on Nowhere"—immediately after graduating from high school. Subsequent television dramas in which he appeared include "To Climb a Mountain," "Making the Grade," and "In the Custody of Strangers."

Estevez made his motion picture debut in "Tex," a film based on a novel by best-selling author S.E. Hinton. He next appeared in "The Outsiders," another screen adaptation of a Hinton novel. Following "The Outsiders," he earned a starring role in the 1984 film "Repo Man," in which he portrayed a young punker working as an apprentice to a group of Los Angeles automobile repossessors. According to Thomas Wiener in *American Film*, "Repo Man" was "a flop in its initial theatrical release, [but it] found a second life on videocassette and was then miraculously revived in theaters like New York's Eighth Street Playhouse, where it ran for months."

When Estevez first read the script for "Repo Man," he was immediately drawn to the film's leading character, he told

Wiener. However, he was unfamiliar with the punk rock scene and felt he needed to understand it better in order to prepare for the role. "So I started listening to the music and going to the clubs, and I began to understand what the punk movement is all about," he explained to Wiener. He also went out on a couple of occasions with a real repo man. Asked by Wiener if he had feared being typecast as a rebel kid, Estevez answered: "Not at that point in my career. I didn't think I was perceived by the public as being a punk or a type. And I didn't feel that it would be detrimental in any way for me to be seen as such."

In "Repo Man," which Vincent Canby of the *New York Times* described as a "neo-Surreal, southern California fable," Otto (Estevez) works for the Helping Hands Acceptance Company under the guidance of Bud, one of the company's veteran employees. Bud "is a fast-talking, beat-up looking guy with a worry line for every vehicle repossessed," observed Canby. The *New Yorker*'s Pauline Kael felt that "L.A. is the perfect setting for a movie about men who take out their frustrations by confiscating other people's cars." Kael concluded: "The movie gives you the feeling that you've gone past alienation into the land of detachment. It takes place in a different dimension—a punkers' wasteland where you never really know where you are, and nobody cares to make things work, and everybody you see is part of the lunatic fringe. A movie like this, with nothing positive in it, can make you feel good."

In his next film, "The Breakfast Club," Estevez portrayed a high school varsity letterman, a role quite unlike the one he played in "Repo Man." The action in "The Breakfast Club" occurs in a suburban high school library during a day-long detention that the film's five leading characters have been sentenced to serve. The movie focuses on the interaction among the characters, each of whom represents a different teen stereotype. There's a prom queen, a rebel, a kooky artist, a brain, and Estevez's champion wrestler. As the film opens, the five are strangers to one another. But "in the course of the day, under the prodding of the rebel and mellowing effect of the marijuana he provides, they peel off layers of self-protection, confess their problems with their parents, and, after much shedding of tears, are stripped down to their true selves," summarized Kael in her review of the movie.

"The Breakfast Club" is a film about "Identity and False Facades and Relationships, and as the characters undress their souls, the camera moves in for the kill," wrote David Denby in *New York*. Denby had mixed feelings about the movie as a whole, but declared that "the performers are all high-powered." He was particularly pleased with Estevez's portrayal of Andy, whom he described as a "self-punishing jock" and a "decent boy whose father has got him wound so tight around the fantasy of being a winner that he can barely breathe." Estevez "has got the jock moves down cold," Denby continued. "His Andy seems to react to everything with his shoulders, and he uses his physical strength as if it were a moral policeman, put on earth to keep everyone else in line. Estevez is a touching actor—he can make this boy's macho intensity seem corny and noble at the same time."

Other critics who were impressed with Estevez's performance in "The Breakfast Club" include Janet Maslin, who wrote in her *New York Times* review that "Emilio Estevez

has an edgy physical intensity," and Kael, who especially enjoyed Andy's "long monologue about his father's always telling him to 'win, win.'" Describing his character for *Teen* magazine, Estevez said: "Andy has a lot of turmoil. Everyone rides him. It's an intolerable burden. He really wants to break out, but he's conditioned not to. If a wrestler lets down his defenses, he loses. So he can't and won't be vulnerable."

"St. Elmo's Fire," released just a few months after "The Breakfast Club," again featured Estevez as one of several young actors in an ensemble cast. "St. Elmo's Fire" explores the relationships among its seven leading characters—a group of close friends who've recently graduated from college and are trying to adjust to post-college life. Estevez's character, a law student named Kirbo, is infatuated with a medical student several years his senior. She, in turn, "thinks he's cute but bananas," observed Jack Kroll in *Newsweek*.

"The acting cannot be faulted, although sometimes the script gets in the way," declared Catharine Rambeau in her review of "St. Elmo's Fire" for the *Detroit Free Press*. "Occasionally the film takes itself too seriously, and . . . its characters are limited to very specific types," Rambeau continued. "So audiences who are not particularly curious about the life-styles of young urban professionals may find the picture of limited interest." Like Rambeau, Jack Kroll had misgivings about the movie, but he too was impressed with its cast. "Estevez brings a maniacal comic touch to the pursuit of his startled quarry," he wrote. Kroll concluded that "you can feel the high voltage of friendship crackling between these kids."

Late in 1985, Estevez appeared in "That Was Then . . . This Is Now," a film for which he also wrote the screenplay. The movie is based on a novel by S.E. Hinton that Estevez had first read in 1981 during the filming of "Tex"—another screen adaptation of a Hinton novel. After reading *That Was Then . . . This Is Now*, Estevez contacted the author, and she agreed to his offer to adapt it for the screen. "I don't necessarily want to be a screenwriter," Estevez told *Teen*. "But I came across a project that I became passionate about. I wanted to bring it to the screen because it's a film about young people that's honest. Hopefully, my vision will be captured."

Unlike the novel, which is set in the sixties, Estevez's film version is set in contemporary Minneapolis-St. Paul. It concerns the relationship between two teenage boys whose long-time friendship is threatened when one of them falls in love. "No pals could be more dissimilar, and that's part of the key to their bond," wrote Peter Rose in the *Detroit News*. "Mark [Estevez] is impetuous, with a hearty dash of the criminal. Byron [played by Craig Sheffer] is the proverbial good kid." Discussing his "That Was Then" character with the *Chicago Tribune*'s Robert Blau, Estevez reflected: "There's probably a lot of him in me, the alter ego screaming to get out every once in a while. Fortunately, I was able to vent it in a film and not in real life."

Estevez "is a raw and realistic actor, and he translates that angry edginess into his writing, which often suits the Hinton story quite well," asserted Rose. A *People* magazine critic proclaimed Estevez an "impressive" actor but felt that the dialogue in "That Was Then" was "full of clunkers." Catharine Rambeau was more favorably impressed with Estevez's writing. She commented: "As a screenwriter, Estevez has the kind of accurate ear for dialogue idiosyncracies that recalls [mystery novelist] Elmore Leonard's work. Although it's obvious "That Was Then . . . This Is Now" is aimed straight at the hearts and minds of young men, it is compelling enough to touch plenty of others."

Estevez admits that he enjoys writing. He told *American Film*'s Thomas Wiener that if he weren't an actor, he'd probably be interested in journalism or some other writing-related field. As it is, he's done a significant amount of writing in the movie industry. In addition to "That Was Then," he's written three original screenplays, including a contemporary drama called "Wisdom," which is slated for a 1986 release and which will mark his directorial debut. He's also completed a screenplay entitled "Clear Intent," which he hopes John Hughes (director of "The Breakfast Club") will agree to direct.

Estevez enjoys acting as well, because it "gives you a license to be crazy," he told *Teen*. "I can be a doctor, a hoodlum, an athlete or whatever. The possibilities are endless." But he's through playing teenagers, he says. "I think *That Was Then* was my swan song to high school films," he told Wiener. Sometime in the future, he hopes to co-star with his father, actor Martin Sheen, in "The Subject Was Roses." Father and son have worked together in the past—they co-starred in the television movie "In the Custody of Strangers" in 1982 and on stage in a Burt Reynolds Dinner Theatre production of "Mr. Roberts." But Estevez is reluctant to align himself professionally with his famous father; he's eager to make his own way in the industry. Thus his decision to retain the family name, rather than use Sheen, his father's stage name. "I'm not ashamed of him in any way," Estevez said when discussing that decision with Wiener. "But a lot of times . . . it's not Emilio Estevez on the street, it's Martin Sheen's son, and I think the more I disassociate myself, the more the public sees Emilio Estevez without that identification following him." "Besides," he told *Teen*, "Emilio Sheen sounds stupid anyway. Emilio Estevez sounds more romantic."

Being the son of an actor has its advantages, Estevez admits. "I've been around sets my whole life," he told *Teen*. "As a kid, I thought they were boring, but I didn't realize how much information I was absorbing. It was like being in school." His father wanted him to be a doctor or a lawyer, Estevez revealed to *Teen*. "He thought becoming an actor was the dumbest thing I could do because he knew what I

was getting myself into." Nonetheless, Estevez reports that his father has been "extremely supportive" of his career decisions. Sheen also helps his son keep his growing fame in perspective: "The most significant thing my father taught me is that my job is no more or less important than someone else's," Estevez told *Teen*. "When I realize there are a billion people in China that don't know I exist, any flightiness is swept away."

Still, Estevez admits, fame has its drawbacks. His attempts to lead a private life are often futile. "Notoriety has made it hard for Estevez to do things like go out to restaurants or movies," reported Blau. "It's also hard to find privacy with his fiancee, actress Demi Moore." Moore, whom Estevez describes as "the love of my life," was one of his "St. Elmo's Fire" co-stars, and they've been dating steadily ever since making that picture. Estevez lives in a condominium in Malibu, California, not far from his boyhood home. When he's not acting, he's often busy at home—writing screenplays on his portable computer. Asked about his long-range career plans, Estevez told Wiener: "Longevity is in the stars for me. I'm not the kind of guy who's going to be in there for a couple of shots; I don't ever want to be on one of those shows, 'Whatever Happened to . . . ?' "

SOURCES:

PERIODICALS

American Film, March, 1985.
Boxoffice, February, 1986.
Cosmopolitan, June, 1983.
Detroit Free Press, June 28, 1985, November 8, 1985, November 11, 1985.
Detroit News, October 29, 1985, November 12, 1985.
Films in Review, May, 1985.
Hollywood Reporter, October 16, 1985.
Maclean's, February 18, 1985.
Nation, December 15, 1984.
Newsweek, August 2, 1982, February 25, 1985, July 1, 1985.
New York, February 18, 1985.
New Yorker, August 6, 1984, April 8, 1985.
New York Times, September 28, 1982, July 6, 1984, February 15, 1985.
People, February 18, 1985, September 16, 1985, November 25, 1985.
Rolling Stone, March 14, 1985.
Teen, September, 1982, March, 1985, July, 1985.
Washington Post, February 15, 1985.

—Sidelights by Mary Sullivan

Patrick Ewing

1962-

PERSONAL: Full name, Patrick Aloysius Ewing; born August 5, 1962, in Kingston, Jamaica; came to United States in 1975; naturalized citizen; son of Carl (a mechanic and hospital worker) and Dorothy (a hospital dietician) Ewing. *Education:* Georgetown University, B.F.A., 1985.

ADDRESSES: Office—New York Knicks, Madison Square Garden, 4 Pennsylvania Plaza, New York, N.Y. 10001.

OCCUPATION: Professional basketball player.

CAREER: U.S. Senate, Washington, D.C., worked as page for Senate Finance Committee and for Senator Robert Dole of Kansas; professional basketball player for New York Knicks, 1985—.

AWARDS, HONORS: Named Big East defensive player of the year, 1982, 1983, 1984, 1985; gold medal, 1984 Summer Olympics; "Patrick Ewing Day" established by city of Cambridge, Mass., October 12, 1984.

SIDELIGHTS: Some sports fans were dismayed when twenty-three-year-old basketball player Patrick Ewing graduated from Georgetown University in the spring of 1985 and reportedly asked for a $30-million, ten-year contract prior to joining the New York Knicks as a professional. The average National Basketball Association (NBA) salary is $330,000 per year. Ewing's requested salary—an average of $3 million per year—would have made him, even as a rookie, one of the highest-paid athletes in the world.

UPI/Bettmann Newsphotos

But shortly after those demands surfaced, the *New York Times* did a little bit of arithmetic to see what Ewing was worth in terms of extra revenue to the franchise. Ewing wasn't just an ordinary rookie. Most experts considered him to be the best college basketball player available to the professional league in several years, perhaps since fellow center Kareem Abdul-Jabbar (then known as Lew Alcindor) graduated from UCLA in 1969 and joined the Milwaukee Bucks. According to the *New York Times*, the demand for season tickets at Madison Square Garden increased from 5,000 to 10,000—and perhaps more—when the Knicks acquired the rights to pick first in the National Basketball Association draft lottery. With the average season ticket to Knicks games costing $600, the increase in season seats sold would bring an extra $3 million to the team before the start of the season. And this total didn't include interest on the money, increased revenues from concessions, extra tickets to be sold at road games, or the increased value of the team's television rights. In the jargon of American professional sports, Ewing—like Alcindor—was "the franchise."

Financial considerations aside, Ewing's bosses seemed certain that he would bring success to the team in competition. "Patrick Ewing will help us, he might even lead us to a

championship," Knicks team president Jack Krumpe told the *New York Times* after the Knicks won Ewing's rights. Coach Hubie Brown said he was "overjoyed for the franchise and the city."

Ewing's is an American success story. Born in Jamaica, he went to high school in Cambridge, Massachusetts. He earned great success as a collegian at Georgetown University in Washington, D.C., and he was a star on the American Olympic basketball team that won the gold medal in 1984 at Los Angeles. "My coming to America fulfilled a lifelong dream of my mother's," he said in a *Time* magazine interview. "She told us America is the land of opportunity. I enjoy being an American, but I still miss the natural beauty, the waterfalls and the landscapes of Jamaica." He returned there for a visit in August of 1985 and was observed by a *New York Times* reporter as the airplane approached Montego Bay. "Now that's real water down there," he said, looking at the clear white beaches and crystal blue waters of the island's northern shore. "Ya, mon, Reeeel wa-taah."

Patrick Aloysius Ewing was born August 5, 1962, in Kingston, Jamaica, the fifth child in a family of seven children of Carl and Dorothy Ewing. His father had been a mechanic in Kingston. His mother, Dorothy Phipps Ewing, left the family home in 1971 to move to the United States, where she worked in the dietary department at Massachusetts General Hospital. The Ewing children and their father followed over a period of several years. Patrick arrived on Jan. 11, 1975.

It was not until he reached America that Ewing even saw a basketball. In Jamaica, he had played goalie, with modest success, on a soccer team. Basketball intrigued him immediately. "I'd watched and seen the object was to put the ball in the basket," Ewing recalled in an interview with *Sports Illustrated*. However, he found, "it was more difficult than I could have imagined." He played basketball for Rindge and Latin High School in Cambridge; the school won three state championships during Ewing's years. While there, he struggled with some studies, partly because of the unfamiliar dialect of English spoken in the United States. He became a naturalized American citizen during his junior year of high school.

Ewing's position, center, is usually regarded as the most important position on a five-man basketball team and is often played by the tallest, best athlete available. Because Ewing was so tall (7 feet) and skilled in high school, he was recruited by many colleges, so many that Ewing's high school coach, Mike Jarvis, sent letters to 150 schools telling their coaches the rules for recruiting Ewing. The letter said that Ewing, in college, might need special educational considerations, including tutoring.

The winner of the recruiting competition was John Thompson of Georgetown, one of few prominent black college coaches in the country. As a professional player, Thompson had been a backup center on the Boston Celtics to Bill Russell, who is considered by some to be the greatest center ever to play the game. Thompson had seen Ewing play in the tenth grade during a state championship final between Rindge and Latin and Boston Latin at Boston Garden. After watching, according to *Sports Illustrated*, Thompson told his former coach, Red Auerbach of the Boston Celtics, "Get me him and I'll win the national championship."

His first year at Georgetown, Ewing led the team to a 30-7 record, to a Big East Conference tournament championship, and to the final game of the post-season, National Collegiate Athletic Association post-season tournament, (The Georgetown Hoyas lost, 63-62, to North Carolina in the final at New Orleans.) In his sophomore year, Ewing's team had a 22-10 record and made it to the regional round of the tournament. In his junior year, Georgetown finished 34-3, won the Big East regular season championship, won the Big East tournament, and won the NCAA tournament, beating Houston, 84-75, in the championship game. Between his junior and senior seasons, Ewing played on the United States Olympic basketball team and won a gold medal in the 1984 Summer Olympics. In his senior year, the Hoyas won the Big East season championship and the league's post-season tournament. Many observers expected them to win the NCAA tournament again, but they lost the final, 66-64, to Villanova, to finish the season with a 35-3 record. In Ewing's four years with Georgetown, the team was 121-23.

Ewing graduated in the spring of 1985 with a bachelor's degree in fine arts, but his athletic and academic careers had their troubled moments. In 1981, columnist David S. Broder, writing in the *Washington Post*, questioned the fact that Ewing was admitted to Georgetown University "despite an acknowledged 'reading deficiency' and 'slowness in writing.' " In another article, Broder speculated on whether Ewing's admission was due to "affirmative action"—special consideration for blacks who had been historically denied opportunity for education—or to athletics, which tend to increase the prestige and the revenue of the school. "There will be no squawks from . . . anyone . . . so long as affirmative action is confined to 7-foot centers who want only an undergraduate education and are no threat for a faculty job or any other position a better-educated white might want," Broder wrote.

In the 1981 high school championship game between Ewing's school and Boston College High, said a *Sports Illustrated* report, the opposing fans chanted "Ewing can't read!" In February of 1982, the *Washington Post* reported that fans of Georgetown's foes often taunted Ewing. A sign at Villanova said "Ewing is an Ape." One fan wore a T-shirt saying "Ewing Kant Read Dis." During a pre-game introduction, someone tossed a banana peel on the court. And under the Providence basket, someone raised a sign that said "Ewing Can't Read."

"The enmity is based on a sad misunderstanding of a superb athlete," wrote Howard Husock in the *Boston Observer*. "And make no mistake about it: It is also based on race." The Rev. Timothy J. Healy, president of Georgetown, told the *Washington Post*, "No one on the face of the Earth can tell me if Patrick were a 7-foot white man that people would still carry those signs around."

Some of the harassment was more serious than the derisive placards. The *Washington Post* reported that on March 8, 1982, Georgetown received a telephoned death threat against Ewing. "It scared the hell out of me," coach Thompson said. "You can say it's pretty common. But it was pretty common last year when the president of the United States was shot, wasn't it?"

In addition, the play of Ewing on the court—and that of his teammates—drew criticism from some who felt that the Hoyas at times lacked sportsmanship. "Whether it is deserved or not, Ewing and his teammates are perceived as Big East Bullies, players who will use their elbows to establish position and a menacing look to keep an opponent in his place," Peter Alfano wrote in the *New York Times*. According to this article, Syracuse guard Dwayne Washington had been treated with rudeness when he tried to prevent a pass to Ewing. "I tried to step in front of him," said Washington, "but he took a swipe at me with an elbow to the jaw like the one he gave [Chris] Mullin." The week before, Mullin of St. John's of New York was elbowed in the jaw by Ewing while moving without the ball, the *New York Times* reported. "This isn't the first time a Georgetown game has provoked a fight," Alfano wrote. "Ewing has traded punches with Kevin Williams of St. John's, Michael Adams of Boston College and now, Washington in his four collegiate seasons."

During his college career, Ewing, his teammates, and particularly coach Thompson developed a team personality that critics called "Hoya Paranoia," based, in part, on Thompson's rules making himself and his players available very rarely to the news media. Some said Ewing seemed to be a scowler on the basketball floor, something Thompson refuted as a superficial judgment. "Patrick is judged by his facial expression too often," he told the *Detroit Free Press*. "People say he never smiles. If he grinned and showed his teeth and went around with a pocket of sand and threw it on the ground and danced on it, everyone would think he's a great kid. He isn't like that when he's on the court."

Much of the controversy was not of Ewing's making. In May, 1984, the Portland Trail Blazers of the NBA were fined $250,000—the largest fine in league history—for improper contacts with Ewing and Houston collegian Akeem Olajuwon. They sought to offer them pro contracts while they were still amateurs. In January, 1983, coach Thompson had sparked debate by proposing that Ewing leave college, turn pro early, and take the available money because officials were making decisions that Thompson thought were unfair to Ewing.

Not all his troubles were quite so serious. On the lighter side, Ewing stood out in a crowd not only for his height and ability, but also because he wore a gray T-shirt beneath his standard, sleeveless Georgetown basketball jersey. Even that created controversy in 1982, when Ewing wore a shirt with a patch bearing the logo of the Nike shoe company, on the sleeve. Critics claimed he was promoting the product.

A final controversy came in Ewing's senior year, when Mullin of St. John's was named the winner of the John Wooden player of the year award, chosen by the United States Basketball Writers Association. "Once again, the armchair sociologists cried racism," Alfano wrote in the *New York Times*. (Mullin, a shorter man who plays the guard position, is white). In the same article, University of Kansas basketball coach Larry Brown was quoted as saying "Ewing is the best player in America by far. That is no slap at the other kids. He is just a greater player."

In general, however, Ewing's college career was filled with success and acclaim. In the 1981-82 season, as a freshman, Ewing made 183 of 290 two-point field goal attempts, 103 of 167 one-point free throw attempts, and averaged 7.5 rebounds and 12.7 points per game. In the 1982-83 season, as a sophomore, he was 212 of 372 in field goals and 141 of 224 in free throws; he averaged 10.2 rebounds and 17.7 points per game. In the 1983-84 season, as a junior, he was 242 of 368 in field goals and 124 of 189 in free throws; he averaged 10 rebounds and 16.4 points per game. In the 1984-85 season, as a senior, he was 220 of 253 in field goals and 102 of 160 in free throws; he averaged 9.2 rebounds and 14.6 points per game. For his total college career, he averaged 9.2 rebounds and 15.3 points per game.

More than his offensive statistics, Ewing was known for his defensive abilities. He blocked opponents' shots with startling regularity and often, by virtue of his size and ability, forced them to change their natural technique when he guarded his basket. In four years, Ewing blocked 493 shots. "The first thing coach Jarvis taught me was defense," Ewing told *Sports Illustrated*. "But I'm not Superman—I can't

block every shot. The one thing Bill Russell suggested was to use my mind of defense."

Many compared him to former college and professional great Bill Russell, as well as Wilt Chamberlain and Kareem Abdul-Jabbar, also centers. "Patrick doesn't just beat you," St. John's coach Lou Carnesecca, told the *Detroit Free Press*, "he tears you up." Knicks coach Hubie Brown said Ewing had the potential to be as great, but cautioned in the *New York Times*: "You must always wait. Those three did it year in and year out for more than 10 years. Kareem and Russell were the ultimate most valuable players. But to put it in perspective, Bill Walton came into the NBA with more hoopla than Patrick Ewing does now, but Bill Walton put together only one and a half great seasons. Injuries curtail potential."

So great was his ability, and the resulting desire of many professional teams to draft him, that the NBA changed its rules, creating a lottery for the first time in 1985. It was conducted among the seven teams that had failed to make the NBA post-season playoffs after the 1984-1985 season and was undeniably Ewing-inspired. The NBA created the

Patrick Ewing (number 33) exhibits his outstanding defensive ability in a Big East conference playoff game against the University of Connecticut, March 7, 1985. AP/Wide World Photos.

lottery to discourage teams from losing purposely to gain high draft status as they could under the old system, which allowed teams to pick collegians according to inverse order of their won-lost records.

To negotiate his first pro contract, Ewing signed with agents Donald Dell and David Falk of ProServ, a Washington, D.C., sports agency. He turned down Bob Woolf, a Boston lawyer who represents Larry Bird of the Boston Celtics, among others. "In New York, I think he's going to have a particularly high impact," Falk told the *Detroit Free Press.* "And also with the league being centered in New York, he's going to have an entertainment impact on the entire league."

Thus, with extraordinarily high expectations, the stage was set for Patrick Ewing's rookie season in the NBA. The pressure was on for him not only to perform well on the court, but also to resurrect an ailing basketball team single-handed, and even to improve the fortunes of the whole league. He began his professional career by displaying some of the same aggressiveness that had become his trademark in college. In what Jack McCallum of *Sports Illustrated* called "the utter refusal of Ewing to act like a rookie," Ewing was ejected from four preseason games for arguing with referees and fighting with opposing players. And despite his having taken some knocks in the press for cooperating only grudgingly with reporters, the Knicks' fans loved him; in his debut performance at Madison Square Garden, he received a two-minute standing ovation. Ewing responded admirably. He was expected to be a fine defensive player, but, as Walter Leavy reported in *Ebony,* "in the NBA so far, it's his offensive ability that has everybody talking. He has unveiled a virtually unstoppable 15- to 18-foot jump shot that seems to slip into the basket as softly as a hen sits on her eggs, and his thundering slam dunks have brought even the most reserved spectators out of their seats to give each other 'high fives.' If there was ever any doubt about Patrick Ewing making an impact in the NBA, forget about it. 'The people with talent and ability to be superstars also have the ability to make an immediate impact,' says Knicks coach Hubie Brown. 'And believe me, Patrick's got it.'"

So Ewing proved he could play in the NBA and bring out the fans—on the road as well as in the Garden. But how much did he help improve the team? In the *Sporting News,* Jan Hubbard stated that Ewing learned "the same lesson that Michael Jordan learned last season and that Ralph Sampson learned two years ago: It takes more than one great rookie to turn a franchise into a contender." Hubbard pointed out that through 37 games of the 1984-85 season,

the New York Knicks had posted a 13-24 record. In the same number of games in 1985-86, with Ewing, their record was again 13-24. But, as Hubbard admitted, "Ewing has had to carry a team that has played without injured Bernard King and Bill Cartwright," a situation for which Ewing can hardly be held responsible. In the final analysis, as Leavy wrote, "the only promise Ewing has made to the Knicks is that he will do the best he can. And he *has* performed heroically. What the Knicks hoped he would be, he has been. What the team has asked him to do, he has done. Unfortunately, that hasn't been enough."

And when Ewing injured his knee late in the season—one more in a long list of injuries for the Knicks—it appeared that the team's hopes for an immediate turnaround in their fortunes were put to rest. Still, as in all sports, there's always another season, and if the Knicks can get their entire squad healthy at the same time, there's a good chance that they can improve dramatically and perhaps become an NBA power-house once again. Said Leavy: "Ewing's arrival signals the beginning of a new era [for the Knicks], one that could rival the memorable days when Madison Square Garden was the stage for Walt Frazier, Earl (The Pearl) Monroe and Willis Reed. If Ewing can somehow lead the Knicks back to respectability and to that elusive championship, the chants of 'Patrick! Patrick!' will ring in his ears."

SOURCES:

PERIODICALS

Boston Observer, May, 1984.
Detroit Free Press, July 12, 1984, May 13, 1985.
Ebony, February, 1986.
Newsweek, April 12, 1982, December 13, 1982, March 25, 1984, April 3, 1984, April 16, 1984, July 1, 1984, July 29, 1984, March 29, 1985, April 1, 1985, May 27, 1985.
New York Times, December 8, 1980, March 29, 1982, January 14, 1983, March 9, 1985, March 17, 1985, May 13, 1985, May 19, 1985, August 2, 1985.
People, March 23, 1981, March 5, 1984.
Sporting News, January 27, 1986.
Sports Illustrated, August 10, 1981, December 28, 1981, January 3, 1982, November 29, 1982, December 20, 1982, March 19, 1984, January 7, 1985, March 25, 1985, May 6, 1985, May 20, 1985; October 28, 1985.
Time, March 14, 1983, July 8, 1985, July 29, 1985.
Washington Post, March 8, 1981, February 10, 1982, March 8, 1982, March 29, 1982.

—Sidelights by Joe LaPointe

Nanette Falkenberg
1951-

PERSONAL: Born April 27, 1951, in Scranton, Pa.; daughter of a small business owner. *Education*: Bucknell University, B.A., 1973.

ADDRESSES: Office—National Abortion Rights Action League, 1424 K St. N.W., Washington, D.C. 20005.

OCCUPATION: Social activist; political organizer.

CAREER: Senate campaign worker in Nevada and Oregon prior to 1973; AFL-CIO, American Federation of State, County and Municipal Employees (AFSCME), union organizer, beginning 1973, associate director of political action, beginning 1979, liason to National Democratic Party; currently executive director of National Abortion Rights Action League, Washington, D.C.

MEMBER: Phi Beta Kappa.

SIDELIGHTS: In the arena of women's issues—a political realm filled with outspoken feminist authors, born-again ministers, and controversial politicians of all stripes—Nanette Falkenberg is something of a surprise. She describes herself as a hard-headed, no-nonsense political strategist for the cause of legal, accessible abortions for every woman who wants one. In this way, she cuts a figure that is often quite at odds with others in the emotionally charged war being waged over abortions in the United States.

This soft-spoken, articulate woman is *the* national spokesman for abortion rights in this country. She appears on talk shows—often squaring off against a fundamentalist minister or Catholic priest or anti-abortion housewife. She is frequently contacted by news magazines for her views on some new development, be it the rash of bombings of abortion clinics or some unexpected turn in the legislative effort for a constitutional amendment to ban abortions. She and her organization, the National Abortion Rights Action League (NARAL), counter nearly every major anti-abortion pronouncement with their own news releases and public statements, in order to give their position on abortion the widest possible currency.

In the eighties, as the battle over abortions is waged in the legislatures and in the courts, Nanette Falkenberg is likely to be the single most influential "pro-choice" figure on the national scene. Since the future of legal, accessible abortions is now in question, especially if President Reagan chooses to appoint anti-abortion justices to the Supreme Court and other federal benches, Falkenberg and NARAL will have their hands full in their efforts. Indeed, the availability of abortions in this country may come down to just how effective a political strategist Falkenberg is.

AP/Wide World Photos

She appears to be up to the job. Although she has been a supporter of legal, accessible abortions throughout her life, she was hired as executive director by NARAL for her political skills, largely gained as a worker on political campaigns, as a union organizer and political strategist for union interests. Even now Falkenberg prefers to think of herself as a strategist more than a "pro-choice" ideologue. She says no heart-rending personal experiences molded her stand on abortion. "I don't think I came to this job because of any personal experiences," she told CN, but "because of my personal potential to create political influence" on behalf of the pro-choice cause.

Falkenberg has been busy creating this influence throughout much of her life. Born in 1951, the only child of a small businessman in Scranton, Pennsylvania, she attended public schools there and, later, Bucknell University. During college, she briefly considered becoming a lawyer, a profession that would certainly have been suited to her predilection for rational analysis over histrionics and emotionalism. But while still a student, working on the George McGovern campaign in 1972, Falkenberg was smitten by politics and thereafter would never really separate herself from this area. She graduated Phi Beta Kappa in political science from

Bucknell in 1973, worked on senate campaigns in Nevada and Oregon, and then was hired, in 1975, as union organizer for the American Federation of State, County and Municipal Employees, a branch of the AFL-CIO. "I did a lot of straight union organizing there," Falkenberg recalls. But she soon gravitated to work that was more clearly "political," rising through the ranks to become associate director of political action in 1979. Her job then was to coordinate AFSCME efforts on behalf of sympathetic candidates in the state and municipal campaigns. She also served as the union's liaison to the National Democratic party.

Though hired by NARAL more for her skills than for her ideology, Falkenberg could hardly be called a political mercenary. She has invariably worked for causes that she believed in. On the abortion issue, Falkenberg maintains that the whole question is not as black and white as the anti-abortionists contend, and her stance is this: Since there is no agreement on exactly when human life begins, a decision on whether to have an abortion should be made by the pregnant woman. "And while there is no consensus on when life begins" she explained to *CN*, "there is a very clear consensus among the American people that the decision on abortion ought to be left to the individual woman. . . . And I think the strength of that position is that, if an individual believes that life begins at conception, and that it would be difficult if not impossible for her to have an abortion, then she can choose not to have one."

Ms. Falkenberg has said repeatedly that, if abortions were made illegal in this country, abortions would still be common, and widespread flouting of the laws would take place. She does favor better birth-control education in this country to diminish the number of abortions performed each year but points out that even the most effective birth control means, the oral contraceptive, is only 98 percent effective. "Even if every woman used the pill, there would still be 200,000 unwanted pregnancies each year from pill failures."

Obviously, the one thing that Falkenberg and NARAL would least like to see is a ban on abortions. The organization remembers the time of illegal abortions all too clearly. NARAL itself has its roots in an organization, the National Association for the Repeal of Abortion Laws, that was founded in 1969, four years before the Supreme Court made abortion legal in its historic *Roe vs. Wade* decision. Since 1973, the renamed organization has endeavored not only to keep abortions legal, but also to make them accessible to all women, even very poor ones. This has meant lobbying at the level of state legislatures for financing of abortions for welfare recipients and the indigent. The organization also lobbies members of Congress, makes campaign endorsements, and provides some funding of the campaigns of candidates sympathetic to their cause. In the 1982 presidential election year, spending totalled $700,000.

NARAL therefore plays a preponderant role in the pro-choice battle. It is the only national organization whose sole purpose is assuring what it considers to be the abortion rights of women, although it has some allies in this task: the National Organization for Women, Planned Parenthood, and the American Civil Liberties Union. NARAL's opponents include Right to Life, an anti-abortion group, the hierarchy of the Roman Catholic church, the Moral Majority, and President Ronald Reagan, who favors a ban on all abortions, except those undertaken to save the life of the mother. Statements in NARAL literature have termed the president's positions on abortion-related issues—especially his decision to have the firearms and tobacco enforcement agency and not the FBI investigate bombings at abortion clinics—as "callous" and "dangerous."

Within NARAL, Falkenberg's role is that of spokesperson and strategist. She says she especially enjoys working out the broad outlines of NARAL strategy. "I'm not a detail person. I delegate. I'm learning to delegate," she told *CN*. One priority is building up the organization's membership, and Falkenberg says she is proud of the fact that the number of NARAL members has just topped 200,000 nationwide. (She indicates that one of the reasons that she was hired in 1981 was to add members to the group as effectively as she did as a union organizer for AFSCME.) During the recruiting of volunteers, trained NARAL speakers hold informal meetings in private homes. Once on board, the members perform tasks such as compiling lists of pro-choice individuals and then, in turn, recruiting them for letter-writing campaigns, fund-raising, and other activities.

Another important activity is lobbying. Falkenberg says her greatest accomplishment since joining NARAL was the recent campaign to convince legislators that a pro-choice stance on abortion does not hurt them at the polls—something NARAL says was proven in the 1984 state and national elections. "I think on the hard political stuff, we have done very well," Falkenberg says. "The people's inclination in this country, after all, has been pro-choice, and I think we have helped political candidates learn about this." Another lobbying function is the training of grassroots members to lobby for abortion rights on the state and local level.

In mid-1985, however, NARAL went on the defensive in the battle for U.S. public opinion when Dr. Bernard Nathanson, an ex-abortionist who had a change of conviction, produced the anti-abortion movie "Silent Scream," a sonogram of a fetus being aborted that quickly garnered national publicity for his cause. Falkenberg and NARAL responded on an equally emotional level. A new ten-week, $200,000 campaign was mounted to show that women with unwanted pregnancies are victims, too. Thousands of women were urged to "go public" and tell the story of their decision to have an abortion. The campaign marked a shift in the pro-choice effort, especially for Falkenberg. "We [previously] had a conscious desire to de-emotionalize the issue," she told *CN*, "and I don't think that we can play it that way anymore. . . . We have to say, 'You want emotion, we'll give you emotion.' "

Even with this response, the film had clearly taken its toll. Falkenberg was disturbed by the fact that "Silent Scream" showed the fetus, but not the mother who had chosen to have an abortion. At one point, according to *Boston Globe* columnist Ellen Goodman, Falkenberg asked a reporter in a burst of frustration, "Do you think the fetus is housed in a Tupperware jar?" The debate over "Silent Scream" was clearly taking the abortion debate in a direction that Falkenberg did not want it to go. "We won't fight the fetus fight with them," Falkenberg later told Goodman. "Instead we want to remind people that the fetus is carried by a living, breathing, thinking woman."

But the biggest test of Ms. Falkenberg's political savvy may be yet to come: Twenty-nine states have proposed legislation to ban or restrict abortions, and demonstrations and even violence have begun erupting at many abortion clinics. Worst of all for the pro-choice movement, President Reagan may soon have the opportunity to appoint new justices to the U.S. Supreme Court—the body that made abortions legal in the first place. At last count, six of the nine justices agreed with the 1973 decision, but five justices are over seventy-five and may soon retire. Thus, by virtue of his powers to appoint them, Mr. Reagan may soon have the opportunity to shape judicial opinion on abortion for the next forty years. It is not a prospect that Falkenberg and NARAL relish.

SOURCES:

PERIODICALS

Boston Globe, January 31, 1985.
Ms., August, 1982.
New York Times, June 12, 1983, June 6, 1984, January 12, 1985.

—*Sidelights by Gary Hoffman*

Trevor Ferrell

1972-

BRIEF ENTRY: Born 1972, in Gladwyne, Pa. American youth, whose campaign to aid Philadelphia's homeless has received national attention. Trevor Ferrell's self-described "mission" began in December of 1983 when he saw a television news report on the city's street people. Shocked at the sight, he asked his parents if the problem was as serious as the report stated. His father, a successful businessman, volunteered to show him firsthand. Young Ferrell brought along a blanket and pillow, which he gave to a man lying on a subway grate. Since that night the family has regularly returned, bringing coffee, hot meals, and clothing.

Ferrell's efforts were first reported by suburban newspapers and local television stations; soon the national media picked up the story. Public reaction has been overwhelming. The Ferrells have received nearly $50,000 in contributions. Churches, synagogues, men's clubs, restaurants, and supermarkets have donated various goods and services. New Jersey's Fort Dix Army Training Center sent one hundred surplus overcoats. A Volkswagen van and a thirty-room boarding house have also been donated. The Ferrell family has received several awards, plaques, and city council commendations, and they have been approached by movie companies and book publishers eager to tell their story.

In spite of public support and official praise, the Ferrells find it increasingly difficult to maintain their operation. Trevor's father, Frank, temporarily closed his electronics sales and service business to work full time on his son's campaign. The family has exhausted its savings and now depends on their church and friends for financial support. Moreover, Trevor's mother, Janet, was attacked by a street person in 1984. The family remains devoted to the project, however, and they are not without hope. Resources for Human Development, a nonprofit organization, is furthering their cause, and they continue to receive contributions from across the country.

Young Ferrell refers to Philadelphia's homeless as "my friends." They, in turn, call him "little buddy," "John Boy," and "little Jesus." *McCall's* writer Maryann Bucknum Brinley comments: "He never judges the street people for their inability to make a living wage or to stay sober. All he wants to do is help. When the first man lying on the grate

AP/Wide World Photos

said, 'God bless you,' thanking him for the blanket, [his mother explains,] 'Trevor couldn't wait to do it again.'"

Address: Trevor's Campaign, Resources for Human Development, 120 West Lancaster Ave., Ardmore, Pa. 19003.

SOURCES:

PERIODICALS

McCall's, January, 1985.
New York Times, March 12, 1984.
People, March 26, 1984, December 24, 1984.

Mel Fisher

1922(?)-

PERSONAL: Full name, Melvin A. Fisher; born c. 1922 in Hobart, Ind.; father was a poultry farmer; mother's name, Grace; previously married; current wife's name, Dolores; children: (first marriage) Terry; (second marriage) Dirk (deceased), Kim (son), Kane (son), Taffi Quesada (daughter). *Education:* Degree in engineering from Purdue University.

ADDRESSES: Office—Treasure Salvors, Inc., 200 Green St., Key West, Fla. 33040.

OCCUPATION: Treasure hunter.

CAREER: Former poultry farmer in California; proprietor of Mel's Aqua Shop, Torrance, Calif., until 1961; host of television program on diving; in marine salvage business in Florida since 1961; founder and president of Treasure Salvors, Inc., Key West, Fla., 1963—. *Military service:* Served in U.S. Army during World War II; participated in Normandy invasion, June, 1944.

AWARDS, HONORS: NOGI Award in sports/education from Underwater Society of America, 1980; honored by Queen Sophia of Spain.

SIDELIGHTS: Mel Fisher, the founder and president of Treasure Salvors, Inc., has been called a dreamer, an incredible optimist, and a charlatan. For seventeen years he patiently searched the waters off the Florida Keys for the wreck of the *Nuestra Senora de Atocha*, a seventeenth-century Spanish galleon that sank with a fortune in cargo on board. During his quest, Fisher battled the state of Florida and the U.S. Government, suffered personal tragedy, and faced near-financial ruin. The long and costly search ended in the summer of 1985, when Fisher discovered the *Atocha*'s hull—and an estimated $400 million worth of gold, silver, and jewels. It is considered the largest treasure ever recovered from a shipwreck. "People called Mel a fake. They said he was luring investors with ridiculous claims, but he was right," exclaimed diver Pat Clyne to Montgomery Brower of *People*. "This is what Robert Louis Stevenson meant to write about. Now kids'll grow up on Mel Fisher stories."

Born in Hobart, Indiana, Fisher was raised on tales of adventure and sunken treasure. At the age of eleven he made a diving helmet from a paint can and a bicycle tire pump and nearly died testing it. "I always wanted to do something adventurous, although the treasure hunting grew on me very gradually," Fisher told Brower. "I remember reading everything I could about pirates and treasure. I'd get my homework done in the morning and do my research on Blackbeard and Laffite in the afternoon." Fisher majored in engineering at Purdue University and later designed bridges for the Army during World War II. After the war he briefly

tended chickens on his father's California farm, then opened his own business, Mel's Aqua Shop, one of the country's first diving stores. He hosted a television show on diving, produced the first scuba training film, and pioneered the art of underwater cinematography. He also started a salvage diving club; each week the group would explore a different shipwreck. In 1961 Fisher and his wife decided to hunt for treasure full time. They sold the business, moved to Florida, and, in 1963, formed Treasure Salvors in Key West.

Fisher began his search for the *Atocha* five years later, after reading of the wreck in *The Treasure Diver's Guide*. The flagship of a twenty-eight galleon fleet, the *Atocha* and her sister ship, the *Santa Margarita*, left Havana, Cuba, for Spain on September 4, 1622, carrying gold, silver, and jewels taken from the Indian empires in Mexico and South America. Two days after they set sail, a hurricane struck. Nearly 400 people died in the shipwrecks, and only seventy-two survived. According to the ships' manifests, the *Atocha* carried forty-seven tons of silver coins and bars, as well as 600 pounds of gold. The *Margarita* also held a sizable bounty: Thirty-four gold bars and disks, 118,000 coins, and 419 silver ingots. Moreover, historical records indicate that forty-three wealthy Spaniards were on the *Atocha* and may have stored their personal valuables on board. The loss of the *Atocha* caused a depression in Europe and proved disastrous to Spain's economy, which relied heavily on revenue from the New World. Spain sent crews to retrieve the riches, but seventeenth-century salvage equipment was primitive, and very little treasure was recovered.

Fisher resumed the search some 350 years later, examining centuries-old shipping records and survivors' reports. According to his research, the *Atocha* lay near two islands in the Florida Keys, the Upper Matecumbe and the Lower Matecumbe. His divers combed the area but found nothing. In 1970 a friend of Fisher's, Eugene Lyon, discovered the original salvor's report at the Spanish archives in Seville. The document placed the wreckage near the Marquesas Keys, thirty-five miles west of Key West. Fisher then sent his crews to investigate an underwater reef ten miles off the Marquesas, speculating that the *Atocha* had been forced onto the reef and broke apart. In 1973 Fisher's oldest son, Dirk, found the ship's anchor and three silver bars in shallow waters a few miles from the reef. The crew fixed their search in this area. Though they brought up thousands of artifacts and millions of dollars worth of treasure, the ship's hull, and the bulk of her cargo—the "mother load"—eluded them. Later, Fisher realized that the recovered

Mel Fisher (left, holding champagne bottle) offers a toast as son Kane hoists a bar of silver recovered from the wreck of the Spanish galleon Nuestra Senora de Atocha, *July 1985. AP/Wide World Photos.*

objects had been scattered from the main structure by a second storm that struck the area shortly after the *Atocha* sank. "I wish we had never found them," lamented Treasure Salvors' vice-president Bleth McHaley to Amy Wilentz of *Time.* "It was a false lead that cost us years."

Fisher encountered a number of setbacks in his pursuit of the *Atocha.* Throughout the 1970s he battled Florida and the Federal Government over ownership rights to the treasure. Florida claimed 25 percent of his find; the United States demanded all of it, contending that the wreck and her cargo are a national legacy. These legal contests all but bankrupted Treasure Salvors. Meanwhile, Fisher came under fire for his fund-raising and salvaging techniques. Some critics accused him of seducing investors with inflated estimates of the treasure's worth. Archeologists charged that his salvage methods were "destructive" and "piratical," recounts Philip Trupp or *Smithsonian.* Ross Morrell, the director of Flordia's Division of Archives, History, and Records, voiced a similar opinion to the *Wall Street Journal*'s L. Erik Calonius: "It's the looting of our own heritage for fun and profit. He's blowing the sites apart with blowers, grabbing the goodies." Countered Fisher: "The treasure isn't a natural resource. It's the cargo of a shipwreck. If it's abandoned, it belongs to the finder."

The search for the Spanish galleon also came at a high personal cost. On July 20, 1975, Dirk Fisher, his wife, Angel, and diver Rick Gage drowned when their salvage ship capsized. One week earlier Dirk had located nine of the *Atocha*'s bronze cannons. Upon his son's death, Fisher considered abandoning the quest. "I thought, 'Maybe it just ain't worth it,'" he recalled to Brower. "But my son would have wanted me to complete the search, so I said, 'Okay, I'll keep it up until I find her.'"

Fisher's luck began to change in 1980, when he discovered the wreckage of the *Margarita* and retrieved $20 million in gold and silver. Two years later U.S. Supreme Court denied Florida's and the Federal Government's claims to Fisher's cargo, ruling that Fisher and his investors were entitled to all of the treasure and artifacts he salvaged. In the spring of 1985 Fisher knew that he was finally closing in on the *Atocha.* On Memorial Day his divers picked up thirteen gold bars, a seven-foot gold chain, over one dozen large emeralds, and 400 silver coins. On July 20, 1985—exactly ten years after Dirk's death—two divers found the hull of the ship and what Fisher's younger son, Kane, describes as "a reef of silver bars." The vessel lay forty miles west of Key West, near the site Fisher had named fifteen years earlier. Thus far, crew members have removed close to 1,000 silver ingots, each weighing from 70 to 100 pounds; mahogany chests filled with silver coins and bricks of gold; and thousands of artifacts, including silver candelabra and pitchers and gold cups and bracelets. The wreck itself is of great historical value, according to R. Duncan Mathewson III, Treasure Salvors' chief archeologist. The ship's hull and stern are well-preserved and in good condition. Mathewson considers the wreck "a virgin time capsule," quoted *Newsweek*'s Mark Starr and Ron Moreau, "as important as Pompeii or King Tut's Tomb."

Fisher's personal share of the treasure, which he does not plan to sell, is 5 percent. His employees will also receive a percentage. The rest will be divided among Treasure Salvors' hundreds of investors. There is some controversy over the method of distribution. No investor will receive cash; instead, each will be paid with actual treasure, the value of which will be determined by Fisher and his staff. As *Money*'s William C. Banks points out, "Fisher's valuations. . . are debatable, based as they are on what he gets for similar items retailed through his museum shop." He continues: "What the market will bear depends a great deal on location, and Fisher's museum gift shop is the retail bull's-eye. Recently, the shop was selling silver pieces of eight for as little as $180 to as much as $1,200, depending on the quality of their markings. Yet Joel Rettew's Rare Coin Gallery in Beverly Hills, which tends to be frequented by serious collectors as opposed to giddy tourists, is currently selling pieces of eight picked up along the trail that finally led to the Atocha for $85." Banks also notes that "if the Atocha's estimated cache of 225,000 pieces of eight hits the market all at once, the price could drop precipitously." However, Jerry Burke, an investment banker who sells limited shares of Treasure Salvors, states that most small investors do not expect to realize a fortune from their investment. They buy into Fisher's expeditions because it's "fun and exciting" and because it provides a tax shelter. "It's the only investment I have ever seen that can change the most sophisticated, hard-nosed businessman into a little boy," Burke told Starr and Moreau. "Some want the gold, some would like a piece of pottery, . . . and some just want the thrill, never expecting to get their money back."

Fisher apparently has no set plans for the future. He has been deluged with offers from book publishers, television networks, and film producers for the rights to his life story. Meanwhile, he hopes to set up an exhibit of the *Atocha* once she and her cargo have been completely excavated, cleaned, and catalogued. He has said that he plans to sell Treasure Salvors and retire. He has also said that he would like to search for the wreck of the *San Roman*, near Vera Beach, Florida, and for galleons that sank en route from the Philippines to Japan. "You have to be an eternal optimist to do this for a living," Fisher declared in *Nation's Business*. "But once it gets into your blood, you're hooked for life." Fisher's daughter, Taffi Quesada, agrees. "Life's been real exciting," she remarked to Brower. "We've always been broke, always struggling, and, of course, everyone thought we were rich. . . . We were raised by my father never to lose faith, to have confidence. 'Today's the day,' he always said. Then, at sunset, he'd tell us, 'Tomorrow's the day.' He doesn't have to say that anymore."

SOURCES:

PERIODICALS

Christian Science Monitor, November 8, 1982.
Detroit Free Press, July 25, 1985, September 1, 1985.
Detroit News, August 23, 1985.
Fortune, August 19, 1985.
Los Angeles Times, July, 21, 1985.
Maclean's, August 5, 1985.
Money, September, 1985.
National Geographic, March, 1983.
Nation's Business, August, 1980.
Newsweek, August 5, 1985.
New York Times, July 21, 1975, March 20, 1978, June 23, 1978, March 16, 1980, June 23, 1981.
Oceans, September, 1982.
People, August 12, 1985, December 23, 1985.
Rolling Stone, January 30, 1986.
Skin Diver, October, 1980.
Smithsonian, October, 1983.
Time, April 11, 1983, August 5, 1985.
USA Today, September 20, 1985.
U.S. News & World Report, August 5, 1985.
Wall Street Journal, June 24, 1982.
Washington Post, July 2, 1985.

—Sidelights by Denise Wiloch

Robert M. Fomon

1925-

PERSONAL: Born 1925, in Chicago, Ill.; son of a plastic surgeon; married first wife, Marilyn (divorced); married Sharon Kay Richie (a former Miss America; divorced); children: (first marriage) one son, Robert; one daughter. *Education:* University of Southern California, bachelor's degree, 1947, graduate study.

ADDRESSES: Office—E.F. Hutton & Co., One Battery Park Plaza, New York, N.Y. 10004.

OCCUPATION: Investment banker and business executive.

CAREER: E.F. Hutton & Co., trainee in Los Angeles, Calif., beginning 1951, vice-president, beginning 1962, member of board of directors, beginning 1967, senior vice-president, beginning 1969, president and chief executive officer in New York, N.Y., 1970-77, chairman of board of directors and chief executive officer, 1977—, president of E.F. Hutton Group, Inc., 1982-85.

SIDELIGHTS: Regarded by employees as an autocratic ruler and by some rivals as a hunter prowling for more profits, Robert M. Fomon has never been one to be intimidated by the size of a competitor. Under Fomon's guidance, E.F. Hutton & Company challenged giant Merrill Lynch, Pierce, Fenner & Smith for leadership of the brokerage business and nearly succeeded, climbing from the number eight spot to number two among retail brokerage houses. That the competition sometimes views him as a predator is appropriate; as William G. Shepherd, Jr., reports in the *New York Times*, Fomon delights in "ptarmigan shoots in Spain" and has a taste for "collections of hunting scenes, and large volumes with titles such as 'Birds of Prey.'. . . Mr. Fomon is so much the hunter, in fact, that to mark his first decade as Hutton's boss, Hutton employees . . . gave him an elegantly engraved pair of English Purdey bird guns."

Fomon spent seven years in college without knowing what he wanted as a career. There were four years of undergraduate studies at the University of Southern California and three years of graduate school in law, anthropology, archeology, and English. Notes Robert Cole in the *New York Times*, "When he left school, he had completed enough English studies for a master's degree except for the required thesis."

In 1951, Fomon started his first job and his business career with E.F. Hutton as a trainee in Los Angeles. Advancing up Hutton's management ladder, Fomon became a vice-president in 1962, responsible for West Coast corporate finances, syndicate, and institutional departments. By 1967, he was a board member and two years later senior vice-president.

The *New York Times* related how Fomon was elected president and chief executive officer in 1970: "Keith S.

UPI/Bettmann Newsphotos

Wellin, president of Hutton in 1970, was the logical choice to become chairman and chief executive the following year on the retirement of then chairman Sylvan C. Coleman. But Wellin ran into opposition." Fomon recalled that "The majority of the board felt that the way to solve it was to elect someone else president. They felt Al Jack [Alec R. Jack, then senior vice-president in charge of the Southern California office] was the logical person to be president. But Al said he was too old [he was 64] and recommended me. I was a compromise candidate."

As president, Fomon moved to the firm's New York headquarters and led an expansion push that by 1973 made Hutton the number two brokerage firm in sales. Desiring even greater profitability, Fomon reported in the *New York Times* that his firm believed its future strength "may come in part from its ability to engage in businesses broader than those it presently conducts." For the first time, member firms of the New York Stock Exchange, including Hutton, formed holding companies to gain greater flexibility and diversity of operations. E.F. Hutton Group, Inc. was organized as a holding company owning all of the stock of its respective firms, which became sole subsidiaries.

Never afraid to tangle with a competitor, Fomon told Cole of the *New York Times* that Merrill Lynch had accused Hutton of proselytizing Merrill salesmen in a small Michigan office and then raiding its customers. Said Fomon, "If they can't hold their own employees, that's their problem; if they were running their business well, there's no way we could hire their employees." Fomon was also proud of Hutton's clout in the marketplace when a company wished to sell securities: "When we're chosen to be co-managers with Merrill Lynch, we're not chosen by Merrill Lynch. We're chosen by the issuer. They want that distribution."

In 1977, Fomon was rewarded for his highly successful leadership by being elected chairman of the board. Unworried by rumors that Hutton would be a likely target for a takeover in a merger, he stated flatly to Shepherd of the *New York Times* that Hutton could generate all the growth it needed internally. He continued, "We think of ourselves as being in the business of investment." Hutton puts its excess capital into companies that represent attractive investments in their own right but that can also provide products for Hutton's brokerage customers. According to the *New York Times*, Hutton adopted "the European merchant-banking practice of acquiring or investing in outside companies for the firm's own account. That approach has gained them a variety of innovative products from the popular new 'universal' life insurance policies to funds for investing in timber properties." This successful marketing strategy is enhanced by Hutton's lean management ranks with everybody having fast access to others in the organization. Fomon told Shepherd that he creates a contagious "eat-em-alive" spirit within the company and spends most of his off-hours socializing with Hutton employees. "We do not aspire to be the largest," Fomon said to Shepherd, emphasizing his interest in profitability. "I frankly don't care about growth in revenues." Fomon's work has made him personally wealthy, but he continues at his job "just because I want to stomp the competition."

Business Week reported that Fomon keeps Hutton focused on selling, and according to one competitor, "Bob is smart enough to see that Hutton's forte is not in trading or positioning but in distribution." Fomon concentrates on keeping costs down. In 1970, after being elected CEO, he fired 600 people to reduce losses that had reached $1 million a month. In the bear market of 1974, he acquired twenty brokerage offices of Du Pont Walston to boost Hutton's revenues and make its back office operation more cost efficient. Hutton has formal contingency plans for cutbacks in staff and spending but is aggressive in taking risks that attract an affluent clientele according to *Business Week*. Hutton was the first Wall Street firm to develop a substantial tax shelter department, and it started a fee-service financial planning program to assist clients with their investments and insurance. Even in the face of this growth, Fomon watches costs.

From 1977 to 1982, George L. Ball assisted Fomon as president but resigned, according to the *New York Times*, "to head a new Prudential Insurance Company subsidiary that includes the Bache Group and other brokerage and investment operations." Fomon was named president of E.F. Hutton Group, Inc., and its subsidiary E.F. Hutton & Company and reported to the *New York Times* that "it feels very challenging" to get back into "the retail end of the

business, which was always my first love and the part of the business that I have been in the longest." When asked whether he had taken up another new hobby—at various times he has been interested in dogs, horses, macaws, cockatoos, and parrots—he replied crisply, "Just Business."

Fomon added another jewel to his crown in 1984 by having Hutton sign a long-term lease for a thirty-story office building to be constructed on West 53rd St. as its new headquarters in midtown Manhattan. Hutton will move from its current downtown headquarters at One Battery Park Plaza after the new building is completed in 1986. Fomon reported to the *New York Times*, "This new headquarters and its location in midtown Manhattan is a declaration of our intent to be more closely associated with our clients." Another tribute to Fomon came in the October, 1984, issue of *Architectural Digest* in which his Fifth Avenue apartment was described as "a Deft Touch of ceremony, comfort and formality in New York City." One of the outstanding features of the decor was his collection of nineteenth-century English sporting paintings.

In December, 1984, in the midst of Fomon's tremendous success, a scandal shocked the financial community. According to the *New York Times*, the Securities and Exchange Commission (SEC) censured E.F. Hutton & Company for not disclosing to mutual fund investors and directors that Hutton was earning interest on investors' money during a five day "float" period. Hutton agreed to return $191,000 to the mutual funds without admitting or denying liability. Hutton then amended the mutual funds' prospectus and proxy statements to report the float. But there were other problems that were not so easily repaired. On May 2, 1985, according to the *Wall Street Journal*, Hutton pleaded guilty to Federal fraud charges of operating a check-writing scheme to obtain money from many of its 400 banks without paying interest. The firm pleaded guilty to 2,000 counts of mail and wire fraud and agreed to pay a $2 million fine and make restitution to the aggrieved banks. Attorney General Edwin Meese said the scheme involved checks totaling billions of dollars written between July, 1980, and February, 1982. Justice Department representatives said Hutton systematically overdrew hundreds of its own accounts in banks across the country and moved money between banks to artificially delay collection of certain funds. Prosecutors said Hutton was thus able to use interest-free money that totaled as much as $250 million on some days.

Hutton obtained a temporary exemption from a securities law that would automatically disqualify the company as an investment adviser or principal underwriter for several mutual funds and unit investment trusts. Under the Investment Company Act of 1940, any company convicted of criminal misconduct in connection with its investment advisory activities, securities trading, or underwriting is automatically debarred. The exemption was granted after Hutton agreed to cooperate with any SEC investigation of fraudulent practices. Fomon, as reported by the *Wall Street Journal*, said, "The practices in which the company pleaded guilty didn't in any way jeopardize the security of customer or client funds."

According to the *Wall Street Journal*, prosecutors said that more than twenty-four Hutton employees, including some senior company officials, were involved in the scheme.

However, immunity was given to nearly half of them during the three-year investigation, and criminal prosecution of the company and employees was dropped as part of a plea agreement presented to the court. A Hutton background document, described by the *Wall Street Journal*, said that compensation for Hutton branch managers is partly tied to the profitability of their offices. One of the factors in determining profitability is interest income, which became particularly important during the period of rising interest rates in 1980 and 1981. The *Wall Street Journal*, citing documents filed in court, reported that Hutton officials "frequently" misused bank accounts for Hutton branches by writing checks for amounts "unrelated to and in excess of the volume of customer funds deposited" in those accounts. In some cases, prosecutors said, local Hutton officials arbitrarily multiplied by ten the actual balance in those accounts before drawing down the funds for transfer to the company's central accounts. Hutton said it would take "appropriate" action against certain employees.

Also, the *Wall Street Journal* reported that Hutton pleaded guilty to extending the "float" time during which checks are cleared by setting up a chain of transfers between branch accounts. This scheme was carried out illegally "without the prior agreement or consent of the banks involved."

These activities, according to Hutton, violated company policy and procedures, and they were immediately halted early in 1982, when senior Hutton management learned about them. Fomon told the *Wall Street Journal*, "E.F. Hutton covered every check it wrote." A letter signed by him was sent to hundreds of bankers with whom Hutton had accounts from July, 1980, to early 1982 apologizing for its cash management practices and offering them full restitution. The letter told bankers that the firm had instituted internal controls "to assure that such events can never happen again."

The *New York Times* reported that a few individual Hutton stockholders started lawsuits against Hutton. Fomon and other officers contended that the check-writing inflated Hutton stock, defrauding its buyers and benefiting financially top officers of Hutton, and that the fines and court costs hurt investors.

Hutton named former Attorney General Griffin B. Bell to lead the inquiry to determine who at Hutton should be held responsible for defrauding banks in the check-writing scheme. Fomon, according to the *Wall Street Journal*, assumed ultimate responsibility for the fraud scheme but said he didn't intend to take a pay cut (his 1984 salary and bonus totaled $975,000) or reduce his role in Hutton's management. Fomon added that Hutton would recover from its branch managers in the check-writing scheme the "small portion of their annual compensation" derived from the illegal practice during the period investigated. Fomon reported in the *Wall Street Journal* that Bell would conduct a "thorough review of the practices to which the company pleaded guilty, determine how those practices evolved, identify those individuals who bear personal responsibility, and make recommendations with respect to those individuals."

In an interview with the *New York Times*, Fomon admitted, "If I had to do it over again, the company would not have taken full responsibility for the scheme, but could have allowed individuals to be charged, if that was called for." He added: "I would have pleaded guilty on behalf of the company. The individuals involved would have stood by themselves." He also noted that he did not yet know which individuals were involved but agreed that it was "incredible" to think that no high-level executives were aware of the fraud.

Some states were conducting inquiries into whether Hutton's brokerage license should be revoked as a result of its guilty plea to the fraud scheme. Fomon said that Hutton would work with the states to allow it to continue its business but would resist heavy penalties which other states might demand.

Hutton's employees suffered morale problems because of the cloud hanging over the company. "The employees want to see a purge. They want to see the bad ones go," said Fomon. He found it difficult to perform his regular job function while dealing with the problems of the investigation. However, the job frustration might prolong his stay at Hutton. He reported to the *New York Times* that "Even if I were tired of the job, I'm not going to move now until this is cleared up, and then stay some. I couldn't retire now because it would look like I was involved, which I wasn't."

Despite the damage done to Hutton's reputation, writes Anthony Bianco in *Business Week*, "the scandal also has had the beneficial effect of jolting Robert Fomon . . . into altering his management approach—a move that may get the company moving again" after slipping from number two among retail brokers to number five. Among other changes, Fomon surprised financial observers by appointing Robert P. Rittereiser, a former Merrill Lynch executive, to the presidency of Hutton. Rittereiser is very highly regarded as one of the new breed of professional administrators who contrast sharply with old-line industry executives who traditionally came from the ranks of brokers and investment bankers. In addition, Bianco observes, "Hutton's retail system remains strong. The firm is a power in public finance and still the only brokerage house that has figured out how to make money selling life insurance." Fomon's resourcefulness, combined with fresh input from Rittereiser, should give Hutton a good chance of reestablishing the reputation for excellence that it enjoyed in previous years. The firm, Bianco says, may even "emerge from the trauma of scandal significantly improved."

SOURCES:

PERIODICALS

Architectural Digest, October, 1984.
Barron's, May 6, 1985.
Business Week, January 19, 1981, May 20, 1985, June 3, 1985, June 17, 1985, July 15, 1985, February 24, 1986.
Forbes, April 13, 1981.
Newsweek, May 13, 1985, May 20, 1985, July 22, 1985.
New York Times, March 15, 1973, March 30, 1975, July 15, 1975, September 2, 1975, September 28, 1975, June 2, 1977, April 30, 1980, June 23, 1981, August 16, 1981, September 6, 1981, July 22, 1982, May 8, 1984, December 13, 1984, May 10, 1985, July 11, 1985, July 29, 1985, July 31, 1985, August 14, 1985, September 29, 1985.

Time, May 13, 1985, June 10, 1985, July 1, 1985, July 15, 1985, July 22, 1985.

U.S. News and World Report, July 29, 1985.

Wall Street Journal, March 12, 1984, May 3, 1985, May 6, 1985, May 7, 1985, May 20, 1985, May 28, 1985, June 4, 1985, June 20, 1985, June 21, 1985, July 1, 1985, July 8, 1985, July 10, 1985, July 11, 1985, July 12, 1985, July 16, 1985, July 25, 1985, August 2, 1985, August 9, 1985, August 15, 1985.

Washington Post, June 4, 1985, July 17, 1985.

*—Sidelights by William C. Drollinger,
William C. Drollinger, Jr.,
and Steven C. Drollinger*

Steve Fonyo

1965-

BRIEF ENTRY: Full name, Stephen Fonyo, Jr.; born June 29, 1965, in Montreal, Quebec, Canada. Canadian marathon runner who crossed Canada to raise money for cancer research. In late spring of 1985 Steve Fonyo, who lost a leg to cancer, completed a trans-Canada run to benefit cancer research. He began his fund-raising mission, named "Journey for Lives," on March 31, 1984, in St. John's, Newfoundland. Fonyo, who averaged twenty to twenty-five miles a day, endured snow, freezing rain, and high winds throughout his effort. Fourteen months—and 4,924 miles—later he reached Vancouver Island and the end of his run. When it was over, "Journey for Lives" had raised $10 million.

Fonyo was twelve when doctors discovered he had bone cancer; his left leg was amputated to stop its spread. His recovery, physically and psychologically, was slow and painful. As a teenager he drew inspiration from fellow Canadian Terry Fox, also a cancer victim, who attempted to run the width of his country. Fox's effort ended in 1980, when he succumbed to the disease. Three years later Fonyo decided to take up the challenge. He pursued his goal in spite of initial opposition from the Canadian Cancer Society, which did not want to take away from Fox's achievement, and from his parents, who feared for his health. Undaunted, Fonyo solicited private donations to finance his run and began training. Eventually, his parents and the Cancer Society supported the project.

Fonyo, however, faced yet another hurdle—the press. During the early stages of his run he was frequently, and usually unfavorably, compared to his predecessor. Fox, college educated, articulate, and personable, had captivated the Canadian media and public. Fonyo, a high school dropout, was less polished and frequently outspoken. The press depicted him as arrogant and sullen. As the run progressed however, Fonyo grew more adept at handling media and public pressures. Moreover, as Jane O'Hara of *Maclean's* notes, when he passed the point that marked the end of Fox's run, Fonyo "symbolically began to run his own race." Up to then, Fonyo tells her, "I was seen as just the second guy coming down the road. Now I am making my own path." *Address:* National Cancer Institute of Canada, 77 Bloor St., Suite 401, Toronto, Ontario, M5S Canada 2V7.

SOURCES:

PERIODICALS

Maclean's, April 8, 1985.
Time, June 10, 1985.

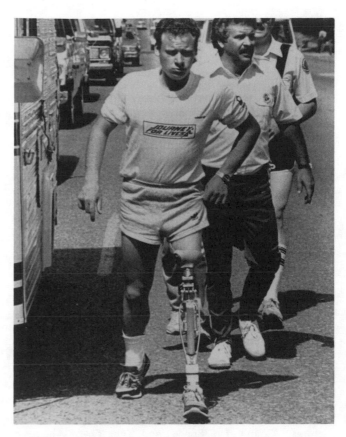

Reuters/Bettmann Newsphotos

Phil Foster

1914-1985

OBITUARY NOTICE: Name originally Fivel Feldman; born March 29, 1914, in Brooklyn, N.Y.; died following a heart attack, July 8, 1985, in Rancho Mirage, Calif.; buried at Eden Hills Memorial Park, Mission Hills, Calif. Comedian and actor. Best known as the gruff but kindhearted Frank DeFazio, on the television comedy series "Laverne and Shirley," Foster began his entertainment career as a stand-up comedian. He developed a comedy routine during his World War II Army service, and he later practiced it daily on the handball courts at Coney Island. A man he met on the courts one day was impressed with Foster's comedic talents and offered to train him as a partner. That led him to his first appearance in the RKO Amateur Show and subsequently to a string of nightclub dates. During the 1950s Foster played the Borscht Belt, in New York's Catskill Mountains, and he later performed in such celebrated clubs as the Copacabana in New York, the Fontainebleau in Miami Beach, and the Sands in Las Vegas. "Laverne and Shirley" producer Garry Marshall described Foster as "one of the first comedians not to tell jokes but to tell true experiences from the floor instead."

Foster's first television break came in 1955, when he appeared on "Caesar Presents," hosted by Sid Caesar. In the years that followed, he made numerous appearances on Jack Paar's "Tonight Show" and on the "Ed Sullivan Show" and made his dramatic television debut in "Strike." In 1965 Foster played the lead in the Off-Broadway production of "The Day the Whores Came Out to Play Tennis," and later Neil Simon selected him for a lead role in the first road version of "The Odd Couple." He performed in two motion pictures, "Conquest of Space" and "The Great American Traffic Jam." Joining "Laverne and Shirley" in 1976, Foster remained in the cast until its last show in 1983. He reportedly often joked that the only steady jobs he had ever held were "Laverne and Shirley" and World War II.

UPI/Bettmann Newsphotos

SOURCES:

BOOKS

Who's Who in America, 41st edition, Marquis, 1980.

PERIODICALS

Chicago Tribune, July 10, 1985.
Newsweek, July 22, 1985.
New Yorker, June 11, 1966.
New York Post, July 9, 1985.
New York Times, July 9, 1985.
TV Guide, August 6, 1983.

Martin Galvin

1950(?)-

AP/Wide World Photos

BRIEF ENTRY: Born c. 1950, in Long Island, N.Y. American attorney, political activist. Galvin, a lawyer for the New York City Sanitation Department, is the publicity director and a member of the board of directors of the Bronx-based Irish Northern Aid Committee (NORAID). NORAID was founded in 1970 to raise money for families of slain or imprisoned Irish Republican Army (IRA) supporters. Irish, British, and American officials, however, charge that NORAID is the IRA's major foreign source of funds and weapons. As NORAID's youngest board member (the others are in their eighties), Galvin has become the movement's chief—and most controversial—spokesman.

Galvin became an avid IRA supporter upon his first visit to Northern Ireland at the age of twenty. His wife and grandparents are natives of the country. He joined NORAID in the early 1970s, shortly after it was formed. In 1983 Galvin and other NORAID members attended an IRA rally in Belfast. One member was wounded and another arrested for "riotous behavior" at the meeting. In April of 1984 Galvin again traveled to Northern Ireland, delivering a speech in which he professed to be "encouraged" by an IRA attack that left one British soldier dead. Three months later the British Government issued an order barring Galvin from the United Kingdom. Nevertheless, Galvin, in disguise and aided by IRA members, stole into Belfast in August of 1984. When he appeared at a rally, the police, firing plastic bullets, moved to arrest him. Galvin escaped, but one man was killed and two dozen people were injured in the fray.

Several days of rioting followed the incident. Galvin, who had made the trip while on vacation from his job at the sanitation department, returned to New York. According to the *New York Times*, Galvin "told reporters that he felt regret but 'no responsibility' for the dead and wounded at the rally." Michael Flannery, NORAID's director, commented to Michael Brooke of the *New York Times*, "[Galvin] has accomplished what we wanted him to and that is sufficient."

SOURCES:

PERIODICALS

Maclean's, August 27, 1984.
Nation, September 1, 1984.
New York Times, August 14, 1984, August 22, 1984, October 3, 1984.
Time, August 27, 1984.

Indira Gandhi

1917-1984

OBITUARY NOTICE: Born November 19, 1917, in Allahabad, India; assassinated, October 31, 1984, in New Delhi, India; cremated and ashes scattered over the Himalayan Mountains. Politician. In 1966 Gandhi was elected prime minister of India, becoming the third person to head the government of the South Asian nation since its establishment as an independent republic in 1947. Gandhi was only twelve years old when she began working to free her country from British colonial rule, an effort that continued throughout her years as a student at Oxford University and eventually led to her imprisonment for subversion in 1942. After the British withdrew from India, Gandhi's father, Jawaharlal Nehru, became prime minister, and Gandhi served as his official hostess and political aide. In 1959 she was elected president of the Congress party, and, when Nehru died in 1964, she was elected to the Upper House of the Indian Parliament as minister of information and broadcasting under Nehru's successor, Bahandur Shastri. Following Shastri's death in 1966, Gandhi came to power as prime minister after defeating rival Mararji R. Desai in the 1967 national elections.

Gandhi instituted within India such policies as strong population control, nuclear and space research, and a friendly stance toward the Soviet Union. Internationally known, Gandhi enjoyed relatively wide acceptance in her own country during her first years as prime minister, but by 1975, in the midst of government economic woes and severe droughts, she came under attack by critics who charged her with corruption within her organization and abuse of authority. Responding to the widespread demand for her resignation, she declared a national state of emergency, censoring the press, jailing thousands of opponents, and curtailing civil rights. In March of 1977, after nearly two years of totalitarian rule, Gandhi called for elections. She lost to Desai, but, after reorganizing her supporters to form a new party, called the Indira Congress, she won the 1980 general elections in a landslide victory and was restored as India's prime minister. The events leading up to her assassination involved escalating tensions and violence between the Moslem, Hindu, and Sikh religious sects. In June of 1984 Gandhi, a Hindu, ordered the government takeover of the Sikh's Golden Temple in Amritsar, which was being used as a terrorist arsenal. As a result, large numbers of both Sikhs and Hindus were killed. Four months later, Prime Minister Gandhi was assassinated on the grounds of her New Delhi compound by Sikh members of her own security staff. Immediately following the attack Gandhi's son, Rajiv Gandhi, who was sworn in as India's Prime Minister, urged restraint among Hindus retaliating violently against Sikh adherents.

AP/Wide World Photos

SOURCES:

BOOKS

Current Biography, Wilson, 1966, January, 1985.
Dictionary of Politics, revised edition, Free Press, 1974.
The International Who's Who, 48th edition, Europa, 1984.
1000 Makers of the Twentieth Century, David & Charles, 1971.

PERIODICALS

Detroit Free Press, November 1, 1984.
Detroit News, November 1, 1984.
Los Angeles Times, November 1, 1984.
Newsweek, November 12, 1984.
New York Times, November 1, 1984.
Time, November 12, 1984.

Marc Garneau

1949-

PERSONAL: Born February 23, 1949, in Quebec City, Quebec, Canada; son of Andre (a career army officer) and Jean (Richardson) Garneau; married Jacqueline Brown, October 6, 1973; children: Yves and Simone (twins). Education: Royal Military College, Kingston, Ontario, bachelor of engineering physics, 1970; Imperial College of Science and Technology, London, Ph.D. in electrical engineering, 1973; also attended Canadian Forces Command and Staff College, 1982-83.

OCCUPATION: Canadian naval commander and astronaut.

ADDRESSES: Home—Ottawa, Ontario, Canada. *Office*— Royal Canadian Navy, Department of National Defence, Ottawa, Ontario, Canada; and c/o National Research Council of Canada, Building M58, Montreal Rd., Ottawa, Ontario, Canada K1A 0R6.

CAREER: Royal Canadian Navy, 1974—, present rank, commander; United States National Aeronautics and Space Administration (NASA), astronaut, beginning 1984. Combat systems engineer, HMCS *Algonquin*, 1974-76; instructor in naval weapons systems, Canadian Forces Fleet School, 1976-77; project engineer in naval weapons systems, 1977-80; member of naval engineering unit, 1980-83; design authority for all naval communications and electronic warfare equipment and systems, 1983—.

MEMBER: Association of Professional Engineers of Nova Scotia, Association of Old Crows.

UPI/Bettmann Newsphotos

SIDELIGHTS: On October 5, 1984, French-Canadian Marc Garneau joined Americans Sally Ride, Kathryn Sullivan, Robert Crippen, Paul Scully-Power, Jon McBride, and David Leestma aboard the space shuttle *Challenger* to become his country's first astronaut. One of more than 4300 applicants in a nationwide competition for the opportunity to fly on the shuttle, Garneau survived an intensive screening process that resulted in the naming of six candidates in December, 1983. Three months later, shortly after he and his colleagues had begun their rigorous training program, the thirty-five-year-old Quebec native learned that he had been chosen to make the actual first flight. Describing his selection as "the realization of a dream" and "an absolutely fantastic thrill," an elated Garneau declared himself "quite ready" to be the first Canadian in space. "It's a great honor, and I'm a very lucky person," he concluded. Backup choice Robert Thirsk heartily agreed with this self-assessment, praising Garneau as "the essence of the Canadian astronaut program." Thus, endowed with a $4.5 million budget and a personable, well-educated, and highly-motivated shuttle crewman-to-be, Canada at last had "a toe in the manned-space door," as Robert Miller observed in *Maclean's* magazine.

Garneau's dream first began to take shape in July, 1983, when he spied a "help wanted" advertisement for Canadian astronauts in the Ottawa *Citizen*. Thinking it over for only a moment, he announced to his wife that he intended to apply. "I thought it was sort of a joke," Jacqueline Garneau later recalled. "But Marc said, 'This could be a dream come true.'"

With his background as a naval commander, engineer, and design specialist in communications and electronic warfare, Garneau was just the type of scientist/astronaut that Canada and the U.S. National Aeronautics and Space Administration (NASA) had hoped to find. Canada, on the one hand, seeking ways to boost its share of the lucrative high-tech industries market, views its participation in the shuttle program as a means of testing Canadian-built scientific equipment, specifically the invention known as Canadarm, a robotic space arm designed to assist in manipulating cargo and constructing a future space station. (Its successful debut aboard the second flight of the shuttle *Columbia* in November, 1981, paved the way for Garneau's more sophisticated experiments.) NASA, on the other hand, having witnessed the gradual shift of space defense budget dollars away from its own programs to those of the military, is aggressively trying to regain that lost territory. Garneau's military experience in testing new equipment under field conditions made him the ideal choice for both parties.

As a payload specialist, Garneau devoted most of his time during the eight-day shuttle mission to a variety of Canadian-sponsored experiments judged critical to future space flights. Among them were preliminary tests intended to enhance the capabilities of Canadarm's "space vision system" and studies in human adaptation to zero gravity, including research on motion sickness, a problem that has plagued many of the shuttle astronauts (but not non-pilot Garneau). In addition, Garneau conducted the first in-flight testing of a new instrument, the solar photometer, a device Canadian scientists designed to measure levels of solar radiation in the atmosphere. (Findings of the photometer are essential to studies of acid rain and the earth's ozone layer.) He also monitored other atmospheric phenomena, photographed the mysterious red "shuttle glow" observed on previous flights, and noted changes in samples of possible construction materials exposed to the radiation, vacuum, and temperature extremes common in outer space. When not occupied with his own tests, Garneau assisted the American astronauts with their experiments and even helped prepare meals for the crew, the largest ever to be sent into space. Upon his return, reported a writer for *Apogee*, the Canadian described his time in the shuttle as "an experience that will indelibly mark me for the rest of my life. . . . I could have spent two months up there, I loved it."

While Canada hopes for a major boost in its various high-tech industries as a result of the successful flight, Garneau himself admits to a passion for politics that might one day tempt him to run for office. And according to Paul Tisdall in *Maclean's*, the possibility is not all that far-fetched. "The Canadian astronauts are already becoming heady with the larger-than-life mythology of the glamor that already surrounds their U.S. counterparts," the reporter observed.

"[Garneau] is articulate and charming with a gentle self-mocking humor in both official languages. If he eventually does launch a political career, [he] may prove to be a truly formidable politician."

In the meantime, Garneau is busy giving talks throughout Canada on his trip, preparing reports on what he accomplished during the flight, and working with fellow Canadian astronauts and engineers on improvements to Canadarm's space vision system, which is scheduled for its next critical shuttle test in early 1986. Through it all, Garneau has repeatedly expressed his commitment to Canada's goal of becoming a leader in space technology—a commitment he believes he can best share with the Canadian public via the lecture circuit. "I get the greatest satisfaction seeing people get enthused about [the program]," he says. "I have a particular concern trying to expand the Canadian manned involvement in space. I hope it's a program that's going to grow."

AVOCATIONAL INTERESTS: Sailing (in 1969 and 1970, he sailed across the Atlantic in a 59-foot yawl with twelve other crewmen), flying, jogging, scuba diving, swimming, wine-making, working on car and home repairs, playing squash and tennis.

SOURCES:

PERIODICALS

Apogee (bulletin of the Canadian space program), January, 1985.
Aviation Week and Space Technology, April 16, 1984.
Los Angeles Times, October 11, 1984.
Maclean's, December 12, 1983, March 26, 1984, October 8, 1984.
New York Times, October 6, 1984.

—*Sketch by Deborah A. Straub*

David Geffen

1943-

PERSONAL: Born February 21, 1943, in Brooklyn, N.Y.; son of Abraham and Batya (in the corset and brassiere manufacturing business) Geffen. *Education:* Attended University of Texas and Brooklyn College of the City University of New York.

ADDRESSES: Home—New York, N.Y.; and Los Angeles, Calif. *Office*—David Geffen Co., 9130 Sunset Blvd., Los Angeles, Calif. 90069.

OCCUPATION: Record, film, and theatrical producer.

CAREER: Studio usher, Columbia Broadcasting System, Inc. (CBS), New York City; William Morris Agency, New York City, 1964-68, began as mailroom worker, became talent agent; talent agent with Ashley Famous Agency, beginning 1968; executive vice-president and talent agent with Creative Management Associates; founder, with Laura Nyro, and president of Tuna Fish (music publishing company), until 1969; founder, with Elliott Roberts, of Geffen-Roberts Agency, Los Angeles, Calif.; founder, with Roberts, and president of Asylum Records, Los Angeles, 1970-73; Warner Communications, Los Angeles, president of Elektra-Asylum Records, 1973-76, vice-chairman of Warner Bros. Pictures, 1975-76, executive assistant to chairman of the board, 1977; instructor in music business courses at University of California, Los Angeles, and Yale University, 1978-80; founder and president of Geffen Records, Los Angeles, beginning 1980; currently chairman and chief executive officer of David Geffen Co. (encompassing record, film, and theatrical production companies), Los Angeles.

SIDELIGHTS: One of the most influential people in the contemporary entertainment industry, David Geffen is a man of many opinions and such an unabashed propensity for sharing them that he's been called the Billy Martin of the record business. The stable of musicians Geffen has feuded with includes such luminaries as Bob Dylan and Stephen Stills. In *Esquire* magazine, Geffen was quoted as saying about rock superstar Mick Jagger: "Who gives a shit? D'ya know what I mean? I mean who is this? At his last concert here he was practically taking off his clothes. He reminded me of a male stripper."

A lithe, curly haired former *wunderkind* who earned his first million at age twenty-five, Geffen has dated such high-profile celebrities as Laura Nyro, Marlo Thomas, and Cher. He is in large part responsible for the careers of such stars as Joni Mitchell, Jackson Browne, Asia, Quarterflash, Madness, Jennifer Holliday, and the Eagles. The original cast recording from his stage musical "Dreamgirls" has sold more copies than any original cast album since "Hair," and his Tony Award-winning Broadway show, "Cats," was greeted with rave reviews. If there ever was someone with a Midas touch, David Geffen would seem to be he. "You gotta bet on a winner like David," Warner Brothers chairman Mo

Ostin told *Esquire.* "Someone like that, he's driven. He's just gotta succeed. You know whatever he touches is going to turn to gold."

Geffen was raised in a small, three-room apartment in Brooklyn by a father who never worked and a mother who supported the family with the "Chic Corsetry by Geffen" corset and brassiere company, which she originally ran out of the family living room. The company expanded into a full-scale manufacturing business occupying a store on nearby 13th Avenue, and Batya Geffen eventually bought the entire building and became a landlord. Geffen credits his mother for inspiring him with her entrepreneurial spirit. "I was a terrible student," he told the *New York Times.* "I learned my lessons by watching her. She taught me to tell the truth, to make sure that whatever I put out was good stuff. Coming from a relatively poor family was a great motivation for me. My parents would take me to the movies in Times Square and I could see for myself there was a better life. I wanted it."

Geffen attended New Utrecht High School, barely graduating with a sixty-eight average. But his major goal was not school. It was to flee to the west coast, which he fell in love with after a drive through Beverly Hills. While visiting his brother on the law school campus at the University of California, Los Angeles, Geffen was cast as a high school freshman in a movie called "The Explosive Generation." Soon after he saw the movie, Geffen had his nose fixed. Shortly thereafter, he flunked out of the University of Texas. Then he returned to California, where his brother was engaged to rock promoter Phil Spector's first wife's sister. He was almost hypnotized by Spector and told *Esquire* that the record executive "was my idol. He was God." Geffen would later drop out of Brooklyn College of the City University of New York and be fired from his first job at CBS as an usher; he was subsequently discharged from a second minor job there for being "too aggressive."

In 1964 he got a job as a mailroom clerk at the William Morris Agency in New York. His mother's credo regarding honesty notwithstanding, he lied to his future bosses that he had graduated from UCLA, and when he learned that the agency planned to check out his story, he went into the office early every morning for four months, searching for the university's reply. When it finally arrived, he took it to a printer, had the letterhead forged, and rewrote the letter.

"I was desperate," Geffen told *Esquire*. "I would have killed—well, not really—to keep my job there. I mean, do you know what it was like? You can't be sick a day. Because if you are sick that day, and [the letter] comes in that day, well, it was just terrifying. Well, finally one morning it came and I opened it and replaced it with a letter saying I had graduated from UCLA." He told the *New York Times:* "It was either give William Morris what they wanted or give up my dreams. . . . I just don't believe in taking no for an answer."

That quickly became evident from the litany of successful rock stars Geffen began signing from within the confines of the agency's mailroom, including Laura Nyro and Jesse Colin Young and the Association. In 1968, he moved to the Ashley Famous Agency, whose music division he helped build into the industry's second-largest. But Geffen found it difficult to work in a structured setting and soon left, after several acrimonious bouts with agency chief Ted Ashley, to take a position as executive vice president of another major talent agency, Creative Management Associates. There he met Elliott Roberts, his secretary, with whom he soon entered into a partnership to form Geffen-Roberts, which was to become one of the industry's largest music management agencies. While at Geffen-Roberts, he tried to interest Ahmet Ertegun, the president of Atlantic Records, which was owned by Warner Communications, in various singing groups. Instead, Ertegun convinced Geffen to start his own record company, and in 1970 Geffen and Roberts founded Asylum Records.

Within two years, Warner Communications, recognizing a successful company and serious competition, bought Asylum for $7 million and signed Geffen to a seven-year contract. "Seven million dollars was more than I could imagine," Geffen told *New York* magazine. "They more than made their money back in six months. I said, 'Oh shit! I gave the company away. Seven million dollars is nothing.' But Steve Ross, the head of Warner Communications Inc., made a new deal with me because it was clear to him that they made such an incredible deal that it wasn't right for me and that it would not inspire me to keep working if they didn't compensate me correctly." (In between his stints at the Ashley and Creative agencies, Geffen and Nyro had started a successful music publishing company called Tuna Fish, which they sold to CBS in 1969 for $4 million.) It was Warner chairman Ross who, in 1973, asked Geffen to merge Asylum with another Warner division, Elektra Records. That sparked the creation of one of the conglomerate's most profitable divisions. "I dropped 90 percent of their new artists, made new deals, and out of forty record releases thirty-eight were hits," Geffen recalled in the *New York Times.* "We had a 25 percent pretax profit the first year I was there."

Thus, in 1975, when Geffen told Ross that he wanted to run a movie studio, Ross agreed. And the next year Geffen, at age thirty-three, became vice-chairman of Warner Brothers Pictures. "When I was a kid in Brooklyn I dreamed of being in the movie business," he told the *Los Angeles Herald Examiner.* "I had reached the top of my profession in the music business, so maybe it was a matter of greener pastures.

"After two weeks at the studio I turned to my secretary Linda and I said, 'Oh my God. I've really screwed up this time.' " Despite some successful pictures, the media mogul with the Midas touch had finally stumbled. "The movie business became a nightmare," Geffen told *New York* magazine. "I'd gone from running my own company to having a big title but not really running the company." Geffen oversaw the production of such films as "Oh God," "Greased Lightning" and "The Late Show," but he admitted to *New York* that he "was just f—-ing up constantly because I didn't realize you had to check with this person and send a carbon to that one and all the stuff people learn growing through the ranks of a big company. . . . By the end of the year, I had stepped on so many toes, without intending to do so, that the relationships were so warped that I had to get out. And did."

It was during this professional nadir that Geffen was told he had cancer. He had checked into Cedars-Sinai Medical Center in 1976 for what was supposed to have been a relatively minor operation. When he regained consciousness, doctors told him a tumor on his bladder was malignant.

He bundled up his business affairs, moved back to New York, and proceeded to live life with a vengeance. "I started visiting museums and art galleries," he told *Esquire*. "I traveled. I went to Barbados five times in a year. I did a lot of things. I learned a lot about myself, about having a balance, and the impact I have on people. . . . And, I thought it was very important to get laid as much as possible. I mean, they said I'd have to lose my bladder at some point. You lose your bladder, you end up with a bag. You end up with no sex life, let me assure you. I thought I'd rather be dead than walk around with a bag."

For about four years Geffen drifted along. He became a regular at New York's Studio 54 disco. He taught music business courses at Yale and U.C.L.A. He also spent the time making another $23 million by investing the $7 million he made in the Asylum Records sale in California real estate.

Then, in 1980, Geffen suddenly discovered that he was not going to die of cancer. He recalled to *Esquire:* "I check into another hospital, a New York hospital, with a New York doctor, and when I wake up, this New York doctor says it's all a mistake. That there's nothing wrong with me. That there never has been anything wrong with me. . . . When I told Marlo [Thomas], she wanted me to sue [the Beverly Hills doctor who had made the original diagnosis]. As a service to the community, you know? My mother wanted me to go smash him in the head with a baseball bat. Me, I never wanted to hear that word [cancer] again."

Geffen was buoyant but bewildered. "Four years is a long time," he told *Esquire* of his self-imposed retirement. "I thought, 'How do I start again?'. . . Then Lorne Michaels and Paul Simon and I went off to Barbados to have one of these, 'Let's figure out what David can do' conversations. And finally Paul said something to me that sort of connected. He said, 'You've got to begin. Who knows where it will end, but you have to make a commitment to start'. . . . So when I got back, I called Steve Ross [chairman of Warner Communications] and Mo Ostin [chairman of Warner Brothers Records] and said, 'Look, I'm gonna go back to work.' And, literally, a deal was made within two days. And funnily enough, the phones started ringing. Your biggest fear is that the phones won't ring, but they started ringing. And Donna Summer called me, and Elton John I ran into at a party, and then I got a call from Yoko Ono. And. . . . "

If anything, Geffen's comeback catapulted his career even higher than it was before his self-imposed hiatus. He has been responsible for such theatrical hits as "Master Harold. . . and the Boys," "The Little Shop of Horrors," "Dreamgirls," and "Cats." Geffen films include "Personal Best," starring Mariel Hemingway, and the summer hit "Risky Business," starring Tom Cruise. Recent successes on the music end of Geffen's stable include "Double Fantasy," by John Lennon and Yoko Ono, and Asia's debut album, both of which were number one albums. He also represents Elton John, Neil Young, and Joni Mitchell, in addition to such newer stars as Quarterflash and Johnny Hiatt.

"I don't believe in market surveys or target audiences," Geffen told the *New York Times.* "If I'm an expert, I'm an expert at my own taste. I figure if I enjoy something, others will too. I run on instinct." How much longer Geffen can run on instinct is uncertain. "A lot of people feel I've peaked," he admitted to the *Los Angeles Herald Examiner.* "I look at it this way. I want to point myself in every musical direction. As long as something's good, that's what I'm interested in. I'm out there looking for artists and they're out there looking for me."

A millionaire several times over, Geffen says he knows his winning ways cannot last forever. And, one can argue, it doesn't matter all that much if Geffen backs a few losers, given his golden touch so far. But the bi-coastal media mogul says that even if he loses some, he'll be back in there the next day. Winning is as much a part of his personal regimen as the ninety-minute daily workouts in the personal gym in his Los Angeles tudor mansion or the Perrier water that is never far from his arm. "It's impossible to be successful without failing," Geffen told the *New York Times.* "All I want is to be allowed to work in any area that I choose. I like the theater, films, records. I like real estate, art. I don't like television. I know what I like. I like money. People who say they don't are full of it."

AVOCATIONAL INTERESTS: Collecting art.

SOURCES:

PERIODICALS

Calendar, December 12, 1982.
Detroit Free Press, December 31, 1983.
Esquire, February, 1975, November, 1982.
Forbes, April 14, 1980.
Los Angeles Herald Examiner, September 5, 1980.
Newsweek, November 20, 1972.
New York, May 17, 1982, January 24, 1983.
New York Times, October 3, 1982, October 31, 1982.
New York Times Magazine, July 21, 1985.
Rolling Stone, May 15, 1980, January 22, 1981, March 5, 1981.
Sound and Music, November, 1980.
Time, February 25, 1974.
Washington Post, May 6, 1982.

—*Sidelights by Stephen Advokat*

Bob Geldof

1954(?)-

PERSONAL: Born c. 1954, in Dublin, Ireland; son of an import-export businessman; children: Fifi Trixibelle.

ADDRESSES: Home—London, England. Office—c/o Columbia Records, 51 West 52nd St., New York, N.Y. 10019.

OCCUPATION: Singer; actor; famine relief activist.

CAREER: Worked at a variety of jobs, including butcher, bulldozer operator, photographer, and writer; correspondent for *Melody Maker* (British music magazine); lead singer with band Boomtown Rats (originally called Nightlife Thugs), 1975—. Actor; appeared in "Pink Floyd—The Wall," 1982, and "Number One," 1984. Organizer of relief efforts on behalf of African famine victims, 1984—; organized Band Aid project, 1984, and Live Aid concerts, 1985; took part in USA for Africa project, 1985.

AWARDS, HONORS: Nominated for Nobel Peace Prize, 1985; Congressional Arts Caucus Award, 1985.

DISCOGRAPHY:

RECORD ALBUMS; ALL WITH BAND BOOMTOWN RATS; PRODUCED BY COLUMBIA RECORDS, EXCEPT AS INDICATED

The Boomtown Rats, Mercury Records, 1977.
A Tonic for the Troops, 1979.
The Fine Art of Surfacing, 1980.
Mondo Bongo, 1981.
Ratrospective, 1983.
In the Long Grass, 1985.

SIDELIGHTS: "You know," Bob Geldof told 72,000 people cheering him at London's Wembley Stadium, "I just realized that this is the best day of my life." Few would argue with that assessment. Geldof and his band, the Boomtown Rats, were the third act featured in the British Live Aid concert, part of a joint concert staged simultaneously in England and at JFK Stadium in Philadelphia in an effort to raise money to fight hunger in famine-plagued portions of Africa.

The show, which reached an estimated 1.5 billion people watching it on television and listening to it on radio, was the product of Geldof's ideas and execution. He was, in fact, responsible for the whole concept of the international pop music industry adopting African famine relief as its special cause. And even though his band has never been a major force in the pop mainstream, Geldof has established a rather luminous reputation for his charitable efforts and has received a Nobel Peace Prize nomination. "He's a saint in my eyes," one of the publicists who worked on the Live Aid concerts told the *Detroit Free Press.* "Before this he was a monsignor. Now he's definitely a saint."

AP/Wide World Photos

Lofty words about a rock musician of modest means. Born and raised in Ireland, Geldof worked as a butcher, a bulldozer operator, a photographer, and a writer before eventually landing a job as a correspondent for Britain's prestigious *Melody Maker* music magazine.

The Boomtown Rats—named after a gang in a Woody Guthrie song, "Bound for Love"—didn't get their start until 1975, when Geldof and a friend, guitarist Garry Roberts, got together in Roberts's kitchen in Dun Laoghaire, Ireland. Originally known as the Nightlife Thugs, the group also included keyboardist Johnny Fingers, bassist Pete Briquette, drummer Simon Crowe, and guitarist Gerry Cott. They began playing around Ireland, becoming a popular live attraction largely because of Geldof's impassioned singing.

The group eventually changed their name and raised their goals. By 1977—at the start of the punk rock movement—they were signed by an American company, Mercury Records, looking for its own entry into this new pop music form. But the Boomtown Rats didn't hit it off with the rest of the punk community at first. While Geldof's peers denounced the rich, selfish rock stars that were dominating radio playlists, the *Detroit Free Press* reported that Geldof announced his ambition to become one—to, in fact, "get rich, get famous and get laid."

"I think that makes sense," he maintained. "If you've never had money, you'd like to. If you're anonymous and you want not to be, then you'd want to be famous. And if you want to go to bed with other people, then why not? I never understood the hue and cry that followed."

In England, at least, Geldof was getting what he wanted. The Rats' first single, "Looking After No. 1," went to number eleven on the British charts, and by 1981 the group had scored nine consecutive top fifteen singles in that country. However, they weren't part of the small cache of punk/new wave bands that experienced success in the more lucrative American market. Their most successful single—1980's "I Don't Like Mondays"—peaked at number seventy-three in the United States.

But that song brought with it a great deal of press attention because of the controversy surrounding its subject matter. Geldof got the idea during a 1979 promotional tour of the United States, when he read a newspaper account of Brenda Spencer, a seventeen-year-old San Diego high school student who went on a shooting spree, killing one person and injuring several others. Her explanation: "I guess I just don't like Mondays."

"To me," Geldof told an Associated Press reporter, "it was a song about not needing a reason to do anything, not even the most extreme human act of all." But many observers felt such a tragic incident was not a suitable subject for a rock and roll song, and the record was pulled by a number of radio stations. At one point, Spencer's family even threatened—but never filed—a lawsuit. "I don't regret writing it," Geldof explained. "I regret the barks that followed it. I regret that it wasn't a hit because I'd love to have a hit in America, for financial reasons if not for anything else."

The first important critical notice Geldof received in this country, however, came not from his band but from his starring role in the movie "Pink Floyd—the Wall," a dark, intense work that dealt with a man's retreating into himself as a defense against unpleasant experiences in his life. Geldof played the part of Pink, the brooding, introspective hero, to perfection, in the opinion of many reviewers, and his screen debut was generally regarded as a success.

On the docks at Tilbury, England, Bob Geldof observes the cargo ship Band Aid I *being prepared to depart for Africa with a load of food and supplies for famine victims, April 26, 1985. AP/Wide World Photos.*

Then one evening in 1984, Geldof watched a news report about people dying of hunger in Ethiopia. Thus was born the Band Aid project. "I can't sit in front of the TV and watch people die and not do anything about it," Geldof told a *Detroit Free Press* reporter at the time. "I felt disgusted and ashamed by what was going on in Africa, and I felt that if I didn't do something, I was taking part in some crime. It wasn't enough to simply put my hand in my pocket and give money." Rats drummer Simon Crowe recalled to the reporter: "Bob came into the studio one day and said, 'Did you see the thing on the TV last night?' Everyone said, 'Yeah, horrible, wasn't it?' He said, 'Let's do something about it.' "

What Geldof did was get on the phone, start calling friends in the music business, and ask them to participate in a special recording session. Geldof's friends included people like Boy George, Paul McCartney, Phil Collins, Paul Young, Sting, and members of such high-profile pop bands as Duran Duran, U2, and Kool & the Gang. In many cases, he had to ask them to make sacrifices. Spandau Ballet flew in from Japan, Boy George and Culture Club flew in from New York, and Duran Duran cancelled a television appearance to do the session. "I wanted the people who sell the most records in the world to do this," Geldof explained to the *Detroit Free Press*. "I just phoned everybody up, and they said, 'Absolutely.' There were a million efforts made because they felt the same way I did."

The much publicized Band Aid session lasted twenty-four hours and produced "Do They Know It's Christmas?," an uplifting song released just in time for the 1984 Christmas season. In ten days, it sold more than two million copies in England, and it sold more than a million copies during its first week out in the United States, making it one of the fastest selling records in history. American singer Dionne Warwick started a minor fad by buying several dozen and sending them out as Christmas cards.

"It's so morally correct to [buy this record]," Geldof said, "that you don't have to think about it. Even if you don't like pop music, you have to root for this, say, 'Shut up, just buy it!' People in England have bought fifty copies and given forty-nine back to the record stores to sell again."

To distribute the money, Geldof set up the self-contained Band Aid Foundation, to take full control of the funds rather than turn them over to inefficient and potentially corrupt governments or relief agencies. In January of 1985 he even traveled to Africa to find out, first-hand, how the food was distributed and what else was needed. Later that month, Geldof delivered a fiery oratory about his trip to a group of American performers gathered to do a U.S. version of Band Aid. According to a *Detroit Free Press* account, he told them: "You walk into one of the corrugated iron huts and you see meningitis and malaria and typhoid buzzing about the air. And you see dead bodies lying side by side with the live ones."

The subsequent American USA for Africa project featured Michael Jackson, Bruce Springsteen, Lionel Richie, Tina Turner, Kenny Rogers, and almost forty other performers who got together in a Los Angeles studio to record a song entitled "We Are the World." Although there were a number of other Band Aid spinoffs—country and gospel

singers in America, pop stars in Canada, Germany, and Australia—USA for Africa became the most profitable Band Aid imitator, raising more than $40 million through the sales of the single, album, and related merchandise.

Geldof feels the goodwill had an artistic price, however. "I didn't realize we were going to spawn some of the worst songs ever written," he told the Associated Press at one point. "They're awful. 'We Are the World,' [which, incidentally, Geldof sang on] sounds too much like the Pepsi generation."

Despite his reservations about the quality of these musical efforts, Geldof continued to play an active role in the famine relief movement. He told the story of a cabdriver in New York who gave him free fare and a ten dollar donation. And he told a *Detroit Free Press* interviewer that, when walking down a street in England, he was constantly approached by people wanting to give money to Mr. Band Aid. "I can't even walk from one end of the block to the other without winding up with £120 in my pocket," he said.

For Geldof, the Live Aid concerts, according to a *Rolling Stone* report, were "the ultimate expression the pop industry can make." Between London and Philadelphia—as well as smaller shows in Australia, Germany, Holland and Russia— he convinced more than sixty acts to play for free and to cover their own expenses. Through sales (of tickets, merchandise and media rights) and a telethon staged simultaneously, the concert raised more than $50 million and was still taking in donations several weeks later.

Geldof was certainly rewarded for his efforts during the British show. Unshaven and wearing a denim jacket and jeans, he sat next to Prince Charles and Lady Diana—an achievement for any Irishman, much less for a rock star. His performance at the concert was cheered as loudly as that of any of the superstars, and at the show's conclusion he was hoisted onto the shoulders of Paul McCartney and Who guitarist Pete Townsend.

"A lot of Doubting Thomases feel Bob might have done it to sort of further his own career," the Rats' Crowe told the *Detroit Free Press*. "He definitely did it for all the right reasons." In fact, Geldof told *Rolling Stone*, the Band Aid activities forced his group to postpone the release of their 1985 album, "In the Long Grass," so that "it wouldn't seem like we were capitalizing on [Band Aid's] success."

With Live Aid over, Geldof—who lives in London with his girlfriend, Paula Yates, and their two-year-old daughter Fifi Trixibelle—is adamant about concentrating once again on his musical career. "I'd love to just turn the running of this thing over to professionals and get on with my music," he told *Record* magazine. "But it's all become so personalized. It's too closely associated with me. Do you think I like spending my days negotiating grain contracts?"

SOURCES:

PERIODICALS

Associated Press, June, 1985.
Detroit Free Press, December 15, 1984, July 12, 1985, July 16, 1985.

Detroit News, July 24, 1985.
Los Angeles Times, July 21, 1985.
Musician, August, 1985.
Newsweek, June 3, 1985, June 24, 1985, July 15, 1985, October 28, 1985.
New York Times, January 26, 1985.
People, October 25, 1982, December 23, 1985.
Record, August, 1985.
Rolling Stone, March 14, 1985, March 28, 1985, July 4, 1985, July 18, 1985, August 15, 1985, December 5, 1985.
Time, July 22, 1985.
United Press International, June, 1985.
Washington Post, December 18, 1984.

—Sidelights by Gary Graff

Kirk Gibson

1957-

Photograph by Kathy Marcaccio

PERSONAL: Full name, Kirk Harold Gibson; born May 28, 1957, in Pontiac, Mich.; son of Robert (a tax auditor and high school mathematics teacher) and Barbara (a high school theater and speech teacher) Gibson; married JoAnn Sklarski (a model and dancer), December 21, 1985. *Education:* Attended Michigan State University, 1975-78.

ADDRESSES: Home—Grosse Pointe, Mich. *Office*—Detroit Tigers Baseball Club, Tiger Stadium, Michigan and Trumbull, Detroit, Mich. 48216.

OCCUPATION: Professional baseball player.

CAREER: Baseball player in minor leagues, 1978-79, and in major leagues with Detroit Tigers, 1979—.

SIDELIGHTS: Baseball player Kirk Gibson of the Detroit Tigers made a major impression on the American sports scene during the final game of the 1984 World Series, when he hit two home runs to lead his team to an 8-4 victory over the San Diego Padres, the final victory in a five-game Series triumph. After circling the bases for the second time that dark, cool, misty Sunday afternoon, the 6-foot, 3-inch, 215-pound Gibson—his heavily-whiskered face beaming with joy and his shaggy blond hair blowing freely from his hatless head—ran toward the Tiger dugout and thrust his clenched fists skyward while more than 50,000 Detroit fans cheered and the cameras from national television and print media captured the moment.

For the 27-year-old Gibson, the triumphant scene on the national stage marked a high point in a baseball career that has been at times successful, at times frustrating, and often controversial. The pose seemed to sum up all the fury and ability within him. "I may not be the next (Mickey) Mantle," he told *Sports Illustrated,* "But I'll tell you one thing: I'll be remembered."

The next year, the 1985 baseball season, was to be a pivotal year in his career. Unable to come to terms with the Tigers on a long-term contract, Gibson signed for one year at a salary of $675,000. While that wage is higher than that paid most American workers, it is modest for baseball stars, some of whom make between $1 million and $2 million per year on long-term contracts. Before the 1985 season, Gibson announced that he would not negotiate with the Tigers during the playing season and that he intended to make himself available for baseball's free-agent draft before the 1986 season.

The free-agent draft, for veteran players, is an annual process by which some players change teams after choosing among bids from teams drafting them. For Gibson, who had played only with Detroit in the major leagues, the decision was a major step not without risk. Although touted for years for his potential and although he had been outstanding in 1984, he had not—up until that point—been able to put together two consecutive successful baseball seasons.

In 1983, for instance, Gibson batted a weak .227 and was frequently booed by the hometown fans. "He was booed mercilessly," a *Sports Illustrated* reporter wrote. "There were rumors about booze, broads and drugs, the three deadly sins of professional sport. His response to the acrimony was to lose his temper in public and private. . . . " Gibson agrees: "I had vendettas out against the fans, the press, everybody." After his performance in the World Series finale—which included five runs batted in and scoring the winning run with a dash from third base to home plate—Gibson told the *New York Times,* "I don't want to dwell on the bad times, they're behind me now."

Born in Pontiac, Michigan, on May 28, 1957, and raised in the northern Detroit suburb of Waterford, Gibson was a football star from 1975 through 1978 at Michigan State University, where he earned All-America honors as a flanker who caught forward passes. In his four seasons with the Spartans, he set MSU records with 112 catches, 2,347 yards and 24 touchdown receptions. Football scouts believed him to be a sure bet as a pro star, and Gibson was drafted by the St. Louis Cardinals football team as well as by the Tigers. But instead of football, Gibson chose baseball, where careers are often longer and higher-paying, even though he had played only one year of baseball at the college level.

An intense, strong-willed and competitive person, Gibson played less than two seasons in the Detroit minor league system before breaking in with the Tigers in September of 1979. Jack Billingham, a Detroit pitcher at the time, recalled Gibson's tense mood before that 1979 debut in an interview published in the *Detroit Free Press*. Gibson was undergoing a pre-game trainer's massage in the team's Tiger Stadium medical room when Billingham, a veteran, began to tease the rookie. "I was saying 'What's the matter, you nervous?' and he didn't even smile," Billingham said. "He yells, 'Jack, just leave me alone, just leave me alone' and I saw a look in his eyes of fire, so I stopped. . . . Fifteen or 20 minutes later, I'm going through those swinging doors of the trainer's room and he comes walking through again and I say 'Geez, you can't stay out of there, can you?' And he comes at me with a flying body block, knocks me 10 feet! I don't think it's too funny to have an ex-football player charge me. I was no fool, so I stayed away from him after that. But I said 'Relax,

Kirk. If you're going to play this game and you stay that tense, you're gonna go crazy.' "

In the following years, Gibson developed a reputation for dramatic clutch hitting, dramatic batting slumps and demonstrative temper tantrums. He missed more than half of the 1980 and 1982 seasons with wrist injuries. When he was healthy and playing—and even when injured—he was a very visible star in his home town and he became known for his visits to nightclubs and bars. Fans in Detroit occasionally complained of his reluctance to sign autographs. Gossip columnists and other reporters on Detroit's major newspapers published stories about Gibson's public behavior, which often included loud cursing.

Stories chronicled, among other things, his snub of a retarded child who requested an autograph when Gibson was injured and out of uniform at Tiger Stadium and his failure to show for a promised appearance at a Christmas party for a Detroit-area orphanage. In 1984, even while en route to the best season of his career, he stormed out of Tiger Stadium after a frustrating game, started up his red Jeep Renegade and tried to get home ahead of heavy traffic. Instead, he crashed into another vehicle. And after the World Series victory parade in downtown Detroit, when

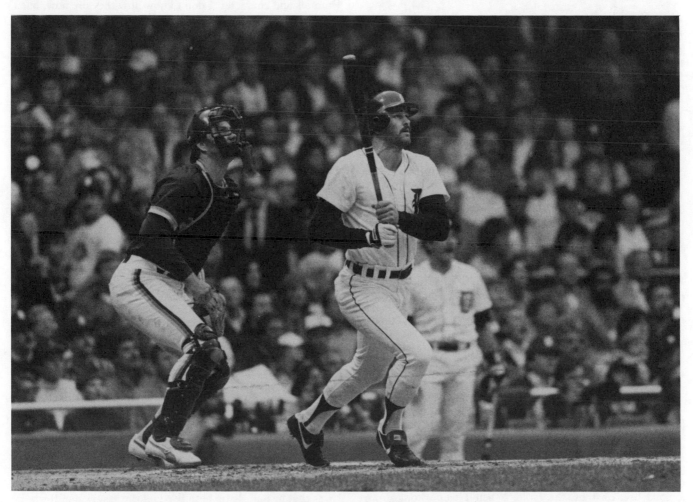

As San Diego Padres catcher Terry Kennedy (left) looks on, Kirk Gibson hits a two-run homer at Tiger Stadium in the first inning of the fifth and final game of the World Series, October 14, 1984. AP/Wide World Photos.

Gibson and teammate Dave Rozema were driving home to suburban Grosse Pointe, their vehicle overturned after an accident with another car.

"The basic way I've changed is I'm much more rational now," Gibson said in an interview with *Monthly Detroit* magazine. "Hey, lookit—I did a lot of stupid, irrational things. I admit it. I did some embarrassing things. I was like push-pull. It's called the low low concept. Lock on, lock out. But to grow, you have to learn by your mistakes. I used to have too big an ego and I know I'm a very arrogant person. But now I know why I do what I do, and I know what I want and I'm going to succeed."

In 1984—with no injuries, 149 games played, 27 home runs, 91 runs batted in, and a batting average of .282—Gibson obviously enjoyed the most successful season in his first six. But in the previous years, he had shown dramatic flashes of talent. Two of the most remarkable episodes came on June 14, 1983, in a game at Tiger Stadium against the Boston Red Sox. Early in the game, Gibson hit a home run that cleared not only the right-field fence but also the right-field grandstand and stadium roof. It landed outside the ball park, on the roof of a building across the street. It was later estimated that the ball traveled 540 feet.

That feat alone made for a remarkable performance, but Gibson wasn't finished. Later in the game, he hit a ball over the head of Boston center fielder Tony Armas. The ball bounced off Armas's glove and hit the center field wall 440 feet from home plate, the deepest part of the playing field. Tiger teammate Lou Whitaker, who started the play at first base, was tagged out at the plate by catcher Rich Gedman. When home plate umpire Larry Barnett stated to signal Whitaker out, he was knocked to the ground by Gibson, who unexpectedly had caught up almost behind Whitaker and had continued on to the crowded scene at home plate. "I was chasing Lou home and I was going to try to jar the ball loose," Gibson said after the game. "It was a great relay, and I was surprised the ball was there. Hell, I was out by 10 feet. I figured my only chance was to try and plow him [Gedman] over." The collision knocked the umpire unconscious. First base umpire Ken Kaiser had to make a ruling on the play, so he called Whitaker "out" and Gibson "safe."

Skilled in more than one sport, Gibson at times inspires admiration in men of other athletic professions. On May 10, 1985, he hit a ball over the roof in right field at Chicago's Comiskey Park. The blast was witnessed by hockey star Wayne Gretzky of the defending Stanley Cup champion Edmonton Oilers, who asked a *Detroit Free Press* reporter, "Holy cow! Does he do that often?" And Oiler teammate Kevin Lowe asked: "Can he skate? He's big enough to play defense."

As a boy, Gibson was greatly encouraged by his father, Bob Gibson, a former tax auditor who later became a math teacher. The elder Gibson spent lunch hours at home so he could throw footballs and baseballs to his son, and encouraged the boy to shoot baskets in the winter. "He drilled me," Gibson told the *New York Times*. "When I woke up, he had a good breakfast on the table. When I came home from school, he was waiting to play basketball. When I was down the road, he'd call me: 'Time to play catch.' I didn't always

like it, but I did it. I suppose he wanted me to do the things he didn't have a chance to do."

In an interview with the *Detroit Free Press*, Bob Gibson said of his son: "We played a lot of catch. And I'd hit him ground balls and fly balls. I hung up a baseball on the old clothesline post and I hung up an old tire for him to throw through, ideas I got from baseball coaching clinics. I probably made him play ball at times when he probably wouldn't have wanted to. I felt it kept him active and kept him out of trouble."

Of the negative publicity his son had received, Bob Gibson said: "It used to bother us. Every once in a while, we hear negative comments from people. The things about signing autographs bothers me. I don't know if Kirk always handled it well. Sometimes he may get a little gruff. I remember when he used to climb that wall in Lakeland [the Tigers Florida training camp] to avoid people. But you have to understand what it's like for him. We have 300 letters for him here right now in the house, baseball cards with stamped, self-addressed return envelopes, from all over the country, all over the world, really. His mother really puts the thumb on him and sits on him and makes him do it. His mother made him behave more than I did as far as his morals and character. I don't know how they are now, but I know she keeps on him. Basically, he's pretty good."

Gibson is the youngest of three children and the only boy. His sister Jocelyn is six years older than he; his sister Christine is five years older. In an interview with *Sports Illustrated*, Gibson said "My parents never made me work. When I grew up, all we did was screw around with motorcycles and water skiing. I had it pretty easy."

Gibson's parents later were divorced. His mother, a teacher at a suburban Detroit high school, said in a television interview on Detroit's WJBK-TV that she gets nervous and excited at ball games. "Maybe that's where Kirk gets it from," she said of her son's obvious nervous tension. "He tends to get violent about throwing his bat and his helmet. . . . I think he's grown up a lot. . . . He's a lot of fun."

Gibson also discussed his maturation in an interview with *Monthly Detroit*. "Before, I lived day to day like a party and I was comfortable going out and getting drunk every night, being in the bars, the social scene," he said, "I never cared about my family. I never cared about a relationship with any chick. Chasing women was just a big game to me. Now, if I go out, I go out with my lady to dinner with a bottle of wine." The lady of whom he spoke is JoAnn Sklarski, whom Gibson married on December 21, 1985. The ceremony was a double wedding, involving Dave Rozema, Gibson's friend and ex-teammate, who married Sandy Sklarski, JoAnn's sister.

A friend of Gibson, Detroit auto dealer Joe Ricci, told *Sports Illustrated*: "Kirk has grown up a lot in the past two years. And JoAnn has had a lot to do with it. When they started hanging out together, he wouldn't let you go home until it was five o'clock in the morning. I think much of the problem was that he and Rozie both lived on the east side of town, in Grosse Pointe. Grosse Pointe is older money. It's tradition. Anything they did seemed to contrast with that."

Gibson also credits much of his new attitude to training he received at the Pacific Institute in Seattle, Washington, where—among other things—he learned to practice positive thinking. "You create a picture of what you want to happen in your creative subconscious," he told Marney Rich of *Monthly Detroit.* "And you make an affirmation. Like: 'I'm going to hit a home run.' And you see yourself doing it. . . . What you're doing is changing your state of mind. . . . In '83 I thought I was a piece of crap. I had a bad picture then. I was out of my comfort zone. So, one of my affirmations for then was: The negative attitudes and opinions of people don't affect me." Tiger manager Sparky Anderson agrees that today's Kirk Gibson is far removed from the 1983 version as a result of this change in attitude: "He let a lot of outside people cause him animosity," Anderson commented to Rich. "He no longer lets people crucify him or crucify himself." Summarizes one of Gibson's friends: "The changes have been fabulous. . . . In the span of one year he went from goat to hero. He's gone both ends of the spectrum."

Gibson declared his free agency status following the 1985 season, during which he batted .287 with 29 home runs, 97 runs batted in, and 30 stolen bases. Gibson asked $8 million for a five-year contract, but Tiger management refused, making a counteroffer of $4 million for a three-year pact. In what Gibson's agent Doug Baldwin and players' union head Donald Fehr characterized as a prearranged agreement among club owners, Gibson received no offers from other clubs. Club owners and Baseball Commissioner Peter Ueberroth denied any collusion, but none of the other twenty-five free agents received offers from any but their original teams. And none were offered long-term pacts.

Gibson repeatedly vowed not to accept any contract offer except the one outlined in his original request. In December he announced that once he left on his honeymoon to Australia and New Zealand following his December 21 wedding no further negotiations would take place prior to the January 8 deadline. If Gibson remained unsigned by the Tigers at that date, Detroit would not be able to sign him until May 1986, well into the baseball season. And without offers from other clubs, Gibson would be forced to miss spring training and the first month of play. Many sports observers viewed Gibson as the test case, the player where the line was drawn on long-term, multimillion-dollar deals. On January 8, 1986, minutes before the negotiations deadline, Gibson, calling from a pay phone in New Zealand, accepted the Tigers' original offer of $4 million for three years.

AVOCATIONAL INTERESTS: Hunting, fishing, boating.

SOURCES:

BOOKS

Anderson, Sparky, *Bless You Boys: Diary of the Detroit Tigers' 1984 Season,* Contemporary Books, 1984.

PERIODICALS

Detroit Free Press, August 8, 1978, September 3, 1982, December 16, 1982, April 10, 1983, June 15, 1983, October 17, 1984, May 13, 1985.
Monthly Detroit, April, 1985.
New York Times, October 5, 1981, March 28, 1982, October 15, 1984.
People, December 28, 1981.
Sports Illustrated, March 24, 1980, August 31, 1981, December 10, 1984, March 4, 1985.
Time, October 8, 1984.

—*Sidelights by Joe LaPointe*

Bernhard Hugo Goetz

1947(?)-

PERSONAL: Born c. 1947 in New York, N.Y.; father worked as a book binder, dairy farmer, and land developer; divorced. *Education:* New York University, B.S. in electrical and nuclear engineering, 1969.

ADDRESSES: Home—New York, N.Y.

OCCUPATION: Electronics engineer.

CAREER: Worked in father's land development company in Florida, beginning 1965; Electrical Calibrations Laboratories, New York, N.Y., proprietor and electronics engineer, beginning 1975.

SIDELIGHTS: It came as a shock to his neighbors when they learned that Bernhard Hugo Goetz, then thirty-seven, had surrendered to police in Concord, New Hampshire, and confessed to shooting four young black men on a New York City subway. They found it hard to believe that the self-employed electronics engineer was the same man the media had dubbed the "subway vigilante." Yet by the time Goetz was returned to New York there was little doubt. Goetz told police that he shot the youths because they tried to rob him and because he felt physically threatened. The youths contend that they asked Goetz for a few dollars, that they meant him no harm, and that he fired without provocation. These conflicting accounts of the incident are but one example of the many contradictions and complexities surrounding this case, which was presented to two grand juries. The second grand jury indicted Goetz on four counts of attempted murder, assault, reckless endangerment, and criminal possession of a weapon. Before a New York Supreme Court justice dismissed the attempted murder and assault charges, the case drew international attention and sparked heated debates over a citizen's right of self-defense.

By most accounts Goetz is an unlikely subject for such controversy. His neighbors describe him as a quiet-spoken, somewhat intense loner who enjoys playing with children and is concerned—some say obsessed—with the welfare of his neighborhood. Goetz was raised in upstate New York on a 300-acre dairy farm run by his father, a German immigrant. He entered New York University in 1965 and graduated with a degree in electrical and nuclear engineering. (To avoid serving in the military during the Vietnam War, he feigned mental illness.) After graduation he joined his family, who had moved to Florida, in their land development business. He entered into a short-lived marriage and returned to New York following his divorce.

In 1975 he started his own business, specializing in calibrating electronic equipment. He ran the business from his apartment on the outskirts of Greenwich Village. Goetz devoted most of his spare time to neighborhood improvement projects and became an active member of his local

neighborhood association. He frequently petitioned city agencies to take action on the litter, abandoned structures, winos, and drug dealers that plagued his street. In a subway station in January of 1981 Goetz was mugged and badly beaten by three black teenagers. Two of the muggers escaped. One was captured by the police and held for less than three hours, while Goetz was detained for six. Outraged at what he called "the incompetence" of the New York Police Department, Goetz tried to secure a handgun permit. His request was denied. He later purchased a revolver in Florida.

Several commentators suggest that the 1981 mugging and Goetz's subsequent frustration with the police were crucial to what took place on December 22, 1984. On that afternoon, Goetz boarded a relatively empty subway car, taking a seat across from the door through which he had entered. Sitting in the same area of the car were Troy Canty, Darrell Cabey, and James Ramseur, all 19, and Barry Allen, 18. Canty asked Goetz how he was doing. Goetz replied that he was fine. According to Goetz, the youths got up and began to move towards him. Eventually, he was surrounded. Goetz states that Canty then said, "Give me five dollars." Goetz says that he rose, unzipping his jacket, and asked

Canty to repeat what he had said. Canty did so, while one of the others indicated, with a gesture, that he was armed. Goetz asserts that at this point he was certain of their intention to harm him. He pulled the gun from his jacket and opened fire, wounding all four. He then checked their injuries; when he came to Cabey, who was not bleeding, Goetz told police that he fired a fifth shot, saying, "You don't look so bad, here's another." Cabey is now paralyzed from the waist down as a result of that shot.

When the train came to a stop, a conductor entered the car and asked Goetz if he was with the police. Goetz replied that he was not and added, "They tried to rip me off." Goetz jumped onto the subway tracks and disappeared into the tunnel. He rented a car and fled to Vermont, then to New Hampshire, where he surrendered nine days after the shooting. He gave the police a four-hour confession, two of which were videotaped. Before surrendering, Goetz phoned his neighbor Myra Friedman. Friedman, a writer, taped their conversation and later recounted it in *New York*. "He was, by turns, frightened, sickened, confused, ashamed, and outraged," she recalls. "His primary concern seemed to be his privacy. He said he simply desired to resume a 'normal life.' " During their long conversation Goetz made the following remarks: "I responded viciously and savagely. . . . If you corner a rat and you are about to butcher it, okay? The way I responded was viciously and savagely, just like that, just like a rat. . . . The people are looking for an easy answer. They're looking for a good guy defending himself, or a Clint Eastwood. Or if they want to condemn it, they're looking for someone who was looking for trouble. . . . I think what I did was appropriate or reasonable. . . . Just appropriate and reasonable under the circumstances. . . . I saw what was going to happen. And I snapped. . . . Myra, in a situation like this, your mind, you're in a combat situation. Your mind is functioning. You're not thinking in a normal way. Your memory isn't even working normally. You are so hyped up. Your vision actually changes. . . . Myra, what I did—I turned into a monster, and that's the truth. But if most people, a lot of people, would have been in my shoes, they would have done the same thing."

Initially, the public reaction to the shooting was overwhelmingly favorable. The youths all proved to have criminal records, and two of them were carrying sharpened screwdrivers. Police, journalists, and radio talk-show hosts all reported hundreds of calls and letters praising Goetz and offering money for his legal defense. Goetz's story touched a "raw nerve in the American psyche," notes Ed Magnuson of *Time*. He came to represent "an Everyman: even people who deplored what he did felt they could understand why he did it." Prior to Goetz's surrender, people drew halos over police sketches of the then unknown "subway vigilante." Psychiatrist Alfred Messer believes that the public's response stemmed from feelings of fear, anger, and helplessness. Goetz "symbolically accomplished what we couldn't do and were taught not to do," Messer told Magnuson. "He is seen as striking a blow for all of us."

The official response was quite different, however. New York City Mayor Edward Koch called the shooting and the public's support of it "animal behavior," according to *Newsweek's* Pete Axthelm. "If you allowed instant, self-meted-out justice, we would have crimes committed against

innocent people." New York Governor Mario Cuomo agreed: "If we're talking about vindication, or impatience with using the judicial system, we're talking about attempted execution. The people supporting this guy should think of it that way—unilateral execution without trial."

On January 3, 1985, Goetz was arraigned in Manhattan Criminal Court on charges of attempted murder and illegal gun possession. A racially mixed grand jury read police reports of the incident, viewed the videotapes of Goetz's confession, and heard the taped conversation between Goetz and Friedman. Goetz consistently maintained that he felt "cornered" and that he "snapped." (Neither Goetz nor the men he shot testified in person before the jury.) On January 25, the grand jury found that Goetz had acted in self-defense; he was indicted only on the charge of illegal weapon possession.

Shortly after the decision, public support began to waver. Details from the videotaped confession became widely known, particularly Goetz's statement to Cabey before firing the fifth shot. Moreover, Goetz's post-grand jury behavior created misgivings. *Time's* Richard Stengel explains: "Goetz seemed slightly intoxicated by his notoriety. He recommended that more civilians be trained to carry guns. He showed up at the funeral of a slain cabby. Every other day he seemed to give another 'exclusive' interview. His soapbox preaching rebounded against him, redoubling the calls for a new investigation. Says his lawyer Barry Slotnick: 'It took him out of the light of the humble, decent Bernie Goetz and made him a public figure who was pontificating on things.'. . . The man the public had proclaimed a hero had called himself a monster, and people wondered whether he might not be right."

In March, District Attorney Robert Morgenthau announced a new grand jury investigation into the shooting. Morgenthau said his office had uncovered "new evidence" against Goetz, but he has refused to disclose its nature. Two of the youths shot by Goetz testified before the second grand jury after they were granted immunity from prosecution. Goetz, according to Stengel, "practically begged to testify, but he balked when Morgenthau insisted that he sign a complete waiver of immunity." On March 27, Goetz was indicted on four counts of attempted murder, four counts of assault, one count of reckless endangerment, and one count of criminal possession of a weapon. Goetz publicly denounced the jury's decision. Tom Morganthau of *Newsweek* quotes from an article Goetz wrote for the *New York Post:* "Justice appears to have been thrown out the window. . . . What's laughable is that these four young men are criminals. They get immunity. Can you imagine? The criminal gets immunity and the victim gets nothing except another day before the court."

The young men, however, contended that they, not Goetz, were the victims on December 22. They said that Canty, acting alone, asked Goetz for a match, the time, and five dollars to play video games. They did not demand the money, surround Goetz, or threaten him. Moreover, observers noted that although the youths were carrying sharpened screwdrivers, there is no indication that Goetz saw or was aware of the tools. (Police speculate that the screwdrivers were not carried as weapons, but were used to pry open video game machines to steal coins.) There were other questions, such as, why were two of the youths shot in the back, and why did Goetz, by his own account, shoot Cabey twice? An eyewitness to the shooting, Victor Flores, stated that Canty and his friends were noisy but nonthreatening. Flores also said that he neither saw nor heard Goetz fire the fifth shot at Cabey. Canty, Ramseur, and Allen do not remember the shot, either.

Despite the new evidence, on January 16, 1986, New York State Supreme Court Justice Stephen G. Crane dismissed the attempted murder and assault charges against Goetz. According to a *New York Times* report by Robert D. McFadden, Crane "said he was dismissing the charges because of 'prejudicial error' by a prosecutor who instructed the second grand jury in the case last March, and because statements by two of the shooting victims before that grand jury now 'strongly appear' to have been perjured. 'The integrity of the second grand jury was severely undermined to say the least,' Justice Crane said in his 35-page decision."

New York law states that a person must avoid a confrontation unless he "reasonably" believes that he is in physical danger. According to the *New York Times*, Justice Crane felt that the prosecution's main error "centered on what [an assistant district attorney told the grand jury] about the 'reasonableness' of Mr. Goetz when he used deadly force to defend himself. [The assistant district attorney], the justice said, neglected to state that Mr. Goetz might have 'reasonably believed that unlawful physical force was about to be used against him.'" In addition, noted Bob Drogin of the *Los Angeles Times*, Crane also said that "prosecutors did not present evidence from a police officer. . . who said the wounded Canty had told policemen that 'we were going to rob' Goetz. Another [shooting] victim, Darryl Cabey, confirmed that account in a subsequent hospital room interview with the *New York Daily News*. Crane said that Canty 'strongly appears' to have perjured himself before the grand jury."

The possibility still exists that Goetz's case could come before yet another grand jury, but that would be a very rare occurrence. And while the Manhattan District Attorney's

Office announced that it intends to appeal Crane's ruling, and even though Goetz is still open to charges of reckless endangerment and criminal possession of a weapon, for which he could face up to eight years in prison, his lawyers are convinced that their side has won the battle. Attorney Barry Slotnick, quoted in the *Los Angeles Times*, announced at a press conference: "We've won a great legal victory. Certainly, this is the most unusual case of the century." As for Goetz, said Slotnick, "he hopes the nightmare is over. . . . It's been a very painful year. Now, he just wants to regain his anonymity. He'd just like to go back to work, earn some money and become the introverted, quiet individual he was before this began." And, according to the *Los Angeles Times* report, 'Goetz recently said that he no longer rides the subways."

SOURCES:

PERIODICALS

Detroit Free Press, March 3, 1985, March 6, 1985, March 13, 1985, March 28, 1985.
Los Angeles Times, January 17, 1986.
Newsweek, January 7, 1985, January 14, 1985, February 4, 1985, April 1, 1985, January 27, 1986.
New York, February 18, 1985.
New York Times, January 1, 1985, January 4, 1985, January 23, 1985, January 25, 1985, January 26, 1985, January 28, 1985, February 7, 1985, February 8, 1985, February 22, 1985, February 24, 1985, February 25, 1985, February 26, 1985, February 28, 1985, March 1, 1985, March 3, 1985, March 23, 1985, March 24, 1985, March 25, 1985, March 27, 1985, March 28, 1985, March 29, 1985, April 5, 1985, June 28, 1985, July 10, 1985, July 28, 1985, August 14, 1985, January 17, 1986.
Time, January 14, 1985, March 11, 1985, April 8, 1985, January 27, 1986.
Washington Post, January 19, 1985, January 26, 1985, February 8, 1985, March 2, 1985, March 28, 1985, March 29, 1985.

—*Sidelights by Denise Wiloch*

Dwight Gooden

1964-

PERSONAL: Full name, Dwight Eugene Gooden; born November 16, 1964, in Tampa, Fla.; son of Dan (a chemical plant laborer) and Ella Mae (a nursing home aide) Gooden. *Education:* Attended high school in Tampa, Fla.

ADDRESSES: Home—Tampa, Fla.

OCCUPATION: Professional Baseball Player.

CAREER: Selected as a pitcher by the New York Mets in the first round of the 1982 free-agent draft; played for the minor league teams in the Mets' farm system, including Lynchburg of the Carolina League, where he was named Pitcher of the Year for 1983; began major league career with New York Mets, 1984—.

AWARDS, HONORS: Named National League Rookie of the Year, 1984; winner of National League's Cy Young Award, 1985; named *Baseball Digest*'s Player of the Year, 1985.

WRITINGS: Rookie: The Story of My First Year With the Major Leagues (with Richard Woodley), Doubleday, 1985.

SIDELIGHTS: In his first season playing major league baseball, pitcher Dwight Gooden of the New York Mets set more records and won more acclaim than most pitchers do in their entire careers. Named National League Rookie of the Year for 1984, Gooden made a spectacular debut in the majors with a won-lost record of 17-9 in thirty-one starts and an earned-run average of 2.60. He pitched three shutouts, including a one-hitter against the division-winning Chicago Cubs, and was the first Met to pitch consecutive shutouts since Pat Zachry in 1980. Gooden accomplished all this when he was only nineteen years old—the youngest player in the National League.

Perhaps most outstanding was Gooden's strikeout record. Dubbed "Dr. K" by Mets fans, who hang red "K" signs over the outfield railing whenever Gooden gets a strikeout (a K is used by baseball scorekeepers to indicate a strikeout), Gooden led the majors in 1984 by striking out 276 batters. That record far exceeded the previous all-time rookie strikeout record of 245 set in 1955 by Herb Score of the Cleveland Indians. Gooden's strikeouts were earned in just 218 innings pitched, which made his ratio of strikeouts per nine innings pitched a phenomenal 11.39. He gave up only 73 walks with a strikeout/walk ratio of 3.78 to 1. The young right-hander also set a league record in September, 1984, by striking out 32 batters in consecutive games—16 against the Pittsburgh Pirates and 16 against the Philadelphia Phillies. And in neither game did he give up a walk. "You really can't pitch any better than that," Mets pitching coach Mel Stottlemyre told *Sports Illustrated.* "One thing that was clear by the end of the year was that teams weren't able to

handle his pitches any better the second or third time they saw him than they were the first time. He kept getting better and better and better."

Just two years before winning Rookie of the Year honors, Gooden was a high school senior in Tampa, Florida. He was the Mets' first-round selection in the June, 1982, amateur draft after his outstanding last season at Hillsborough High School. In 1983, the pitcher's record was 19-4 in the Mets' Class A farm team in Lynchburg, Virginia. After playing in only 40 games in two seasons in the minor leagues, Gooden expected to start the 1984 season with the Mets' Triple-A club in Tidewater, Virginia. Days before the season began, however, Mets manager Dave Johnson informed him that he would be in the Mets' four-man starting rotation at the start of the season.

What impressed observers immediately was the poise and control Gooden exhibited game after game. Even his facial expression remained consistently impassive whether he won or lost a game. As Stottlemyre commented in the *New York Times:* "The thing about Dwight is his poise. He's not going to beat himself. Other young pitchers panic or lose control in tight situations. He'll never do that. Man on third, no out, he usually makes the big pitches. That's a very unusual trait."

Gooden learned control the hard way, he told the *New York Times.* "I used to always get mad and always ended up making a fool of myself. When I was 14, I felt I was supposed to get everybody out. I got hit hard once, and lost my temper. I banged my hand up against something and hurt it, which messed me up even more. That's when I learned about control."

Gooden's dazzling fastball has been clocked at 93 m.p.h., his curveball has been described as "virtually unhittable" by teammate Rusty Staub, and Gooden, unlike many other pitchers, can throw the ball inside to great advantage. He has been compared to such pitching greats as Tom Seaver, Jim Palmer, and Steve Carlton. After facing Gooden for the first time in spring training, Seaver told *Sports Illustrated:* "What impressed me about him were his mechanics and control. I wouldn't mind having his curveball either."

In the midst of Gooden's first season, strikeout pitcher Nolan Ryan of the Houston Astros offered this assessment to the *New York Times:* "At 19, Dwight Gooden is much farther advanced than I was at that age, or Seaver or Carlton. He has control and command of his pitches, and he

gets his curveball over. And you won't find a strikeout pitcher who doesn't have a good curveball to complement his fastball." The young right-hander "is so far advanced," Ryan continued, "there's no advice I could give him. The only thing I see in him is that he throws his fastball high, and the hitters chase it. But if you pitch up and make a mistake, you can get hurt. I'm not saying he can't survive up there. But the hitters adjust."

Gooden expressed surprise that major league hitters struck out so easily on his fastballs. As he told E.M. Swift of *Sports Illustrated,* "They kept telling me they'd lay off that pitch in the big leagues. But they didn't. Power hitters like that high pitch. It looks real good to them up there where they can see it. They like it, but they can't catch up to it." Perhaps the only thing that Gooden has consistent trouble with is holding runners on base. In 1984, for example, 47 of 50 runners stole bases while he was on the mound.

The 6-foot 4-inch, 190-pound pitcher combines physical grace with nearly flawless technique. Kinetics specialist Bob Toski was awestruck the first time he watched Gooden pitch, he commented to the *New York Times.* "That kid," Toski exclaimed, "has perfect synchronization of his body action when he pitches. Not just good—perfect. I couldn't take my eyes off him. He has perfect balance with his feet, legs, hips, shoulders, arm and head. He's so smooth, he

Dwight Gooden in action against the Los Angeles Dodgers, August 28, 1984. He struck out twelve batters in the game, which the Mets won 5-1. AP/Wide World Photos.

doesn't even look like he's throwing as hard as he is." That Gooden is well-versed in the technical aspects of his craft was attested to by Johnson, who managed Gooden his first year in the minors. Johnson told the *New York Times:* "One day I asked him: 'How do you throw your fastball?' He said: 'I hold the ball across the seams when I want it to rise, and along the seams when I want it to sink or break.' He was 17 then. Most guys that age don't even know how to grip the ball. But here he was, going into a 15-minute lecture on the different ways he throws his hard one."

Among the many highlights of Gooden's rookie year was being chosen to play in the 1984 All-Star Game with three of his Mets teammates, Darryl Strawberry, Keith Hernandez, and Jesse Orosco. Gooden was the youngest player ever chosen to play in the All-Star Game. When Gooden entered the game in the fifth inning the National League was ahead 2-1. As Gooden described the experience in *Playboy,* he walked out to the pitcher's mound telling himself that it was just like any other game, and all he had to do was throw strikes. "But," he related, "it wasn't just like any other game. In a regular game, I try to pace myself, but in the All-Star Game, with just two innings to pitch, I wanted to air it out and throw every pitch with everything I had. I wasn't thinking strikeouts, but I wanted to throw strikes, and I didn't want to give up any runs and lose the lead, and I didn't want to do anything like throw a wild pitch all the way to the backstop."

The first pitch he threw to Detroit Tiger catcher Lance Parrish was a fastball that Parrish took for a strike. Next Parrish fouled off a fastball to make the count 2-2. Then, Gooden commented in *Playboy,* "I decided to try to get him right there. I threw the fastball high, and he went for it and missed. I had a strikeout." Gooden used the same formula— fastballs, curveballs, and fastballs—to strike out the next two batters, Chet Lemon of the Tigers and Alvin Davis of the Seattle Mariners. By the end of Gooden's two-inning turn, he had given up only one hit and no runs. Gooden described his reception in *Playboy:* "When I walked off the mound, the crowd was standing and cheering, and it was like I was walking on air. Everybody in the dugout shook my hand and gave high fives. These were some of the best players in the game, congratulating me."

Because Gooden seems to have been born to play baseball, it's not surprising that his involvement with the sport started when he was just a toddler. Gooden's father, Dan Gooden, was formerly the coach of the Tampa Dodgers, a local semi-pro team. He introduced his son to baseball before he could even throw a ball: Dodger players would toss the ball to the three-year-old and he would roll it back. By the time the youngster started playing on teams, he was so much better than the other boys that he almost quit playing in frustration. He joined his first little league team at the age of ten as an outfielder but soon was moved to third base to take advantage of his strong arm. Gooden began pitching at the age of twelve and by fifteen was seriously considering a professional career.

Gooden was strongly encouraged by his mother Ella Mae. She told Swift: "That's all he cared to talk about, his

baseball. The day he turned 17, I says to him, 'This the year for you to decide what you want to be. You can be a drug addict; you can be a drunk; you can be a nice young man and stay in school; you can be a baseball player. You decide.' He says, 'I know that.' A little later he tells me he wants to get a job at the Wendy's and what did I think. I tell him, 'you need money, you ask for it. Don't steal. But you got no time for a job. You got to play ball.' "

Unlike many other sports stars Gooden has not let success go to his head. He used part of his $400,000 rookie salary to buy a house for his parents in Tampa. He still plays catch with the neighborhood kids when he's back home, and he recalled for the *New York Times* how his high school teammates turned out to cheer him in the majors. "It was kind of unbelievable. I threw batting practice to them, and they're coming to see me throw against major league hitters. It was amazing to them. . . . I played with these guys, and now they're coming to watch me. It's something to think about."

Gooden followed up his spectacular rookie season with an even more impressive sophomore showing in 1985: he led the major league in strikeouts (268), games won (24, against only four defeats), and earned run average (1.53) on his way to winning the National League's Cy Young Award. In September, twenty-year-old Gooden won his twentieth game, becoming the youngest player in modern baseball history to accomplish the feat.

Despite his rapid rise to stardom, Gooden is determined not to rush himself. He knows that it takes more than strikeouts to sustain a pitching career. As he told the *New York Times:* "Right now I'm just concentrating on learning the hitters. I'm not a great pitcher yet. I haven't proven myself." Manager Johnson has total confidence that Gooden will prove himself. "Truthfully," he commented to the *New York Times,* "I have run out of adjectives to describe Dwight. You pick a word, and it applies. He is just going to keep getting better and better as the years go by."

SOURCES:

BOOKS

Gooden, Dwight and Richard Woodley, *Rookie: The Story of My First Year With the Major Leagues,* Doubleday, 1985.

PERIODICALS

Baseball Digest, December, 1985.
Chicago Tribune, February 16, 1986.
Newsweek, September 2, 1986.
New York Times, February 20, 1984, April 20, 1984, May 3, 1984, May 7, 1984, June 18, 1984, July 6, 1984, July 15, 1984, July 16, 1984, July 18, 1984, August 7, 1984, September 9, 1984, November 20, 1984.
People, December 23, 1985.
Playboy, May, 1985.
Sports Illustrated, April 15, 1985, September 2, 1985.
Time, September 24, 1984.

—Sidelights by Barbara Welch Skaggs

Mikhail Gorbachev

1931-

PERSONAL: Full name, Mikhail Sergeevich Gorbachev; born March 2, 1931, in Privolnoye, Stavropol, U.S.S.R.; married Raisa Maksimovna. *Education:* Moscow State University, law degree, 1955; Stavropol Agricultural Institute, graduate, 1967.

ADDRESSES: Central Committee, Communist Party of the Soviet Union, Kremlin, Moscow, U.S.S.R.

OCCUPATION: Soviet politician.

CAREER: Agricultural worker in Stavropol Krai, U.S.S.R., 1946-50; Stavropol City Committee, Komsomol (Young Communist League), member, beginning 1956; Stavropol City Committee, Communist Party of the Soviet Union, first secretary, 1956-58, 1966-68, second secretary, 1968-70; Stavropol Krai Committee, Komsomol, second secretary and first secretary, 1958-62, first secretary, 1970-78; deputy to U.S.S.R. Supreme Soviet, beginning 1970; Central Committee, Communist Party of the Soviet Union, member, 1971—, secretary for agriculture, beginning 1978, general secretary, 1985—. Candidate member of Politburo, 1979, full member, 1980—; chairman of Foreign Affairs Committee of U.S.S.R., beginning 1984.

SIDELIGHTS: On March 11, 1985, Mikhail Sergeevich Gorbachev became one of the most powerful men on earth when his selection as general secretary of the Communist Party of the Soviet Union placed him in command of one of the two great superpowers. He leads a nation of 273 million people whose land area covers more than one-seventh of the globe. The armed forces of the Union of Soviet Socialist Republics exceed in size and weaponry that of any other single nation and are matched only by the alliance of the United States and Western Europe. His nation, along with the United States, has fielded missiles and bombers armed with nuclear weapons sufficient to destroy civilization on much of the globe. Literally, the future of human civilization rests in part with the actions of Mikhail Gorbachev.

As general secretary, Gorbachev will be the dominant figure of the Communist Party's Politburo (Political Bureau), a self-perpetuating body of ten to fourteen men who hold supreme power in the Soviet state. Although the position of general secretary is no longer the absolute personal dictatorship it was under Joseph Stalin, when Stalin's whim had the force of law, Gorbachev's personal power will be enormous. He and his Politburo colleagues are not subject to free elections, and they control all of the major institutions of Soviet society: the armed forces, the police, the media, the schools, and the bureaucracy of the state-controlled economic system. Gorbachev's personal discretion far exceeds that available to any Western leader.

Gorbachev was nearly unknown to the West until 1982. Then, at the time of the death of long-time Soviet leader Leonid Brezhnev at age seventy-six, Gorbachev was rumored to be a possible candidate for the top position in the Soviet government. Gorbachev, then fifty-one, was the youngest member of the Politburo. The fact that he was even a possibility for general secretary meant that the long anticipated transfer of power to a younger generation of Soviet leaders might be underway. But the job went to Yuri Andropov, the sixty-eight-year-old head of the KGB, the Soviet secret police. Although chronology made Andropov one of the older generation of Soviet leaders, in the early months of his reign he called for internal Communist renewal. The renewal shook up Soviet society by cracking down on corruption, by replacing long-entrenched Communist Party and government officials, by ordering increased social discipline through a drive against worker absenteeism and inefficiency, and by expanding the power of the KGB. Gorbachev emerged in this period as Andropov's chief lieutenant and supervised implementation of Andropov's reforms. Andropov's renewal program slowed, however, when his health deteriorated. He died fifteen months after taking office.

After Andropov's death, Gorbachev was considered one of the major contenders for the succession. The Politburo, however, chose Konstantin Chernenko. Chernenko, at age seventy-two, had been close to Brezhnev and did not share the desire of Andropov and Gorbachev for an attack on the ossification of Soviet society that had developed in the latter years of Brezhnev's rule. By selecting Chernenko, the Politburo slowed the transition to a younger leadership that Andropov had begun. Nonetheless, Chernenko's age and his poor health suggested that his tenure would be relatively short; Moscow rumors held that Gorbachev was the heir apparent.

After Chernenko's selection, Gorbachev undertook an official visit to Great Britain. His career in Soviet politics had been almost entirely concerned with domestic matters. This tour served both to introduce Gorbachev to the West and to demonstrate to Gorbachev's Politburo colleagues that he could perform well on the international stage. And, indeed, his performance was superb. The West had grown used to Soviet leaders who were extremely old and often in poor health, intellectually unimpressive, and harsh or even crude in manner and speech. Gorbachev, however, was middle-aged, healthy, intelligent, and charming. Even as harsh a critic of the Soviet Union as Prime Minister Margaret Thatcher of Great Britain found Gorbachev to be a reasonable man. "I like Mr. Gobachev," said Thatcher. "We can do business together."

Gorbachev and his wife, Raisa Maksimovna, at age fifty-one, were also well dressed in the Western manner (unusual among Soviet officials) and were dubbed the "Gucci Comrades" by some Western media. Raisa Maksimovna's role in her husband's tour was also a surprise as wives of high Soviet officials usually avoid media coverage. (The Western press was unsure if Yuri Andropov's wife was even still alive before she attended her husband's funeral.) Mrs. Gorbachev, however, took a prominent role in the tour, proved to be an intelligent conversationalist (she studied philosophy at Moscow State University), and showed herself to be both photogenic and charming.

That Gorbachev was the chosen successor became clear immediately after Chernenko died on March 10, 1985. The Politburo met and announced Gorbachev's selection as General Secretary the next day. Within his first months in office, Gorbachev won full Politburo membership for three close allies. These three appointments to a body which never has more than fourteen voting members gives Gorbachev a solid majority in the Politburo and very likely assures him a long tenure.

Gorbachev was too young to participate in World War II, and that alone makes him unusual among Soviet leaders. Before Gorbachev, virtually all high Soviet officials were of a generation that came to maturity under Joseph Stalin and fought World War II, experiences that produced tough and often brutal survivors. This generation also rebuilt the Soviet Union after World War II, established its domination over Eastern Europe, and raised it to superpower status. The same generation, however, also institutionalized itself into a permanent ruling class. Communist Party officials gained virtual lifetime tenure in office, and the highest levels of the Party and the government, known as the *nomenklatura,* obtained for themselves enormous privileges not available to other Soviet citizens. These privileges included higher salaries, access to special high-quality health care, the use of state goods and workers to build or refurbish a private home and a "dacha" (a cottage in the country), access to special high-quality consumer goods at low prices, admittance to elite vacation resorts, and preferential access to elite schools and colleges for their children.

During Brezhnev's eighteen-year rule, the bureaucratization of Soviet life produced a society that was increasingly resistant to innovation. Soviet economic growth slowed significantly, and Soviet technology and science continued to lag well behind that of the United States, Japan, and Western Europe; in literature and the arts, life in the Soviet Union stifled creativity. Promotion in the upper levels of Soviet society often came through cronyism, and in some areas corruption flourished as Soviet citizens sought shortcuts through the gargantuan governmental bureaucracy.

Soviet leaders have been aware of the negative aspects of Soviet life and have attempted reforms on a number of occasions. These reform campaigns, however, were either blocked or frustrated by Communist cadre resistant to change. In the early 1960s, Nikita Khrushchev called for more rapid turnover in Party leadership. Entrenched Party cadre resented Khrushchev's plans, and, when he persisted, the Politburo deposed Khrushchev from power. Initially, Khrushchev was replaced by a dual leadership of Aleksei Kosygin and Leonid Brezhnev. In the mid-1960's Kosygin attempted to partially dismantle central economic controls. His reforms were also stifled by the bureaucracy, and he was pushed out of the leadership by Brezhnev.

Under Brezhnev, "continuity of cadre," meaning support for the tenure and privileges of the *nomenklatura,* became Soviet policy. Brezhnev recognized, however, the growing inefficiencies of the Soviet economy. On several occasions in the 1970s reform programs to partially decentralize the economy were announced, although in practice little change was noticeable. Gorbachev, in fact, won his promotion to the inner circle of the Soviet Government when he was placed in charge of implementing Brezhnev's program to decentralize agriculture. The program called for shifting control of agricultural planning from Moscow authorities to regional planners and for offering farm workers financial incentives for increased production. The results of this reform program were, however, unclear. In several years grain production fell drastically, a drop Soviet authorities attributed to poor weather. Finally, the Soviet Union stopped publishing crop production figures.

In his first months as general secretary Gorbachev's style of leadership proved to be a marked contrast to other recent Soviet leaders. He has appeared frequently on Soviet television visiting and talking with ordinary citizens and has demonstrated that he is an eloquent speaker, even without a prepared text. His wife has also taken an unprecedented high profile in Soviet media. In terms of substantive actions, Gorbachev has fired, retired, or demoted a number of officials in the Communist Party and in the government. Among those dismissed were two government ministers and nearly a dozen regional Party heads. He is attacking corruption through a reassertion of state police power, harsher and more frequent punishment for violation of economic or social discipline, and expanded KGB surveillance of domestic Soviet life. Thus far, Gorbachev has not made any significant changes in Soviet foreign policy. Nor have there been hints that Gorbachev has any desire to relax the Communist Party's monopolistic control over political and intellectual life or its policy of harsh suppression of dissidents.

Western media sometimes describe Gorbachev as a "reformer." It is an accurate term if it is understood strictly within the context of the Soviet system, a system which is hostile to democratic liberties and human rights in the Western sense. In the late 1950s Khrushchev launched a program of "de-Stalinization" to eliminate the brutal elements of Soviet life that had become institutionalized under Joseph Stalin. The KGB, the central instrument of Stalin's terror, was subordinated to other organs of Soviet government and Lavrenty Beria, Stalin's KGB chief, was executed for his bloody crimes. Other unrepentant aides of Stalin, such as Vyacheslav Molotov, were stripped of Communist Party membership and publicly condemned. For a few years a limited measure of artistic and intellectual freedom was allowed, and dissident writers such as Aleksandr Solzhenitsyn were able to publish openly.

Khrushchev began to cut back on the limited freedoms he had allowed even before his fall, and after he was removed from office a steady "re-Stalinization" took place. The KGB returned to the inner circle of Soviet power with the selection in 1982 of its head, Yuri Andropov, as general secretary of the Communist Party. Gorbachev was one of Andropov's proteges, and one of his first acts on becoming general secretary was to raise the man Andropov appointed to head the KGB to full membership in the Politburo. (By contrast, the head of the Soviet armed forces is only a "candidate" or nonvoting member of the Politburo). Stalin himself has been partially rehabilitated in Soviet history books and old unreconstructed Stalinists, such as Molotov, have been restored to Party membership. KGB harassment of intellectual, religious, and political dissenters has intensified. (Solzhenitsyn, for example, was exiled.) Further, harsh punishments are being imposed on members of non-Russian ethnic groups who resisted "Russification," and Stalin's anti-Semitism has been revived in the form of a campaign against "Zionism." There has not, however, been any use of Stalin's practice of mass terror.

Gorbachev's major concern since taking office has been the stagnation of the Soviet economy. In June, 1985, the Western press reported that Gorbachev had rejected the proposed five-year economic plan drafted by incumbent Soviet ministers. In a speech to the Central Committee, Gorbachev criticized several long-entrenched economic planners and other high economic officials associated with the Brezhnev generation. He called for revisions of the economic plan to provide for more emphasis on the quality of products, equipping plants with more modern machinery, and greater investment in research and development. Such open criticism of incumbent officials by a General Secretary is highly unusual in the Soviet Union. The *Wall Street Journal* quoted one Western expert on the Soviet economy who felt that the speech showed that Gorbachev "continues to portray the image of the new broom who comes in and really shakes thing up, a useful and dynamic person who is going to change things."

Gorbachev is reported to be sympathetic to the economic reforms suggested by the economic institute in Novosibirsk. This Soviet think-tank calls for decreased bureaucratic control of state enterprises and more flexibility for managers of these plants. In an interview with the *Wall Street Journal*, a spokesman for the institute asserted that the central planning agencies in Moscow "follow the work of enterprises too closely, and sometimes this undermines the initiative of the enterprise." In the area of agriculture, the *Washington Post* reported that Gorbachev had ordered the distribution of small plots of land to a million peasants for their private use in hopes of improving food production. Earlier, the *Washington Post* also reported that Gorbachev had asked for information on Lenin's New Economic Policy, a program in the early 1920s that allowed limited private enterprise within the Soviet economy.

Nonetheless, the same *Wall Street Journal* story citing the Soviet advocate of decentralization also quoted a spokesman for the Soviet economic planning agency, Gosplan. The Gosplan spokesman said that Gorbachev's innovations, while allowing greater flexibility and use of financial incentives to reward efficient workers and managers, will not threaten central control of the economy. Nor, it was emphasized, would Soviet economic reforms use a market mechanism to set prices, as has been done by the Communist government in Hungary. Gorbachev's speeches, although sharp in criticism of individuals, have been vague about any changes in the system of central economic control.

Gorbachev is, himself, a product of the system he wishes to revitalize. He was born in 1931 to a peasant family in Privolnoye, a village in the Stavropol territory, a farming region north of the Caucasus mountains. He graduated from law school at the Moscow State University in 1955 but never practiced law. He was admitted to the Communist Party in 1952 and served as Komsomol (Young Communist League) organizer at law school; his first professional post after graduation was as first secretary (executive head) of the Stavropol City Komsomol. He did well as a professional Party "apparatchik" and in 1958 became first secretary of the Stavropol Krai (territory) Komsomol. Then he moved further up into the Party hierarchy when he became first secretary of the Stavropol City Communist Party Committee. In 1970, he became the first secretary of the Stavropol Krai Communist Party Committee. Arkady Shevchenko, the highest ranking Soviet official ever to defect, noted in his book *Breaking with Moscow,* that Gorbachev had "earned a reputation as an energetic regional Party leader and manager . . . . He was also known as a reasonable man, with less arrogance than most professional Party apparatchiki." Shevchenko, who had met Gorbachev, described him personally as "intelligent, well educated, and well mannered."

The leadership of the Party organization in Stavropol Krai was an important post, and also a fortunate one for Gorbachev. The Stavropol region is a popular recreation area, and many high Soviet officials vacation there at elite resorts. Gorbachev, as the head of the local Communist Party, played host to these officials. Furthermore, Stavropol was the home region of Mikhail Suslov, a long-time member of the Politburo, a rigid Marxist-Leninist ideologue, and one of the leaders of the coup that forced Khrushchev from power. Suslov's patronage and Gorbachev's intimacy with many Moscow officials allowed Gorbachev to gain membership on the Central Committee of the Communist Party in 1971.

It is evidence of Gorbachev's conscienciousness that after he became Stavropol Communist Party chief that he undertook the study of agricultural issues because of the importance of farming in the local economy; in 1967 he earned a degree from the Stavropol Agricultural Institute. When the post of agricultural secretary of the Central Committee became vacant in 1978, Gorbachev was available to assume the post and move to Moscow. His work as agricultural secretary and the political allies he had developed won him full membership in the all-powerful Politburo in 1980.

Gorbachev is, then, a professional Communist functionary. His career is based upon the Communist Party's domination of the Soviet state and its monopoly of political, economic, and social power. It is unlikely that he has any desire to fundamentally change that system. What he appears to want to do, however, is to revitalize it by eliminating its corrupt and ossified elements, to bring in fresh and younger leaders, and to reduce the drag of bureaucracy on economic growth.

SOURCES:

BOOKS

Shevchenko, Arkady N., *Breaking with Moscow,* Knopf, 1985.

PERIODICALS

Detroit Free Press, March 4, 1985, March 12, 1985, March 13, 1985, March 17, 1985.
Foreign Affairs, spring, 1985.
Newsweek, June 3, 1985.
New York Times Biographical Service, March, 1985.
Time, March 25, 1985.
Wall Street Journal, May 23, 1985, June 12, 1985.
Washington Post, June 4, 1985.

—Sidelights by John E. Haynes

Tipper Gore
1948-

PERSONAL: Full name, Mary Elizabeth (Aitcheson) Gore; born August 19, 1948, in Washington, D.C.; married Albert Gore, Jr. (a U.S. Senator), May 19, 1970; children: Karenna, Kristin, Sarah, Albert III. *Education:* Boston University, B.A., 1970; George Peabody College for Teachers of Vanderbilt University, M.A., 1976. *Religion:* Baptist.

ADDRESSES: Home—Route 2, Carthage, Tenn. 37030; and Arlington, Va. *Office*—Parents' Music Resource Center, 1500 Arlington, Suite 300, Arlington, Va. 22209.

OCCUPATION: Photographer, consumer advocate, and social activist.

CAREER: Tennessean (daily newspaper), Nashville, Tenn., employed in photography department, 1971-76; chairperson of Congressional Wives Task Force, 1978-79; Parents' Music Resource Center, Arlington, Va., co-founder and vice-president, 1985—; free-lance photographer. Member of board of directors of Capitol Children's Museum and of Center for Science in the Public Interest; served on American Academy of Pediatrics' Task Force on Children and Television.

SIDELIGHTS: In early 1985 Tipper Gore was shocked to discover that in the "Darling Nikki" cut on the *Purple Rain* album she had purchased for her twelve-year-old daughter, pop star Prince rhapsodized a girl he knew with the couplet: "I guess you could say she was a sex fiend/I met her in a hotel lobby masturbating with a magazine." Gore, the wife of U.S. Senator Albert Gore, Jr. (D-Tenn.), expressed her anger and fear to friends and found that other mothers within the group, informally called the "Washington Wives," shared her concern about the potential harm to their children from some of the more explicit aspects of popular culture, specifically rock lyrics.

In May, 1985, Gore co-founded the Parents' Music Resource Center (PMRC) with Pam Howar, wife of a Washington, D.C. businessman, Susan Baker, wife of Treasury Secretary James A. Baker III, and Sally Nevius. The group, with Howar serving as president, Baker and Gore as vice-presidents, and Nevius as treasurer, launched a campaign to alert educators, ministers, the press, and parents in general to the problem of what Gore described as "raunchy rock." Spearheaded by Gore and Baker, members of the PMRC appeared on talk shows, wrote magazine articles, and presented examples of rock lyrics, album covers, and music videos they found objectionable.

On May 31, 1985, the PMRC wrote a letter to the Recording Industry Association of America (RIAA), in which they proposed a rating system for records. Intended as a consumer information guide for parents, the system was envisioned to feature labels to be attached to records, tapes,

and videos to indicate objectionable material in the separate categories of violence, profane or sexually explicit lyrics, references to drugs or alcohol, and themes on the occult. Left unclear were details of exactly what constituted the objectionable material and who would serve as arbiter of any disputes arising from the system.

In July, 1985, the RIAA made a counterproposal to the PMRC in which the record industry agreed to voluntarily place a nonspecific blanket discretionary warning label on albums with explicit content, a proposal the PMRC rejected as unacceptable. The Parent-Teacher Association (PTA) joined the PMRC in their efforts and it was announced that the Senate Committee on Commerce, Science, and Transportation had placed the matter on its agenda, with a hearing scheduled for September 19.

As the PMRC campaign grew through the summer of 1985, the elements of celebrity, sex, and children captured the attention of the press and caused supporters and critics of both the PMRC and the music industry to draw battle lines. The PMRC was against censorship, they claimed, and saw the problem as one of rights: the right of parents to be aware of and have control over what their children see and hear versus the performers' right of artistic freedom. Rock musicians, on the other hand, viewed the PMRC's efforts as the latest attempt on the part of the established culture to outlaw the art form.

Rock's roots in Hillbilly music and black rhythm and blues stigmatized it as being too lowbrow for mainstream American respectability in the 1950s and outraged religious fundamentalists and white supremacists, who focused their attention on the "evil beat" of the music. As David Zucchino noted in *Rolling Stone:* "Ever since white hillbillies merged 'race music' into rock & roll, purists have sought to outlaw, pressure or rein in rock records and lyrics. In 1956, *The Ed Sullivan Show* refused to televise Elvis Presley below the waist. In 1963, the FBI and FCC replayed the Kingsmen's 'Louie, Louie' at different speeds to try to detect dirty words. Conclusion: they couldn't make out the lyrics. In 1970, Spiro Agnew called rock music 'blatant drug-culture propaganda' and warned that it 'threatens to sap national strength unless we move hard and fast to bring it under control.' "

In a statement read by Baker and Gore at the Senate hearing they stressed that "the material we are concerned about cannot be compared with 'Louie, Louie,' Cole Porter, Billie Holliday, etc. . . . There is a new element of vulgarity, violence, and brutality to women that is unprecedented. While a few outrageous recordings have existed in the past, the proliferation of songs glorifying rape, sadomasochism, incest, the occult, and suicide, by [a] growing number of bands illustrates an escalating trend that is alarming. . . . Some rock artists actually seem to encourage teen suicide, Ozzy Osborne sings 'Suicide Solution'; Blue Oyster Cult sings 'Don't Fear the Reaper'; AC/DC sings 'Shoot to Thrill.' Just last week in a small Texas town a young man took his life while listening to the music of AC/DC. He was not the first."

Despite assurances from the committee that no regulatory legislation was being considered at that time and assurances from the PMRC that none was being requested, members of the record industry were not mollified. PMRC critics argued that many of the examples presented by Gore, Baker, and PMRC consultant Jeff Ling were by obscure or unknown performers, that interpretation of lyrics was a highly subjective practice, often open to error.

Musician Frank Zappa asked the committee about the potential of a conflict of interest: Gore's husband was a member of the committee and the wives of four others sitting on the committee were members of or actively associated with the PMRC. Zappa also accused the RIAA of abandoning the cause of artistic freedom in order to strike a deal to insure the enactment of the Blank Tape Tax, long sought by record manufacturers who feel they are losing revenues to individuals who buy blank tape in order to illegally record off the radio or friends' albums; the proposed tax on all blank tape sold would go into their pockets. Songwriter John Denver spoke to the committee about Nazis and censorship and about how misinterpretation of his song "Rocky Mountain High" resulted in its being banned and labeled a drug-oriented song. Others appeared before the committee, including Twisted Sister's Dee Snider, who stressed his belief

that it is the responsibility of parents, not the government, to monitor the listening tastes of their children.

On November 1, 1985, the RIAA announced that it had reached an agreement with the PMRC-PTA coalition. According to the agreement, twenty-two of the RIAA's forty-four members, responsible for about 80 percent of the records released in the United States, had voluntarily agreed to label their releases with the warning "Explicit Lyrics—Parental Advisory" or to display the lyrics on the record jacket if they are considered to contain "explicit sex, explicit violence, or explicit substance abuse"—virtually the same proposal the PMRC had rejected in July. Despite several unclear areas, including rock videos and the labeling of cassettes (which account for about 60 percent of all record sales but are physically too small on which to reasonably display the lyrics contained within), both the RIAA and the PMRC-PTA, which proclaimed the agreement a victory, expressed satisfaction with the accord.

CN INTERVIEW

CN interviewed Tipper Gore by telephone on November 25, 1985.

CN: First of all, in order to establish a point of reference, I was wondering what your personal tastes in music are? Have you ever been a rock and roll fan?

GORE: Yes, and I still am. I'm serious! I like classical, jazz, pop, rock. I like light rock a little better now than I like hard rock, but I am a rock and roll fan still.

CN: Parents' Music Resource Center co-founder Susan Baker told the Senate Commerce Committee that rock lyrics are at least partly responsible for teenage pregnancy, teen suicide, and rape. Isn't it possible that rock lyrics merely reflect the presence of these phenomena in our society rather than cause them?

GORE: Well, that's not exactly accurate. In fact what she said—after outlining the new trend that we feel is in the music towards violence and explicit sexuality—was that there is a proliferation of songs glorifying rape, sadomasochism, incest, the occult, and suicide by a growing number of bands, illustrating an escalating trend that is alarming. Now someone suggested that the records in question are a minute element in music, but we are saying that these records are selling millions of copies. Prince's *Purple Rain* has sold 14 million copies with the explicit song "Darling Nikki" on it; Judas Priest's *Defenders of the Faith* has a song about forcing oral sex at gunpoint and has sold 2 million copies; Quiet Riot has one called *Let's Get Crazy*, which has sold over 5 million copies, with explicit sexual references; and Motley Crue's *Shout at the Devil* has sold 2 million copies. These are just some examples.

Some say there is no cause for concern, but we believe there is. We are painting a picture of the climate—part of the climate—that teenagers grow up in. Teenage pregnancy and teenage suicide rates are at epidemic proportions. This is true. We go on to say [in the Senate Testimony] that the Decker Report states that the U.S.A. has the highest teenage pregnancy rate of any developed country, 96 out of 1000, and in the latest FBI statistics rape is up 7 percent. The suicide rate of youths between sixteen and twenty-four has gone up 300 percent in the last three decades, while the adult level has stayed the same. Now this at a time when you have a number of songs glorifying suicide. You have Ozzy Osbourne's "Suicide Solutions," Blue Oyster Cult's "Going through the Roof," AC/DC's "Shoot to Thrill," "Gimme a Bullet." I mean we can go on with more examples. There are certainly many causes for these ills in our society, but it is our contention that pervasive messages, aimed at children, which promote and glorify suicide, rape, and sadomasochism have to be numbered among the contributing factors.

CN: To what do you attribute the extraordinary influence that rock seems to have on teenagers?

GORE: Well, I think that rock has always been, and always will be, music that is counterculture music, music that speaks through rebelliousness—breaking away from home and the values that you've learned—and it's always been very sexual. We recognize that. I think that's perfectly normal, and we're not trying to contend that point at all but to talk about new trends in the music which have a more specific and more violent tone to them and to mention that fact and point out to people that this music is now available to younger and younger kids. Grade school kids are listening to Twisted Sister and Motley Crue, third, fourth, fifth graders! We're simply trying to point this out, and the things we're saying are in some senses very delicate and very sensitive. Talking about very fine points like that can tend to get lost out in the media where they like to see things in black and white and really not dwell on the nuances or the bridge between one sentence and another; but that bridge can be very, very important. We're not trying to say that a rock song about rape has caused rape to go up. What we're talking about is a general climate and trend, and we think it is one factor. It's a small factor, but it can be a factor. It should be considered when you think about the overall environment that our kids are growing up in and their music, which is particularly important to them at a certain point in their life. All of which, I think, is a rather reasonable and moderate statement.

CN: Rock and roll seems to owe a good deal of its mystique and popularity to its ability to withstand periodic attacks from critics. Are you ever concerned that the PMRC's efforts will only serve to strengthen the popularity of these types of rock?

GORE: Well, you see, this is not anti-rock. I mean, it may *sound* like its anti-rock, but it's not. What we're talking about is anti-violence and anti-brutality in the lyrics of the music. Rock music should withstand any attack. We're not anti-rock music, per se. If this trend, if this development, were in pop music we'd be talking about pop music today. It just so happens that it's in rock music. Most rock music is very positive and fine. There's nothing in it that I think even a group of concerned parents would be troubled about. But parents with younger kids can't help but notice the trend toward explicitness in the music. You know, if you have your ten year old jumping rope and singing along with [Sheena Easton's] "Sugar Walls", it makes you say, "Whoa, what's going on here?"

CN: Do you feel that the explicit depiction of sex and violence is a growing trend in other aspects of popular culture, particularly television and films?

GORE: Yes, I do. I think that television and films have led the way—particularly television—in desensitizing people to violence and to sex. Now, because we have been subjected to it on the screen, on television and in the films, we tend to become desensitized and to require more to be shocked. I think that is something that has been going on in the adult population, and now we're seeing that inability to draw a line, an inability to seem to be shocked, reflected in the fact that so many of these outrageous scenes continue to push the edge in the music that is particularly appealing to our young people. And I think the adult population has a responsibility to at least discuss some sort of line, like some sort of parameter, that we would approve or not approve. That does not mean anything other than a system of values attached to—well we disapprove of songs extolling violence going to young kids. They're still there, the artists have the right to express that and to sell it, etcetera, but we are saying, "Hey don't think this is the greatest thing in the world."

CN: Filmmakers have used a rating system for a number of years now, and some of them seem to feel that a G rating actually can hurt a film's chances at the box office, which seems to act as an incentive for them to include material that will get their films rated PG or R. Isn't it possible that warning labels or a rating system might have the same effect on records, encouraging the inclusion of the very material you want to see eliminated?

GORE: Well, again, it's not so much that we want to see it eliminated. We want a mechanism by which to make an informed choice in the marketplace. For those people who want explicit recordings, let them have them, but give *me* a warning, either by a label or by making lyrics available on the product in the marketplace, so that if I want to avoid buying it unwittingly I can do so. That's our whole point. We're not trying to restrict it necessarily, at all.

CN: Why couldn't the PMRC establish its own standards, rate records using any system it liked, and then publish the ratings—as the Catholic Church has done for films—thereby informing interested consumers about the lyrical content without requiring record companies to place labels or lyric sheets on the record?

GORE: Because we don't feel that it is unreasonable to ask a $4 billion industry that has allowed these excesses to develop in the marketplace to assume corporate and artistic responsibility over their own product. Particularily when, in a lot of people's opinions, it has become explicit. Let's let that include violence and other things. It's become explicit, okay? The second ingredient that is causing us concern is that it is going to elementary-school-aged children in addition to the traditionally older audience. Now, is it okay to sit back as a society and condone the explicit lyrics—singing about "Sugar Walls," singing about "Darling Nikki," singing about rape, incest—going to eight-, nine-, ten-, eleven-year-old kids? I think not, particularly when they use the public airwaves to promote, advertise, the product in order to get people to go into the record store and buy it. They use the broadcast airwaves to do that.

Now, the broadcast airwaves, whether they are radio or whether they are TV, are the public's; and these super entities are being lent this scarce national commodity with an understanding that they will exercise responsibility to their audience. You have a number of people within the community at large who all own a part of the airwaves saying, "You're supposed to broadcast with the public interest, and you're not." We are raising the question of how much it is in the public interest to broadcast "Sugar Walls," "Darling Nikki," etcetera. Because it's available to younger and younger kids, we're raising this question. We're saying this to you [the recording industry]: We don't think that's responsible. We think that's irresponsible. We think that you are doing it in your pursuit of promotion and advertising so that people will come in and buy your product, and we would like to ask you to exercise some self-restraint and exercise the responsibility that you are supposed to be exercising as you use the public airwaves.

CN: The record industry doesn't seem too eager to go along willingly. Do you think some of their resistance is primarily a concern for artistic freedom or is it really economic?

GORE: Are you kidding me? Twenty-two companies have agreed to either put a warning label or lyrics on their products that they deem explicit. That's 80 percent of recorded music in America.

CN: So, you feel, then, that you are making quite a bit of progress?

GORE: Oh, absolutely! We're very delighted with the agreement that the PMRC, the PTA, and the RIAA jointly announced on November 5, [1985]. It represents, like I said, twenty-two companies, RIAA members, 80 percent of recorded music saying: "You have a legitimate complaint, a legitimate concern as parents of younger kids. We will respond to that concern by voluntarily either labelling or making lyrics available on all products that we deem explicit." That's a very terrific first step. It's very similar to what some companies are already doing. I don't know if you are familiar with the new Marvin Gaye album released by Columbia, *Dream of a Lifetime*? If you turn it over, the back of the album has a box description that tells you that the album contains explicit lyrics that might be objectionable. And indeed "Masochistic Beauty" is an extremely explicit song. But that's great; I mean, you were informed about that in the marketplace, and it's up to you whether or not you want to go ahead and purchase that. Everybody has different considerations. That is exactly the kind of generic inscription that we have asked them to put on the back of albums that they think are explicit. And they made this decision. I think that's a very positive step that the companies have pledged to take to provide consumer information.

CN: When you appeared before the Senate Commerce Committee, you said that you didn't feel there was a need for any legislation at that particular time. Do you still feel that way?

GORE: Yes. We have never recommended legislation as a remedy to the problem. The problem is one of excess. The industry, a $4 billion industry, has allowed those excesses to develop in the marketplace for whatever reason. *They* are the proper entities to address it, and they in fact are taking the first step to address it. And the way to address it— balancing the rights and needs of the artists, the producers, and the parents of younger kids out in the consuming public—is, we think, by providing additional information, consumer information, on the product. We think that is the way to go.

CN: How did the PMRC get this issue on the agenda of the Senate Commerce Committee?

GORE: The PMRC did not get the issue on the agenda of the Senate Commerce Committee. The Senate Commerce Committee got the issue on the agenda. That would be better answered by Senator John Danforth who is the chairman of the Commerce Committee.

CN: His wife has been described as being "connected with" the PMRC.

GORE: That's right.

CN: And you, of course, are the wife of another Committee member, Senator Albert Gore. Are you saying that this had no influence on the decision of the committee to conduct these hearings?

GORE: I'm saying that *I* didn't have any. Some people have suggested that I was able to get this hearing through my husband. Those are people that have no understanding of how Washington works and who sets up an agenda for a hearing. My husband is a freshman minority member of the Commerce Committee. He cannot establish the agenda for hearings, as much as he'd like to. It just doesn't work that way. I think the reason there was a hearing is because the Danforths had an interest in this issue, and I happen to also be involved in the issue.

CN: You've become something of a national celebrity, a status that many people find difficult to relinquish. Do you plan to remain in the public spotlight, perhaps in politics?

GORE: I have been involved in many issues in the nine years that I have been the wife of a political person here in Washington. Many many issues. It just so happens that this particular issue struck a chord, I think, among people and among the media, so therefore I was thrust into the public spotlight. It happened that way much to my surprise.

CN: Have you enjoyed your time in the spotlight?

GORE: I can't answer that. What I would say is that I feel very strongly about the issue, obviously, or I wouldn't be involved in it. And I think that it's good that the media were able to present the issue to the American people and spotlight or highlight the discussion around it from all sides for people who had a different viewpoint than mine. I think it is very important and very good that there was a general public debate in many instances about this particular issue. All that is for the good. I'm very glad that the issue was able to gain as much attention as it did, because I think it's important, and I think the reason is because it's a very credible issue. Many people all across the country were interested in it, and that was one of the reasons that you had all the attention focused on it. But it was a surprise to me.

CN: Do you have any future plans that you'd like to share with us?

GORE: As far as what the PMRC is planning on doing now, we're simply going to go along with the national PTA, with whom we have a coalition, monitoring to see how this works out in the marketplace—this proposed solution, which we think is a positive first step but not a perfect solution by any means. We'll see how that works in the marketplace. An issue that I began working on in earnest at the same time that I began working on this issue is the plight of the homeless, which I think is a growing national crisis. And I will continue to work on that.

One other thing which might fit me in context for you is that back in 1977 and '78, I helped form a congressional wives' group which for one year studied the issue of violence on television, particularly the violence on television that children were exposed to and the lack of quality programming for children. We were a bipartisan/bicameral group of seventy wives who wrote a report at the end of the year. We formed a coalition with ACT [Action for Children's Television], the American Medical Association, and the National Academy of Pediatrics, the American Dental Society, etcetera. At that time there was a lot of public outcry about the highly sugared cereals and candy advertisements during children's programming. And at that time the Federal Trade Commission was considering a rulemaking on that issue, and we were involved in that. There were some shows—thirty-minute cartoon shows, thirty-minute shows designed for children—which carried as much as twelve-and-a-half minutes of advertising, all of it for highly sugared products.

It seemed [that the same question was at issue]: Are children fair prey for commercial interests? It seems like somebody in this society periodically has to kind of reflect the sentiment that, you know, "Hey, children cannot be considered completely fair game." They *do* deserve some sense of protection or some call to the businesses that have become excessive in their zeal in selling products to the kids to exercise some self-restraint. I think this is a periodic need, apparently. We were able to reduce, through this coalition, some commercial time down to nine minutes, which was considered a great victory at that time back in '77-'78. I have a master's in psychology, so I'm interested in the effects of media on children, and I think it's very different, and you have to look at it in a different way. You have to realize that children process reality and images on the screen differently; a six year old is going to be different than an eight year old, and an eight year old is different from a twelve year old, etcetera. And that's something that the adult population, I think, tends to overlook and forget sometimes.

CN: So you feel that at times adults—particularly businesses, which would include rock bands—exploit children for financial gain?

GORE: Well that's a harsh statement. I think that what happens is that they are so focused, perhaps, on their financial gain that they are not as sensitive as they should be or could be about younger kids. Yes, I think that's right without making a broad-brush statement because some people are very sensitive and some are not. That's true. But the whole focus of our concern is on younger children and how they seem to be approached by what are business interests. I mean there could be other interests involved, too; obviously with the music there are artistic considerations, etcetera. But the bottom line is that these people selling products, basically, are in many instances mainly targeting a younger and younger audience to sell their product to, whether it's sugared cereal or whether it's rock music. We need to be reminded that they can't, or they shouldn't, apply the same techniques to such a vulnerable population in our society. I mean children *do* deserve special protection. Right

now we're just hoping that by articulating these concerns, and by the pressure of public opinion, we will get the desired reaction.

For example, Morris Day has already said: "Hey, because of the publicity about this issue, my next album is going to be cleaned up a bit. I am going to be sensitive to younger kids. I'm not going to be quite as explicit." Are you familiar with him?

CN: He's with the Time, the band put together by Prince, isn't he?

GORE: Well, he did an album called *Ice Cream Castle*, and there was a hit from it on the radio called "Jungle Love," which was fine; there's nothing wrong with that song. But if you like that, and you go and you buy the Morris Day and the Time album *Ice Cream Castle*, which a lot of eleven, twelve, thirteen year olds did, you got a song called "If the Kid Can't Make You Come," which is a sexually explicit song. We think that what he is doing is ideal. He's doing it on his own in response to the publicity about the issue. It's got him thinking about the fact that lots of younger kids do like his stuff and do buy his stuff, and maybe it's not really appropriate to have songs quite that explicit available to them. And he's deciding that himself in saying that he's going to clean up his next album.

CN: How widespread is this attitude? Is this something you feel that a lot of performers are going to be more conscious of now?

GORE: I would hope so. What you expressed in one of your questions, maybe some of them will say, "Well, I don't care, and I'm just going to be more explicit in my next album." Of course if that's their reaction, then so be it. But at least put on a warning label telling the person in the marketplace that it is explicit. That's the whole focus of our organization: just to know. Because many people, unless they can keep up with every group, are buying these things for their kids and finding out at home after they've played it that it's not appropriate for them. They would like to make that decision in the marketplace, and all you need to do that is just that kind of information.

CN: One last question, how did you come by the nickname Tipper?

GORE: Well, when I was young my mother gave me that nickname. It was supposed to be temporary, because Mary Elizabeth is my name and it is rather long, so she thought Tipper was kind of cute and shorter for somebody that was about a year old and that she would go back to calling me Mary Elizabeth. But that just never happened. It's a temporary nickname that stuck like thousands of others that people have gotten stuck with.

SOURCES:

PERIODICALS

Chicago Tribune, September 23, 1985.
Detroit Free Press, November 2, 1985, November 5, 1985.
Detroit News, October 9, 1985.
High Fidelity, December, 1985.
Los Angeles Times, November 2, 1985.

Los Angeles Times Calendar, August 25, 1985, November 10, 1985.

Maclean's, October 14, 1985, October 21, 1985.

Musician, December, 1985.

New York Times, October 13, 1985.

People, September 16, 1985, November 4, 1985.

Rolling Stone, September 12, 1985, September 26, 1985, October 10, 1985, November 7, 1985.

Time, September 30, 1985.

U.S. News & World Report, August 26, 1985, October 28, 1985.

Washington Post, September 15, 1985.

—Sketch and interview by Michael L. LaBlanc

Chester Gould

1900-1985

OBITUARY NOTICE: Born November 20, 1900, in Pawnee, Okla.; died of congestive heart failure following a long illness, May 11, 1985, in Woodstock, Ill. Cartoonist. The creator of "Dick Tracy," Chester Gould was considered a pioneer in the field of the cartoon comic strip. Gould demonstrated his talent and interest long before the debut of his most famous character. At the age of twelve he won his first cartoon contest; while in high school he enrolled in a cartoon-art correspondence course. Gould was a cartoonist for the *Tulsa Democrat* and the *Oklahoma City Daily Oklahoman* before moving to Chicago to attend Northwestern University. Upon graduation in 1923, he joined the staff of the *Chicago American*, where he introduced "Fillum Fables," a comic strip satirizing Hollywood movies of the day. In the spring of 1931 he created the hawk-nosed, square-jawed detective that was to become his trademark. Gould drew his character with the picture of a young, modern Sherlock Holmes in mind. He sold the series, which he had titled "Plainclothes Tracy," to the *Chicago Tribune-New York Daily News* Syndicate. Joseph Patterson, publisher of the *New York Daily News*, rechristened the strip "Dick Tracy," deriving the first name from the slang word for detective. "Dick Tracy" premiered on October 4, 1931, in the *Detroit Mirror*.

Gould's inspiration came from his, and the general public's, frustration with Prohibition-era gangsters and crime. Gould wanted to create "a symbol of law and order, who could 'dish it out' to the underworld exactly as they dished it out—only better,"he explained in *Comics and Their Creators*. "An individual who could toss the hot iron right back at them along with a smack on the jaw thrown in for good measure." Yet "Dick Tracy" proved to be more than a vent for public frustration. It became the first successful, present-day adventure comic strip. Unlike his predecessors, Gould treated topical issues and set his stories in modern locales; he was the first cartoonist to depict—sometimes graphically— urban violence. Moreover, the series introduced the average reader to the concepts of two-way wrist radios, closed-circuit television, space shuttles, and heart transplants.

The strip's most popular feature, however, has been its panoply of characters, from the moody but devoted Tess Trueheart and the dull but faithful Pat Patton to such villains as B-B Eyes, Mumbles, Flattop, and Peaches de Cream. Gould received numerous awards and citations for "Dick Tracy," including the National Cartoonists Society's Reuben Award and the Mystery Writers of America's Edgar Award. He retired in 1977, leaving the comic strip to his proteges Dick Locher and Max Collins. "He pioneered our

AP/Wide World Photos

field," Locher told Wes Smith and Kenan Heise of the *Chicago Tribune*. "You could walk into his pictures and be part of his strip. When Gravel Gertie talked to B.O. Plenty, you could smell [him], and when he spit tobacco, you wanted to jump out of the way."

SOURCES:

BOOKS

Horn, Maurice, editor, *The World Encyclopedia of Comics*, Chelsea House, 1976.
Sheridan, Martin, *Comics and Their Creators*, Hyperion Press, 1971.

PERIODICALS

Chicago Tribune, May 12, 1985, May 13, 1985.
Newsweek, May 20, 1985.
Time, May 20, 1985.

Donald Graham

1945-

PERSONAL: Full name, Donald Edward Graham; born April 22, 1945, in Baltimore, Md.; son of Philip L. (a newspaper executive) and Katharine (a newspaper executive; maiden name, Meyer) Graham; married Mary L. Wissler (an attorney) January 7, 1967; children: Liza, Laura, William, Molloy. *Education:* Harvard University, B.A., 1966.

ADDRESSES: Home—Washington, D.C. *Office*—The Washington Post Co., 1150 15th St. N.W., Washington, D.C. 20071.

OCCUPATION: Newspaper executive.

CAREER: Metropolitan D.C. Police Department, Washington, D.C., patrolman, 1969-70; *Washington Post*, Washington, D.C., reporter, advertising salesman, and night production manager, 1971-74, assistant managing editor, sports, 1974-75, assistant general manager, 1975-1976, executive vice-president and general manager, 1976-79, publisher, 1979—; member of board of directors, The Washington Post Co. Reporter and writer for *Newsweek* magazine, 1973-74; member of board of directors, American Press Institute, 1976, and Bowaters Mersey Paper Co. Ltd.; trustee, Federal City Council, 1976. *Military service:* U.S. Army, Air Cavalry, 1967-68; served in Vietnam.

MEMBER: American Antiquarian Society, Phi Beta Kappa.

SIDELIGHTS: Having grown up as the heir apparent to the *Washington Post* media empire, Donald Graham finally assumed the title of publisher in January, 1979. Graham had trained long and hard at the *Post* for his opportunity. He had covered news and written headlines, sold ads and overseen production during the bitter 1975 strike. He had unbundled newspaper at 3 a.m. He had even worked for more than a year as a foot patrolman for the Washington, D.C., police in order, he said, to learn the city's grittier realities. He has instituted few changes thus far as publisher. Rather, he has hewn to the course steered by his predecessors: his mother Katharine, his father Philip, and his grandfather Eugene Meyer. At the *Washington Post*, family tradition is more than merely the backdrop for what Graham calls "the best job in the world." It is, rather, the yardstick—the standard for measuring success—against which everything the publisher does must be judged.

The paper's executive editor, Benjamin Bradlee, told *Esquire* magazine that "things are going well for Don here. The paper is making more money than it ever did when Katharine ran it. We reached our circulation penetration goal for 1990 last year [1984]." The *Post*'s operating income has risen from $35.4 million to $94.6 million since Graham took over, and The Washington Post Company's annual revenue has jumped from $593.3 million to $984.3 million.

AP/Wide World Photos

The *Post* has solidified its position as a reliable and sophisticated chronicler of the capital's political machinations, has strengthened its business coverage, and has survived a scandal in which a Pulitzer Prize-winning feature article was discovered to be a fabrication. At the same time, Graham has emerged as one of Washington's most influential players despite his carefully maintained low profile and preference to stay out of power politics. He currently stands first in line to follow his mother and run The Washington Post Company, the parent company of the *Post*, a media conglomerate that owns such holdings as *Newsweek* magazine. Yet his attention seems squarely focused on the newspaper, as it has been since he became publisher.

Donald Graham is the fourth family member in three generations to publish the *Post*, which his grandfather bought in 1933 and turned over to Donald's father, Philip, in 1945. Raising the family, including older sister Sally and two younger brothers, was Katharine's job, as Philip devoted his hours to the newspaper, political maneuvering, and—more and more—fighting off his private demons. Dinners at home were frequently taken in the company of the country's chief decision-makers: Roosevelt New Dealers in the thirties and forties and, during Graham's childhood and adolescence, the Kennedy inner circle. Graham's summer reading list was compiled by national columnist Joseph Alsop; a school paper on the Supreme Court meant giving Justice Felix Frankfurter a phone call.

Throughout childhood and youth, the *Post* cast a long shadow over Graham's life. He was nine years old when his grandfather bought out the morning competition and, according to *New York* writer Maureen Orth, remarked, "The real significance of this event is that it makes the paper safe for Donny." The three Graham brothers attended St. Albans, and all wrote for the school newspaper. Don manifested "an intense interest in journalism," his younger brother Bill recalled years later to Toby Thompson in an *Esquire* article. Elsewhere in that article, Katharine Graham reminisced: "Journalism was what [Donald] liked. So I guess there was an assumption that since that's what he wanted to do, that's what he would do."

As an undergraduate at Harvard, Graham delved deeper into journalism, learning the production and the financial sides of the business. There were summer internships, including one under *New York Times* Washington bureau chief James Reston. During his senior year Graham ran the *Harvard Crimson*, an independent daily that had repeatedly closed every year in the red. Under Graham it turned a $27,000 profit. Yet back home reaction to this achievement was mixed. Katharine Graham recalls her husband urging their son to learn other fields besides newspaper publishing.

If the son had been inclined to muse over this ambivalent response to his precocious publishing success, any such tendency disappeared after August 3, 1963. That day Philip Graham put a shotgun to his head and pulled the trigger. The publisher had been under psychiatric treatment for the past six years or more, and at the time he was home on leave from a psychiatric hospital. According to *Esquire*'s Toby Thompson, Philip Graham "was depressed. In recent years he had drunk heavily, flaunted a series of public romances, and stormed against Meyer [his father-in-law], Kay and the children." Classmates recall the impact the tragedy had on Donald, then eighteen. "People will tell you about a wall, a shell—that's when I first noticed it," Marty Levine, managing editor of the *Crimson* when Graham was its president, told Maureen Orth of *New York* magazine. Orth also interviewed a former *Post* managing editor, Alfred Friendly Sr., who recalled trying to offer support: "I wanted to do whatever I could as a substitute father." But, Friendly said, Graham remained distant.

Donald Graham was something of an enigma to his classmates. "Analyzing Graham became almost an intramural sport at Harvard," Levine quipped. His right-of-center political attitudes left him targeted for teasing; classmates gave him a live hawk during his valedictory dinner as *Crimson* president. Graham's attitudes, points out Thompson in her *Esquire* profile, were formed after listening firsthand to the opinion of his father's chums, the architects of U.S. foreign policy. Writes Thompson: "What had been Kennedy's war was now Johnson's, and Johnson had been Phil Graham's man. Don knew Kennedy, McNamara, Mac Bundy, and the rest; they were guests at his parents' table."

Donald Graham graduated from Harvard and—noticeably out of step with much of his generation—promptly enlisted

in the army to serve in the Vietnam War. He reported to Fort Bragg and later was assigned to a Nike missile base near Pittsburgh. Then he was shipped to Vietnam as an information specialist with the First Air Cavalry. His duty was to churn out upbeat, "Our Boys In Service" copy for hometown newspapers. Privately, he says, his disillusionment raged. "My view of the war changed totally the day I got there," he asserted to *Esquire*.

Graham left the service to find that his mother was hardly waiting to hand over the reins of the *Post*. Upon the death of her husband, Katharine Graham had assumed the corporate suite on the eighth floor, and under her management, the business was flourishing. Rather than beginning his apprenticeship at the newspaper, Graham chose to work for the Metropolitan D.C. Police Department. In an interview in *Gentleman's Quarterly*, he recalled the year 1968: "The Washington riot had just taken place. I had been away for six years, and I knew that I did not know enough about what life in this city was all about. I thought about working in one of the local poverty programs, where the demand for young, well-meaning whites. . . wasn't very high. I thought about being a teacher, but there were some pretty severe requirements for teaching credentials. The police, though, were desperate for people." It began on a shaky note—Thompson notes that the lieutenant introduced him as "Donald Graham, who graduated from Harvard." Yet co-workers recalled that he was accepted quickly. Graham still values the experience highly, saying it taught him about day-to-day realities far outside his previous personal experiences. The precinct he patrolled was the Ninth, a tough one, and he patrolled it on foot.

In January 1971 Graham turned in his badge and reported for work at the family business. His mother was still distressed, this time because he chose to start as a city reporter. She would have preferred him to work on the business side and felt that he already had enough news experience. As Graham explained to Thompson: "She was always pushing me to move up in the hierarchy before I wanted to. I had come off the police force feeling very strongly that the place to learn about an organization is at the ground level."

Despite his democratic declarations, Graham still faced an uphill struggle convincing *Post* employees that he was not just a well-heeled blueblood claiming the publishing empire through primogeniture. Yet co-workers discovered that he seemed to know everyone by name and know everybody's spouse by name, too. As he had on the police force, he quickly eased resentment. "Don worked hard around this building and earned people's respect and friendship." Meg Greenfield, then deputy editor of the editorial page, told *Esquire*.

As a reporter, Graham covered a police beat, reviewed novels, wrote a series on alcoholism, and reported on political events. He got the plum job he had long coveted: he was made sports editor. (According to Thompson, Graham calls that "my one glorious year.") He kept moving up the ladder, training in various departments. He handled home circulation, sold advertising, worked in accounting, and did news makeup. By 1975 he was assistant general manager. That was the year of the pressmen's strike, an event his mother called a war, which proved to be his baptism by fire.

Approximately $200,000 damage was done when the strike began in October; a foreman was beaten; Katharine's figure was burned in effigy; and at one point a sign was hoisted proclaiming "Phil Shot The Wrong Graham." "It was hard mentally, emotionally, psychologically," Graham told Maureen Orth. "I remember the first day and the last day. The rest is a kind of blur." Insiders remember Graham sleeping nights in his office, losing twenty pounds, and putting out the newspaper with a skeleton crew. Orth quotes an unidentified executive as saying, "After the strike, Don no longer simply inherited the paper, he had earned it."

Ben Bradlee remembers Katharine Graham fretting over the timetable by which she would install her son in the publisher's chair. "I think Donnie was dying to be publisher but he would have deferred to her for years," Bradlee told *New York.* "It's not in his nature to rebel." Announcing the changing of the guard to *Post* employes, writes Thompson, Graham declared: "Today, as in the rest of my life, my mother has given me everything but an easy act to follow." Katharine—whom he calls Kay—remains active as president of the newspaper's parent company and is routinely consulted on prospective changes and political endorsements.

While insisting that he is open to change and desirous of continually improving working conditions at the *Post,* Graham is seen as loathe to change a philosophy and business strategy that clearly has been working. Whatever changes he has brought with him have been more evolutionary than revolutionary. "If you came on as publisher of *The Washington Post* and your first instinct was to put your imprint on it, or to do something to make it fundamentally different so that people would say that you did it, you would have to have a screw loose," he told *Business and Real Estate Washington.* Yet there have been changes, of course, beginning in 1978 with his first major decision: to remove Phil Geyelin as editorial-page editor. Yet what truly served notice of the young publisher's arrival was his outmaneuvering of Time Inc., which had purchased his floundering rival, the *Star,* a year earlier, promising to bankroll the paper into fiscal solvency. The *Star* folded despite Time Inc.'s, resources, and the *Post* picked its bones for staff, circulation and advertising. It seemed an echo of Graham's grandfather's merger of the *Post* with the *Times-Herald,* the merger "that made the *Post* safe for Donny."

There have been a few blemishes on Graham's tenure as publisher, most noticeably in 1981 when a Pulitzer Prize-winning story by Janet Cooke was discovered to have been fabricated. The paper also apologized formally to President Carter that year for publishing an unfounded rumor about him. Yet the overall assessment by media watchers is that the *Post*'s influence has been increasing among a readership that is already considered the most elite of any daily.

Graham elaborated on his publishing philosophy in an interview with the *Washington Journalism Review*: "I have always seen the *Post* as trying to serve an intelligent, sophisticated audience that wants complexity, details in what it reads in its news coverage, while remaining a mass newspaper. Plainly, the *Post* readership is heavily influenced by the fact that Washington is a government town." To an interviewer from *Business and Real Estate Washington,* he summarized: "The basic job of a newspaper is to make sense of the world for its readers. The more a newspaper acts like a newspaper, the better a newspaper it's going to be. I think that if a newspaper starts thinking about how much clout it has, it's going to be distracted from its basic job. . . [which is] a completely honest report of the day's news."

Physically, Graham's appearance reminded former *Washington Post* writer Rudy Maza of a "faceless Washington bureaucrat; a dark-eyed, brown-haired man with country-and-western singer's sideburns down to his earlobes." Maureen Orth limns him as "wearing the uniform of regulation WASP: bright and enthusiastic in the face of huge responsibilities and far more ambitious than he lets on."

Graham is married to his Harvard sweetheart, the former Mary Wissler, a lawyer. There are four children: Liza, Laura, William, and Molloy, ranging in age from infancy to early adolescence. Graham shuns the Washington social circuit, although his mother is an "A" list regular. "Mary and I try—and fail, in all honesty—to spend three out of five nights a week at home having dinner with the kids," he told *Gentleman's Quarterly.* "I'm usually [working] one or two nights a week. I try to leave for home by 5:30 or 6." He takes the bus to and from work and often surprises new *Post* employees who are shocked to learn their boss commutes by public transportation.

SOURCES:

BOOKS

Halberstam, David, *The Powers That Be,* Knopf, 1979.
Kelly, Tom, *The Imperial Post,* Morrow, 1983.

PERIODICALS

Business and Real Estate Washington, October, 1980.
Business Week, September 22, 1980.
Esquire, April, 1985.
Forbes, September 29, 1980.
Gentleman's Quarterly, January, 1984.
New York, August 27, 1979.
New York Times, January 10, 1979, January 11, 1979, June 26, 1984.
Time, November 2, 1981.
Wall Street Journal, April 19, 1982.
Washingtonian, September, 1980, May, 1981.
Washington Journalism Review, April-May, 1979.

—Sidelights by Warren Strugatch

Amy Grant

1961(?)-

PERSONAL: Born c. 1961 in Augusta, Ga.; daughter of Burton (a radiologist) Grant; married Gary Chapman (a musician and songwriter), June, 1982. *Education:* Attended Furman University and Vanderbilt University.

ADDRESSES: Home—Nashville, Tenn. *Office*—c/o A & M Records, 1416 North LaBrea, Los Angeles, Calif. 90028.

OCCUPATION: Singer.

CAREER: Vocalist and recording artist, 1976—; has performed in concert throughout the United States and abroad.

AWARDS, HONORS: Four Grammy Awards, including one for gospel album of the year, 1983, for *Age to Age*, and one for female gospel vocalist of the year, 1985, for *Unguarded*; five Dove Awards from Gospel Music Association.

DISCOGRAPHY:

RECORD ALBUMS; PRODUCED AND DISTRIBUTED BY WORD RECORDS, EXCEPT AS INDICATED

Amy Grant, 1976.
My Father's Eyes, 1977.
Never Alone, 1978.
Amy Grant in Concert, 1979.
Amy Grant in Concert II, 1980.
Age to Age, 1983.
A Christmas Album, 1983.
Straight Ahead, distributed by A & M Records, 1984.
Unguarded, distributed by A & M Records, 1985.

SIDELIGHTS: Courting the fifteen- to thirty-year-old-record-buyer, who is the archetype consumer of pop music, Christian rock singer Amy Grant has launched a crusade to expand her audience by trying to move her albums from the record-store purgatory known as the "Religious" bin to the commercial heaven of the "Rock" and "Pop" categories. Backed by a producer and a manager who share her faith in the mass market, Grant's crusade has racked up a line of impressive marketing victories. The breakthrough year was 1984, when she sold out Radio City Music Hall in New York City, performed before half a million fans overall, and grossed $1.3 million. And her message still focuses on Jesus, although the evangelism has been softened to allow the crossover into the mainstream to proceed as easily—and speedily—as possible.

Grant's music is known as "Christian contemporary," essentially white gospel music that, as *Rolling Stone* writer Michael Goldberg observes, "fuses spiritual lyrics to various types of pop and rock." Grant's career success marks the crest of a wave of popularity and market penetration for Christian pop-rock recordings. In 1984—at the start of

Grant's effort to cross over into mainstream markets—Christian record sales climbed over $75 million, surpassing the jazz and classical categories. Her album *Age to Age*, sold over a million copies; her 1985 release, *Unguarded*, flirted with a hard-edged trendy sound that Grant said, in a *Rolling Stone* interview, "would fit musically right between Madonna and Huey Lewis."

Grant sees herself as the performer who will bridge the gap between inspirational music and rock, and she is quick to refute charges from either side that she has compromised her principles to sell albums to the audience that supports such decidedly secular performers as Madonna and Michael Jackson. The Gospel Music Association has recognized her accomplishments with five Dove Awards, and the record industry establishment has given her three Grammy Awards. She received the most recent Grammy wearing the New-Wavish, leopard skin jacket she sported on the cover of *Unguarded*, thus announcing her intention to compete head-on with such pop idols as Madonna (who strips onstage to lacy underwear) and Prince (whose working togs are often comprised of a purple bikini). "I want to play hardball in this business," Grant told *Star* correspondent Angela Fox Dunn. "I'm trying to look sexy to sell a record. But what is sexy? To me it's never been taking my shirt off or having my tongue sticking out. I feel that a Christian young woman in the 80s is very sexual." The message, her husband and bandmate Gary Chapman adds, "is that it's OK to be a Christian and have fun."

Grant's blend of inspirational lyrics with a beat you can dance to got a massive boost in June 1985, when her record label, Word, signed an agreement with giant A & M Records (whose roster includes the band The Police among many other rock stars) to distribute select gospel artists. Grant's *Unguarded* LP was "launched in June with a marketing push that included posters, buttons, stand-up cardboards of the artist, saturation retail distribution, and a 40-date national summer tour," Robert K. Oermann reported in a profile in the *Tennessean*. For the first time in her career, major decisions were being made by people who were outside, as she puts it, "the family of God." She told Oermann: "The pop poster comes out, and I might not like it or see the point in it. But maybe the marketing group is saying, 'This makes sense! To you, a poster is embarrassing and mundane, but to a 13 year-old who values what you say and your songs, that is your credential.'"

Grant's credentials in the much more insular world of Christian music date back to 1976, when the Texas-based Word Records released her debut album on its Myrrh label. "It was," reported *Rolling Stone*, "an immediate hit in the Christian community, selling some 50,000 copies. From the start, however, her managers had an eye on the pop market. 'We never played many churches with Amy,' says [manager Dan] Harrell. 'That was the way everyone else had done it, and nobody had [successfully penetrated the mass market.]'" The singer got involved with the recording company at a time when music was just entering her life. A growing interest in Bible studies, coupled with a frustration at not being able to find songs that appealed to her, led to early songwriting efforts at the age of fourteen. Writer Richard Harrington, profiling the performer in the *Washington Post*, describes Grant as having pursued "her faith non-musically—she wasn't even in a choir. At one point she volunteered to perform at a vespers service, and a solid reaction from her fellow students convinced her to continue."

Grant's first job in the recording studio consisted of sweeping the floor and demagnetizing tapes. Being at the right place at the right time, Grant used the facilities to make a tape of her original compositions, while she played accompaniment on her guitar. "I made the tape for my parents," she recalled in an interview with *Family Weekly*. "And without my knowing it, someone called Word Records took the tape, and Word Records said, hey, this is contemporary Christian music. I didn't know what I was doing was contemporary Christian music. Then they called me and said, 'We want you to do an album.' And I thought it was a practical joke. We never thought it would go anywhere. We were probably five or six albums into it when I realized, hey, you know, I'd kind of like to do this as my life."

For the next few years, Grant was kept busy trying to juggle her education and her blossoming recording career. She attended Harpeth Hall girls' prep school, then majored in English literature at Furman University in South Carolina. She transferred to Vanderbilt University but dropped out in

her senior year to marry songwriter Gary Chapman, whom she had met after hearing a cassette tape of his song "Father's Eyes," which she recorded herself not long after. The two met in person at an industry gathering in 1979 and began dating. Today Chapman plays rhythm guitar in her ten-piece touring band.

At first, Grant played churches: just herself, her voice and her guitar. She recalled how she felt leaving that context in an interview in the *Gavin Report*: "The only time I felt myself changing was when I got my first band, then I quit playing churches. But it wasn't a moral decision. It's just that churches are built for a man to stand on a pulpit and to speak and be heard. You get eight people up there with amplifiers and everything else and it doesn't sound good. So we made a decision based on a musical problem and some people say, 'Oh, no!' And that's when it can appear that you're trying to be a maverick." Grant's managers (including Harrell, her brother-in-law) began suggesting that interested churches sponsor the band in a civic hall or at colleges. "It was helpful for all of us to meet on neutral territory," Grant asserted in the *Gavin Report* interview.

Even though a performer's career is often seen as a succession of album releases, Grant's has been an evolving effort to meet the American record-buying public in the pop music arena. Richard Harrington quoted her self-evaluation at the time of the release of *Unguarded*: "[Although] I don't want to sound like everybody else, I [do] like what's happening musically. I want to be relevant." Critical opinion of just how "relevant," and how musically innovative, her music has been have been varied. Early reviewers placed her voice in the Olivia Newton-John/Carol Carpenter/Carole King style. When Grant made her effort to slide into the pop categorization, one critic, Bryan Munson of the *Houston Post*, found it "hard to understand what all the fuss over her cross-over is about. Grant's voice has never been better and her lyrics still reflect the same honest approach to her faith in God they always did. Gone is the shy, tentative singing she displayed on her first album, and in its place is a mature Christian voice that deserves to be heard by everyone. The beauty of Grant's music, he added, "has always been her emphasis on living your faith and dealing with the realities of life at the same time."

Mainstream critics have, in general, been sparser in their praise, possibly because Grant's music is aimed at a different sensibility than their's. Bob Claypool, music critic at the *Houston Post*, described *Unguarded* as "an extremely well-produced—in fact, overproduced—product that trots out virtually every pop-rock cliche imaginable. There's some very good stuff here, but it certainly isn't very adventurous as pop music—sort of the middle of the middle of the road." Concerning the lyrics, he found that "Grant's testifying is very subtle and intentionally veiled in places. The name of Jesus does not crop up very often, and unless a listener pays very close attention, he'd think these were merely secular love songs." Indeed, some are, including one love song for her husband.

Grant says that the purpose of her music is not necessarily to proselytize—a concept that causes brows to furrow in some of the more conservative elements of the born-again Christian world. "For me," Grant declared to Harrington of the *Washington Post*, "the best way to communicate is to be available emotionally to the mainstream and to realize that everybody is human. Whether or not you believe in God or in Jesus there is a fellowship of man that often the church tends to ignore. It's a fellowship of people, and Jesus often referred to the family at large, brothers and sisters of any kind. Sometimes we [evangelical Christians] alienate ourselves, become exclusive and say we're better."

Born in Augusta, Grant was raised in a Nashville family that attended services regularly at the local Church of Christ; today she shies away from discussing the religious atmosphere in her parent's home. In his *Washington Post* profile, Harrington describes Grant's childhood as "comfortably middle class," as "one of the four daughters of a prominent Nashville radiologist. Her earliest musical experience was. . . singing stern old hymns at the local Church of Christ." Grant got both religious and musical training when she attended Harpeth Hall, an exclusive girl's prep school. Then one summer, away at camp, she was mesmerized by a fellow camper who played John Denver songs on the guitar. She cut her nails and convinced the friend to give her lessons. She's never had a formal music teacher. During her early teens Grant followed her older sister's boyfriend into his Bible study group. At first her intentions were somewhat short of sanctity. "He was oh, so cute, I thought: 'Honey, I'd go anywhere with you,' " she confessed to Bob Niedt of the Syracuse Herald *American Stars Magazine*. The apparent sincerity of the group members, however, changed her way of thinking. "The way they talked, it seemed they knew God was listening. I flipped. This is what my insides were aching for. I thought, I want my Christianity to be a living, thriving thing."

Her original audience, now dwarfed by millions of rock listeners who share their most successful musical emissary, sometimes complains that Grant has forgotten the evangelical roots of their community. Critics from church publications have charged that she "softsells Jesus." Grant responded in *The Washington Post* that "love (and not just love for Jesus) has value. If we could get over that hump in our songwriting we could still communicate Christ." Grant

insists that her music can fill the need that teenagers and young people have for the rebellious element of rock without encouraging drugs or premarital sex. She told *Rolling Stone* that following a studio listening session of the *Unguarded* material, she proclaimed: "What we're trying to do is take Christian principles and make them understandable. Even if it doesn't say Jesus, it doesn't matter. For someone whose heart is open—some kid sitting in his room at night, lonely, just thinking 'My world is bleak'—that's the time we hope this record can say something deeper than, 'Hey, pull down your pants; I'm going to show you what love really is.' "

SOURCES:

PERIODICALS

Boston Phoenix, June 18, 1985.
Christian Herald, September, 1981, December, 1982, May, 1984, September, 1984.
Detroit News, July 24, 1985.
Esquire, November, 1985.
Family Weekly, August 11, 1985.
Gavin Report, June 7, 1985.
Houston Post, June 10, 1985.
Life, November, 1984.
Los Angeles Times, April 1, 1984.
Newsweek, August 19, 1985.
New York Times, April 8, 1984.
People, April 18, 1983, June 24, 1985.
Rolling Stone, June 6, 1985.
Star, August 13, 1985.
Stereo Review, July, 1985.
Syracuse Herald American Stars Magazine, June 16, 1985.
Tennessean, August 3, 1985.
USA Today, February 26, 1986.
Variety, February 29, 1984, November 14, 1984, December 12, 1984.
Washington Post, November 2, 1982, December 11, 1983, June 9, 1985.
Wilmington Journal, August 19, 1985.

—Sidelights by Warren Strugatch

Charity Grant
1974-

BRIEF ENTRY: Born 1974, in Iowa City, Iowa. American youth who stirred national controversy when she refused an award from a local club that bans women from its membership. Charity Grant was ten years old and in the fourth grade in 1984 when she was offered, and subsequently refused, the "good reading award" from the Coralville Noon Optimist Club, citing as her reason the organization's men-only membership policy.

This seemingly unremarkable act—the refusal by a ten-year-old of an obscure award given by a small club in Iowa—drew a surprising amount of national media attention and resulted in Grant receiving a great deal of mail, both pro and con, from around the country. A woman from West Virginia wrote to say that refusing the award was impolite and that Grant had displayed bad manners. Grant's response, according to *Ms.* writer Julie Gammack: "It's good she did that, she expressed how she felt. . . . That's her point of view." Grant also received crank calls, and some of her schoolmates teased her after the news stories started coming out. Grant says: "That's their problem. . . . They've got to be pretty insecure."

Overall, most of the response to the incident has been positive. Grant has received numerous letters from people—mostly women—praising her for her courage and for her sensitivity to discrimination. Her parents, too, have been supportive of her stand. They told Gammack that they feel this experience has made their daughter more "thoughtful" and "aware." Grant is convinced that by the time she reaches adulthood women will have attained equality. "I think that with all the women fighting for women's rights," she stated to Gammack, "discrimination will probably stop." In the future, Grant says, she intends to run for political office, "probably as a Democrat."

SOURCES:

PERIODICALS

Ms., January, 1985.

AP/Wide World Photos

Maurizio Gucci

1948(?)-

BRIEF ENTRY: Born c. 1948 in Florence, Italy. Italian fashion executive. Until September of 1985 Maurizio Gucci seemed the heir apparent to his family's prestigious fashion firm, the House of Gucci. The previous November he had been named president of the parent company, Guccio Gucci; located in Italy, and chairman of its American branch, Gucci Shops, Inc. He appeared to be the favorite of his uncle, Aldo Gucci, the family patriarch. He planned to modernize the organization, streamlining the firm's operations by creating divisions for each product, such as purses and shoes, and placing a new emphasis on marketing.

His plans were cut short when Aldo and two of his sons, Giorgio and Roberto, accused Maurizio of wresting control of the company by forging his late father's signature on a stocks document. Maurizio's father (Aldo's brother and business partner), Rodolfo, died in 1983, supposedly leaving his share of the fashion empire—fifty percent—to his son. Not so, according to Aldo and his sons, who have filed suit in Italy. They claim that Maurizio induced a secretary to forge Rodolfo's name on the bequest, making Maurizio majority shareholder (Aldo, Giorgio, and Roberto together own 46.6 percent of the company stock). An Italian judge has impounded Maurizio's shares pending a settlement of the case.

The Gucci's are not unused to such bitter family conflicts. One of Aldo's sons, Paolo, once the company's chief designer and vice-president, has filed a number of suits against his father. During one court hearing Paolo implied that the elder Gucci was guilty of tax evasion, which prompted an investigation by the Internal Revenue Service. In another case Paolo charged his father and brothers with assault, claiming that they beat him up when he tried to tape record a board meeting. Aldo's oldest son, Giorgio, now a loyal member of the clan, has also battled his father. As Uli Schmetzer of the *Chicago Tribune* notes, "For years the Gucci family rivalry has contained all the ingredients of a soap opera."

For his part, Maurizio Gucci seems to be taking this latest dispute in stride. In a press release, quoted by Schmetzer, he calls the charges levelled against him by his uncle and cousins "an evident expression of an organized personal

AP/Wide World Photos

attack, the scope of which is easily imaginable." *Address:* Gucci Shops, Inc., 685 Fifth Ave., New York, N.Y. 10022.

SOURCES:

PERIODICALS

Chicago Tribune, September 15, 1985.
Detroit News, September 29, 1985.
New York Times, August 11, 1985.
People, September 6, 1982.
Time, September 23, 1985.

Marvelous Marvin Hagler

1954-

PERSONAL: Name originally Marvin Nathaniel Hagler; legally changed in 1980; born May 23, 1954, in Newark, N.J.; son of Robert James Sims and Ida Mae Hagler; married Bertha Joann Dixon, June 21, 1980; children: Gentry, James, Celeste, Marvin, Charelle. *Education*: Dropped out of school in ninth grade. *Religion:* Baptist.

ADDRESSES: Marvelous Enterprises, Inc., P.O. Box 336, Brockton, Mass. 02403.

OCCUPATION: Professional boxer.

CAREER: Worked in a toy factory after dropping out of school at age fourteen; worked at a variety of jobs while boxing as an amateur; professional boxer, 1973—, World Boxing Association middleweight champion, 1980—.

MEMBER: World Boxing Association, U.S. Boxing Association, World Boxing Council, Kiwanis.

SIDELIGHTS: The place was a boxing ring in the parking lot of the Caesars Palace hotel and casino in Las Vegas, Nevada. The date was April 15, 1985, income tax day for most Americans and a payday in more ways than one for a bald, ambidextrous, Massachusetts-based boxer legally named Marvelous Marvin Hagler. By defeating Thomas Hearns with a third-round, technical knockout in a vicious middleweight boxing title defense that warm night at the gambling oasis in the desert, Hagler had earned not only a $5.7 million purse but also something less tangible and, perhaps to him, more precious. He'd finally earned, at the age of thirty and after fifteen years as a boxer, respect from the world of his sport, the admission of its intelligentsia that he was one of the best of his generation at his profession. In the immediate reaction after the bout, the national news media declared his victory over Hearns to be one of the most savage and exciting championship bouts of the modern era. "Without a doubt, this fight—which Hagler had predicted would be a 'war'—will be remembered, despite its brevity, as one of the great ring classics of recent years," the *Detroit Free Press* wrote. "A screaming throng of 15,128 roared from the opening bell to the finish as Hearns and Hagler traded awesome, crushing blows."

Until then, Hagler wasn't unanimously admired in the boxing world. Although a champion since 1980, he had scored an unimpressive victory over Roberto Duran on November 10, 1983, seventeen months before his bout with Hearns. Even though he had successfully defended his 160-pound, middleweight title against Duran, he did it with a fifteen-round decision, not a knockout. *Sports Illustrated* magazine had headlined its story, "Marvin Was Something Less Than Marvelous" and had said in the concluding paragraphs of its article, "The winner stepped out of the ring with $8 million and his image diminished."

AP/Wide World Photos

Before the fight with Hearns, Hagler told the *New York Times*: "I have a lot to prove. People have not been giving me the credit I deserve. Thomas Hearns has been lucky. He can make the big money, he can move to different divisions. But I can take anything Tommy Hearns can deliver. He's going to have to hit me with that ring post to knock me out. . . . This fight comes down to who can take the hardest shot, who can take the most punishment. I've been through the bumps and bruises and I don't think he has." Over the years, Hagler had been frustrated with his lack of recognition and the time he had to wait to get a title fight. According to a *People* report, Joe Frazier, the former heavyweight boxing champion, once told him that his biggest problems were "You're black, you're a southpaw and you can fight." Hagler, it seemed, was too dangerous for most talented boxers to risk fighting. "I used to think, 'What do I have to do, kill somebody to get the notoriety?,' " Hagler said in a *New York Times* interview. "It's a terrible thought, but what I learned is, you have to keep trucking, you have to keep the faith. This fight [with Hearns] is at the right time because I'm mature enough to want it, mature enough to handle it."

Although he had beaten Hearns to the canvas, Hagler had not escaped the bout without sustaining physical damage. In fewer than eight minutes of boxing, he had been hit by 94 of Hearns 166 punches. (He'd hit Hearns 96 times in 173 attempts). Moments after Hearns had been carried to his corner, Hagler stood for an interview in the center of the ring, blood streaming down his face from two cuts as his three-year-old daughter, Charelle, was handed to him. She wore a pink dress. Hagler lifted her into his arms, pointed out his wounds and said to her: "Hi, baby. See Daddy's boo-boos?" He resumed his interview with Home Box Office television by saying his future plan for the child compels him to do what he does. "I'm waiting to send her to school, to college one day," Hagler said as he kissed the baby and handed her gently back to her mother. "So I gotta keep it up. In ten years, who knows what the money will be to go to school?"

Hagler, although he has said he still wishes to pursue higher education, dropped out of high school in Brockton, Massachusetts, to pursue a career in boxing. He was born in Newark, New Jersey, the first child of Ida Mae Hagler and Robert Sims. His father left the family when Hagler was a child. Hagler also had a brother, Robbie, and four sisters, Veronica, Cheryl, Genarra and Noreen. His mother moved the family to Brockton after Newark's civil disturbances of 1967 and 1969. Hagler recalled the race riots in an interview with the *Detroit Free Press*. "It was funny," he said. "Like a free-for-all. Bunch of hatred. Lots of innocent people hurt. People walking into stores and taking things. Lot of bad feeling between black and white."

Hagler, in some stories, has been portrayed as one who did not mingle with other children. "Hagler was a fatherless loner who turned Ida Mae's back porch into a clinic for wounded birds and a coop for raising and training pigeons," *Sports Illustrated* reported. "A turtle lived on the fire escape, and to Ida Mae's dismay, Marvin even let it swim in the family tub." Hagler called the animals "Maybe the only friends I really liked. I was always by myself."

In 1970, he met his current boxing handlers, brothers Guareno (Goody) Petronelli and Pascuale (Pat) Petronelli, partners in a Brockton construction company. Goody is officially listed as the trainer, Pat as the manager. He first met the Petronelli brothers in Brockton when he was fifteen years old, and he first boxed professionally in Brockton in 1973, after winning fifty of fifty-two amateur fights. He also worked for the Petronellis, digging ditches and cutting down trees. Brockton is the hometown of former boxing champion Rocky Marciano, and the Petronellis had known him as a youth.

As a young fighter, Hagler was known as brash, and confident, and motivated, despite the small wages he earned at the time. In a *Sports Illustrated* article, Hagler told why he wanted a fight against Don Wigfall, another boxer from Brockton. The two had exchanged angry words at a party when Hagler was sixteen years old. When the men stepped outside to settle their differences, Hagler said he tried to take off his leather jacket. "Before I could get my jacket off, he'd decked me," Hagler said. "I rolled under a car, my jaw was swollen." In their official bout, three years later, at Brockton High School gymnasium, Hagler won a decision in eight rounds. "Every time I had the chance to put him out, I let

him back into the fight," Hagler said. "I whupped him, right in front of all the people who had seen him deck me that night." It was his fourth pro fight, and he earned $1000.

He lost two consecutive fights in 1976. One was to Bobby (Boogaloo) Watts, in Philadelphia. Two months later, Willie (the Worm) Monroe defeated Hagler in a ten-round decision. Hagler later defeated Monroe twice in rematches. Their third bout, on February 15, 1977, gave Hagler the confidence he would carry in later bouts. "That was the fight that made him," said Philadelphia promoter J. Russell Peltz. By his fiftieth bout, against Vito Antuofermo for the middleweight championship in 1979, he was called by his fans "the uncrowned middleweight champion of the world." Antuofermo retained his title that night on a draw, but after Antuofermo lost his title to Alan Minter, Hagler defeated Minter in London later that year for the title. Before the fight with Minter, Minter had been quoted in the British press as having said he wouldn't lose the title to a black man. Hagler bloodied Minter above both eyes, and the fight was stopped in the third round as Hagler dropped to his knees in thanks. When he defeated Minter, a shower of bottles and other debris fell on the ring. But when he arrived back home in Massachusetts, a crowd of 10,000 cheered for him at Brockton City Hall.

Hagler makes for an imposing physical figure. He is 5 feet, 9½ inches tall and about 160 pounds, and he has a 70-inch "reach." His body is lean and muscled. He has medium-brown skin and a Fu Manchu mustache. His head is shaved of hair. He has a deeply scarred right eyebrow, covered much of the time by sunglasses.

In 1982, he drove a white Cadillac Fleetwood Brougham with a license plate that said "CHAMP M.H." Instead of a horn, the car played a recording of the song "La Cucaracha." "It's good for the kids," he told the *Detroit Free Press*. Hagler has said he wants to take business courses, to be a movie star, and to appear in public-service messages on television aimed at young persons. His mother said she thought Hagler would grow up to be a social worker because "he loved little kids."

His regular training camp is in Provincetown, Massachusetts, a small town on the tip of Cape Cod. It is known for, among other things, its ocean location, its homosexual community, and its artistic sense. He prefers the traditional boxing training method of getting away from all distractions for a monastic existence before a big bout. The Petronelli brothers, who train him, call it "going to jail." "I get mean here," he told *Sports Illustrated*. "I've gotten meaner since I've become champion. They're all trying to take something from me that I've worked long and hard for, years for, and I like the feeling of being champ. There's a monster that comes out of me in the ring. I think it goes back to the days when I had nothing. It's hunger, I think that's what the monster is, and it's still there." In Brockton, at the door of his gym, a sign says "No women allowed." When he does his situps in training, his handlers play "Theme from Rocky" on a speaker system. At home, he sleeps in a bed with a blue velour bedspread and a gold headboard. He still raises homing pigeons. He trains by running five to fifteen six-minute miles each dawn in heavy electrician's boots. He has said his favorite color is red because "that's the blood color." He wears red boxing gloves. He is a left-handed boxer who

An elated Marvelous Marvin Hagler raises his arms in celebration after his victory over Thomas Hearns (left, being supported by the referee) in their world middleweight championship bout in Las Vegas, April 15, 1985. AP/Wide World Photos.

can switch his stance, a tactic that seemed to confuse Hearns in their showdown.

Hagler had entered the bout with Hearns with a career record of 60-2-2. Fifty of Hagler's victories had been achieved by knockout. He had not lost a fight since 1976, when he lost two consecutive bouts, the only two defeats of his professional career. Hearns was 40-1-0, with 30 knockouts. They had been scheduled to fight in 1982, but the bout was canceled when Hearns announced he had an injured finger. Hagler said often afterward that Hearns, more highly publicized and better-paid at that point, had avoided Hagler because of fear. When they eventually met, the bout lasted only seven minutes and forty-nine seconds.

Although Hearns didn't fall to the floor until the third round, Hagler may have won the bout in the first, when he began to get the best of Hearns, who had broken a bone in his right hand by hitting Hagler. A computer counted that 165 punches had been thrown in the round, 82 by Hagler, 83 by Hearns. "It was a sensational opening round," *Sports Illustrated* reported. "Both fighters were rocked during the violent toe-to-toe exchanges, and midway through the round the champion's forehead over his right eye was ripped open either by a Hearns right hand or elbow. With Hagler not

bothering with defense, Hearns went for the quick kill. His gloves became a red blur as he rained punch after punch on the champion's head—and it would prove his undoing." As Emanuel Steward, Hearns's manager and trainer, said later of Hearns, "He fought twelve rounds in one."

Despite the edge Hagler held going into the third round, Hearns still had a good chance to win due to the condition of Hagler's facial cuts. In the third round, referee Richard Steele called time out and asked Dr. Donald Romeo, the chief physician of the Nevada State Athletic Commission, to examine the cut on Hagler's forehead and another under the eye. He asked Hagler if he would be able to continue. "No problem," said Hagler. "I ain't missing him, am I?" Less than a minute later, Hearns had been chased across the ring, hit with a series of punches, and had landed, eyes rolling, on his back.

By mid-1985, his actions had convinced the skeptics. Among his earlier admirers is Reg Gutteridge, author of *The Big Punchers*. In the book, Gutteridge wrote: "Marvin Hagler can box or brawl ambidextrously, a consummate pro who destroys the belief of the misinformed boxing followers that the men of the eighties cannot match the old-timers. . . . The accuracy of Hagler's hitting has not been surpassed by any champion. . . . He destroys (opponents) with a versatility that not only hurts but also humiliates."

SOURCES:

BOOKS

Gutteridge, Reg, *The Big Punchers*, Hutchinson (London), 1983.

PERIODICALS

Detroit Free Press, April 23, 1982, April 16, 1985, April 17, 1985, March 11, 1986.
Detroit News, April 16, 1985.
Newsweek, January 1, 1979.
New York, November 14, 1983.
New York Times, December 1, 1979, December 2, 1979, February 17, 1980, April 18, 1980, September 28, 1980, June 16, 1981, October 5, 1981, October 31, 1983, October 21, 1984, October 22, 1984, December 14, 1984, April 14, 1985, March 9, 1986.
People, November 14, 1983.
Sports Illustrated, April 17, 1978, October 6, 1980, January 26, 1981, June 22, 1981, October 18, 1982, November 8, 1982, February 21, 1983, June 6, 1983, November 21, 1983, November 14, 1983, April 8, 1985, April 22, 1985.
Time, November 21, 1983.

—Sidelights by Joe LaPointe

Margaret Hamilton

1902-1985

OBITUARY NOTICE: Born September 12, 1902, in Cleveland, Ohio; died of a heart attack, May 16, 1985, in Salisbury, Conn. Actress. Margaret Hamilton struck fear into the hearts of generations of children with her effective portrayal of the Wicked Witch of the West in the 1939 film version of L. Frank Baum's *The Wizard of Oz.* Her fame for this role is somewhat ironic, as in her private life Hamilton was known as a particularly gracious woman who loved children, even working for many years as a kindergarten teacher. Her first acting experience, a high school play, inspired her to make the stage her career. Her parents urged her to enter a more practical field, however, and she was trained as a schoolteacher. While teaching in Cleveland, Hamilton appeared in many productions at the Cleveland Play House. One of these, entitled "Another Language," went to Broadway where it enjoyed a one-year run, and when it was filmed in Hollywood in 1932, Hamilton traveled West to recreate her role, thus beginning an enduring career in motion pictures.

In over fifty years as an actress, Hamilton appeared in seventy-five films, one hundred plays, and countless radio and television broadcasts. Her razor-sharp features usually cast her in the part of the hard-bitten maid, the shrewish spinster, or the meddlesome town gossip. She was also seen in television commercials as Cora, the no-nonsense Yankee shopkeeper who only sold Maxwell House coffee. But despite her many other roles, the public continued to identify Hamilton most closely with the green-skinned witch who terrorized Judy Garland's Dorothy and her companions on the road to Oz. Aided by evil, winged monkeys, the witch cruelly mocked Dorothy's frightened cries for Auntie Em, hurled fireballs at the Scarecrow, and kidnapped the little dog, Toto, all in her quest to obtain Dorothy's ruby slippers. She was vanquished only when Dorothy accidentally splashed her with water, causing her to melt. This was probably Hamilton's most famous scene; she withered away into a specially-built trap door underneath her witch's gown, moaning, "What a world, what a world! Who would have believed an innocent little girl like you could destroy all my beautiful wickedness!" Hamilton turned down many offers to resurrect the witch in a sequel to "Oz," although she often appeared in stage versions of the musical. "Little children's minds can't cope with seeing a mean witch alive

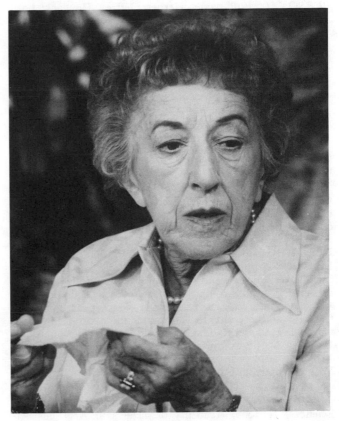

AP/Wide World Photos

again," she explained. "It's as though they think maybe I'm going to go back and cause trouble for Dorothy again."

SOURCES:

PERIODICALS

Chicago Times, May 18, 1985.
Los Angeles Times, May 17, 1985.
New York Times, May 17, 1985.
People, June 3, 1985.
Washington Post, May 17, 1985.

Herbie Hancock

1940-

PERSONAL: Full name, Herbert Jeffrey Hancock; born April 12, 1940, in Chicago, Ill.; son of Wayman Edward and Winnie (Griffin) Hancock; married Gudrun Meixner, August 31, 1968. *Education:* Attended Grinnell College, 1956-60, Roosevelt University, 1960, Manhattan School of Music, 1962, and New School for Social Research, 1967. *Religion:* Nichiren Shoshu Buddhist.

ADDRESSES: *Agent*—William Morris Agency, 151 El Camino Blvd., Beverly Hills, Calif. 90212.

OCCUPATION: Jazz pianist; composer; record producer; music publisher.

CAREER: First performed with Chicago Symphony Orchestra in 1952; while attending college, formed a big band, composed and performed music; played with various musicians in Chicago, including Coleman Hawkins; pianist with Donald Byrd group, New York City, 1960-63, and with Miles Davis Quintet, 1963-68; since 1968, has fronted his own sextet, quartet, and trio, played with a wide variety of musicians, and has composed music for record albums, film, and television; has performed in concert at numerous theaters and concert halls around the world, including Carnegie Hall and Radio City Music Hall. Owner-publisher, Hancock Music Co.; president, Harlem Jazz Music Center. Producer of record albums by a number of artists, including Wynton Marsalis.

MEMBER: National Academy of Recording Arts and Sciences, National Academy of Television Arts and Sciences, Jazz Musicians Association, Broadcast Music Club, Pioneer Club (Grinnell College).

AWARDS, HONORS: Citation of Achievement, Broadcast Music Club, 1963; Jay Award, *Jazz* magazine, 1964; *Down Beat* critics' poll, named Talent Deserving Wider Recognition, 1967, first place in piano category, 1968, 1969, 1970, composer award, 1971, named Jazzman of the Year, 1974; All-Star Band New Artist Award, *Record World*, 1968; named Top Jazz Artist, *Black Music* magazine, 1974; received awards from *Cash Box* and *Playboy*, 1974; Grammy Award for Best Rhythm and Blues Instrumental, 1984, for "Rockit"; received five awards in First Annual MTV Video Music Awards, including Best Concept Video and Most Experimental Video, all 1984, for "Rockit"; D.H.L., Grinnell College.

WRITINGS/DISCOGRAPHY:

RECORD ALBUMS; PRODUCED BY CBS RECORDS, EXCEPT AS INDICATED

Takin' Off, Blue Note, 1963.
My Point of View, Blue Note, 1963.
Herbie Hancock, Blue Note, 1964.
Empyrean Isles, Blue Note, 1964.

UPI/Bettmann Newsphotos

Inventions and Dimensions, Blue Note, 1965.
Maiden Voyage, Blue Note, 1966.
Speak Like a Child, Blue Note, 1968.
Blow Up (film score), MGM, 1968.
Mwandishi, Warner Bros., 1971.
Crossings, Warner Bros., 1972.
Sextant, 1972.
Headhunters, 1974.
Thrust, 1974.
Best of Herbie Hancock, Blue Note, 1974.
The Prisoner, Blue Note, 1974.
Succotash, Blue Note, 1974.
Fat Albert Rotunda, Warner Bros., 1974.
Treasure Chest, Warner Bros., 1974.
Live in Japan, 1975.
Water Babies, 1975.
Death Wish (film score), 1975.
Man-Child, 1975.
Secrets, 1976.
Live Under the Sky, 1976.
Kawaida, DJM, 1976.
Flood, 1977.
Herbie Hancock Trio, 1977.
Quintet, 1977.

V.S.O.P., 1977.
Sunlight, 1978.
Tempest in the Colosseum, 1978.
Feets Don't Fail Me Now, 1979.
In Concert, 1979.
Direct Step, 1979.
An Evening With Herbie Hancock, 1979.
Monster, 1980.
Mr. Hands, 1980.
Hancock Alley, Manhattan, 1980.
Magic Windows, 1981.
Lite Me Up, 1982.
Future Shock, 1983.
Sound System, 1984.

Has performed on numerous albums with a variety of musicians, including over a dozen with the Miles Davis Quintet.

OTHER

Composer of scores for films, including "Blow Up," MGM, 1967, "Death Wish," Paramount, 1974, and "A Soldier's Story," 1984; also composer of music for television program "Hey, Hey, Hey! It's Fat Albert."

SIDELIGHTS: With music as energetic and buoyant as the dismembered robots dancing in his smash "Rockit" music video, pianist and composer Herbie Hancock has paved a new road in electronic jazz, gathering along the way countless fragments of ideas from his work with other great jazz performers in the music industry. From his early days as a member of Miles Davis's jazz band in the 1960s to rapping out a beat for 1980s break dancers, Hancock's voracious appetite for experimentation with new ideas, effects and rhythms has fused a musical style that is both comprehensive and unique. In the words of *Musician* magazine, Hancock is "a man for all seasons, be they heavy or lighthearted, hip jazz or hip-hop, natural or digital."

Born on the south side of Chicago in the heart of blues and jazz country, Hancock first drew audiences at the age of eleven, performing a Mozart piano concerto with the Chicago Symphony. Later, he attended Grinnell College and Roosevelt University and by his early twenties had taken his musical talents to New York as a protege of trumpeter Donald Byrd. Byrd introduced Hancock to a select group of musicians recording for the Blue Note label, and Hancock found himself with a foot firmly wedged in the door leading to his goal to be a professional musician.

Hancock first gained prominence on the jazz music scene with the composition of "Watermelon Man," a piece combining gospel and funk that was made popular by Mongo Santamaria. The exposure from this hit earned Hancock the attention of jazz great Miles Davis, and in 1963, Hancock's talent and hard work were rewarded with a call from Davis, asking Hancock to join his quintet for a rehearsal. Hancock was asked back a second time, and then Davis asked him to play on a record the group was cutting entitled "Seven Steps to Heaven." Still wondering if he had a job or not, Hancock joined the band for recording sessions. "Miles told us we were going to do a record in two days. I was wondering what was going on—he hadn't even told me whether I was in the group or not," Hancock said in an interview with *Down Beat* magazine. When he finally asked

Davis whether his playing was good enough for a steady job with the group, Davis said, "You made the record, didn't you?" Although Hancock had been hired, he was not completely satisfied. "He had me jumping through the hoops," Hancock told *Down Beat*. For the next five years, those hoops encircled Hancock and kept him secure as Davis's only pianist.

Bringing imagination and new ideas to the Davis quintet, Hancock initiated a number of innovations in the group. Melodic constraints were loosened, and solos, themes and phrases would appear at one interval only to be echoed and perhaps subtly changed a few bars later. While Davis was the master and Hancock the pupil, Hancock's chordal accompaniments added a richness to the group that Davis found allowed for departure into new harmonies. As Hancock's style developed during his years with Davis, so did his musical ingenuity and a desire to incorporate several musical ideas into one. Hancock recorded several albums with the Miles Davis group, including *Miles in the Sky* and *Filles de Kilimanjaro*, and a new element began to filter into his music in the form of electric piano, the prelude to electronic jazz.

It was Hancock's fascination with the electronic piano that spurred him to spread his wings and emerge as a leader of his own band and creator of his own musical sound. He left Davis's group in 1968, and soon formed his Mwandishi band, which provided him with a firm yet flexible foundation for integrating synthesizers into his music. The result was a unique blend, quite different from Hancock's previous piano playing, yet still deeply rooted in his musical background. Hancock told *Down Beat* that "getting into synthesizers was a natural evolution for me, not only because I'm fascinated with the possibilities of creating new sounds and colors, but because I have a streak in me that loves electronics."

The journey into jazz-rock waters with the Mwandishi band also revealed a religious direction to Hancock that he incorporated into his life and his music. Hancock was converted to Nichiren Shoshu Buddhism and adopted Mwandishi, the Swahili word for composer, as his Buddhist name. Hancock said he was becoming a musical snob by not deeply involving himself in his music, and the devout practice of Buddhism gave him a "whole spectrum" to work with in his music. Hancock described to *Time* magazine the chanting that is integral to the religion as a low rhythmical prayer "you can do if you have a problem, or if you want something to happen or not to happen. It's you you are chanting to. It's just like adding fire to yourself."

Through reaffirming old rhythms as well as creating new ones, Hancock's music has evolved into a combination of rhythm and blues, jazz, funk, and even pop. He has embraced the musical ideas of such performers as Sly Stone, Marvin Gaye, Stevie Wonder and Earth, Wind, and Fire, and emerged with a hybrid style some call jazz rock, others call pop rock, and some followers call pure funk. Encouraged by the 1973 success of his *Headhunters* album, which produced the smash hit "Chameleon," Hancock became "convinced of the validity of fusion and its electronic future," wrote David Fricke in *Rolling Stone* magazine.

But Hancock found popularity fleeting and did not have an easy task maintaining the freshness of the *Headhunters* album that had made him a pop star. It was back to the drawing board of musical ideas for Hancock, who began experimenting with disco, rock, and television and film musical scores. He regathered elements of past success with reunions of former members of the Miles Davis quintet and called the new group the V.S.O.P. band.

The quintet members put aside leadership of their own bands to embark on a nationwide tour and spend some time in the studio recording songs. To both new and old fans, the group brought back the music that had made them popular and that retained its vitality over the years, some critics said. Wrote Conrad Silvert of *Down Beat* after hearing the group perform: "All five musicians were obviously savoring the occasion to play, as a unit, the music that was so much a part of their early careers, and the music which is as vital today as it was during its inception. But they were also a little piqued by critics who have insisted on drawing boundary lines between the jazz they played in the '60s and the music they're making today."

Pleasing the critics was not always easy for Hancock, who by branching into new musical styles and then weaving them into his music has disappointed some followers in the music industry who lament his departure from pure jazz. But Hancock told *Musician* magazine he could not have developed his career if he had written music to please critics or old fans clamoring for songs from his Miles Davis days. "People are no longer surprised when I come out with something different," Hancock said. "I've done it enough now. That's what I've wanted all this time."

But neither Hancock nor the critics were prepared for his startling fusion of synthesized funk and record scratching (rubbing the needle the wrong way) that catapulted him into the hearts, souls, and feet of break dancers and into popularity once again.

The 1983 *Future Shock* album contained the Top Ten hit "Rockit," which became the biggest-selling twelve-inch single in Columbia Records' history, according to *Rolling Stone*. Combining a driving beat with electronic special effects and jazz improvisations, Hancock created a record that both pleased and disappointed music critics but fed a portion of listeners ever-hungry for dance music. While Steve Futterman of *Rolling Stone* called *Future Shock* a "sterile, joyless album full of mechanical rhythms and digitally manipulated instruments and voices" and an "outgrowth of soul music" that is "soulless," *People* magazine said that the album "throbs with immediacy" and that "Hancock has caught up with what's happening in black dance music: electronics and the rhythms of rap."

"Rockit" won Hancock a Grammy Award, and also broke through into music video's early days with a video of dismembered robots jerking and dancing to the beat. The "Rockit" video swept the first annual Music Television (MTV) Awards, winning a total of five awards. It was Hancock's "scratch and funk" formula, combined with the inventive video, that helped him "regain his street edge," wrote Bill Milkowski in *Down Beat*.

Hancock's 1984 follow-up album, *Sound System*, contained many of the same ingredients that created success for *Future Shock* and added new musical flavors through Hancock's continuing experimentation with instruments and sounds. Milkowski said in *Down Beat* that although "aging r&b fans may be put off by all this cold-blooded technology," the *Sound System* album contains Hancock's blend of "something for everybody, at least on one cut, and all the parts fall neatly into place without calling undue attention."

Commissioned by ABC-TV to write the "Junku" selection from the *Sound System* album for the 1984 Olympic field events, Hancock told *Musician* magazine that he "wanted to do a piece of music that had an international flavor to it. I wanted to write something that had an ethnic undertone, with a kind of American thing on top." Although the intertwined ethnic rhythms might disappoint the jazz purists Hancock attracted in his days with Miles Davis, the musician is not bothered that old fans may not like the new Hancock. He prefers to maintain his interest in several music camps: jazz, pop, blues and rock. Although he admits a risk in losing part of his old following, Hancock has a love for all forms of music. He told *Musician* magazine's Bill Flanagan, "I decided a while ago that if there's any marriage, it's to music and not jazz. It's open-ended. I can do what I want. Since I like all kinds of music, why not play 'em?"

The electronic element that fuses all of Hancock's music together also represents his future. From the musician who majored in electrical engineering in college to the pioneer in electronic jazz, Hancock is anxious to have his fusion of musical forms accepted as an art form. Continually expanding his horizons as a musician, composer, performer and producer, Hancock has combined talents with fellow jazz pianist Chick Corea and trumpeter Wynton Marsalis on several occasions, as well as preserving performance ties with Miles Davis alumni.

Hancock's popularity has not gone unnoticed by the music industry, and he has gained recognition of his "potential as a media star," said Bill Flanagan in *Musician* magazine. "Hancock, a Nichiren Shoshu Buddhist who radiates bigger-than-life enthusiasm just walking into a room, is delighted to take his record company's advice about dressing sharp and projecting an 80s image," Flanagan writes. "Herbie Hancock's experience proves that rules are meant to be broken."

Breaking rules by mixing pop music with jazz has earned Hancock the title of "crossbreed," but he maintains that won't stop him from creating more musical hybrids. "When we have life, we have music. Music can be manifest in many different forms, and as long as they all have purpose they shouldn't be pitted against each other as one being more important than the other. That's stupid. That's like apples and oranges," Hancock told *Musician*. "I only feel musically fulfilled when I can do both."

SOURCES:

PERIODICALS

Down Beat, September 8, 1977, May 17, 1979, September, 1982, April, 1984, November, 1984.
Musician, January, 1985, March, 1985.

New York Times, May 22, 1983, July 6, 1983, August 31, 1983, November 9, 1983, August 29, 1984, September 1, 1984.
People, March 13, 1978, October 17, 1983.
Philadelphia Bulletin, April 12, 1984.
Rolling Stone, March 23, 1978, September 29, 1983, October 25, 1984.
Stereo Review, November, 1978.
Time, July 8, 1974.

—Sidelights by Amy C. Bodwin

Chris Haney
1949(?)-

Chris Haney (center) with co-inventors of Trivial Pursuit John Haney (left) and Scott Abbott. Courtesy of Chris Haney.

BRIEF ENTRY: Born c. 1949 in Canada. Canadian newspaper photo editor and inventor of Trivial Pursuit. While playing Scrabble together, newspaper reporter Scott Abbott and Chris Haney were inspired to invent a board game. In 1979, Trivial Pursuit was born, based on, as Haney says in *Esquire,* "the kind of questions we knew from being in the news business, being attuned to small details." Haney then enlisted his brother John, an ex-hockey player, to help organize their plans, and another friend, Ed Werner, to provide legal advice. By 1984 their invention had outsold all other board games two to one, and the inventors had pocketed $10 million each after taxes.

Targeted at "people like us"—according to Haney, the baby-boom generation—Trivial Pursuit combines modern-day love of disconnected facts and the desire to socialize. Trivial Pursuit has become a "cultural artifact,. . . buried in a time capsule along with Michael Jackson's Thriller album." Haney and crew have produced several editions now, including the original Genus I, Sports, Silver Screen, Baby-Boomers, and a new Genus II edition. But its creator, who almost suffered a breakdown trying to put the game together, is taking his success in stride. All he wants is to "go to Dorset and watch the sheeps."

SOURCES:

PERIODICALS

Esquire, March, 1985.
New York Times, January 15, 1984.
Time, September 3, 1984.

Patricia Roberts Harris

1924-1985

OBITUARY NOTICE: Born May 31, 1924, in Mattoon, Ill; died of cancer, March 23, 1985, in Washington, D.C. The daughter of a railroad-car waiter and a schoolteacher, Patricia Roberts Harris became the first black woman to serve as a U.S. ambassador and to hold a cabinet post. A graduate of Howard University and George Washington University Law School, Harris actively supported the civil rights movement, participating in sit-ins and other demonstrations while a student. From 1960 to 1961 she was a trial lawyer with the Justice Department. President Lyndon Johnson appointed her ambassador to Luxembourg in 1965, a position she held until 1967, when she returned to Howard University as a professor of law. Harris was named dean of the Law School in 1969, but she resigned that same year after a series of confrontations with students. In 1977, after seven years as a partner in a Washington law firm, Harris became secretary of Housing and Urban Development (HUD) under President Jimmy Carter, and from 1979 to 1980 she served as secretary of Health, Education, and Welfare (HEW).

Harris made an unsuccessful bid for mayor of the District of Columbia in 1982. Shortly before her death she was a professor of law at George Washington University. Harris received numerous awards and honorary degrees, including the Black Enterprise Achievement Award and LL.D.s from Tufts University, Johns Hopkins University, and American University. Frequently characterized as a diligent, shrewd, tough, and blunt-spoken administrator, Harris was credited with restoring order and direction to HUD and HEW.

AP/Wide World Photos

SOURCES:

PERIODICALS

Chicago Tribune, March 25, 1985.
Newsweek, April 1, 1985.
New York Times, March 24, 1985.
Time, April 1, 1985.

Christie Hefner

1952-

UPI/Bettmann Newsphotos

PERSONAL: Full name, Christine Ann Hefner; born November 8, 1952, in Chicago, Ill.; daughter of Hugh Marston (founder and publisher of *Playboy* magazine) and Mildred Marie (Williams) Hefner. *Education:* Brandeis University, B.A. in English literature (summa cum laude), 1974. *Politics:* Democrat.

ADDRESSES: Home—Chicago, Ill. *Office:* Playboy Enterprises, Inc., 919 North Michigan Ave., Chicago, Ill. 60611.

OCCUPATION: Publishing and entertainment company executive.

CAREER: Boston Phoenix, Boston, Mass., reporter, 1974-75; Playboy Enterprises, Inc., Chicago, Ill., special assistant to the chairman of the board, 1975-77, vice-president, 1977-82, president, 1982—, chief operating officer, 1984—. Member of board of directors, Playboy Foundation; member of national advisory board, National Women's Political Caucus.

MEMBER: American Civil Liberties Union (member of president's committee), National Organization for Women, Committee of 200, Brandeis National Women's Committee (life member), Economic Club, Phi Beta Kappa.

SIDELIGHTS: "She is simply the most remarkable twenty-nine-year-old I've ever met. We think very much alike." With these words, *Playboy* magazine founder and publisher Hugh Hefner explained his decision to turn over the day-to-day operations of Chicago-based Playboy Enterprises to his eldest child and only daughter, Christie Hefner. A Phi Beta Kappa graduate of Brandeis University, the personable and articulate young executive had enjoyed modest success during her seven years with the company, most recently as publisher of the magazine's consumer guides to fashion and electronic entertainment systems. Though her age and lack of experience made some observers doubt her ability to provide the type of management Playboy needed to rid itself of a potentially disastrous case of financial doldrums, Christie Hefner has since proven herself to be a savvy, candid, no-nonsense businesswoman.

Only ten years before, few observers would have guessed that a second Hefner would one day emerge to lead the Playboy empire. Hugh Hefner and his wife, Mildred, were divorced when Christie was still a baby. Very much involved with launching his new magazine, he rarely saw Christie or her brother, David, who lived with their mother and stepfather (whose surname they used at the time) in suburban Chicago. Even though Christie and her father got along well during their infrequent encounters, they were not especially close. Then, at the end of her junior year in college, Christie made an important decision. Newly elected to Phi Beta Kappa and facing the breakup of her mother and

stepfather's marriage, she made up her mind to reaffirm her connection to her father by once again using his name. As she explained to Lally Weymouth in *New York* magazine: "I guess the combination of the separation from my stepfather and the impending graduation and feeling very honored by the Phi Beta Kappa thing and knowing that I was going to have this certificate that I was always going to keep—somehow it combined in my mind to make me feel that this was maybe the time to go back to 'Hefner.' " Hugh Hefner was delighted and touched by her decision, and their relationship flourished.

After graduation, Christie got a job with an alternative Boston newspaper, the *Phoenix*. Though the thought had crossed her mind, she had not wanted to work for *Playboy*—at least, not yet. Being the boss's daughter, she told Weymouth, "if I turned out not to write very well, no one would tell me, and it would be this terrible embarrassment." When Christie was sure that she could indeed write, she quit her job in Boston and headed for Chicago and the *Playboy* offices. Though she had originally wanted to be involved in the creative process, she soon found herself gaining experience in a variety of other fields, including finance, management policy, marketing, and public relations.

Soon Christie discovered that she "enjoyed not just journalism but publishing." And gradually she began to believe that "rather than wanting to be involved in some part of the company. . . what I'd really like to do someday was run the company. And, simultaneously, I think my father increasingly became interested and intrigued with the possibility of having a second generation to take the company over. So while there was no moment when we sat down across the table and said, 'Okay, here's the plan,' increasingly he would make reference to my running the company someday. . . . And if people asked me was I the heir apparent, I would say, 'Well, yes, someday I do hope to run the company.' "

The company Christie Hefner was given to run that spring of 1982 when she became president was far from cash-poor, yet its future was shaky and uncertain at best. The 1970s had dealt several blows to the sprawling Playboy empire, namely a decrease in circulation (from a peak of 6.5 million in 1973 to slightly less than 5 million in 1980) and multi-million dollar losses in various affiliated ventures (movie theaters, hotels, clubs, and television productions). Hugh Hefner, characteristically slow to act in such situations ("business doesn't light my fire," he has often admitted), did not make a move to stem the tide of these losses until 1976, when he hired former Knight-Ridder Newspapers vice-president Derick Daniels to restore order and profits to Playboy Enterprises. Daniels immediately set out to shed some of the unprofitable parts of the empire, including the record division and the movie theaters; he also trimmed the corporate staff by more than one hundred employees.

Soon the magazine began to bounce back, and with hefty profits from the Playboy gambling casinos in Great Britain continuing to roll in as they had throughout the 1970s (accounting for about 80% of the company's profits), Hugh Hefner was lulled into a false sense of security. Losing propositions such as the book publishing division, resort hotels, and the new magazine *Oui* (a venture designed to compete with *Playboy's* racier rival, *Penthouse*), were subsidized by the millions brought in by the casinos. The number of employees swelled once again, partly to accommodate Daniels's detached style of management, a move he defended as necessary in order to give the company a more structured chain of command.

The bottom fell out of the reorganization effort in 1981, when two major defeats dealt a severe blow to Playboy's financial outlook. Amid charges of illegal corporate interference and violation of certain gaming laws, Playboy was forced to sell all of its British gambling operations after it was denied renewal of the required licenses. The repercussions of this scandal cast a shadow on the casino licensing hearings then in progress in Atlantic City, N.J., and Playboy eventually had its application for a license to run a casino there rejected by state officials.

Its gambling revenues suddenly gone, Hefner and Daniels were forced to deal quickly with high overhead costs and unprofitable divisions. Early in 1982, they sold the book publishing arm of Playboy Enterprises as well as several resort hotels. Though cash reserves from such sales eventually totaled some $32 million (after all debts had been paid), morale at the company was low, and its chances for long-term financial success were unsure.

Into this near-crisis atmosphere stepped the boss's daughter. As perhaps no one else could or would, she told her father what had gone wrong with Playboy Enterprises, backing her declarations with figures showing that, had it not been for the gambling revenues, the company would have lost money steadily during Daniels's presidency—a fact of which the elder Hefner was unaware. By April, Daniels and Playboy had parted company. "He's done a fine job for us," said Hugh Hefner, attempting to dispel rumors of bitterness between them. "This just seemed like the right time for a change." Commenting on his daughter's promotion, he described it as "a natural transition. She has certainly been well prepared for this move." When asked to explain the nature of the new setup, he explained that "the major decisions—the destinations—will be largely established by me. Getting us there will be in the hands of Christie and the other executives."

One of the first problems Christie faced as the new president of Playboy was the apparent contradiction involved in having a woman serve as one of the chief officers of a company whose stock-in-trade is a magazine that features female nudity. An avowed feminist and supporter of various liberal causes, Christie denies that *Playboy* is a sexist publication. Although she is quick to point out that she has never had editorial control of the magazine (her father retains that, including the responsibility of choosing each month's centerfold and reviewing covers and cartoons), she does not believe it exploits women. In a 1983 speech to the Washington chapter of Women in Communications, she described herself in her role at Playboy as an oxymoron—a contradiction. "Like jumbo shrimp. Or for those who travel a lot, airline food. Some people think being a woman president of Playboy Enterprises is an oxymoron. Being president of Playboy is not as easy or ideologically pure as editing *Ms.* But. . .from my point of view it's not as hard as being a Republican woman right now." Besides, she went on to note, "no matter how you feel about erotic pictures, [Playboy is] a company that has a pretty good track record on women's issues."

The Playboy Foundation, the corporation's gift-giving arm, has supported a variety of groups and organizations, including the American Civil Liberties Union, the Institute for Policy Studies, and several national abortion rights and women's groups. Some praise the Hefners for their generosity; others regard it as "blood money" or an attempt at making reparations. As one California philanthropist observed in Weymouth's article, Hugh Hefner "wants it to appear what he's doing isn't sleazy—after all, he says, he's defending the First Amendment!"

For her part, Christie insists that the foundation sets an example in corporate contributions to worthy causes. "It's the issues Hef believes in—abortion, the First Amendment, gay rights, drug-law reform, police surveillance, and government misconduct," she explained to Weymouth. "Playboy has been more supportive of feminist politics and philosophies than most other companies I know of—in its attitude toward hiring and promotion of women, through its editorial and financial support of the Equal Rights Amendment and abortion. . . . I think people who make the leap that because it chooses to picture women as sexually attractive that that somehow goes hand in hand with thinking women are stupid, or women belong in the bedroom, are people who

Christie Hefner (left) with her father, Hugh Hefner, founder of Playboy Enterprises. AP/Wide World Photos.

are making a leap of faith that has nothing to do with anything that's in the magazine. . . . [Criticism from women's groups] seems like misplaced energy. I'm living in a country where the president wants to make abortion a crime, and some segment of the women's movement is suggesting that the major enemy in society is *Playboy*. I think that's crazy. If we don't all fight the real enemy, we're likely to lose what we've won in the last decade. If you don't want to look at the pictures, then don't buy the magazine."

In the years since she succeeded Daniels as president of Playboy Enterprises, Christie has worked swiftly and decisively to transform her father's company into a more efficient and profitable operation. Although she characterizes herself as being just like her father—"we have an uncannily similar sense of humor, of style, of analyzing problems," she once remarked in *Fortune*—she is very much *unlike* him in areas that matter most to the survival of Playboy. Notes Shawn Tully in another *Fortune* article: "Christie has a zest for spading deep to turn up facts and for reshaping the organization chart to make a business whir. In contrast to 'Hef,' she has an affinity for balance sheets, a tolerance for daylight office hours, and a gregarious personality. She also shows an admirable willingness to confront people and to fire and promote without years of soul-searching."

Under Christie's direction, Playboy has concentrated primarily on its best assets: the magazine itself and the solidly profitable licensing and marketing of products (ranging from clothing to golf balls) displaying the familiar bunny emblem. She has also invested much time and hope in the company's entry into cable and pay television, the Playboy Channel, a joint venture with a firm that already owned the satellite and other expensive equipment needed to offer such a service. ("We've already reinvented the wheel too many times," says Christie of her decision not to squander money on rampant diversification or risky new businesses.) Begun in 1982, the Playboy Channel, a station that features sex-oriented news programs, talk shows, and serials, now has more than 650,000 subscribers nationwide. Its progress has been slower than expected, however, due to the tendency of some cable operators to balk at the idea of offering it in certain communities and risk losing their licenses. Nevertheless, Christie is pleased that profitable spin-offs such as video cassettes, movies, and a hotel channel have enabled Playboy to devote more money to improving programming and (ideally) attracting more subscribers (one million is her goal).

On the management front, Christie's overall strategy for the immediate future is to grant more power and freedom to the division managers, reduce corporate overhead, and collect interest on the cash obtained from the sale of unprofitable enterprises. The company posted its first profit with Christie at the helm in the quarter ending December 31, 1983, prompting some to speculate that Playboy is on its way back.

As far as Christie is concerned, however, Playboy cannot yet declare itself in the clear. Though encouraged by the magazine's fairly stable circulation figures (4.1 million in 1983), the promising video operations (the cable television channel and home video cassettes), a new policy governing the dozen or so Playboy Clubs still in existence (establishing them as franchises rather than company-owned businesses), and the nearly $60 million in cash expected to filter in through 1990 (from the forced sale of its share of the Atlantic City casino), she is leery of making any extravagant predictions. "There's no upside in it," she told *Forbes* reporter Jill Bettner. "And if you're wrong, they nail you to the wall." Nevertheless, Christie Hefner seems comfortably ensconced in her executive position and cautiously optimistic about the future. "We're going to be much smarter than we were before," she said to Bettner. "We were a seat-of-the-pants company for years and years. Some of that worked out

very well. But when you back into a lot of businesses, the odds of getting winners are very low. . . . We've come through a very difficult time, but with our existing businesses and important new businesses, this is a company that ought to be growing dramatically the next couple of years. It has the resources to do it."

SOURCES:

PERIODICALS

Forbes, March 26, 1984.
Fortune, August 23, 1982, October 3, 1983.
Newsweek, May 10, 1982.
New York, June 21, 1982.
New York Times, March 25, 1984.
Time, May 10, 1982.
Wall Street Journal, February 21, 1984.
Washington Post, May 25, 1983.

—Sketch by Deborah A. Straub

Willie Hernandez

1954-

PERSONAL: Full name, Guillermo Villanueva Hernandez; born November 14, 1954, in Aguada, Puerto Rico; son of a sugar-cane worker and a housekeeper; married Carmen Rivera; children: Xavier, David, Guillermo.

ADDRESSES: Office—Detroit Tigers Baseball Club, Tiger Stadium, Michigan and Trumbull, Detroit, Mich. 48216.

OCCUPATION: Professional baseball pitcher.

CAREER: Pitched in minor leagues, 1974-76; drafted by Chicago Cubs, 1976, played with Chicago, 1977-82; traded to Philadelphia Phillies, 1982, played with Philadelphia, 1982-84; traded to Detroit Tigers, 1984, with Detroit, 1984—.

AWARDS, HONORS: Winner of Cy Young Award as best pitcher in American League, and named Most Valuable Player in American league, both 1984.

SIDELIGHTS: When Willie Hernandez won the Cy Young Award as the best pitcher in the American League in 1984 and the league's Most Valuable Player award, it was recognition that he had a season like few other pitchers in baseball history.

Hernandez is a left-handed relief pitcher who specializes in working only the last couple innings, when the game is on the line. In baseball jargon, he is known as a "stopper" or "short man." In 1984, Hernandez had 32 saves in 33 save opportunities, an almost-unheard-of statistic. He also had a very low earned-run average of 1.92, plus a 9-3 record and 112 strikeouts in 140 1/3 innings. He played a major role in the Detroit Tigers' capture of the World Series in a season that the team started by winning 35 of their first 40 games—a major league record. In the off-season, Hernandez continued to make news when he signed a contract that makes him one of the highest paid Tigers ever.

Hernandez, a native of Puerto Rico, was not even a Tiger until the last week of 1984 spring training. He was traded to Detroit by the Philadelphia Phillies, along with first baseman Dave Bergman, for outfielder Glenn Wilson and utility man John Wockenfuss. Hernandez started pitching almost immediately. An hour after arriving in the Tigers' training camp in Lakeland, Florida, he was warming up in the bullpen. He had driven to the park during the third inning. "I put my uniform on, and I sent a message to the big man," Hernandez told the *Detroit Free Press*, referring to Tiger manager Sparky Anderson. "What inning am I pitching?" He pitched one inning, retiring the St. Louis Cardinals in order on six pitches. The Tigers won the game.

It was new then, but Hernandez's trips to the mound became a familiar scenario to millions of Tigers fans, who watched their team accomplish the rare feat of spending the entire

UPI/Bettmann Newsphotos

season in first place. His walk from the bullpen became a sure sign that the Tigers were going to win. Hernandez became the team's missing link. The Tigers had the hitters and the fielders and the starting pitchers, but in Hernandez they discovered a winning, left-handed relief pitcher.

Hernandez is 6-foot-2, 185 pounds. His look is menacing, and his attitude toward hitters is often arrogant. He has an assortment of pitches that includes the only left-handed screwball in the American League and a cut fastball that breaks sharply toward the hitter. Some managers stopped "platooning" against him during the 1984 season, meaning they no longer bothered to use right-handed batters, a supposed strategic advantage against left-handed pitchers. They felt his imposing array of pitches nullified the advantage.

Hernandez's success stunned his teammates. "I said he'd be a good acquisition, but I never knew he'd be this good," pitching coach Roger Craig told the *Free Press* in August, 1984.

While Hernandez became one of the most talked-about pitchers in baseball during the summer of 1984, he noted that it was an accident that he became a pitcher at all. Growing up in Aguada, Puerto Rico, Hernandez was a baseball rarity: A left-handed third baseman. He was also an outfielder and a "good hitter," he recalled. As a kid, the youngest of nine children, he did odd jobs to help what he described as a poor, but happy, family. "My parents would buy me things, but I could help pay for the bills," Hernandez told the *Free Press*. "I wanted a bike for Christmas, but they couldn't afford it. I would look out the window at the kid on his new bike. My [late] mother told me, 'Don't worry about it. One of these days you're going to have enough money to buy what you want.' "

That day was a long time coming, but Hernandez set the events in motion as a teenager, playing semipro double-headers on Sundays. The team would practice on Saturdays, and Hernandez would often pitch batting practice. "I got a good fastball and a good breaking ball," he said. "But I don't know how to pitch. One time, somebody got suspended, somebody else got hurt. We don't have a pitcher. My manager give me the ball." The manager, Hernandez recalled, asked him: "Do you think you can pitch?" "Yeah," Hernandez replied.

He pitched a seven-inning shutout but lost the game 1-0. Still, he estimates that he was throwing a 100-mile-per-hour fastball and an 85-mile-per-hour breaking ball. "It would just drop over the plate," he recalled to the *Free Press*. I pitched for a month and a half then went to Italy with the Puerto Rico national team. I beat the United States, the first time Puerto Rico ever beat the United States. But I lost to Japan, 1-0, for the championship."

It was not long before Hernandez had a professional contract. Philadelphia originally signed him in 1974, but he spent his first three pro seasons in the minors. He was drafted during the winter of 1976 by the Chicago Cubs, and he spent 1977 in the majors as rookie.

For most players, making the majors is the end of a long and difficult journey, but Hernandez remembers that his trouble was only beginning. "I've been through a lot," he commented to the *Free Press*. As recently as 1981, there were whispers that his career was over. He was a reliever for the Cubs, who at the time were a team that lost more games than they won. Although he pitched often, Hernandez never had more than four saves until 1982, when he had ten. "When you pitch that much, it's weird that you don't have that many decisions," Hernandez said. "People were talking behind my back, saying I'm through."

One of the problems was that Hernandez belonged to a staff that included Bruce Sutter, the bullpen ace who earned 31 saves in 1977. "I was pitching a lot, doing great," said Hernandez. "They take me out and put Bruce Sutter in for one inning, and he'd get the save. I was just a kid. I didn't know what was going on." Hernandez felt he was slighted at contract time by the Cubs' front office, which had told him his work was appreciated. He was earning the minimum salary of $19,000. "I said, I'm a poor man. I got to eat." When the Cubs offered him $100,000 for two years, Hernandez demanded $140,000 but didn't get it. "My attitude changed," said Hernandez. "The next year, I wanted out of there."

Hernandez was 8-2 in 1978 and 4-4 in 1979. He was still in the shadow of Sutter. By 1981, Hernandez's career really appeared to be in trouble. He was in the minors after having a 1-9 record the previous summer. It was a bad time. Hernandez claims the Cubs were playing games with his mind after several years of shorting him in contract talks. "I make a lot of people rich," he said.

"I was struggling," Hernandez admitted to the *Free Press*. "My attitude was bad. They send me down [to the minors]. That was the year of the strike. They say they need a starting pitcher. They bring me up three days before the strike start. They didn't talk to me. Nobody was talking to me. I was in the [dog] house. They were [messing] with me."

When the professional baseball players' strike came, Hernandez refused to work out in Chicago and returned to Puerto Rico, angry. After the strike, the Cubs sent him back to the minors, where he finished the season with a losing record. "My attitude was real bad," he remarked. "I said, 'You give me a release. I don't want to go nowhere.' "

Hernandez received a new lease on life in 1982. The Cubs were sold, and a new management—led by Dallas Green— took over. Hernandez liked Green, but Green traded Hernandez to the Philadelphia Phillies for Dick Ruthven and Bill Johnson because the Cubs had Lee Smith to play the role as bullpen stopper. With the Phillies, Hernandez turned in his first winning season since 1978 (he was 8-4 after going 1-0 in Chicago before the trade) and helped the Phillies to the World Series, where they lost to the Orioles. He also signed a three-year contract worth $1.7 million, plus bonuses.

The Tigers had been eyeing Hernandez for three years, but something always came up to block the trade. In 1984, the Toronto Blue Jays—one of the Tigers' chief rivals—had also been after Hernandez, but the Phillies wanted Jesse Barfield in return. The Blue Jays refused and suffered through the summer with a poor bullpen. Finally, first-year Tiger general manager Bill Lajoie made the deal that sent Glenn Wilson and John Wockenfuss to Philadelphia in exchange for Hernandez and Dave Bergman.

At first, the trade was unpopular among Detroit fans because Wilson and Wockenfuss had become favorites. But the Tigers finally had their much-needed left-handed reliever, someone who could spell right-handed reliever Aurelio Lopez, who had faltered in some earlier seasons.

Hernandez caused controversy late in 1984 when he began agitating again for a new contract, even though his pact still had a year to run. Even during the World Series, Hernandez said there was a "50-50" chance he would not return for 1985. After the Series, Hernandez demanded a trade, then entered into negotiations that would take three months to complete. At first, he represented himself. Later, he hired an agent, Brian David of Chicago. Finally, on a bitterly cold day in January, Hernandez flew to Detroit and signed a contract that will keep him a Tiger through 1989. The agreement is believed to average in excess of $1 million a year, reportedly the richest in club history.

"I'm just happy and thank God everything's over," Hernandez told the *Free Press.* "My toes are frozen. I'm ready to go back to Puerto Rico. I always thought I would sign with the Tigers. I know they want to keep me around."

SOURCES:

PERIODICALS

Detroit Free Press, March 26, 1984, August 26, 1984, January 19, 1985.
New York Times, October 14, 1984, October 31, 1984.
Sports Illustrated, September 10, 1984.
Sporting News, April 2, 1984.

—Sidelights by Bill McGraw

Jack Horner

1946-

PERSONAL: Full name, John R. Horner; born 1946, in Shelby, Mont.; divorced; children: Jason. *Education:* Attended University of Montana for seven years.

ADDRESSES: Office—Museum of the Rockies, Montana State University, Bozeman, Mont. 59715.

OCCUPATION: Paleontologist.

CAREER: Princeton University, Princeton, N.J., fossil preparator in museum, 1975-82; Montana State University, Museum of the Rockies, Bozeman, curator of paleontology, 1982—. *Military service:* U.S. Marine Corps; served in Vietnam.

WRITINGS: Contributor of articles to journals, including *Nature* and *Scientific American.*

SIDELIGHTS: Because of his discoveries of dinosaur nesting sites and fossilized eggs, paleontologist Jack Horner has called into question long-held scientific beliefs. Since 1978, Horner has uncovered more than four hundred fossilized dinosaur eggs and eight dinosaur nesting sites at an archeological dig in northwestern Montana. His finds suggest that dinosaurs cared for their young, a discovery that contradicts what science has believed about dinosaurs for many years. Until Horner's discovery, it was assumed that dinosaurs, like present-day reptiles, simply laid their eggs and abandoned them. To find nesting sites implies that dinosaurs had some sort of family structure and were capable of forming social groups. Horner even speculates that dinosaurs may have been warm-blooded animals. His conclusions, writes David Quammen in *Esquire*, are "a little like announcing, five hundred years ago, that the earth isn't flat after all."

A native of Montana, Horner came by his profession naturally. Since the 1850s, Montana has been the site of some of the world's most important finds of dinosaur fossils. It is ideal country for fossils. During the Cretaceous Period, Montana formed the western shore of a great sea. It was country favored by many species of dinosaur. When the sea withdrew from the area, dinosaur remains were preserved in the remaining sediments. Horner found his first dinosaur fossil—which he still has—at the age of eight, and his interest in paleontology began. In school, Horner did well in the sciences but dropped out of the University of Montana because of problems in completing his nonscience requirements. Horner explains to Steve Byers of *People* that he "hated the other stuff, which seemed to have no relevance to my life." Nonetheless, in 1975 he found a job with the Princeton University museum doing what he loves to do best—working with fossils. Each summer, Horner manages to return to Montana for independent fossil digs.

Photograph by Dan Root/Missoulian

Since 1978, Horner and fellow paleontologist Robert Makela have been uncovering fossils at a site in Montana called the Willow Creek Anticline. This site is unique because it appears to have been a rookery—an area where many dinosaurs gathered to lay their eggs, much as some species of birds do today. Over four hundred dinosaur eggs of three different species have been found. "At this site," Horner writes in *Scientific American*, "unlike most other places where dinosaur remains have been found, most of the eggs are in the exact position where they were laid and most of the skeletons are in the position and apparent location where the animal died." Of special interest are the skeletons of juvenile dinosaurs, which show that young dinosaurs stayed near their mothers until they were able to fend for themselves. "Some form of extended parental care was administered," Horner and Makela write in an article for *Nature*, "for, if the young were confined to the nest, food must have been brought to them." This new species of parental dinosaur was named *Maiasaura peeblesorum* by Horner and Makela. *Maiasaura* means "good-mother reptile," while *peeblesorum* is in honor of the Peebles family, on whose land the dig is located.

"Throughout the whole history of fossil collection," Quammen states, "dinosaur eggs and juveniles have remained breathtakingly rare; no other nest full of hatchlings has *ever* been found." Already the discovery has necessitated changes in books about dinosaurs and in the way dinosaurs are depicted in natural history museums. Despite his lack of a college degree, Horner has become one of the country's leading paleontologists and one of three, along with John Ostrom and Robert Bakker, whose work was drastically transformed scientific beliefs about the dinosaurs.

Working now at Montana State University's Museum of the Rockies, Horner teaches and writes during the winter months and spends his summers at the fossil site with a crew of volunteers. Living in tepees and stocked with such supplies as "a rented jackhammer, short-handle picks, ice picks, delicate brushes, and 150 cases of beer," as Quammen observes, Horner's excavation team digs throughout the summer. "I couldn't be lured away from here by any amount of money or promised notoriety," Horner explains to Byers. Speaking to Quammen, Horner adds: "Dinosaurs are *really neat* animals."

SOURCES:

PERIODICALS

Esquire, December, 1984.
Nature, November 15, 1979.
New York Times, October 11, 1981.
People, August 27, 1984.
Scientific American, April, 1984.

—Sketch by Thomas Wiloch

Rock Hudson

1925-1985

OBITUARY NOTICE: Real name, Roy Fitzgerald; born November 17, 1925, in Winnetka, Ill.; died October 2, 1985, in Beverly Hills, Calif. of lymph cancer resulting from acquired immune deficiency syndrome (AIDS). American actor and leading man. Hudson got his start in the film business following service in World War II. After being discharged from the Navy, he worked as a piano mover, mail carrier, and truck driver, but he wanted to break into the movies, so Hudson hung around Hollywood film studio gates, hoping to be noticed. He was discovered and groomed by agent Henry Willson, who gave him the screen name Rock Hudson. His first film was "Fighter Squadron" in 1948, while his first starring role was in "Magnificent Obsession," with Jane Wyman as his leading lady.

Although he was never particularly highly regarded for his acting ability, Hudson received popular acclaim in the light romantic comedies he made with Doris Day in the late 1950s and early 1960s: "Pillow Talk," "Send Me No Flowers," and "Lover Come Back." These films highlighted his strong sense of comedic timing and easy, natural manner. Hudson was also nominated for an Academy Award for his role as Texas rancher Bick Benedict in the film "Giant," which co-starred Elizabeth Taylor and James Dean. Other films in which Hudson appeared include "Something of Value," and "A Fairwell to Arms." His final feature film was the 1980 movie "The Mirror Crack'd," adapted from an Agatha Christie mystery. In later years he also appeared in theatre.

He starred on the television series "McMillan and Wife" in the 1970s and began "The Devlin Connection," although production on that series was shut down when Hudson was hospitalized for a quadruple heart bypass operation. Looking quite gaunt, he later made several appearances as a love interest for Linda Evans on the "Dynasty" series. The announcement that Hudson had AIDS, a fatal disease passed primarily by male homosexual contact, was made the July before his death at a press conference in Paris, where he had gone to receive treatment with an experimental viral drug. It was subsequently noted in the press that Hudson had long been a homosexual despite a studio-arranged marriage in 1955 to his agent's secretary, Phyllis Gates. That marriage was dissolved in 1958.

The announcement of Hudson's condition is credited with drawing attention to the AIDS illness. Hudson donated $250,000 to a foundation he established for AIDS research, and he also pledged to the foundation his share of the advance and royalties from the book on which he was working at the time of his death. That book, co-authored and since expanded by Sara Davidson, is entitled *Rock Hudson: His Own Story.*

SOURCES:

BOOKS

Hudson, Rock, and Sara Davidson, *Rock Hudson: His Own Story,* Morrow, 1986.
Miller, Edwin, *Seventeen Interviews,* Macmillan, 1970.
Parish, James Robert, and Don E. Stanke, *All-Americans,* Arlington House, 1977.
Schickel, Richard, *Stars,* Dial, 1962.
Shipman, David, *Great Movie Stars,* A & W Visual Library, 1976.

PERIODICALS

Chicago Tribune, October 6, 1985.
Films in Review, May, 1975.
Life, September 6, 1954, October 3, 1955, February 16, 1962.
Look, March 18, 1958.
Maclean's, October 14, 1985.
Newsweek, October 14, 1985.
People, October 21, 1985.
Saturday Evening Post, September 27, 1952, July 23, 1960.
Time, February 2, 1976, October 14, 1985.
U. S. News & World Report, October 14, 1985.

Mark Hughes

1956-

PERSONAL: Born 1956, in Lynwood Calif.; married Kathryn Perry (divorced, January, 1984); married Angela Mack, December, 1984. *Education:* Dropped out of school in the ninth grade.

ADDRESSES: Office—Herbalife International, P.O. Box 80210, Los Angeles, Calif. 90009.

OCCUPATION: Health and personal care products company executive.

CAREER: Salesman of diet products for Seyforth Laboratories, beginning 1976; sold a variety of items, including clothing and health-care products, until 1980; Herbalife International, Los Angeles, Calif., founder and president, 1980—.

SIDELIGHTS: To some people, Herbalife International founder Mark Hughes is a prime example of the American enterprise system—a handsome school dropout who has worked his way into millionaire ranks selling weight loss and nutrition products. To others, who claim to have shed pounds and regained good health with his Herbalife formulas and diet plan, he is a savior. But to some medical experts and government agencies, Mark Hughes is a huckster with a company that makes unproven claims for its products and uses an illegal method for selling them. One thing is certain: entrepreneur Hughes has attracted a great deal of attention in a very short time.

Hughes was born in 1956 in Lynwood, California, to parents who were divorced by the time he was one year old. Hughes's mother lived on welfare payments and fought her life-long battles with obesity and tension through diet and sleeping pills. Hughes dropped out of high school in the ninth grade and turned to drugs, which got him "in trouble with the law," he told *People* magazine.

At sixteen, he was sent to Cedu, a private residential school for emotionally troubled teenagers in Running Springs, California. It was at Cedu that he got his first taste of the art of selling and learned the value of work and being in a caring environment. As part of his rehabilitation at Cedu, he raised money for the school by selling raffle tickets. A quick study, he became Cedu's top salesman, selling tickets door-to-door in Los Angeles, at times even garnering corporate cash.

Three and one-half years into his stay at Cedu, Hughes's mother died from an overdose of diet pills. Hughes found the turning point in his life; the death of his mother became the cornerstone of his dedication to nutrition. In an account in *Herbalife Journal*, a company publication, Hughes described how he discovered "a vital interest in nutrition, and a fervent desire to find a product that would enhance and

build health while allowing an individual to take off weight safely and sensibly."

In 1976, Hughes began selling diet products for Seyforth Laboratories, a multilevel sales organization that went out of existence in 1979. In the years that Hughes sold Slender Now diet products for the company, he became one of its top 100 salespeople, he told *Forbes* magazine. Other sales jobs followed, including one where Hughes met his first wife, Kathryn Perry. Perry says he "sold himself" to her when he was selling an herbal weight control product distributed by a company called Golden Youth. Perry helped Hughes to set up a health products business after attending a sales meeting for a now-defunct weight loss program from which they bought samples. By hiring a manufacturer to produce a line of diet and nutrition pills and powders similar to the defunct line, Herbalife was formulated.

Now divorced from Hughes, Perry told the *Los Angeles Times* that Hughes had learned to "sell just about anything." Although Hughes doesn't deny wanting to make money, he maintains that financial lure was not what drove him to make Herbalife a success. Insisting that his primary goal has always been to promote basic nutrition, Hughes has built his enterprise into a company with annual sales of more than $500 million, and more than one million customers in the United States, with 700,000 distributors spanning the United States, Canada, Australia and the United Kingdom. According to the *Herbalife Journal*, top Herbalife salespeople can earn $25,000 and more marketing the products. Hughes owns more than half the company himself and pays himself a salary of five percent of gross sales, or more than $1 million a month, he told *People* magazine.

For Hughes, the fruits of his labors at Herbalife are sweet. He owns a $7.3 million mansion in Bel Air that once belonged to Kenny Rogers, and he vacations at a beachfront home in Hawaii. When he remarried in 1984 to a twenty-three-year-old former Swedish beauty queen named Angela Mack, he entertained the 300 wedding guests with comedian David Steinberg, singer Wayne Newton, and Doc Severinsen and the "Tonight Show" orchestra. Hughes owns two Rolls-Royces, a Mercedes, and a Toyota and dresses in finely-tailored suits accented with diamond and gold jewelry, including custom-made gold cuff links shaped in Herbalife's three-leaf logo.

In all, Herbalife International's slogan, "Lose weight now/ Ask me how," has netted Hughes an opulent lifestyle and a faithful following that continues to grow. But the fervor with which he and his distributors sell their products is overshadowed by public and governmental concerns regarding the products' safety, whether the company's success claims can withstand laboratory scrutiny, and whether the method of marketing, which has propelled the company on its course of rapid growth, is legal.

Hughes insists that his products can help people lose weight—up to ten to twenty-nine pounds per month—boost energy levels, and cure a wide variety of ailments ranging from asthma and baldness to venereal disease. On the Slim and Trim plan, dieters take a variety of Herbalife pills and powders. Herbalife users are allowed one 1000-calorie meal per day, which is supplemented with two low-calorie skim milk shakes containing the company's cream-colored protein powder. Dieters also take various herbal vitamins and minerals each day. Ingredients in the products include Vitamin B6, lecithin, senna leaves, kelp, chickweed, and dandelion.

At national conventions held throughout the country, Herbalife followers praise these products with revival-tent fervor, proudly claiming substantial weight loss, improved energy, and the disappearance or improvement of such health problems as allergies, depression, hyperactivity and blood clots. Herbalife distributors also claim that by increasing meals to two a day and cutting back to one skim milk shake, the products can be taken for weight gain. In addition to weight control products, the company markets Cell-U-Loss, which is purported to help attack cellulite, Herbal Aloe juice, which is said to aid digestion and flush out the system, skin-care products, shampoo, and herb-based food supplements intended to combat premature aging.

At what cost are these herbal potions available? In all, Herbalife users spend about $300 a month on various pills, powders and liquids. Separately, the Slim and Trim package

sells for around $29.95 for a month's supply, Cell-U-Loss is about $12.95 for ninety tablets, and a quart of Herbal Aloe costs $11.95, according to figures the company reported to the *Detroit News*. And attorneys for some governmental agencies allege that consumers are not getting their money's worth, that the products contain no special ingredients for weight loss or for alleviating any other medical conditions. "The whole impression behind the product is that these are some kind of magic elixirs that are going to solve all sorts of problems one way or another," said Herschel Elkins, senior California assistant attorney general, in the *Los Angeles Times*. Elkins believes that the reported weight loss is simply the result of cutting back to one meal per day and that the Herbalife products do "nothing whatsoever."

But the pocketbook expenditures are not the only costs of the programs, some who have tried Herbalife have found. The U.S. Food and Drug Administration (FDA) has received numerous reports of adverse reactions to Herbalife products, ranging from constipation, diarrhea, and nausea to headaches and allergic reactions. (One pregnant woman reportedly collapsed and went into shock shortly after taking Herbalife.) While physicians and nutritionists argue that Herbalife's pills and powders contain powerful laxatives and diuretics, Hughes insists that the natural ingredients cleanse impurities from the body and prepare it to more easily absorb nutrients. But the FDA has found that some ingredients are not so harmless.

In 1982, the FDA sent Herbalife a "Notice of Adverse Findings," in which it stated that one of the Herbalife products contained ingredients considered unsafe for food use. One of the ingredients, mandrake, was used at one time as a suicide drug among American Indians, the FDA said. Mandrake and pokeroot were both voluntarily removed from Herbalife formulas. But the company currently has a suit pending against it claiming, among other things, that Herbalife fails to disclose caffeine as an ingredient in its NRG (Nature's Raw Guarana) tablets.

Aside from unpleasant side effects or unknown ingredients, questions have been raised about how the products are tested and are determined to be fit for human consumption. Hughes says the answer is simple. He tests them himself, along with his staff. "After we develop a product," he told *People* magazine, "we test it ourselves. Normally we will get a group of people together and have them start using the product. Then we put it out." Of the lawsuits filed against his company, he says that at least some are attributable to his competitors. "If people are skipping two meals a day and getting healthier, they're hurting the food and medical industries. There's no doubt we're getting some pressure from out there," he told *People*.

Whether or not the lawsuits are prompted by competitors, Herbalife's legal hurdles are mounting in number. The California attorney general, along with the state Department of Health and a district attorney, has filed a civil lawsuit against Herbalife. The suit alleges that the company uses an illegal "pyramid" or "chain" scheme to sell its products and supports some of its products with false medical claims. In addition, the suit maintains that Herbalife fails to disclose that the NRG tablets contain caffeine. The company is the subject of inquiries by two congressional panels, and the FDA has cited Herbalife for six violations of the Food, Drug and Cosmetic Act and is continuing its investigation. Canada has also placed the company under close scrutiny. In November, 1984, the Canadian Ministry of Health and Welfare cited Herbalife of Canada for twenty-four violations of that country's Food and Drug Act.

The Herbalife marketing plan is central to much of the controversy surrounding the company. Herbalife uses a multilevel sales approach, in which independent distributors handle all pills, powders, juices and other Herbalife products. To earn money, the distributors sell Herbalife to retail customers as well as take a percentage of the sales from distributors they have recruited to sell Herbalife, who will in turn recruit others. Claiming that it is not impossible for an Herbalife distributor to make $1 million a year, Hughes has not had trouble finding recruits to keep his company profitable and growing. To allegations by the California attorney general's office that this type of marketing scheme is illegal and will collapse when it runs out of new recruits, Hughes says Herbalife has become "the biggest hit target in the country." He told the *Los Angeles Times*, "As far as I'm concerned, if they think they're going to scare us, they've got another thing coming."

The sales techniques are powerful. Car bumpers, buttons, and many cable television channels all carry the Herbalife message: "Lose weight now/Ask me how." Hughes's enthusiastic and flashy approach to marketing his products—and keeping the faith of his distributors and followers—has been compared to "tent-show preaching" and has caused the company, *Newsweek* says, to "acquire the trappings of a cult." Millions of Americans viewing two- to three-hour Herbalife programs on the USA Cable Network and inde-

pendent cable channels see "slickly-produced" shows "full of inspiring testimonials from common people and resemble old-style revival meetings in their fervor," says *Forbes*.

And with the same energy that he displays when firing up distributors, Hughes is ready to do battle with the forces that seek to put his rapidly-growing company under a regulatory microscope. He has filed a lawsuit against the FDA and the Department of Health and Human Services, charging them with defamation. He continues to refuse to have Herbalife products analyzed by medical experts, a suggestion by a public relations agency that has since been dismissed from Hughes's hire. And to those who say the products contain ingredients harmful to health, he insists that sound nutrition is what Herbalife is all about. "I don't have to go out and get an independent study from anybody," Hughes told the *Los Angeles Times*. "Our independent study is the fact that this company is the biggest, the best, and it's helped more people lose weight than any other institution in the world."

SOURCES:

PERIODICALS

Detroit News, May 20, 1985, May 27, 1985.
Forbes, February 25, 1985.
Los Angeles Times, April 4, 1984.
Newsweek, April 8, 1985.
People, April 29, 1985.
Public Management, October, 1982.
USA Today, April 24, 1985.

—*Sidelights by Amy C. Bodwin*

Charlotte Hullinger
1935(?)-

BRIEF ENTRY: Born c. 1935. American legal secretary, college teacher, and social activist. Charlotte Hullinger has gained notoriety as the founder of Parents of Murdered Children, an organization dedicated to the proposition that grief must be shared. After her nineteen-year-old daughter Lisa was bludgeoned to death by an ex-boyfriend in 1978, Hullinger "had a tremendous need to talk about what had happened but. . . found few people were able to listen," she recalls in *People*. Even her husband, Robert, a Lutheran minister in Cincinnati, felt inadequately prepared to deal with the violent death of his own daughter and his wife's sense of loss. Through a priest who had done extensive work with the grieving, Charlotte obtained the names of two other couples who had had children murdered and asked the parents to meet with her.

From a coffee klatsch involving just these three couples in 1978, Parents of Murdered Children has grown into a nationwide network of twenty chapters that publish newsletters, lobby for new victim's rights laws, and conduct sensitivity-training workshops for clergy, lawyers, and psychiatrists. But the primary focus of each chapter remains the monthly meeting where members share their feelings and experiences, because, as Hullinger says, "Violent death brings anger so intense most people can't stand it. We find that those who would normally be helpful, like people in the Church, especially don't like these unacceptable emotions and will try to smooth them over with platitudes. . . . I think the most helpful thing to say to all that is 'Baloney!' People have to be allowed their anger. Those feelings are there."

Photograph by Thomas S. England

SOURCES:

PERIODICALS

Newsweek, April 12, 1982.
People, March 16, 1981.

Joel Hyatt

1950-

PERSONAL: Surname originally Zylberberg; name legally changed; born May 6, 1950, in Cleveland, Ohio; son of David and Anna Zylberberg; married Susan Metzenbaum (an attorney), August 24, 1975; children: Jared. *Education:* Dartmouth College, B.A., 1972; Yale University, J.D., 1975. *Politics:* Democrat.

ADDRESSES: Office—Hyatt Legal Services, 4410 Main St., Kansas City, Mo. 64111.

OCCUPATION: Attorney; entrepreneur.

CAREER: Paul, Weiss, Rifkind, Wharton & Garrison (law firm), New York, N.Y., associate, 1975-76; manager, with wife, of successful Senate campaign of Democratic Senator Howard Metzenbaum of Ohio, 1976; Hyatt Legal Services, Kansas City, Mo., co-founder, president, and chief executive officer, 1977—.

MEMBER: Phi Beta Kappa.

SIDELIGHTS: The television and radio media are increasingly becoming home to a number of goods, services, and businesses that are entering the advertising ring for the first time. In the legal profession, the emergence of advertising has caused such a stir that even a U.S. Supreme Court ruling could not quell arguments among lawyers, who are divided on the ethics of legal advertising. In the center of the controversy is Joel Hyatt, the young legal entrepreneur who founded Hyatt Legal Services, the firm that has blazed a trail for radio and television advertising.

One of Hyatt's earliest commercials for his string of legal clinics began in a straightforward, low-pressure fashion: "My name is Joel Hyatt. And I'm an attorney with the Hyatt Legal Clinics. We're a new law firm specializing in legal services for people, not businesses or corporations. And we offer these services at very reasonable fees." The commercial first ran in 1978 in Cleveland, Ohio, Hyatt's hometown. The ad, which was aired when Hyatt Legal Clinics consisted of four offices around metropolitan Cleveland, was the result of Hyatt's success in helping to convince the Ohio Supreme Court to sanction television advertising for the legal profession. Nearly eight years later, in 1985, about fourteen percent of the approximately 640,000 lawyers in the country have tried advertising, and many say they will stick with it, according to the American Bar Association in Chicago. "There is an unmet need for legal services, and a great deal of middle-America that does not know how to find legal aid," Adrian Foley, Jr., past chairman of the ABA's Commission on Legal Advertising, told *CN.* "The ABA did studies that show that legal advertising, if done properly, can change people's perception of the law practice," Foley said, and Joel Hyatt agrees. "Most Americans don't have a lawyer, and they don't know how to find one,"

Photograph by William Coupon

Hyatt told the *New York Times.* "Using television advertising, I have developed a way to give these people access to legal services."

Born on May 6, 1950, Hyatt is the only son of a Jewish father who left Poland prior to World War II. As he grew up in Cleveland, he developed a strong belief in the teachings of Robert Kennedy and formed ties with the Democratic party. A 1972 Phi Beta Kappa graduate from Dartmouth College, Hyatt enrolled in Yale Law School, attracted by the large number of previous Yale graduates who were members of the U.S. Justice Department under Attorney General Robert Kennedy. While at Yale, Hyatt met his wife, Susan Metzenbaum, daughter of Ohio Democratic Senator Howard M. Metzenbaum. They married in 1975, the same year Hyatt graduated from Yale. Susan, who Hyatt described in the *Washington Post* as his "best friend, supporter and adviser," is a full and equal partner in Hyatt Legal Services. Working side by side with his wife drew some cautionary comments from friends, Hyatt admits, but he didn't pay much attention. "I've had close friends take me aside and go, 'What are you doing, you fool? Let me give you some advice. Don't work with your wife. I mean, that's the start of big trouble,'" Hyatt told the *Washington Post.* Hyatt and his wife together managed the 1976 U.S. Senate election campaign of Senator Metzenbaum, and even with close to 200 offices around the country, Hyatt refuses to take lengthy business trips unless his wife and their son can accompany him.

His legal and business ambitions currently overshadow his political ambitions, but Hyatt admits that he would not mind entering the political arena someday, as long as the office fits his desired notch on the political totem pole. "I would not leave what I'm doing for something less than the Senate," he told *Business Week*. But being U.S. attorney general also might fit; Hyatt said: "I'm running the largest private law practice in the country. As attorney general, I would be running the largest public one."

When Hyatt opened his first legal clinic in Cleveland in 1977, his goals were not nearly so ambitious. Leaving the prestigious New York City law firm of Paul, Weiss, Rifkind, Wharton & Garrison, Hyatt had the goal of serving a majority of the public that he felt were going unserved by the law because they could not afford lawyer's fees. He said leaving corporate law to do divorces and wills didn't make much sense to many of his legal colleagues, but Hyatt didn't care if they thought there was no prestige involved in opening a legal clinic. He did not expect to market to $200,000-a-year executives. "We're appealing to the middle seventy percent of the population, who normally don't have access to a lawyer because they're not rich enough to afford one and not poor enough to get one from a legal-aid society," Hyatt said in *Esquire*. "What drives the bar crazy," he added "is that for fifteen dollars we bring people in and tell them what we think their problem is, how we can solve it, and what it will cost. Most lawyers like to just nod their heads and say 'I'll do what I can,' and keep the whole thing a mystery, including the work involved and the bill."

One of the first things Hyatt realized when he started the clinics was that he would have to advertise. That realization brought him sharply out of line with the legal tradition, and head-to-head with fellow lawyers and bar associations who felt that legal advertising was undignified and could lead to abuse. To some, it was bad enough that Hyatt was opening legal clinics, but to advertise on radio and television in addition was enough to enrage many traditional practitioners. Hyatt's determination and belief in advertising have won him support from the Ohio Supreme Court—his first opponent—and even from some of his critics who acknowledge that Hyatt has set a course that the legal profession might be well-advised to take notice of. One critic, who had once recommended that growth of electronic ads be slow, told *Esquire* that "the [Hyatt] clinics are degrading the law, but it may be a proper type of degrading that forces us to come off our pedestal."

In 1976, the U.S. Supreme Court determined that legal advertising was protected by First Amendment rights. The American Bar Association, which represents 300,000 lawyers around the country, suggested to all states that legal advertising be struck down. When Hyatt began planning his clinics following the U.S. Supreme Court ruling allowing lawyers to advertise, he decided that he would run radio and television ads even if the Ohio state court ruled against him, and if he faced disciplinary action, he would take his appeal back to Washington. At an October, 1977, Ohio Supreme

Court hearing held to determine if legal pitches on radio and television would be allowed, Hyatt showed up armed with a "sample" ad he had produced to convince the justices that legal ads served a public interest. He argued that lawyers had the constitutional right to advertise, and that bar associations should no longer be allowed to infringe on that right. The ads, he said, inform the public that legal service can be provided at very reasonable fees. The court ruled to prohibit only deceptive radio and television ads or those using music or actors, and Ohio became the first state to sanction television ads for lawyers.

Recent studies by the ABA have found that fourteen percent of all lawyers in the country have tried advertising, double the seven percent that had tried it by 1979. And of those lawyers that have tried advertising, the ABA says, about eighty percent have found it successful and will probably use it again. That does not mean that the ABA endorses advertising, however. Foley, former chairman of the association's Commission on Legal Advertising, told *CN* that, officially, the ABA "neither favors nor disfavors advertising." Foley said that lawyers are divided on the issue of legal advertising and that the Hyatt ads may be the most well-known of any legal ads. According to the ABA, Hyatt spent more than $3 million on legal advertising in 1984.

Since the original U.S. Supreme Court decision, other rulings have followed, which have fueled a growing barrage of legal advertising. In 1985, the Supreme Court ruled that as long as advertisements are nondeceptive, a state may not ban them even when the attorney is soliciting a specific kind of case or client. This ruling, Hyatt said in *Time* magazine, may cause his firm and others to be bolder when looking at expanding into states where restrictive ad policies may now be threatened. As of mid-1985, there were 188 Hyatt Legal Services clinics in twenty-two states and the District of Columbia, with further growth planned.

Due to its heavy expansion, profits have been low at Hyatt Legal Services. And although Hyatt has become a millionaire, he told *Business Week* that he doesn't "define greatness in terms of monetary wealth." The chain's fast-paced growth has kept client volumes high while keeping fees—and lawyer's salaries—low. In contrast to starting salaries of nearly $50,000 garnered by lawyers at top Wall Street firms, a beginning Hyatt lawyer with a minimum of two years experience may receive around $18,000. The fees, which are fixed in advance, are also substantially lower than standard lawyers' fees, which are usually computed by the hour. At a Hyatt Legal Services office, a standard will may run between $45 and $65, an uncontested divorce will cost around $275 and a personal bankruptcy costs between $350 and $375. At these prices, some lawyers argue, quality may suffer. But Hyatt points out that quality and sophistication do not deteriorate in response to a high volume/low profit approach. In most of the areas in which the Hyatt lawyers practice, sophistication and accompanying steep fees are not necessary, Hyatt believes.

In 1985, Hyatt settled a two-year-old lawsuit filed against him by the Hyatt Corporation hotel chain, charging him with the infringement of the Hyatt name. His original name is Joel Zylberberg, which he had changed even before he decided to start Hyatt Legal Services because "having a last name that was not phonetic and not pronounceable was burdensome," Hyatt said in the *Washington Post*. While keeping his name, Hyatt Legal Services agreed to place a statement at the bottom of its ads specifying that it "is named after its founder, Joel Z. Hyatt."

Hyatt has recently gone after, and won, pre-paid legal plans as a customer source. As legal service plans become a growing fringe benefit for union workers, Hyatt is tapping into the market by offering lower rates and convenient neighborhood offices for union members to visit. In 1983, he reached an agreement with the Sheet Metal Workers' union under which locals can negotiate free legal benefits through the Hyatt chain. "If we do succeed in making pre-paid legal services the next major fringe benefit, that will be terribly important," Hyatt said in the *New York Times*. "It would mean access to lawyers for hundreds of thousands of workers. And of course, it would be financially important for us."

Hyatt also has a working relationship with the H&R Block income tax firm, which began to consider the integration of nontax businesses as tax plans became simpler. In 1980, Block agreed to provide marketing and administrative services to the Hyatt Legal Clinics. The two companies agreed to open clinics nationwide as a joint venture and house them in quarters shared with Block's tax preparation offices. For Block, the law offices could provide the impetus for the tax preparation company to maintain a targeted fifteen percent annual earnings growth. For Hyatt, the venture represents a means by which to expand rapidly and take advantage of Block's marketing and administrative muscle. "What Block did for income tax preparation, we are trying to do for legal services," Hyatt said in *Business Week*.

Looking back on the success he has achieved, both monetarily and personally in terms of recognition and credibility, Hyatt says his commitment to the role of law in society was idealistic but has now become a reality that he would not alter. The original idea stemmed from a commitment to make legal services available, and it was this commitment that landed Hyatt at his first legal clinic in Cleveland instead of devoting his energies to corporate law in New York City. "It turns out it is now a big business and we are doing very well, and it is terrific for my large ego," Hyatt said in the *Washington Post*. "But it started out [as] idealism."

SOURCES:

PERIODICALS

Business Week, December 8, 1980, January 21, 1985, June 17, 1985.
Corporate Report, February, 1982.
Esquire, May 9, 1978, December, 1984.
Florida Trend, August, 1984.
Forbes, April 13, 1981, October 25, 1982.
Money, March, 1982.
National Law Journal, November 1, 1982, August 1, 1983, August 6, 1984, April 15, 1985.
New York Times, June 5, 1980, September 2, 1982, May 9, 1983, March 12, 1985.
Plain Dealer (Cleveland), August 5, 1978, April 28, 1982.
Playboy, April, 1985.
Success, February, 1984.
Time, June 10, 1985.
USA Today, February 15, 1984, July 10, 1985.
Wall Street Journal, April 26, 1983, July 14, 1983.
Washington Post, February 12, 1984.

—Sidelights by Amy C. Bodwin

Rick Inatome
1953-

PERSONAL: Born July 27, 1953, in Detroit, Mich.; son of Joseph T. and Atsuko Nan (Kumagai) Inatome; married Joyce Helen Kitchen, August 18, 1979; children: Dania Lynn. *Education:* Michigan State University, B.A., 1976.

ADDRESSES: *Home*—5726 Sussex, Troy, Mich. 48098. *Office*—Inacomp Computer Centers, Inc., 1824 West Maple, Troy, Mich. 48084.

OCCUPATION: Computer sales executive.

CAREER: Computer Mart, Inc., Troy, Mich., founder, vice-president, and general manager, 1976-82; Inacomp Computer Centers, Inc., Troy, president and chief executive officer, 1982—.

Lecturer on computers; instructor at Marygrove College, Detroit, Mich., and Macomb County Community College, Warren, Mich.; has appeared on national television and radio programs. Computer consultant; president of Microsoft Dealer Advisory Board; member of several other advisory boards, including *Computer Merchandising* and *PC Retailing* magazines.

MEMBER: American Management Association, Data Processing Management Association, Association for Computer Machinery, National Office Machine Dealers Association, Association of Better Computer Dealers, Economic Club of Detroit, Engineering Society of Detroit, Phi Delta Theta.

AWARDS, HONORS: Outstanding Young Man Award, Michigan Jaycees, 1983; listed as one of twenty-five most influential executives in the personal computer industry by *Computer Retail News*, 1983; named Computer Merchandiser of the Year by *Computer Merchandising* magazine, 1983 and 1984; Excellence in Oral Presentation Award, Society of Automotive Engineers, 1984; listed as one of top five software dealers in the country by *Software Review* magazine, 1984; named Michiganian of the Year by *Detroit News*, 1985.

Photograph by Andrew Sacks

SIDELIGHTS: Rick Inatome, dubbed a "new breed of tycoon" by *U.S. News and World Report,* has led an offbeat, storybook business life as the founder and chief executive officer of Inacomp Computer Centers, Inc., one of the nation's largest independent chains of retail computer stores. At age thirty-two, Inatome is noteworthy for being one of the youngest chief executive officers in the country at a time when the average age of CEOs is increasing (to fifty-two), according to *Forbes* magazine. But he is becoming the stuff of business legends for more than his youth. Inatome oversees a $95 million business with more than fifty stores—half of them owned by the company he founded in 1976 at age twenty-three—with a management style that is unique and innovative by most business school standards. Noted a

Detroit Free Press article: "Inatome is hustle personified, but his is the kind of cool business hustle that separates the boys on the sales floor from the boys in the boardroom."

Inatome has been photographed for national magazine stories holding impromptu board meetings in the indoor pool and Jacuzzi of the 5,200-square-foot home he built next to his banker in Troy, Michigan, not far from Inacomp's headquarters. Midnight brainstorming sessions at the company's home office in Troy are typically a weekly occurrence, usually accompanied by takeout pizza. And the boss does not adhere to a nine-to-five routine. Employes usually do not count on seeing Inatome before noon. "I go in whenever I wake up," he explained to *U.S. News and World Report* and added, "If I worked for somebody else, I'd be a total failure."

Inatome got into the business on the cutting edge of the boom in home computer sales after graduating from Michigan State University with a degree in economics and a minor in computer science. With $35,000 borrowed on his father's life insurance policy, Inatome began the business—initially called Computer Mart—and turned a $12,000 profit the first year; he promptly spent the money on a new sports car. "I was building machines from kits in the basement at night and selling them by day," Inatome recalled in an *Inc.* magazine interview. "We did $400 the first month, but it took off from there and just kept going." By 1981, five years later, sales had jumped to $9 million; in fiscal 1983, revenues ballooned to more than $36 million and then soared to more than $60 million in fiscal 1984. In the interim, Inatome's salary rose from $70 a week in 1976 to more than $200,000 a year.

On the surface, Inatome's early success—he was a multimillionaire at age thirty—may seem like all fun and games. It wasn't. Inatome had to cope with an initial lack of credibility, serious illness (internal bleeding) brought on by stress and overwork, and the accidental death of one close friend who also made it big in computers at an early age. Because of his youth, he had difficulty initially raising funds to expand the business. Inatome told *Forbes* magazine: "I had a lot of trouble being taken seriously. . . . I went to the bank to borrow money and was told, 'We don't give lines of credit to businesses.' Instead, [the banker] suggested that I open up a Visa account. Those are the kinds of things that happened from day one."

Inatome had a difficult childhood, growing up as the son of Japanese-American parents in a blue-collar Detroit suburb. He says his most enduring childhood memories are of racial prejudice and being an outsider. Inatome's father was interned in a Utah camp for Japanese-Americans during World War II and was released after winning a scholarship to study mechanical engineering at Detroit's Wayne State University in 1943. Inatome was born in 1953, and as the eldest son, had the imperative to excel instilled in him from an early age. Besides coping with that demand, Inatome learned about prejudice firsthand when eggs were thrown at his family's modest ranch house in suburban Warren and neighborhood children spat on him.

Inatome told the *Detroit News*: "Between first and sixth grade, I was an egghead. I was far-sighted and had thick glasses, short hair. The teacher would say, 'Why can't you kids be more like Rick?' At recess, the kids would all. . . you know." Inatome tried hard to revamp his image and eventually captured the "Best Dressed" award at Warren's Cousino High School. At Michigan State University, he told the *Detroit News*, "I really didn't make a career choice. I spent the first three years in a premed curriculum, and I knew I wasn't going to get into med school or anything. In my junior year, I didn't know what I wanted to be, and I took an aptitude test. The No. 1 thing was to be a funeral home director, and No. 2 was a life insurance salesman."

He considered opening a stamp and coin shop, but when his father offered to bankroll the computer venture, Inatome rented a small shop in Royal Oak, Michigan and began to assemble computer kits at night with two friends, both of whom went on to become Inacomp executives. His early sales were strictly to computer hobbyists. "The only guys that would come in then were electronic wizards because they were the only ones who could build the kit and make it work," Inatome said in a *Detroit Free Press* article. "It was like a special, elite club when we started out. But if we still had a business that catered to those guys, we'd be out of business now."

Today, Inatome is highly respected by his peers in the computer industry. Among other honors, he is a member of the IBM and Apple dealer advisory boards and, in 1983, he was named one of the most influential executives in the personal computer industry in a *Computer Retail News* survey.

Customer relations play a large part in Inatome's success. He has lectured on computers at several Detroit-area schools and colleges, and his Inacomp stores offer special computer training classes to buyers. "It's my equivalent to the Colonel's eleven herbs and spices or the Big Mac's special sauce," he told the *Detroit News*. A subsidiary company, Inacomp Systems Support, was spun off two years ago to provide classes, troubleshooting, and even house calls to handle problems with home systems. One of the company's goals, according to Inacomp vice-president Ronald Baker, is to "eliminate the fear of purchasing a computer. . . . We want to make sure the customer feels comfortable, and we provide the support services."

Inatome has established a reputation as the master of a hip, high-growth company that is constantly expanding into new sales operations and geographic regions. His firm has been ranked for several years running by *Inc.* magazine among the country's fastest-growing businesses. Much of the company's growth in the past two years has been through acquisitions of smaller regional chains with strong local reputations and solid management. But the computer industry has been jittery—weathering a slump on Wall Street and the shakeout of several major home-computer manufacturers—since Inacomp merged in 1983 with Computer City, a California-based computer chain, and Inatome took the new company public in early 1984. "You have to develop a completely different mentality to run a public company," he told an interviewer for *Inc.* magazine. "You have to fight against getting too low—or riding too high—over things you can't control. You have to stop feeling victimized, stop internalizing anxiety that really comes from outside sources. People's perceptions affect us, sure, but those aren't the realities of our industry or our company."

Inatome has big plans for the future. In a *Detroit News* interview, he said: "My goal is to make the [Inacomp] franchise comparable to the McDonald's franchise, or better. I've heard that the people who started in the first McDonald's shops now are millionaires. I want my people and my franchises to be millionaires." He told *Inc.*: "There are three phases of management in any company—the entrepreneurial, the transitional and the professional." Ultimately, he believes, "six or seven national chains will dominate the computer retail market, and we plan to be on top of that group."

Inatome remains a workaholic. "Right now, he's really ambitious," noted his father, Joseph, to the *Detroit News*. "It kind of overwhelms me. . . . As you grow, you're afraid you're going to lose it all so you become conservative. He wipes that away by saying, 'Hey, I've got nothing to lose because I started with nothing.' He's not afraid of risks." Inatome himself told the *News*: "Certain types of people reach a position and then see something else they have to accomplish. Now, I've got to build a company worth a billion dollars."

Inatome told the *Detroit Free Press*: "I don't think, at least in the next ten years, that I'll ever feel so comfortable that I could afford to take a lot of time out. There's too many things I want to accomplish. I can go and talk to General Motors vice-presidents, and you can see the anguish in their faces; they wish they had gotten out and done something like this. They had all the prerequisites. They were sharp guys. They had ambition. They were highly motivated. . . . They feel a remorse or a sense that they didn't accomplish as much as they could have." He concluded: "If I don't make the most out of it in every way,. . . . I'll live the next fifty years of my life kicking myself in the rear end and saying, 'You know, you had an opportunity, and you blew it.' I don't want to grow up like that."

SOURCES:

PERIODICALS

Detroit Free Press, May 24, 1982, August 10, 1983, December 1, 1983, June 28, 1984, July 4, 1984, November 8, 1984, November 29, 1984, April 8, 1985.
Detroit News, December 26, 1982, June 3, 1984.
Forbes, April 8, 1985.
Inc., December, 1984.
New York Times, October 21, 1983, June 28, 1984.
PC Week, March 5, 1985.
U.S. News and World Report, December 27, 1982, April 2, 1984.
Wall Street Journal, June 26, 1984, June 28, 1984, February 27, 1985.

—Sketch by Anita Pyzik Lienert

Bobby Ray Inman

1931-

PERSONAL: Born April 4, 1931, in Rhonesboro, Tex.; son of Herman H. and Mertie F. (Hinson) Inman; married Nancy Carolyn Russo, June 14, 1958; children: Thomas, William. *Education:* University of Texas, B.A., 1950; graduated from National War College, 1972.

ADDRESSES: Office—Microelectronics and Computer Technologies Corp., 9430 Research Blvd., Austin, Tex. 78759.

OCCUPATION: Computer research executive; retired admiral and intelligence officer.

CAREER: U.S. Navy, 1952-82, commissioned ensign, 1952, served on U.S.S. *Valley Forge,* beginning 1952, assistant naval attache, U.S. Embassy, Stockholm, Sweden, 1965-67, executive assistant to vice-chief of naval operations, 1972-73, chief intelligence briefer to commander-in-chief, U.S. Pacific Fleet, 1973-74, director of Naval Intelligence, 1974-76, vice-director of Defense Intelligence Agency, 1976-77, director of National Security Agency, Fort Meade, Md., 1977-81, deputy director of Central Intelligence Agency, McLean, Va., 1981-82, retiring as admiral; Microelectronics and Computer Technology Corp., Austin, Tex., chairman, president, and chief executive officer, 1983—. Congressional adviser to House Select Committee on Intelligence, 1982. Lecturer on college campuses, 1982.

AWARDS, HONORS—Military: Defense Distinguished Service Medal; Navy Distinguished Service Medal; Legion of Merit; Defense Superior Service Medal; Meritorious Service Medal; National Security Medal; Joint Services Commendation Medal.

SIDELIGHTS: "Because he is unusually quick witted, rapier tongued, and in the spy business, people have always suspected [Bobby Ray] Inman of being something more than he appeared," *Omni* magazine declared in 1984. First as a high-level member of the intelligence community, then as the head of a trailblazing computer and microelectronics research consortium, Inman has drawn fascination, respect, and praise from many different, sometimes opposing, quarters. During Inman's career with U.S. intelligence agencies, for instance, members of the press, congressmen, conservatives, and liberals all spoke highly of him, commending, according to Robert Sam Anson in an article for *Playboy,* such qualities as Inman's "brilliance,. . . integrity,. . . guts,. . . brains, [and] wisdom." These qualities, observers have noted, are responsible for Inman's uniquely broad appeal. As *Time* magazine's Ed Magnuson explained: "Inman's bipartisan popularity stems largely from his straight talk and incisive mind." In summing up Inman, *Newsweek* termed him "a superstar in the intelligence community," while, as Anson reported, Delaware's Democratic Senator Joseph Biden deemed Inman "the most quality guy in the

Federal Government" and former U.S. Secretary of Defense James Schlesinger appraised him as "a national asset."

Inman apparently displayed intellectual gifts early in his life. While Anson was unable to confirm portions of an official Central Intelligence Agency (CIA) biography that state that Inman was born in Rhonesboro, Texas, and graduated in 1950 from the University of Texas, Anson did manage to ascertain that as a child Inman was one of radio's popular "Quiz Kids." He reportedly read a great deal in his youth and demonstrated nearly perfect recall of what he read. "His brain," asserted Anson, "is an intimidating storehouse, crammed with every imaginable fact." Inman joined the U.S. Navy in 1952, beginning a career with opportunities he seemed in a favorable position to seize. As Magnuson recounted, Inman's "virtually photographic memory and workaholic habits pushed him to the top of a career in military intelligence." According to *Omni,* Inman "rose quickly after a brilliant performance in analyzing Arab and Soviet moves during the Yom Kippur War of 1973" in the Middle East, and in 1974 he was named director of U.S. Naval Intelligence. He next served for one year as vice-director of the U.S. Defense Intelligence Agency before becoming, in 1977, director of the National Security Agency.

Based in Fort Meade, Maryland, the National Security Agency (NSA) monitors electronic communications throughout the world and breaks foreign codes, using, Magnuson noted, "satellites, sophisticated monitoring techniques and more employees . . . than the CIA." As director, Inman enjoyed a good relationship with the press. "During his time at NSA," Anson wrote, "exposes of the agency all but disappeared." In addition, Inman, who received a Distinguished Service Medal—the Navy's highest noncombat decoration—for the high quality of his congressional testimony, maintained a high reputation with Congress. *Newsweek*'s John Brecher quoted Congressman Albert Gore, Jr., who observed that "Inman's greatest talent is to take complicated issues and 'clarify, clarify, clarify.'" And Anson noted that after just "two tight paragraphs" of testimony by Inman, an interrogating Senator "would have what he had been after, with maybe a lesson in Russian history or English literature in the bargain." Also while director of the NSA Inman was awarded the National Security Medal by U.S. President Jimmy Carter.

When Carter's successor, Ronald Reagan, took office in 1981, he persuaded Inman to serve as deputy director of the CIA. Termed by Inman "the smoothest job of arm twisting I've ever encountered," according to Magnuson, Reagan's offer involved Inman's promotion to four-star admiral. The promotion made him not only one of the youngest full admirals in history, but also, in Anson's words, "one of the very rare non-Annapolis, non-blue water, full, four-star admirals in U.S. naval history." At the U.S. Senate hearings to confirm Inman's appointment as the CIA's deputy director, the *U.S. News and World Report* related, Arizona's veteran Republican Senator Barry Goldwater, serving as chairman of the Senate Intelligence Committee, told Inman: "If there's any such thing as the right man for the job at the right time, you're that man. I don't know of a man in the business who is better than you."

Characterized by *Newsweek* as "a key player in rebuilding the CIA," Inman articulated goals for his new post that included reestablishing competitive intelligence analysis, improving the agency's ability to forecast trends in political events, and streamlining the agency's bureaucracy while increasing intelligence manpower. These goals involved Inman's efforts to make greater use of university consultants for analysis work and to persuade experienced former agents to rejoin the CIA. In addition Inman wanted to concentrate more agency attention on the Third World, increase counterintelligence measures, and maintain cordial relations with Congress.

Inman's activities as deputy director of the CIA, according to Anson, encompassed most of the agency's efforts: "What he does is everything. It is Inman who runs the agency's day-to-day operations; Inman who coordinates the activities of the 'intelligence community'; Inman who prepares the critical 'national intelligence estimates'; Inman who evaluates the data flowing in from spy satellites; Inman who protects CIA from flak on Capitol Hill; Inman who has the next-to-last word on every CIA undertaking, from planting a blonde in the boudoir of a Hungarian vice-premier to

shipping arms to the Afghan rebels. He is, in the very deepest sense, the man who keeps the secrets."

Among the secrets Inman was concerned with keeping were research results in scientific and technological fields. Urging voluntary restrictions such as prepublication censorship, Inman conceded in an article for *Aviation Week and Space Technology* that "restrictions on science and technology should only be considered for the most serious of reasons." In the same article Inman pointed to cryptography, or code making and breaking, as a field of research in which self-regulation would be extremely desirable. In addition he identified "other fields where publication of certain technical information could affect the national security in a harmful way. Examples include computer hardware and software, other electronic gear and techniques, lasers, crop projections and manufacturing procedures." Inman later defended his position on self-censorship in an interview with Philip J. Hilts for *Omni*: "I was trying to indicate that there would be an enormous focus on technology transfer [to the Soviets] by the government, and that the U.S. research community had better start thinking about how to deal with it—or else we would find ourselves with regulations that would be very hard to live with."

Other issues addressed by Inman during his tenure with the CIA, including policy on domestic spying and foreign convert ventures, sparked conflict with Reagan's staff. At his Senate confirmation hearings, Inman had denied that the Reagan administration intended to lift restrictions, imposed by the previous administration, on CIA spying within the United States. But in March, 1981, the White House produced the draft of an executive order that would allow the CIA to engage in domestic spying through such means as clandestine wiretaps and warrantless searches. Inman denounced the proposed executive order, later telling Margie Bonnett in an interview for *People* magazine: "The CIA's role is abroad, on a foreign intelligence and counterintelligence mission, and the FBI's role is to do the counterintelligence job in this country. Where American citizens in the U.S. are concerned, the CIA has no role." Though Inman was unable to block the executive order entirely, his efforts did result in revisions that clearly limited the CIA's domestic activities.

In discussing covert action, another major subject of conflict between Inman and the Reagan administration, Inman provided *U.S. News and World Report* with an outline of the CIA's areas of activity. "The CIA," he said, "performs three functions: Foreign intelligence—espionage in other nations; counterintelligence—blocking some other nation's espionage effort; and covert action." "Covert action," Inman explained to Bonnett, "is when you're trying to influence events in another country, and you don't want your own activities to be acknowledged. I think one can make a good case for covert action to offset Soviet use of force outside their borders. But when you move beyond that, I'm not persuaded, in looking back over history, that our efforts to change governments have served our interests in the long term." Inman elaborated in his interview with Hilts: "Every administration considered using covert action—whether they initially rejected it or arrived in office very enthusiastic about it. Why do they all come to it? My judgment is that they use it out of frustration when they don't get what they want from diplomacy and they still don't want to use overt force. . . . We talk about lessons learned in Vietnam. I think we may have learned the wrong lessons or failed to learn things we should have. The critical lesson I would draw is that although it is very difficult to deal with unfriendly governments, it is even harder to prop up governments that you helped install in power and who lack a base to govern. . . . I'd prefer to be forward looking and attack problems with economic means before they explode into fighting." Inman's commitment to controversial views such as these led a U.S. senator to declare in the fall of 1981, reported Anson, "Bobby is the conscience of the [CIA]. Without him, the deluge."

While lauded in most circles, Inman's convictions produced clashes with those under whom he served. "Differences over the CIA's role at home and abroad," *People* revealed, "led to friction with CIA Director William Casey and with the White House." When Casey came under suspicion of alleged business improprieties, some factions called for Inman to replace the CIA director. The White House countered with a threat to oust Inman if Casey were asked to resign, thus forcing Inman to display support for his superior. Magnuson reported that, in addition, "Inman often clashed with the staff of Reagan's National Security Council, particularly with former National Security Adviser Richard Allen." Allen left his post in January, 1982, continued Magnuson, "after disclosure that he had accepted gifts from a Japanese magazine." But Allen's resignation did not eliminate the fields of conflict between Inman and the Reagan administration. In an article for the *New York Times*, Wallace Turner related that Inman was "concerned with damage to intelligence gathering by publication of details that revealed sources and methods." Inman's concern deepened when the Reagan administration came under attack for its Central American activities and responded by disclosing sensitive intelligence reports. Magnuson explained: "Inman was said to have been upset by White House leaks that sought to buttress Administration policies in Central America. . . . He felt that [the] disclosures about U.S. surveillance of the region compromised CIA intelligence-gathering methods." Nevertheless, when Inman announced on April 21, 1982, that he was leaving the CIA, becoming what *Newsweek* called "the first major defector from the Reagan Administration's national security ranks," he denied that the move was prompted by any climate of discord. As quoted by Magnuson, Inman claimed that "all the stories that are running around about major policy differences and personality disputes are just plain false."

In accepting Inman's resignation, President Reagan affirmed that Inman had left the intelligence community "in a strengthened and enhanced posture," the *U.S. News and World Report* related. The same article quoted U.S. Senator Joseph Biden's reaction to Inman's move: "Inman believed the nation can have both effective intelligence agencies and civil liberties. Without him, the intelligence agencies may be given license to try all kinds of questionable things both here and abroad." Confirming his assertions that he left the agency to spend more time with his family, Inman spent two months in the summer of 1982 touring the United States with his wife and two sons. That fall he resigned as a part-time congressional adviser to the House Select Committee on Intelligence because, explained Robert D. Hershey, Jr., in the *New York Times*, "he had not been consulted about the publication of what he regarded as a partisan study of

intelligence activities in Central America." *People* confirmed that Inman resigned the advisory post "because he feared what he calls 'politicization' of its watchdog function." The same article noted that Inman had turned to lecturing on college campuses about U.S. intelligence and the Soviet Union.

"Since leaving the CIA, Inman has spoken of U.S. weaknesses in tracking political and economic trends and anticipating Third World upheavals," wrote William H. Inman (no relation to Bobby Ray Inman) in an article appearing in the *Detroit News*. The article went on to reveal Admiral Inman's judgment that U.S. surveillance "does poorly in monitoring competition for raw materials, natural resources and markets. America also needs to [keep] closer tabs on the fervor of religious movements, he added." *Omni* spelled out the emphasis Inman places on information access: "Inman is convinced that intelligence gathering is necessary for the survival of democratic governments: Information is crucial to making decisions. 'Articles saying I'm a master spy are pure garbage. I've never run a clandestine operation. But I am an avid user of what they produce,' he hold the *Washington Post*. He relished the analysis, the puzzle to be solved." Describing his enjoyment of intelligence analysis, Inman informed Hilts: "You look at scraps of evidence; you work up a jigsaw puzzle of information. You really are doing the same sort of thing as a reporter. You pick up bits and pieces of information and pursue it until you suddenly get the whole story." Inman endorses the intelligence field as a career choice, prompting some observers to speculate that he has not entirely ruled out a return to intelligence work. In 1982 *Newsweek* reported that "few in the intelligence community would be surprised if [Inman] returns to a top national-security job in some future Administration," but a year later the magazine quoted Inman's continued resolve to remain outside the intelligence arena: "Intelligence work tends to focus on defining the problem; . . . you reach a stage in your life when you are interested in the solution of the problem."

For Inman, the solution of the problem lies in computer technology, a field in which he occupies a prominent position since becoming, in January, 1983, the chief executive officer of Microelectronics and Computer Technology Corporation (MCC), a research operation jointly funded by some of America's top computer firms. The computer field, observers have noted, shares characteristics with Inman's former career. In his government work, the *Detroit News* article pointed out, Inman "created electronic espionage networks . . . to crack enemy codes, monitor foreign communications and shield U.S. secrets." "For Inman," *Omni* declared, "spy wars have become computer wars." *Omni* further remarked that "throughout his NSA and CIA tenures, Inman was concerned about the technology race with the USSR and other countries," and quoted Inman's view that, concerning technology transfer, "you can impede the Soviets but only if you do it on a multinational basis, since much of the technology of interest to the Soviets is also being created in Japan and Western Europe." Thus, Inman argues, "one answer is for the United States to run faster" in the technology race, a goal he has identified as a major force behind MCC. "To Inman," asserted the *Detroit News*, "the mission is as important as many he undertook for the government and the need for speed and secrecy is just as vital." Described by *Time* as "no stranger to high-stakes research in the face of a tough challenge from abroad," Inman told Hilts: "I was really eager to see if some of the same techniques, the same approaches that worked in managing large operations in the government, would work in industry. That is clearly one of the major attractions of MCC. And also MCC is unique. It has never been done."

"I was approached about something brand-new, something never before tried in this country—putting together a consortium to do long-range research, pooling talent from several companies, as the Japanese have done," Inman explained to Hilts. Some of the companies involved in the MCC cooperative, which was founded in August, 1982, are Honeywell, Sperry, Control Data, RCA, Motorola, United Technologies, Boeing, and Lockheed. MCC's member corporations loan research personnel to MCC and contribute annual fees ranging from one hundred fifty thousand to ten million dollars to sponsor specific projects. As Inman informed Hilts, MCC was intended as "a joint research venture within the letter and the spirit of the antitrust laws so long as they kept a wide, visible furrow between the research and the marketplace." "So," he continued, "we put together a joint venture that would go all the way through the research phase to a prototype, but would never design, manufacture, or market the actual product."

Concern about antitrust violations evoked by MCC's formation was extenuated, in part, by Inman's reputation. *Newsweek*, for instance, remarked that "the consortium raises troubling antitrust questions, but Washington is going to feel more comfortable with the squeaky-clean Inman in charge." And Inman himself told John Walsh of *Science*: "I am absolutely confident that we are within the letter of the antitrust law. If we thought we were violating the law we wouldn't be here. But there are ambiguities." When asked about proposed legislation that would exempt such ventures as MCC from antitrust action, Inman, according to Walsh, replied that he would welcome such legislation, "so that I wouldn't have to worry about the diversion of attention. But I'm much more interested in how to encourage other industries to do this kind of research to get the most out of our investment and talent."

Another sensitive area for Inman as head of MCC involves dealing with people he knew in other contexts during his tenure with the government. In fact, Inman had previous dealings with some of MCC's member corporations and, according to Hershey, "was hired despite the fact that he was 'pretty tough' with several sponsors for cost overruns when he was procuring vast quantities of technological equipment for the Government." In addition, Inman indicated that MCC would not seek government contracts. This decision is due to Inman's desire to avoid business contacts with former government associates. "I simply decided," he told Hershey, "I was not going to go back and deal with people in a business way who were in any way indebted to me for their promotions."

"Computer war was officially declared in 1981," *Omni* reported, "when Tokyo announced that under the leadership of [Japan's] Ministry of International Trade and Industry (MITI), they would create a new [generation] of intelligent computers within ten years." With the Japanese enjoying government subsidy in their challenge to America's prominent place in the computer field, MCC is seen, according to *Omni*, as "one of America's strongest responses to the challenge, an experiment unlike anything in the history of American business." "The race," the *Detroit News* article declared, "is to unlock the secrets of thinking machines,. . . superfast computers that can simulate the human brain by absorbing data and applying it to solve problems." Sometimes called "fifth generation" computers, these artificial intelligence machines, experts claim, will be perhaps thousands of times more powerful than present computers, with the ability to infer from data, to make accurate judgments, and to take instructions in human languages like English or Japanese. While MCC was formed to pursue research on artificial intelligence, Inman described a wider field of inquiry for the consortium. "I try to avoid the appellation *fifth generation*. I try to focus on the variety of areas in which a major increase in computer performance, access, and ease of operation may be doable," Inman informed Hilts.

MCC's focus emphasizes four areas of interest: advanced computer design and architecture, computer software technology, integrated circuit packaging, and computer-assisted design and manufacturing systems. Inman revealed to Hilts that he was particularly excited about the potential of parallel processing, in which a group of machines works independently and simultaneously to solve a problem. "If we can find a way to use parallelism in computing, enormous gains in both cost and speed should be available to us," Inman noted. Displaying a wariness perhaps typical to one with his background, Inman further confessed to Hilts that he does not entirely trust his competitors in the race to develop artificial intelligence: "I must tell you I worry a little about the uncharacteristic fanfare in Japan for the fifth generation. If you'll forgive me, that's some of my past thirty years cropping up. Perhaps this wonder computer is a red herring that the Japanese are using to lure us all into rushing down the artificial-intelligence trail as the single solution, while they in fact have a much broader-based program." In the words of the *Detroit News* article, "the retired spy master still tries to outfox his competitors."

After selecting Austin, Texas, for the development of MCC's headquarters, Inman's next task was to staff the project. Inman told Walsh that when he was approached by the member companies to head MCC, he wanted to be assured that sponsors would commit high-quality personnel to the joint effort, recalling that he "kept tugging at the question of talent to insure I wouldn't be running a retirement home, a turkey farm, in the vernacular." When Inman felt that, in fact, sponsors were not sending their best, the *New York Times* reported, Inman recruited researchers from outside the consortium. The great number of applicants that responded to Inman's recruiting efforts allowed Inman to be extremely selective in hiring. Called "America's elite research pool" in the *Detroit News*, MCC employed two hundred scientists and engineers by January, 1985. Salaries are said to be competitive and security tight; MCC requires employees to sign secrecy agreements to protect the research. In the *Detroit News* article Inman identified "a strong sense of ethics" and "peer pressure" as important in the maintenance of MCC's security.

When Inman joined MCC, Hershey predicted that "Admiral Inman could become enmeshed in corporate maneuvering every bit as fierce as that he left behind," and *Omni* later confirmed that "in MCC's first 18 months, Inman is reported to have spent much of his time battling to save the consortium from the competitive jealousies of its participants." Part of Inman's responsibility at MCC is to insure that member corporations enjoy equal access to the results of the consortium's research efforts. As Inman told *Time*, "The ability of the partners to believe they are going to share equally and fairly is critical." Hershey articulated the skepticism of MCC's critics, noting, "Some think it can't be done, that . . . when the gloves come off and it's time for the individual partners to contribute jointly to an effort that may help a competitor make millions" rivalries will surface within MCC. "We would never want to constrain the individual entrepreneur," Inman acknowledged to *Forbes* magazine's Jerry Flint, but, continued Inman, "you are not going to get those breakthroughs that compete with the concentrated Japanese effort by the single individual entrepreneur," The *Detroit News* article quoted an optimistic Inman, who asserted: "One thing we have proven indisputably is that this is the way to meet the competition—a collaborative research effort. We have already made great headway on our projects. . . . We still have a long way to go before we see results. But we know now this was the way to do the job."

The importance that Inman attaches to his efforts at MCC is evident in his remarks to interviewers. "Technology and its commercialization," he told Hilts, "has been a critical factor in the development of the American economy." Moreover, Inman stated in the *Detroit News* article, "Our success or failure here will affect the long-term security of the United States and its economic viability." Agreeing with the contention that knowledge will be the future measure of wealth in the world economy, Inman informed Hilts: "We have every reason to expect information handling to be a trillion-dollar worldwide industry in the early Nineties. Well, that is a big, big market to go after." With such potential in the balance, Inman seems to have convinced onlookers that he is the best trustee of America's stake in the profits expected from the impending information age. For, according to Anson, a former CIA director once said of Inman, "Bobby understands information. He knows it is power. He knows how to use it," while a former U.S. secretary of defense admitted, "I'm just glad that guy's on our side."

SOURCES:

PERIODICALS

Aviation Week and Space Technology, February 8, 1982.
Detroit News, January 13, 1985.
Forbes, April 25, 1983.
Newsweek, February 16, 1981, May 3, 1982, July 4, 1983.
New York Times, April 28, 1982, March 8, 1983.
Omni, November, 1984.
People, November 22, 1982.
Playboy, May, 1982.
Science, June 17, 1983.
Time, May 3, 1982, February 7, 1983.
U.S. News and World Report, March 2, 1981, May 3, 1982, December 20, 1982.

—Sketch by Diane L. Dupuis

Robert K. Jarvik

1946-

PERSONAL: Full name, Robert Koffler Jarvik; born May 11, 1946, in Midland, Mich.; son of Norman Eugene (a surgeon) and Edythe (Koffler) Jarvik; married Elaine Levin (a journalist), October 5, 1968 (divorced); children: Tyler, Kate. *Education*: Syracuse University, B.A. (zoology), 1968; attended University of Bologna (Italy) School of Medicine, 1968-69; New York University, M.A. (occupational biomechanics), 1971; University of Utah, M.D., 1976.

ADDRESSES: *Office*—825 North 300 W., Salt Lake City, Utah 84103.

OCCUPATION: Physician; inventor.

CAREER: University of Utah, Salt Lake City, research assistant in Division of Artificial Organs, 1971-76, assistant director of experimental laboratories, 1976-82, assistant research professor of surgery, 1979—. President, Kolff Medical, Inc. (artificial organ company), Salt Lake City, 1981—. Inventor; holds patents on a number of surgical instruments as well as first artificial heart implanted in a human being.

MEMBER: American Society of Artificial Internal Organs.

AWARDS, HONORS: Named Inventor of the Year by Intellectual Property Owners, 1982, and by National Inventors Hall of Fame, 1983; John W. Hyatt Award from Society of Plastics Engineers, Golden Plate Award from American Academy of Achievement, Gold Heart Award from Utah Heart Association, and Brotherhood Citation from Utah Chapter of National Conference of Christians and Jews, all 1983; D.Sc., Syracuse University.

WRITINGS: Author of more than sixty technical publications, 1972—. Section editor, *Journal of Artificial Organs*, 1979—.

SIDELIGHTS: In December of 1982 Robert K. Jarvik and Barney Clark made international news when Clark, a retired dentist, became the first human recipient of a permanent artificial heart designed by Jarvik, a physician and biomechanical engineer. The artificial heart, named the Jarvik-7, is slightly larger than the human heart and consists of two hollow chambers of polyurethane and aluminum. It is powered by a 300-pound compressor that pumps air to the heart through two plastic hoses. As an alternative to the heart transplant, the artificial heart holds two distinct advantages: No foreign human tissue is implanted in the recipient, which eliminates the possibility of rejection; and the artificial heart can be manufactured on a large scale, making it readily available and ending the long, often futile, wait for a heart from a suitable donor. In the United States alone, the artificial heart could benefit an estimated 50,000 people annually. Yet the Jarvik-7, despite its advantages, is

AP/Wide World Photos

not without its critics. The cost of the operation and the recipient's quality of life after surgery are frequently targeted, and some observers argue that such high-technology procedures divert funds and public attention from less dramatic, albeit more significant, long-range efforts. Nevertheless, as *Time*'s Otto Friedrich points out, the Jarvik-7 has "seized the world's imagination, arousing once again a sense of . . . awe at the incredible powers of technology, a sense that almost anything is possible, almost anything that can be imagined can be done."

Jarvik, whose father was a surgeon, showed an early interest in medicine and "the design of surgical tools," according to Bayard Webster of the *New York Times*. Jarvik also harbored a keen interest in the arts, especially sculpting, and once considered art as a career. Medicine prevailed, however, and in 1976 he received his medical degree from the University of Utah. After graduation he remained with the university, serving as an assistant to Willem Kolff, a highly respected pioneer in artificial heart research. Jarvik's predilection towards this field was occasioned by his father's death from heart disease. "Today," Webster recounts, "Dr. Jarvik says that event led him down the newly opened path of artificial heart research."

Jarvik is first to acknowledge that the work of many scientists, past and present, made the Jarvik-7 possible. In particular, he credits the research conducted by Kolff and various associates during the 1950s and 1960s. The results of these early experiments, performed on dogs and calves, were modest but encouraging. At the time, Jarvik notes in a *Scientific American* article, "the surgical techniques for implanting an artificial heart were poorly developed, so that survivals of even a few hours were a considerable accomplishment." As medical knowledge and techniques improved, so did the survival times of the animals. By the early 1970s survival periods of up to two weeks had been achieved. Despite these advances, several problems remained, including excessive clotting, uncontrolled bleeding, and what Jarvik describes as "[right ventrical] failure resulting from the poor fit of the artificial device to the natural anatomy." In 1972, with these deficiencies in mind, Jarvik designed the Jarvik-3, which slightly lengthened the period of survival. Two years later he improved the heart by fitting it with a flexible, three-layer diaphragm. Jarvik explains the significance of this development: "Earlier hearts had had a single-layer diaphragm of polyurethane, which had ruptured too easily. . . . The heart with the three-layer diaphragm soon increased survival times to as much as four months." Jarvik continued to refine the device, and in 1979 he introduced the Jarvik-7. This heart, which is designed to fit the human anatomy, was first implanted in a calf. The animal lived a record 221 days.

In 1981 Jarvik and colleague William De Vries applied to the Food and Drug Administration (FDA) for permission to implant the Jarvik-7 in humans. The agency denied their initial request, citing problems that ranged from the drastic nature of the procedure to the adequacy of the patient consent forms. Yet the FDA made it clear that their decision was a provisional one. "They are going to come through with an acceptable proposal," Melvin Cheitlin, chief of the advisory panel that evaluated the heart, predicted in *Time*. "I don't see any problem that it will eventually be granted."

A revised application was accepted by the FDA, and in 1982 Clark became the first human to receive the Jarvik-7. To qualify for the mechanical heart Clark and his successors, William Schroeder and Murray Haydon, had to meet several criteria. All were in the final stages of terminal heart disease and ineligible for heart transplants, which are limited to persons 50 and younger. Moreover, they demonstrated a strong will to live and a firm grasp of the considerable risks involved during and after surgery. Clark was 61 and suffering from emphysema as well as heart disease when he received the Jarvik-7 at the University of Utah Medical Center. Shortly after the operation he experienced a series of disabling brain seizures. Clark died 112 days after the heart implant.

Schroeder, 52, and Haydon, 58, are younger and somewhat healthier than their predecessor (though Schroeder is diabetic and has advanced arteriosclerosis). Schroeder's surgery took place in November of 1984 at Louisville's Humana Hospital. His early recovery was swift and encouraging. Within hours of receiving the Jarvik-7, Schroeder was able to breathe on his own and speak. Several days later he tested a portable air compressor developed by a West German engineer. The following month, however, Schroeder suffered the first of a series of debilitating strokes that impaired his memory and left him partially paralyzed and unable to speak. Haydon suffered lung damage after his surgery and since March 1985 has been on a respirator.

In spite of its success, the Jarvik-7 has generated a storm of controversy. As Friedrich of *Time* comments: "In what should be a time for congratulations and rejoicing, it may seem carping to raise questions about the value of such spectacular operations, yet that is exactly what a number of medical experts were doing. . . . They did so because they feel serious doubts about the whole course of high-technology medicine, doubts about cost, ethics, efficiency and simple justice." Clark's, Schroeder's, and Haydon's procedures cost $200,000 each. While Humana has promised to pay for the first 100 implants, many observers agree that the burden will eventually fall to the government. They explain that most insurance firms consider such operations experimental and refuse to foot the bill; they add that few individuals can afford the expense on their own. "To some theorists the real danger with artificial hearts is that they will work," state *Newsweek*'s Jerry Adler and George Raine, "presenting the unwelcome choice of saving the lives of only those who can afford the operation or making them available to everyone, at a potential cost of billions." Moreover, such critics fear that should the state agree to pay, the staggering price will force it to impose restrictions or rationing measures. Still others argue that the funds earmarked for implant study and surgery would be better spent on preventive medicine, such as public education programs and drug research.

Cost is not the only issue. Critics of the artificial heart allege that its recipients are little more than human guinea pigs. They emphasize the experimental status of heart implants, and they question the patient's quality of life, particularly in light of the brain seizures suffered by Clark and Schroeder's stroke. According to Claudia Wallis of *Time*, "Clark had complained to psychiatrists that he wanted to die, that his 'mind was shot' and that he found it enormously disappointing to wake up and find that he was still alive with the artificial heart pounding away in his chest." Schroeder, too, has been described as "confused" and sometimes "despondent" since his stroke. Some experts object to the very principle that underlies artificial organs and organ transplants. Kenneth Vaux, a University of Illinois professor of ethics and medicine, worries that science is in quest of immortality. "We are going to have to temper our ambitions and learn to accept the inevitability of disease," he tells Friedrich, "the inevitability of death itself."

Notwithstanding the concerns and protests voiced by opponents to "expensive novelties like the artificial heart," Friedrich asserts, "very few scientists see any possibility of retreating from high-tech medicine, which has the glamor that attracts talent, money and publicity." He continues: "Very few think such a retreat desirable. Most argue that a number of now standard procedures were once regarded as extravagant. . . . The artificial kidney, by now commonplace, was attacked 20 years ago in the *Annals of Internal Medicine* in words much like those now being applied to the artificial heart." Finally, and most importantly to its recipients, the Jarvik-7 offers a last chance at life. As Adler and Raine comment, "While authorities in the field of medical ethics gravely weighed his 'quality of life,' [Schroeder], irrelevantly glad just to be alive, was toasting his recovery with a can of beer." Later, they record De Vries's response to those who claim that Clark paid too great a price, physically and psychologically, for an extra 112 days: "To say to only live an additional 112 days is unsuccessful is ridiculous. His case was successful because he was going to die that day, and he saw Christmas and his birthday and his anniversary."

The debate is certain to continue. Jarvik himself appreciates the drawbacks of the artificial heart. In his *Scientific American* article he touches on the "ethical, social and economic considerations" attending the procedure. Nevertheless, he is at work on the Jarvik-8, designed to fit women and small-framed men (the current heart is intended for average- to large-sized men). Ultimately, Jarvik hopes to render his invention inconspicuous, so that future recipients will enjoy near-routine lives. "If the artificial heart is ever to achieve its objective, it must be more than a pump," Jarvik writes. "It must also be more than functional, reliable and dependable. It must be forgettable."

AVOCATIONAL INTERESTS: Skiing (cross country and downhill), weight-lifting, poetry.

SOURCES:

PERIODICALS

Fortune, June 29, 1981.
Maclean's, May 9, 1983.
Newsweek, December 13, 1983, December 10, 1984, March 4, 1985, April 15, 1985.
New York Times, December 3, 1982, June 11, 1985, July 9, 1985, November 12, 1985, November 26, 1985, December 3, 1985, December 26, 1985.
People, December 16, 1985.
Science News, February 19, 1983.
Scientific American, January, 1981.
Time, April 6, 1981, December 10, 1984, December 17, 1984, March 4, 1985, April 15, 1985.
Washington Post, February 12, 1983.

—Sidelights by Denise Wiloch

Pierre Marc Johnson

1946-

PERSONAL: Born July 5, 1946, in Montreal, Quebec, Canada; son of Daniel (a politician) and Reine (Gagné) Johnson; married Marie-Louise Parent, June 30, 1973; children: Marc Olivier, Marie-Claude. *Education:* College Jean-de-Brébeuf, B.A., 1967; Université de Montreal, LL.L., 1970; Université de Sherbrooke, M.D., 1975. *Religion:* Roman Catholic.

ADDRESSES: Home—16 Roskilde St., Outremont, Quebec, Canada H2V 2N5.

OCCUPATION: Canadian politician.

CAREER: Called to Bar of Quebec, 1971; admitted to Quebec College of Physicians, 1976. Member of board and of various committees, OXFAM (Oxford Committee for Famine Relief) Canada and OXFAM Quebec, 1969-76; elected member of national assembly, representing riding (district) of Anjou, 1976; member of national executive council, Parti Quebecois, 1977-79; Quebec minister of labour and manpower, 1977-80; Quebec minister of consumer affairs, cooperatives, and financial institutions, 1980-81; Quebec minister of social affairs, 1981-85; leader of Parti Quebecois; premier of Quebec, September, 1985-December, 1985; opposition leader, December, 1985—.

SIDELIGHTS: Quebec politician Pierre Marc Johnson is the ideal personification of French Canada's new conservative mood. After a decade of separatist inspired political unrest that included bombings and kidnappings, the Quebec electorate has turned its back on the issue of independence. And even though Johnson is leader of the separatist Parti Quebecois (PQ), he insists he is now prepared to work within the federal framework. Most residents of the largely francophone province don't mind the inconsistency. Like Johnson, they are now more interest in bread-and-butter economic issues.

Johnson has become one of Quebec's most popular politicians because of his ability to read the mood of the people. He turned around the failing fortunes of his party in just a few short months after succeeding René Lévesque as leader of the PQ. The PQ had first gained power in 1976 when it argued Quebec had to separate from Canada if it wanted to maintain a French cultural and linguistic identity. But the separatist movement was badly shaken in 1980 when a province-wide referendum on separatism was defeated. By late 1984, its popularity had slipped to less than 20 percent. When Johnson took over from Lévesque in September 1985, he declared he would no longer fight for the province's independence. And, predictably, the party's popularity soared to within points of the competing Liberal party.

Johnson called an election just weeks after he was named premier. Political pundits were surprised because the party

stood much lower in the polls than the Liberals headed by former premier Robert Bourassa. In the final analysis, the Parti Quebecois was too far behind to be able to beat the Liberals. On December 2, 1985, the Liberals swept 99 of the province's 122 ridings. Still, every poll showed that Pierre Marc Johnson was personally more popular than Bourassa. In fact, Bourassa was unable to win his seat. Johnson now sits in the Quebec National Assembly as leader of the opposition rather than as premier, but at thirty-nine years of age his political career is hardly over.

The son of respected former Quebec premier Daniel Johnson, Pierre Marc was touted as the heir apparent almost as soon as he entered politics. Pierre Marc's admirers say he inherited his father's patience and understanding. When Johnson was first named a cabinet minister in 1976, Brian Mulroney, who was later to become Canada's prime minister, said: "Johnson's nomination is a brilliant one. He's got all the charm and all the good judgement of his old man. He's first class—they don't make them any better."

Johnson is the sort of politician people look up to. He is one of only a handful of North Americans who is licensed to practice both law and medicine. He has a formal, almost regal manner, that some describe as arrogant. But for the most part, the assessments are admiring. As Alycia Ambroziak wrote in *Maclean's*, "Johnson, in contrast to the unpredictable Lévesque, is a poised authoritative politician with a calm and sometimes eloquent speaking style." Added one of Johnson's colleagues, "He may not stir crowds the same way Lévesque does, but he's unbeatable on a one-to-one basis."

But no one active in Quebec's volatile political scene is free from detractors, and Pierre Marc Johnson is no exception. His critics agree he is his father's son—to the extent that he is ideologically uncommitted and politically ambiguous. The senior Johnson wrote a book called *Equality or Independence* and flirted with the idea of independence without committing himself. Pierre Marc's critics say he too has refused to commit himself to the philosophy of separatism. What his admirers call political adroitness, his critics call opportunism. "Pierre Marc Johnson, like his father Daniel, practices the art of verbal ambiguity. His rhetoric promises much but reveals little," wrote columnist Jeffrey Simpson in the Toronto *Globe and Mail*. A Liberal member of the National Assembly nicknamed Johnson "hovercraft" in an attempt to describe his ability to skim over sensitive issues. Some critics also point to Johnson's formal manner as a barrier keeps him removed from ordinary people.

Politics was the stuff of dinner conversations when Johnson was growing up. Daniel Johnson's influence, in fact, propelled both of his sons into politics. Pierre Marc's brother, Daniel, now sits across from him in the Quebec assembly as a member of the Liberal party. But there was a time when Pierre Marc swore he would have nothing to do with politics. That was in 1968 after his father died at a relatively early age. Pierre Marc was disgusted to see the graveside politicking for Daniel's successor. And from his father's regular absences during his childhood, Johnson knew politics exacts a heavy toll on family life. Now, Johnson tries to live as quietly as possible with his wife, Marie-Louise Parent, and their two children.

Pierre Marc was six months old when, in 1946, his father was first elected to the province's assembly as a member of the Union Nationale. The Union Nationale was an anti-urban, anti-intellectual and anti-labour party. Like all Quebec parties at that time it was nationalist but not separatist. In 1961, Daniel Johnson became leader of the party and served as premier from 1966 to 1968. Despite his loyalties to his father and the Union Nationale, Pierre Marc felt drawn to the Quebec independence movement of the 1960s. As a young law student, he found himself influenced by two key events. In 1969, the Union Nationale government adopted a law giving Quebeckers free choice in the language of education. He was outraged that the party his father had led would weaken the position of French in the province. So he resigned from the party. Then, in 1970, Canada's federal government sent tanks and troops into the streets of Montreal in response to two terrorist kidnappings in Quebec. Civil liberties were withdrawn across the province, and all separatists were described as terrorists. Johnson told *Saturday Night* magazine he realized Quebec couldn't negotiate with the federal government for French rights. "I asked myself how was it possible to negotiate with people who saw no difference between the horrifying acts of terrorists and the democratic process pursued by nationalists." And so Johnson joined the Parti Quebecois.

In 1974, the party asked the young student to run in a by-election in his father's old riding (district). Johnson declined, determined to complete his medical studies. But he was prepared in 1976 to give up his fledgling career as a hospital emergency ward doctor to run in the next general election campaign. He easily won the riding of Anjou by more than 8,000 votes.

In 1977, Premier Lévesque appointed Johnson to the cabinet as labour and manpower minister. It was a particularly precarious cabinet position; three men had held the post in less than a year. But Johnson hung on for three years without making a serious mistake. In fact, he earned a reputation as a reformer when he introduced measures prohibiting the use of strikebreakers, improving construction workers' job security, and setting minimum collective bargaining standards. But Johnson climbed into the hot seat when, after a long and bitter dispute, he ordered striking public employees back to work. And in 1981, as minister of social affairs, he was forced to administer Draconian cutbacks in health and social services. Yet despite these unpopular tasks, Johnson seemed invulnerable. In 1983, 30,000 public sector employees demonstrated against the government and hung several cabinet ministers in effigy. Johnson was not one of them.

Johnson travelled across Quebec in the summer of 1984 with his seven-year-old son, Marc Olivier, to assess the mood of the people. He came home convinced the Parti Quebecois had to drop the issue of independence in the next election and resume negotiations with the federal government for a new agreement for Quebec. "Most Quebeckers now believe that progress is not necessarily tied to the idea of independence, that it can exist within a Canadian context," Johnson told *Saturday Night*.

He said the same thing to René Lévesque. And he told the party he wouldn't run in the next election if it were fought on independence. In late 1984, Lévesque announced that independence would no longer be the primary platform of the Parti Quebecois. His announcement sparked a series of resignations by senior cabinet ministers and other avowed separatists in the PQ. But at a convention in January, 1985, party members agreed with Johnson that separatism was, at least for the present, an irrelevant issue. After Lévesque resigned, Johnson was elected the new leader with the support of 60 percent of party members.

The party's decision to turn to Johnson's way of thinking marked the end of an era. Gone were the hot emotions of the 1960s and early 1970s. Now, the Parti Quebecois was prepared to deal with the more mundane issues of economic performance and administrative ability. "The quest for political sovereignty must not become an obsession that obscures the concrete, everyday concerns of our fellow citizens," Johnson told an applauding audience during the election campaign.

Pierre Marc Johnson has, in many ways, created a new party without having to leave the Parti Quebecois. As a leader of the new, more conservative Quebec, Johnson has vowed to keep separatism on the shelf and work within the framework of Canada. But that doesn't mean he has lost his early concern for the protection of French culture and language in Canada. As he told *Maclean's* magazine, "My first allegiance is to the people of Quebec."

AVOCATIONAL INTERESTS: Swimming, music.

SOURCES:

PERIODICALS

Christian Science Monitor, June 24, 1985.
Detroit News, September 30, 1985.
Financial Post, January 5, 1985.
Globe and Mail (Toronto), February 4, 1985, September 27, 1985, September 30, 1985, October 1, 1985.
Maclean's, January 21, 1985, July 1, 1985, September 23, 1985, October 7, 1985, October 19, 1985, November 4, 1985, November 18, 1985.
Montreal Gazette, January 26, 1985.
New York Times, October 6, 1985.
Saturday Night, August, 1985.
Time, October 19, 1985.
Toronto Star, August 29, 1985.

—Sidelights by Ingeborg Boyens

Arthur A. Jones

1924(?)-

PERSONAL: Born c. 1924 in Arkansas; son of two physicians; married fifth wife, Terri Brantner (a model); children: four (previous marriage). *Education:* Dropped out of school after ninth grade. ("I should have dropped out in the sixth grade," Jones told *Forbes* magazine.)

ADDRESSES: *Home*—Ocala, Fla.; and Lake Helen, Fla. *Office*—Nautilus Sports/Medical Industries, 305 Ohio Ave., Lake Helen, Fla. 32744.

OCCUPATION: Inventor and entrepreneur.

CAREER: Worked as a pilot in Central America and Africa; tracked, captured, and transported big game from Africa to zoos and research facilities; independent film maker; producer and host of television program "Wild Cargo" in the 1960s; inventor and developer of Nautilus exercise equipment and chief executive officer of Nautilus Sports/Medical Industries, Lake Helen, Fla. Also inventor of numerous other items, including photographic vehicles and camera mounts and lenses. *Military service*: Bomber pilot in World War II.

SIDELIGHTS: "Every single innovation in the field of exercise since the barbell has come from Nautilus," Arthur Jones, inventor of the Nautilus exercise machine, told *Newsweek.* "Anybody who says otherwise is either a liar or a fool." Such statements are typical of Jones, who is also a big-game collector, moviemaker, entrepreneur, researcher, syndicated television show host, pilot, and multimillionaire.

Jones is presumed to be in his early sixties, although he steadfastly refuses to reveal his exact age. He was born in Arkansas and raised in Tulsa, Oklahoma, during the Depression. Both of his parents were physicians; his mother completed medical school while Jones was still a child. He quit school at age fifteen, contending that he had learned all that the educational system had to offer. He traveled—rode the rails—for a time before serving as a bomber pilot during World War II.

Jones began working to improve the barbell method of body building in 1948. He was living in the Tulsa YMCA at the time, and it was there that he built his first exercise machine. He continued to rebuild and modify his invention until 1970, when he introduced the perfected product at a Los Angeles weight-lifting convention. He named his machine Nautilus after the nautilus seashell, which resembles the kidney-shaped cam that proved to be the breakthrough development for Jones's improved exercise machine.

Barbells are good for building only part of the muscle, Jones told *Playboy.* "A barbell provides one-directional resistance—straight down as the result of the force of gravity. But human beings are rotational animals. . . . We move by

Ron Lindsey/NYT Pictures

rotating around the axis of the body joint. . . . So the first requirement when it came to improving the barbell was to design a device that provided rotational resistance for exercise. . . . Another problem with movement is that the strength of a human being changes. It varies as your advantage of leverage gets better or worse. With a barbell, as a consequence, you're limited to the amount of weight that you can handle in your weakest position."

Creating his specially shaped cam, which applies constant pressure to the muscle as its position changes, was no simple task. "I started out trying to solve the problem of adding variable resistance to the barbell by adding chain to one," he told *Playboy.* "At the start of the movement, most of the chain would be lying on the floor, so that as you lifted the barbell, more of it came into the air, thereby adding weight. That helped but it didn't solve the problem because in some cases you need a decrease in the weight."

Jones was living in Africa when he took the first step toward the critical discovery. He described an idea for a cam to an employee over the telephone one evening and told the man to deliver the finished product by eight o'clock the next morning. "We installed it and it did not work," he recalled. "It was a total, absolute abysmal failure. But it failed so obviously that for the first time I understood why." Refining and improving through trial and error eventually brought success.

There are now thirty-seven different models of exercise machines for fitness centers, and two for home use, produced by Nautilus Sports/Medical Industries. The firm, which is owned by Jones, is based in Lake Helen, Florida, and has plants in Independence, Virginia, and Houston and Maria, Texas. It is the biggest single producer of exercise machines in the United States.

According to *Time,* Jones has manufactured more than 400,000 machines selling for an average price of $2,640. His firm has estimated 1984 sales of $300 million. Sales can only be estimated because Jones, with his usual maverick spirit, shares the figures with no one—not even the federal government for a while. But the Internal Revenue Service took exception to that practice and in 1981 indicted Jones for failing to pay federal income taxes for 1974 through 1976. He paid the taxes and fines immediately.

Jones's singular style has helped him become very successful at marketing his products. In addition to exercise equipment, Nautilus Sports/Medical Industries also produces video exercise cassettes, a line of sports clothing, and sells its name to franchised workout centers. The firm's colorful founder packs a Colt .45, which he is fond of talking about, and, according to *People,* often refers to his political beliefs as being "64,000 miles to the right of Attila the Hun." He refers to his competitors, reports *Newsweek,* as "thieves, frauds, fakes, slanderers and incompetents."

He and his twenty-three-year-old wife, Terri, spend a great deal of time at their mansion on a 600-arce spread in Ocala, Florida. The estate is home to ninety elephants, three rhinos, a gorilla, 300 alligators, 400 crocodiles and three Boeing 707 jet airliners, which Jones pilots. They also maintain an apartment over Jones's $70 million television production studio in Lake Helen, Florida. Terri is the fifth of Jones's wives, all of whom he married when they were between the ages of sixteen and twenty. As he has told numerous interviewers, the things that make life worthwhile are "younger women, faster planes, and bigger crocodiles."

In addition to its general-use machines, Nautilus Sports/ Medical Industries has recently added to its inventory special machines for hospital and laboratory use. In 1983 the firm first produced a "lower-back" machine that was developed to help diagnose and cure back ailments. In 1985 it introduced a $30,000 computerized Nautilus machine for doctors and clinics, which is designed to aid physical therapy by measuring strength.

The firm is very heavily involved in research, says Jones. Nautilus gave $3 million to the University of Florida to help develop the lower-back machine, and it is estimated that Jones has thus far donated a total of more than $11 million to medical research. In addition, the Nautilus staff is busy with a wide variety of their own research projects—including physiological testing and animal studies—at several locations. It is possible, however, that Jones was given to

slight exaggeration when he told *Newsweek* that Nautilus is doing "over 500 times more research than everybody in the world put together in the area of exercise physiology and anything related to it."

The next field Jones intends to conquer has already been designated as video production. Although an interview-entertainment show he sponsored—to be hosted by friend G. Gordon Liddy, ex-FBI agent and convicted Watergate planner—failed to materialize, he continues to work on the development of his latest enterprise: the Nautilus Television Network. Jones is no stranger to television production. He spent twelve years capturing and transporting big game from Africa to zoos, pet stores, and research facilities on his own fleet of World War II planes. He filmed many television specials on his hunts, which were shown in the States. Eventually his exploits became the subject of a television series, produced and hosted by Jones himself, called "Wild Cargo."

After roaming the jungles of the world for many years, *Newsweek* said of Jones, he almost lost his life when he entered a lion's cage to save a co-worker. The angry animal bit him through the neck and left his right shoulder three inches lower than his left. "It would not have gone through my mind to do anything else," Jones told *Playboy* of the incident. "There's a tendency to not want to get involved, which I suppose is fear of some sort. I don't consider myself brave. . . . But if you lead an active life, if you get around the country or around the world, you're going to have adventures."

Adventure seems to follow wherever the outspoken Jones travels. In 1968 the Rhodesian government took exception to his wild-game business and seized all his assets in that country, including, Jones told *Playboy,* "seven ground vehicles, two aircraft, a brand-new helicopter, cameras, weapons, ammunition, family records going back two centuries, my wife's insect collection and children's toys."

Jones has four children from previous marriages whom he has already told will receive no inheritance from him. "Leaving [money] to people destroys them," he told *People.* His daughter Eva told the magazine that her father is a "gentle giant" who has an insatiable hunger for knowledge. Jones, who in typically humble fashion describes himself as a genius, has taught himself, among other things, physiology. Eva, a New York physician, said he learned that particular subject by studying cadavers. "We always had an arm or something in the freezer," she told *People.* Perhaps the only thing Jones has not succeeded in learning is to stick to the healthy regime he recommends to those using his machines. He drinks coffee by the potful, chain smokes, nibbles from bowls of Hershey Kisses and cheese puffs that are always placed within his reach.

Jones usually dresses in baggy, rumpled outfits that he sometimes doesn't change for days. His interest in collecting unusual animals continues; in addition to the big game, he has an indoor menagerie that includes scorpions, tarantulas, and twenty-five varieties of poisonous snakes. He has a plan for further testing of new exercise machines, says *Newsweek,* in an undisclosed South American country, where "it's easier to find research subjects." According to *People,* he has installed forty-eight video monitors in his office, many of which are trained on his own staff, and he "often tests his associates' stamina with meetings that adjourn at 2 a.m." *Forbes* quoted him as saying, "The one good thing about Communists is that when they take over a country the first thing they do is kill all the lawyers." Regarding his rather strange behavior and outspoken nature, Jones told *Time*, "When I was broke, I was crazy; Now that I am rich I am eccentric."

SOURCES:

PERIODICALS

Forbes, September 26, 1983.
Newsweek, April 21, 1980, August 15, 1983.
New York Times, July 25, 1982.
People, March 7, 1983.
Playboy, March, 1983.
Science Digest, May, 1984.
Time, June 10, 1985.
Washington Post, September 29, 1983.

—Sidelights by Mary Solomon Smyka

Henry E. Kloss

1929(?)-

BRIEF ENTRY: Born c. 1929. American electronics executive and inventor. Henry E. Kloss is a major name in the home entertainment industry. He has invented several of its most important products, and he has helped to found four of its more successful companies. Among his inventions are the acoustic-suspension speaker and the large-screen projection television.

Kloss discovered his flair for enterprise while a student at the Massachusetts Institute of Technology during the early 1950s. There, he and some friends designed the first acoustic-suspension speaker, considered an audio breakthrough that popularized high fidelity sound. The invention's success prompted Kloss to drop out of school to start his own manufacturing firm, Acoustic Research. Later, Kloss and two partners formed a second concern, KLH, where Kloss redesigned his previous effort and eventually created the KLH Model Eleven, the world's first compact, portable stereo. When Kloss and his associates sold KLH, the inventor turned his attention to the growing video market. In 1967 he co-founded Advent with the goal of producing projection televisions. To finance this project, the company manufactured and sold loudspeakers. Kloss introduced his first projection television in 1973. Six years later he became founder and president of Kloss Video Corp., which manufactures one of his latest inventions, the Novatron tube and two-piece projection screen system. The Novatron system, experts agree, provides the clearest picture available in the large-screen projection television market.

For the most part, Kloss credits his success to the shortsightedness of his competitors and to his own ability, as *Rolling Stone*'s Susan March points out, "[to combine] possibilities in ways no one else seems to envision." Referring to the projection television, Kloss told March that he intended to "develop a more desirable and commanding picture, something I guess that would resemble the movies. . . . The elements were there; I just brought them to bear."

AP/Wide World Photos

SOURCES:

PERIODICALS

Fortune, June 29, 1981.
New York Times, December 25, 1982.
Rolling Stone, January 24, 1980.

Bobby Knight

1940-

PERSONAL: Full name, Robert Montgomery Knight; born October 25, 1940, in Orrville, Ohio; son of Carroll (a railroad worker) and Hazel (an elementary school teacher; maiden name, Menthorne) Knight; married April 17, 1963; wife's name, Nancy Lou (divorced, 1985); children: Timothy Scott, Patrick Clair. *Education:* Ohio State University, B.S., 1962. *Religion:* Methodist.

ADDRESSES: Office—Basketball Office, Assembly Hall, Indiana University, Bloomington, Ind. 47405.

OCCUPATION: Basketball coach.

CAREER: Cuyahoga Falls High School, Cuyahoga Falls, Ohio, assistant basketball coach, 1962-63; United States Military Academy, West Point, N.Y., assistant basketball coach, 1963-65, head coach, 1965-71; Indiana University at Bloomington, head basketball coach, 1971—. Coach of United States national basketball teams at Pan American games, San Juan, Puerto Rico, 1979, and at Summer Olympics, Los Angeles, Calif., 1984. Public speaker; conductor of seminars for basketball players and coaches. *Military service*: Served in U.S. Army.

MEMBER: National Association of Basketball Coaches (member of board of directors).

AWARDS, HONORS: Named Big Ten coach of the year, 1973, 1975, 1976, and 1980; named national coach of the year by Associated Press and *Basketball Weekly*, 1976; gold medal, 1984 Summer Olympics.

WRITINGS: Author of several booklets on playing and coaching basketball.

SIDELIGHTS: In his twenty-year career as a college basketball coach, Bobby Knight has become one of the most successful, and certainly one of the most controversial, figures in the game. His statistics since 1966 denote a record-setting pace: 417 wins to 157 losses, two National Collegiate Athletic Association (NCAA) championships, one National Invitational Tournament (NIT) championship, seven Big Ten conference titles, and an Olympic gold medal. As coach of the Indiana Hoosiers since 1971, Knight has achieved an added measure of notoriety due in large part to his repeated temperamental outbursts on- and off-court—outbursts that have included grabbing and shoving his own players, throwing chairs, breaking clipboards, verbally abusing officials, and, in one instance, assaulting a police officer. Knight's tempestuous behavior has led *Newsweek* writer Pete Axthelm to characterize him as "a boiling blend of brilliance and loyalty, fanaticism and temper."

Even Knight's critics admit, however, that his coaching credentials are extraordinary for a man his age. He is the youngest coach ever to win three hundred games and one of only three coaches to win an NCAA championship, an NIT championship, and an Olympic gold medal. He is the only person to have both played on and coached an NCAA championship team, and he has sent a record eleven assistant coaches to head coaching jobs on the collegiate level. His commitment to basketball has led Axthelm to declare: "It is both the glorious destiny and the curse of Bobby Knight that he must dominate all he surveys. He wears his uncompromising passion for excellence on the sleeves of his bright plaid sports jackets." Frank DeFord, writing for *Sports Illustrated*, adds, "Some of his esteemed predecessors—mythic men of basketball lore—see Knight as the very keeper of the game."

According to DeFord, Knight "always wanted to be Coach Knight, officially expressing this desire in an autobiography he wrote when he was a junior in high school." The only child of a railroad man and an elementary school teacher, Knight grew up in Orrville, Ohio, a town of five thousand at a major railway junction. As a child, Knight was closest to his maternal grandmother, who lived with the family. DeFord writes: "Knight always had an ally in his grandmother. She was the one who followed his basketball closely." In high school Knight played all the major sports—basketball, football, and baseball. DeFord describes the especially close relationship between the young Knight and his high school basketball coach, Bill Shunkwiler: "When other kids were hanging out, chasing, Bobby would come by Shunkwiler's house, and the two of them would sit and have milk and cookies and talk coach talk."

Knight's days as a basketball player continued at Ohio State University, where he served as sixth man on the 1960 national championship team that included teammates Jerry Lucas and John Havlicek. DeFord says of Knight's ability, "He didn't amount to a hill of beans as a player." But DeFord sees this less-than-stellar playing career as one of Knight's assets: "Knight the failed hero has not only served as the challenge for Knight the coach, but also Knight the disappointed hero is the model for the Everyplayer Knight coaches." While he may have since profited from only having started two games in three years with the Ohio State varsity team, Knight chafed under the restraint at the time. His complaints ultimately reached his coach, Fred Taylor, who in turned labelled Knight "the Brat from Orrville."

After graduating from Ohio State in 1962, Knight was offered two coaching jobs at high schools in Ohio. The most lucrative of these involved coaching both basketball and football. The other, an assistant coaching position offering less salary, was exclusively basketball. Knight chose the latter because, as he later told *Sports Illustrated*, "I thought, if I'm going to be a basketball coach, I can't be diverted. I wanted vertical concentration." This singlemindedness benefitted Knight almost immediately. Within a year he became assistant basketball coach at the United States Military Academy (enlisting in the Army to get the job), and two years later, at age twenty-four, he was elevated to head coach—a promotion that, according to DeFord, "stunned everybody." The youthful coach proceeded to take Army, "hardly a basketball power," according to *Time*, to four NIT playoffs in six years. Ending his tenure at West Point with a highly respectable 102-50 record, Knight moved on to Indiana University in 1971.

The Indiana Hoosier basketball squad, a member of the intensely competitive Big Ten conference, prospered under Knight's tutelage. Within ten years, his teams had won six Big Ten titles, as well as one NIT and two NCAA championships. It is at Indiana that Knight's presence as a coach began to make the news. In 1976, he drew national criticism by pulling guard Jim Wisman off the court by grabbing his jersey. Knight had by that time already established a reputation as one who, according to *Time*, "succumbs to his hot temper and starts kicking the nearest

A familiar scene: Bobby Knight disagrees with a referee's call—and receives a technical. AP/Wide World Photos.

chair." While the incident with Wisman—having occurred in a nationally televised game—brought Knight's emotional behavior to a wider audience for the first time, the reaction to it in Indiana was relatively mild. "When I grabbed Jimmy by the shirt on national t.v.," Knight told *Sport* magazine, "the first person who said anything about it was Jimmy Wisman's mother. She said, 'If I had been there, I would have grabbed him too.' "

Answering his critics in the media further, Knight told Axthelm of *Newsweek*: "I may be overreacting when I kick a chair or holler at an official, but, hell, everybody's entitled to overreact once in a while. If I was the raving maniac I keep reading about, I don't think we'd win so many games." Knight's remarks came during a fifty-six consecutive game winning streak that included a perfect 32-0 season and an NCAA championship. Axthelm, among others, was willing to rationalize Knight's behavior as a product of "the agonizing profession that he dominates."

Some of the rationalizations ended abruptly when, at the Pan American games in 1979, Knight was arrested in Puerto Rico for assaulting a police officer. As the United States basketball coach at the international competition, Knight "turned the basketball court into a stage for a whole hemisphere's worth of Ugly American scenarios," according to Axthelm. Knight was ejected from a game on a technical foul with only seconds remaining and his team winning by thirty-five points. The altercation with the police officer, later described by Knight as a "reflex action," came during a dispute over the use of a practice gym. Though outwardly repentant (he offered to resign from his position at Indiana and penned a letter of apology to Puerto Rico's governor), Knight was quoted in *Sport Illustrated* as saying of the Puerto Rican people, "F——'em, f——'em all. . . . The only thing they know how to do is grow bananas."

Seeking an explanation for Knight's behavior in Puerto Rico, DeFord suggests that the coach was concerned for the safety of his wife and two sons, who were in attendance at the Pan American games. Nancy Knight told *Sports Illustrated*: "[San Juan] was terrifying. We had to change apartments. I couldn't sit in my seat at the games. I feared for my life and my children's." Knight's anxieties for his family were compounded by his "frenzied. . . drive for success," according to Axthelm in *Newsweek*, as well as anti-American sentiment at the games. As DeFord notes in *Sports Illustrated*, "Knight perceived, correctly or not, that the three things he values most in life were being menaced—his family, his country, and his team."

Returning to Indiana, Knight "kept his mean streak going," according to *Time*, but he also continued to win. The tradition of success at Indiana, in DeFord's view, now became self-fulfilling: "Knight's players have a high success rate because only success-oriented types would select Indiana basketball in the first place. In other words, the twigs only grow as they were bent a long time ago." Knight's coaching techniques revolve around his definition of discipline, as told to *Sports Illustrated*: "Discipline: doing what you have to do, and doing it as well as you possibly can, and doing it that way all the time." Knight told *Time* that he counsels his players: "Wherever you start life, there will be others above you. Get used to it now."

Hoosier basketball practices are conducted in complete privacy, off limits to the media and fans alike. Knight explained his reasons for this isolation to *Sport*: "I'm a teacher. And therefore I've got to have the right conditions under which to teach. One of those is a quiet situation where I'm not in competition with anyone else in terms of what's being said, taught, and learned."

Knight's basic strategy involves three elements: an aggressive man-to-man coverage on defense, a disciplined, relentlessly intense offense, and a system of teamwork designed to "discourage the individual," in the words of ex-Indiana guard Isiah Thomas, who plays professionally for the Detroit Pistons. Knight's demands upon his players, furthermore, do not end at the gymnasium door. He expects acceptable scholarship and regular attendance at classes, and he is careful to recruit athletes who will be bona fide college students. In 1982 he told *Sport*, "We've had thirty-eight players who I have recruited since I've been here [at Indiana]. Thirty-two of them have played for four years. Of these, thirty-one have degrees. That's way above the national average for regular students, let alone athletes."

Probably the greatest recruiting job Knight has had to face involved the selection of twelve basketball players to represent the United States at the 1984 Summer Olympics. Knight hand-picked the final team from a pool of seventy-two players by watching drills from atop a scaffold above the Bloomington, Indiana, basketball court. Still making the news for shoving a rival fan into a garbage can after the 1981 NCAA finals, Knight was restrained before the press during the Olympic trials, stressing his fundamental principles of discipline and desire to win. When asked about his suitability as a representative of the United States before the world, Knight responded to Axthelm in *Newsweek*: "The average fan doesn't want diplomacy. He wants to know whether we'll win."

The United States Olympic basketball team did indeed win the gold medal, remaining undefeated throughout the games, which were boycotted by the Eastern-bloc nations. The paucity of competition from the countries that competed in the Olympics led Axthelm to comment that Knight's intrasquad practice games "give the Americans the strongest competition in Los Angeles." Fears that Knight's volatile behavior would reflect badly upon the United States proved to be unfounded as he joked with the press and his players. Axthelm said of Knight: "Of course, he is driving his team relentlessly and telling his public that a careless defeat is possible. But that is the least convincing part of his routine. The comedy is more compelling. Enjoy it. . . General Patton as Johnny Carson."

After garnering the gold medal in 1984, Knight began yet another season of college basketball with the Indiana Hoosiers, a season that would be marred by multiple crises and suggestions that he was suffering from "coaching burnout." In a close game against Purdue, Knight protested a foul on one of his players, then swore at an official when another of his players was charged with a foul. Before play could resume, Knight picked up a chair and threw it across the court, drawing his second technical foul of the game. More swearing occasioned his third technical and his ultimate ejection from the contest, which Purdue won, 72-63. Trouble with players followed, including his dismissal of starting forward Mike Giomi. Indiana center Uwe Blab commented upon Knight's reactions to the 1985 season in *Sports Illustrated*: "During all the turmoil, he hasn't been screaming and yelling. And the moment Coach Knight doesn't scream and yell, you know there's a problem. It was like he had given up." Southern Methodist University coach Dave Bliss, a former assistant under Knight, was quoted by the *Detroit Free Press* as saying: "They talk about player burnout from the Olympics, but sometimes I think that Bob is the only one burned out. . . . He's the one who needs to slow down a little."

Rather than slowing down, Knight has taken on a new project in recent years: the restructuring and modification of the athletic recruiting system. He has introduced a plan aimed at curbing the abuses that allow virtual non-students to play intercollegiate sports. His ideas, as he told *Sport*, have been less than enthusiastically received by the NCAA: "People want to talk about what to do about academics and how to clean up college basketball, but when it comes down to having a chance to do something, I just don't think anybody is really very big on that."

As far back as 1976, rumors circulated that Knight would eventually leave his coaching position for a career in politics. In 1982, Knight himself indicated that he had given strong consideration to a contract with the CBS college basketball broadcasting team. Ultimately, however, Knight reaffirmed in *Sport*, "a definite commitment on my part to college coaching. I think I resolved what I'm going to do for quite a while." The man who had been called "a prodigy in search of proportion," by Frank DeFord in *Sports Illustrated*, told DeFord: "I just love the game of basketball. The game! I don't need the 18,000 people screaming and all the peripher-

al things. To me, what's most enjoyable is the practice and the preparation." As DeFord notes, "Those who would survive at Indiana, much less succeed, must subjugate themselves to the one man and his one way." But the ultimate goal Knight has set for himself, aside from his "frenzied. . . drive for success," is outlined by Pete Newell, a former coach and mentor of Knight's, in *Sports Illustrated*: "What [Knight] does do is the single most important thing in coaching: he turns out educated kids who are ready for society."

SOURCES:

PERIODICALS

Detroit Free Press, January 20, 1984, February 26, 1985, March 5, 1986.

Esquire, June, 1985.

Newsweek, December 29, 1975, July 23, 1979, May 7, 1984.

New York Times, April 1, 1971, March 13, 1975, April 9, 1975, December 2, 1975, December 27, 1975, December 13, 1978, December 16, 1978, December 18, 1978, July 4, 1979, July 9, 1979, July 10, 1979, July 11, 1979, July 12, 1979, August 23, 1979, August 24, 1979, August 25, 1979, September 11, 1979, November 13, 1979, December 2, 1979, December 30, 1979, November 23, 1981, March 20, 1983, March 27, 1984, April 22, 1984, June 23, 1984, July 15, 1984, July 23, 1984, March 27, 1985.

Sport, February, 1982.

Sports Illustrated, February 3, 1975, July 23, 1979, January 26, 1981, February 28, 1983, March 5, 1984, February 11, 1985.

Time, March 22, 1976, April 13, 1981.

—Sidelights by Mark Kram

Philip H. Knight

1938-

PERSONAL: Born February 24, 1938, in Portland, Ore.; son of William W. and Lota (Hatfield) Knight; married Penelope Parks, September 13, 1968; children: Matthew, Travis. *Education:* University of Oregon, B.B.A., 1959; Stanford University, M.B.A., 1962. *Politics:* Republican. *Religion:* Episcopalian.

ADDRESSES: *Office*—Nike, Inc., 10300 Southwest Allen Blvd., Beaverton, Ore. 97005.

OCCUPATION: Shoe manufacturing executive.

CAREER: Importer of athletic shoes, beginning 1964; Nike, Inc., Beaverton, Ore., co-founder, president, and chairman, 1967-83, 1984—, chairman and chief executive officer, 1983. Certified Public Accountant. Director, Metheus Corp.; member of board of directors, National Council on U.S.-China Trade and Asian Business Council. Trustee, Reed College; member of advisory council, Stanford University Graduate School. *Military service:* U.S. Army, 1959-60; became first lieutenant.

MEMBER: American Institute of Certified Public Accountants.

AWARDS, HONORS: Named Oregon Businessman of the Year, 1982.

SIDELIGHTS: In 1960, Philip H. Knight, then a graduate business student at Stanford University, was given a routine class assignment: devise a plan for a small business. Knight was an avid runner and a former miler of some accomplishment at the University of Oregon, so it was natural that the small business he chose to profile was a running shoe company. More than twenty-five years later, Knight is still developing corporate strategies for the production and marketing of athletic footwear, as well as an entire line of sports and leisure clothing. His company, Nike, with sales in excess of $900 million per year, has succeeded in making its mark in a U.S. market formerly dominated by the West German Adidas firm.

Nike got its start, according to Cynthia Jabs in a *New York Times* article, with a research paper written by Knight, in which he theorized that Japanese manufacturers "could do for athletic shoes what they were doing for cameras, that is, edge out other giant foreign competitors in the business." Following graduation, Knight embarked on a world tour and, while in Tokyo, stopped in at the offices of the Onitsuka company, makers of the Tiger running shoe, a product that Knight admired and one he believed could become a big seller in the United States. He left Japan as the sole U.S. distributor of Tigers and quickly began selling the shoes himself out of the trunk of his car at track meets.

Soon Knight acquired a partner, former Oregon track coach Bill Bowerman, the man who is credited with making the University a running powerhouse. Bowerman had long been critical of American athletic shoe design, saying the domestic product was too heavy and clumsy. The partners each put up $500 for a shipment of three hundred pairs of Tigers, which they stored in Knight's father's basement. Before long, they were marketing the shoes nationally.

Some eight years later, Knight and Bowerman found themselves embroiled in a dispute with Onitsuka. The Japanese firm, in light of the increasing popularity of jogging in the United States, had decided to end the exclusivity of its contract with the pair in order to promote wider distribution of Tigers. In response, Knight and Bowerman decided to manufacture their own running shoes, contracting the actual construction out to a number of firms in the Far East.

They shipped their first batch of Nikes (the word rhymes with "psyche" and is the name of the Greek goddess of victory), emblazoned with the now familiar "swoosh" emblem, to the United States just in time for the 1972

Olympic track trials in Eugene, Oregon. They managed to convince a number of distance runners to try the new shoes and later, in a clever advertising campaign devised by Knight, were able to boast that four of the top seven marathoners wore Nikes; as a *Time* writer points out, the ads conveniently "neglected to mention that runners wearing West Germany's Adidas shoes placed first, second, and third." And so Nike was off to a strong start. They expanded their line to include tennis and basketball shoes and were able to bring at least a portion of their manufacturing process to the United States with the opening of their first domestic plant in Exeter, New Hampshire.

Yet Bowerman's main interest had been in designing a new *kind* of running shoe. "He was always trying to figure out ways to make a shoe lighter," Knight told Jabs. "He figured carrying one extra ounce for a mile was equivalent to carrying something like an extra thousand pounds in the last fifty yards." He also felt that most of the available shoes lacked proper cushioning and that sole design could stand some improvement. Bowerman's dissatisfaction with existing shoe design led him to try a variety of homemade experimental alternatives. Eventually he got the idea of a waffle-patterned sole. To test his latest thesis, he cooked some urethane rubber in the family waffle iron, ruining the appliance but producing Nike's first revolutionary development. The little rubber studs of the waffle sole resulted in a newfound springiness, and, as *Time* reports, the new shoe "was soon grabbed by the army of weekend jocks suffering from bruised feet."

In addition to weekend athletes, many more serious competitors have achieved a great deal of success wearing Nike shoes. One early devotee, Sebastian Coe, set a world's record for the mile in Nikes (to commemorate the occasion, Knight gave his employees a day off work), and he went on to set another record in the 1500-meter event. Another Nike wearer, Kenyan runner Henry Rono, set records in the 3000-, 5000-, and 10,000-meter runs and the 3000-meter steeplechase.

In the ensuing years, of course, many other athletes—amateur and professional—have worn Nikes to victory. And the company has made an effort to encourage the use of their products, particularly by well-known professional athletes, and has capitalized on the endorsements of these athletes in a number of highly successful advertising campaigns. "The best shoes on the best guys" is the way Nike marketing vice-president Neil Goldschmidt sums up the company's sales pitch. *Fortune* writer Myron Magnet states that "there's nothing newfangled about the use of endorsements in marketing, but Nike uses them to a fare-thee-well, spending a bundle to get the most charismatic feet into its shoes. A tennis star like John McEnroe can net over $100,000 annually for lacing them on; some basketball players charge over $25,000. . . . Most amateur luminaries don't get money, but like the pros they get painstakingly custom-crafted shoes from Nike and a cascade of equipment—all bearing the familiar 'swoosh' logo that resembles a stylized vapor trail. Doubly invaluable to Nike, all this keeps the company in touch with what its market wants."

But Nike's increasing market in the 1970s consisted not only of professional and serious amateur athletes. Mostly, it was made up of the millions of health-conscious Americans who took up jogging. As Magnet notes, "Knight was an early believer in jogging, but even he never envisioned the speed and vastness of the nation's conversion to the pastime in the mid-1970s, nor could he imagine that the 'jogging look' would become so fashionable that non-athletes would sport Nikes by the million. Yet by 1975 Nike's kind of shoe had become part of the official uniform for what writer Tom Wolfe dubbed the Me Decade." Warmup suits and running shoes send out a message that says the wearer is physically fit and youthful. And, whether or not one is a jogger, one does—according to the marketing strategy—want to *appear* healthy and youthful. In order to promote this image, Nike and other sports equipment manufacturers do as much as possible to encourage highly visible young people to use their products. This is why, Magnet points out, Nike employs two full-time promoters in Los Angeles to "inundate rock stars, movie costumers, and TV and film actors with Nike shoes."

While the jogging trend—among both those who jog and those who want to *look like* they jog—has been responsible for much of Nike's success in the United States, the company has experienced varying degrees of difficulty in getting its products accepted throughout the rest of the world. In Japan, where jogging is as popular as it has been in the United States, Nike has become a big seller in the athletic shoe market. But in Europe the company has been less successful. For one thing, there are Common Market trade agreements that inhibit the importation of footwear from Asia where most Nikes had been manufactured. Thus, the company was forced to set up European subsidiaries and begin producing shoes there. But the cost of making shoes in Europe is considerably higher than in the Far East, and Nike has had trouble competing in that market.

Another problem with marketing in Europe is that the jogging craze never hit there with the same impact as in America. Magnet quotes British critic Peter Conrad, who says that in England, for example, jogging "is not a national phenomenon. The English don't have the mad, ambitious striving—the questing Puritan fanaticism—that it takes to make a whole country run. It's really a religion, this quest for self-perfection. People don't have that here." "Nor do they have it in the rest of Europe," writes Magnet, "and without it the Nike mystique loses force." Still, even though they may not have experienced the growth explosion in running that we have in the United States, Europeans have an existing market for sportswear, and Nike has certainly made some impressive advances into that market, taking a significant share of the sales away from Adidas and other European firms.

With manufacturing sites in Asia (including China), Europe, and North America, and with marketing and distribution throughout most of the world, Nike production increased steadily, and the company enjoyed many years of continuous growth. But in 1984 Nike announced that it had experienced its first year ever of lower profit than the preceding year. Sales had increased 6.1 per cent (from $867 million to $920 million), but stock earnings dropped 28.8 per cent. At the same time that this announcement was made, Knight—who had given up the presidency of the firm a year earlier to concentrate more on long-range planning—announced that he was resuming his duties as president and indicated that he intended to take a more active part in the day-to-day running of the company.

The jogging craze appears to have levelled off to the point where only the more serious runners continue. And for those who are only interested in the image, there are dozens of companies manufacturing athletic footwear today, much of which sells below the price of a typical pair of Nikes. Still, Knight and the staff at Nike continue to think of themselves primarily as runners, and they continue to design and manufacture shoes for athletes. As Knight told a *Time* reporter, "We are just a bunch of guys selling sneakers."

SOURCES:

PERIODICALS

Forbes, October 22, 1984.
Fortune, November 1, 1982, November 12, 1984.
Los Angeles Times, April 20, 1984.
New York Times, August 19, 1979, September 24, 1984.
Time, June 30, 1980, February 15, 1982.
Wall Street Journal, September 21, 1984, November 6, 1984.

—Sketch by Peter M. Gareffa

Ray Kroc

1902-1984

OBITUARY NOTICE: Full name, Raymond Albert Kroc; born October 5, 1902, in Oak Park, Ill.; died of heart failure, January 14, 1984, in San Diego, Calif. Restaurateur, baseball club executive, and philanthropist. When Ray Kroc opened his first McDonald's in 1955, he revolutionized the restaurant industry by applying assembly-line production techniques to food preparation. By providing fast service and inexpensive food to an increasingly mobile American society, Kroc eventually parlayed his first successful restaurant into a worldwide network of franchises, numbering over seven thousand restaurants by 1984, and a business empire that included the San Diego Padres baseball team. Prior to opening his first McDonald's in Des Plaines, Ill., Kroc worked for the Lily Cup Company for seventeen years, sold real estate, and marketed his Multi-mixer milkshake machine.

The overwhelming popularity of McDonald's provided Kroc with the means to become a philanthropist. In 1969, he established the Kroc Foundation, which is dedicated to research on diabetes, arthritis, and multiple sclerosis. In the mid-1970's, McDonald's restaurants and several professional sports teams banded together and raised funds to build Ronald McDonald Houses at children's hospitals throughout the United States. These houses provide temporary shelter for the families of seriously ill children being treated at the hospitals.

SOURCES:

PERIODICALS

Esquire, December, 1983.
Los Angeles Times, January 15, 1984.
New York Times, January 15, 1984; October 5, 1984
Time, January 23, 1984.

AP/Wide World Photos

Kay Kyser

1906(?)-1985

OBITUARY NOTICE: Full name, James King Kern Kyser; born June 18, 1906 (some sources say 1897 or 1905), in Rocky Mount, N.C.; died of a heart attack, July 23, 1985, in Chapel Hill, N.C. Musician, bandleader, church official, and radio personality. As the host of radio's "Kollege of Musical Knowledge" Kyser developed a format of dance music, comedy routines, and quiz questions that attracted record audiences from 1933 to 1949. Even in high school and college Kyser demonstrated a natural inclination toward showmanship by assuming his nickname and by gravitating toward activities that put him in the spotlight, including cheerleader, class president, yearbook editor, and member of various scholastic societies. Additionally, as a student at the University of North Carolina in the 1920s, Kyser found time to organize a band whose steadily growing popularity yielded playing dates well beyond Chapel Hill. The band's success eventually led Kyser to redirect his career from law to music.

The first few years after college were lean ones for Kyser until 1934, when he and his band, who called themselves Kay Kyser's Kampus Klass, were hired for a radio program that was broadcast from Chicago's famed Blackhawk Restaurant. The show quickly acquired a large local following and in early 1938 was sold as a network series to the American Tobacco Company. As "Kay Kyser's Kollege of Musical Knowledge," each weekly broadcast blended comedy and clowning with sweet swing and a musical quiz in which "old perfesser" Kyser, dressed in academic cap and gown and brandishing a pointer, posed true-false questions to contestants drawn from the studio audience and awarded prizes to nearly all answers. Working with Kyser was a succession singer-comics, the best known of whom was Ish Kabibble, a trumpeter whose real name was Merwyn A. Bogue and who performed novelty numbers such as "Mares Eat Oats and Does Eat Oats and Little Lambs Eat Ivy" and "Three Little Fishes in an Itty Bitty Pool." Other notable performers included Harry Babbitt, Ginny Simms, Michael Douglas (later known as television talk show host Mike Douglas), and Georgia Carroll, whom Kyser married in 1944. While Ish Kabibble's tunes provided the laughs, Kyser's more conventional vocalists sang the songs that made his band among the most popular in the country— "Who Wouldn't Love You," "On a Slow Boat to China," "There Goes That Song Again," and the wartime favorite, "Praise the Lord and Pass the Ammunition." During World War II, Kyser took his musicians to hundreds of service camps, bases, and hospitals.

At the height of his popularity, however, Kyser quit his radio show, resuming his career briefly in 1949 to bring his

"Kollege of Musical Knowledge" to television, then retiring for good from show business in 1951. With his wife he moved to Chapel Hill, in his native North Carolina, and devoted his energies full time to his Christian Science religion as a teacher and practitioner. In 1974 Kyser and his wife took up residence at the Christian Science headquarters in Boston, where he produced films for the church. In 1983 Kyser was named president of the Mother Church of the First Church of Christ, Scientist, in Boston, an honorary title rarely awarded a member.

SOURCES:

PERIODICALS

Detroit Free Press, July 24, 1985.
Los Angeles Times, July 24, 1985.
New York Times, March 17, 1940, July 24, 1985.
Time, August 5, 1985.

Pat LaFontaine

1965-

PERSONAL: Born February 22, 1965, in St. Louis, Mo.; son of John (a Chrysler Corp. plant manager) and Jay LaFontaine. *Education*: Graduate of Waterford Kettering High School.

ADDRESSES: Home—Waterford Township, Mich. (summer). *Office*—New York Islanders, Nassau Veterans Memorial Coliseum, Uniondale, N.Y. 11553.

OCCUPATION: Professional hockey player.

CAREER: Member of New York Islanders hockey team, 1983—. As an amateur, played with Detroit Compuware Midgets, 1981-82, Verdun, Quebec Major Junior Hockey League, 1982-83, and with U.S. National and 1984 U.S. Olympic hockey teams.

SIDELIGHTS: In the spring of 1983, his eighteenth year, Pat LaFontaine was tearing up a Canadian hockey league long considered too tough for Americans. By the summer of that year, he became the first player selected by the New York Islanders, four-time defending champions of the National Hockey League, in the annual NHL draft. And by the fall, he was playing with the 1984 United States Olympic team that would be trying to match the glory achieved at Lake Placid four years earlier. Following that, he participated in the Stanley Cup finals with the Islanders in May 1984, something many NHL veterans have never experienced. And the Islanders were already convinced that LaFontaine was "the most famous American-born player to ever perform in the NHL," according to their media guide for the 1984-85 season.

That would put a lot of pressure on most nineteen year olds trying to make the grade in a professional sport. But LaFontaine thrives on it. "I'm just honored to be part of this organization," he told the *New York Daily News* before playing his first game for the Islanders in Winnipeg on February 29, 1984. "A lot of guys were giving me words of advice. I'm only nineteen, and any time they do that, I surely appreciate it. Everything has happened so fast. It seems like only yesterday I was fifteen. But it took so fast for all of it to happen, I'm sure it will go by just as fast."

As a youngster, LaFontaine dreamed of playing professional hockey. His father steered him to the game, buying him skates at age three and becoming his coach. Every winter John Sr. would set up a hockey rink on Williams Lake near Pontiac, Michigan, where the LaFontaines lived in a nine-room, split-level house. With snow banks piled up for sides of the rink, two hockey nets, and eight spotlights, Pat and his older brother, John Jr., would play all night if they could. His mother, Jay, said the boys would often skate until 11 p.m. on school nights and later on weekends. Some nights she would have to switch the lights off to get them to bed,

AP/Wide World Photos

she told the *New York Times.* "There were a couple of times . . . I had to put my foot down," Mrs. LaFontaine said. "There were times I thought they were overdoing it and they would never make it to school the next day."

Besides endless practice honing his skating and shooting skills in junior hockey, LaFontaine improved his game through observation. "When I watch a pro game, I try to watch three or four players, see what they do, and try to go out on my own and see what works for me," LaFontaine told the *New York Times.* "You might see one move, like the way Mike Bossy [of the Islanders] takes a shot, and you say, 'I wonder if I could do that . . . anticipate like that . . . some little trick.' "

At age fifteen, while playing with Compuware—a team sponsored by a Birmingham, Michigan, computer firm—LaFontaine was already being considered as a pro prospect by NHL scouts. But the seed had been planted for his Olympic dream on the night his fifteenth birthday, February 22, 1980, as he watched the U.S. hockey team defeat the Soviet Union, 4-3, at Lake Placid, New York. He remembered having a poster of the 1980 gold medalists in his bedroom. "Those guys were my idols," he said. "After watching the 1980 Olympics, this had become a dream of mine," LaFontaine told *Sports Illustrated*. "My family wanted me to do it. It's the experience of a lifetime."

With such lofty goals at a tender age, LaFontaine sought the quickest route to attain them. At Compuware it became obvious that he was playing in a class above everyone else; he was averaging more than two goals per game. In the 1981-82 season he scored 175 goals and 149 assists in 79 games. His father told Pat that, if he was serious about hockey as a career, he would have to get out of Detroit. So at sixteen he left home to play for a team in Verdun, a French, middle-class suburb of Montreal. The team was a member of the Quebec Major Junior Hockey League, one of the three best leagues in North America and a chief source of NHL talent.

In one season LaFontaine stunned Canadians and Americans alike who had doubts that he could dominate play as he had in the Detroit midget leagues. In 70 games he led the Quebec league in scoring with 104 goals and 130 assists for 234 points. He added 11 goals and 24 assists in the playoffs. During this amazing spree, LaFontaine broke junior records held by two of his NHL idols, Mike Bossy of the Islanders (most points by a rookie) and Guy Lafleur of the Montreal Canadiens (43-game consecutive scoring streak). Lafleur

presented LaFontaine with the puck that broke the 12-year-old record. "I figured that was the only way I'd get to meet him," LaFontaine said.

His other statistics did not go unrewarded. At the season's end, LaFontaine was named the Quebec league's first team all-star center and most valuable player for the regular season and playoffs. As an even greater achievement, he was named 1983's Canadian Major Junior Player of the Year, beating out more than 800 players nationwide.

In addition, he had become a media star. "I've never seen a kid loved like him," Verdun general manager Eric Taylor told the *Detroit Free Press* in March, 1983. "His face has been in all the papers, on all the talk shows, on thousands of buttons and posters," the *Free Press's* Bill McGraw reported. "His phone rings constantly. Young female admirers write messages in the dust on his car. He signs autographs for up to 45 minutes after games."

There was no doubt that LaFontaine's stock had risen among NHL scouts by the time of the June, 1983, amateur draft. Some were worried about his 5-foot-10, 180-pound size, believing that he might be too small for the NHL. The Islanders weren't worried—they selected him third overall. "He's never going to be a six-foot giant, but he hangs tough

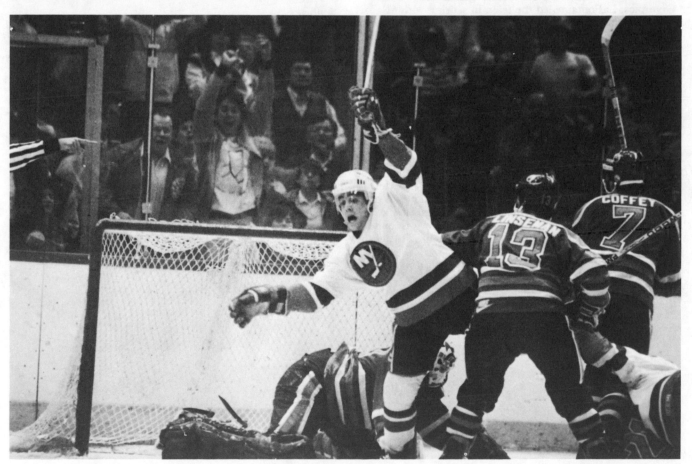

Pat LaFontaine (in white jersey) celebrates a New York Islanders goal against the Edmonton Oilers in the Stanley Cup finals, 1984. AP/Wide World Photos.

in front of the net," Islanders general manager Bill Torrey told the *New York Times*. "If he does get knocked down, then he bounces right back up."

LaFontaine was ecstatic over being selected by the Islanders, although, if they had passed him, he might have stayed closer to home, since the Detroit Red Wings had the next pick in the draft. "My heart was [in Detroit]," he told the *Free Press*. "But when the Islanders called my name, it was a shock. I'm very happy." LaFontaine always appears happy. He's been described as bubbly, vivacious, sincere, and as a "Donnie Osmond lookalike." Off the ice, he's known as "Bugs," short for Bugs Bunny because he likes to greet everyone with his favorite expression: "What's up?"

After the draft, what was up for LaFontaine was a tough decision: turn pro immediately or first pursue his Olympic dream. "Bill Torrey never put any pressure on me to sign," LaFontaine told *Sports Illustrated*. After three weeks of deliberating, he chose the Olympics. "My family wanted me to do it. It's the experience of a lifetime," LaFontaine said. "It gives you a chance to see the world . . . while at the same time you're learning and developing as a hockey player." Unfortunately, LaFontaine's dream of helping the United States win another Olympic gold medal at Sarajevo, Yugoslavia, did not come true. The team failed to win any medal. But during 58 exhibition games and 6 in the Olympics, LaFontaine led the team in scoring with 61 goals and 60 assists. Some of his teammates said they wanted to forget the Olympics as soon as possible, but not LaFontaine. "I don't look at it that way," he told the *Free Press*. "Sure it's a disappointment to lose, I wish we could have done better, but . . . as long as you do your best, you should be happy."

With his Olympic experience still fresh, LaFontaine came upon the NHL scene with a splash, scoring 13 goals and 6 assists in the Islanders' last 15 regular season games. But disappointment quickly struck again. The Islanders, seeking their fifth straight championship, lost the Stanley Cup to the Edmonton Oilers, 4 games to 1 in a best-of-seven series. In the final game at Edmonton, LaFontaine scored New York's only goals in a 5-2 loss. The experience was bittersweet. "Getting a taste of that Stanley Cup fever was quite a feeling," he told the *Hockey News*. "Now we have to get the Cup back."

LaFontaine is one of the Islanders' building blocks back to glory—as long as misfortune doesn't continue to follow him. He suffered a knee injury in August, 1984, preparing to play for the U.S. team in the six-nation Canada Cup Tournament, and he missed the tournament and the start of the regular NHL season. In January, 1985, he was lost to the Islanders for another dozen games with a bout of mononucleosis. But by mid-February, 1985, he was back in action; through 46 games he had 13 goals and 29 assists—not the scoring pace he had enjoyed in junior hockey, but he would be turning just 20 years old February 22, and he's remained optimistic. "If you start thinking about it too much, then you might do worse," LaFontaine told the *New York Times*. "You have to learn to pay the price a little, I guess. It's not an easy league. . . . It's a long year, and I knew there'd be an adjustment. I've just got to keep working hard."

He also works hard outside the ice arena for charities and the Amateur Hockey Association of the United States, which called LaFontaine "America's Hockey Hero" and named him honorary chairman for National Youth Hockey Week in 1985. "I'd like to see every young hockey player have the chances I've had to become a pro," LaFontaine said in an association newsletter. "Hockey has been good to me, and I won't forget that."

SOURCES:

BOOKS

Halligan, John, senior editor, *NHL Guide and Record Book, 1984-85*, National Hockey League, 1984.
Wagner, Les, executive editor, *New York Islanders 1984-85 Media Guide*, Sports Programs, Inc., 1984.

PERIODICALS

Amateur Hockey Association of the United States, Newsletter, February, 1985.
Detroit Free Press, March 10, 1983, June 9, 1983, November 30, 1983, December 8, 1983, March 1, 1984.
Hockey News, September 28, 1984.
New York Daily News, February 28, 1984.
New York Times, February 6, 1984, December 17, 1984, January 10, 1985, February 2, 1985.
Sports Illustrated, December 12, 1983.

—Sketch by John Castine

Marc Lalonde

1929-

PERSONAL: Born July 26, 1929, in Ile Perrot, Quebec, Canada; son of J. Albert and Nora (St. Aubin) Lalonde; married Claire Tetreau, September 8, 1955; children: Marie, Luc, Paul, Catherine. *Education*: St. Laurent College, Montreal, Quebec, B.A., 1950; University of Montreal, LL.L., 1954, M.A. (law), 1955; Oxford University, M.A. (economics and political science), 1957; University of Ottawa, diploma of superior studies in law, 1960; also attended Oxford University. *Politics*: Liberal. *Religion*: Roman Catholic.

ADDRESSES: *Home*—5440 Legare, Outremont, Quebec, Canada H3T 1Z4. *Office*—Room 515-S, House of Commons, Parliament Bldgs., Ottawa, Ontario, Canada K1A 0A6; and Stikeman-Elliot, Montreal, Quebec, Canada.

OCCUPATION: Canadian politician, economist, and lawyer.

CAREER: Called to the Bar of Quebec, 1955, created Queen's Counsel, 1970; University of Montreal, Montreal, Quebec, professor of commercial law and economics, 1957-59; served as special assistant to the Canadian minister of justice, Ottawa, Ontario, 1959-60; Gelinas, Bourque, Lalonde & Benoit (law firm), Montreal, partner, 1960-68; Canadian Federal Government, Ottawa, policy adviser to Prime Minister Lester B. Pearson, 1967, principal secretary to Prime Minister Pierre E. Trudeau, 1968-72, elected to House of Commons, Montreal-Outremont seat, 1972, later reelected, minister of national health and welfare, 1972-77, minister responsible for the status of women, 1975-78, minister of state for federal-provincial relations, 1977-78, minister of justice and attorney general for Canada, 1978-79, minister of energy, mines, and resources, 1980-82, minister of finance, 1982-84; in private practice with the law firm Stikeman-Elliot in Montreal, 1984—. Member of board of directors of the University of Montreal's Institute of Public Law, 1960-64; director of Canadian Citizenship Council, 1960-65; lecturer in administrative law at the University of Montreal and Ottawa University, 1961-62; member of Committee on Broadcasting, 1964. Counsel before various royal committees, including the Royal Committee on Great Lakes Shipping and the Royal Committee on Pilotage.

AWARDS, HONORS: Dana Award from the American Public Health Association, 1978.

WRITINGS: Author of *The Changing Role of the Prime Minister's Office*, 1971.

SIDELIGHTS: When Marc Lalonde announced retirement as Canadian minister of finance in July, 1984, an era in Canadian politics came to an end. As lieutenant and strongman to Pierre Trudeau, Lalonde had worked side-by-side with the prime minister for nearly twenty years.

UPI/Bettmann Newsphotos

Together they had sought recognition of the French fact in Canada, nationalization of the oil industry and patriation of the Canadian constitution from England. After Trudeau had stepped aside earlier that year, Lalonde predictably concluded that he too had fulfilled his political aspirations.

During his years in Ottawa, the political economist and law professor had earned a reputation as a determined and disciplined pragmatist. He had served as Trudeau's principal secretary, his patronage lieutenant in the province of Quebec, minister of health and national welfare, minister of federal-provincial relations, minister of energy, and finally, during the critical recession of the early 1980s, minister of finance. "The Prime Minister needs someone who'll deliver the goods, and he knows I'll deliver," he explained to one interviewer.

Although his role as architect of the contentious National Energy Program won him few friends, his critics say he did earn their respect. "It is entirely possible to loathe things that he does with his power," wrote W. A. Wilson in the *Winnipeg Free Press*, "become deeply convinced that they are dead wrong and damaging, and yet not lose personal regard for the man himself. He is, in fact, a very considerable person."

Even Lalonde's Liberal colleagues stood in awe of him. No judges were appointed, no candidates nominated, no contracts awarded in Quebec without the stamp of approval from "le boss." Quebec Liberals were regularly told to "clear it with Marc." He was the party enforcer. Yet despite his considerable powers, Lalonde never fell victim to them. He left Ottawa, according to Ian MacDonald of the *Montreal Gazette*, "as a man who has exercised great power without being personally or intellectually corrupted by it."

Lalonde's pragmatic approach to politics was first developed when he left the shelter of the family farm on Ile Perrot just outside of Montreal, Quebec, for a rigorous Catholic schooling with the Fathers of the Holy Cross. As a young man, he worked as a volunteer for the Catholic Action Movement, a post-war social reform movement that became the forerunner of the 1960s unrest. Catholic Action taught its followers "voir, jugir, agir"—to see, to judge, to act. This was an adage Lalonde was to follow throughout his political life.

He entered law school at the University of Montreal on the advice of a young Quebec intellectual and bureaucrat, Pierre Trudeau. Lalonde soon became an avid reader of Trudeau's editorials in Quebec's influential intellectual journal *Citeá Libre*. In 1964, Lalonde collaborated with Trudeau and several other federalists to publish a manifesto denouncing Quebec's increasing nationalism and lauding the principles of an equal partnership of regions in a federal system. Later, in Ottawa, he would have his chance to transform these ideas into reality.

Armed with three scholarships, Lalonde went on to Oxford to study law and economics. Ironically, upon his return in 1959, the man who would later become a powerful Liberal took a job as a research assistant to Conservative Justice Davie Fulton. He soon returned to Montreal to practice law but kept his hand in the federal political scene by serving on several royal commissions. By 1967, he had committed himself to the Liberal cause and worked as a policy advisor to then Prime Minister Lester Pearson.

In 1968, it was Trudeau's turn to be advised by Lalonde. On his friend's counsel, Trudeau let his name stand for the leadership of the Liberal party. Lalonde's real influences in Ottawa began when Trudeau took power as prime minister. He was appointed principal secretary to Trudeau, quickly gaining a reputation for tough, ruthless efficiency in difficult times. It was Lalonde, for example, who advised the imposition of the War Measures Act when terrorists threatened the stability of the Quebec government in October, 1970.

Lalonde took the final step into politics in 1972, running for office in the upper-class Montreal riding of Outremont. He was rewarded with an appointment as minister of health and national welfare. Although a political newcomer, Lalonde quickly displayed the interest in bold, sweeping programs that would characterize his political career. In this case, recalling his Catholic Action social reform teachings, he proposed to narrow the gap between Canada's rich and poor. He developed plans for a guaranteed annual income supplement, but financial concerns killed the proposal at the cabinet table.

Lalonde attained his pre-eminent position in Liberal Ottawa after the province of Quebec elected a separatist government in 1976. He was the chief antagonist for Rene Levesque's new Parti-Quebecois government as he and Trudeau believed in a bilingual country under the direction of a strong central government. Their dispute with Quebec separatists became a battle in which hostilities on both sides were barely masked. In 1979, for example, when the Liberals met in Quebec City, Levesque complained about the "foreigners" in town.

Lalonde came up with Ottawa's proposal for full-scale constitutional reform in 1978 as a means of countering the separatist sentiments. His continuing struggle for the preservation of Confederation abated only with the unsuccessful 1980 Quebec referendum on separatism.

The battle naturally turned Lalonde to the West where provinces were reaping the benefits of a massive resource boom. Again, with the concepts of federalism at heart, Lalonde waged battle for the sake of economic nationalism in the oil industry. It was Lalonde as minister of energy who unveiled the controversial National Energy Program in October, 1980. The program had two objectives: to increase the federal government's share of oil and gas revenues and to encourage Canadian businesses to take over foreign natural resource holdings. The ultimate aim of the program, described by many as the government's most radical plan ever, was to see fifty per cent of Canada's oil industry in Canadian hands by 1990.

Unfortunately, Lalonde's timing was poor. The NEP was announced just before an oil glut sent prices tumbling. The oil industry, investment circles, and U.S. observers claimed the subsequent decline in exploration, the failure of megaprojects like the Alsands tar sands project, the souring of Canada-U.S. relations and a new reliance on oil imports could all be blamed on Lalonde's energy program. The president of one oil company compared the energy plan to the action of Nazi brownshirts. Lalonde's deeply-felt concern had developed into a civil war of words between the Trudeau administration in Ottawa and the Western provinces. "In this palaver, one man, the Honorable Marc Lalonde, has come to symbolize all that is thought to be arrogant and arbitrary about the Liberal Party and Pierre Trudeau's Ottawa," wrote Robert Collison in *Today* magazine.

But, characteristically, Lalonde made an impressive comeback as finance minister in 1982 when Canada was entering its worst economic downturn in half a century. The business community was aghast that the man who had generated the fear and loathing of the oil industry was to be Canada's new minister of finance. One observer said his appointment was much like choosing Attila the Hun as moderator of the United Church.

But within two months, Lalonde had somehow won over business representatives with a careful, consultative economic statement. "Lalonde had seemingly taken a political deathtrap, the finance portfolio, and turned it into a wonderfully convenient launchpad for economic and political revival," said Deborah McGregor in the *Financial Times*. The Toronto *Globe and Mail* concurred: "Since Marc Lalonde moved to the Finance portfolio last September, he has almost singlehandedly carried the Government on his back and recent signs that Liberal political fortunes may have begun to turn are almost solely the result of his labors." So, Lalonde's appointment to the finance portfolio saw his surprising transformation from economic nationalist to free enterpriser. "I have never had any dogmatic approach to state intervention," he told *Saturday Night*. "I like to look at those issues in a very pragmatic way." His success was once again testimony to his practical approach.

Lalonde is a shrewd man who made few mistakes in his political career. He had slipped once in his first months in office when he accepted a free flight to Israel on a jet owned by a liquor company. But he never forgot the lesson. Years later, he noted the criticism heaped on a former finance minister who had hosted a three-hour food extravaganza, complete with cigars and liquor, for reporters at a budget briefing. When it was his turn, Lalonde provided pizza and beer.

At a photo-opportunity session with the press just before the release of his 1982 economic statement, Lalonde inadvertently revealed part of his budget to the television cameras. When details of the slip-up hit the press, Opposition MPs demanded Lalonde resign for breaking budget secrecy. Yet Lalonde was not rattled. He insisted the documents had not been the final version of the budget. On budget night, he coolly presented a plan that proposed spending $200 million more than the one revealed by the leaked documents.

Lalonde was always prepared to go on the offensive. In January, 1984, he suggested that when Conservative Party leader Brian Mulroney (now prime minister) had been president of the Iron Ore Company he had written letters to Lalonde lobbying for tax changes to benefit the rich. The incident sparked charges that Lalonde had abused his privilege as finance minister by making private correspondence public. Lalonde's allegations proved to be unfounded when the finance department could not produce any letters from Mulroney.

He was evidently prepared to risk the wrath of the U.S. government, first through the National Energy Program and then by criticizing American interest rate policies. His tough talk may ultimately have cost him a job after his resignation from politics. He competed in 1984 for the position as secretary-general of the Paris-based Organization for Economic Cooperation and Development. However, he withdrew from the race when it became clear he could not get the support he needed from the United States and some other member states.

Lalonde had earned a star billing on the federal stage despite his own decision to play a supporting role to Trudeau, so he would have had a part to play in Ottawa even after his prime minister's retirement. Trudeau's successor, John Turner, did, in fact, re-appoint Lalonde minister of finance when he assumed the helm of the Liberal party in the summer of 1984. He also called on Lalonde to sit on the national election planning committee in preparation for the September, 1984 election.

But the ever-pragmatic Lalonde felt it was time to move on. He and Trudeau had fulfilled their dream by patriating a Canadian constitution and holding the separatists in Quebec at bay. As he told an interviewer in 1979: "I have never planned on committing myself for much more than two years ahead. Modern man must be mobile." Lalonde was clearly one of those men who went into politics to do something, did it, and accepted the consequences without, so far as anyone knows, ever once losing a night's sleep.

Since his resignation, Lalonde has joined the highly-regarded Montreal law firm Stikeman-Elliot. Now, once again, he and Trudeau are embarked on parallel paths—working lawyers in Montreal. Their concurrent return to private life is proof positive that an era in Ottawa has ended.

SOURCES:

BOOKS

McCall-Newman, Christina, *Grits: An Intimate Portrait of the Liberal Party*, MacMillan (Canada), 1982.

PERIODICALS

Financial Post, September 25, 1982.
Financial Times, December 27, 1982.
Globe and Mail (Toronto), July 16, 1983, June 9, 1984, July 19, 1984.
Montreal Gazette, October 2, 1982, July 20, 1984.
Saturday Night, June, 1981.
Today, March 28, 1981.
Winnipeg Free Press, July 24, 1984.

—Sidelights by Ingeborg Boyens

Toni Lander
1931-1985

OBITUARY NOTICE: Real name, Toni Pihl Peterson; born June 19, 1931, in Copenhagen, Denmark; died of cancer, May 19, 1985, in Salt Lake City, Utah. Danish ballerina, Toni Lander was known for the unparalleled dancing style, bravura, and charm she exhibited throughout her lifelong career in ballet. A student of the esteemed Royal Danish Ballet from the age of seven, Lander first gained public recognition for her impromptu performance in a dance production by one of the school's most revered members, nineteenth-century choreographer August Bournonville. Her premier leading role, created by her husband Harold Lander in his "Etudes" in 1950, won critical acclaim worldwide and launched the dancer's career as an international ballerina.

After leaving the Royal Danish Ballet in 1951, Lander danced with several other leading ballet companies, including the original Ballet Russes and the London Festival Ballet of Anton Dolin and Alicia Markova. Periodically over the years she returned to Copenhagen and performed as guest ballerina of the Royal Danish Ballet, and in 1957 she was created a Knight of the Dannebrog by Denmark's King Frederik IX. By 1960 Lander joined the American Ballet Theatre (ABT), performing major roles in "Swan Lake," "Miss Julie," "Theme and Variations," "La Sylphide," and "Coppelia," to name a few. Lander's farewell stage performance came with ABT's premiere of "The Moor's Pavane," in which she played Desdemona.

Following her retirement as a dancer, Lander moved to Salt Lake City in 1976. There she joined her second husband, Bruce Marks, on the staff of Ballet West, where previously both had danced in "The Nutcracker." During the next nine years of her career as principal dance instructor, Lander also staged several ballets for other dance companies and regularly conducted a three-week international Bournonville seminar in Copenhagen. Lander's last project was her collaborative recreation of the long-forgotten Bournonville ballet "Abdallah," which critics agreed owes its extremely successful revival to the combined skill, experience, imagination, and art of Lander—hailed by the *New Yorker* as "one of the great Sylphs of modern times."

AP/Wide World Photos

SOURCES:

PERIODICALS

Chicago Tribune, May 22, 1985.
Los Angeles Times, May 24, 1985.
Newsweek, May 20, 1985.
New Yorker, May 27, 1985.
New York Times, January 18, 1985.
Times (London), May 21, 1985.

Cyndi Lauper

1953-

PERSONAL: Born June 20, 1953, in Brooklyn, N.Y. *Education*: Received high school equivalency certificate; studied art at several colleges.

ADDRESSES: *Home*—New York, N.Y. *Office*—c/o CBS Records Division, 51 West 52nd St., New York, N.Y. 10019.

OCCUPATION: Pop singer.

CAREER: Singer with Doc West (disco band), beginning 1974, with Flyer (rock band), and with Blue Angel (rockabilly band), 1977-81; solo performer, 1981—.

AWARDS, HONORS: Named one of twelve Women of the Year by *Ms.* magazine, 1984; received eight nominations in first annual MTV Video Music Awards and seven nominations from National Academy of Video Arts and Sciences, both 1984, for videos; received Grammy Award nominations for Album of the Year, for *She's So Unusual*, Record of the Year and Best Female Pop Vocal Performance, both for "Girls Just Want to Have Fun," Song of the Year, for "Time After Time," and Best New Artist; Grammy Award for Best New Artist, 1985.

DISCOGRAPHY:

Blue Angel (with band Blue Angel; includes "Maybe, He'll Know," "Anna Blue," "Can't Blame Me," "Late," "Cut Out," "Take a Chance," "Just the Other Day," "I'm Gonna Be Strong," "Lorraine," and "Everybody's Got an Angel"), Polydor, 1980.

She's So Unusual (solo album; includes "Girls Just, Want to Have Fun," "All Through the Night," "Time After Time," "She Bop," "Witness," "I'll Kiss You," "He's So Unusual," "Yeah Yeah," "Money Changes Everything," and "When You Were Mine"), Portrait Records, 1983.

SIDELIGHTS: Early in 1984, Cyndi Lauper burst onto the national music scene with a solo debut album entitled *She's So Unusual*. The album proved to be an ideal showcase for her unique and wide-ranging vocal ability, and—with the help of some innovative, award-winning videos—it became one of the biggest rock sensations of the year. Remarking on Lauper's sudden rise to stardom in a *Rolling Stone* article, Kurt Loder states that "no one who'd heard her sing doubted the brilliance of her freakish, four-octave voice. . . . But less than two years ago, . . . she seemed a pop character without a context: a never-was, and edging toward thirty. Then an astonishing thing happened—astonishing to everyone, that is, except Lauper and her circle of long-haul supporters. At the very nadir of her career, the dream finally came true. . . . *She's So Unusual* turned into a platinum-bound Top Ten hit."

AP/Wide World Photos

Like that of many "overnight sensations," Lauper's success is the culmination of years of hard work and sacrifice. She was born in Brooklyn, New York, and raised in a working-class neighborhood in nearby Queens. Her parents divorced when she was five, and her mother supported the family—Cyndi, a brother, and a sister—by working as a waitress in local diners. "It was really the pits," Lauper told Loder. "She looked like she was killing herself." Watching her mother work so hard to support the family was a radicalizing experience for Lauper; it made her determined to make a better life for herself and to escape the endless cycle of birth, courtship, marriage, pregnancy, and child-rearing that was the destiny of most of the women she saw around her.

Having been expelled from the local Catholic school, Lauper was sent to a Catholic boarding school in upstate New York, where she quickly found herself at odds with the authorities. "I realized that nuns and God could not have anything to do with each other," she stated to Loder. "These women were trained by Nazis, I think. . . . If you talked to a boy, they'd slap you as hard as they could in the face. I remember one time I scratched this girl's back in the middle of the night—I was, you know, nine, and she was twelve, and she asked me to scratch her back. A nun ran in, ripped me off her back, threw me against the lockers, beat the shit out of me and called me a lesbian. I didn't know what a lesbian was." She is still bitter about the experience and particularly about her mother's continued faith in the institutions that Cyndi found intolerable. "It was all traditional," she says, "the church, the family, the government. And you know what I learned? Those are the three biggest oppressors of women that will ever come along."

Her stay at the convent lasted only six months. (Lauper was thrown out after asking the nuns if they menstruated.) She returned to Queens and entered the local public school. In his book *Cyndi Lauper*, K. K. Willis Jr. notes that about this time she began to look different from the other kids: "By the time she was twelve she was dying her hair garish colors and wearing outrageous makeup and clothes in an effort to change her life and become somebody—*anybody*—else. It was a conscious decision to indulge her individuality, to ignore the kids and teachers who criticized her for being different, to recognize and, if possible, avoid the institutions of oppression." Her mother frequently lit candles to Saint Jude, patron saint of desperate cases, in the hope that her daughter would abandon her sometimes too unusual ways. But "no matter how hard I tried to look normal," Lauper told *Newsweek*'s Cathleen McGuigan and Peter McAlevey, "there was always something that wasn't right. I'd put on false eyelashes and one would always curl up." Finally she gave up even trying to look "normal," and to this day her public persona, her self-image, and her music seem to grow out of the fierce independence that is exemplified by her unique clothing, jewelry, and hairstyle.

About this time, too, Lauper started to become increasingly interested in singing, a talent that she says she realized she possessed as early as age five or six. And like many musicians and vocalists of her generation, Lauper points to the arrival of the Beatles as a turning point in her life and cites the group as a major source of inspiration. "I was really fascinated by John Lennon's low harmony," she told Loder. "I would copy that when my sister and I harmonized as we did the dishes." Unfortunately, Willis points out, as much as she admired them, she was unable to sound very much like Lennon or any of the Beatles. So she acquired a guitar and hopped on the folk music bandwagon, enjoying moderate success singing in parks and at other neighborhood venues with a friend.

Lauper was, according to *People* writer Jim Jerome, a "wild" and sometimes "self-destructive teenager who experimented with alcohol and drugs, "survived several car wrecks as a passenger, [and] endured bouts of dehydration and malnutrition." She became fed up with life in Queens. Willis reports that "everywhere she looked she saw women as losers: Her mother wasting her life waiting on tables, other women turning old before their time from the slavery of supporting their families and raising a bunch of kids." At seventeen she left. "I was packin' since I was fourteen, so it was time, you know?" she explained to Loder.

In addition to music, Lauper had displayed considerable talent as an artist, and friends convinced her that art offered her a better chance to earn a living than did singing. Thus, after leaving Queens, she attended a string of art schools and, according to David Frankel in *New York*, "flunked out of all of them." For a while she supported herself by

working at odd jobs, including waitress, housekeeper, kennel attendant, and race-horse hot-walker. After nearly a year on her own, Lauper found herself back in the old neighborhood, dejected but still determined to find an outlet for her creativity. It was at this point that she decided to ignore the advice to the contrary and pursue a career as a vocalist. She began singing on street corners in Greenwich Village, but by 1974 she had joined a professional band, Doc West, a group that played cover versions of disco hits on the Long Island bar circuit. Lauper's primary job was that of backup singer, but she gradually began to sing lead on a few numbers and eventually became fairly well known locally for her medley of Janis Joplin songs.

But Lauper considered herself a rock and roller at heart, and singing disco music for a living was not making her happy. In addition, writes Willis, "her Joplin act was getting out of control—not only was she beginning to feel haunted by Janis's spirit, but the people around her were starting to mention that Cyndi's singing was sounding exactly like Joplin's." She left Doc West and helped found Flyer, another Long Island band, but one more suitable to her musical taste. Flyer also played cover versions of popular songs, but now at least Lauper was singing rock and roll. Unfortunately she had trouble being accepted as a rock and roller by the Long Island bar crowd. She didn't dress like a rock star and, with her high and heavily Queens-accented speaking voice, didn't sound like a rock star. She found that audiences reacted to her dress and her speaking voice rather than to her singing, and she found herself once again frustrated and unable to express herself creatively. Finally, after three years of straining her voice night after night, trying to sound like someone else, her vocal chords gave out. She quit Flyer and sought medical help.

Doctors said Lauper would probably never sing again; she had damaged her voice beyond repair. But a singer friend recommended that she consult Katherine Agresta, a well-known and highly regarded opera singer and voice coach who had done some work with rock singers. Agresta, reports Loder, taught Lauper "about vocal exercises and warm-ups, diet and the damage that drugs and alcohol can do—not that Lauper was a serious abuser in either category. And slowly but surely, over the course of a year, Cyndi started singing again."

She performed at a small Manhattan club while working at odd jobs to pay the rent. Before long she had a manager, Ted Rosenblatt, who introduced her to songwriter/musician John Turi. They became friends and within a year had formed a fifties-style rockabilly band called Blue Angel. The group played a mixture of rock and roll classics and original music, and this time Cyndi and the band clicked. They were headlining at some of the best clubs in New York, and as Willis puts it, Lauper "was playing the songs *she* wanted to play, singing the way *she* wanted to sing, jumping around the stage the way *she* liked to jump around the stage, and dressing the way *she* liked to dress." She was happy, and the audiences accepted her. Blue Angel became one of the hottest local bands in the area.

In early 1979, Steve Massarsky, manager of the Allman Brothers Band, heard a Blue Angel demo tape and, according to Loder, declared it "terrible. . . . The songs were bad, the playing was bad. There was something interesting about the singer's voice, but that was all." Still Massarsky was moved to go see the group in a live performance at Trax, a popular Manhattan rock club. He still felt the band was bad, but as for Lauper, "she opened her mouth to sing, and it was magic. I'd never heard anything like it. I fell in love." He immediately bought the group's contract from Rosenblatt for $5000. Massarsky was primarily interested in Lauper as a solo artist, but she could not be persuaded to leave the group. They continued to perform and write their own material, and as their popularity increased, critics and recording industry insiders began to take notice. In 1980, a record offer came from Polydor, a division of Polygram Records, and Blue Angel cut their first and only album.

They toured Germany with Joe Jackson and, while there, appeared on German television with Hall and Oates. Critics were impressed, but the record, as Lauper often quips, "went lead." She told Frankel: "We were starving. We used to go to a gig and look at the deli tray as the meal for the day. We'd look at each other and say, 'Is this really happening to us?' After a while we just couldn't keep fighting it." Blue Angel broke up in 1982, and Lauper decided to go it alone.

The band had split with Massarsky in the middle of a lawsuit in which the manager charged that they owed him $80,000. Several of the band members, including Lauper, filed for bankruptcy. In the winter of 1983, she was officially declared bankrupt, she was without a band for the first time in nine years, and she had no business manager. She found work at a Japanese piano bar where, writes Willis, her job was "singing classics,. . . singing Japanese songs phonetically, and dancing with the inebriated businessmen who patronized the place." At the same time, she worked at a vintage clothing store and continued her vocal lessons with Agresta.

Lauper's current manager, David Wolff, entered her life in an unusual manner. She maintains that she heard a voice in her head that said, "Find Dave, find Dave." But she didn't know anyone named Dave at the time. Then one night, while she was performing, a man came up to her and said, "Hi, my name's Dave." Their relationship began on the spot. And as luck would have it, Wolff was a rock and roll manager. "And so," Willis sums up, "with the support of a new manager who also happened to be her boyfriend, Cyndi was ready to get her career rolling again." One of Wolff's client bands had a contract with Portrait Records, a subsidiary of CBS, and he felt that this would be the ideal company to record a solo album by Lauper: it was small enough to allow her the personal freedom to put together the kind of record she wanted; but it could draw upon the resources of the larger parent company for advertising and promotion.

The head of Portrait Records, Lennie Petze, was enthusiastic about Lauper, and he introduced her to producer Rick Chertoff. "Soon," writes Loder, "a solo album started taking shape, with Chertoff calling in two friends, Eric Bazilian and Rob Hyman of Philadelphia's Hooters, to help out with the music. Songwriter Jules Shear also took part, as did drummer Anton Fig and bassist Neil Jason, two crack sessionmen. The resulting album, *She's So Unusual*, was probably the most exuberant vocal debut of 1983. And some of its better tunes were cowritten by Lauper." She takes co-

author credit on "Time After Time," "She Bop," "Witness," and "I'll Kiss You"; for the other six cuts on the album, she explains in a Portrait Records press release, "producer Rick Chertoff and I selected songs that enabled me to keep my integrity, and that meant something to me."

An example is the album's biggest hit, "Girls Just Want to Have Fun." Chertoff had heard the song performed by its author, Robert Hazard, long before he had heard of Cyndi Lauper, but when *She's So Unusual* was in its early stages, Chertoff expressed the opinion that they should include it on the album. Unfortunately, when Lauper first heard the song she hated it, feeling that it was "an ode to sexism," Willis reports. Lauper says, "It was originally about how fortunate he was 'cause he was a guy around these girls who wanted to have 'fun'—with *him—down there*, of which we do not speak lest we go blind." But Chertoff persisted, and eventually Lauper changed her mind; she made only a couple minor alterations to the lyrics and, "with a few deft strokes of her pen," Willis states, "the song was transformed into the magnificent, happy, liberating anthem that would soon catch the world's fancy and make Cyndi Lauper a household word."

But, notes Loder, "it was the video for 'Girls' that really made Cyndi Lauper a star." Lauper agrees that the song did not take off until the video began getting heavy play on MTV, the rock video cable network. According to Willis, she says: "Maybe it's because if you just hear it, this weird girl voice, you don't understand what I'm trying to say. Maybe it took the video to capture it." And maybe the video so accurately captures Lauper's interpretation of the song because, unlike many performers, she exercised a great deal of control over the production of the video. *People* writer Jim Jerome explains that "Lauper, behind her goofy getups, is a shrewd tactician who sees videos as electronic canvases on which she imposes her own design and her own handpicked cast of characters," including her mother, David Wolff, and an assortment of relatives and friends. David Frankel, in his *New York* article, notes that the video "reflects the artistic impulse Lauper set aside in favor of music. She attended to the visual details, even picking the set's wallpaper. ('This was an artist's video,' she asserts, 'not a video with an artist in it.')"

Despite the upbeat melody of "Girls Just Want to Have Fun," and despite the giddy atmosphere of the video, critics caution against taking the song—or Lauper—too lightly. In honoring Lauper as one of the Women of the Year for 1984, *Ms.* writer Ann Hornaday writes: "If Helen Reddy's recording of 'I Am Woman' was about anger and a newfound collective pride, 'Girls Just Want to Have Fun' is about a newer, defiant joy and the celebration of our strength." Willis asserts that the song gave Lauper a long-awaited chance to "say something positive about women. Explaining that she's a feminist,. . . she says that listening to the lyrics while you watch the video will make it clear that the song is a subtle feminist statement. Her favorite line in the song, she says, is 'I want to be the one to walk in the sun'; she loves overhearing young girls walking down the street singing the line." And Dave Marsh, writing in the *Nation*, says that on the surface "Girls," with its "patronizing title, suggests the predominant fantasy figure of rock— the round-heeled cheerleader, the good girl unleashed by the beat to become a sexual dynamo devoted to instant (male) gratification. But Lauper has a gift for subversiveness and like many great pop records, 'Girls Just Want to Have Fun' is not about its surface but about the contradictions just beneath. It would be silly to say that Cyndi Lauper uses her hit to demolish the stereotype it defines, but it is not at all silly to claim that Lauper uses [the song] to wreak some damage on the image of women in pop music."

In addition to "Girls Just Want to Have Fun," other songs from *She's So Unusual* have spawned videos, including "Time After Time," "She Bop," and "Money Changes Everything." All have received a great deal of play on MTV and have proven extremely popular with rock fans and critics alike. Altogether, Lauper's work on her first solo album has resulted in numerous awards, including eight nominations in the MTV Video Music Awards, five nominations for Grammy Awards, and a Grammy for Best New Artist. Lauper is hard at work on an anxiously awaited second album, she is reportedly going to come out with her own line of clothing, she has been a big hit on the talk-show circuit, and there are rumors that she has been offered a part in at least one motion picture.

People's Jerome wonders how much difference success has made to Lauper's everyday life and whether it's true, as the cut from her album says, that "Money Changes Everything." Lauper says that she and Wolff hope to move to a large loft in Manhattan and that she doesn't have much time for her favorite hobby, painting, any more; but she still finds time for "junking" expeditions for jewelry and clothes. Altogether, "nothing has changed much," she maintains. "I don't want a Porsche, a Rolls. My gift to society is not getting a driver's license. I have trouble concentrating on the road. And I ain't buying no cocaine. . . . After watching *Lifestyles of the Rich and Famous*, I decided on all linoleum floors, maybe even the kind that look like brick. Forget parquet. Linoleum you wax and it shines. You don't get splinters."

AVOCATIONAL INTERESTS: Professional wrestling (manager of World Wrestling Federation champion Wendi Richter).

SOURCES:

BOOKS

Willis, K.K., Jr., *Cyndi Lauper*, Ballantine, 1984.

PERIODICALS

Ms., January, 1985.
Nation, June 30, 1984.
Newsweek, March 26, 1984, March 4, 1985.
New York, December 26, 1983.
People, September 17, 1984.
Rolling Stone, May 24, 1984.
Time, March 4, 1985.

—Sketch by Peter M. Gareffa

Robin Leach

1942(?)-

BRIEF ENTRY: Born c. 1942, in England. British-American television producer, host. Robin Leach is host and executive producer of one of the most popular syndicated television shows in America, "Lifestyles of the Rich and Famous," carried by nearly 200 stations across the country. One hour each week viewers are offered a glimpse of the homes, clothes, cars, haunts, and habits of the world's wealthiest and most glamourous people. Leach's subjects include celebrities, movie and television moguls, business tycoons, and royalty.

"Lifestyles" debuted in 1983 as a limited series of specials. It became a weekly series one year later. Leach, who also produces "The Start of Something Big," hosted by Steve Allen, hopes to introduce "Run Away with the Rich and Famous" in 1986. The new series proposes to travel with celebrities to the world's most exclusive vacation spots.

Leach is most interested in the self-made members of the rich and famous set; he rarely profiles those who were born into wealth. Leach's own life resembles a rags to riches story. He came to the United States in the early 1960s, taking a job as a shoe salesman at a New York department store. He later worked for several newspapers before television's Entertainment Tonight" hired him as a reporter. As a result of his work on that show, Leach was picked to host "Lifestyles."

Critics frequently use the word "fluff" when discussing Leach's efforts. He agrees. "We're not *20/20* and we're not *60 Minutes,*" he told Marc Gunther of the *Detroit News.* "We're the People and Us magazines of the television generation. My job is to entertain people." Leach also has a response for those who accuse him of pandering to his audience's baser tendencies, such as envy and voyeurism. "If we did a show called 'Lifestyles of the Poor and Unknown,'" he pointed out to Bettelou Peterson of the *Detroit Free Press,* "we'd never make it." *Address:* TPE, 875 Third Ave., New York, N.Y. 10022.

SOURCES:

PERIODICALS

Detroit Free Press, August 17, 1985.
Detroit News, August 7, 1985.
Newsweek, April 2, 1984.
New York Times, January 30, 1984.
People, April 22, 1985.
Variety, November 30, 1983.

Annie Lennox
1954-

PERSONAL: Born December 25, 1954, in Aberdeen, Scotland; father was a shipyard worker; married Radha Raman, March, 1984 (divorced, 1985). *Education:* Studied flute, piano, and harpsichord at Royal Academy of Music, London, England, for three years.

ADDRESSES: Home—London, England; and Switzerland. *Office*—c/o RCA Records, 1133 Avenue of the Americas, New York, N.Y. 10036.

OCCUPATION: Singer and musician.

CAREER: Former factory worker and waitress; vocalist and musician; member of groups Catch and Tourists, 1977-80; founder and member of Eurythmics, 1980—. Actress; appeared in film "Revolution."

DISCOGRAPHY:

ALL WITH EURYTHMICS; ALL RELEASED BY RCA RECORDS

In the Garden (never released in the United States), 1980.
Sweet Dreams (Are Made of This), (includes "Sweet Dreams [Are Made of This]," "Wrap It Up," "Jennifer," and "Love Is a Stranger"), 1983.
Touch (includes "No Fear, No Hate, No Pain [No Broken Hearts]," "Cool Blue," "Who's That Girl?," "Regrets," "Touch," "Right By Your Side," and "Here Comes the Rain Again"), 1984.
Eurythmics: 1984 (For the Love of Big Brother), (includes "For the Love of Big Brother," "Sexcrime," "Julia," "Room 101," "I Did It Just the Same," "Winston's Diary," and "Greetings from a Dead Man"), 1984.
Be Yourself Tonight (includes "There Must Be an Angel," "Sisters Are Doin' It for Themselves," "Adrian," and "Here Comes That Sinking Feeling"), 1985.

Also recorded three albums with group Tourist; appeared, with Eurythmics, on video disc *Eurythmics: Sweet Dreams* (includes "Sweet Dreams [Are Made of This]," "Prologue," "This Is the House," "Never Gonna Cry Again," "Take Me to Your Heart," and "I've Got an Angel"), produced by Pioneer Artists, 1984.

SIDELIGHTS: She has been called a David Bowie imitator. She is said to have borrowed heavily from the stage persona of Grace Jones. And *Time* magazine has placed her at the head of "the second British invasion" of pop music stars into America. Annie Lennox of the duo Eurythmics is at the forefront of what *Time* calls "England's strange new world of pop," a new British scene that "reflects a heady sense of adventure, irreverence and playful passion, with music and fashions to match."

AP/Wide World Photos

The fashion—in hairstyle and clothing—of this second invasion, as exemplified by Lennox and Boy George, among others, is decidedly androgynous. Indeed, these performers have become as well known for their looks as for their considerable vocal talents. In Lennox's case, the style was developed, at least in part, by accident. She felt there were already too many blonde female rock singers performing in the 1970s and early 1980s, and, not wanting to be lost in the crowd, she cut and dyed her hair. But when the time came to take the stage at Heaven, a popular London nightclub, with Eurythmics partner Dave Stewart, she decided at the last minute to don a long, black wig. In the middle of the act, however, an overzealous fan climbed onto the stage and tore the wig from her head revealing her own flaming orange, greased-back crew cut. The crowd went wild, and Lennox adopted the masculine look.

By blurring sexual boundaries, like Bowie, Jones, and Boy George, Lennox raised the interest and attention given to Eurythmics almost overnight. "Of course we're conscious of our image," she told *Time.* "The image is a kind of disposable wrapper,. . . something that will draw people in." In a *Rolling Stone* interview, Lennox made the point that "when I started wearing mannish clothes onstage, it was to detract from what people had come to expect from women singers, the height of which was Debbie Harry [of Blondie], who I loved. But I felt I couldn't be a sex symbol. That's not me. So I tried to find a way to transcend that emphasis on sexuality. . . . I wasn't particularly concerned with bending genders. I simply wanted to get away from wearing cutesy-pie miniskirts and tacky cutaway push-ups."

Lennox grew up in a musical home, a two-room flat with outside toilets in the coastal town of Aberdeen, Scotland. Her father was a bagpipe playing shipyard worker. And it was at home that she first learned to play piano and flute. For much of her childhood, Lennox planned to become a classical musician, and after graduation from Aberdeen High School for Girls, she was awarded a scholarship to London's Royal Academy of Music. But while there, she realized she would never embark on a classical career. "I hated it," she told *Rolling Stone* of the Academy. "I spent three dreadful years there trying to figure a way out." And to *Spin* magazine Lennox later said, "All the boys were gay and all the girls thought they were Maria Callas." So, just three days before final exams, Lennox simply left.

She drifted through a series of odd jobs for the next three years, waiting on tables and singing with a string of anonymous groups. Then, in 1977, Dave Stewart walked into the health food restaurant where Lennox worked. Stewart, a frazzled-looking, small Englishman who claims heritage from the Duke of Northumberland, had heard rumors about a fantastic singing waitress and wanted to see for himself.

Unlike Lennox's modest upbringing, Stewart had seldom gone wanting. His mother was a child psychologist, his father an accountant. Yet Stewart embarked on the struggling musician path by choice. His love affair with rock music started in 1964 when, at the age of twelve, he was hospitalized after he broke his knee in a soccer match. "Someone brought me a guitar in the hospital and as I couldn't walk, I started learning it," Stewart told *Rolling Stone.* "Then someone else brought me a leather jacket, and I hung it up at the bottom of the bed. I used to look at this leather jacket and play the guitar, and wish I could get out of the hospital."

When Lennox first met Stewart, "He looked like he'd been through a hedge backward," she recalled to *Rolling Stone.* "But he's a very special person, I soon recognized that." Lennox rushed Stewart back to her small apartment and accompanied herself on her giant wooden harmonium. "She just sat there like the Phantom of the Opera," Stewart told *Rolling Stone.* "She was straight from classical. She didn't know anything about pop groups. But I heard her sing and we started celebrating. Then we went out to this club, and from that moment on, Annie and I lived together, and we made music together, for about four years."

Joining with guitarist Peet Coombes, they started a group called Catch and later the Tourists, with whom they experienced modest success. With Coombes doing most of the writing, the Tourists toured all over the world and recorded three albums. But they still didn't make any money. The Tourists' only bona fide hit came in 1979 with their remake of the Dusty Springfield tune "I Only Want to Be with You." Ironically, that single commercial hit proved to be their undoing. Reviewers panned them, criticizing the group for catering to the oldies market rather than recognizing the song for the whimsical tribute to the singer that it was. Their credibility as a rock group destroyed, the Tourists disbanded in 1980.

When the Tourists broke up, Lennox and Stewart decided upon a philosophy for their collaboration. "We were never going to do anything again that we didn't like doing," Stewart told *Rolling Stone.* "We said, there's two of us and we always want to keep fresh and never have this thing where you're just touring around and round with the same people in a band, so that every night you have to pretend you're really into it. . . . We were getting really frustrated anyway. . . . During the punk movement, Annie and I bought a synthesizer, and we were doin' the opposite thing to the punks, we were getting more into sequencers and the mixture of soul feeling with electronics. We'd sit in hotel rooms and Annie would sing and I'd play the synthesizer and we started comin' up with the whole 'Sweet Dreams' concept."

"Sweet Dreams (Are Made of This)," a cut from the second Eurythmics album, became their first top ten hit. It is a melodic, almost eerie mix of synthesized pop music, to which Lennox contributed lyrics. "Dave and I were in the studio and we'd had a terrible argument," she told *Interview* magazine. "We weren't talking to each other. Dave said, 'Would you mind if I programmed the drum computer?' and I said go right ahead. He programmed the rhythm to 'Sweet Dreams' and I started to get interested. I found the riff and the words came and that was that."

Their first album, *In the Garden,* was never released in the United States and failed to do much on the English charts. Part of the problem was a lack of promotion. Stewart, who had been in a car crash years earlier, perennially suffered from a collapsed lung and needed surgery around the time the album was released. For eight months he was unable to promote the LP, and it died. So, too, did their romantic interest in one another, although Lennox and Stewart were determined to keep Eurythmics together and to continue working with one another. They remain good friends, or, as they often put it, now enjoy a brother-sister relationship.

In March 1984 Lennox had thought she'd found a second sweet dream, this time in the unlikely person of Radha Raman, a short, heavy, retiring German dedicated to the Hare Krishna movement. She met Raman in 1984 while the Eurythmics were in the middle of a world tour. Lennox, whose bouts with depression were well known, was also having trouble with her throat at the time. While the Eurythmics were in West Germany, Raman and a group of Krishnas made a vegetable dinner for them and prepared a special homopathic medicine for Lennox. The Eurythmics brought the Krishnas with them through Europe, Lennox and Raman spent more and more time together, and they were married in a spur-of-the-moment ceremony in New York.

After fourteen months of marriage, they separated. Lennox admitted to *People,* "Perhaps I was a bit impetuous." And she vowed, "I'm having a sabbatical from all religious forms." "I would say that I'm very good friends with him," she told *Spin* magazine, "and I just hope that we'll continue to be. But sometimes people just develop at different rates, and that's what happened with us—I think we've just gone in slightly different directions."

Although Lennox and Stewart often collaborate on the music, it is Annie Lennox who dominates the duo's performances, exuding an onstage burst of energy that some have compared to Bruce Springsteen. With bright red hair and deep blue eyes, she provides a fetching on-stage presence. She is "a singer of huge range and emotional power," said one London *Times* reviewer, after hearing her soar from operatic highs to gutteral lows at a concert.

Despite becoming well known for her androgynous persona, Lennox was voted "one of the ten most beautiful women in the world," by *Playboy* magazine in 1983. "The reason I come on a little masculine is to put down the sexual, feminine thing visually, and to allow my real sexuality to come through," she told *Interview* magazine. "I feel that when I wear clothes—it's a wrapped presentation. It could be anything. I could look one way and people think, 'Oh, she's that kind of person.' It's only a visual facet—not a real indication of the person who's really there. So I have to play with visual imagery."

Lennox capped the androgynous image at the 1984 Grammy Awards show by appearing on stage in full Elvis Presley

Annie Lennox with Eurythmics partner Dave Stewart. AP/Wide World Photos.

drag. Since that time, says *Rolling Stone* writer Brant Mewborn, she has "hung androgyny in the closet for now, but only so she can slip on other costumes. If people find the latest Lennox persona more feminine and less threatening, sexier and more real, then fine." But, maintains Lennox, "I'll just play with [the new image] as long as I want to. I'll play with what I want! I always will. It's just natural for me to do that. I mean, it's not like, 'Oh, God, I must be seen as a sex goddess now!' "

Despite the tremendous success she has achieved, Lennox remains troubled by the loneliness and depression that she says have haunted her all her life. "Obviously, someone that performs and writes music like that and does the things that I do is not going to be exactly the most even-keel person in the world," she told *Spin.* "I have been prone to a great deal of very bad depression. I've suffered from a history of depression which I hope that as I get older, I come more and more to terms with."

In an attempt to deal with the problem, Lennox consulted two psychotherapists. The first "didn't help at all," she related to *Musician* interviewer Barbara Pepe, "just sat and looked at me. I felt completely tongue-tied, like I was filling in all the spaces with words. I was more freaked out when I left than when I came in." But recently she has seen a Los Angeles therapist who has proven considerably more supportive. "She was so helpful to me," Lennox told Pepe, "just in terms of going and talking to her and asking 'Am I mad? Am I going to go insane, or am I all right, really?'. . . . We are living in this crazy, super fast, hyped-up society. There's this superconsciousness, which before, we never really had. We just did what we were doing and didn't ask too many questions. Now we're full of self-doubt. Neurosis is a common disease. We used to have scurvy, now we have neurosis."

In the *Spin* interview, she described her feeling as being similar to "adolescent depression that you get when you're about fifteen, and it never quite leaves you. It's always there and it's also been the source of my creativity, as well, to a great degree; at least in the sense that I sense this awful sort of angst and greyness about existence. Part of the reason why I've written songs was to deal with that, to express what was inside, which was just something so awful."

Still, there seems to be far more good going on for Lennox than bad. Despite her divorce and a flap surrounding the movie "1984," for which the Eurythmics were commissioned to do the soundtrack and later dropped from the project, Lennox and Stewart are riding high. The duo's "Sweet Dreams (Are Made of This)" in 1983 and their 1984 hit "Here Comes the Rain Again," both were top ten singles. A new album, *Be Yourself Tonight,* reached the stores in 1985. Lennox is signed to star in several videos and recently landed a cameo role in the film "Revolution," starring Al Pacino and Nastassia Kinski.

"I actually embrace the idea of being happy now," Lennox told *Rolling Stone.* "I've had my share of pain and probably will in the future. But I guess it's molded me into the person I am today. There was a time when I looked to other people for recognition because I didn't have enough confidence in my own judgment. Now I'm not looking for reassurance because I realize how fickle people are. . . . My own strength is the best strength I can have."

SOURCES:

PERIODICALS

High Fidelity, April, 1985.
Musician, July, 1985, November, 1985.
New York Times, February 5, 1984, August 3, 1984.
People, August 22, 1983, December 19, 1983, March 12, 1984, May 20, 1985, June 10, 1985.
Playboy, April, 1984.
Rolling Stone, June 23, 1983, September 29, 1983, October 24, 1985.
Spin, August, 1985.
Stereo Review, October, 1984, September, 1985.
Time, June 23, 1984, September 30, 1985.
Wall Street Journal, January 19, 1984.
Washington Post, March 21, 1984, January 10, 1985.

—Sidelights by Stephen Advokat

Candy Lightner

1946-

PERSONAL: Born May 30, 1946, in Pasadena, Calif.; daughter of Dykes C. (a career serviceman in the U.S. Air Force) and Katherine (an exchange system employee for the U.S. Air Force; maiden name, Karrib), Doddridge; married Steve Lightner (an officer in the U.S. Air Force; divorced); children: Carime Anne (died, 1980) and Serena (twins), Travis. *Education:* Attended American River College, Sacramento, Calif., beginning 1966.

ADDRESSES: Home—Hurst, Tex. *Office*—Mothers Against Drunk Driving, 669 Airport Fwy., Suite 310, Hurst, Tex. 76053.

OCCUPATION: Social activist.

CAREER: Dental assistant in various cities, 1964-72; real estate agent in Fair Oaks, Calif., 1979-80; Mothers Against Drunk Driving (MADD; formerly Mothers Against Drunk Drivers), Hurst, Tex., founder, president, 1980–85, consultant, 1985—. Member of board of directors, National Commission on Drunk Driving. Guest lecturer at numerous conferences, seminars, and symposia, including the National Judicial College Presentation on Victims' Rights and Alcohol and Traffic Safety, the International Symposium on Alcohol, and the International Commission for the Prevention of Alcoholism and Drug Dependency's Fifth World Congress. Member of advisory board, National Sheriff's Association.

MEMBER: National Commission Against Drunk Driving, Parents of Murdered Children.

AWARDS, HONORS: Named one of Five Outstanding Californians by California Jaycees, 1982; Jefferson Award from American Institute for Public Service, 1983; President's Volunteer Action Award, 1983; named One of the Top One Hundred Women in America by *Ladies' Home Journal*; Individual Achievement Award from Freedom Foundation; Human Concern Award for outstanding contribution to the protection of life or property from Western Insurance Information Services; Dr. Hum., St. Francis College (Pennsylvania), 1984; Epilepsy Foundation award, 1984; named Woman of the Year by Baylor University Mortarboard Society, 1985; Human Dignity Award from Kessler Institute for Rehabilitation, 1985; Black and Blue Award from Thomas Jefferson University Hospital Emergency Medicine Society.

WRITINGS: Contributor of articles to several publications, including *Abstracts and Reviews, Judges Journal,* and *USA Today.* Member of editorial board, *Abstracts and Reviews.*

SIDELIGHTS: Giving a driver's license back to a drunk driver, Candy Lightner believes, is like giving the murder weapon back to a murderer. Take the case of the driver who

killed Lightner's 13-year-old daughter, Cari, on May 3, 1980: prior to killing Cari he had been convicted of drunk driving twice before, and at the time of Cari's death he had been out of jail on bail from a third drunk-driving arrest only two days. But he was driving with a valid California license.

That spring day, Lightner tragically learned the truth about drunk drivers and the law when a policeman told her it was highly unlikely that her daughter's killer would receive a jail sentence. She came face-to-face with an attitude explained by Bennett H. Beach in *Time* quoting a California motor vehicle official who said, "We still laugh at Charlie driving home drunk and just barely missing someone, rather than consider it a shocking thing." "The public doesn't perceive drunk driving as a crime," Lightner declared in a *McCall's* report, "yet more people are killed each year in this manner than they are by handguns." The death of her daughter and the leniency often shown to drunk drivers by the legal system led Lightner to start Mothers Against Drunk Driving (MADD), an organization aimed at maintaining a strong public voice on behalf of the victims. Indeed, according to *People,* Lightner considers the victims of drunk drivers to be her "constituency."

Lightner was enraged by Cari's needless death, but the thought that her murderer could go virtually unpunished was more than she could bear. The anger that inspired her to found MADD transformed her from an apolitical real estate agent—she wasn't even registered to vote—into a one-woman dynamo, head of a non-profit organization of over 50,000 members with a budget of over $10 million. She became a political force with whom civic leaders nationwide from former California Governor Jerry Brown to President Ronald Reagan dealt.

Ironically, MADD was founded in a cocktail lounge. On the eve of her daughter's funeral, Lightner sat with friends in a restaurant's lounge waiting for a table. She recalls in a *Time* article, "I remember sitting in the bar with all these people and saying out loud, 'I'm going to start an organization. . . .' There was a big moment of silence, and then my girlfriend pipes up and says, 'And we can call it Mothers Against Drunk Drivers.'" (The name of the organization was changed in October 1984, to Mothers Against Drunk Driving to better reflect its aim—to change attitudes toward impaired driving rather than exact revenge from the individuals involved.) And, the one-woman group formed that night has grown with startling speed.

Lightner quit her real estate job and used her savings plus insurance money from Cari's death to finance almost 60 percent of the organization's expenses its first year. Her first stop was Sacramento, California's state capital, to ask Governor Brown to appoint a state commission to study drunk driving. He refused to see her. Undaunted, Lightner called a press conference to express her concern to the people of her state. Victims of drunk drivers from all over the country began to contact her. MADD's first out-of-state chapter was formed by Cindy Lamb of Maryland whose daughter, Laura, became a quadraplegic at the age of five months when a drunk driver hit Lamb's car.

By October 1980, there were four MADD chapters in California and a staff of three volunteers at the national headquarters, including Lightner and her father. While providing counseling for victims of drunk drivers, the organization lobbied for state laws requiring mandatory sentencing for convicted drunk drivers and for national reforms, including the establishment of a standard legal definition of intoxication nationwide, more sophisticated record-keeping techniques (which would enable law enforcement officials to keep better track of habitually drunk drivers), and mandatory prison terms and license suspensions for repeat offenders.

In a desperate effort to be heard, Lightner began going to Governor Brown's office daily. Finally, in the fall of 1980, the governor agreed to meet with her. As a result of their meeting, Brown established a statewide task force on drunk driving and appointed Lightner its first member. She cried when she heard the news. By the time the task force made its final report public, about a year later, MADD had had its first membership drive and boasted twenty-five chapters in five states. From a small California organization, MADD was becoming a nationwide presence.

That same year, new laws to help get drunk drivers off the highways were approved in nine states. This new legislation allowed law enforcement officials to pursue the drunk driver more rigorously than before. Legislators in Michigan, for example, passed a law that allowed police officers to detain drivers whom they suspected of drinking; previously, officers had to see an incident or have witnesses to it before pulling the person off the road. Due to this and other measures, Michigan police were able to increase drunk-driving arrests by 21 percent in a year-and-a-half period. In Maryland, lawmakers petitioned for and received a $150,000 federal grant that paid state troopers to work overtime, particularly weekend nights when drunk drivers were more likely to be out. Maryland drunk-driving arrests went up 10 percent in the year after the patrols were increased.

At her urging, Lightner's own state of California passed one of the nation's toughest drunk-driving codes. It established, among other provisions, a mandatory forty-eight-hour jail sentence for the first drunk-driving conviction with only minor exceptions. Also, as part of the California law, persons involved in two drunk-driving fatalities were liable for up to four years in prison. Drunk-driving arrests and traffic deaths fell dramatically in California after the laws went into effect.

Coincidentally, just a month earlier, the California Supreme Court, deciding that drunk driving is malicious, ruled that a drunk driver could be charged with second-degree murder. Traditionally, the court had held that a drunk driver could not be considered a murderer because drunk driving itself was not socially malicious. The social acceptability of being drunk while driving was starting to change; Lightner's dream of highways free of drunk drivers was coming closer to fruition. She told a *Time* reporter: "We've kicked a few pebbles, we'll turn a few stones, and eventually we'll start an avalanche."

The avalanche already appears to have begun. In two successive years, 1980 and 1981, Lightner asked President Ronald Reagan in two Washington, D.C., press conferences to establish a national commission on drunk driving. After Reagan expressed reluctance to start such a commission, believing it would interfere with states' rights, Lightner and two cooperative members of the House of Representatives gathered 303 signatures of congressmen and congresswomen who supported the idea. In April, 1982, Reagan not only established the commission but also appointed Lightner to serve as a member. The thirty-member commission coordinates anti-drunk-driving efforts in an attempt to focus more public attention on the problem.

Figures gathered by this and other groups have demonstrated the overwhelming size of the problem. During the seventies, 250,000 Americans were killed in alcohol-related accidents. In the first two years of the eighties, more Americans died in alcohol-related traffic accidents than died in Vietnam; an average of three Americans are killed, and eighty injured, by drunk drivers each hour of every day.

These staggering statistics touched the conscience of the nation. Just two years old in 1982, MADD had eighty-nine chapters in twenty-nine states. It had eight paid employees and was supported by a $100,000 grant from an anonymous donor and a $60,000 National Highway Traffic Safety Administration grant. In 1982, the California Jaycees recognized Lightner as one of their Five Outstanding Californians. She was the first woman ever to receive the honor.

That same year, twenty-seven states toughened their drunk-driving laws. The majority of these laws reflected goals for which MADD had been striving since its inception. In most states, the new laws held that anyone caught with a .10 percent or higher blood-alcohol content had already committed a crime. Formerly, this was merely considered evidence of guilt. New legislation made certain alcohol-related offenses punishable by mandatory jail sentences, where previously sentencing was left to the discretion of judges. In many states, drunk-driving convictions could no longer be expunged from the driver's record. Older laws had provided that drunk drivers, even those who seriously injured others by their actions, could go through an alcohol education program and emerge with a clean record.

States reported new successes with each new law passed. In Maryland, drunk-driving arrests by state police went up 45 percent, while highway fatalities decreased 20 percent. Maine recorded a 47 percent reduction in alcohol-related fatalities. And in an effort to make sure that everyone who purchases alcoholic beverages helps to pay for the increased cost of keeping drunks off drunks off the road, Maine included a new tax on liquor in its legal package. The monies raised by the new tax were destined to finance centers for the treatment and prevention of alcohol problems.

One of Lightner's major concerns has always been the high incidence of alcohol-related traffic fatalities involving young people. Between 1974 and 1984, it is estimated that 50,000 teenagers died in drunk-driving accidents. Alcohol-related traffic fatalities became the largest killer of Americans between the ages of eighteen and twenty-four during the same period. Through the mid-seventies, after many states lowered their legal drinking age to eighteen, the problem of young people's drinking and driving reached crisis proportions. After Michigan lowered its drinking age in 1972, for example, accidents associated with drunk driving increased between 18 and 20 percent. In New Jersey, the number of people killed by eighteen-to-twenty-year-olds in traffic accidents climbed 176 percent after the state lowered its drinking age. Teenagers commuting across state borders to drink caused an increase in accidents along the borders of neighboring states with differing drinking ages. For instance, although Illinois raised its drinking age to twenty-one in 1980, with a resultant 28 percent decrease in highway deaths among eighteen-to-twenty-year-olds in the state, drunk-driving deaths were up 10 percent in the two Illinois counties adjacent to Wisconsin, which had a lower legal drinking age.

These statistics on young people led Lightner to found the first Students Against Drunk Drivers (SADD) chapter in August, 1980. Although she is not officially affiliated with the current SADD groups, many of MADD's own programs are also aimed at youth education. MADD sponsors "Project Graduation," which strives to make students particularly aware of the danger of drinking while driving after their proms or graduation activities. It also has an annual National Poster and Essay Contest, open to elementary-through high-school-age students, focusing on changing youth attitudes toward drinking and driving. The contest allows youngsters to express themselves creatively while increasing their knowledge of America's drinking and driving problem. MADD also has material available that it sends students who wish to start student groups on their campuses.

But by far the most important youth-related activity in which Lightner has been involved is her campaign to raise the drinking age across the nation to twenty-one. Lightner doesn't buy the idea of "old enough to fight, old enough to drink." In *People*, Margie Bonnett Sellinger notes Lightner's explanation: "There are different age limits for different levels of responsibility: thirty-five for President, thirty for Senator, twenty-three for FBI agent. We just don't feel that kids at eighteen, many of whom are just learning how to drive, should be allowed to drink too."

Her lobbying efforts won Lightner her first Congressional success in October 1982, when Congress passed a bill providing monetary incentives for states to raise the drinking age to twenty-one. The bill, however, proved to be ineffective. Although twenty-three states considered raising the drinking age, only four actually did. In her organization's newsletter, Lightner blamed the states' liquor lobbies for the failure of the bill.

A few months later, in March 1983, Lightner received national television coverage when the National Broadcasting Co. (NBC) produced a made-for-television film about her life. The film, "Mothers Against Drunk Drivers: The Candy Lightner Story," was shown as an NBC "Movie of the Week."

By July 1983, MADD had 184 chapters in thirty-nine states and Lightner had already begun discussing strategies for the passage of a new Congressional drinking-age bill. She hoped to come up with a measure that would be more effective than the previous bill. In September, Congressman James Florio of New Jersey called a press conference in which he and Lightner announced the introduction of a bill to prohibit the sale of alcoholic beverages to anyone under twenty-one if the beverage had travelled over state lines. One month later, Lightner testified before the Subcommittee on Commerce, Transportation, and Tourism in favor of the bill and a federal minimum drinking age of twenty-one. Subsequently, Senator Richard Lugar of Indiana introduced a bill into the Senate that was similar to the one Florio had introduced in the House.

On December, 13, 1983, in Washington, D.C., the Presidential Commission on Drunk Driving, of which Lightner was a member, released its final report. Included in the report was a recommendation that Congress deny federal highway funds to states that fail to set the minimum drinking age at twenty-one. Among other recommendations were enactment of programs to assist victims of traffic accidents involving drunk driving, requirements that repeat offenders must receive medical screening for alcoholism, prohibition of open alcohol containers or the consumption of alcohol in automobiles, and stricter enforcement of drunk-driving laws, including mandatory suspension of first offenders' drivers' licenses for at least ninety days. In the *New York Times*, John A. Volpe, the commission chairman, echoed the feelings of Lightner and other MADD members when he said, "If we hope to reduce the number of alcohol-related highway tragedies, we must make it socially unacceptable to drive after drinking."

Buoyed by the commission's report, Lightner lobbied for a new bill sponsored by Representative James Howard of New Jersey (one of the sponsors of the 1982 incentives bill). This new bill called for withholding an escalating percentage of federal highway funds from states whose drinking age was not twenty-one. The bill also provided increased highway safety funds for states that enacted mandatory minimum sentencing for persons convicted of drunk driving. If passed, the states would have two years in which to comply with the law.

In March 1984, New Jersey, a state whose legal drinking age was raised to twenty-one on January 1, 1983 (after extensive campaigning by the state's newly organized MADD chapter), reported figures favorable to MADD's position on the raising of the drinking age. In the year after New Jersey's new law went into effect, there were 25 percent fewer drunk-driving convictions among eighteen-to-twenty-year-olds and the number of drunk-driving-related highway fatalities in that age group also dropped.

In May, MADD staff members gathered with members of other safety-oriented organizations at the National Highway Traffic Safety Administration's third annual Lifesavers Conference in Orlando, Florida, to discuss traffic safety. The organizations decided to combine their efforts and form the "Save Our Students" coalition. Together, they could lobby for legislation to curb the growing menace of drunk-driving accidents involving young people. They set June 13th as the day they would announce their effort in a press conference on the east steps of the U.S. Capitol. They did not know at the time what a busy month June would be for MADD and its founder.

June was the highlight of 1984 for MADD. For the entire month, Lightner spent eighteen-hour days gathering research, meeting with legislators, and working with the media in her effort to get "21" (as Howard's bill came to be known) passed. She worked relentlessly to convince leery legislators of the importance of the bill. Jane Perlez reported on the impact of Lightner's work in the *New York Times*: "Now and then an issue takes the Capitol by surprise, and the link between teen-age drinking and road fatalities is such an issue. While teen-age drunken-driving is a hot issue in many states, including New York, it had hardly raised a murmur here before Mrs. Lightner arrived."

Lightner's work brought swift passage of the House measure. Support for the bill grew so strong that when the House voted on it on June 7th, Lightner told *People*, "There were Congressmen standing three and four deep on the floor speaking on behalf of the measure."

The next step was to get a similar bill passed in the Senate. Senator Frank Lautenberg of New Jersey introduced a companion bill in the Senate, and the drive to get it passed began. On June 13th, Lightner appeared at the "Save Our Students" press conference along with members of MADD and the thirty-eight co-sponsoring organizations. After Lightner's address, in which she reiterated the need for "21" legislation, Secretary of Transportation Elizabeth Hanford Dole spoke. She revealed to the delighted crowd that President Reagan, reversing his former position, had decided to support the bill. According to MADD's newsletter, Dole noted, "The sanction sends a clear message: Americans will

no longer tolerate drunk driving." She also thanked "citizen groups like MADD for awakening America to the menace of the drunk driver."

A few days later, the Senate Subcommittee on Alcoholism and Drug Abuse heard testimony for and against "21." Lightner and Lautenberg were among those testifying. Lautenberg's own special reason for backing the bill was reported by Steven V. Roberts in the *New York Times*. "We see the need for this legislation in New Jersey," the congressman declared, "because our young people are overrepresented in fatal alcohol-related accidents in the four counties of New York [which has a lower drinking age than New Jersey] which border my state." Conservative lawmakers, however, spoke out against the bill, saying that the issue should be left up to the states. Representatives of student groups and restaurant owners also voiced opposition, declaring that the law would discriminate on the basis of age and that restaurant revenues would decrease because of it. Conflicting testimony delayed the bill over a week in the committee before it got to the Senate floor for a vote.

Finally, on June 26th, debate and voting on the bill was scheduled to take place. At 2:00 p.m. Lightner and other supporters of the bill gathered in the Senate gallery to await the final outcome. Several senators had again proposed a bill to substitute incentives for sanctions against states that failed to raise their drinking age. After four hours of debate, the bill granting incentives was defeated and the time had come for the vote on Lautenberg's bill. The final outcome: the bill passed by an eighty-one-to-sixteen margin.

Two days later, the bill returned to the House for final approval. Representative Howard called for a vote on the bill shortly after midnight as Lightner watched the proceedings on a television monitor in a room near the House floor. Howard decided to call for a voice vote even though House rules state that only one vote against a bill in a voice vote would mean that it has to be voted on again under normal voting procedures. So, with only about twenty members of the House present, debate was started. Only one representative, William Carney of Suffolk, New York, raised any objections. But, when the votes were called for, Carney did not vote against the measure, and it passed.

Irvin Molotsky reported in the *New York Times*, "Carney, recognizing that Mr. Howard had enough support to gain its passage under normal voting, did not vote against it." Carney said: "I entertained thoughts of voting against it, but Howard had the votes. I don't think it is the proper thing to do legislation by blackmail, but I'm a good counter." He also mentioned that his major objection to the bill was the fact that New York State would lose federal funds if it passed, since the New York Assembly had recently defeated an attempt to raise the state's drinking age to twenty-one.

According to MADD's national newsletter, when Lightner heard that the bill had passed, she said, "It means a lot of lives saved, it means that grassroots organizing works—and it means I can go home." What had begun as a five-day trip to organize the "Save Our Students" press conference had turned into a month-long stay in Washington, D.C., for Lightner as she saw "21" through Congress from start to finish. On July 17, 1984, President Reagan signed what was officially known as the National Minimum Drinking Age

Act of 1984 into law. Lightner was at his side. Molotsky called the bill, "the first significant Federal move against drinking since Prohibition."

Reflecting on the passage of the bill in her column, "Founder's Message," in MADD's national newsletter, Lightner wrote: "Our intent was not to punish the minority, the youth of our nation who are under twenty-one. We hope instead to give them a chance—an even better opportunity to live, to prosper, and to enjoy all that life has to offer."

Nineteen eighty-four offered other triumphs for MADD. In May, the U.S. Supreme Court rejected an appeal to declare unconstitutional the California law stating that having a .10 percent blood-alcohol content is a crime. Lawyers had argued the law was too vague because drivers had no way of knowing when they reached the limit. In June, the New Jersey Supreme Court ruled that a host could be sued for injuries caused by an automobile crash of a guest, if the host allowed a guest to leave a social gathering intoxicated. Michigan law-makers passed a bill calling for special coding on drivers' licenses of people under twenty-one. Such marking should make it easier to spot underage individuals trying to buy alcohol. The Ohio Liquor Commission placed a ban on bartenders serving more than one drink at a time to a customer. By the year's end, MADD had moved to new headquarters in Hurst, Texas, and had 325 chapters in forty-seven states.

But 1985 witnessed a reversal of Lightner's administrative fortunes. The *New York Times* reported that in the spring of that year "the Council of Better Business Bureaus, an Arlington, Va., umbrella organization for 169 local bureaus and branches, and the New York-based National Charities Information Bureau, which monitors the finances of more than 400 nonprofit charitable groups, said MADD's spending did not meet their standards. The council's standards call for at least half of an organization's total income to be spent on programs, with no more than 35 percent going for fund raising. The bureau's standards call for 60 percent of the revenue to be spent on programs, with no more than 30 percent for fund raising."

In October 1985 Lightner was separated from her administrative position in MADD by the organization's six-member executive committee. Robert D. McFadden, writing in the *New York Times*, reported that Lightner's "removal appeared to reflect dissatisfaction by MADD's board of directors with her performance as leader and financial manager of the group." And *USA Today* asserted that Lightner "lost executive powers when negotiations broke down over her request for a $10,000 bonus to her $75,000 salary." Lightner refused to leave the organization and was given the titles of founder and consultant.

SOURCES:

PERIODICALS

Car & Driver, January, 1985.
Christian Century, June 2, 1982.
Detroit News, December 31, 1984.
Glamour, February, 1985.
Ladies' Home Journal, February, 1985.
McCall's, September, 1982.
Mothers Against Drunk Driving National Newsletter, fall, 1984, winter, 1984.
Newsweek, September 13, 1982.
New York Times, April 4, 1982, May 23, 1982, February 27, 1983, July 14, 1983, July 17, 1983, August 14, 1983, October 2, 1983, December 14, 1983, December 18, 1983, December 23, 1983, March 8, 1984, June 4, 1984, June 9, 1984, June 13, 1984, June 20, 1984, June 27, 1984, June 29, 1984, October 4, 1985.
People, June 29, 1981, July 25, 1983, July 9, 1984.
Time, August 3, 1981, January 25, 1982, April 26, 1982, January 7, 1985.
USA Today, October 4, 1985.
U. S. News & World Report, June 25, 1984.

—*Sketch by Marian Walters Gonsior*

Pelle Lindbergh

1959-1985

OBITUARY NOTICE: Full name, Per-Erik Lindbergh; born May 24, 1959, in Stockholm, Sweden; immigrated to United States, 1980; declared brain dead following an automobile accident, November 10, 1985, pronounced clinically dead, November 12, 1985, in Stratford, N.J. Swedish-born professional hockey player. Lindbergh became the first European ever to win the Vezina Trophy as the top goaltender in the National Hockey League (NHL) when he led the league with forty wins during the 1984-85 regular season. His superb goaltending helped guide the Philadelphia Flyers into the Stanley Cup finals where they were defeated, four games to one, by the Edmonton Oilers.

Drafted by Philadelphia in the 1979 NHL entry draft, Lindbergh played for the Swedish Olympic team that won the bronze medal at Lake Placid, N.Y., in 1980 before joining the Flyers organization later that year. He made his NHL debut with Philadelphia during the 1981-82 season and was the Flyers' number one netminder from the next season on. By posting a 40-17-7 record in 1984-85, Lindbergh established himself as only the third goalie in Philadelphia history to win forty or more games in a single season. He had become "without question one of the greatest goalies," former Flyer superstar goaltender Bernie Parent told the *Sporting News.*

After a night of celebration following a Flyers victory early in the 1985-86 season, Lindbergh crashed his car into a concrete wall at a Somerdale, N.J., school and suffered severe brain and spinal cord injuries. Declared brain dead, he was kept alive by a respirator until doctors, at the request of Lindbergh's parents, removed his organs for transplant. Following the removal surgery Lindbergh was taken off the respirator. He died shortly thereafter and his body was returned to Sweden for burial.

SOURCES:

PERIODICALS

Chicago Tribune, November 12, 1985, November 13, 1985, November 17, 1985.

AP/Wide World Photos

Hockey News, November 22, 1985.
Newsweek, November 25, 1985.
New York Times, April 8, 1985, April 20, 1985, November 12, 1985, November 13, 1985, November 24, 1985.
Sporting News, April 22, 1985, May 6, 1985, May 27, 1985, June 10, 1985, November 18, 1985, November 25, 1985.
Sports Illustrated, November 25, 1985.
Time, November 25, 1985.
Washington Post, November 11, 1985, November 12, 1985.

Andy Lipkis

1953(?)-

BRIEF ENTRY: Born c. 1953, in California. American environmentalist. Best known as the founder of the Los Angeles-based action group TreePeople, Lipkis is dedicated to the conservation and growth of forests. Discovering at the age of fifteen that 80 percent of the pines in the San Bernardino National Forest were destined to succumb to smog by the turn of the century, the concerned high school student determined to challenge fate and the system. Defying resistance and staggering odds, Lipkis has managed, since 1970, to rally a coalition of nearly two thousand volunteer members to counter pollution's threat to Southern California's tree population. The organization, inspired by the enthusiasm and optimism generated by its founder, conducts mass plantings of smog-tolerant saplings at various needy locations.

People of all walks of life have joined the tree crusade, proving that ecology is not just a private concern. Celebrities such as Gregory Peck, Jack Nicholson, and Johnny Carson have given generous support to Lipkis and the TreePeople project through personal appearances, advertisements, broadcasts, and donations. Warner Brothers movie studio co-sponsored the organization's first annual TreeRun, which awarded milk carton-potted seedlings to its three thousand participants. Media coverage from across the nation as well as from foreign countries, including France, Sweden, Australia, and Japan, has greatly contributed to the environmental program's momentum. In addition, several politicians have responded to the immense public support behind the TreePeople cause by endorsing its work. Lipkis announced that he anticipates a show of interest from President Reagan also.

Although TreePeople's primary thrust originally was to preserve and replenish existing West Coast forest lands, Lipkis is fostering other ecology-minded plans. One is a city-wide planting project that would turn Los Angeles into a veritable urban forest. Another is a small-scale power plant that will convert tree trimmings into a clean, efficient energy supply. As Lipkis points out, trees serve numerous valuable functions, from filtering impurities out of the air to providing alternate sources of energy—evidence of his belief that "a tree does make a difference."

SOURCES:

PERIODICALS

American Forests, November, 1981.
Christian Science Monitor, April 20, 1983.
National Wildlife, June-July, 1981.
Omni, June, 1984.

Photograph by Mark Wexler

Harry H. Lipsig
1901-

PERSONAL: Born December 26, 1901, in Poland; son of David and Rose Lipsig; married Mildred Slonim, September 14, 1924. *Education:* Brooklyn Law School, LL.D., 1926.

ADDRESSES: Home—860 U.N. 10017. *Office:* Lipsig, Sullivan, Mollen & Liapakis, 100 Church St., New York, N.Y. 10007.

OCCUPATION: Attorney.

CAREER: Admitted to Bar of U.S. Supreme Court and to Bar of State of New York; former member of faculty, New York University Law School; currently senior partner, Lipsig, Sullivan, Mollen & Liapakis (law firm), New York, N.Y. Lecturer on legal topics.

MEMBER: International Bar Association, International Academy of Trial Lawyers (fellow), American Bar Association, Federal Bar Council, American Association of Trial Lawyers, Public Awareness Society (president), Puerto Rican Bar Association, New York State Bar Association, New York State Trial Lawyers Association, New York Criminal and Civil Courts Bar Association (member of board of directors), New York Criminal Bar Association, New York Women's Bar Association, New York County Lawyers Association, Association of the Bar of the City of New York, Metropolitan Trial Lawyers Association, Association of Trial Lawyers of the City of New York (member of board of directors), Brooklyn-Manhattan Trial Lawyers Association, Brooklyn Trial Lawyers Association, Bronx Bar Association, Bronx Women's Bar Association, Queen's Women's Bar Association, Kings County Criminal Bar Association.

AWARDS, HONORS: Outstanding Leadership Recognition Award, International Academy of Estates Attorneys, 1960; Anti-Defamation League Appeal Award, 1971; Law Day award, New York State Trial Lawyers Association, 1979.

WRITINGS: Contributor of articles to professional journals.

SIDELIGHTS: New York lawyer Harry Lipsig, one of the preeminent personal injury attorneys in the country, "has done more for the lame and afflicted than the Statue of Liberty has done for the tired and the poor," a reporter for the *"New York Times"* commented in a profile of Lipsig's lengthy career. For six decades Lipsig has specialized in the branch of civil law known as negligence law. He represents individuals who allege that they have suffered harm through the negligence of corporations, municipalities, or other persons.

Born in Poland in 1901, Lipsig later immigrated to New York City. He graduated from Brooklyn Law School in

1926 and began his career by seeking out cases that other lawyers felt they could not win. Establishing himself as a winner early in his career, Lipsig won the first twenty cases he tried. His phenomenal record of success has continued unabated to the present. In the two decades prior to 1979, Lipsig received only three jury verdicts in which his client received nothing, the *New York Times* reported.

Lipsig's trial successes have made him a very wealthy man. In a field of law where million-dollar awards are not unknown, the attorney usually receives one-third of the total award or settlement. Lipsig staunchly defends the large verdicts he garners for clients. As he told reporter Alan Richman of the *New York Times,* "I never get more vicious than when I talk to people who criticize large verdicts when they have never spent a day with a cripple who is imprisoned for life in his living, but dead, body."

A master of courtroom strategy, Lipsig recognizes the importance of using psychology and staging in presenting his clients' cases at trial. "Trial preparation has nothing to do with what you learn at law school," Lipsig explained to the *New York Times.* "Just because you've read all the plays doesn't mean you can direct a play. Staging a trial is like staging an important drama. It's up to you to be in control."

Several of Lipsig's cases have led to the development of important legal principles. One such case involved a woman who had a surgical clamp sewed inside her during an operation. The cause of her medical problems was discovered only after the statute of limitations period had expired. According to the law at that time the statute of limitations period began to run at the time the malpractice occurred regardless of when it was discovered. Lipsig attacked the inherent unfairness of that rule as applied to his client's situation and successfully argued that the statute of limitations should begin to run in such cases only when the malpractice was actually discovered. In another case, Lipsig represented a child who was injured by the rear of a moving vehicle when the child ran into the street. The courts accepted Lipsig's theory that drivers, and not children, are expected to exercise due care as they travel on public roads.

For the past several years, Lipsig has been involved in a case brought by the widow of a young photographer who was killed when he was struck by a falling cable on the Brooklyn Bridge. The 600-foot cable, which was apparently corroded by salt air or pigeon droppings, snapped as Akira Aimi walked across the bridge. He was struck in the head, sustained a fractured skull, and died from his injuries a week later. When the victim's widow sought Lipsig to represent her, Lipsig was excited by the challenge the case presented. "Tragic as it may be for a client, for a lawyer it's a honey of a lawsuit," he commented to the *New York Times*.

Lipsig filed the lawsuit in January of 1982. The suit seeks $50 million in damages and names eleven defendants, including the City of New York, which is responsible for maintenance of the bridge. Damages sought include $1.9 million for the victim's pain and suffering, $100,000 for the widow's loss of her husband's "services, society and companionship" during the week before his death, $10 million for his anticipated lifetime earnings as a photographer, and $38 million in punitive damages for the defendants' "willful, egregious, callous and wanton disregard of their obligation to the life and safety of the public at large," according to the lawsuit.

Attorneys for the City of New York estimate that the value of the suit is well below one million dollars. However, assessing the impact of the case on jurors, Lipsig believes that the suit "could easily bring in $2 million, because of the dramatic nature of it." He explained to the *New York Times:* "So many jurors would feel at home with the Brooklyn Bridge, and would wonder what would have happened if they'd been walking the bridge themselves. If I can get them to put themselves in the place of the man who was executed, then I'm at home and it's two million bucks. Maybe four million."

SOURCES:

PERIODICALS

New York, April 5, 1982.
New York Times, May 20, 1978, February 2, 1979, April 25, 1979, August 24, 1979, October 8, 1984.

—Sidelights by Barbara Welch Skaggs

John Lithgow

1945-

PERSONAL: Full name, John Arthur Lithgow; born October 19, 1945, in Rochester, N.Y.; son of Arthur (a theatrical producer) and Sarah L. (an actress) Lithgow; married Jean Taynton (a teacher), September 10, 1966 (divorced, 1976); married Mary Yeager (a history professor) 1981; children: Ian (first marriage); Phoebe, Nathan (second marriage). *Education:* Graduated magna cum laude from Harvard University, 1967; additional study at London Academy of Music and Dramatic Art, 1967-69.

ADDRESSES: *Home*—Los Angeles, Calif. *Agent*—Lund Agency, 6515 West Sunset, Los Angeles, Calif. 90028.

OCCUPATION: Actor on stage and in motion pictures; theatrical director.

CAREER: Made dramatic debut in 1951; acted in fifteen plays produced by Great Lakes Shakespearean Festival in Ohio, 1963-64; Royal Court Theatre, London, England, actor and director, 1967-69; director of five Broadway and Off-Broadway productions, 1968-70; actor in eleven Broadway and Off-Broadway productions, 1973-82; actor in motion pictures, including "All That Jazz" and "Rich Kids," both 1979, "Blow Out," 1981, "The World According to Garp" and "Dealing," both 1982, "Twilight Zone—The Movie," "Terms of Endearment," and "Footloose," all 1983, "The Adventures of Buckaroo Banzai" and "2010: Odyssey Two," both 1984, and "Santa Claus—The Movie," 1985. Has also appeared in a variety of television shows. Performed on his own program, "Under the Gun," WBAI-Radio, New York, N.Y., 1972-73.

WRITINGS: Author of one-man show "Kaufman at Large."

AWARDS, HONORS: Tony Award from League of New York Theatres and Producers, 1973, for "The Changing Room"; Academy Award nominations for best supporting actor, from Academy of Motion Picture Arts and Sciences, 1982, for "The World According to Garp," and 1983, for "Terms of Endearment."

SIDELIGHTS: Versatility—the ability to play off-beat roles ranging from a psychopathic killer to a transexual ex-football player to a fiery country preacher—helped John Lithgow become one of Hollywood's most sought-after character actors by the mid-1980s. He attained prominence in his thirties, after years of respected work on Broadway. But even after his career took off through roles in films like "Terms of Endearment" and "The World According to Garp," more people knew Lithgow by face than by name. "I wouldn't mind being an unrecognized actor so long as people who know about acting know me," Lithgow told the *New Yorker* in 1977. "My reputation is extremely important. My face is not."

Lithgow was born into an acting family. His mother, Sarah, was an accomplished thespian. His father, Arthur, headed Princeton University's McCarter Theater before moving the family to Ohio as a regional theater producer during John's infancy. John made his stage debut at age six in "Henry VI, Part Three," and throughout his childhood was regularly cast in the Shakespeare plays produced by his father. Still, Lithgow's earliest ambition was to become a graphic artist. He was awarded a scholarship to Harvard University and helped pay college expenses by selling his own woodblock Christmas cards. He also continued acting on the side and, by the time he earned a Fulbright scholarship to the London Academy of Music and Dramatic Art in 1967, his love for the stage was rekindled. While in England, he acted and directed with the Royal Shakespeare Company and the Royal Court Theatre.

Lithgow returned to the United States at age twenty-two to direct plays for his father's company. In 1971, he moved to New York City with his first wife, Jean Taynton, a teacher of emotionally disturbed children. After two years of struggling with bit parts, he landed his first big role as a British rugby player in the Broadway production of David Storey's "The Changing Room." Lithgow won a Tony

Award for his performance in the play, which included the only nude scene of his career.

Over the next eight years he drew enthusiastic reviews for his performances in respected Broadway and Off- Broadway productions such as "Comedians," "Once in a Lifetime" and "Anna Christie," in which he co-starred with actress Liv Ullmann. He also wrote and starred in "Kaufman at Large," a one-man show about playwright George S. Kaufman. Reviewing the play in the *New Yorker* in 1982, Edith Oliver criticized the way "in which the sardonic, unsentimental Kaufman is misleadingly portrayed as emotional and occasionally tender." Still, she allowed, "For all my objections, I was not bored or depressed, but only because Mr. Lithgow is an engaging fellow to watch under any circumstances."

Lithgow's film career began in the 1970s with what were considered forgettable roles in inconsequential films such as "Dealing," "Obsession," and "Rich Kids." But he drew notice for his performances as an envious stage director in "All That Jazz" in 1979 and a psychopathic killer in "Blow Out" in 1981. His big film break came in 1982 in "The World According to Garp," George Roy Hill's adaptation of John Irving's novel, in which Lithgow played Roberta Muldoon, a one-time tight end for the Philadelphia Eagles who underwent surgery to become a woman. He was nominated for an Oscar for best supporting actor for that work, but, ironically, Dustin Hoffman won the best actor Oscar the same year for his role as a female impersonator in "Tootsie."

In an article for *Mademoiselle* in 1982, Lithgow—a six-foot-four hulk of a man—wrote that playing a woman in "Garp" was the most challenging role of his career. "It's so much fun pretending to be another person," he commented. "But this was something else again. For those nine weeks [of filming] I contemplated one of life's basic mysteries: What does it really feel like to be a member of 'the other sex'? It was as if I was lurking around in disguise, inside the borders of some forbidden country—a spy behind the lines. . . . It was quite an experience: comical, secretive, sexy, and from time to time, more than a little confusing."

While promoting "Garp" on television, Lithgow said he would like to act in a movie directed by Steven Spielberg. When he returned home, he found a note from the famed director, offering him a part in the film version of "The Twilight Zone." The film—actually four separate episodes within one movie—was plagued from the start. A helicopter accident killed actor Vic Morrow and two Vietnamese children acting in the movie. Production was held up for two months, lawsuits were filed over the deaths and, when it was finally released, "Twilight Zone—The Movie" received poor reviews. "The deaths had such a devastating effect on the film," Lithgow told *People* magazine. "It never recovered from the dark shadow that ended three lives and ruined others."

Still, Lithgow won critical praise for his performance as a fear-crazed airline passenger who sees a space monster. *Newsweek*'s Jack Kroll called him "a human earthquake," and *Rolling Stone* declared him "a virtuoso of hysteria." In a self-analysis of his performance for a Warner Brothers press release, Lithgow said, "I wanted the character to be simply prostrate with fear—capable of anything—but it's not purely theatrics. This a man who loses any semblance of rationality at 20,000 feet up in the air but who, when down on the ground, is completely normal." Later he called his work in the film "the best thing I've ever done."

Lithgow followed in 1983 with a small, but much-noticed role as Midwestern banker Sam Burns, who has an affair in "Terms of Endearment," a film that earned him his second Oscar nomination as best-supporting actor. In a diary of the making of "Terms" he wrote for *Film Comment*, Lithgow described his character as "shy, bumbling, faintly hayseed, but goodhearted and dignified. . . . I actually sobbed when I read the scene where they say goodbye and thought to myself, 'The audience will just die when they see this scene.' " Lithgow's diary further reflected on his chosen career: "Acting, for all its essential frivolity, is such emotionally intense and involving work that you cannot do it (or do it well, anyway) without thinking you're working on something great and important. This is why we're often deluded about the worth of a project, and why we go on and on about the incredible impact of some little moment or how the audience will just die when they see this scene. We have to believe in what we're doing, or doing it is worse than pointless; and once in a while, where we're lucky, we're right."

Lithgow's next film performance was the highly acclaimed supporting role in "Footloose," in which he played a fire and brimstone country preacher who thought the road to hell was paved with rock and roll records. Writing for *Film Comment*, Lithgow described "Footloose" as "a curious mixture of rock movie and torrid domestic drama—a sort of cross between 'Fame' and 'Rebel Without a Cause.' " Of his own character, Reverend Shaw Moore, Lithgow wrote: "I needed to be born again, in three short weeks, if I was to give this man some plausibility, dignity and sympathy. Otherwise, I'd end up the unsubtle black side of a black-and-white tale."

Lithgow made two film appearances in 1984, in "The Adventures of Buckaroo Banzai" and in "2010: Odyssey Two." In "Buckaroo Banzai," a science fiction/rock and roll fantasy, he played Dr. Emilio Lizardo, an eccentric Italian physicist possessed by the mind of an evil alien. For the role, he wore two sets of false teeth and three layers of clothes, and he acquired an accent by spending weeks mimicking an Italian tailor at MGM. Lithgow told the *Washington Post* that the film, which was a box office flop, was "the weirdest thing I've ever done." In "2010," a sequel to the tremendously successful 1968 film "2001: A Space Odyssey," Lithgow played an aerospace engineer. The film was a critical and financial failure, although Lithgow's performance was not panned by critics.

For all his success, Lithgow has yet to land the lead in a feature film but retains hope that he may, still. "I read a script in which I'm offered the third part and I say, 'Damn it, why don't they give me the first part? I can play the hell out of this,' " he told *Newsweek* in 1984. "And I think before too long they will." He told *People* magazine, however, that he does not expect to play a romantic figure. "My hairline is receding," he said. "So my days as a romantic lead—even though I've never had them—are behind me." But if he is not regarded as a star in the traditional Hollywood sense, Lithgow's work is nonetheless respected. *Newsweek*'s Jack

Kroll, for example, calls him "an actor's actor, like Robert Duvall, a guy who can play the hell out of any part."

In 1984, Lithgow took a break from Hollywood to co-star with Richard Dreyfuss as the punch-drunk fighter in "Requiem for a Heavyweight" at Connecticut's Long Wharf Theater. The performance was very satisfying, he told *Newsweek*. "You had the sense you were transfixing the audience and you were part of that transaction. A movie is different—I once said I don't think God ever intended actors to see themselves." He plans to return to films but says he will be more selective about his roles. "My agent warned me, 'You're going to be offered lots of things that need you more than you need them,'" he told the *Washington Post*.

In a *Newsweek* article, Lithgow explained his approach to acting: "You just do the best you can from shot to shot, and when you get to the end forget you were ever in it. Don't store up any hopes, don't go snooping around the editing room and don't go to early screenings because you're bound to be disappointed by the way you've been used. In this business you have to acknowledge the fact that you are just being used and all you can hope for is to be well used." He also told *Newsweek* what he hopes for in his future: "I want to retain my capacity for surprising people. And I want life to retain its capacity to surprise me. And I hope I don't lose too much hair." In addition, Lithgow has chosen an epitaph for himself. He told *People* that he wants his tombstone to read: "He was the best thing in it."

AVOCATIONAL INTERESTS: Cooking, collecting old furniture, playing the banjo.

SOURCES:

PERIODICALS

Film Comment, November-December, 1983.
Mademoiselle, September, 1982.
Newsweek, March 19, 1984, December 2, 1985.
New Yorker, January 21, 1977, January 11, 1982.
People, July 4, 1983, December 9, 1985.
Time, December 9, 1985.
Washington Post, February 21, 1984.

—Sidelights by Glen Macnow

Henry Cabot Lodge

1902-1985

OBITUARY NOTICE: Born July 5, 1902, in Nahant, Mass; died of congestive heart failure following a long illness, February 27, 1985, in Beverly, Mass. Politician, diplomat, lecturer, journalist, and author. Descended from a prestigious family that included in its history six U. S. senators, a secretary of state, a secretary of the Navy, and a governor of Massachusetts, Lodge held various crucial post–World War II positions in the United States under both Republican and Democratic administrations. He began his political career in 1932 when, after nine years as a journalist, he was elected to the Massachusetts state legislature. Four years later Lodge won a U. S. Senate seat, maintaining an isolationist philosophy until, in 1942, he resigned from his second elected Senate term to participate in World War II combat in the European theater. In doing so Lodge became the first U.S. Senator since the Civil War to resign for armed service; he was much decorated for his wartime activities. When he returned to the Senate in 1946, Lodge displayed an avowed internationalism, supporting such policies as the Marshall Plan—or European Recovery Program—which provided for aid to European countries devastated by World War II, and the North Atlantic Treaty Organization (NATO), an allegiance of nations for collective self-defense of the Atlantic community against possible Soviet aggression. Influential in the 1952 election of Dwight D. Eisenhower as thirty-fourth U. S. president, Lodge that year lost his Senate seat to fellow Massachusetts politician John F. Kennedy.

Lodge subsequently became Eisenhower's ambassador to the United Nations (UN), where he spoke out against the Soviet Union, negotiated an agreement concerning the peaceful use of outer space, and helped to calm turmoil in the Middle East. Lodge remained U. S. ambassador to the UN until 1960, when he campaigned as Richard M. Nixon's running mate on the unsuccessful Republican ticket in that year's presidential election. The election's winner, thirty-fifth U. S. president John F. Kennedy, in 1963 named Lodge U. S. ambassador to South Vietnam, where, some analysts speculate, Lodge encouraged the overthrow of the corrupt and repressive regime of South Vietnamese president Ngo Dinh Diem. In 1964, without campaigning, Lodge won the New Hampshire Republican presidential primary election as a write-in candidate, defeating his party's eventual nominee, Barry Goldwater. The following year President Lyndon B. Johnson again sent Lodge to South Vietnam for another two-year stint as U. S. ambassador. As American involvement in the Vietnamese conflict deepened, Lodge attempted to negotiate a peace settlement and arrange a U. S. withdrawal. In 1969 President Richard M. Nixon, Lodge's former running mate, posted Lodge to Paris, where peace talks were convened between parties involved in the fighting in Southeast Asia, but Lodge resigned after a ten-month deadlock in the proceedings. He had served from 1968 to 1969 as ambassador to West Germany, and from 1970 to 1977 acted as special envoy to the Vatican. In his later years,

AP/Wide World Photos

he lectured at colleges in Massachusetts. A contributor of articles to such publications as *Atlantic Monthly, Life, Reader's Digest*, and *Saturday Evening Post*, Lodge wrote several books, including *The Storm Has Many Eyes*, published in 1973, and *As It Was*, published in 1976.

SOURCES:

BOOKS

Contemporary Authors, Volume 53-56, Gale, 1975.
Current Biography, Wilson, 1954.
The International Who's Who, 48th edition, Europa, 1984.
Who's Who, 136th edition, St. Martin's 1984.
Who's Who in American Politics, 7th edition, Bowker, 1979.
Who's Who in the World, 8th edition, Marquis, 1984.

PERIODICALS

Chicago Tribune, March 1, 1985.
Esquire, October, 1983.
Newsweek, March 11, 1985.
New York Times, February 28, 1985.
Time, March 11, 1985.

Shelley Long

1950(?)-

AP/Wide World Photos

PERSONAL: Born c. 1950, in Fort Wayne, Ind.; daughter of two teachers; married Bruce Tyson (a stockbroker), October, 1981; children: Juliana. *Education:* Attended Northwestern University.

ADDRESSES: Office—National Broadcasting Corp., 30 Rockefeller Plaza, New York, N.Y. 10020.

OCCUPATION: Actress.

CAREER: Left college to become an actress and model; during the early 1970s, worked as writer, associate producer, and co-host of local television program "Sorting It Out," and member of "Second City" improvisational troupe, both in Chicago, Ill.; made several guest appearances on network television, including "That Thing on ABC," "The Love Boat," "Family," and "M*A*S*H"; regular on National Broadcasting Corp.'s "Cheers," 1982—. Has appeared in several feature films, including "A Small Circle of Friends," United Artists, 1980, "Caveman," United Artists, 1981, "Night Shift," Warner Bros., 1982, "Losin' It," Embassy, 1983, and "Irreconcilable Differences," Warner Bros., 1984.

AWARDS, HONORS: Three Emmy Awards for local programming, for "Sorting It Out"; Emmy Award for Outstanding Actress in a Comedy Series, National Academy of Television Arts and Sciences, 1983, for work on "Cheers."

SIDELIGHTS: In a number of films and in her highly regarded role as Diane Chambers on the NBC comedy series "Cheers," Shelley Long has established herself as a subtle, sophisticated comedienne. Diane is a former graduate student turned cocktail waitress who finds herself in a constant battle of wits with the regulars at Cheers, the Boston bar in which the show is set. Her relationship with the bar's owner Sam Malone, a former big-league pitcher, also provides humorous situations. As director James Burrows told Peter Kerr in the *New York Times,* "We wanted to create a show around a Katherine Hepburn-Spencer Tracy-type relationship." On "Cheers," Sam is a dumb jock, and Diane is a self-assured intellectual. "Diane has put her whole life into her brain," Long told Paul Corkery in *People.* "She's not in touch with her gut, so she can't fully enjoy life. That's something I've had to learn myself. I'm a lot gutsier. I love to see Diane get some street sense."

Though set in a bar, "Cheers" offers a brand of humor beyond typical barroom jokes. NBC entertainment division president Brandon Tartikoff told Peter Kerr, "'Cheers' is a very important comedy for us. It is classy, sophisticated and for adults." Kerr observes, "The dialogue on the show at times reaches a sophistication that is rare on network television." As Diane, Long's wit often includes references to authors, philosophers, and other "great thinkers." Since its premier in 1982, critics have commended the series, evidenced by its strong showing in the annual Emmy Awards. Concludes James Wolcott in *New York,* "['Cheers'] is smartly written and even more smartly cast."

SOURCES:

PERIODICALS

Maclean's, October 22, 1984.
Newsweek, October 8, 1984.
New York, October 25, 1982.
New York Times, April 8, 1983, September 26, 1983, November 29, 1983.
People, April 4, 1983.
Playboy, February, 1984.
Time, October 8, 1984.
TV Guide, March 26, 1983.

—Sketch by Bryan Ryan

Madonna

1958-

PERSONAL: Full name, Madonna Louise Ciccone; born August 16, 1958, in Bay City, Mich.; daughter of Silvio (an engineer) and Madonna Ciccone. *Education:* Attended University of Michigan for two years; studied dance in New York with the Alvin Ailey American Dance Theater and with Pearl Lang; studied voice in Paris.

ADDRESSES: Office—c/o Sire Records, 165 West 74th St., New York, N.Y. 10023.

OCCUPATION: Pop singer; actress.

CAREER: Drummer with band Breakfast Club in New York City for one year; formed and performed with a number of bands in New York City; currently solo performer. Actress in motion pictures, including "A Certain Sacrifice," 1979, "Desperately Seeking Susan," 1985, "Vision Quest," 1985, and "Shanghai Surprise," 1986.

AWARDS, HONORS: Grammy Award nomination for best female pop performance, for "Crazy for You," 1986.

DISCOGRAPHY:

RECORD ALBUMS, PRODUCED BY SIRE RECORDS

Madonna (includes "Lucky Star," "Borderline," "Burning Up," "I Know It," "Holiday," "Think of Me," "Physical Attraction," and "Everybody"), 1983.
Like a Virgin (includes "Material Girl," "Angel," "Like a Virgin," "Over and Over," "Love Don't Live Here Anymore," "Dress You Up," "Shoo-Bee-Doo," "Pretender," and "Stay"), 1984.

OTHER

Recorded "Crazy for You," from the soundtrack of the film "Vision Quest," and "Into the Groove," from the soundtrack of the film "Desperately Seeking Susan"; has also recorded several twelve-inch discs.

SIDELIGHTS: She has made the belly button fashionable again. She has put rosaries and crucifixes back around the necks (and in the ear lobes) of teenage and pre-teenage girls. "Boy Toy," a legend she wears on her belt buckle, has become a symbol of tease and titillation. Through a tongue-in-cheek song called "Material Girl," she has made the pursuit of instant gratification something to be proud of. She's Madonna Louis Ciccone—Madonna to most people. And as a result of two albums, several rock videos, and a hit movie, she is the latest in trends, following Boy George, Michael Jackson, Prince and Cyndi Lauper in the line of succession for pop stardom.

She has become the siren and the scourge of American popular culture. Feminists particularly have charged her with setting their movement back in time by exploiting her

AP/Wide World Photos

body and espousing archaic, sex-kitten values. Fans, meanwhile, cheered her cheeky, carefree attitude that—during her spring, 1985, concert tour—manifested itself in an onstage challenge: "Do you believe in yourselves?" "She personifies what people would like to be but are afraid to be," explained her Los Angeles-based manager, Freddie DeMann, to the *Detroit Free Press*. "Everyone would like to be her, but they don't have the guts." Or, as Madonna herself told *Time* magazine, "My image to people, I think, is that I'm this brazen, aggressive young woman who has an OK voice with some pretty exciting songs, who wears what she wants to wear and says what she wants to say."

According to friends, teachers, and co-workers, that's the way Madonna has been all her life. She was born August 16, 1958, in Bay City, Michigan, to Chrysler/General Dynamics engineer Silvio "Tony" Ciccone (pronounced "Chick-onee" in Italian but Americanized to "Gi-kone") and his wife, who gave her own distinctive first name to her daughter. In all, there were six children from this union; Madonna was the third child, behind Anthony and Martin; following her were Paula, Christopher, and Melanie. On December 1, 1963—after the family had moved to Pontiac, Michigan—Madonna's mother died, and shortly thereafter, her father shocked

232

the family by announcing he would marry their housekeeper, Joan. "It just didn't make any sense to me," Madonna told *Rolling Stone* magazine. "I'm sure I felt a lot of anger, . . . and I'm sure I took it out on my stepmother." One of her academic counselors, however, said the second marriage—which produced two more children, Jennifer and Mario—didn't cause any unusual tension. "[Madonna] had several different roles in her family, but she seemed to take pride in being able to do them all," she told the *Detroit Free Press*.

A popular story that now follows Madonna is that the Ciccone family lived next door to rock star Bob Seger and his family. They did live in the same neighborhood in Pontiac, but the only contact friends can remember was one incident when Seger had car trouble and stopped at the Ciccone house for assistance.

The family, for its part, now tries to keep a low profile in the wake of Madonna's success. "I get so many calls on this," said her father to a *Detroit Free Press* reporter. "Basically, I'm happy for her success, but I don't want to say any more about this; it could be taken out of context, as so much has been." He did however, consent to take part in Madonna's stage show, dragging her offstage as a taped voice boomed over the speakers, ordering the star to "come home this instant."

It seems hard to find anyone from Madonna's past who's surprised at her success. Even during her early school days—at St. Frederick's in Pontiac and St. Andrews and West Junior High in Rochester, Michigan—Madonna, one teacher told the *Detroit Free Press,* "had this attitude like, 'Yeah, I'm gonna be somebody. You all just watch me.' " Agreed Carol Lintz, a French teacher at Rochester Adams High School: "She never bothered with the whole peer thing, other than, 'I'm gonna be somebody.'. . . Her . . . personality was well on its way to forming by the time she was here."

No matter what she may have dreamed for her future, Madonna kept herself in a college preparation program all through high school. She was often on the honor roll (her record is mostly A's and B's), scored well on the SAT tests, and scored in the top 10 percent on a verbal intelligence test. Counselor Nancy Ryan Mitchell's recommendation on a scholarship application to the University of Michigan described her as having an "extremely talented, dedicated, motivated, sparkling personality." Her record is also filled with extra-curricular activities, including junior-varsity cheerleading, choir, Latin club, swimming instructor at the Rochester community pool, and volunteering in Help-A-Kid, a variation of the Big Brother program. She ended up graduating early, in the middle of the 1975-76 school year.

"She spent her high school years zipping out of here," Mitchell recalled in the *Detroit Free Press*. "I didn't counsel her; she came to me and told me what she was going to do. At that time she talked mostly about dance. She knew she was good and wanted to be famous and would work hard to make it." Many teachers at Rochester Adams remember Madonna's dancing. At school dances, she would just get out on the floor and start dancing by herself. "She'd be in front of the cafeteria, just really letting it loose," said Carol Lintz. "The other kids would walk up to me and say, 'Who's

Madonna dancing with?' The music started and her whole body filled with it, like she was alone with the music." Madonna was also active in starting the school's Thespian Society, a theater troupe that performed several skits and one play, "Dark of the Moon." During her tenure, she won the club's first Outstanding Senior Thespian award and also came up with the first fund-raising idea—a pie sale. Yearbook pictures from her final year also show Madonna's shift from neat, suburban grooming to what was then considered a more natural appearance, wearing little make-up and letting her hair grow. As choir teacher Alan Lintz told a *Detroit Free Press* writer, "She had a real European kind of attitude, a real cosmopolitan flair. She dared to be different."

Some of that attitude can be traced to Madonna's out-of-school education, hours spent with private dance instructor Christopher Flynn, who ran the Christopher Ballet in Rochester until it closed in 1976. Flynn and Madonna—who started studying with him in 1972—struck up a friendship outside of class as well. The two would go for long drives or catch the latest fashions, music, and dances at local Detroit clubs. "We used to go mostly to the gay bars because the disco dancing was so good," Flynn, fifty-four, recounted in the *Detroit Free Press.* "She could very quickly attune to any atmosphere. She'd be totally relaxed and get into it, then come out and be a totally different person. . . . To me, what's so interesting is this incredible image that's up there. They see the obvious, the bare midriff, the sleaze, . . . which is fine, because that's what the image is about. I know her behind that, not a different person, but a complete person."

Both Madonna and Flynn ended up in Ann Arbor, Michigan, in the fall of 1976, Madonna to study and Flynn to teach in the University of Michigan dance department. One of her roommates was Whitley Setrakian, a dance department student who had transferred from a small college in upstate New York and was looking for someone to share a room with. "One of the first things I noticed was she really said what was on her mind," said Setrakian (now artistic director for an Ann Arbor dance troupe) to the *Detroit Free Press.* "The first day she looked at the apartment, I was really depressed and she immediately said, 'Whitley, you don't look very happy.' She just plunged into being really, really direct."

The two had much in common. Both worked at an ice cream parlor, " 'til our arms were raw," and they enjoyed reading poetry. Setrakian called Madonna "My Little Bowl of Bear Mush" after a whole-grain cereal she ate, though she could just as often be found eating large amounts of popcorn. At night, they and a third friend, Linda Alaniz, would hit Ann Arbor clubs such as the Blue Frogge and the Ruvia. "It was crazy," said Alaniz, now a photographer with Martha Swope Studio in New York. "We'd dance six hours at school, then go home and eat, then dance another four hours at night. The woman just loved to dance."

Madonna and Alaniz were in a University production called "Stations of the Cross," based on the religious ritual, and were rehearsing in a nearby church. "During one of the breaks, Madonna got up on the pulpit and started singing, 'Good golly Miss Molly, sure like to ball,' " Alaniz remembered. "The teacher just screamed at her, 'Madonna, stop that! It's sacrilegious!' " Alaniz also remembered going back to Madonna's dormitory room in Stockwall Hall—where she lived shortly before moving in with Setrakian—after finishing work at Dooley's Bar. One of the first things she would do is put her tips into a book about the New York Ballet. "Every time I'd come she'd open this book and show me how much money she had," Alaniz remembered. "She was getting ready to come to New York, getting her kitty together for the real world. It's such a change to think of Madonna worth millions of dollars when I used to buy her salad."

The millions—multi-millions actually—were still in the distant future when Madonna got off the bus in New York carrying a rag doll during the fall of 1978. She didn't have immediate plans, but she was able to get some modeling jobs (during which were taken the nude photographs that were later sold—amid much publicity—to *Penthouse* and *Playboy* magazines). And she eventually won a work-study scholarship and took classes with the Alvin Ailey American Dance Theater's third company, which *Rolling Stone* described as "a little like getting a tryout for the sub-junior-varsity team." Still, "I thought I was in a production of 'Fame,'" Madonna told *Rolling Stone*. "Everyone was Hispanic or black, and everyone wanted to be a star." She left Ailey's troupe after a few months and hooked up with Pearl Lang, who used to work with choreographer Martha Graham. But about the same time, she discovered an interest in rock and roll music through Dan Gilroy, who lived in an abandoned synagogue with his brother Ed. He taught Madonna the rudiments of guitar and drums, and before long she was singing with their group, Breakfast Club.

Before long, however, Madonna was whisked away to Paris to sing backup and dance for disco star Patrick Hernandez. The trip was a bust, and Madonna returned to New York to work once more with the Gilroys. By 1981 she was out of that group again due to internal disagreements. She eventually sought out Steve Bray, a former boyfriend from Michigan, and they began writing songs together and formed a number of bands, including the Millionaires, Modern Dance and Emmy.

The club gigs caught the attention of one music mogul who put her on salary and gave her a place on New York's Upper West Side. Madonna and Bray formed a new band—named simply Madonna—playing funkier, more danceable material. It was Mark Kamins of Danceteria, a trend-setting Manhattan club, who brought a tape of her songs to Sire Records. The record company signed her, and the marketing of Madonna began in earnest.

The original strategy, according to Michael Rosenblatt—then in charge of signing and developing new acts for Sire—was to introduce Madonna through the dance clubs. "I thought we had something special here, so I didn't want to throw out just another great album by another great new artist," Rosenblatt explained to the *Detroit Free Press*. "Instead of recording an album very fast, we did it slowly. We put out a 12-inch [one song on an album-sized disc; very popular in dance clubs], and when that worked, we put out another." The strategy for that first song, "Everybody," according to Bobby Shaw, then head of national dance promotion for Warner Bros. Records—which distributes Sire—was to "get the record played in the clubs, then cross

it over from clubs to radio." And it worked; the song was a number three hit on the dance charts and was played on urban contemporary radio.

The same thing happened with the next twelve-inch discs— "Burning Up/Physical Attraction" and "Holiday"—but Madonna still wasn't getting the kind of attention Shaw and Rosenblatt thought she deserved. "They were selling like crazy, but nobody at Warner Bros. seemed to care about it at the time," Shaw told the *Detroit Free Press*. "A lot of record companies won't push an artist until an album's out."

Once the first album, *Madonna,* came out in early 1983, it was evident that Madonna needed a high-powered manager to guide her career. She asked Rosenblatt who the best was; he told her Freddie DeMann, who at the time was busy guiding Michael Jackson's *Thriller* to history-making proportions. Something about her appealed to DeMann. As he explained to the *Detroit Free Press:* "What she has is undefinable, in my opinion. Very few of our stars have it. Michael Jackson has it, and Madonna has it." DeMann set about turning whatever it was into one of the hottest female acts of the eighties using an innovative and effective music-video coupling.

The first step was to cross Madonna over from the dance to the mass audience. In "Borderline," they had a song Shaw said "was more a pop and not as much a dance record as the others." And for "Lucky Star," according to DeMann, "we did this inexpensive performance video, and she came across so tantalizing, she just drove everybody crazy." Indeed, it was the video for the latter—which featured Madonna purring and puckering to the camera between shots of her bare belly-button—that pushed her way to the top. "I couldn't be a success without also being a sex symbol," she told *Spin* magazine. "I'm sexy. How can I avoid it?" To *People,* she said, "Bruce Springsteen was born to run. I was born to flirt."

The combination of her come-hither personality plus her above-average skills in dance and singing spurred sales of more than two million copies of her first album and made her fare for every music and popular magazine, from *People* to *Rolling Stone* to the *National Enquirer*. Her romances— most notably with producer John "Jellybean" Benitez and actor Sean Penn (to whom she is now engaged)—have been widely chronicled, and she was chased by photographers at parties and at restaurants.

Feminists, meanwhile, screamed that her seductive tactics were setting the image of women backwards, and other detractors wrote her off as a pre-programmed star who was more style than substance. "I think people want to see me as a little tart bimbo who sells records because I'm cute, and record companies push 'em because they know they can make a quick buck on my image," Madonna told *Record* magazine. "I try to have thick skin, but every once in a while I read something that someone says about me, and it's so slanderous and moralistic and it has nothing to do with my music. . . . The fact of the matter is that you can use your beauty and use your charm and be flirtatious, and you can get people interested in your beauty. But you cannot maintain that. In the end, talent is the only thing. My work is the only thing that's going to change any minds."

Regardless of what people thought, Madonna stormed into 1985 with twice the momentum she had the previous two years. The *Like a Virgin* album and single, which had debuted on the MTV Video Awards program a couple months earlier, shot straight into the top ten; the album eventually sold more than four million copies. DeMann, meanwhile, channeled Madonna's career towards the silver screen. He wanted her to have the lead role in "Vision Quest," but by the time he put his bid in, all that remained was the part of a nightclub singer. Good enough, he thought, and all the better, in that the film was scheduled for a fall, 1984, release, just as the *Like a Virgin* album would be coming out. Then came the title role for the film "Desperately Seeking Susan," a part DeMann said was made for Madonna: "The character Susan, that's exactly what Madonna is. There's almost no acting involved there. That's her—her personality, her lifestyle, her dress."

So the plan was set—a movie cameo in the fall, followed by an album at Christmas, then another movie in the spring and, finally, her first tour. Things went awry, however, when "Vision Quest" was postponed and became an early 1985 release, not too far in front of "Susan." In a five-month period, then, Madonna had songs on three new albums and her face in two new movies. "Suddenly, I had a lot of music to contend with," DeMann said. The danger of which, he pointed out, was fragmenting interest in the songs. "I want all our records in the top five, top ten for sure. Anything less I consider a failure."

Excess, in this case, meant success, however. "Material Girl," the second single from the *Like a Virgin* album, hit number one, as did "Crazy for You" from "Vision Quest." Both, in fact, were in the top five at the same time. The follow-up single from the album, "Angel," also glided up the charts, and a song from "Desperately Seeking Susan," entitled "Into the Groove," became all the rave at dance clubs.

Her next step was to conquer the nation's concert stages, and it barely took any effort. DeMann originally wanted the "Like a Virgin" tour to play small, three-thousand-seat halls so they'd "still leave people waiting, and that way create a hot ticket." But those small venues sold out in minutes, and one promoter told DeMann he could have sold another 36,000 tickets. So later dates of the tour were upgraded to large arenas, and Madonna sold them out with ease; indeed, she became the hot ticket for the first half of 1985, just as Michael Jackson and Prince had split ticket sales in 1984.

DeMann says that after all the hype and hoopla, Madonna's future remains bright. And few disagree with him. Even the publication of the nude photographs in the September, 1985, issues of *Penthouse* and *Playboy* failed to diminish her popularity as some early observers suspected it might. Madonna was honest about the photos right from the beginning, maintaining that she saw no reason to be ashamed of them, and her career appears not to have suffered in the slightest from the controversy. Said Rosenblatt, "She's more dimensional than just a recording artist. When I signed her, I thought her boundaries were limitless. She could become like a Barbara Streisand for this generation. She'll be around a long, long time."

SOURCES:

PERIODICALS

Detroit Free Press, May 19, 1985, May 24, 1985.
Mademoiselle, December, 1983.
Newsweek, March 4, 1985.
New York Times, April 14, 1985.
Playboy, September, 1985.
People, March 11, 1985, December 23, 1985.
Penthouse, September, 1985.
Record, March, 1985.
Rolling Stone, November 22, 1984, May 9, 1985, May 23, 1985, December 19, 1985.
Spin, May, 1985.
Time, March 4, 1985, May 27, 1985.
Washington Post, November 25, 1985.

—Sidelights by Gary Graff

J. Willard Marriott

1900-1985

OBITUARY NOTICE: Full name, John Willard Marriott; born September 17, 1900, in Marriott, Utah; died of a heart attack, August 13, 1985, in Wolfeboro, N.H.; buried at Parklawn Cemetery in Rockville, Md. Restaurant and motel executive and philanthropist. In the course of a career that spanned nearly fifty years Marriott parlayed a nine-stool root beer stand into a $3 billion food and lodging empire. Born in the Utah town that was established in 1847 by his Mormon great-grandfather, John Marriott, and that now bears his name, J. Willard Marriott grew up on a sheep and cattle ranch. By the time he was twenty years old, he had fulfilled a two-year Mormon missionary obligation, traveling in New England. In 1927, a year after graduating from the University of Utah, Marriott drove east with his bride, Alice Sheets, and, with twenty-five hundred dollars in savings and loans, bought one of the first A & W root beer franchises, in Washington, D.C. Within a few months Marriott added Mexican food to the menu and renamed the restaurant Hot Shoppe. In 1932 Marriott began an expansion that by the end of World War II resulted in the establishment of Hot Shoppes all along the highways from New York to Florida. During this time he also launched a catering service to airlines, prompted by his observation of passengers at a Washington airport carrying food on board from a nearby Hot Shoppe. In 1957 Marriott opened his first motor hotel, the Twin Bridges Marriott, in Washington, D.C.

In 1964 Marriott turned over to his son, J. Willard Marriott, Jr., the presidency of his corporation and in 1972 transferred to him also the post of chief executive officer. An active Mormon all his life, Marriott contributed 10 percent of his income to the church and generously endowed Brigham Young University and the University of Utah. He was also a loyal supporter of Republican political causes and candidates, among them former presidents Dwight D. Eisenhower and Gerald R. Ford and former governor of Michigan and fellow Mormon, George Romney. Marriott served as chairman of both of President Richard M. Nixon's inaugural committees. At the time of his death, Marriott's original investment had grown into a conglomerate whose 140,000 employees operated 143 hotels and resorts in 95 cities, 1400 restaurants, and 90 flight kitchens serving more than 150 airlines worldwide. Recipient of three honorary doctorate degrees, Marriott was eulogized by President Ronald Reagan as "a living example of the American dream."

UPI/Bettmann Newsphotos

SOURCES:

BOOKS

O'Brien, Robert, *Marriott: The J. Willard Marriott Story,* Deseret, 1977.
Who's Who In America, 37th edition, Marquis, 1972.

PERIODICALS

Los Angeles Times, August 18, 1985.
Newsweek, August 26, 1985.
New York Times, August 15, 1985.
Time, August 26, 1985.
Washington Post, August 18, 1985.

J. Willard Marriott, Jr.

1932-

PERSONAL: Full name, John Willard Marriott, Jr.; born March 25, 1932, in Washington, D.C.; son of John Willard (a business executive) and Alice (Sheets) Marriott; married Donna Garff, June 29, 1955; children: Deborah, Stephen Garff, John Willard, David Sheets. *Education:* University of Utah, B.S. in banking and finance, 1954. *Religion:* Church of Jesus Christ of the Latter-day Saints (Mormon).

ADDRESSES: *Office*—Marriott Corp., One Marriott Dr., Washington, D.C. 20058.

OCCUPATION: Business executive.

CAREER: Marriott Corp., Washington, D.C., worked in architectural department while in high school; Marriott Hot Shoppes, Inc., Salt Lake City, Utah, vice-president, 1959-64, executive vice-president, 1964; Marriott Corp., president and member of board of directors, 1964—, chief executive officer, 1972—.

Chairman of board of directors, Citizens Choice; member of board of directors, Business-Industry Political Action Committee; member of executive committee, President's Council on International Youth Exchange; member of national executive board, Boy Scouts of America. Member of advisory council, Stanford University Graduate School of Business; U.S. trade representative, Services Policy Advisory Committee. *Military service:* U.S. Naval Reserve, 1954-56; became lieutenant.

SIDELIGHTS: "I am pleased to report that we have had another year of strong growth. Growth has been virtually constant for our company throughout its. . . existence. But I can assure you, we do not take it for granted, and we never will." These remarks were made by J. Willard Marriott, Jr., at an April 1985 annual meeting for the nation's premier company in lodging, hospitality, and related business areas: the Washington, D.C.-based Marriott Corporation. The company, which has built its business from a small root beer stand to the ownership of hotels, cruise ships, theme parks, and airline flight kitchens—to name a few—has been called one of the best-managed firms in the country. A central reason for the company's success is Marriott, Jr., son of J. Willard Marriott, who founded the company in 1927.

J. Willard Marriott, Jr., called Bill to distinguish him from his father, was born in Washington, D.C., on March 25, 1932, the elder of two sons. His parents, who came to Washington from Utah, were strict Mormons. They instilled in their sons the work ethic that has kept the company on a prosperous road. In Washington, the family opened a nine-seat root beer stand on 14th Street called the Hot Shoppe. Today, the name still lives on Marriott cafeterias and restaurants around the country. The elder Marriott's drive to make the fledgling stand a successful venture was passed

on to his son. "My father couldn't stand to see me idle," the younger Marriott told *People* magazine. "He always had a list of things for me to do—even chopping wood. Father pushed and Mother consoled. It would have been terrible to have two unforgiving parents."

Marriott attended St. Albans prep school and graduated in 1954 from the University of Utah with a bachelor's degree in banking and finance. He experienced his first job with the family business when he was in high school, working summers in the company's architectural department. He got involved in the day-to-day foodservice operations when he was at the university and worked the fountain at a Hot Shoppe in Salt Lake City. He reported for work at 4 a.m. and learned every station of the restaurant—from making french fries to milk shakes. As the company branched into the hotel business, Marriott went to Washington to manage Marriott's Twin Bridges Hotel, the first of a more than 60,000-room chain. Additional Marriott hotels opened, and at the age of thirty-two, Bill Marriott became president of the company, which then had annual sales of $85 million. In 1972, Marriott succeeded his father as chief executive officer, but the elder Marriott's presence and pressure to run a tight ship remained. "My father, always afraid of going broke, is extremely cautious and conservative," Marriott said in a 1978 *People* interview. "We have a delicate balance. I've not pushed the company as much as I would like, and I have not let him hold me back as much as he would like."

Marriott's father died in August 1985 of a heart attack. Eleven days later, the younger Marriott was severely burned in a boathouse explosion at the family's summer home. He received first- and second-degree burns in the accident but was soon reported in stable condition. Bill Marriott is married, has four children, and enjoys spending time taking his family to a movie or one of the company's Farrell's Ice Cream Parlors. True to family tradition, the Marriott children have worked summers at Marriott operations, although Marriott says he is closer to his children and a less demanding parent than his father was with him.

Marriott's belief in developing capable, well-trained hotel management has led him to become an active recruiter of graduates of Cornell University's School of Hotel Administration—one of the leading hotel management training schools in the country. Without the right management, Marriott says, a hotel or restaurant will not be an efficient, well-run business. "Our prime concern in management development is to get our people to respond quickly," he said in *Nation's Business*. "We are heavily people-oriented. You can build the best hotel in the world, but if you haven't got friendly people in the front desk, the customer is not going to come back. The key elements for Marriott people are hard work and a dedication to excellence."

Hard work and dedication have paid off for the company of more than 120,000 employees. Sales for the 1984 fiscal year were more than $3.5 billion. Net income increased 21 percent to $139 million, and earnings per share rose 25 percent. In all, Marriott's sales and profits have doubled since 1980 and increased tenfold since 1971. The key, Marriott maintains, is controlling expenses and keeping the company's name and reputation solid. "This is a penny business," Marriott said in *Dun's Business Month*. "We hold no patents; all we have is our name. So we watch our expenses." For example, there are some sixty-six prescribed steps chambermaids must follow in making up a room and some 6,000 recipes for food portions and preparation. While it would be impossible for Marriott to keep a constant watch on all of the company's hotels and resorts, flight kitchens, cruise ships, and popular-priced restaurants, he does an impressive round-the-clock job.

Marriott logs some 200,000 miles a year traveling to various company locations and is involved in every level of operation, from dedicating a new hotel to inspecting a flight kitchen, testing the softness of new furnishings, checking the size of vegetables in a salad, and making sure braille elevator numbers are accurate. His seemingly endless stamina comes from a reliance on enterprise and faith in morality. An acknowledged workaholic, Marriott neither smokes nor drinks, and is a devout Mormon. He devotes several hours each week as a counselor, and in every Marriott hotel room the Book of Mormon sits alongside the Gideon Bible. He is not concerned with the wealth that accompanies the head of a giant company and dresses for simplicity and wear, shunning designer labels. He drives himself to work and usually flies coach when he is called away on a business trip. But his attention to economy and cost-control in his hotels

does not mean that quality, comfort, and the guest's satisfaction are compromised. While visiting a new hotel in Austin, Texas, wrote a *People* reporter, Marriott remarked to hotel employees: "There are not enough lights out front. Somebody was trying to skimp."

Although he avoids the political party circuit in Washington and shuns the political and social connections that accompany it, Marriott has taken several stands in the political arena. He devotes time not only to the Mormon church and causes such as the Boy Scouts, but also to a grass-roots political arm of the U.S. Chamber of Commerce called Citizen's Choice. Serving as the chairman of that 75,000-member body, he has pushed for a reduced federal role in the economy. Of particular concern to Marriott are proposals to increase the minimum wage, which would directly affect his company's labor-intensive operations. In the Washington area, for example, the corporation shut down several properties because of the wage increases mandated by new laws. Food service operations would also be affected, Marriott believes, and such departments might be forced to initiate price increases that could cause customers to turn away from restaurants and cafeterias in favor of buying at the grocery store and eating at home. "What the government is doing is seriously affecting our company," Marriott said in the *New York Times*. "If we don't stand up and fight for what we believe in, for the free enterprise system, we'll just go down the road like England and Sweden, to economic disaster." Big government could be reduced, he believes, either through a constitutional amendment requiring a balanced budget or through new presidential power to veto individual items in appropriation bills. "I think that we have too much government, that we pay too much tax," he said in *Business Week*. Marriott is also a director of the Business-Industry Political Action Committee, which advises corporated Political Action Committees which candidates to support with campaign donations.

The company has steered away from casino gambling and nightclub operations that many of the nation's other large hotel chains have entered in quest of profits. Through the Explorers arm of the Boy Scouts, Marriott has worked to promote heightened moral values and to preserve marital commitments. He acknowledges that at times he may be giving up a short-term business interest but believes the ultimate benefit of long-term social gain is the overriding concern. Thus, when the Explorers took a stance to fight teenage drinking, Marriott admitted the campaign might hurt his hospitality business, but he believed it would ultimately build the credibility of his company. The ethic of hard work and clean living is a source of pride for Marriott. "This is a business where it is very easy to get into trouble, with all the bars and nightclub operations," Marriott said in *People*. "Marriott employees are very conservative. All the senior guys are good family men with good character and good habits and dedication to hard work. They stay away from enticements. We're a bunch of squares."

Marriott considers himself conservative, and that quality has made him a natural to star in commercials for his hotels. He has joined fellow top executives like Chrysler's Lee Iacocca, Eastern Air Lines' Frank Borman, and Schlitz head Frank Sellinger as company spokesperson, exuding credibility. The risk of putting a top executive on television commercials is high and could cause some viewers to question the ego of the spokesperson and the desperation of the advertising agency to come up with a catchy campaign. If the commercial message is viewed in a positive light, Marriott and his companions may be viewed as gutsy, down-to-earth officers that are not afraid to step out of the corporate shadows and face their largest audience.

Marriott's plans for corporate growth do not rely merely on advertising. The company is continually re-evaluating its operations—strengthening them and enlarging them in some areas, while weeding out other divisions that no longer fit the company's master plan. In 1984 it sold its profitable Great America theme parks, and the specialty restaurant operations of Casa Maria Mexican and Dinner House restaurants. Both were described by Marriott as not fitting the company's long-term growth objectives; and all the sales were profitable—a credit the company is proud of. "Over the past twenty years, we have not invested in one thing we did not sell at a profit," said Executive Vice President Gary Wilson, Marriott's chief financial officer, to *Dun's Business Month.*

Marriott is the nation's largest hotel operator, boasting occupancy rates as high as 80 percent, at least 10 percent above the industry average. But Bill Marriott envisions many more beds before the company's growth will slow. "There are some 2.3 million hotel rooms in the U.S.," he said in *Dun's Business Month,* "and we have only about 2 percent of them." The company plans to add some 25,000 rooms, most of which are already under construction, by 1988. Marriott is plunging more than $3 billion into developing four new markets for the company over the next five years. One of the ventures is in the low-overhead, moderate price segment that is showing signs of being a profitable area.

Courtyard hotels by Marriott, first successfully tested in Georgia, are being planned for a national rollout of more than 350 hotels by the early 1990s. The hotels are designed to look like contemporary country inns and have rates ranging from $40 to $60 per night, placing them in the moderately-priced market that represents about 45 percent of all hotel rooms in the United States. The hotels are targeted at the highly desirable business traveler and offer amenities designed to promote a residential feel in the approximately 150-room properties. The Courtyard hotels are designed to go head-to-head with other national lodging chains like Holiday Inn, and Marriott hopes to steal business from its competitors. The concept is also economical for the company, because the Courtyards have three basic designs and use common management teams, enabling Marriott to keep rates low and reduce overhead.

In the higher end of the lodging market, Marriott has announced plans to build all-suite hotels. The Marriott Suites will feature about 250 suites per hotel at a cost of between $70 and $90 per night. The company plans to build about a dozen of the hotels by 1988 and hopes the higher revenues generated by the suites will result in higher overall profit margins. Marriott is not the only entrant in the all-suite market, which has become increasingly popular as guests opt for a suite over a traditional hotel room.

As a way of capturing more of the vacation traveler's dollars, Marriott is moving his company into time-share vacation condominiums. Marriott acquired a leading company in the time-sharing field with properties on Hilton Head Island, South Carolina, and has decided to develop a second project on the grounds of the Marriott resort being built near Disney World in Orlando, Florida, to be completed in 1986. While analysts say pure time-sharing is a risky proposition for a hotelier, they say Marriott may succeed because the company is doing it in conjunction with its other resorts. The idea is that the time-share customers will dine at the resort restaurants, and attract prospective time-share buyers from the resorts. The Marriott name will lend credibility to the time-share properties, Marriott says. "We've got to leverage our name," he said in *Business Week.* "We've got a good name going."

Marriott also is in the process of developing lifecare retirement communities which would build on the company's lodging and food service experience and expertise. The company initially plans to build three prototype communities of 300 units and additional nursing beds in each community for residents that may need care. The first venture is in northern Virginia and will offer independent living, food service, health service and recreational facilities. Although the lifecare market is presently dominated by nonprofit organizations, the Marriott Corporation believes its managerial experience and financial foundations will allow the company to provide a more attractive alternative.

Through these new segments, and through existing operations, Marriott hopes to grow at a rate of 20 percent a year—an outlook that Bill Marriott believes is both realistic and proven by the company's past track record. "There's always been a considerable amount of skepticism, and we've always been able to do it," he told *Business Week.* "It's always been our strategy to have enough new things going on and enough things going on in each area to make it all work."

SOURCES:

PERIODICALS

Barron's, August 25, 1980, November 10, 1980.
Business Week, September 24, 1984, October 1, 1984, November 5, 1984, January 21, 1985, June 28, 1985.
Christian Science Monitor, June 19, 1984.
Dun's Business Month, December, 1984.
Forbes, July 5, 1982, August 16, 1982.
Fortune, February 18, 1985, August 5, 1985.
Nation's Business, October, 1979.
Newsweek, May 22, 1972.
New York Times, May 18, 1977, August 25, 1977, August 6, 1978, July 13, 1982, December 18, 1984, December 19, 1984, January 14, 1985.
People, April 17, 1978.
USA Today, August 26, 1985.
Wall Street Journal, May 12, 1982.
Washingtonian, March, 1981, October, 1984.
Washington Post, April 22, 1983, December 19, 1984, January 14, 1985, August 26, 1985.

—Sidelights by Amy C. Bodwin

Christa McAuliffe
1948-1986

OBITUARY NOTICE: Full name, Sharon Christa McAuliffe; born September 2, 1948, in Framingham, Mass.; killed in the in-flight explosion of the space shuttle *Challenger,* January 28, 1986, off the coast of Florida. Teacher. McAuliffe, a high school teacher of social studies in Concord, New Hampshire, was chosen from among 11,000 candidates for the honor of being America's first private citizen in space, a decision that NASA hoped would revive the public's interest in the space program.

Faced with almost-certain Congressional budget cuts and growing competition from outside competitors, NASA had prepared an ambitious schedule of fifteen shuttle launches during 1986 and had begun efforts to popularize the shuttle program by using ordinary citizens on its flights. McAuliffe's highly publicized training had garnered positive press coverage and piqued public interest in the flight, which was the twenty-fifth shuttle mission in the program's five-year history. During her five months of training at the Johnson Space Center in Houston, McAuliffe was spotlighted as being representative of the future of the space program: average citizens living and working in space. "I realize there is a risk outside your everyday life," she observed during her training, "but it doesn't frighten me."

On January 28, 1986, after several days of weather delays, McAuliffe and the other six crew members, mission commander Francis Scobee, pilot Michael Smith, shuttle payload specialist Gregory Jarvis, and astronauts Ronald McNair, Ellison Onizuka, and Judith Resnik, boarded *Challenger* for the flight. Seventy-four seconds into the launch, with McAuliffe's family members and friends in attendance at the Kennedy Space Center at Cape Canaveral, Florida, the shuttle craft exploded in a giant fireball to the horrified astonishment of millions of television viewers around the world. Slow-motion videotape replays of the tragedy seemed to indicate that the giant, sixteen-story external fuel tank containing a half-million gallons of liquid hydrogen and liquid oxygen ruptured and exploded, disintegrating *Challenger* and initiating a shower of debris that prevented rescue workers from entering the down-range area off the Florida coast for nearly an hour. The cause of the explosion that claimed the lives of the first Americans to die in space was not immediately known.

McAuliffe had intended to keep a journal of her flight and told David H. Van Biema of *People:* "I liken what I'm going to do to the women who pioneered the West in . . . wagons. They didn't have a camera; they described things in vivid detail, in word pictures." She had also planned to conduct lessons from space via television hook-up with classrooms across the nation. A six-month personal appearance tour for NASA was slated for her return, a chance for her to share her impressions of life in space with other average Americans, but she was most looking forward to returning to teaching and settling back into the familiar routine of family life with her husband, Steven, and children Scott and Caroline.

Courtesy of NASA

In the aftermath of the tragedy President Reagan, whose remarks during a 1984 speech suggesting putting a teacher in space prompted NASA to initiate the program that led to McAuliffe's selection, promised the nation that America would never forget the "seven heroes," and spoke directly to the millions of schoolchildren who had followed McAuliffe through her training and watched her final moments: "I know it's hard to understand, but sometimes things like this happen. It's all part of the process of exploration and discovery. It's all part of taking a chance and expanding man's horizons. The future doesn't belong to the faint-hearted. It belongs to the brave."

SOURCES

PERIODICALS

Chicago Tribune, January 26, 1986.
Detroit Free Press, January 29, 1986.
Detroit News, September 29, 1985, January 29, 1986.
New York Times Magazine, January 5, 1986.
People, August 5, 1985.

William McGowan

1927-

PERSONAL: Full name, William George McGowan; born December 10, 1927, in Ashley, Pa.; son of a railroad union organizer. *Education:* King's College, Wilkes-Barre, Pa., B.S., 1952; Harvard University, M.B.A., 1954.

ADDRESSES: Office—MCI Communications Corp., 1133 19th St. N.W., Washington, D.C. 20036.

OCCUPATION: Entrepreneur; communications company executive.

CAREER: Worked in film business in Hollywood, Calif., helping produce movies for Michael Todd and George Skouras; inventor of several electronic devices and founder of a number of electronics and computer firms in the 1960s; MCI Communications Corp., Washington, D.C., chairman and chief executive officer, 1968—. Director of N-Triple-C, Inc.

SIDELIGHTS: William McGowan doesn't seem to mind that people thought he was a little crazy for wanting to challenge American Telephone & Telegraph's comfortable monopoly of the country's telephone system. The costly years of litigation seem to McGowan a small price to pay for the prize of breaking up the AT&T monolithic hold on the telephone marketplace and nourishing a fledgling phone company to a full-grown aggressor in long-distance service. And the fun is just beginning, McGowan says. "I went all the way around the world in one direction," he told a *Newsweek* reporter, "and then went all the way around again in the other. Then I decided that I preferred the working world."

Born in Ashley, Pennsylvania, in 1927, McGowan grew up in the coal country of eastern Pennsylvania, the son of a railroad union organizer. Working his way through college, he won a scholarship to Harvard Business School, where he gleaned the business knowledge that was to become invaluable to him years later as an entrepreneur. The glamour of Hollywood captured his interest, and he went to work for movie moguls Michael Todd and George Skouras, helping to produce films that included "Oklahoma." But he abandoned the glitter of Hollywood lights for business of a new kind: working with dollars and figures as a management consultant and venture capitalist. He even turned inventor and learned to transform adversity into advantage—a practice that was to serve him well in his battle against AT&T.

One of McGowan's early inventions was an ultrasonic beeping device that he was convinced would be of great benefit to the U.S. Navy. The beeping, he believed, would serve to repel sharks from pilots downed at sea. However, the device did not work quite as he planned. Instead of fending off the sharks brought in for the demonstration to Navy brass, the beeping prompted the predators to tear the

device apart. Undaunted, McGowan wondered whether the Navy would be interested in a shark aphrodisiac.

McGowan launched several firms in electronics and computers, and, retiring a rich man at thirty-nine, took a trip around the world. The trip didn't cure his restlessness for new venture capital opportunities, and he returned to the business environment to scout them out. That was how he happened on a small Illinois-based company that was struggling to enter the communications business. It was building a single microwave radio link between St. Louis and Chicago to carry long-distance telephone calls. Nearly bankrupt, Microwave Communications of America had what McGowan thought were invaluable assets: a method of transmitting calls inexpensively by using microwave transmission instead of copper cables, and a chance to challenge AT&T by offering discount long-distance service to corporate customers. "Challenging the monopoly had one irresistible element," McGowan told *Time*. "It had never been done before."

Because he was not an expert on the telephone industry, what others called an impossible task did not deter McGowan. It was simply a matter of logic, he said. "We looked over the papers in the Federal Communications Commission library, and we couldn't find anything that said AT&T had the rights to a monopoly in telephone service," he recalled to *Time*.

For $50,000, McGowan bought half of the fledgling company and has seen the worth of his shares balloon to around $50 million. The company was reincorporated as MCI Communications Corp. After raising $107 million from private investors whom McGowan was able to sell on his revolutionary idea, construction on microwave transmission towers began, paving the way for what McGowan saw as the future highways of long-distance phone service. Anticipating possible regulatory roadblocks, he moved the company headquarters to Washington, where lobbying efforts could be more effectively carried out and the company would be under the watchful eyes of the federal agencies whose approval was essential to give life to MCI. "I didn't concern myself with the technology, just the regulation of the industry," McGowan said in *Time*.

The technology, however, was no insignificant matter. It was the element that sent many long-distance carriers rushing into the market to achieve cost or quality advantages over AT&T. Analysts predict that as the shakeout in the burgeoning long-distance market occurs over the next few years, the key to survival will be owning, rather than leasing, a communications network. McGowan was quick to see the cost and efficiency advantages of microwave radio transmission over copper cable and built a cross-country network of—at last count—more than 14,500 circuit miles, second in size only to AT&T's network. By sending most calls over its own network rather than buying or leasing transmission facilities from AT&T, MCI has kept overhead low and has been able to offer 30 percent to 50 percent reductions in the cost of long-distance service.

Concentrating on the business client, McGowan's first move with his new company was into the high-density, inner-city market. In 1972, MCI rolled out its telephone service to businesses in a few selected high-traffic cities including New York, St. Louis, and Chicago. Expanding its service around the country, MCI beams calls by microwave to about 80 percent of the nation's telephones; to reach their final destination, calls are transferred to local Bell System lines and carried to customers. Remote areas not serviced by the microwave network can be linked up by leased local lines, a practice that has not received the blessing of Bell System officials who have fought the industry upstart.

During the trial for an antitrust suit brought against AT&T by MCI, George Saunders, a senior attorney for Bell, said in the *New York Times* that MCI's business strategy was to " 'skim the cream' off the most profitable long-distance markets while avoiding obligations to serve lesser, out-of-the-way markets," a practice that he said could eventually "lead to price increases for the public."

Before MCI's service could be established, the company filed lengthy pleas with the Federal Communications Commission and entered into court battles with AT&T that became milestones for the growing industry and opened the door for competition in the long-distance market. In landmark decisions in 1969 and 1971, the FCC broke the Bell System's

fifty-year monopoly on the long-distance market by authorizing McGowan's MCI to build facilities that enabled the company to offer long-distance private-line links between St. Louis and Chicago. In 1971, that decision was expanded to allow other competition to enter the private-line long-distance market and battle AT&T for a share of its 85 million customers. In the 1971 decision, AT&T was ordered by the FCC to provide local facilities for other long-distance companies to use to complete long-distance calls. For McGowan, who compared MCI's challenge to Bell as "a flea crawling up the leg of an elephant" in *Newsweek* magazine, the early FCC victories were just the first shots in an all-out war against AT&T.

Following the FCC's 1971 decisions, MCI began fighting the Bell System for the intracity connections it needed to complete the long-distance calls that moved over the MCI microwave network from city to city. Without the vital connections, MCI could not offer the advantages over AT&T that it had promised. In 1975, AT&T acquiesced to a court order and reluctantly provided the connections—but not before McGowan vowed that his company would be compensated for the lost business in those four years. In a landmark suit that finally sprung open the hinges on AT&T's monopoly and precipitated the breakup of the Bell System, McGowan filed against giant AT&T for $900 million in damages. In 1980, a twelve-member jury in the Chicago Federal District Court found the Bell System guilty of dragging its feet and illegally delaying action on the MCI requests for local connections. The jury awarded MCI $1.8 billion in damages, the largest antitrust judgement in the country's history. MCI attorneys figured that the total amount of the award, with trebling, would come to $5.8 billion. A federal appeals court, however, ordered a retrial on damages which reduced the amount of the award to just $37.8 million, $113 million after trebling. The reassessment of damages was a financial blow to MCI, who had staked many of its plans for future growth on anticipation of receiving the original $5.8 billion award.

MCI was also facing financial difficulty with several of its ventures. In 1983 McGowan had launched MCI Mail, an electronic mail service designed to convey information between computers and to customers without computers. After three years and $40 million, the system has not been profitable and, according to *Business Week*, is being quietly phased out of existence. MCI Airsignal, the division responsible for paging and cellular-mobile phone services, was also slow in showing indications of potential profitability and was sold in 1985 for $120 million. And the company's difficulties extended to its bread-and-butter long distance service. As the two-year "equal access" period draws to a close and as MCI's cost advantages are eliminated, the company is shifting its efforts from its unsuccessful attempts to sign residential customers (a *Business Week*/Harris Poll showed that 72 percent of customers electing long-distance service have opted for AT&T; only 11 percent have chosen MCI) to a campaign to capture commercial clients.

The problems MCI faces in competing with AT&T in the long-distance business market were summarized by *Business Week* writers John Wilke and Mark Maremont: "Changing MCI's image won't be easy. The [*Business Week*] poll shows that AT&T has staked out quality and reliability as its own trademark: 59% of those surveyed believe AT&T's service is superior. And despite MCI's claims that its network has improved, many customers still complain. Manufacturers Hanover Corp. recently discontinued using MCI private lines in four large cities because of what David K. Ross, the bank's senior technical officer, describes as 'terrible transmission quality' that had 'deteriorated substantially.' ''

To change this perception and to provide needed cash resources, MCI in 1985 purchased IBM's long-distance service, Satellite Business Systems, for 16 percent of MCI's stock, making IBM MCI's largest shareholder. Amid rumors that IBM plans to buy up all of MCI, speculation dismissed by McGowan, *Business Week* noted: "IBM's involvement can only be a boon to MCI. But in the end, MCI's success will turn on whether it can stay leaner, meaner, and better-managed than its larger rival. MCI will have to do all that—just to stay afloat. If anyone can pull it off, it's Bill McGowan."

SOURCES:

PERIODICALS

Business Week, October 10, 1983, November 5, 1984, July 8, 1985, February 17, 1986.
Forbes, January 30, 1980.
New York Times, October 8, 1976, July 18, 1979, June 13, 1980, June 15, 1980, June 16, 1980, February 12, 1984.
Newsweek, June 23, 1980, July 25, 1983.
Time, February 23, 1981, January 7, 1985.

—Sidelights by Amy C. Bodwin

Martin McGuinness

1950(?)-

PERSONAL: Born c. 1950; married Bernadette Canning, November 21, 1974. *Religion:* Roman Catholic.

OCCUPATION: Northern Irish politician and activist.

CAREER: Former butcher's assistant; active in Northern Irish republican movement since 1970; member, or former member, of outlawed Irish Republican Army (IRA); currently serving as an elected member of Northern Ireland Assembly; one of the leaders of the Sinn Fein political party.

SIDELIGHTS: Martin McGuinness, a butcher's assistant who had become a leader of the Irish Republican Army (IRA) by the time he turned twenty-one, was largely unknown outside England and Ireland until the British Broadcasting Corporation made him famous by keeping him off the air. In August 1985, the BBC succumbed to British government pressure and decided not to broadcast a documentary film featuring McGuinness, alleged to be the chief of staff of the outlawed Irish Republican Army. The film was eventually shown with some minor modifications in October, but its broadcast prompted far less reaction than its suppression.

Controversy surrounding the documentary, called "Real Lives: At the Edge of the Union," was touched off in July after a BBC magazine published excerpts from the show. The forty-five minute film provided profiles of McGuinness and Gregory Campbell, a Loyalist politician known for his outspoken views in support of Northern Ireland's continued membership in the United Kingdom. McGuinness, an elected member of the Northern Ireland Assembly, is a leader of Sinn Fein, the political arm of the IRA. (While membership in the IRA is against the law, Sinn Fein—pronounced Shin Fane—is a legal political party.) The BBC publication *Radio Times*, ran pictures of each man and extensive excerpts from the film's interviews with them. The BBC cancelled the scheduled August 7 broadcast in response to a request from Home Secretary Leon Brittan, who was acting at the direction of Prime Minister Margaret Thatcher. Thatcher told the *Sunday Times* of London that she would "utterly condemn" the BBC for showing the program. "I do not believe that any great body like the BBC should do anything which might be construed as furthering the objectives of terrorists," she said. "I feel extremely strongly about it." The cancellation, according to the *New York Times*, prompted the Association of British Editors to label the BBC's action "a betrayal of its own best traditions," and to say it had handed the IRA "one more victory in the propaganda war."

It has been a long war. The British first sunk themselves into the Irish bog in the twelfth century, when Henry II invaded the country and turned it into a British colony. England had little to do with the colony, however, until Henry VIII became worried in the sixteenth century that Catholic

France or Spain might seek an alliance with Catholic Ireland and threaten Protestant England. In 1530, England began installing various military and bureaucratic representatives of the crown on Irish soil. The Irish resisted the takeover then, and the resistance has continued.

The struggle turned especially violent in 1919, and Britain applied a compromise it had used with restless colonies before: partition. Under a treaty signed in 1921, the predominantly Catholic twenty-six counties of southern Ireland became an independent nation, the Republic of Ireland, while the country's predominantly Protestant northern six counties, known as Ulster, remained a part of the United Kingdom. The conflict between the Loyalists, the mostly Protestant backers of the British in Northern Ireland, and the Republicans, the mostly Catholic advocates of reunification with the Irish Republic, has escalated over the past sixteen years. Since 1969, some 2,500 people have been killed and more than 19,000 wounded in what has come to be known as The Troubles.

McGuinness told the BBC he "became involved in the republican movement in late 1970." As is often the case with activists operating at the periphery of—or behind the scenes of—guerilla campaigns, it is difficult to pin down McGuinness's precise role in the Irish republican movement. His role was less cloudy back in 1972, when he freely acknowledged his leadership role with the Provisional wing of the IRA—the faction most involved in bombings and armed conflict—in Londonderry. Republican forces had sealed off the Roman Catholic section of the city known as the Bogside, and McGuinness was the Provisional IRA leader in charge. "The job, as far as I'm concerned," he told the *New York Times* in April 1972, "is fighting the British Army. Ours is an offensive role. No one likes to kill. I don't. But we're at war. These people are invaders."

In an interview published in April 1972, McGuinness told the *Irish Times* of Dublin: "It seemed to me that behind all the politics and marching, it was plain as daylight that there was an Army in our town, in our country and that they weren't there to give out flowers. Armies should be fought by armies. So one night I piled into a black Austin, me and five mates, and we went to see a Provo [IRA guerrilla]. . . . " After the British introduced the practice known as internment (picking up and holding suspected IRA members without trial), McGuinness told the *Irish Times:* "The Provos in Derry were ordered into fulltime military action. I gave up my job working in the butcher's shop." Responding to charges by Catholic moderates that violence only makes The Troubles worse, McGuinness said: "I know they're wrong. I know it and I feel it when I go round the barricades and see the men they called wasters, and the fellows that used only to drink, doing things now they really believe in. Protecting the area, and freeing Ireland and freeing themselves." In 1976, the *Economist*, the British weekly magazine, theorized that McGuinness, then twenty-six, was being forced out of the IRA and that the organization's leadership was in disarray. But hard evidence of such theories is hard to come by.

Not much has been published about McGuinness's personal life. According to the *Belfast Telegraph*, he was married on November 21, 1974 to Bernadette Canning in a quiet ceremony in a village church just across the Irish Republic border in County Donegal. The wedding was about a week after his release from a nine-month jail term he served following conviction on charges of IRA membership.

He and another man had been acquitted in a Dublin court in 1973 of charges of possessing 250 pounds of explosives and 4,757 rounds of ammunition. McGuinness refused to recognize the court but declared: "In Derry City [republicans routinely drop the "London" from Londonderry] it is a known fact that every civilian killed has been killed by British Army or the Royal Ulster Constabulary. For over two years I was an officer in the Derry Brigade of the IRA. We have fought against the killing of our people. My comrades have been arrested and tortured and some were shot unarmed by British troops." Three years later, in 1976, a Belfast Magistrate's Court dropped charges of IRA membership. McGuinness was quoted by the *Belfast Telegraph* as saying: "I am a republican, a socialist republican, but being a republican and a member of the IRA are two different things."

While active on the political front, McGuinness has never left much doubt about his views of what it will take to bring real change to the North. Interviewed in May 1985 about Sinn Fein's successful showing in local government elections in Ulster, he said: "The results are good, but at the end of the day it will be the cutting edge of the IRA which will bring freedom." Asked in November 1985 about the negotiations between London and Dublin aimed at devising a role for the Republic of Ireland in the affairs of the North, he rejected such an arrangement. "Settlements that ignore reality, that ignore history, that do not confront the real issue," he told the *New York Times*, "are not solutions at all, but devices that enable Britain to refine its repression of republicans and its partition of Ireland."

Campbell, the hardline Loyalist profiled in the documentary, said of McGuinness during a rally filmed by the BBC: "The man was described by a Fleet Street newspaper as the chief of staff of the IRA. Martin McGuinness. The man is a craven coward because he's the same as the IRA murderers. He's a yellow-bellied coward at heart." McGuinness's mother told the BBC: "I worry all the time about his safety. Any mother would worry about her son involved in a political struggle. I worry about him and his whole family. Martin is a man. He can use his own judgment. I never tried to influence him one way or the other. I know that we have suffered. But there are lots of people in Derry and the six counties that suffered a lot more than we did. They've had their husbands killed, their sons killed and their little children killed." Said his wife, interviewed while their children played in the background: "I don't like to see anybody shot, but they [the British] shouldn't be here, you know. It's our country." She said she believes "the ballot box is the only solution," but added: "I don't think they should give up the Armalite [rifle] either."

When the *Sunday Times* of London described him in July 1985 as the IRA's chief of staff, McGuinness told the *Irish Times*, published in Dublin, that the claim was unsubstantiated and part of a British plan to have him assassinated. "I have consistently denied these libellous claims, yet British Government Ministers and others have continued to repeat this allegation. If any evidence existed to back those claims I would have been arrested. The whole matter is deeply sinister and I am convinced that these allegations are part of a plan by the British establishment to have me assassinated."

The *Sunday Times* article was published shortly before the BBC documentary was scheduled to appear. The documentary includes extensive footage of both McGuinness and Campbell with their families at home in Londonderry. Asked about his role in the IRA, McGuinness told the BBC interviewer: "It's no secret to the people of these areas that I was actively involved against the British involvement in Ireland and the British forces of occupation. I have no regrets whatsoever." Asked if he had been involved in military action, he said: "I was involved actively on behalf of my people against the British forces of occupation. That's as much as I'm prepared to say." Elsewhere in the documentary, McGuinness said: "They [the British] partitioned this country against the overwhelming wishes of the Irish people. They must pick up the tab, not the people of Ireland. Republicans don't glory in death. We believe that the only way the Irish people can bring about the freedom of their country is through the use of arms—if someone could tell me a peaceful way to do it, I'd gladly support them, but no one has done that yet. Take the British presence away and there will be peace in Ireland. I believe that."

Loyalist Campbell offered BBC viewers an opposing, and no less violent, point of view: "You either be killed by the IRA or kill them, and I want to see them dead. If the British government withdraws, there will be the worst civil war ever seen in Ireland—untold violence, horrendous bloodshed. We would have reached a doomsday situation. All the Protestants have worked for, voted for, campaigned for, would be thrown on one side. There would be no alternative—no way further politically—but taking up the gun." *Time* magazine reported that the producer of the film, Paul Hamann, who has made seven previous documentaries about Northern Ireland, defended his film as giving "a unique insight" into what is happening in Ulster. Both Campbell and McGuinness, said Hamann, live in constant fear of assassination. He described them both as "ostensibly nice people, but there was a 5% unspoken ruthlessness of personality, and when it showed, it was frightening." According to *Time*, Hamann said each man displayed his own justification for killing people and a fanaticism that defied rationality.

SOURCES:

TELEVISION DOCUMENTARY

"Real Lives: At the Edge of the Union," produced by the British Broadcasting Corp., 1985.

PERIODICALS

Belfast Telegraph, November 21, 1974, March 2, 1976, August 1, 1985.
Detroit Free Press, May 3, 1981.
Economist, February 14, 1976.
Financial Times, September 6, 1985.
Irish Times, April 19, 1972, July 30, 1985.
New York Times, April 27, 1972, July 31, 1972, May 31, 1983, May 19, 1985, August 1, 1985, November 3, 1985.
Time, July 31, 1972, August 12, 1985.
Wall Street Journal, August 14, 1985.

—Sidelights by Bill Mitchell

Jim McMahon

1959-

PERSONAL: Full name, James Robert McMahon; born August 21, 1959 in Jersey City, N.J.; son of Jim and Roberta McMahon; married; wife's name, Nancy; children: Ashley, Sean. *Education:* Attended Brigham Young University, 1977-82.

ADDRESSES: Home—Northbrook, Ill. *Office*—Chicago Bears Football Club, Inc., 55 East Jackson, Chicago, Ill. 60604.

OCCUPATION: Professional football player

CAREER: Member of Chicago Bears football team, 1982—.

SIDELIGHTS: In the autumn of 1985, when the Chicago Bears took the National Football League by storm, they were paced by one of the most talented and colorful assortments of athletes in the modern history of the professional game. On offense, their star running back was Walter Payton, an eleven-year NFL veteran who has gained more than 14,000 yards en route to what was likely to be enshrinement in the league's Hall of Fame. After serving more than twice the career span of most pro running backs, Payton was still gaining 100 or more yards in most games and 1,000 or more yards per season. He ran with a fury and aggression rare for his profession and especially rare for a veteran, often delivering the blow—crashing into defensive players before they could crash into him—sometimes sticking stiff arms into the masks on their faces or onto the sides of their helmets. His fans and teammates call Payton "Sweetness."

On defense, the Bears were unusual in that they employed a 308-pound rookie lineman named William Perry, a pear-shaped man who was one of the largest in the sport. He said that in college, at Clemson, he once ate $28 worth of fast food in a single dinner at a McDonald's restaurant. He claimed he once drank forty-eight cans of beer in a single night while celebrating a victory. What made him especially unusual in 1985, however, was that the Bears used him not only on defense but also on offense, to try to help the Bears score by carrying the ball and by blocking for Payton and others. In a game against Green Bay, he even caught a pass for a touchdown. Perry was dubbed "The Refrigerator," and the man who threw him the pass was quarterback Jim McMahon, perhaps the most colorful Chicago Bear of all.

McMahon doesn't have a nickname, but his behavior on and off the field is anything but commonplace. A beer-drinking, tobacco-chewing Catholic who attended a strictly religious Mormon college, Brigham Young University, McMahon seems to be especially eccentric in a sport that often tolerates unusual behavior. Early in the 1985 season, in a 45-10 victory over the Washington Redskins, McMahon threw three touchdown passes and caught one himself—from

UPI/Bettmann Newsphotos

Payton, on a trick play. It is rare for quarterbacks to catch touchdown passes (they are generally paid to throw them and, once in a while, run for one); McMahon's behavior afterward was even stranger: He ran to the sidelines and began banging his helmeted head into those of larger teammates. "I'm excited and I'm having fun, it doesn't bother me," he told the *Detroit Free Press*. "They [the Redskins] were just in our way and we had to step on 'em."

The aforementioned helmet covered one of the stranger haircuts in pro sports. During training camp prior to the season, McMahon was tired of his long hair curling up under his helmet during practice. He tried to give himself a haircut, made a mess of it, became frustrated, and got a teammate to give him what was described by observers as a "punk Mohawk." If that didn't make him appear different enough in civilian clothes, the look was complemented by a pair of sunglasses McMahon wore almost everywhere, including indoors and on cloudy days.

The glasses were necessary, he said, to protect from bright light a right eye made sensitive by his poking a fork into it in a childhood accident. He was six years old and playing cowboys and Indians with his brother when McMahon found a knot in the leather string tying his holster to his leg. "So I'm trying to get the knot out," he told the *New York Times*, "and 'Wham!' " He spent the next two weeks in the hospital. The doctors thought he might have severed the retina. He hadn't, but his dark pupil spread over his blue iris. That limits his ability to block out brightness; hence, the sunglasses. In that he had to wear them anyway, McMahon often chose those with mirrors or wrap-around styles with slits through which to see.

His tendency toward injury—not just the normal sprains and muscle-pulls common in professional football, but often unusual and frightening injury—has continued into his adult life. In a 1984 game against the Los Angeles Raiders, McMahon, already playing with a bruised back and a broken bone in his throwing hand, sustained a severe and rather odd injury: a lacerated kidney. The helmet of one Raider hit him in the back as the helmet of a second opponent hit him in the ribs, causing his kidney to get wrapped around a rib and putting him out for the rest of the season.

After the first two games of the 1985 season, McMahon spent two days in the hospital with a sore neck, back spasms, and a swollen shin. He didn't start the third game, but he entered it in the third quarter with Chicago trailing the Minnesota Vikings, 17-9. On his first play, McMahon threw a 70-yard touchdown pass to Willie Gault. His second play was a 25-yard touchdown pass to Dennis McKinnon. The next time the Bears got the ball, he moved them downfield for five plays then threw a 43-yard touchdown pass to McKinnon. Just six minutes, forty seconds after McMahon entered the game, Chicago had taken the lead, 30-17; the Bears went on to win 30-24, and McMahon was credited with turning the game around with both his outstanding throwing arm and his leadership ability.

Such dramatic achievements have been a common feature of McMahon's career in sports. Kevin Lamb of the *Sporting News* wrote that McMahon "did things in high school and college that should appear only in comic strips or Disney movies." For instance, in a high school baseball game, with his team trailing 8-4 in the bottom of the ninth inning of a state tournament, he hit a grand-slam home run. In a basketball game, with his team behind by a point and only five seconds left on the clock, he "stole an inbounds pass and scored the winning basket." And in football, when he moved from San Jose, California, to Roy, Utah, during his sopho- more year of high school, he won the starting quarterback position from two older, more established players. One of the most famous moments in McMahon's college football

Jim McMahon (number 9) rolls out on a pass play against the Minnesota Vikings. AP/Wide World Photos.

career came in the 1980 Holiday Bowl. His BYU team trailed SMU, 45-25, with only four minutes, seven seconds left to play. On fourth down his coach called for a punt. "Jim came charging off the field," Lamb reports BYU wide receiver Dan Plater recalling. "He was yelling at LaVell [Edwards, the coach], 'What are we gonna do? Blankin' quit?'" Edwards changed his mind. McMahon threw three touchdown passes in the closing minutes of the game, including a 46-yarder for the last play of the game, and Brigham Young won 46-45.

McMahon was born in Jersey City, New Jersey, and raised in San Jose, California. His father was a Catholic, his mother a Mormon. Having been raised a Catholic himself, McMahon wanted very much to play football for Notre Dame, but at 6 feet, one inch tall and 190 pounds was considered too small; so he ended up at Brigham Young in Provo, Utah. There, he threw 84 touchdown passes and broke 71 NCAA records. He was also "considered a hell raiser," he told the *Sporting News*, after he was spotted drinking a beer while playing golf at a school where alcohol, caffeinated beverages, and tobacco are prohibited. "I was on probation my whole time," conceded McMahon.

Lavell Edwards, the BYU coach, says he had "to get on Jim at times" but believes his demeanor in Utah was much milder than it was to become in Chicago. Still, there was no denying the young quarterback's flair for the unusual. As the team's specialty punter, McMahon improvised in a spectacular way during a game against Hawaii during his junior year. A snap from center went over his head. He turned and chased the ball, grabbed it, and pivoted to see some Hawaii tacklers approaching from his right. McMahon, who is right-handed and right-footed, punted with his left foot and kicked the ball 33 yards to the Hawaii two-yard line. (He also baffles Chicago coach Ditka at times by throwing the ball left-handed in practice.)

McMahon was the fifth player—and the second quarterback—selected in the first round of the 1981 pro football draft. He arrived at his first professional press conference in a limousine, wearing sunglasses and carrying a can of Budweiser. In business terms, his 1985 contract with the Bears was worth $600,000, up from the reported $190,000 he was paid in 1984. Like a businessman, he often carries an expensive leather briefcase. But in it, McMahon usually packs sandwiches, bags of potato chips, and packaged fruit pies.

The 1985 season was his fourth year in the league, and many wondered how long he would play, given his tendency toward injuries. He played eight games in 1982, fourteen in 1983, and nine in 1984 before his serious kidney injury. In 1982, he had the NFL's highest passing rating ever for a rookie. In 1983, the Bears were 5-2 in games started by McMahon, who shared playing time with Vince Evans. In 1984, in the nine games that McMahon started, the Bears were 7-2. He failed to finish four of them due to injuries. Many observers have noted his tendency to take chances—running upfield when many quarterbacks would head toward the safety of the sidelines—in a position that is one of the most vulnerable in sports.

McMahon's attitude is the sort that football coaches generally appreciate: the willingness to play with pain. But his relationship with Ditka has been trying, at times. "Oh, he's different," Ditka told the *New York Times*, "He thinks he's the best passer, the best runner, the best blocker there is on the team. A lot of players wouldn't do what he does. A lot shouldn't. I just wish he would be more discreet about some of the things he does." McMahon has been known to mimic coaches when they point out the mistakes of players in film sessions. Ditka has a rule that all players must wear shirts with collars on travel days; McMahon complied on two occasions by wearing a Roman Catholic priest's collar. "He [Ditka] understands me now," McMahon told a *New York Times* reporter. "At least, I think he understands me. Well, sometimes I don't even understand myself. Seems like I do something weird every day."

One thing he does quite regularly is run different plays than the ones Ditka sends in. "You tell him to go 'Bang, bang, bang,'" Ditka told *Newsweek*, "and he goes 'Bang, boom, boom.' He shocks the s—— out of me sometimes, but somehow he makes it work." As Don Pierson of the *Chicago Tribune* points out, it is this ability to improvise that both "maddens and gladdens coaches who spend hours plotting strategy only to watch their quarterbacks turn play specifications into playground spontaneity. For all its intricacy and sophistication, football remains simple and basic. The quarterbacks who can't turn bad plays into good ones lose." And that, Bears wide receiver Ken Margerum says, is why McMahon is "a great quarterback," writes Lamb in the *Sporting News*. Explains Margerum: "Defenses have all these computer printouts of what you're going to do on first-and-10 and second-and-long and third-and-three, and Jim just goes against all convention of what he's supposed to do. A lot of big plays go to a completely different receiver than the one that was planned. You can't defend that."

Of ten representative McMahon touchdown passes during 1985, only two followed exactly the play sent in from the sidelines. On five of them, he scrambled out of the pocket before throwing. On four he did not throw to primary receivers. On three he called audibles—changing the play at the last minute at the line of scrimmage. Bears defensive coordinator Buddy Ryan, who was a member of the New York Jets staff when the legendary Joe Namath quarterbacked the team, compares McMahon favorably to Namath. "It's the same feeling I had when I was with the Jets," Ryan told Ed Sherman of the *Chicago Tribune*. "Even if the [opposing] defense played great, it didn't matter because we had Namath. The score didn't matter because we knew the guy could get hot and get you back into the game. McMahon's the same way."

McMahon remained hot throughout the 1985 season despite a serious shoulder injury that forced him to miss several games midway through the Bears' successful drive to the Super Bowl. The Bears charged into the playoffs with only one loss in an otherwise perfect campaign and shut out both the New York Giants and the Los Angeles Rams to secure a Super Bowl berth against the New England Patriots. Along the way to postseason play McMahon's antics both off and on the field made him a national celebrity, a rebel folk hero who was at all times his own man. Much of this perception resulted from football commissioner Pete Rozelle's ordering McMahon not to wear a headband sporting the Adidas company name during televised games. McMahon responded by wearing a headband with the inscription "ROZELLE" scrawled on it during the playoff game against Los Angeles. His act of defiance created a stir in the press, and speculation ran wild as to what he would display on his headband during the Super Bowl.

McMahon was the star of the weeklong pregame press coverage in New Orleans, the site of Super Bowl XX, and helped to insure the largest Super Bowl television audience in history. A music video the Bears had made for charity received wide airplay, and the ire of the women of New Orleans was raised when it was reported on a local radio station that McMahon had made uncomplimentary remarks about the virtue of the women of that city. (The report was later proven untrue.) When Super Sunday arrived television cameras scanning the Bears' sidelines viewed McMahon wearing a variety of inscribed headbands throughout the game, including one showing support for the cause of the MIAs and POWs believed to still be in Vietnam and one supporting the Juvenile Diabetes Foundation. McMahon's performance on the field led the Bears to a relatively easy 46-10 victory over New England and brought the city of Chicago its first major professional sports championship since 1963.

McMahon's tremendous ability, combined with his offbeat attitude and growing mystique, has given him a charismatic quality among his teammates. On more than one occasion he has been credited with inspiring the Bears by his mere presence on the field. "When he's in," one teammate told Lamb, "we're a different ball club." Unlike most quarter-backs, however, who spend much of their leisure time courting the receivers and running backs who gain yardage for them, McMahon's best friends on the team are the offensive linemen. This makes good sense—it is the offensive linemen who protect him from enemy defenders. But the truth is that McMahon *likes* linemen. He goes out to dinner with a group of them once a week during the season, and some of them feel he's really a lineman at heart. "He always wants to be one of the guys," offensive tackle Keith Van Horne told a *New York Times* reporter. "He likes to get down in the trenches with us, get dirty or get turf burns. He wants marks on his helmet."

SOURCES:

PERIODICALS

Chicago Tribune, October 13, 1985, January 5, 1986.
Christian Science Monitor, November 7, 1984.
Detroit Free Press, September 30, 1985.
Newsweek, October 21, 1985.
New York Times, September 29, 1985, October 13, 1985.
People, January 6, 1986.
Rolling Stone, March 13, 1986.
Sporting News, October 14, 1985, October 28, 1985, January 27, 1986.
Sports Illustrated, November 30, 1981, October 21, 1985, October 14, 1985, January 20, 1986, February 3, 1986.
Time, January 27, 1986.

—*Sidelights by Joe LaPointe*

Vince McMahon, Jr.

1945(?)-

PERSONAL: Born c. 1945; son of Vince McMahon (a wrestling promoter).

ADDRESSES: Office—TitanSports, P.O. Box 4520, 81 Holly Hill Lane, Greenwich, Conn. 06830.

OCCUPATION: Wrestling promoter.

CAREER: Wrestling ring announcer during the 1970s; currently head of TitanSports (wrestling promotion firm), Greenwich, Conn., and head of World Wrestling Federation. Host of wrestling talk-show "Tuesday Night Titans" (TNT), on USA cable network.

SIDELIGHTS: Wrestling promoter Vince McMahon, Jr., has accomplished a feat unrivalled even by his performers in the ring: He has given professional wrestling—an activity that detractors say is neither professional nor wrestling—the cloak of respectability. For years wrestling had been relegated to a twilight world somewhere between sports and entertainment. No self-respecting sports publication (other than a few special-interest fan magazines) would cover it with any regularity, and wrestling bouts and television shows drew only the most rabid, fanatical audiences. But McMahon, scion of a family of wrestling promoters changed all that.

Now such celebrities as Andy Warhol, Brian DePalma, and Joe Piscopo have been spotted ringside at Madison Square Garden viewing the antics of Rowdy Roddy Piper, Hulk Hogan, and the Iron Sheik—all denizens of the World Wrestling Federation stable run by McMahon and his company, TitanSports. McMahon has orchestrated one of the most massive, multifaceted promotions ever, bringing this quasi-sport onto Saturday morning cartoon shows, into ever-increasing numbers of huge sports arenas, and onto cable television, where wrestling programs routinely out-draw college basketball games.

Detroit Free Press television critic Mike Duffy has called McMahon a "promotional genius" for all he has accomplished. WWF announcer Mean Gene Okerlund noted to *Sports Illustrated* that "there's that fine line between genius and insanity, and [McMahon] walks it." Undoubtedly some of the features of McMahon's style of wrestling promotion border on the tasteless and the odd, if not the insane: racial slurs and xenophobia in the ring; a Johnny Carson-type talk show, hosted by McMahon and featuring highly excited wrestlers as guests; and a much-vaunted promotional strategy known as the "rock 'n' wrestling" connection that has catapulted rock star Cyndi Lauper into the unlikely role of wrestling manager.

The guiding force behind this mania is a man who, until recently, showed little sign of revolutionizing the industry.

Steve Taylor/Titan Sports

During the 1970s McMahon, then known simply as Junior among wrestlers, was earning a living as a ringside announcer at WWF bouts in the northeast United States, often flanked by "color commentators" like former wrestler Bruno Sammartino. McMahon's father ran the WWF at the time, commuting from his home in Florida to the federation's main venues in New York and other East-Coast cities. Bill Apter, editor of the *Wrestler* fan magazine, described the elder McMahon to *CN* as "a laid-back, polite business-man who had many friends in the business." His profile was so low that he garnered no more than three lines in *Sporting News* when he died of cancer in the spring of 1984, and no mention at all in the *New York Times*, the largest newspaper in the city where his matches had filled Madison Square Garden to capacity for generations. While his father ran the WWF, Vince, Jr., "grew up in the business," a spokesman for McMahon told *CN*, doing everything from commentary at ringside to interviews with wrestlers to selling tickets. Promotion was a family tradition; his grandfather had been a boxing promoter in the 1930s.

Vince McMahon, Jr., came into his own in the early 1980s, when he bought out his father's shares in the company and took over as president. He immediately exhibited a promotional flair and aggressiveness that, uncharacteristic as it may seem in an industry bent on mock mayhem, had been lacking in business competition between rival wrestling federations. In the elder McMahon's day, wrestling associations had been happy to monopolize their particular region of the country; the Northeast, for instance, had always been considered WWF turf. But the younger McMahon unhesitatingly went after a national market—via cable and network television shows and thus exceeded the limits of the traditional family fiefdom. McMahon admits that these moves ran counter to his father's philosophy: "Had my dad known at the time what my plans were," he told *Sports Illustrated*, "he never would have sold his stock to me." But the plans were well underway by the time his father died at the age of sixty-nine.

McMahon's decision to move into the national market is considered a cheap shot by rival promoters. His critics say he is trying to blanket the media, the fan magazines, cable television, and network television with WWF wrestlers like Hulk Hogan and thereby dry up demand for their own stars. But McMahon sees the move as the destiny of the WWF. "We had been very successful in the northeast, and I felt that we could be equally successful elsewhere," he told *Sports Illustrated*. "Even when I was a kid, if I wanted something and somebody else told me that I could not have it, the worst that could happen was I might get the hell kicked out of me. So we decided to disassociate ourselves from the other promoters and make a lot of enemies all at once. I must say we've been very successful at that." The rivals, of course, have retaliated by invading the WWF's East Coast territory with wrestling events of their own and by putting on their own national television events.

But the WWF is still on top in this competition, largely because of the connection with rock and roll. Cyndi Lauper has been the mainstay of this strategy, especially in her role as manager of "good girl" wrestler Wendy Richter in matches against heavies Lellani Kall and her mentor the Fabulous Moolah. In these events, Lauper typically screams a lot and performs numerous ringside antics—apparently to good effect, since her wrestler has done quite well. Lauper also has featured wrestlers in her music videos and once managed a Hulk Hogan match. The TitanSports spokesman told *CN* that this was a typical example of McMahon's genius: "He took Cyndi Lauper at the height of her career and Hulk Hogan at the height of his career and put them together."

McMahon is now best known to wrestling fans as host of the weekly cable television talk show "Tuesday Night Titans" (TNT), which appears on the USA network. He plays the straight man while his guests alternately turn outrageous, silly, or violent. Once he looked on as Kamala the Ugandan Giant supposedly ate a live chicken. (The cameras cut to a commercial as Kamala pounced on the chicken's cage and later cut back to a close-up of the Giant with feathers sticking out of his mouth.) And the *New York Times* reported another noteworthy event in "TNT" history: "When Paul (The Butcher) Vachon was married on TNT, . . . George (The Animal) Steel ate the floral decorations."

The behavior of WWF wrestlers in the ring is often even more outrageous—something critics have attributed to McMahon's penchant for the freakish. White wrestlers have called their black opponents "boy." Bouts featuring the Iron Sheik are said to have fanned anti-Iranian prejudices left over from the U.S. hostage crisis. Observes David Meltzer in *Sports Illustrated*, "All of this is not new to wrestling, but the WWF exploits racism more than any promoter I've ever seen." The WWF even appears to be encouraging such criticism by purging all-American type wrestlers from its rosters. According to *Sports Illustrated*, perennial nice guy Bob Backlund's image was just too cleancut for the WWF: "By the time the elder McMahon died. . . and his son Vince Jr. decided to push the WWF into the bigtime, Backlund's days were numbered." Ironically, by firing Backlund pro wrestling jettisoned one of its last small claims to legitimacy as a sport; Backlund was the 1971 NCAA college wrestling champion.

Like what is going on in the ring, much of what passes for wrestling promotion is pure illusion, too. The new, supposedly broader appeal to higher income, highly educated groups is probably restricted to the New York area, and it may just be the passing fancy of blasé Manhattan thrillseekers. In fact, the manipulation of the media and public sentiment about wrestling may come easily to an industry that has been manipulating what happens within the ring for years. A TitanSports news release from McMahon's headquarters makes this point. It says, "Hulk Hogan exploded into international prominence on January 26, 1984, by beating Iran's feared Iron Sheik for the WWF title," when in fact Hogan became best known to the general public for his role as Thunderlips in the movie Rocky III. This surely gave him more prominence than his match with the Iron Sheik, the much-vaunted, new popularity of wrestling notwithstanding.

No one is sure where all the promotion and hype will end. In 1985, TitanSports was rapidly becoming the next frontier in professional wrestling. Already firmly established in regular cable television programming, WWF wrestling was moving into something called pay-per-view television. In this type of programming, the viewer pays extra for each wrestling program that he sees. (Payment is made by calling a special number or filling out a subscription card in advance.) By mid-1985, numerous pay-per-view wrestling events—dubbed Wrestlemania—were already scheduled for 1986. In news conferences, McMahon went out of his way to assure cable television operators that pay-per-view wrestling was good for their industry; in particular, he quieted their fears that the special shows might be followed by free programming of the same events several weeks later—something that would doom the new program to failure. No one wants to pay for something that he can get for free in just a week or two. The question of whether pay-per-view wrestling will catch on raises the issue of just how much wrestling television audiences will watch. Some observers think it may already be reaching the saturation point, although *Wrestler* editor Bill Apter told *CN* that so far "everything seems to be flourishing pretty well."

In the end, McMahon and the WWF may emerge victorious in the battle between the promoters of professional wrestling. Or perhaps the unprecedented media hype may give a boost to the entire industry and increase everyone's profits. Or it could be that the new look of WWF-style wrestling— including the celebrity fans and the rock connection—may prove to be merely a passing fad. Such is the view of Apter, who suggests that the old-guard, diehard wrestling fans will still be loyal to the old-fashioned, traditional version of the sport long after today's recent converts lapse in their faith. Ultimately, it's possible that the WWF's rivals could emerge even stronger than the WWF, he believes. But it's also possible that the unpredictable McMahon may have a few more bits of promotional wizardry left in his bag of tricks.

SOURCES:

PERIODICALS

Detroit News, July 28, 1985.
Los Angeles Times, March 8, 1985, April 1, 1985.
Newsweek, March 11, 1985.
New York Times, March 14, 1985.
People, May 27, 1985.
Sports Illustrated, September 17, 1984, April 29, 1985.
Texas Monthly, February, 1985.

—Sidelights by Gary Hoffman

Josef Mengele

1911-1979

OBITUARY NOTICE: Born March 16, 1911, in Guenz-burg, Bavaria, Germany (now West Germany); drowned after suffering a stroke while swimming, February 7, 1979, in Bertioga, Brazil; buried in Embu, Brazil; remains were disinterred for medical identification, June 6, 1985. Physician. Mengele became interested in Alfred Rosenberg's theories of Aryan racial superiority while a philosophy student in Munich during the 1920s and later, during his medical studies at the University of Frankfurt am Main, began to formulate his own theories about the possibility of breeding humans to produce a race of Aryan giants.

Mengele enlisted in the German Army in 1939 and joined the Waffen-SS as a medical officer. In 1943, Gestapo chief Heinrich Himmler named Mengele chief medical officer at the Auschwitz-Birkenau concentration camp, where Mengele's duties included determining which incoming prisoners would be assigned to work details and which would be sent to death in the gas chambers. Mengele also devised ghastly medical experiments to perform on the camp's inmates, usually without the benefit of anesthetics. These included the sewing together of children to produce artificial Siamese twins, injecting dye into childrens' eyes to change their eye color, and ripping the limbs from living children. Known as the Angel of Death among the camp's inmates, he is estimated to have been responsible for the deaths of 400,000 people between the time of his arrival at Auschwitz in 1943 and his disappearance in December, 1944.

After World War II Mengele became a prime target for Nazi hunters seeking to bring war criminals to justice. But despite being within the grasp of the Allies several times, Mengele reportedly made his way from a British internment hospital to Rome, where he secured false identity documentation, to South America. Over the course of the next forty years Mengele was the subject of an ongoing manhunt. The search ended in 1985 when an Austrian-born couple, Wolfram and Liselotte Bossert, told Brazilian police that they had sheltered Mengele for several years prior to his death during a swimming holiday in 1979. They said that Mengele had used the cover name Wolfgang Gerhard.

Following disinterment of the remains, a team of international medical and document experts examined the body believed to be Mengele's and compared it to Mengele's service medical records. The team's preliminary report stated that the skeleton unearthed in Brazil was "within a reasonable scientific certainty" that of Mengele. The scien-

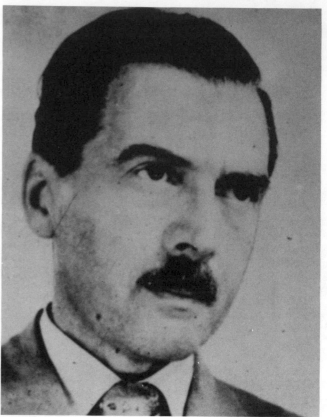

UPI/Bettmann Newsphotos

tific report was backed by handwriting analysis, dental and radiological findings, and the testimony of members of Mengele's family.

SOURCES:

BOOKS

Encyclopedia of the Third Reich, McGraw, 1976.

PERIODICALS

Chicago Tribune, June 19, 1985, June 22, 1985, June 23, 1985, June 30, 1985.
Detroit Free Press, June 12, 1985.
New York Times, June 7, 1985, June 10, 1985, June 11, 1985, June 19, 1985, June 20, 1985, June 22, 1985, June 23, 1985, June 27, 1985.

Sue Mengers

1938-

PERSONAL: Born September 2, 1938, In Hamburg, Germany; brought to United States in 1938; daughter of Eugene (a salesman) and Ruth (a bookkeeper) Sender; married Jean-Claude Tramont (a screenwriter and director), May 5, 1973. *Education*: Attended public schools in New York, N.Y.

ADDRESSES: International Creative Management, 8899 Beverly Blvd., Suite 721, Hollywood, Calif. 90048.

OCCUPATION: Motion picture talent agent.

CAREER: William Morris Agency, New York City, secretary, 1956-61; Music Corporation of America, New York City, 1961-63, began as receptionist, became secretary; Korman & Associates, New York City, talent agent, 1963-68; Creative Management Associates, Los Angeles, Calif., talent agent, 1968-75; International Creative Management Associates (formed by merger of International Famous Agency and Creative Management Associates), Los Angeles, talent agent, 1975—, senior vice-president and co-chairman of department of motion pictures, 1977—.

WRITINGS: Member of editorial board, *Horizon* magazine.

SIDELIGHTS: "Larger than life" is a phrase that is often applied to Sue Mengers. Agent to motion picture superstars and hostess of fabled Hollywood parties, Mengers has acquired a reputation as a highly visible, volatile, tough, and smart businesswoman, able to handle movie-star egos and multi-million-dollar contracts with equal aplomb. A *Time* writer calls her "a throwback to the more flamboyant flesh-peddling days of the studio moguls. At 5 ft. 2 1/2 inches and 160 pounds, usually billowing in a sea of muumuus and caftans, she is sometimes seen as a cross between Mama Cass and Mack the Knife. She has the soft, breathy voice of a little-bitty girl, the vocabulary of a mule-skinner and the subtle approach of a Sherman tank."

In contrast to their popular image as fast-talking wheeler-dealers, Hollywood agents must in reality act as sales people, deal-packagers, legal counsel, best friends, and devil's advocates for the talented—but often neurotic and unpredictable—stars of the big screen. And Sue Mengers represents only the cream of that dream-maker crop, people like Barbra Streisand, Gene Hackman, and Ryan O'Neal, whose names can make or break a motion picture and who earn more for a single film than most people could make in two lifetimes.

Born in Hamburg, Germany, in 1938, Mengers was brought to the United States that same year as her parents fled the Nazi onslaught. Her father committed suicide when she was eleven years old, a fact, she told *Ms.,* that she has "blocked out."

Immediately after graduation from a New York City high school, Mengers joined the staff of the William Morris Agency as a $135-a-week secretary. From there she moved to Music Corporation of America (MCA), where she worked first as a receptionist and later as a secretary. She remained at MCA until 1963 when she and a partner, Tom Korman, formed their own agency, Korman & Associates. In a typically candid statement, Mengers told a *Time* writer, "It dawned on me that I could handle people better than the schmucks in the agency making $100,000."

From the beginning of her career as an agent, Mengers was never shy or subtle in collecting stars for her stable. Story after story has been told in the media about her enthusiasm and her brazen persistence. There's the time she dropped her business card in Tom Ewell's soup at Sardi's, the posh Midtown Manhattan restaurant. She pursued Richard Benjamin and his wife Paula Prentiss even while Prentiss was hospitalized with a nervous breakdown. For eight months, Mengers hounded Tony Perkins, wining and dining him until he finally agreed to sign a contract. And one well-known tale relates the time she pulled up next to Burt Lancaster in traffic, honked her horn, and offered to be his agent. The stories have the glitzy ring of Hollywood hype.

But Mengers, "known around Hollywood as The Hottest Agent in Town" and "the most talked-about woman in the industry," according to *Ms.,* maintains that they are not only true but typical.

Adding to the glamorous, gregarious image are the famous Sue Mengers parties—the Hollywood parties of endless movie-magazine reports, where actors, directors, and writers meet and mingle. Carefully arranged guest lists provide Mengers's clients with the maximum opportunity for meeting the right people. "On a scale of 1 to 10," she told *Time,* "I'd say that entertaining has contributed 5 to my success. It is harder for someone to screw you if they've had dinner at your house."

In addition to the parties at her Beverly Hills *palazzo,* Mengers conducts an incredible amount of business by phone. With fourteen telephones and a WATS line in her home, *Time* says she is able to curse and cajole eighty or more people every day. And she reportedly spent a good deal of her honeymoon "in telephone booths on various Greek islands."

The audience appeal of her dynamic, high-profile lifestyle has not escaped the attention of writers. A character based on Mengers appeared in the 1973 film "The Last of Sheila" and in the Gwen Davis novel *The Pretenders,* while Mengers as Mengers swept through the pages of William Murray's novel *The Dream Girls.*

Mengers, at one time, had ambitions toward the other side of the agent-client relationship. As a child she took elocution lessons, and in her young adult years she had the svelte, sophisticated good looks of an ingenue. But, she told *Ms.,* she changed her mind one day while at an acting class. "Everyone there was better looking and more talented," she recalled. "My practical streak told me, 'There goes that dream.'"

Having established a reputation as an aggressive and effective agent, Mengers left Korman & Associates to join Creative Management Associates (CMA), one of the top firms in the country. In 1975, CMA merged with the International Famous Agency to form International Creative Management, a division of Martin Josephson Associates, Inc. At the time of the merger, rumors circulated that Mengers would leave and join Paramount. This change never materialized, but the thought of losing Mengers made the agency heads more than a little nervous. Freddie Fields, her boss at CMA, and Josephson of International Famous Agency, were reportedly furious over the rumors. She was already a star among agents, and no talent agency likes to lose stars—whether agent or client.

It was while she was at CMA that Mengers met another agent who, along with Fields, is credited with giving her career a boost—David Begelman. When the merger took place, Begelman was Fields's partner and served as agent to Barbra Streisand. But it was not for his expertise as an agent that Begelman found fame. It was later, in 1977, when as studio chief at Columbia Pictures he confessed to improprieties involving $80,000 of company funds that he found notoriety.

In the end, that incident (which became known as the Begelman Affair) was found to be only the tip of the proverbial iceberg as far as questionable Columbia practices went. Eventually there were probes by the Internal Revenue Service and the Securities and Exchange Commission, as well as government investigations into possible ties between the movie industry and organized crime.

Sue Mengers's name was brought into the scandal at least once. Columbia Pictures president Alan Hirschfield told the *New York Times Magazine* that Mengers and producer Ray Stark had tried to use their considerable influence to save Begelman's job by making threats against the studio. They created an atmosphere, said Hirschfield, in which it looked as though "the studio was going to collapse if Begelman didn't get back in. . . . Stark and Mengers started the horror stories. Stark was leaving. . . . Streisand would never sign another picture with Columbia. The atmosphere was: We wouldn't be able to hire anybody. We wouldn't be able to sign any pictures." An indication of Mengers's influence is that Hirschfield, the head of a major studio, felt that she could help create a climate in which "directors would walk. Producers would walk. Stars would walk. The world was coming to an end. There wouldn't be a company left to run."

In 1973, Mengers married screenwriter and director Jean-Claud Tramont whose work includes "Ash Wednesday" and "All Night Long." The latter, directed by Tramont, starred two of his wife's clients, Barbra Streisand and Gene Hackman, and almost cost Mengers her personal and professional relationship with Streisand, according to accounts in *People.*

Streisand was apparently coaxed into taking the role—and second billing to Hackman—as a personal favor to Mengers. Unfortunately, despite the efforts of two such talented actors, "All Night Long" was greeted with primarily lukewarm reviews. Streisand, at a star-studded New York screening party hosted, not surprisingly, by Mengers, was obviously cool and talked to no one but Tramont and Hackman.

Still, most film deals clinched by Mengers have proven tremendously lucrative for her clients. Streisand, for instance, is said to have netted almost $10 million for her 1976 film "A Star Is Born." And, a few years earlier, Mengers had pulled off a coup in starring no less than three of her clients—Peter Bogdanovich, Streisand, and Ryan O'Neal—in the Warner Brothers comedy "What's Up Doc?" It is this deal that Mengers is most proud of, and Warner Brothers president John Calley told *Ms.* that it was "a thirty-five to forty million dollar picture for us. If it hadn't been for Sue there wouldn't have been any picture, and I'm forever grateful to her for it. Without her faith in it when it was an amorphous project, without her ability to keep her clients hanging in there, the whole thing would have gone up in smoke."

An enviable as her glamorous career might seem, Mengers minces no words about her priorities. She told *Cinema* magazine: "My relationship with my husband is the most important facet of my life . . . . My career is a terrifically nice thing that I enjoy a lot, . . . but if I lost my career, my husband could fill the void for me, . . . but if I lost my husband, my career could not replace him."

This attitude has not, however, kept her from becoming one of the most financially successful agents in motion picture history. From her $135-a-week secretarial job in the early sixties, Mengers rose to a solid six-figure income by the middle seventies. And in 1977 *Time* reported her salary at $300,000 plus an additional $40,000 expense account for those all-important parties. With a list of clients that includes such stars as Tatum O'Neal, Cybil Shepherd, Sidney Lumet, Arthur Penn, Nick Nolte, Michael Caine, and Robin Williams, the superagent's fame continues to grow at a record pace, and the sky that is the limit for ordinary mortals may be just another challenge for Sue Mengers.

SOURCES:

PERIODICALS

Los Angeles, December, 1980.
Ms., June, 1975.
New York Times Magazine, February 26, 1978.
People, March 23, 1981.
Time, June 13, 1977.

—Sidelights by Mary Solomon Smyka

Justine Merritt

1924(?)-

BRIEF ENTRY: Born c. 1924. American peace activist. At one time, Justine Merritt's primary goal in life was, in her own words, to be "the perfect wife and mother." Now, writes Mary McGrory of the *Washington Post,* the former school teacher aspires "to needle the mighty of the United States to stop the arms race and rid the world of nuclear weapons." Merritt was the founder and prime motivator of an unusual group called The Ribbon that on August 4, 1985, looped a fifteen-mile-long banner through the streets of Washington, D.C., encircling the Capitol Building and the Pentagon. The giant ribbon consisted of 23,000 cloth panels—each approximately eighteen inches high and thirty-six inches long—that were hand made by people from all fifty states and a dozen foreign countries, including the Soviet Union. Some of the panels were embroidered, others were appliqued, tie-dyed, silk-screened, quilted, woven, or painted; their common theme, according to a *People* magazine report: "What I cannot bear to think of as lost in a nuclear war." Recurrent subjects on many panels were scenes representing home, family, and friends, as well as the word "peace," which appeared in several languages. Other ribbon sections depicted landscapes, sunsets, pets, wild animals, and even picnics complete with ants.

At one time Merritt seemed to be an unlikely peace activist. She graduated from Northwestern University and married her high school sweetheart. They settled in suburban Illinois and raised five children in a house with a two-car garage, four bedrooms, and two baths. McGrory says Merritt joined the PTA and "baked marvelous cakes." But the killing in 1969 of two Black Panthers by Chicago police officers changed her life. "I wondered about the good Germans during the Nazi Reich," she told the *Washington Post* columnist, and she wondered if she, too, was turning her back on problems that called for individual action. She was shocked to realize that she was "living in a world where you can murder two black kids in their beds and life goes on." She quit her suburban teaching job and began working as an unpaid worker in a Chicago social service agency. A year later, she and her husband divorced. She joined a commune and took a job teaching at a Catholic girl's school on the impoverished South Side of the city. Then, in 1975, according to *People,* "she experienced a spiritual awakening." Merritt says she accepted God and became a devout Catholic. She moved to Denver and taught a few courses at the University of Colorado while working as a counselor for juvenile delinquents.

The ribbon, Merritt told a *People* interviewer, "was God's idea." She had been deeply moved by the Peace Memorial Museum, which she had visited on a trip to Hiroshima, Japan, and she was troubled about the effect that a nuclear war would have on her seven grandchildren. "As a little girl," she told the *New York Times,* "I used to tie a string around my finger to remember something," and she thought

AP/Wide World Photos

a ribbon around the Pentagon would serve as a reminder to the country's leaders that people are truly concerned about nuclear war. She sent notes to people on her Christmas card list asking them to contribute sections to the ribbon and to spread the word to people on their own mailing lists. The project mushroomed so that by 1985—the fortieth anniversary of the atomic bombing of Hiroshima—there were enough banners to encircle not only the Pentagon but also the Lincoln Memorial, the Capitol, and the Ellipse behind the White House. The Ribbon of Peace, Merritt told McGrory, was a reminder to the government that "we love babies and butterflies and Mozart, and that all those things would be destroyed in a nuclear war."

SOURCES:

PERIODICALS

New York Times, July 1, 1985.
People, July 8, 1985.
Time, August 19, 1985.
USA Today, August 5, 1985.
Vogue, February, 1985.
Washington Post, August 4, 1985.

Barbara J. Millard

1958-

BRIEF ENTRY: Born 1958. American business executive. When she took over as president and chief operating officer of the ComputerLand Corporation, the nation's largest chain of franchised computer stores, Barbara J. Millard became one of the youngest corporate executives in the country. Appointed president in 1984 by her father, William H. Millard, founder of the privately-held company, Millard was in charge of some 800 retail stores in twenty-five countries with annual sales of $1.5 billion.

ComputerLand was founded in 1976 and was considered at the time to be a risky business venture. The home computer field was small and limited, and it was widely assumed that a store chain catering to that market was doomed to failure. But with the microcomputer boom of the late 1970s came skyrocketing growth for the young company, and ComputerLand emerged as the leader of the computer sales field.

Millard first entered the family business in 1979 as business manager of IMS Associates, the holding company for ComputerLand. In 1982 she was named a vice president of IMS and moved to the presidency in 1983. In November of 1984 her father named her president of ComputerLand Corporation, bypassing "four division presidents who had been with the company much longer," Pauline Yoshihashi reports in the *New York Times.* Although some company executives and franchise owners at the time voiced their private concern that Millard was not qualified for the position, she was confident of her ability to perform well. "I know I can do the job," Yoshihashi quotes Millard as saying, "and I'm ready."

Jeff Reinking/NYT Pictures

But in October, 1985, in a move engineered by disgruntled franchisees, the Millards were forced to relinquish control of ComputerLand to long-time associate Edward E. Faber, a former president of the firm. The franchise holders cited reasons ranging from the Millards' refusal to lower their royalty fees (which varied from 5 percent to 8 percent) to their failure to honor a commitment to sell computer equipment at cost to the dealers. Although the Millard family continues to own more than 95 percent of the company and is expected to be keeping close tabs on Faber, William and Barbara Millard are no longer involved in day-to-day operations.

In spite of this sudden upheaval, there is little likelihood that Barbara Millard will find herself out in the street. As a result of the tremendous success of ComputerLand, the Millards are worth in excess of $500 million, and she is generally regarded as a savvy, experienced business executive with a creditable track record. Still, even though she helped to secure a promising future for ComputerLand, Millard's own position in the company remains tenuous. In a *Los Angeles*

Times interview, however, she commented on a possible return to the presidency: "I don't think it's outlandish reasoning at all. . . . What we agreed [with Faber] was that we didn't know where this would go or how long it would be. He will stay for as long as that's the right thing to do. It's important that the [franchise] network knows that we didn't just put him in there and are waiting in the wings. . . . I will certainly continue to be involved in a substantial way in the family business. I love working with my father and I love business."

SOURCES:

PERIODICALS

Business Week, September 2, 1985, October 14, 1985.
Los Angeles Times, March 31, 1985, October 20, 1985.
New York Times, November 8, 1984, December 16, 1984.
Rolling Stone, March 28, 1985.
Savvy, February, 1985, July, 1985.
Time, October 14, 1985.
Wall Street Journal, November 8, 1984.

Joan Miro

1893-1983

OBITUARY NOTICE: Born April 20, 1893, in Barcelona, Spain; died of heart disease December 25, 1983, in Palma de Mallorca, Spain. In spite of fierce loyalty to his Catalonian roots, Miro was best-known as a member of the French school of surrealistic painters formed in Paris in the 1920s. His paintings, ceramics, tapestries, sculptures, and other creations, variously described as "bizarre," "playful," "spontaneous," and "fanciful" by critics, were testimony to the surrealists' attempts to remove their art from the rational world. But, although characterized as a surrealist throughout his life, Miro insisted on his independence from any group or style. "Yo soy yo," he told a *New York Times* reporter. "Joan Miro is Joan Miro."

The artist's first public showing of his work came in 1918. The following year he visited Paris for the first time where he met compatriot Pablo Picasso. Soon, Miro's name became linked with the innovative art movements of the time: cubism, dadaism, and surrealism. He participated in all the major surrealist exhibitions of the 1930s and regularly contributed to the movement's principal literary organ, *Minautore.* Although, later disenchanted with the group's political and doctrinal leanings, he preserved the surrealists' love of imagination in art in his work for the rest of his life.

The earliest recognition of Miro's talents, outside his friends and relatives, came from Americans, and today U.S. museums house more significant Miros than any other country in the world. During the Franco era in Spain, when the artist was officially ignored in his native country, New York's Metropolitan Museum of Art, in 1941, staged the first Miro retrospective. His work has had considerable influence on many American artists, including sculptor Alexander Calder, and painters Jackson Pollock, Adolphe Gottlieb, and Robert Motherwell. Art critic and historian, Barbara Rose, wrote of this influence in *Miro in America*: "Miro. . . was actually the channel through which the genuinely innovative forms, techniques, and attitudes we identify as 'Surrealist' passed into American art." Several American cities boast monumental outdoor Miro sculptures, including Houston's 55-foot tall "Personage and Birds."

SOURCES:

BOOKS

Rose, Barbara, *Miro in America,* Museum of Fine Arts (Houston), 1982.

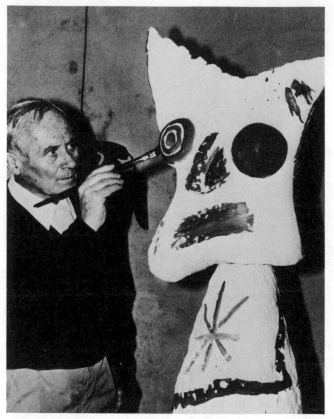

AP/Wide World Photos

PERIODICALS

Chicago Tribune, December 26, 1983.
London Times, December 27, 1983.
Los Angeles Times, December 26, 1983.
Maclean's, January 9, 1984.
Newsweek, January 2, 1984.
New York Times, April 15, 1978, June 2, 1980, June 13, 1982, December 26, 1983.
Time, January 9, 1984.

Issey Miyake

1939-

PERSONAL: Name originally Kazunaru Miyake; born April 22, 1939, in Hiroshima, Japan. *Education*: Attended Tama Art University, Tokyo, Japan, 1959-63, and La Chambre Syndicale de la Couture Parisienne, Paris, France, 1965.

ADDRESSES: Office—3-5-27 Roppongi, Minato-ku, Tokyo, Japan.

OCCUPATION: Fashion designer.

CAREER: Assistant designer for couturiers Guy Laroche, Paris, France, 1966-68, and Hubert de Givenchy, Paris, 1968-69; designer for Geoffrey Beene, New York City, 1969-70; independent designer, 1970—, director of Miyake Design, Issey Miyake & Associates, Miyake On Limits, and Issey Miyake International, all Tokyo, Japan, and Issey Miyake Europe, Paris, and Issey Miyake U.S.A., New York City. Exhibitions of his work have appeared at Seibu Museum of Art, Tokyo, 1977, Musee des Arts Decoratifs, Paris, 1978, Massachusetts Institute of Technology, Cambridge, Mass., 1982, and San Francisco Museum of Modern Art, 1983; permanent collections housed at Metropolitan Museum of Art, New York City, and Victoria and Albert Museum, London, England.

AWARDS, HONORS: Japan Fashion Editors' Club award, 1974; Mainichi Design Prize, 1977; Pratt Institute award for creativity in design, 1979.

WRITINGS: Issey Miyake: East Meets West, edited by Kazuko Koide and Ikko Tanaka, [Tokyo], 1978; *Issey Miyake: Bodyworks*, edited by Shozo Tsurumoti, [Tokyo], 1983.

SIDELIGHTS: Issey Miyake's first name means "one life" in Japanese. And, as if influenced by his name, this internationally-renowned innovator in clothing design displays a remarkable zest and originality in his philosophy and his creations.

After studying art for four years in Tokyo, Miyake set out for the fashion capital of the world—Paris. There he trained in the techniques of couture under famous designers Hubert de Givenchy and Guy Laroche, as assistant designer. Miyake confesses that the ideas behind his original work were formed primarily from the dynamic atmosphere in Paris from 1966 to 1969. Politically active university students in Paris were rebelling against established authority, and the music they listened to reflected their attitude of protest against traditional mores. "Every night, parties! I was so influenced by Janis Joplin, Jimi Hendrix", Miyake told Kennedy Fraser of the *New Yorker*.

© 1983 Eiji Miyazawa/Black Star

Miyake went on to complete his apprenticeship in couture under designer Geoffrey Beene in New York City. He was deeply moved by what he terms the "jeans revolution" brought about by American youth of that era. "Every day I was so *excited*," he recalled to Fraser. "I saw then what it could be—modern life."

"I feel very lucky to have lived when the class system began to crumble, when jeans became the garment for all people," Miyake stated in the *Christian Science Monitor*. "I'm not negative about European couture, but I find clothes of that tradition to be a package that people step into. They are fine and beautiful clothes, but they feel stiff and everyone looks the same in them. . . . I want the body of the wearer, her individuality to make the shape of clothes."

In 1970, Miyake went back to Tokyo to go into business for himself. He worked to develop his own style—a style that would represent modern Japan. "I respect European tradition, but the Europeans do it better," Miyake told Jay Cocks of *Time*. So Miyake drew from his own Japanese tradition. He borrowed the quilted cotton cloth, called *sashiko*, from the Japanese fishermen, farmers, and judo experts. Then he changed the fabric to make it wider, softer, and more sensuous. "It was my denim," Miyake told *Time.*

Miyake also modernized the kimono concept, critics have observed. He took single, rectangular spans of cloth (red silk is one outstanding example) and draped them over his models in freeform fashion. Hilary DeVries noted in the *Christian Science Monitor* that Miyake has raised "the 'wrap and tie' style of dressing beyond mere ethnicity to sophisticated international style that allows the wearer great flexibility." In *Newsweek*, Douglas Davis observed that the designer "opens up space—freedom, in effect for the wearer to reform herself or himself."

Miyake's first Paris show was held in 1973, and he has introduced nearly every collection there since then. But, he stated in the *Christian Science Monitor*, "I hope I am the first and last Japanese designer to have to make my reputation in Paris."

The couturier went on to design cotton jumpsuits reminiscent, in Jay Cocks's view, of *origami*, the traditional oriental art of paper folding. Similarly, Miyake made jerseys out of a ceremonial striped cloth the Japanese used to lead horses. And he transformed the *tanzen*, a Japanese housecoat, into a wool coat with a hood, Cocks reported.

Other Miyake collections have featured "play clothes" such as 1977's boxing trunks and one-piece swim suits with the legs cut high on the thigh. Cover-ups for the latter included skirts, capes, and kimonos. During the same season, Miyake's "bat-winged tops, ballooning pants and loose gauzy dresses, sometimes in two layers," were more "manageable" than in previous years, noted Bernadine Morris in the *New York Times.*

In his 1978 showing, Miyake was "concerned with Japan versus New York," creating "an Oriental view of life in New York City," observed Mary Russell in the *New York Times.* The result was a combination of "kabuki panache and Sony-type organization."

In 1979, Miyake broke tradition and presented his fashions in Milan, Italy, rather than in Paris. Morris commented that Miyake "enlivened things with his Parisian-type presentation." Circumstances brought out his on-the-spot innovative talents when seventeen pairs of pants didn't make it for the show. Miyake simply had the tops modeled over tights. As Morris put it, "the miniskirt was reborn."

The 1980 Miyake collection was shown back in Paris, as were the designs of Claude Montana, Jean Claude de Luca, Castelbajac, Thierry Mugler, and others. Morris wrote in the *New York Times* that "Miyake has style and knows how to make clothes. His show was the best of the day." Morris was not impressed by a "rigid breastplate" of Miyake's design. But she noted that the designer "had some good quilted coats, knitted mini dresses and double tunics of cotton that he meant as dresses. His triangular knee coverings over leg warmers were amusing."

Newsweek writer Jill Smolowe called the Japanese designs of 1982 "bold, flamboyant, even revolutionary. Some are provocative, like Issey Miyake's wool jersey dresses that seem to peel away from the body as a woman moves." Smolowe described Miyake's Issey Sport (now I.S.) collection as "audacious," with inventive combinations like wool and cotton, and the surprise of "magenta zigzags under black flaps."

Miyake's designs for spring, 1984, were called his best up until that time. Featured were "unusual textiles," which included "whisker linen," "cotton embossed by plucking thread," "six-layered woven cotton," and "Japanese paper [raincoat] coated with panlownia oil," reported Hilary DeVries in the *Christian Science Monitor.*

Miyake is regarded as leading the new wave of Japanese designers known as "the Tokyo group." Other members of this coterie include Yohji Yamamoto and Rei Kawakubo, both of design house Comme des Garcons (French for "Like the Boys"). Jenifer Fornaris, who manages a boutique in Rome, told *Newsweek* that this group's "ability, creativity and originality is staggering." Jay Cocks further observed in *Time* that the Japanese designers' clothes "are easy to wear, eccentric only at their most extreme and flattering because they seem to relax around the wearer, not enveloping, containing or constraining the body, but rather exalting its freedom."

Because of the contributions this group has made to the clothing design industry, "Made in Japan" labels on apparel now represent quality rather than mass-production, as they once did, points out Jill Smolowe in *Newsweek.* "Japanese garments have developed a reputation for excellence, from the originality of their fabrics to the durability of their stitchery."

Issey Miyake International is flourishing under the following three labels: Issey Miyake, I.S., and Plantation. The company's gross of $60 million in sales in 1983 represented a 20 percent increase over 1982. In the United States, Miyake's cotton shirts begin at about $50.00. The price tag on a jacket or coat reads around $800.00 (prices quoted in 1983).

Miyake is democratic when it comes to selecting models for his new designs. "I like very much to use real people to show my clothes," Miyake confided to Kennedy Fraser of the *New Yorker.* He often draws from his wide, diverse circle of friends and associates. Whether friends or professional models appear in his shows, Miyake's presentations are "considered unequaled in their theatricality," writes Hilary DeVries in the *Christian Science Monitor.*

The designer himself, however, is a remarkably untheatrical man, thriving in a generally flamboyant milieu. DeVries observed that, dressed in subdued versions of his designs, Miyake "is charming and delightfully unaffected." He has, she said, a "winning personality."

Miyake observed that his idealogy and drive for success developed from the fact that he was born in Hiroshima in the 1930's. "Japan is a very conformist society," he explained in the *Christian Science Monitor.* Miyake and his peers grew up in the "postwar chaos when American and European cultural influences were very great. It hurt me so much not to be proud to be Japanese." It was during this period that Miyake felt compelled to contribute something to the international arena in a way unique and from Japan. "Had I been born 10 or 15 years later, I would not have had as many challenges, but undoubtedly my work would be different," said Miyake.

Designing clothes appears to be not only an expression of idealogy for Miyake, but also of art. He's gifted with an "unparalleled feeling for texture, mass, and volume," noted DeVries in the *Christian Science Monitor*. Critics have likened him to a sculptor, and Miyake himself has said that designing for him is much like "molding clay."

Miyake told Kennedy Fraser of the *New Yorker* that he's "very much influenced by Rauschenberg and Christo as artists—how they think excites me," he said. Commenting about art and the body, Miyake stated: "For me, the body is the most important part of fashion. What I learned in Paris is how the body is beautiful. In Japanese culture, the kimono conceals, transforms the body in a spiritual and philosophical way, makes a package."

But Miyake does not stop with art and philosophy and haute couture. He believes in reaching as many people as he can with his ideas. Miyake innovates for the ready-to-wear market as a way of expressing his democratic views. In addition, he provides new styles of company uniforms and ballet costumes, and he's come out with a line of bed linens.

SOURCES:

PERIODICALS

American Craft, October-November 1983.
Christian Science Monitor, December 15, 1983.
Harper's Bazaar, March 1983.
House and Garden, June 1983.
Metropolitan Home, March 1984.
Newsweek, November 8, 1982, October 17, 1983, April 9, 1984.
New York, March 22, 1982.
New Yorker, December 19, 1983.
New York Times, April 4, 1976, April 6, 1976, October 26, 1976, March 28, 1977, April 10, 1977, October 24, 1977, November 11, 1977, November 27, 1977, April 2, 1978, March 29, 1979, March 31, 1980.
New York Times Magazine, January 30, 1983.
Time, August 1, 1983, October 21, 1985.
Vogue, May 1984.

—Sidelights by Victoria France Charabati

Tom Monaghan

1937-

PERSONAL: Full name, Thomas S. Monaghan; born 1937, in Ann Arbor, Mich.; married Marjorie Zybach, 1962; children: four daughters. *Education:* Attended Ferris State College and University of Michigan. *Religion:* Roman Catholic.

ADDRESSES: Home—Ann Arbor, Mich. *Office*—Domino's Pizza, Inc., 1968 Green Rd., Ann Arbor, Mich. 48105.

OCCUPATION: Businessman.

CAREER: As a teenager, worked at a variety of jobs, including soda jerk, pin spotter at a bowling alley, newspaper circulator, and farm laborer; Dominick's Pizza, Ypsilanti, Mich., co-owner and operator, 1960-65; Domino's Pizza, Ann Arbor, Mich., founder and president, 1965—. Owner of Detroit Tigers Baseball Club, 1983—. Member of board of directors, Michigan National Bank (Ann Arbor), Gelman Sciences, Inc., Clearly College, and WTVS (public television station). Trustee, Michigan Hospitality Industry Political Action Committee. Public speaker; guest lecturer at University of Michigan and Eastern Michigan University. *Military service:* U.S. Marine Corps, 1956-59.

MEMBER: International Franchise Association, National Restaurant Association (member of board of directors).

AWARDS, HONORS: Entrepreneur of the Year award, Harvard Business School of Detroit, 1982; Ph.D., Clearly College, 1982, and Madonna College, 1983.

SIDELIGHTS: Tom Monaghan's forty-four-store pizza business was a long way from being nationally recognized in 1970. Faced with 150 lawsuits and $1 million in debt, he fired most of his executive staff and began rebuilding. That brush with bankruptcy—his fourth—is well behind him now. With more than 1,900 stores, Monaghan's Domino's Pizza is now the second-largest pizza chain in the nation.

Like his hero, the late Ray Kroc, founder of the McDonald's restaurant chain, Monaghan has turned his fast-food success into ownership of a big-league baseball team. In 1983, Monaghan laid down $50 million to buy his boyhood favorites, the Detroit Tigers. A year later, Monaghan's Tigers beat Kroc's San Diego Padres to win the 1984 World Series.

Thus, Monaghan reached one of the goals he had outlined to *Forbes* before the season began: "For the next five years I want to win a pennant, expand this company at a 50 per cent rate, add our 5,000th store and just be an example to others that you can be both honest and successful." Domino's added 700 stores during the year, a 58 per cent increase, and made plans to add an additional 1,000 stores in 1985.

Monaghan showed no early signs of an aptitude for business. His father died when he was four, and Monaghan spent a good portion of his childhood in foster homes, in orphanages, and—as a young teen—on a work farm. He was kicked out of a seminary for "bad behavior"—getting into pillow fights and talking during study hall. After working at a series of odd jobs and a stint in the Marine Corps, Monaghan returned to his hometown of Ann Arbor and enrolled at the University of Michigan. He never finished school.

Instead, in 1960, he borrowed $500 and bought the Dominick's Pizza shop in nearby Ypsilanti with his brother, Jim. After a year, Monaghan traded a 1959 Volkswagen for his brother's portion of the business. With a new partner, Monaghan began expanding—to Ann Arbor and Mt. Pleasant, Michigan, where he met his future wife while making a delivery. By the end of the decade, he had dissolved the Dominick's partnership, founded Domino's, sold the first Domino's franchise, opened a store in Vermont, and toyed with the idea of going public.

In the meantime, Monaghan admits, he learned some lessons. The Dominick's partnership broke up when Monaghan became convinced that his partner was embezzling company funds. And he lost $150,000 in a 1968 Ypsilanti fire because he hadn't paid his fire insurance premiums. Monaghan's biggest jolt, though, came in 1969, when he increased Domino's in size from twelve to forty-four stores in ten months, while trying to catch the eye of Wall Street. In the process, he overloaded Domino's management and lost track of the company's bottom line. Monaghan's bank took over forty-nine per cent of the company, and suppliers filed their lawsuits. Domino's nearly toppled. "I went from being the boy wonder of Ypsilanti to the village idiot," Monaghan told *Newsweek.*

Monaghan regained control of the company by 1971, though, and continued the expansion. By 1975, Domino's had 100 stores and a new problem: a copyright infringement suit from Amstar Corp., makers of Domino Sugar. A five-year battle over the name cost Monaghan $1.5 million and ended when the Supreme Court refused to hear an Amstar appeal of a lower court decision. If Domino's had lost, the chain would be known today as Pizza Dispatch.

With 1,900 stores and 1984 sales of $626 million, Domino's is second only to the Pizza Hut chain (owned by the giant PepsiCo conglomerate), which had 4,450 stores and $1.9 billion in sales in 1984. Among chains that specialize in pizza delivery, Domino's ranks first. Monaghan's own self-discipline—he doesn't drink or smoke, and he jogs five miles and attends church nearly every day—is echoed in the way Domino's does its business. The company ties its success to a promise to deliver a hot pizza within thirty minutes. Domino's also sets a high standard of quality by training franchisees for a year and operating nearly a third of its stores itself.

In early 1985, Domino's secured a $102 million line of credit from nine banks to build 600 additional company-owned stores over the following three years. Other goals include building a store in every U.S. city with a population of more than 10,000. Most early Domino's stores went up in college towns, but now they're being built in residential areas. The company has also announced plans to reach "solid footing" in overseas markets within five years. Domino's currently has stores in the United States, Canada, and Australia.

In a 1984 speech, Monaghan said that running Domino's had become "pretty boring" until he bought the Tigers. When former Tiger owner John Fetzer said it would cost Monaghan between $45 million and $50 million to buy the club, Monaghan immediately offered to pay the higher amount. "I said I don't care what the price is," Monaghan recounted. "I'll pay it." When *Forbes* asked him if the price for the Tigers was too high, Monaghan answered: "No, not for a lifetime dream. There is nothing in this world of a material nature that I wanted more than to own the Detroit Tigers."

Monaghan says he has taken a "non-Steinbrennerian" approach to owning the team. He admits that he's still learning the business and has left most of the operations to the front-office he inherited when he bought the club. In the same manner, he delegates the day-to-day headaches of running Domino's. "People are paid to solve those worries," he told *Forbes.* "People can come to me for advice, but the monkey is on their back."

Monaghan credits baseball with giving him a sudden and invaluable recognition in the business world. A prospering Domino's and the Tigers' World Series victory, however, seem to have put a cap on Monaghan's ambition. "Everything else I've done, I've wanted more," he told *People.* "More pizza stores, a bigger plane, a bigger boat. But now, for the first time in my life, I have something that is the ultimate."

SOURCES:

PERIODICALS

Bay City Times, April 12, 1984.
Forbes, February 13, 1984, October 1, 1984.
Michigan Runner, June, 1984.
Monthly Detroit, April, 1984.
New York Times, June 6, 1984, June 12, 1984.
Newsweek, October 15, 1984.
People, May 7, 1984.
Restaurant Business, January 1, 1984.
Success, August, 1984.
Time, June 25, 1984.

—Sidelights by David Versical

John Moody

1943-

PERSONAL: Born January 15, 1943, in Lorain, Ohio; son of Edward M. (self-employed in school photography business) and Florence (Messmore) Moody; married Vicki L. Wooster; children: James E., Krisan L., Daniel A. *Education:* Attended Cedarville College, Ohio State University, Cleveland State University, and Marquette University.

ADDRESSES: Home—1027 Lochmont Dr., Brandon, Fla. 33511. *Office*—Custom Compactors Corp., 8100 East Broadway, Tampa, Fla. 33519.

OCCUPATION: Mechanical engineer.

CAREER: Worked as a clerk for Texaco Oil Co. and in direct sales; Square D (manufacturing firm), Cleveland, Ohio, designer, 1967-69; P & H (heavy-equipment manufacturing firm), Milwaukee, Wis., 1969-76, began as designer, became development engineer; designer and builder of ultralight aircraft, part time, 1974-76; Ultralight Flying Machines of Wisconsin, Milwaukee, president and development engineer, 1976-84; Custom Compactors (manufacturer of trash compactors and bailing equipment), Tampa, Fla., director of research and development, 1984—.

Courtesy of John Moody

SIDELIGHTS: On March 15, 1975, above a frozen lake southwest of Milwaukee, John Moody, then a thirty-two-year-old engineer, made aviation history by flying a device that looked a little like a noseless and tailless biplane about thirty feet above the ice. As beginnings go, it was a rather inauspicious start of a new form of aviation. But the history of aeronautics is full of inauspicious beginnings that developed into great things. The experience of the Wright brothers, two little-known bicycle makers, along the desolate North Carolina coast is probably the best example of this.

By purely technical standards, it is not easy to define exactly where Moody fits into aviation history. He was not the first person to pilot a hang glider. He was not even the first person to fly a hang glider that had independent propulsion. A Californian named Bill Bennett had earlier strapped a power pack onto his back and had managed to extend his hang glider's long graceful glides by a few thousand feet or so. But Moody was the first person to develop a powered hang glider that could be launched from flat terrain, without benefit of wind, with the pilot merely running along with it until it became airborne. In a sense, what he did was make it possible for man to fly almost like a bird. A *Popular Science* writer put it this way: "If you have ever dreamed, as everyone has, of leaping into the air, circling and soaring like a hawk, and landing on your feet as lightly as thistledown, then John Moody's Ultralight Flying Machine (a hang glider with a motor) may be for you."

John Moody's contribution to aviation is now universally known as the ultralight, and, in a way, it represents a revolution in the philosophy of aeronautics. Almost from its inception, aviation has been basically a business. And it only took a few short years for this enterprise to be taken from inventor-adventurers like the Wright brothers and turned over to governments and businesses to be used for military and commercial purposes. Even today, private planes are expensive enough that relatively few people can afford them for purely recreational purposes. But Moody ushered in the era of the recreational flying machine. Indeed, ultralights are often called ARVs, or air recreational vehicles. In a sense, they are the airborne cousins of snowmobiles, dirt bikes, and all-terrain vehicles.

It was an innovation that was a long time coming. For years, the dream of recreational flight had occupied the thoughts of backyard tinkerers and inventors. One sign of this is the fact that magazines like *Popular Science* and *Popular Mechanics* had long carried articles on do-it-yourself airplanes, known as homebuilts. But these, too, could be expensive, and their pilots had to comply with a whole series of Federal Aviation Administration (FAA) regulations. They certainly did not offer the freedom that ultralights would: the ability to store your plane in a garage and carry it to your take-off point in the back of a station wagon, to feel the wind in your face and along your body, to maneuver in spaces small enough to almost challenge the birds themselves.

Moody's involvement with hang gliders and ultralights came as a result of his speculation about the possibility of human muscle-powered flight. During the early seventies, then an engineer with a Milwaukee manufacturing company, Moody wondered what it would take to win the £50,000 Kremer Prize. This award, eventually won by the now-famous Gossamer Condor, was put up by a British industrialist; it was to be given to the first person to build a human-powered aircraft that could navigate a figure-eight course around two pylons a half mile apart.

To help him understand flight, Moody wanted to fly—or at least glide—himself, and so he took up hang gliding. But he ran into trouble almost immediately. The topography of Wisconsin was not very well suited to hang gliding. In an article in *Sport Aviation* magazine, Moody described his problem humorously: "A hill that looks usable a mile away, invariably, when you get up to it, has six fences across its face, a resident herd of ten bulls who have not seen a cow in six months, and has 150 acres of briars at its base." To the serious flyer, the problem was not a joke; Moody and others did not enjoy traveling hundreds of miles to hang glide, only to find the weather conditions unsuitable.

Once again, necessity gave birth to invention. During the winter of 1974-75, Moody put a ten horsepower go-cart engine on an Icarus II hang glider. The entire package weighed only ninety pounds, including about three quarts of fuel. It could be flown under power for about thirty minutes and actually could spend much more than that amount of time aloft, because the pilot could cut off the engine and soar as high as 2,000 feet—heights most hang glider pilots could only dream of.

To the laymen who witnessed Moody's early flights, the ultralight must have seemed a strange bird indeed. From a distance, it looked like a box kite or a mutilated biplane. Up close, one could see that the pilot sat between the wings with his legs pulled up. *Popular Science* writer E.F. Lindsey once witnessed a take-off. Moody ran with the ninety-pound device suspended on his lower back, starting with a heavy jog and ending with a kind of tiptoed prance as the ultralight became airborne. Then he climbed at the rate of perhaps 125 feet per minute, eventually levelling off at 1000 feet or so above the ground. This was the fun part, according to Moody. "Once you get to altitude and turn the motor off," he told Lindsey, "with the sky unfolding around you, and with the air whispering past wings so close they seem extensions of your arms, there is really nothing like the thrill."

John Moody takes off in his Easyriser ultralight aircraft. Courtesy of John Moody.

Moody maintains that ultralights are far safer than hang gliders. For one thing, he says, hang gliders usually take off from great heights. The ultralight, by contrast, takes off slowly and steadily from the ground, and at any point in the take-off, the pilot can settle back to earth comfortably. For another thing, the cliffs, hilltops and mountainsides that hang gliders frequently use for take-off, often have very rugged terrain—and sometimes water—at their bases. Landing in such spots is tricky, to say the least. But the ultralight pilot can choose the landing site that suits him. In all, these differences are said to make ultralights a great deal safer to use.

With the help of an instruction book entitled *Stick and Rudder*, by Wolfgang Langewiesche, Moody taught himself to fly—something he believed most people were capable of. "A person can teach himself to fly if he is of average intelligence and exercises extreme caution," he wrote in an article in the February, 1976, issue of *Sport Aviation*. That was Moody the rugged individualist. Since that time, he has tempered his earlier opinion and now recommends that any ultralight pilot take formal flight training from an FAA licensed instructor.

Like Moody, the FAA has modified its view over the years and now takes a more lenient stance toward ultralight craft than it originally did. But in the early days, Moody found himself frequently at odds with the FAA. When he first started flying his Icarus II, he discovered that federal authorities considered ultralights to be planes, not hang gliders, and took steps to regulate them as full-fledged aircraft. Moody regarded this as an intrusion of the federal bureaucracy. Had he had sufficient funds, he would have taken the FAA to court. Instead, he grudgingly registered as a student pilot and kept the required student log during his early flying period. But he rallied against the FAA policy whenever he got a chance. In the *Sport Aviation* article, he said: "The vast majority of pilots interested in this type of aircraft will be interested in only relatively low-altitude local sport flying as far away from other air traffic as possible. Who wants to be flying between twenty and fifty miles per hour in the traffic pattern of an airport?" As for the flight instruction, Moody wrote, "I would like to meet the FAA licensed instructor who is genuinely experienced and competent to instruct using a powered tailless hang glider."

While he was dueling with the FAA, Moody's ultralight hobby was rapidly becoming a business. One of his early attempts to promote his new product is destined to go down in aviation history as a classic publicity stunt. In 1976, he contacted Lindsey, a regular contributor to *Popular Science*, and offered to demonstrate the ultralight by landing the craft in a vacant lot across the street from the writer's house. The initial response of Lindsey and his editors was cool. "My commercial aviation background told me that bird-like flight with so little horsepower was unlikely at best," Lindsey wrote. Moody, though, was able to quiet Lindsey's fears, in part by citing some of the powered ultralight's advantages over hand gliders. Finally, Lindsey and the editors consented to Moody's demonstration. In the subsequent *Popular Science* article, Lindsey described the event: "Moody left his local airport after work one evening, flew about twenty miles, landed and refueled at another airport, and appeared over my house at about 2,000 feet, sounding like a chainsaw in orbit and circling with the grace and freedom of an eagle." Minutes later, he made his landing in front of the writer's home.

Needless to say, the article created a windfall for the young engineer. All of a sudden his part-time business was too much for him to handle, so he began manufacturing and marketing ultralights full time. Soon he stopped using the Icarus II hang glider as the basis for his ultralight and started employing another model, dubbed the Easy Riser. It featured an improved airfoil, stronger spars, and easier assembly.

During the seventies, Moody was a frequent performer at airshows. Once he covered 101 miles without refueling, setting a new record. Another time, he narrowly averted catastrophe when he flipped his ultralight and succeeded in righting it just fifty feet above the ground. The novelty of the ultralight, and Moody's exploits, made photographs of him and his machines a common sight in magazines and books. But eventually other, bigger, companies entered the field, and ultralights gradually became more complex, heavier, and were fitted with more sophisticated control systems and landing gear. "They've probably become easier to fly and more forgiving of errors" than the early models, Moody told *CN*. But new ultralights now run between $5,000 and $10,000, and, to the dismay of Moody and other enthusiasts, that cost is prohibitive to the citizen-pilot for whom the ultralights were originally intended. A combination of factors, including increased competition from larger manufacturers and a number of lawsuits, forced Moody out of the ultralight business by 1984.

John Moody is now director of research and development for a manufacturer of trash compactors and bailing equipment in Tampa, Florida, but he harbors few regrets about his experience with ultralights. His place in aviation history is assured. Luis Marden, in a *National Geographic* article, proclaims Moody "the Orville Wright of the new era" in aviation. Moody told *CN* that he still thinks about breaking new ground in the field of aeronautics and often returns to his dreams about human-powered flight. But he insists that his ideas have little in common with the Rube Goldberg-style contraptions of popular conception. Rather, he thinks of the flight of birds and envisions mechanical systems wherein "the movement of lifting surfaces provides the propulsion."

If Moody ever does return to aeronautics he may once again surprise the aviation industry with a still more simple, even lighter aircraft. Ultralight builder John Lasko told Marden that the designer's goal is "to reduce human flight to its essence," to get as close as possible to flying like a bird, rather than flying inside a machine. Moody sees his own pioneer contribution to this effort in the most basic terms. As he commented to Marden, "I didn't mean to reinvent the airplane, I wanted to fly and have fun."

SOURCES:

PERIODICALS

Christian Science Monitor, August 12, 1982.
Model Airplane News, August, 1983.
National Geographic, August, 1983.
People, November 1, 1982.
Popular Science, December, 1976, April, 1984.
Reader's Digest, April, 1983.
Sport Aviation, February, 1976.

—Sidelights by Gary Hoffman

William Penn Mott, Jr.

1909-

BRIEF ENTRY: Born October 19, 1909, in New York, N.Y. American landscape architect, conservationist. Considered an aggressive and dedicated conservationist, William Penn Mott, Jr. was named director of the National Park Service in June of 1985. His appointment has been widely praised by environmentalists, who applaud his theory of parks management, which was quoted by Stephen Labaton in the *Washington Post:* "When in any doubt, we must err on the side of preservation." Mott began his Park Service career in 1933—following training in landscape architecture at Michigan State University and the University of California, Berkeley—during the administration of Franklin D. Roosevelt. In 1967, Ronald Reagan, then governor of California, appointed Mott chief of that state's Parks and Recreation Department. By the end of Reagan's seven-year tenure, Mott had doubled the size of California's park system and substantially increased its revenues.

The current Reagan Administration hopes that Mott will be equally successful on a national level. The country's 337 federally owned parks, monuments, and historical sites are plagued by overcrowding and pollution. According to the U.S. Census Bureau, the number of parks visitors has more than doubled since 1960. Mott plans to impose direct limits on the number of visitors to each park. "Cattlemen know how many cattle you can graze on an acre of land without lasting damage," he explains to T.R. Reid of the *Washington Post.* "It's called 'carrying capacity.' Well, we've got to know the carrying capacity of our parks and start saying, 'After this, nobody gets in this weekend.'" The parks are also understaffed and underfunded. To combat this, Mott wants to double park entrance fees (currently, the admission to Yellowstone for one family for seven days is two dollars) and levy a five-dollar charge on fishing licenses (which have heretofore been free in national parks). He would also place greater restrictions on land and industrial developments at park borders. In addition, Mott has proposed that the Park Service acquire more land.

Mott has his work cut out for him, according to observers. The fiscal budget for 1986 calls for a 30 percent reduction in parks funding; congress regularly vetoes efforts to raise park entrance fees. Mott will also have to battle park concessionaires, who oppose his plans to limit visitors, as well as developers and industry. Nevertheless, Mott remains optimistic, believing that he will win public support. Vacationers journey to the nation's parks in search of a "quality outdoor experience," he told Reid. "When you've got so many people

© *Katherine Lambert, 1985*

in Yosemite that the roads look like the Golden Gate Bridge at rush hour and there's more smoke than in the heart of the city, that's not what people are coming to our parks for." *Address:* National Park Service, Department of the Interior, Washington, D.C. 20240.

SOURCES:

PERIODICALS

Business Week, July 8, 1985.
Newsweek, September 2, 1985.
Parade, November 24, 1985.
USA Today, August 23, 1985.
Washington Post, June 3, 1985, June 8, 1985, June 9, 1985, June 14, 1985.

Brent Musburger

1939-

PERSONAL: Born May 26, 1939, in Portland, Ore.; son of C.C. (in appliance retailing and sheep ranching) and Beryl Ruth (Woody) Musburger; married Arlene Clare Sandler, June 8, 1963; children: Blake, Scott. *Education,* Northwestern University, B.J., 1962.

ADDRESS: *Home*—Weston, Conn. *Office*—CBS Sports, 51 West 52nd St., New York, N.Y. 10019.

OCCUPATION: Sports broadcaster.

CAREER: Professional umpire, Midwest Baseball League, 1959; *DeKalb Chronicle,* DeKalb, Ill., sports editor, 1960; *Chicago American,* Chicago, Ill., copy editor, 1961, sports columnist, 1962-68; WBBM Radio and Television, Chicago, sports director, 1968-74; CBS Sports, New York City, television and radio sportscaster, 1974—, host and managing editor of "NFL Today," host of "Sports Time," "NCAA Today," and "Saturday/Sports Sunday," 1981—. Sports director, KNXT Television, Los Angeles, Calif., 1979-81. *Military service:* U.S. Army, 1960.

AWARDS, HONORS: Named Illinois Sportscaster of the Year by National Association of Sportswriters and Sportscasters, 1971, 1974.

SIDELIGHTS: Brent Musburger is one of the major figures in American commercial television sportscasting in the last quarter of the twentieth century. In 1984, *Sports Illustrated* estimated that Musburger appeared on national television about 275 hours (more than eleven full days) a year. When he signed a new, five-year contract with CBS Sports in December of 1984, the Associated Press reported Musburger's salary to be an estimated $2 million per year, which made him one of America's highest-paid journalists.

Musburger, in addition to hosting pre-game, half-time, and post-game shows for National Football League games on CBS, is also a basketball play-by-play announcer, college football play-by-play announcer, and golf announcer for the Masters Tournament on CBS-TV, as well as a CBS Radio sportscaster. He is a lean man with a full head of hair and bright, even teeth who appears to be somewhat younger than his age. Musburger is one of a small number of "star" television journalists who began their careers as newspaper reporters.

Musburger has always been very confident of his abilities to report and to perform. In 1977, on a visit to Chicago, he told the *Chicago Sun-Times:* "I like to know what's going on. I'd make a great gossip columnist. Every word I say I still believe. I can do anything in sports. I don't worry about images. I've got money in the bank. And I've got the hot hand." Eight years later, he explained his method. "The money doesn't motivate me as much as the competitive

nature of the business," Musburger told the *Richmond Times-Dispatch.* "We have standings in our business, and I'm very upset when we lose. I want to win. Whether ratings are right or wrong, they're the only standings we have to go by, . . . and I really get geared up when we go head to head."

Musburger began in the print medium and moved first to radio and then to television. The story of his debut in radio would, in some minds, fit the image of Chicago reporters, a partially-true stereotype that became secure in the public mind from movies such as "Front Page." Chicago reporters, it is said, often resort to unorthodox methods when aboveboard pursuits are thwarted or unavailable.

According to a story in *Sports Illustrated,* Musburger was working full-time for his newspaper and part-time for WBBM Radio in Chicago, which needed someone to cover the 1968 Olympics in Mexico City. Musburger, *Sports Illustrated* wrote, went as an imposter, pretending to be *Sports Magazine* editor Al Silverman, who hadn't gone to the games and whose credential wasn't being used. When American sprinters John Carlos and Tommie Smith made their famous black-power salute with clenched fists on the medal stand during the playing of the "Star-Spangled Banner," Musburger reached them afterward in an area that was supposed to be off-limits to the media. Musburger got twelve minutes of tape that aired across the country. Soon, he was out of the print journalism business and on to bigger things.

Musburger's career has been aided in a large part by Van Gordon Sauter, a CBS News executive who became attracted to Musburger's style when Musburger was a newspaper writer in Chicago in the mid-to-late 1960s. Sauter, who chose Musburger for major positions as a news anchor at a CBS station in Los Angeles and as managing editor for the CBS Sports national television network, says Musburger prevails for two reasons. "First, and perhaps most important, he's an excellent journalist," Sauter said in a telephone interview for *Contemporary Newsmakers.* "His column in *Chicago American* had an edge. It had an immediacy had it had a consumer attitude way before it became popular. Brent was an advocate for the fan in those days. Most sports columns then spoke to sports from the point of view of the participant. Brent has a tremendous energy level. He is 'up,' he is informed, and he has authority. He's very articulate. It was these same qualities that made Brent an excellent news anchor."

When Musburger's contract with CBS neared its end in 1984, he was approached by rival network ABC. Musburger chose to stay with CBS at the advice of Sauter and others. "I didn't enter the negotiation process, but I called Brent in a fairly unsolicitous fashion," Sauter said. "I gave him my perception of the situation. I did it as a friend and not a company person."

Musburger's greatest visibility is through "NFL Today," which he has hosted in a studio since 1975 with various co-workers. (The show "wraps around" NFL games, telecast regionally in most major markets, and is hosted from a CBS studio in New York City.) Musburger hasn't always gotten along well with co-workers off-camera. A *Sports Illustrated* story in 1984 quoted Musburger as saying that unprepared co-workers "drive you up a wall. . . . . If you want to deal with me directly in that studio, you better be ready. If they say something that's really stupid, yeah, I come unglued on 'em. I get very rude. I can become very nasty."

Although Musburger has shown great ability in the role of studio host for a variety of CBS Sports programming, he has also displayed a certain irritability that may have come with the "cabin fever" of working indoors, away from the big events CBS is telecasting. That is why, midway through his forties he elected in a new contract to get back to the live coverage of events at the scene. "I was getting irritable, yelling at people, making demands, being a big gorilla," he told the *Washington Post.* "It's so demanding mentally. I decided I had to get back on the outside." In the same interview, Musburger said he had become aware of a viewers' perception that announcers talk too much. "I pay attention to criticism," Musburger said, "and everybody I heard was saying that people talk too much on the air. The same thing was striking me. So you talk less. Then when you say something, it means so much more."

Although the trend in sportscasting has been toward ex-players describing action into microphones, Musburger has little active sports experience, outside of his brief umpiring career and his amateur participation in racquetball and swimming. Gary Bender, a CBS sportscaster whose job assignments have been reduced by Musburger's increased duties, said in *TV Guide* that Musburger "is the Joe Namath of broadcasting. He's opened the door for the non-jock play-by-play guys to get into some big money. I think the whole affair [Musburger's big contract] makes network executives begin to think a little harder."

Although many former athletes do indeed find jobs as television sportscasters, there are also many non-athletes populating the broadcast booths. Perhaps the most famous of them is Howard Cosell, a broadcaster for ABC Sports who curtailed his duties greatly in 1984. Musburger told the *Roanoke Times* that he spoke with Cosell at a football game in 1984 and that Cosell asked him, "You still like these games? Don't you see what these really are?" According to Musburger, he told Cosell: "Howard, I could never get that bitter. The day I do, I'm gonna leave it. Of course, I know this isn't important in the overall scheme of things, whatever happens between the Giants and the 49ers or whoever. But, come on, what else do we have to look forward to?"

Musburger has developed an off-the-job personality that is in sharp contrast to his on-air image, which is that of a straight-laced, clean-cut, no-nonsense announcer. He has been involved in two celebrated public fist fights in his career. The first came in 1967 in the press box at Chicago's Comiskey Park. The other party in the altercation was Tom Fitzpatrick, then a Chicago sportswriter. It took place, Musburger told *Contemporary Newsmakers,* after he and Fitzpatrick had agreed to "gang up" on Eddie Stanky, then the manager of the White Sox. Stanky eventually asked for a private meeting with Musburger. During that meeting, Musburger says, he and Stanky decided to deal with each other as individuals. When Fitzpatrick became aware of the agreement, Musburger says, he turned around and insulted Musburger from the front row of the Comiskey Park press box. "Fitz thought I'd double-crossed him," Musburger recalled. "Fitz threw a punch at me and I threw him down and landed a few punches. All hell broke loose."

A better-known fight came in 1980 after a long day working in the CBS studios in New York on the "NFL Today" show. Musburger, host of the show, had curtailed the air time of co-performer Jimmy "The Greek" Snyder. After the show, the two men were drinking in a New York saloon called Peartrees. According to *Sports Illustrated*, Snyder hit Musburger with a glancing blow to the jaw. "My first reaction was, I'm not going to work with this guy again as long as I live," Musburger told *Sports Illustrated.* "But then I cooled off."

The next week, after much newspaper publicity, he and Snyder appeared on camera wearing boxing gloves. It was a theatrical stunt that illustrated a growing trend in Musburger's medium: even the most "straight" reporters had become "stars." Newspapers had covered the Snyder-Musburger fights as if it has involved two major athletes or entertainers.

This coincided with the biggest change in American journalism in the third quarter of the twentieth century, a shift in the strength of the media from print journalism to the "electronic media" of radio and television, especially television. While radio had been a market and opinion force, along with newspapers, from early in the century until after World War II, commercial television didn't become a force in American life until the late 1940s. And it wasn't until the 1960s that television assumed a major role in professional and major college spectator sports.

Musburger says many of the colleagues he left behind in the print business resented the changes in their business and its increasingly subordinate role. "The thing I perceived and, unfortunately, I was right, was that afternoon papers would have a terrible time with distribution because of the traffic snarls" in expanding metropolitan areas, Musburger told *Contemporary Newsmakers.* (In Chicago, Musburger worked for an afternoon paper that went out of business after he left.)

"I always felt the major morning paper would thrive. I turned out to be right. For immediacy, you couldn't beat TV. I knew a lot of writers who wanted to put TV down. I didn't want to continue to beat my head against the wall. I've watched newspapers do this. They haven't come around to realizing TV created more readers, it did not drive them away. The success of the *USA Today* sports section proved that. Less opinion, more fact. Those people [running *USA Today*] have looked toward television, not shied away from it. I pick up a lot of papers. The only thing I see now is rambling opinion of sports writers. As a group, they have gotten away from basic information."

Musburger went on to criticize newspapers for printing gambling information, not on an ethical question, but saying that many young children read sports sections and they don't read them for gambling information. "I think a percentage of the football fans make bets," he said. "But I don't think little kids follow it because of betting." Musburger said, "I'll be damned" if he would agree with the pre-game, football-telecast approach of a rival network, NBC, which gives much more explicit gambling information and opinions than does CBS.

Musburger makes it a point to keep informed about all aspects of sports and sports reporting, but sometimes he finds this difficult to do. He laughed as he told *Contemporary Newsmakers* the story of one such frustration. He was assigned to cover the National Collegiate Athletic Association (NCAA) basketball tournament in the late winter of 1985. Although many of the games were televised on cable stations, Musburger was unable to get cable service in his home because his local cable company ran out of money before it had run the necessary utility wires on his street. And he couldn't receive the games on a satellite dish antenna because the large number of trees on his Connecticut property made the installation of such a dish impossible. Thus, lacking a cable hookup and a satellite dish, Musburger said, "I have to go to a saloon [equipped for cable reception] to do my homework."

SOURCES:

PERIODICALS

Chicago Sun-Times, January 23, 1977.
New York Times, August 24, 1982, May 17, 1983, December 4, 1984.
Richmond Times-Dispatch, January 11, 1985.
Roanoke Times, January 12, 1985.
Sports Illustrated, September 14, 1981, January 16, 1984.
TV Guide, January 19, 1985.

—Sketch by Joe LaPointe

Lloyd Nolan

1902-1985

OBITUARY NOTICE: Full name, Lloyd Benedict Nolan; born August 11, 1902, in San Francisco, Calif.; died of lung cancer, September 27, 1985, in Los Angeles, Calif. Stage, screen and television actor. For over fifty years in the entertainment industry, Lloyd Nolan distinguished himself as an "actor's actor," though formal recognition often eluded him. In 1927, after studying English at Stanford University for three years, Nolan dropped out of school to study acting, and he began his theatrical career by appearing in plays by Shakespeare and Ibsen at the Pasadena Playhouse. Ending up in New England after touring with a production of "The Front Page," he took a job as a stagehand while awaiting his next acting job, which came in 1929 with his Broadway debut in a production of "Cape Cod Follies." He toured briefly in a series of plays before returning to the New York stage as an office boy in "Sweet Stranger," in which he met his first wife, actress Mell Efrid. In 1934 after performing in several Broadway plays, he left for Hollywood with a contract from Paramount Studios in hand.

For the next twenty years, debuting in 1934 with "Stolen Harmony," Nolan made more than seventy films, most notably "Bataan," "Guadalcanal Diary," "A Tree Grows in Brooklyn," "The House on 92nd Street" and "Peyton Place." Though he often found himself acting in "B" movies, usually playing a gangster or cop, he was always credited with giving "A" performances. Formal recognition finally came for his portrayal of Captain Queeg in "The Caine Mutiny Court Martial," for which he won the New York Drama Critics award as outstanding actor in 1954 and an Emmy, the only national award he ever received, in 1955 for the television adaptation of this play. Theatre critic Brooks Atkinson found "Nolan's portrait of fear, desperation and panic a stunning piece of work," but praise such as this was ignored when it came time to put Queeg's insanity on film; the movie role was awarded to Humphrey Bogart.

Living in California with his wife and two children, Nolan's reputation allowed him the luxury of turning down work, a privilege usually bestowed on better-known stars. Though threatening retirement many times, he was easily persuaded to take on new projects. From 1968-1972 he portrayed Dr. Morton Chegley in one of television's first black-oriented programs, "Julia," starring Diahann Carroll. While continuing to act in films, such as "Ice Station Zebra," "Airport" and "Earthquake," Nolan devoted a great deal of time to the

UPI/Bettmann Newsphotos

annual Autistic Children's Telethon, of which he was chairman. In 1972 he finally revealed that his son, Jay, had been diagnosed as autistic and that much of his earnings went to establish a Jay Nolan Autistic Center in Saugus, Calif.

SOURCES:

PERIODICALS

Chicago Tribune, September 29, 1985.
London Times, September 30, 1985.
Los Angeles Times, September 28, 1985.
Newsweek, October 7, 1985.
New York Times, September 29, 1985.
Time, October 7, 1985.

Robert N. Noyce

1927-

PERSONAL: Full name, Robert Norton Noyce; born December 12, 1927, in Burlington, Iowa; son of Ralph B. (a Congregational minister) and Harriet (Norton) Noyce; married Elizabeth Bottomley, 1953 (divorced, 1974); married Ann S. Bowers (personnel director of Intel Corp.), 1975; children: (first marriage) William B., Pendred, Priscilla, Margaret. *Education:* Grinnell College, B.A., 1949; Massachusetts Institute of Technology, Ph.D., 1953.

ADDRESSES: Home—Los Altos, Calif. *Office*—Intel Corp., 3200 Lakeside Dr., Santa Clara, Calif. 95051.

OCCUPATION: Scientist, inventor, and business executive.

CAREER: Philco Corp., Philadelphia, Pa., research engineer, 1953-56; Shockley Semiconductor Laboratory, Mountain View, Calif., research engineer, 1956-57; Fairchild Semiconductor, Mountain View, founder, director, 1957-59, vice-president and general manager, 1959-65; Fairchild Camera and Instrument, Mountain View, group vice-president, 1965-68; Intel Corp., Santa Clara, Calif., founder, president, 1968—, chairman, 1968-75, vice-chairman, 1979—.

Holder of numerous patents in semiconductor device physics; co-inventor of the integrated circuit and inventor of planar process for the manufacture of transistors. Member of board of directors, Rolm Corp., Santa Clara, and Diasonics, Inc., Milpitas, Calif; member of President's Commission on Industrial Competitiveness. Trustee of Grinnell College, 1962—; regent, University of California, 1982—.

MEMBER: National Academy of Engineering, Institute of Electrical and Electronics Engineers (fellow), Semiconductor Industry Association (former chairman).

AWARDS, HONORS: Stuart Ballantine Medal, Franklin Institute, 1967; Harry Goode Award, American Federation of Information Processing Societies, 1978; Cledo Brunetti Award and medal of honor, Institute of Electrical and Electronics Engineers, 1978; National Medal of Science presented by the president of the United States, 1979; Faraday Medal, Institute of Electrical and Electronics Engineers, 1979; Harold Pender Award, University of Pennsylvania, 1980.

SIDELIGHTS: With his invention of the integrated circuit, Robert Noyce helped usher in the age of the computer. Changing forever the lives of millions, his minuscule invention revolutionized nearly every field of engineering and made possible space travel, microcomputers, digital watches, pocket calculators, home computers, robots, and missile guidance systems. He witnessed the birth of the Silicon Valley, which he saw transformed from orchards of

© Chuck O'Rear

pears and apricots to the center of daring entrepreneurship and innovation that *Electronics Week* noted "claims to be the home of more electronics companies than any other. . . [place] in the world." Noyce, sometimes called the mayor of Silicon Valley, founded two of those electronics firms, Fairchild Semiconductor and Intel Corporation, whose defected offspring helped populate the valley. At Fairchild and Intel Noyce oversaw the development of landmark discoveries in the field of high technology. Today, he is seen as an elder statesman of an industry not yet thirty years old.

As a student at Grinnell College in Iowa in the 1940s, Noyce was one of the first persons to study the newly developed transistor. Invented by William Shockley, John Bardeen, and Walter Brattain in 1947 at the Bell Laboratory, the transistor (a shortened form of the phrase "transfer resistance") replaced the cumbersome vacuum tube as a semiconductor and controller of a flow of electrons. It opened up the new field of solid-state electronics. After graduating from Grinnell, Noyce studied at the Massachusetts Institute of Technology, where he earned his doctorate with the dissertation *Photoelectric Study of Surface States on Insulators.* Noyce, a promising young talent in the field, was offered jobs in the research facilities of General Motors, Bell

Telephone Laboratories, RCA, and IBM, but he chose Philco, because, as he laughingly explained to the *New York Times*, "they needed me." The other major companies already "knew what they were doing."

The opportunities Noyce thought Philco offered, however, did not materialize. Philco wanted to build transistors that were of the same caliber as those manufactured at the other large corporations; it was not interested in funding research for further development. Dissatisfied, Noyce resigned after two years and joined the Nobel Prize winner, Shockley, at his newly created firm, Shockley Semiconductor Laboratory, in Palo Alto, California. Noyce explained to Victor K. McElheny of the *New York Times* that he went with Shockley because he "wanted to play in the big leagues."

Shockley had assembled a dozen young Ph.D.s in electrical engineering to research and develop better transistors and diodes. Each day his "Ph.D. production line," as he called his group of young scientists, baked germanium and silicon in kilns to create crystals that could be cut into slices that would then be wired together to create transistors. Shockley offered the young men a chance to do the research they wanted, but before long they grew dissatisfied with the way they were treated by the Nobel Prize laureate. Shockley's management techniques jarred his employees. He published their salaries on a bulletin board and instituted a system in which the scientists regularly rated each other on their work performance. Noyce told McElheny that Shockley sapped his motivation when, after reporting an important result from the laboratory, Shockley called his former co-workers at the Bell Laboratory "to check if I was right." However, it was when Shockley, convinced that a saboteur was operating within his firm, used a lie detector on one of the men that seven of the scientists decided to leave and form their own company.

The seven, Noyce not among them, approached the Wall Street firm of Hayden Stone for the funding they needed to start their business. The man they talked to, Art Rock, felt they lacked a leader. Before he would help them, they would have to find someone to serve as the administrator. The seven turned to Noyce as the natural choice. At only twenty-nine years old, Noyce demonstrated the necessary air of authority. Tom Wolfe described it in *Esquire:* "Bob Noyce projected what psychologists call the halo effect. People with the halo effect seem to know exactly what they're doing and, moreover, make you want to admire them for it. They make you see the halos over their heads." With Noyce on board, Rock approached twenty-two prospective backers before Fairchild Camera and Instrument agreed to provide two million dollars in start-up money for the firm.

The "traitorous eight," as Shockley called them, set up shop in Mountain View, California, about twelve blocks away from Shockley's firm. This group of scientists began a trend that would mark the electronics industry and make it, according to Wolfe, "as wild as show business." In the brain-intensive semiconductor business, which at that time was not hobbled with high production costs, talented scientists had no reason to stay with a firm when they could leave and make more money for themselves. "Defection Capital" became as much a part of the industry as silicon.

The new firm spent about two years doing straight research before Noyce invented the integrated circuit. He did not know it, but a young engineer with Texas Instruments named Jack Kilby had invented a similar device about six months beforehand. However, Kilby's circuit, which was made of germanium, was less efficient and harder to produce than Noyce's, which was constructed of silicon. Noyce's thumbnail-size innovation soon became the industry's standard. Transistors were etched onto the silicon chips, thus eliminating the costly and time-consuming wiring of chips together. As *Time*'s Frederic Golden explained: "Any number of transistors could be etched directly on a single piece of silicon along with the connections between them. Such integrated circuits. . . contained entire sections of a computer, for example, a logic circuit or a memory register. The microchip was born."

Gone forever were the gargantuan computers of the 1940s. ENIAC (Electronic Numerical Integrator and Calculator), a computer created by the army in 1946 to calculate missile trajectories, was, Golden said, "a collection of 18,000 vacuum tubes, 70,000 resistors, 10,000 capacitors and 6,000 switches, and occupied the space of a two-car garage." Wolfe disclosed that "the integrated circuit made it possible to create miniature computers, to put all the functions of the mighty ENIAC on a panel the size of a playing card." Soon, orders poured in for the new integrated circuit. NASA put them in the first computers that the astronauts in the Gemini program used aboard their spaceship. Fairchild Semiconductor stock skyrocketed, and Fairchild Camera and Instrument "got its money back within two years," noted McElheny, "and bought out the $500 original investment of each founder for $250,000." *Management Today* reported that less than ten years later "Fairchild was turning over $150 million a year, and had become the true cutting edge of the semiconductor industry." In the same time period the number of employees grew from the original handful to about twelve thousand.

In the early days of Fairchild Semiconductor, Noyce, as the general manager, sought to avoid the administrative errors Shockley had made. In an effort to create an egalitarian organization, he and his seven partners did not form a corporate structure. There was no hierarchy and no bosses other than the eight partners. New employees were given weighty responsibilities immediately, with no one looking over their shoulders. Noyce wanted the people he hired to be internally motivated. Thus, the demeaning and wasteful surveillance of "management" would be unnecessary. Decisions were made by the person or persons directly involved with a problem; they were not bucked up to increasingly higher levels of the corporate ladder. In addition, parking spots were not assigned nor was a dress code established.

Even with all these precautions against Fairchild becoming a calcified giant of a corporation, Noyce found after about ten years that he wanted to start over, to build a new and better organization. He had made a few management mistakes of his own and wanted to try again. He had let work groups get too big; too many people could veto a project. Noyce told McElheny that "big is bad. . . . The spirit of the small group is better and the work is much harder." He also found that rewarding managers for the profitability of their products served to discourage them from tackling projects that would adversely affect profits for longer than a half year.

So, in 1968 Noyce and Gordon Moore, another of the original defectors from Shockley's laboratory, left the company they had founded. Fairchild had spawned more than fifty "defector" companies in the Silicon Valley, the founders of which Adam Smith called the "Fairchildren." Noyce and Moore went back to Art Rock to obtain start-up capital. Although they had no formal business plan, Noyce and Moore were each willing to put a quarter of a million dollars of their own money into the venture. Rock had no trouble finding the money, given the reputations of the two, and soon Intel (short for integrated electronics) Corporation was in business.

In Intel's first year, Noyce and Moore invested primarily in research, for they had decided to explore the most underdeveloped area of computer technology at that time: memory. They searched for a more efficient mechanism in which computers could store data, hoping to replace the ceramic cores then in use. These cores, which resemble spirals, could only store one piece of information each at any one time. Wolfe reported: "Within two years Noyce and Moore had developed the 1103 memory chip, a chip of silicon and polysilicon the size of two letters in a line of type. Each chip contained four thousand transistors, did the work of a thousand ceramic ringlets, and did it faster." The 1103 memory chip quickly replaced the ceramic cores, and, according to *Management Today*, by 1972 Intel clocked up "sales of nearly $25 million, and in the next year sales almost tripled to $66 million."

Intel quickly followed its success in memory with the introduction of the microprocessor in 1971. A revolutionary discovery made by one of Intel's young engineers, the microprocessor allowed a single silicon chip to contain the circuitry, remarked McElheny, for "both information-storage and information-processing." Because it could "do the work of [the] room-sized computers of 30 years ago," it was dubbed the computer on a chip. Golden elaborated that "with the microprocessor, a single chip could be programmed to do any number of tasks, from running a watch to steering a spacecraft. It could also serve as the soul of . . . the personal computer." With these back-to-back successes, the value of Intel Corporation's stock nearly tripled between 1971 and 1973.

Intel continued to grow rapidly. In 1982 Thomas J. Lueck described the company's amazing success: "Intel's revenues, which were $23.4 million in 1972, grew to $854.6 million by 1980, making it one of the nation's fastest growing companies in the same period. Intel's net income grew from $3.1 million to $96.7 million, while its annual spending for research and development rose from $3.4 million to $96.4 million." During this time, however, Noyce again saw his role change from entrepreneur and researcher to administrator, for him a disagreeable change. He told *Management Today* that he finds "running a large corporation by numbers is less than satisfying to me." As a result, he left his job as president of Intel in 1973 to become the chairman of the board, a position less strenuous on a day-to-day basis. In 1979 he further reduced his responsibilities to the company by becoming part-time vice-chairman of the board.

Free from the daily cares of running a large corporation, Noyce could devote more time to his other projects. He invests in new corporations and businesses with his old friend Art Rock. As a venture capitalist, Noyce has increased his wealth many-fold. *Time* magazine listed him in January 1984 as one of four "financial genies." More important, Noyce has time to work for the industry as a whole. He helped establish the Semiconductor Industry Association and served as its chairman. One of his major concerns is the increasingly stiff competition the U.S. computer industry is encountering from Japan. As Japanese products grasp larger and larger chunks of the American market, Noyce, as one of the spokesmen of the industry, is calling for trade restrictions. He sits on the President's Commission on Industrial Competitiveness and works to protect the industry he helped create. Still, Noyce believes that daring entrepreneurship, well-trained engineers, and strong research programs are ultimately what will save the industry and make it thrive.

SOURCES:

PERIODICALS

Business Week, January 21, 1985, September 2, 1985.
Electronics Week, September 3, 1984.
Esquire, December, 1983.
Forbes, January 4, 1982.
Management Today, July, 1981, February, 1985.
New York Times, March 11, 1976, June 20, 1976, December 10, 1976, December 15, 1976, January 9, 1977, April 19, 1979, February 18, 1980, May 19, 1981, May 24, 1981, December 23, 1982, January 29, 1983.
Time, January 3, 1983, January 23, 1984.
Washington Post, August 4, 1985.

—Sidelights by Anne M.G. Adamus

Akeem Olajuwon

1963-

PERSONAL: Full name, Akeem Abdul Ajibola Olajuwon; born January 23, 1963, in Lagos, Nigeria; came to United States in 1980; son of Alhaji Salaam Olude (a cement broker) and Alhaja Abike (an assistant in the family cement business) Olajuwon. *Education:* Attended University of Houston, 1981-84.

ADDRESSES: Office—Houston Rockets, The Summit, 10 Greenway Plaza, Houston, Tex.

OCCUPATION: Professional basketball player.

CAREER: Member of Houston Rockets basketball team, 1984—.

AWARDS, HONORS: Named Most Valuable Player in National Collegiate Athletic Association (NCAA) playoff tournament, 1984; National Basketball Association (NBA) Rookie of the Year, 1984.

SIDELIGHTS: Akeem "The Dream" Olajuwon became the number one draft choice of the National Basketball Association (NBA) in 1984, when the Houston Rockets won the coin toss and made Olajuwon theirs. At that time, the seven-foot center for the University of Houston had only been in the United States for a few years, and before coming to the States, he had played basketball for a mere matter of months in his native city of Lagos in Nigeria, Africa. Having been selected first in the draft, Olajuwon decided to trade his last year at the University of Houston for professional basketball.

In 1983, Houston had also won the draft and had subsequently picked seven-foot-four-inches-tall Ralph Sampson. Charlie Thomas, owner of the Rockets, commented in the *Christian Science Monitor:* "Even though we already have Sampson, I don't see us trading Olajuwon. It would be something to have Sampson and Olajuwon playing side-by-side."

It *is* something. Olajuwon and Sampson first appeared together, representing the Houston Rockets, in Dallas. Houston won 121-111, with Sampson contributing thirteen rebounds and nineteen points as a power forward. "Olajuwon, who played center, scored 24 points (22 in the second half when he controlled the lane as if he were back in the Southwest Conference playing for the University of Houston against Rice) and had nine rebounds," Jack McCallum reported in *Sports Illustrated.* Ray Patterson, general manager for the Rockets, called the duo "a new phenomenon."

Still, Olajuwon is not considered to have reached his full potential as yet. So when the Rockets signed him for $7 million over a six-year period, they were taking an expensive risk. But, as coach Bill Fitch told *Newsweek,* "Olajuwon has

become a genuine Intimidating Presence—and the best shot blocker on a team that, to the surprise of many, has been among the league leaders in defense."

During the 1985 season, Olajuwon topped everyone in the league in rebounds, even the Philadelphia 76ers' Moses Malone whom he's said to resemble. In February, Akeem The Dream "collected 25 rebounds, including a startling 15 on offense, and scored a team-high 30 points to lead a 113-105 victory over the Knicks at the Garden," wrote Roy S. Johnson in the *New York Times.*

Back at the University of Houston, The Dream belonged to what was widely known as the "Phi Slamma Jamma fraternity." Olajuwon's slam-dunking fraternity brothers included six-foot-seven-inch Clyde "The Glide" Drexler, six-foot-nine-inch Larry "Mr. Mean" Micheaux, and the short guy in the group, six-foot-five-inch Benny "And His Jets" Anders. In 1983, observed Curry Kirkpatrick in *Sports Illustrated,* "Houston had 22 consecutive league victories, the longest Southwest Conference streak in 55 years, and not too many coaches or teams, or fraternities for that matter, were prepared to question the Cougars' right to a high ranking."

Other players have influenced Olajuwon, besides his Phi Slamma Jamma fraternity brothers. A major influence has been Philadelphia center Moses Malone (himself a former Houston Rocket). Working hard against Malone during the summers in Houston earned Olajuwon another nickname: Little Moses. And as gentle as Olajuwon can be much of the time, the man has guts. If he didn't, he couldn't have shouted at Moses (who had just called a foul on Olajuwon) during a practice session, "Aww, no! Dammit, Mo. Be a MON!," as quoted by *Sports Illustrated* writer Curry Kirkpatrick.

Olajuwon has also been influenced by African basketball star Yommy Sangodeyi, whom he met in 1980 at the national basketball camp in Lagos. In Yoruban, an African dialect, Sangodeyi means "god of thunder." Sangodeyi went to Houston in 1981, and enrolled at Houston State. He was restricted to a Division II school because of his age, which was twenty-five at that time. But Olajuwon and Sangodeyi were devoted to cheering each other on at their respective games, even though that meant two hours on the road, round trip.

It was reportedly Richard Mills who first discovered the lanky Olajuwon back in Lagos, Nigeria. Olajuwon was a soccer goalie, attending the Moslem Teacher's College (comparable to a high school in the United States) at that time. Mills, the national basketball coach, stated that Olajuwon was simply too tall for soccer. He coaxed Olajuwon into taking up basketball. Later, Chris Pond, who was working for the United States State Department in Nigeria, spotted Olajuwon playing for the national team. Pond happened to be a good friend of University of Houston coach Guy Lewis. So he set up some meetings for his discovery with Lewis and a couple of other American coaches.

In early October of 1980, Olajuwon flew to the States, landing in New York. The contrast between the tropical climate of Nigeria and the chilly fall weather in New York almost had Olajuwon boarding the next plane back to Lagos. But he decided instead to give Houston, Texas, a try first, foregoing previously planned visits to other places, including Georgetown University in Washington, D.C.

That decision turned out to be a lucky one for Guy Lewis and the University of Houston. Lewis was not aware of his luck at first, however. He tells of how Olajuwon called him from Houston Intercontinental Airport to set up an interview. Because countless newcomers to the States had done the same thing before Olajuwon, with no future in basketball, Lewis did not exactly roll out the red carpet. He told Olajuwon to take a cab.

While it was true that Olajuwon didn't have much experience on the basketball court, Lewis perceived enormous potential in the lean seven footer before him. Trusting his instincts, Lewis signed up Olajuwon with a full scholarship.

At first, Olajuwon did have a hard time of it on the court . He wasn't at all in shape. In fact, he never had been in shape for American basketball. After one dunk, he would grab his back and groan, Lewis remembers. The coach left him out of games most of the time, because in five minutes he'd be exhausted. "He actually hurt us in there. You couldn't play up-tempo when four guys are running and the other is dyin'," commented Lewis in *Sports Illustrated.*

Lewis did not hold back his observations about Olajuwon's inexperience from the press at that time. At one point, Olajuwon was so hurt by Lewis's public rebukes that he went over to the coach's house in tears. But Olajuwon *did* make it through the painful initiation period and improved so much that even Lewis had to admit that he's "the best shot blocker" he's coached in almost three decades at Houston.

Because of his combined talents as a blocker, rebounder, a nd slam-dunker, Olajuwon was voted Most Valuable Player (MVP) in the NCAA tournament in 1983—even though Houston lost to North Carolina State. As Walter Leavy put it in *Ebony,* Olajuwon was being recognized as "the most overpowering, intimidating and dominating figure in the college game."

Akeem Olajuwon (left), in his rookie season with the Houston Rockets, goes up against Cleveland Cavaliers guard World B. Free, 1984. AP/Wide World Photos.

By this time, Olajuwon had already assimilated into American culture to a high degree. He had tossed off his rhinestoned dashiki to don western attire, from jeans to Walkman and headphones. And while at first he hungered for special Nigerian dishes like *fufu* (stew served on baked dough), he soon discovered that Bisquick and American stew tasted just as good. Friends introduced Olajuwon to a new treat, ice cream. Soon he was carting around a cooler filled with Nutty Buddies, Popcicles, and the like.

English wasn't a big problem for Olajuwon. It is the main language in Nigeria, which was a British colony before its independence in 1960. At Baptist Academy and Moslem Teachers College, the two high schools Olajuwon attended in Nigeria, he either spoke English only or paid a fine. He speaks quickly, with a British lilt, and says he has been careful not to pick up locker room slang. In addition to English, Olajuwon speaks French and four of the more than 300 African dialects.

At the University of Houston, Olajuwon majored in Business Technology. And despite the heavy demands of basketball, he was able to keep his grade point average at 2.5. "Our parents have always advocated a strong education above everything," Olajuwon's older brother Kaka told *Sports Illustrated* writer Curry Kirkpatrick. "It is the greatest legacy a chap will have as security against poverty."

Poverty is one thing Akeem does not have to worry about. Although Olajuwon is very private about his business affairs, a writer in *Newsweek* revealed that these affairs include "investments in gas, oil and real estate—not to mention a new white Porsche 944 and a big black Mercedes with a license plate that says 'Dreem.' " Akeem Olajuwon is living up to his surname. In the tribal language, Yoruban, Olajuwon means "always being on top."

SOURCES:

PERIODICALS

Christian Science Monitor, January 27, 1983, April 29, 1983, April 4, 1984, May 3, 1984, May 24, 1984, September 4, 1984.

Ebony, March, 1984.

Jet, June 11, 1984, July 23, 1984, September 3, 1984, November 5, 1984.

Newsweek, November 26, 1984.

New York Times, March 29, 1983, June 20, 1984, February 16, 1985.

People, December 5, 1983.

Sporting News, January 27, 1986.

Sports Illustrated, March 7, 1983, April 4, 1983, November 28, 1983, November 5, 1984.

Time, April 18, 1983.

—Sidelights by Victoria France Charabati

Johnny Olson
1910(?)-1985

AP/Wide World Photos

OBITUARY NOTICE: Born c. 1910; died of complications from a stroke, October 12, 1985, in Santa Monica, Calif. American radio and television announcer, game show host, and performer. Olson began his long show-business career in the 1940s as the host of the talk show "Ladies Be Seated." He went on to host several popular radio quiz shows, including "Break the Bank" and "Whiz Quiz," before moving to television in the late forties.

Olson hosted and announced numerous short-lived television game shows throughout the forties and fifties before becoming a familiar voice to millions in the sixties as the unseen announcer on the popular "Jackie Gleason Show." Olson then announced a succession of highly successful television quiz shows including "What's My Line," "To Tell the Truth," and "The Match Game," before "The Price Is Right" premiered on CBS in September 1972.

"The Price Is Right" made Olson a legend. It was on that show that he coined the phrase "Come On Down" to summon excited contestants from the studio audience; and those words, delivered in his booming, operatic style, became his trademark. Olson also joined host Bob Barker as a performer in comical skits on "The Price Is Right" and warmed up the studio audience with jokes each day before the show began. Olson never missed a taping of "The Price Is Right." He taped his last show on October 2, 1985, just ten days before his death.

Olson was well-liked and highly regarded by those in his own profession. Shortly before his death he was accorded special honors at the daytime Emmy awards in recognition of his forty years in the entertainment industry.

SOURCES:

PERIODICALS

Chicago Tribune, October 14, 1985, October 20, 1985.
Detroit News, October 14, 1985.
Los Angeles Times, October 13, 1985.
Newsweek, October 25, 1985.
Washington Post, October 14, 1985.

Eugene Ormandy

1899-1985

OBITUARY NOTICE: Real name, Jeno Blau; born November 18, 1899, in Budapest, Hungary; died of pneumonia following a long illness, March 12, 1985, in Philadelphia, Pa. Conductor and music director. Considered one of the world's greatest conductors, Eugene Ormandy led the Philadelphia Orchestra for forty-four years, the longest tenure of any conductor in American history. Gifted with perfect pitch, Ormandy displayed his musical talent at a very early age. A violin prodigy at three, he entered the Budapest Royal Academy when he was five, the youngest student admitted. He received his B.A. at the age of fourteen and soon began performing in concerts across Europe. Ormandy came to the United States in 1921, having been promised a $30,000 concert tour. The tour never materialized; Ormandy, penniless and desperate, took a job as second violinist with the house orchestra at New York's Capitol Movie Theater. He was soon promoted to concertmaster and, in 1924, to conductor. This position led to several free-lance engagements, which prompted Ormandy to resign from the theater orchestra and hire an agent. He conducted for various radio programs and traveled the summer outdoor concert circuit until 1931, when he substituted for guest conductor Arturo Toscanini at the Philadelphia Orchestra. Ormandy's performance led to a five-year contract with the Minneapolis Symphony as conductor and music director.

Ormandy formally joined the Philadelphia Orchestra in 1936, serving as associate conductor with Leopold Stokowski. He was named music director two years later and became the symphony's sole conductor upon Stokowski's departure in 1941. Stokowski left behind a highly disciplined ensemble, noted for its sonorous, electric style. Ormandy not only preserved his predecessor's legacy, he refined and intensified it, creating the widely celebrated "Philadelphia sound." Under Ormandy's direction the orchestra became internationally famous for its virtuosity and tonal richness. He was regarded as a demanding conductor, able to perceive the slightest error. The *London Times* described him as "a ferocious but good humoured slave-driver whose perfection demanded as much from him as from the players he controlled." Ormandy led the symphony on extensive concert tours, performing throughout the United States, Latin America, Europe, Japan, and the People's Republic of China. He retired in 1980 and was made the Philadelphia Orchestra's conductor laureate. Ormandy became a U.S. citizen in 1927. He received numerous awards and honors throughout his career, including the Presidential Medal of

AP/Wide World Photos

Freedom, the Order of the British Empire, and the French Legion of Honor.

SOURCES:

BOOKS

Current Biography, Wilson, 1941.

PERIODICALS

London Times, March 13, 1985.
Newsweek, March 25, 1985.
New York Times, March 13, 1985.
Time, March 25, 1985.
Washington Post, March 13, 1985.

Calvin Peete
1943-

PERSONAL: Born July 18, 1943, in Detroit, Mich.; son of Dennis (a farm laborer) and Irenia (Bridgeford) Peete; married Christine Sears (a teacher), October 24, 1974; children: Charlotte, Calvin, Rickie, Dennis, Kalvanetta. *Education:* Dropped out of school in eighth grade; received high school diploma, 1982. *Politics:* Democrat. *Religion:* Baptist.

ADDRESSES: Home—Route 21, Box 81, Tarpon Way N., Ft. Meyers, Fla. 33903. *Office*—Calvin Peete Enterprises, Inc., 2050 Collier Ave., Ft. Meyers, Fla. 33901.

OCCUPATION: Professional golfer.

CAREER: Worked as a farm laborer in Florida, 1957-60; itinerant peddler of a variety of items, including jewelry and clothing, to migrant farm workers, 1961-71; real estate investor; professional golfer, 1971—.

Winner of numerous tournaments, including Greater Milwaukee Open, 1979, Anheuser-Busch Classic, B.C. Open, and Pensacola Open, 1982, Phoenix Open and Tournament Players Championship, 1985; member of U.S. team competing against Japan, 1982-83; member of U.S. Ryder Cup team, 1983; represented United States in World Cup play. Conducts numerous golf clinics and lectures, often for underprivileged or inner-city youngsters.

MEMBER: Professional Golfers Association.

AWARDS, HONORS: Honorary degree from Wayne State University, Jackie Robinson Award for athletics from *Ebony* magazine, and Ben Hogan Award, all 1983; two-time winner of Vardon Award for lowest stroke average on professional golf tour; recipient of awards for driving accuracy and for hitting most greens in regulation number of strokes.

SIDELIGHTS: Professional golfer Calvin Peete is reminiscent of a character from Horatio Alger. A high school dropout who once earned ten dollars a day picking vegetables, Peete has a crooked left elbow (the result of a childhood accident) and never touched a golf club until age twenty-three. Yet he has risen to the height of his profession with eleven career Professional Golfers Association (PGA) victories and has succeeded in his struggle to prove, in the words of Scott Ostler of the *Los Angeles Times*, that "he is no longer Calvin Peete, black golfer, but Calvin Peete, star golfer." Though not the first black to tour with the PGA successfully, he is certainly the richest, earning well in excess of $1,000,000 in his ten-year career.

"How far a man travels, how much he improves his life from start to finish, is a fair gauge of success. By such standards, Calvin Peete is nothing short of exceptional," writes Barry McDermott in *Sports Illustrated*. Born in Detroit in 1943,

Peete lived the first ten years of his life in that city, the youngest of nine children. When his parents separated, Peete chose to live with his father in Pahokee, Florida, an island town on the shore of Lake Okeechobee. His father and stepmother eventually had ten children of their own; so Peete, once the youngest in a large family, became the oldest in an even larger family. "I used to work on weekends to try to help out," he told *Ebony* magazine, "but it wasn't enough, so I dropped out of high school to help with the bills."

For the next four years, Peete worked beside his father in the vegetable fields of south-central Florida, harvesting celery, corn, beans, and other vegetables. "It was very hard work," he told *Sports Illustrated*. "To me, it was very demeaning. It had no standing at all. It was about as low as you could get." But the industrious Peete soon discovered a better way to make a living. At age seventeen, he bought a used station wagon and began to peddle goods to the migrant workers—usually clothing, trinkets and jewelry he had purchased in wholesale houses. He also persuaded a dentist to install two diamond chips in his front teeth, and thereafter he became known as the "Diamond Man." The nickname, and a rash of startled comments upon his appearance, persisted until he had the chips removed and put into a ring in 1980.

By the age of twenty-three, Peete had become friends with Benjamin Widoff, an owner of rental properties in Fort Lauderdale. Widoff sold Peete apartments at reasonable rates, and Peete continued to sell dry goods to migrant workers for capital. "In time I guess I wound up owning maybe $200,000 worth of property he sold me," Peete told *Sports Illustrated*. "He was an awfully good man."

Peete's initiation into golf also came at twenty-three, and the story of his first afternoon on a course has become famous in golfing circles. A group of friends invited him to an afternoon clambake. Peete agreed to go, but on the way to the "clambake," his friends stopped at a municipal golf course. According to *People* magazine, they told him, "Either you play, or you wait until we finish." Peete, who had always thought golf was a game "for sissies," described his first round in *Black Enterprise* magazine: "There were a lot of people ahead of us waiting to tee off. After I watched them for awhile, I realized that some of them didn't know any more about the game than I did. They were topping the ball, hitting behind it, and scuffing it. So I felt a little more relaxed when I got my chance to top it and scuff it." After playing a few holes—one of them for par—Peete was hooked. As he told *Sports Illustrated*, "I thought, 'Hey, it takes more than a notion to get that ball to go where you want it.' It was a challenge. . . . It was my challenge."

Peete bought a set of used golf clubs and began to practice obsessively. He read instruction books by Sam Snead and Jack Nicklaus and Bob Toski, but he refused to take lessons. According to Ira Berkow in the *New York Times*, he was afraid to, "he thought that an instructor would tell him that he wouldn't have a chance to be a top-flight golfer—what with such a late start and a crooked left arm—and to go home." So Peete persisted on his own, wrapping his hands in Dr. Scholl's foot pads when they blistered raw and taking advice on his grip from the salesman who sold him golf gloves. He also developed the technique of recording his stroke on film, using a movie camera mounted on a tripod. McDermott writes: "He was both pupil and professor, . . . Yet he was clearly a 'natural.'" Six months after his first game, he was breaking eighty for eighteen holes, and within eighteen months he was breaking par.

Peete turned professional in 1971, five years after taking up golf. But it was not until 1975 that he earned his PGA card, enabling him to join the tour. Over the next three years he experienced little success, averaging just over $20,000 in winnings each year, barely enough to meet his touring expenses. Says McDermott: "Peete practiced and drove himself so hard, cutting corners on food and accommodations, that friends worried about him. Often he would finish playing and then have to repair his automobile in order to drive to the next pro stop." Discouragement inevitably

Calvin Peete blasts his way out of a sand trap during the Westchester Classic in Harrison, N.Y., June 1985. AP/Wide World Photos.

followed. Peete began to consider quitting the PGA, but his wife, Christine, whom he had married in 1975, advised him to persist. Peete told *Ebony* magazine: "There were a few times when the checks started coming few and far between, and we had to live off what [Christine] was making [as a school teacher]. I was wondering if I had to find something else to do. She was the one that kept encouraging me and saying: 'You just have to work a little harder. It doesn't come easy for everybody, and everything you've ever had, you had to work for. So you just have to keep working.' That's what really kept me going."

The persistence Peete demonstrated was rewarded in 1979, when he won the Greater Milwaukee Open, his first tour victory. After winning only $20,459 and finishing in 108th place in 1978, Peete garnered $122,481 in 1979, for a respectable 27th place finish. "Mostly it was a matter of concentration," he told the *New York Times*. "I went back to studying the films of myself. I studied what it took to hit a bad shot as well as a good one."

"Studying" and "concentration" are words that Calvin Peete uses often. A serious, retiring man, he spends much of his leisure time mentally surveying the next course, the next hole, and his particular approach to each. According to David MacDonald in *Reader's Digest:* "After a fine finish at Miami's Doral-Eastern Open, a reporter asked Peete when he had last broken par on its notorious 18th hole. 'About eleven-thirty last night,' he answered, 'in my room.'" Observers often remark upon Peete's composure during tournaments. "On the course," writes McDermott, "he seems impassive, almost gloomy." Peete told *Sports Illustrated* that he learned to control his excitability in order to improve his game: "I finally came to realize that a round of golf isn't over until the 18th green. I learned to save my emotional reaction, good or bad, for after that."

The outstanding idiosyncrasy in Calvin Peete's game is his crooked left arm, which seems to violate the first cardinal rule for a good golf swing: Keep the left arm straight. Peete fell from a tree when he was twelve and broke his elbow in three places. It will only straighten to 150 degrees, so he must compensate with an unorthodox drive. Peete described his swing in the *Christian Science Monitor:* "My arm naturally stays close to my side on the downswing, which helps me swing the club into the ball from inside the target line. I've hit the ball, my left arm folds naturally. My swing repeats, and that's essential at this level of play." What is also essential at Peete's level is accuracy, and he has been one of the most accurate players off the tee since 1980—and the most accurate overall since 1982. David MacDonald writes: "By keeping his ball in the middle of the fairway, skirting the woods and bunkers where the big hitters come to grief, Peete consistently takes the fewest strokes to reach the green." This accuracy, twice winning Peete the Vardon Trophy for the lowest stroke average on the tour, is especially valuable since Peete's crooked elbow impedes the power of the swing, and since he is by reputation an inconsistent putter.

By 1983 journalists were ranking Peete among the best golfers in America. In 1982 he won four major tournaments and finished in the PGA's top ten in ten out of twenty-six outings. He became the second black man in history to be invited to the Masters Tournament and has subsequently performed in it six times. Now in his forties, he has begun a vigorous program of calisthenics that he insists has added an average of fifteen yards to his drive. In April 1985, when he won the prestigious Tournament Players Championship, his purse of $162,000 was the second largest on the PGA tour. And in January 1986 Peete earned $500,000 by winning the MONY Tournament of Champions at La Costa Country Club with a tournament record score of 267 to open the 1986 PGA Tour. The victory was Peete's eleventh PGA win, his tenth since 1982, setting a new PGA record.

To help achieve his goal of qualifying for the United States' Ryder Cup team, an elite squad of professionals that performs against European teams, Peete studied for, and ultimately passed, his high school equivalency test in 1982. (Ryder Cup rules require that all team members be high school graduates.) He has also been committed to helping young people, especially young blacks, and he has done this by lecturing and offering free golf clinics. In Peete's view, golf is a new option, even for underprivileged youngsters, with the advent of better municipal courses and low-cost equipment rentals. As he told *Black Enterprise* magazine, "Golf is the leading social sport in the country. Some of the most important people in your community—from company presidents to Congressmen—at one time or another rub shoulders with you on a golf course. Sooner or later you're going to run into people who may be able to help your career, and the game lets you meet them easily, casually, on a first-name basis."

Professional golf has been a sport in which integration occurred slowly, but from Calvin Peete's perspective, the transition is nearly complete. He claims little problem with prejudice on tour, though in the early days of his career he did experience an occasional slight. In 1983, he told the *New York Times* that sometimes, "when I go to the clubhouse in the morning before a round, I'm asked who I'm caddying for in order to be let in." And though Barry McDermott feels that Peete and other black golfers are still "semi-curiosities," Peete does not attribute this notoriety to racial prejudice. "In golf," he told *People* magazine, "whites don't discriminate against blacks. They discriminate against lack of money." Still, he admitted to Kenny Moore of *Sports Illustrated* that he's "immensely gratified to hear of galleries calling him 'good for golf.'" "Every athlete feels pride in and protective of his sport," Peete said. "Other than beating a ball around, you want to share, to teach."

At the 1985 Masters Tournament, it was evident that stardom had found Calvin Peete. According to Scott Ostler of the *Los Angeles Times*, "roughly 1,000 fans followed his twosome around the course, and roughly 100 of those fans were black. Just about every black spectator on the course . . . was in Calvin Peete's gallery . . . . It was 'Calvin Peete Day' for many." Though still something of a novelty to spectators and the press because of his race, Peete has nonetheless been accepted, praised, and even envied by his professional peers. That he would adopt golf as a career—and pursue perfection with such persistence and professionalism—has endeared him to the public. "Dorothy's problematic journey in 'The Wizard of Oz' has nothing on his climb to the top of his sport," writes Joe Clerico in the *Christian Science Monitor*. "But for Calvin Peete, three strikes (his age, his race, and his crooked left arm) were not enough to put him out."

SOURCES:

PERIODICALS

Black Enterprise, July, 1983.
Chicago Tribune, January 13, 1986.
Christian Science Monitor, November 23, 1982.
Ebony, July, 1980.
Golf, November, 1982, April, 1983, February, 1984, May, 1984.
Los Angeles Times, August 4, 1983, April 11, 1985, April 12, 1985, January 12, 1986.
New Yorker, July 25, 1983.
New York Times, July 26, 1982, July 30, 1982, January 2, 1983, January 3, 1983, March 6, 1983, March 9, 1983, March 12, 1983, July 25, 1983, June 15, 1984, January 21, 1985, April 1, 1985.
People, June 13, 1983.
Reader's Digest, October, 1983.
Sporting News, January 20, 1986.
Sports Illustrated, March 24, 1980, April 25, 1983, June 27, 1983, January 20, 1986.
Washington Post, March 8, 1983, April 14, 1984, April 1, 1985, April 27, 1985, January 12, 1986.

—Sidelights by Mark Kram

Donald Eugene Petersen

1926-

PERSONAL: Born September 4, 1926, in Pipestone, Minn.; son of William L. and Mae (Pederson) Petersen; married Jo Anne Leonard, September 12, 1948; children: Leslie Carolyn, Donald Leonard. *Education:* University of Washington, B.M.E., 1946; Stanford University, M.B.A., 1949. *Religion:* Episcopalian.

ADDRESS: Home—1953 Woodward Ave., Bloomfield Hills, Mich. 48013. *Office*—Ford Motor Co., American Rd., Dearborn, Mich. 48121.

OCCUPATION: Auto executive.

CAREER: Ford Motor Co., Dearborn, Mich., 1949—, began as product planner, assistant to vice-president, 1965-66, car product planning manager, 1966-69, executive director of administration, engineering, and industrial design, 1969, vice-president for car planning and research, 1969-71, vice-president for truck and recreational products operations, 1971-75, executive vice-president for diversified products operations, 1975-77, member of board of directions, 1977—, executive vice-president for international automotive operations, 1977-80, president and chief operating officer, 1980-85, chairman and chief executive officer, 1985—. Member of board of trustees, Cranbrook Educational Community, 1973—. *Military service:* U.S. Marine Corps Reserve, 1946-47, 1951-52.

MEMBER: Society of Automotive Engineers, Motor Vehicle Manufacturers Association, Engineering Society of Detroit, Mensa, Phi Beta Kappa, Sigma Xi, Tau Beta Phi, Detroit Club, Renaissance Club, Bloomfield Hills Country Club.

AWARDS, HONORS: Distinguished Alumnus Award, University of Washington, 1981.

SIDELIGHTS: The antithesis of the somber, gray-flannel executives who have traditionally populated the U.S. auto industry, Donald E. Petersen is only the second non-family member in eighty-two years to head the Ford Motor Company, the world's second largest automaker. Rather than the classical background in finance, Petersen, who succeeded Philip Caldwell as Ford chairman on February 1, 1985, brings to the chief executive's office an engineer's intimate knowledge of the products and a flair for futuristic styling that is evidenced in Ford's recent designs.

A product planner for much of his automotive career, Petersen is often credited with directing Ford's move away from the crisp, boxy look of its competitors' cars to softer, more rounded, aerodynamic shapes that emulate contemporary European designs. A graduate of the Bob Bondurant School of Performance Driving and one of the chief planners of the original Mustang, Petersen has also helped spearhead Ford's renewed emphasis on sporty and performance cars.

UPI/Bettmann Newsphotos

The *Detroit Free Press* described him in 1984 as "the kind who would rather be test-driving a new car than sitting behind a desk or attending a company board meeting." Added the *Free Press*, "He's the first [Ford] chairman since Henry Ford to love to drive fast cars." James Higgins of the *Detroit News* observed: "Ford now is being run by a certified car nut. . . . [He] has an unashamed passion for cars, [and] he likes car styling that carries some kind of emotional message." David E. Davis, Jr., editor and publisher of *Car and Driver* magazine, notes: "Petersen is totally different from most other car executives. There's an open-minded, ingenuous quality about him that's really refreshing. He's got wide-ranging interests, and shows a willingness to talk to all kinds of people on every kind of subject. That's a wonderful quality for a chairman to have."

A former Marine Corps officer, Petersen is viewed by associates as "a quietly commanding kind of guy," "a stickler for detail" and "a solid team player." One colleague says Petersen is "exceedingly demanding, the most demanding man I've ever worked for." But he can also be refreshingly warm and open. Marcia Stepanek of the *Free Press* describes him as "a shirt-sleeved populist who spends long hours visiting factories, huddling with designers and encouraging employe suggestions on everything from assembly-line changes to dashboard design.''

One telling anecdote, recounted by the *Free Press*, describes how Petersen gave Ford's advertising agency a photo of himself, without a jacket, to accompany a letter to customers in Ford's product brochures. Executives at the agency, J. Walter Thompson, balked and reportedly told Petersen, "[General Motors Chairman] Roger Smith would never appear without a jacket." "Exactly," he replied.

Petersen also copied a page out of Japanese business texts: He hired quality and productivity guru W. Edwards Deming, who worked with the Japanese industry in the 1950's, to help Ford reverse its sagging reputation for quality. The strategy has paid off; recent independent surveys of customers rank Ford products among the highest in quality for both domestic and import manufacturers.

Until recently, Petersen was virtually unknown outside automotive circles. Having spent much of his early career in planning, he had not come to the attention of many business people and business reporters. He held several posts in product planning at Ford in the 1950s and was part of the team that planned the 1964 Mustang under Lee Iacocca, then general manager of the Ford Division. Higgins of the *News* says Petersen played a key role in selling the car to company management: "While Iacocca was the guiding genius behind the Mustang, it was Petersen who had to persuade Ford's top brass that the car would sell." Bell & Howell Chairman Donald Frey, who was Petersen's boss in the early 1960s, told the *Free Press* in a 1984 article that he expects Petersen to follow the same sort of aggressive strategy as chairman: "Pete's a gambler. Under [him], I think you'll see more attempts at innovation, a greater willingness to lead, rather that play it safe. He's not afraid to take risks." Added Robert Hefty, a retired Ford public-relations official, in the same article: "You might have another Edsel or two (under Petersen). But you'll probably see another Mustang or two, as well. I'm not suggesting Pete will flop, but he's not afraid to try something completely different."

During the early 1970s, Petersen gained valuable experience as head of Ford's truck operations then as executive vice-president for Ford's diversified products group—steel, glass, aerospace, electronics and other non-automotive operations—from 1975 to 1977. Remarked one observer: "He's a sharp guy with a well-rounded background who never got the publicity he deserved." *Business Week*, in a 1980 article, called him "a meticulous manager" who, as head of Ford's profitable international operations in the late 1970s, helped offset the cash crunch that plagued the company's North American unit at the time.

Named president and chief operating officer in 1980, Petersen assumed the number two slot in Ford's hierarchy at one of the most critical financial periods in its history. Over three years, from 1980 to 1982, Ford lost a record $3.2 billion. But it returned to profitability in a big way in 1983, with record income of $1.9 billion, then broke its own mark in 1984 with a $2.9 billion profit. For his role in the company's dramatic turnaround—he helped slash overhead by $4 billion while significantly improving the quality of Ford Cars—Petersen has been amply rewarded, with salary and bonus totaling more than $1 million per year.

Petersen has made it clear he's pleased with the success of Ford's so-called "aero" look on such cars as the Thunderbird, Lincoln Continental Mark VII, and Tempo—a dramatic design departure that was viewed by some Ford executives as a major gamble. In a 1985 interview with the *Free Press*, Petersen noted: "I think you'll see this basic, somewhat softer look come into the whole world automotive market. It just makes too much sense. It helps you on your fuel efficiency, helps you on the quietness of an automobile and, as we work with it, we're finding a great many things we can do in terms of handling stability. We're not going to make an obsession out of it, but it's here to stay."

Petersen's background as a product planner and his lack of financial experience don't seem to bother observers. Auto industry analyst Ann Knight, of the Wall Street firm Paine Webber Mitchell Hutchins, says that, given Ford's excellent financial position, "it's not absolutely critical to have a finance man as CEO. It may be an appropriate time to have a car person like Petersen at the helm."

As for the future, in a 1985 interview with the *Detroit News*, Petersen observed: "The progress of the last five years makes a very good point of departure. I think that much of what I hope we can accomplish at Ford for the next five to ten years will be an extension of the process of change you've been watching us undertake now for the last five years."

One of the biggest challenges facing Petersen and and other U.S. auto executives is a massive modernization and retooling of the domestic industry, primarily to improve efficiency and cut costs in order to compete with the imports. "There's no question that we have some very major jobs to accomplish," he told the *News*. "The transition in the whole approach in how we design, develop, manufacture and sell cars is going to be, when it's all finished, a very dramatic transition."

That doesn't necessarily mean all the glamour is gone from the business. As Petersen told Britain's *Car Magazine:* "There are some basic requirements we try to accomplish. One of them is to offer the best value for the money. Our second goal is to be known as the manufacturer of the best-quality automobiles in the world. . . . Then if we can put some excitement and some fun and some other distinctive appeal into out products, we'll be winners."

SOURCES:

PERIODICALS

Automotive News, November 5, 1984.
Business Week, March 31, 1980.
Car Magazine, January, 1985.
Detroit Free Press, March 31, 1984, July 22, 1984, October 30, 1984, November 4, 1984, February 3, 1985.
Detroit News, October 30, 1984, February 1, 1985.
Motor Trend, October, 1980.
New York Times, July 20, 1981, August 20, 1982.
Seattle Times, March 16, 1980.
Time, March 24, 1980, July 18, 1983.
Wall Street Journal, December 1, 1981.

—Sketch by Anita Pyzik Lienert

Christian Petrossian

1943(?)-

BRIEF ENTRY: Born c.1943 in Paris, France. French restaurateur and importer of a variety of gourmet foods, including Russian caviar. By the time he was seven years old, Christian Petrossian had learned to distinguish between the three primary types of top-grade caviar: the gray, large-grained beluga; the golden, medium-grained ossetra; and the stronger-flavored, only somewhat less desirable, sevruga. His sons, Tigran and Stepan, were fed caviar from the age of nine months so that they would begin to develop the sensitive palate essential to the family business. The Petrossians have been leading caviar importers since the nineteen-twenties, when Christian's father, Melkoum, and his uncle, Mouchegh, Armenian-born Parisians, first struck a deal with the Soviet government making them exclusive suppliers of Russian caviar to the large expatriate Russian population in France. (They reportedly made the first phone call from the West to the Soviet Ministry of Foreign Trade shortly after the Russian Revolution.) Until that time, there was little demand for caviar in Western Europe or the United States. Through the years, as non-Russians became familiar with this delicacy, caviar gradually assumed the mystique it now enjoys as the snack food of the rich and famous.

The great expense of top-quality caviar is due, in a large part, to the difficulty in obtaining it. Although virtually any kind of fish eggs are, theoretically, edible, and although many types of roe—including that of salmon and domestic sturgeon—are packaged and marketed in the United States, experts agree that the very finest caviar comes from Caspian Sea sturgeon. And only two countries border on the Caspian Sea: the Soviet Union and Iran. With Iranian caviar exportation disrupted by the political turmoil that has taken place in that country in recent years, only the Soviet Union remains as a source of this rare commodity. As a result of his exclusive contract with the Soviets, Petrossian is able to accompany Russian fishermen on their excursions during the spring and fall sturgeon spawning seasons. He selects the choicest caviar—several dozen tons of it—for shipment around the world. "It is very important that we have the right to choose the caviar ourselves," he asserted to *People* magazine.

After more than sixty years of selling caviar at their Paris store, the Petrossian family crossed the Atlantic in 1980 when Christian and his cousin Armen opened shops in the Bloomingdale's and Neiman-Marcus stores in New York. Four years later, they opened Petrossian's, a midtown Manhattan boutique and restaurant featuring, among other delicacies, imported truffles and paté foie gras. But "the cynosure of the menu," writes a *New York Times* columnist, "is caviar—$49 for 50 grams of beluga, $35 for ossetra, $30 for sevruga," all of which are served with "stunning presentation on. . . black lacquer plates complete with a golden spoon." The presentation, to caviar aficionados, is as important as the texture and taste of the roe itself. Petrossian told William E. Geist, in another *New York Times* article, that "the eggs must be carefully spooned—not spread—so that they remain unbroken until pressed between tongue and palate;. . . mother-of-pearl, ivory, or gold utensils are to be used, because silver often imparts a metallic taste." Petrossian maintains that the eighties mark the "dawning of the age of caviar." He believes that since World War II Americans have experienced the "car phase" of the fifties and the "fashion and wine phase" of more recent years. With a "rapidly growing upper middle class that is striving even higher, now is the time to commence the caviar age."

SOURCES:

PERIODICALS

Christian Science Monitor, September 15, 1982.
New York Times, November 17, 1984, December 21, 1984.
People, March 11, 1985.

John Joseph Phelan, Jr.

1931-

PERSONAL: Born May 7, 1931, in New York, N.Y.; son of John Joseph (a stock exchange specialist) and Edna K. Phelan; married Joyce Catherine Campbell, April 3, 1955; children: John, David, Peter. *Education:* Adelphi University, B.B.A., 1955.

ADDRESSES: Office—New York Stock Exchange, 11 Wall St., New York, N.Y. 10005.

OCCUPATION: Stock exchange executive.

CAREER: Nash & Co. (stock exchange specialists), New York City, member of staff, 1955-57, partner, 1957-62; Phelan & Co., New York City, managing partner, 1962-72; Phelan, Silver, Vesce, Barry & Co., New York City, senior partner, 1972-80; New York Stock Exchange, New York City, floor official, 1967-71, governor, 1971-74, director, 1974-75, vice-chairman, 1975-80, president and chief operating officer, 1980-84, chairman and chief executive officer, 1984—.

Chairman of New York Futures Exchange, 1979-85. Chairman of board of directors, Adelphi University; co-chairman of parents fund, Hamilton College; member of board of directors, Mercy Hospital and Heart Fund. Member of Cardinal's Committee of Laity. *Military service:* U.S. Marine Corps; served in Korea.

MEMBER: Securities Industries Association (member of governing board, 1978-79; member of executive committee, 1979-80; member of board of directors), National Market Association (chairman of operations committee, 1976-77), Creek Country Club, Garden City Golf Club, Cherry Valley Golf Club, Seawanhaka Yacht Club.

AWARDS, HONORS: Named knight of Sovereign Military Order of Malta and of Holy Sepulchre of Jerusalem; Brotherhood Award, National Conference of Christians and Jews; National Youth Services Award, B'nai B'rith Foundation; Stephen S. Wise Award, American Jewish Congress, 1981.

SIDELIGHTS: A former New York Stock Exchange (NYSE) specialist, John J. Phelan, Jr., is credited by *Institutional Investor* with rescuing the Big Board from possible extinction. He brought the NYSE into the electronic age with the development of communications, data processing and trading support systems that today constitute one of the most extensive privately owned computer complexes in the world, enabling the exchange to efficiently handle sustained trading volume of more than 250 million shares a day.

Phelan first went to Wall Street in 1947 at age sixteen as a runner for his father's firm. "I swore I would never work on

UPI/Bettmann Newsphotos

Wall Street again," he recalls in *Institutional Investor*." The pay was low, the trip [from his home in Garden City, Long Island] was terrible, the job was awful. I thought there must be a better way to make a living." However, in 1955, after graduating from Adelphi University's business school and devoting three years to the Marine Corps, Phelan rejoined his father's Wall Street firm and discovered that the floor was more interesting than he previously thought. He is extremely curious about how people, organizations, machines and processes work, and he reported to *Institutional Investor* that "I found there is no magic formula to trading. Trading is an art. You can't trade off a chart or a graph or a statistic." He was dismayed by the floor's outdated mechanical system, and in 1961 his firm became the first to computerize its commission bills and profit and loss statements.

His father was a highly regarded mediator of floor disputes; and, when he died in 1966, Phelan inherited that role. He was, however, more interested in developing methods to handle broad and complex problems. Robert Hall, a computer expert and former NYSE executive vice-president related to *Institutional Investor*, "John has a great ability to mentally disassemble complicated mechanisms and comprehend very complicated interactions within those mechanisms." He combined this technical expertise with a cautious, action approach. Phelan was neither a gambler nor adept at trading, which is too much an art and not enough a science. His avocation centers on information gathering, mostly reading. Phelan told *Institutional Investor* that "if I have a weakness, I could say that I'm somewhat overcautious."

In the years that followed his father's death, there was an absence of leadership at the exchange, and Phelan was ready and anxious to fill the vacuum. He became a floor official in 1967 and a governor of the exchange in 1971. In 1974, he was elected a director and in 1975 became an unpaid vice-chairman at the time when the exchange was under attack. It had been required to abandon its fixed commission rates, and Congress directed that there be a new national market system.

Phelan was instrumental in the removal of James Needham as chairman and in the election of William Batten to replace him. As Phelan recalled to *Institutional Investor:* "The Exchange had been a monopoly, had gotten fat and lazy because of it and had suffered all the net results of that kind of attitude. It had to realize the business wasn't going to come to it on a silver platter any longer and that it had to get out there and fight." He knew change was coming and that "if we didn't work for it, we weren't going to be here much longer."

To obtain lower commission rates, some retail firms sent orders to less expensive, more automated regional exchanges. As a countermeasure, Phelan sought to develop the NYSE as the most efficient marketplace available. He stopped specialist domination of the allocation committee and had floor brokers each quarter evaluate specialist firms. Poorly rated firms merged into better firms cleaning up the bottom and making the whole NYSE process stronger. Phelan also assisted the floor execution functions with numerous small black boxes. He reported in *Institutional Investor* that "what we're really doing is automating as much as possible up to and away from the point of trade." To fulfill the Congressional requirement of a national market system, Phelan developed the "Intermarket Trading System," which connects the NYSE floor with other exchanges, enabling the NYSE specialist to keep any order in New York by equaling a lower regional quote.

To maintain rapport with floor members, Phelan holds small meetings with members and appoints members to committees for information gathering with the goal of not just complaining but doing things better. One official told *Institutional Investor:* "John stays neutral until he thinks he has enough votes, and then he drives hard. Once he's announced a position, it's impossible to budge him." Phelan avoids unpleasant surprises by telling things as they are. A specialist related to *Institutional Investor:* "John likes the lesser-of-two-evils approach. Like he'll say, if we don't change, the regionals will take our business away."

Phelan was vice-chairman until 1980 when the increasing burdens of the job forced him to resign from his firm and accept the full-time position of president and chief operating officer of the NYSE. In May, 1984, he succeeded William Batten as chairman and chief executive officer. Under his leadership, the traditional exchange trading floor has been transformed into an arena likened to a set for a "Star Wars" film. Phelan spurred the exchange's sweeping modernization program and played a key role in the securities industry's planning, development, and implementation of the highly automated National Market System for securities. Phelan stresses the exchange's commitment to a new business-oriented philosophy and corporate goal of being the highest quality, most cost-effective marketplace in the securities industry and maximizing its contribution to strengthening the U.S. capital markets. He advocates prudent exchange diversification spearheading the establishment of the New York Futures Exchange as a wholly-owned subsidiary of the NYSE. He served as chairman of NYFE since that post was created in mid-1979 until mid-1985. Phelan is a spokesman for private enterprise capitalism. He believes that the NYSE is internationally acknowledged to be the focal point of the capital markets system that fuels the growth of American business. He feels that status, achieved over a period of nearly two centuries, demands that the exchange strive to be the strongest possible competitor and that it also confers on the exchange a leadership responsibility that is not open to compromise.

According to *Forbes*, the NYSE coped with the 236 million-share day traded in August, 1984, almost as well as it managed a 100 million-share day the week before. "It couldn't have done so without the high-tech help put in place over the past nine years under John Phelan. Indeed, the trading day could hardly have begun without it." Matthew Schifrin described in *Forbes* how some of the Phelan-inspired technology works: "Before the specialists arrive, a NYSE system called OARS (Opening Automated Report Service) pairs off all 5,099-share-or-less market orders that have arrived electronically while the exchange was closed. At the 10 o'clock opening bell, specialists simply set the price and send the paired orders on their way. That's not a bad way to handle 15% to 20% of a typical day's volume. . . . OARS is just one peripheral program hooked up to Super-DOT, a tandem mainframe with appropriate software that is the exchange's main tech-tool. Super DOT, an improved DOT (for Designated Order Turnaround), electronically routes market order of 1,099 shares or less to the appropriate specialist and summarizes them according to price. Small limit orders are handled in similar fashion. All that's left for the specialist is the pairing and the execution. The round-trip time for a typical Super DOT market order is 75 seconds." The exchange is also doing some automatic execution and reporting in selected stocks. In the past nine years, Phelan has spent more than $80 million improving the efficiency of the exchange's auction market and enabling it to offer more competition to its main high-tech competition, the National Association of Security Dealers (NASD).

Phelan told *Forbes* that his main task is to keep the exchange as the world's "premier" marketplace. He indicated that formerly the exchange existed mostly for the benefit of its members. Now, "its function is to create a liquid market for its listed companies to raise capital. It's necessary to do the first before you can do the second, but you have to do both." In addition to acquiring new listings, Phelan must increase trading hours, suggest new sources of capital for thinly financed specialist firms, and ease the exchange's restrictions on various classes of common stock. Moreover, he must persuade the exchange to accept and market new products such as futures. According to *Forbes*, Phelan wants "a competitive, customer sensitive marketing organization." He has hired salespeople to sign up potential converts for listing, organized forums and conferences to help build rapport between the exchange's listed companies and the federal government and established a committee to review the exchange's common-stock restrictions to help retain companies facing delisting.

Phelan is demanding of his staff, but as he related to *Forbes*, his style is "getting plenty of input and then keying up the nasty issues." His problem is whether his rigorous demands will crumble the morale of his staff. Another area of concern is Phelan's commitment to the specialist. Big-block trading is done by institutions and merely reported on the tape, and most small orders are not processed by specialists. Phelan allows specialists to process medium-sized orders through the semiautomated system hoping to preserve their role with technology. However, some electronics experts say the specialist system will pass away.

Phelan's main strengths are his vision of the future and his determination to act on it. He said to *Forbes*, "My job is to see the changes and then convince others to adjust to them, even if in the short term, it impacts them negatively." He is taking the exchange from a monopoly institution to a competitive company. In reporting to the *Washington Post* on the competitive and technological challenges that face the exchange, he foresaw global twenty-four-hour trading in which the exchange will connect electronically with other exchanges around the world. He thinks the cooperative linking of three market centers—New York, London, and Tokyo—will assure the highest NYSE standards. These exchanges would guarantee the trades within the system and exchange surveillance data. Phelan noted to the *Washington Post:* "I think you can work that out on an international level. And I think that by providing the mechanisms in which the execution [of trades] can take place, you've almost got the entire audit trail there." This means there would be an electronic record of trading.

Phelan is discussing merger with the Pacific Stock Exchange to enable the NYSE to extend its trading hours but doubts that the talks will be successful because of different interests in the two exchanges. Still, Phelan believes that the twenty-four-hour market is gradually becoming part of the mentality of the financial world. He feels that investors with personal computers would like to send in orders at night for execution the next day. And, in an address before the Touche, Remnant & Company International Advisory

Boards Conference in London, he said that today the trader is king, that the name of the game is "volume, creativity and turnover," and that while five years ago major United States brokerage firms had only a few people headquartered in London, they now have hundreds, demonstrating the need for a world-wide system of twenty-four-hour per day stock trading. In addition, he said, staggering advances in communications technology have taken place in recent years, and—unencumbered by the need for sleep or coffee breaks—this new technology operates on a twenty-four-hour basis.

In spite of its numerous problems, and the endless challenges facing it in the near future, "it seems certain that the NYSE will survive in some form," writes a *Time* analyst. "It's still the most efficient market for companies with huge amounts of stock outstanding. . . . And so far, Phelan has been an impressive leader. 'He kept the whole thing from coming apart,' says one broker. Phelan may have been successful so far because of his willingness to change. 'I'm not interested in how things were done yesterday,' he says." As Phelan told *Institutional Investor*, "The longer you hold back change, the more likely it is to sweep you away."

SOURCES:

PERIODICALS

Business Week, January 9, 1984, June 11, 1984.
Chicago Sun Times, December 14, 1984.
Chicago Tribune, December 13, 1984.
Forbes, October 8, 1984.
Institutional Investor, February, 1981.
Investor's Daily, May 23, 1985.
Newsweek, July 15, 1985.
New York Times, October 23, 1975, December 25, 1975, April 28, 1976, February 22, 1977, May 23, 1979, June 3, 1979, February 25, 1980, May 23, 1980, November 7, 1980, November 11, 1980, December 5, 1980, January 1, 1981, September 18, 1983, May 25, 1984, October 14, 1984, December 13, 1984.
Update, May, 1985.
U.S. News and World Report, December 13, 1982, January 14, 1985.
Wall Street Journal, December 20, 1983, December 21, 1983, March 5, 1984.
Washington Post, April 14, 1985, May 31, 1985.

—Sidelights by William C. Drollinger,
William C. Drollinger, Jr.,
and Steven C. Drollinger.

Frederick S. Pierce

1933-

PERSONAL: Born April 8, 1933, in Brooklyn, N.Y.; son of a cabdriver; married; wife's name, Marion; children: Richard, Keith, Linda. *Education:* Bernard M. Baruch School of Business and Public Administration of the City College (now Bernard M. Baruch College of the City University of New York), B.A., 1956.

ADDRESSES: Home—Westchester County, N.Y. *Office*—American Broadcasting Companies, Inc., 1330 Avenue of the Americas, New York, N.Y. 10019.

OCCUPATION: Television network executive.

CAREER: Worked for Benjamin Harrow & Son (public accounting firm), for three weeks in 1956; American Broadcasting Companies, Inc. (ABC), New York, N.Y., analyst in television research department, 1956-57, supervisor of audience measurements, 1957-58, manager of audience measurements, 1958-61, director of research, 1961-62, director of research and sales development, 1962, director of sales planning and sales development, 1962-64, vice-president and national director of television sales, 1964-68, vice-president of planning, 1968-70, assistant to president, 1970-72, vice-president in charge of television planning and development, 1972-74, assistant to president of ABC Television, 1973-74, senior vice-president of ABC Television, 1974, president, 1974-86, chief operating officer, 1983-86, consultant, 1986—; member of board of directors, Capital Cities–ABC, Inc. *Military service:* U.S. Army, Combat Engineers; served in Korea.

SIDELIGHTS: A career employee of ABC Television, Frederick S. Pierce has a button-down demeanor and aversion to personal publicity that for years obscured his rapid ascent up the corporate ladder. Promoted to the presidency of the network on October 22, 1974, Pierce took the network, which had been third in ratings, and masterminded a climb to the top. The ratings primacy has since slipped, but Pierce's strategy had been to keep ABC the most diversified of the three networks and to deliver the biggest share of the coveted eighteen- to forty-nine-year-old audience. By targeting programming to this group, Pierce—a protege of ABC founder Leonard Goldenson—kept the company at the top in terms of advertising revenue.

Pierce's career really took off in 1975 when he unveiled what has been called the "tent-pole strategy" for the pivotal fall 1975 schedule. That year, the "family view hour" was imposed on all three networks: no sex, no violence, between 8:00 p.m. and 9:00 p.m. Pierce realized that the bulk of the viewing audience would start flicking the dial when the hour-long ban ended, and so he dropped his strongest shows into the 9:00 p.m. slot. The strategy worked. Such shows as "Monday Night Football," "The Rookies," "Baretta," "The Streets of San Francisco," "S.W.A.T.," and a pair of movies put ABC at the top of the broadcasting heap. The hard-

working, tight-lipped executive finally began to develop a reputation for programming and management that has withstood the company's shaky performances in the eighties.

The Brooklyn-born son of a New York cabdriver, Pierce is, as Sally Bedell Smith pointed out in *TV Guide,* an organization man, not a showman. "The only flash of showmanship is his [lacquered] fingernails," noted Frank Swertlow in a *New York* magazine profile entitled "The Most Powerful Man in Television." One former colleague said Pierce the broadcasting magnate is very much like Pierce the weekend tennis player: "He doesn't have any flashstrokes, but he is relentless, He's like a bull. He is not graceful, but he'll just stand at the net and pound away, and he winds up the winner."

For Pierce, the pounding away began in 1956 when, as a recent graduate of the Bernard M. Baruch School of Business and Public Administration of the City College, he answered a newspaper ad. He had majored in accounting, but three weeks on the job in an accounting firm provided enough evidence that a career as an accountant would not make him happy. The ad he answered was for a ratings-service clerk in the research department at ABC. It paid $57 a week. The work was drudgery, but it was only the first of many diverse jobs Pierce would hold at ABC, giving him experience in every major area of broadcasting. Steven Flax declared in *Forbes*, "The methodical Pierce has succeeded at every position he has had: research, sales planning and programming." Handed a ratings book by his new boss, Julius Barnatham, Pierce had to ask what it was. As Barnatham told Swertlow, Pierce replied simply, "I guess I'll get to know it."

Barnatham later worked for Pierce as the vice-president in charge of broadcast operations and engineering at ABC. He reminisced to *New York* magazine about how the future president worked around the clock at the job. "Those were the days when we were fighting for our very survival," he related. Characteristically, Pierce's own description of those years is a pragmatic one. "It seem like an exciting business," he told *TV Guide*, referring to the industry that then was in its infancy. "It had some potential."

At night he studied marketing and television. To make ends meet on his meager salary he also peddled $200 sets of Wear-Ever Waterless Cookware door to door. He told *TV Guide's* Smith that this sales experience proved invaluable to his career. He increasingly became aware of "a sense of the different life styles of different kinds of people, and it gave me a little humility. It was a tough way to earn a living. You'd just knock on the door and try to be invited inside." From nine-to-five he was learning about such essentials to the industry as audience flow and program placement, and very quickly the promotions began coming. In 1961 he moved up to director of research. The next year the title of sales development was added. In 1964 he became a vice-president. Over the following four years he worked as a national director of TV network sales, then as head of television planning. Next came a senior vice-presidency, which gave him supervisory responsibilities for the bulk of the network's television operations.

While Pierce's own career was wending upwards, the fortunes of the network itself were lamentable. "ABC was the television industry's spittoon—the butt of many a joke," reported Howard Rosenberg in the *Los Angeles Times*. A typical joke that circulated in those years began with the question, "How do you end the Vietnam War?" The answer: Put it on ABC and it will end in thirteen weeks.

In this environment of gallows humor Pierce received his next promotion—to president of ABC Television. Industry insiders recall that period as the Year of The K, because of the line-up consisting of such weak fare as "Kodiak," "Kolchak" and "Kung Fu." Pierce set to work, trying to light a fire under his program development staff. Then, one night during Christmas week in 1974, he attended a party being given for certain clients. Then it was off for more drinks at the posh "21" Club. At the bar he spied a casual acquaintance, Fred Silverman of CBS. Silverman was then the programming star of the rival network, but while chatting with the man and his wife, Pierce grew certain that Silverman was more than slightly disenchanted with his job. He told Swertlow: "We had an exchange of ideas about how to have gratification out of what you are doing in the business and having some fun while you are doing it. I obviously was full of a lot of piss and vinegar; I was only two months into this new position. I told Silverman we were going to change a lot of things and have a lot of fun."

By the spring of 1975 Silverman had moved over to ABC. The announcement stood the broadcasting world on its head, and ABC stock jumped two points. With Pierce's manipulation of the new family hour rule and Silverman's programming input, ABC soon pushed its way into the number one spot. The two men became the talk of the industry, but Pierce continued to maintain his familiar low profile to the general public, and much of the credit for the network's upsurge went, accordingly, to the flashier Silverman. But Pierce insisted to *New York* magazine's Swertlow that "Everything is under my administration. Fred Silverman does not operate a separate company, believe me." Swertlow concluded: "It was Pierce's schedule that provided the base for ABC's victories. Fred Pierce was the architect, and Freddie Silverman was the contractor."

As architect, Pierce had to redesign the network's basic program philosophy, which was to go after the rural market. Such programs as "Nakia" and "Kodiak", aimed at this market, began to give way to slicker, city-targeted shows such as "S.W.A.T.," "Baretta," and "Barney Miller." Pierce told *New York*, "The philosophy in redirecting ABC was to go back toward urban appeal, young adults, and leading-personality types of shows." And of the strongest shows produced under this philosophy, the most popular were positioned to follow the family hour. This "clothesline" or "ridgepole" concept is Pierce's contribution to broadcasting industry lore.

At that time comedy was a strong suit at the network, and Pierce believes that early evening is the best time for comedy scheduling. When the family hour ban on potentially offensive subject matter was lifted, Pierce pushed such comedies as "Laverne and Shirley," "Three's Company," and "Barney Miller" into the eight-to-nine slot. Viewers took to all three shows. Intent on urbanizing ABC's programming, Pierce insisted on getting strong leading characters who, more and more often, were young, male—and decidedly virile. Pierce had decided to corner the market of women aged eighteen to forty-nine, whose purchasing power was coveted by advertisers. Determined to make daytime television a profit center, Pierce was responsible for ABC's decision to own most of its soap operas, rather then letting advertisers own them. Industry analysts looked favorably on this policy, which in March, 1985, resulted in ABC owning 3½ hours of its five daytime hours. These circumstances bolstered earnings at a time when the network's position in the ratings was slipping.

Pierce, however, was not forgetting male viewers. He was a prime mover in positioning ABC strongly in the sports area, ranging from "Monday Night Football" to coverage of the Olympics. The decision to buy telecast rights to the 1984 Los Angeles Olympic Games for a total of more than $325 million represented a gamble of Olympian proportions itself. The gamble appeared to pay off, however, when the Nielsen ratings showed that nearly one out of four television sets in the nation were turned to ABC's coverage of the games; forty-four percent of all people watching television were watching the broadcasts. Pierce boasted to *Newsweek*, "These games will go down as the major television event in modern television history."

While such reliable sports programming as "Wide World of Sports" encouraged ABC to invest liberally in this niche, some industry experts believe the network doesn't know where to draw the line. ABC is committed to pay $309 million for the rights to the Calgary Winter Olympics in 1988, and the network also carries baseball broadcasts. But so far the biggest black eye has been the continuing unprofitability of ESPN, one of the network's two major ventures into cable television. (The other has already been sold off at a big loss.) ESPN offers mainly sports programming but poses little threat to cable magnate Ted Turner. Turner criticized the network's management to *Forbes* writer Subrata Chakravarty: "I don't think the management of that company is very good. CBS and RCA took their losses and got out of cable quickly. ABC keeps hanging around like the U.S. in Vietnam. They're getting bloodier and bloodier, committing more and more millions of dollars."

Pierce was one of the three men at whom such charges were levelled. Senior management at ABC-TV's parent company, American Broadcasting Companies, Inc., included what one trade editor called "the troika," which, along with Pierce, included Leonard Goldenson, ABC chairman, and Elton Rule, the president. Under this management team, ABC was investing heavily not just in cable but in other state-of-the-art telecommunications technologies. Over the short term these ventures were not paying off; rather, the policy cost ABC over $100 million in this decade.

On January 11, 1983, ABC announced formally that Pierce had been named president and chief operating officer. Talking with the editors of *Broadcasting*, Pierce pointed out at the time of his promotion: "Just by a function of my age I've grown up with the television medium. I've worked for ABC for 27 years as television made its greatest strides." Despite the ratings slippage and critical salvos from some quarters, many in the industry hailed the promotion. "His appointment reinforces the long-time and quite visible stability of ABC's management, arguably one of the strongest in broadcasting," an industry analyst told *Broadcasting*.

There have, of course, been errors in both policy management and programming. During the 1984 summer Olympics—perhaps the coup for which he will be most remembered—a priceless opportunity to promote the fall, 1984, schedule slipped through Pierce's fingers. More than half of the network's promotional time was budgeted for a show, "Call To Glory," that faded fast despite the instant audience the network gave it through the costly promotion. Not only could the time have been sold to advertisers, but it could also have been more evenly distributed among other fall, 1984, programs. When the shows that year wheezed through their first weeks, Pierce conceded that the promotional policy may have been a mistake. As for his former forte, the situation comedy, Pierce told Sally Bedell Smith,

writing in the *New York Times*, "There is some evidence that comedies were more difficult to establish in the last few years."

Pierce found himself under the critical gun as his network struggled to regain its muscle-power of the late seventies. He was sniped at for promoting the so-called "jiggle shows" that feature alluring young actors of both sexes with as much movement and as little clothing as possible. And in her article in the *New York Times*, Sally Bedell Smith said that Pierce had become too high-brow in his programming. Most industry observers, however, give the ABC "troika" credit for successful financial management in regard to cost containment.

Pierce's hopes of succeeding his mentor, Leonard Goldenson, as ABC chairman were set back in March, 1985, when Capital Cities launched a merger with the television network. The merger resulted in the departure from active management of Goldenson, while Pierce remained in the number three position in the new entity, Capital Cities-ABC, Inc. In January, 1986, Pierce resigned from ABC Television, while retaining his position on the board of directors of the parent company. Some industry insiders speculated that Pierce, and other high-ranking officials, will face heavy pressure to rein-in losses resulting from efforts to penetrate the cable market and various high-technology investments that haven't paid off. Pierce told the *Wall Street Journal* that he saw no major stumbling blocks in the merged corporation. Speaking of the corporate histories of both firms, he said: "We both started with nothing and had to fight our way up. We're both entrepreneurs." The merger, he said, "is as good a marriage as you can get. I think everybody would like to be their own boss,. . . [but] I think it's important that you have the financial base to compete with whoever is against you."

SOURCES:

PERIODICALS

Broadcasting, January 17, 1983.
Forbes, July 19, 1982, August 13, 1984.
Los Angeles Times, March 12, 1979.
Newsweek, August 20, 1984, January 20, 1986.
New York, October 10, 1977.
New York Times, July 16, 1981, January 11, 1983, December 23, 1984.
Time, August 6, 1984.
TV Guide, October 13, 1979.
Variety, May 13, 1981, May 20, 1981, May 18, 1983, October 26, 1983, May 16, 1984, August 29, 1984, September 12, 1984.
Wall Street Journal, March 20, 1985.

—Sidelights by Warren Strugatch

Robert W. Pittman

1953-

PERSONAL: Born December 28, 1953, in Jackson, Miss.; son of Warren (a Methodist minister) and Lanita Pittman; married; wife's name, Sandy (a fashion consultant); children: Bo. *Education*: Attended Millsaps College, Jackson, Miss.

ADDRESSES: *Office*—MTV Networks, Inc., 75 Rockefeller Plaza, New York, N.Y. 10019.

OCCUPATION: Cable television executive.

CAREER: WCHJ-FM, Brookhaven, Miss., disc jockey, beginning 1968; disc jockey and programmer at radio stations in Milwaukee, Wis., Detroit, Mich., and Pittsburgh, Pa.; program director, WKQX-Radio and WMAQ-Radio, Chicago, Ill., beginning 1973, and WNBC-Radio, New York City, beginning 1977; Warner Amex Satellite Entertainment Co., New York City, 1979—, director of pay television (responsible for format and programming of The Movie Channel cable television network), beginning 1979, senior vice-president of programming (responsible for planning and development of MTV: Music Television cable television network), currently executive vice-president and chief operating officer of MTV Networks, Inc. (responsible for operation of MTV: Music Television, VH-1/Video Hits One, and Nickelodean cable television networks) and member of corporate board of directors.

MEMBER: International Radio and Television Society (member of board of governors), National Multiple Sclerosis Society (member of board of directors).

AWARDS, HONORS: Album Rock Program Manager of the Year award from *Billboard* magazine, 1977; Program Director of the Year award from *Hall Radio Report*, 1978; Innovator of the Year award from *Performance* magazine, 1981, for development of MTV: Music Television; Humanitarian of the Year Award from AMC Cancer Research Center, award from Council of Fashion Designers of America award, and one of seven runners-up for *Time* magazine's Man of the Year award, all 1984.

SIDELIGHTS: It's morning, and the children and adults are eating their breakfast with the members of Fleetwood Mac televised in the background, traveling through the desert to the tune of "Hold Me," one of their hits. When the kids come home from school, their attention bounces between homework and Twisted Sister, which is tearing through a high school and terrorizing a hapless teacher as "I Wanna Rock" pumps in the background. At the end of the working day, Daryl Hall and John Oates prance through the clouds during "Method of Modern Love" while the viewers eat dinner. Later in the evening, it's Culture Club's Boy George strutting through the street with a pack of children dressed as skeletons and singing "The War Song." Such was the vision of Robert W. Pittman on August 1, 1981, when he

AP/Wide World Photos

flipped the switch that sent Music Television—known to most as MTV, the cable music channel—in stereo to six million cable subscribers.

By its third birthday, MTV was reaching 25.4 million subscribers across America and was turning a profit from its advertising revenue. At the same time, a second station, the adult-oriented VH-1, was hitting 3.4 million subscribers. According to music publicist Howard Bloom—whose clients include pop heavyweights like the Jacksons, Prince, Billy Idol and Kool & the Gang—the concept has become "probably the most important tool to breaking an artist or a song." One Detroit record store reported that about a dozen copies of an album by a band called the Buggles sat unpurchased in its racks for more than two years. When MTV began playing the promotional video for a song from the album called "Video Killed the Radio Star"—the first video aired by the channel—the store sold out of the album within three weeks. The Record Town record and tape chain in Tulsa, Oklahoma, told *Billboard*, the music industry's leading trade magazine, that MTV was responsible for an additional $500 in revenue each week. A manager of the Record Theater in Syracuse, New York, told *Billboard*: "I have the Shoes on re-order because of MTV. Other acts that have picked up since MTV began here are the Specials, Elvis Costello, the Silencers and Rod Stewart, all of whom [MTV] has been featuring a lot. . . . We're considering putting a [video] monitor in the store."

MTV's success, in fact, spurred video software companies like Sony, CBS-Fox and RCA-Columbia to begin marketing music videos for home play. It also convinced several record companies, including A & M and Warner Bros., to form separate divisions to market their own artists' videos. "We were totally amazed with what they were doing with music videos to promote records and artists," explained Andrew Shofer, Sony's director of software marketing. Added director-producer Ken Walz, "We all think MTV when we do these things now. Music video is MTV to the industry."

The influence of MTV has spread beyond the music industry. Political candidates, including 69-year-old Indiana Governor Robert Orr, have run ads on the network. Fashion designers have also discovered the video influence popularized by MTV and are now using tapes of their creations for overseas display. Television commercials have adopted the video format and the editing style has surfaced in motion pictures and television programs. In fact, the original working title of NBC's smash hit "Miami Vice" was "MTV Cops." And musicians who have become video stars are translating their popularity into commercials, television programs, and motion pictures.

Having that kind of influence is nothing new to Pittman. When he was 21, he became the highest-paid radio program director in America. Two years later, he was the victor in an epic battle of New York City's Top 40 radio stations, piloting WNBC above WABC—America's first Top 40 station—for the first time in history. So Pittman seemed like the best choice to launch for the Warner Amex Satellite Entertainment Company (WASEC) a proposed music channel, which was described by Andy Seros, WASEC's vice-president of engineering as "a radio station with pictures,. . . able to play any tune in any order. That meant we had to put it together like a radio station, but the equipment itself had to be TV gear."

In designing MTV, Pittman utilized the same strategies he used to make his radio stations successful, techniques that were pioneered during the late 1960s when FM radio gained popularity and began fragmenting the listening audience. So instead of broadcasting to a wide audience, radio programmers—Pittman among them—began "narrowcasting" to a specific demographic. Rock stations, for instance, began aiming for the 14-25 age bracket, while adult-contemporary (commonly called soft-rock) stations looked for an older age group. With stations attracting those particular demographics, advertisers had more focused outlets to use in order to reach their target audience.

"In the old days [of radio], there were very few radio stations and the audience was at the mercy of the schedule," Pittman told the *Washington Post*. "If Jack Benny was on at 8:30 you had to be there. . . . But radio began to fractionalize. There were all-music stations and all-news stations, and suddenly there were five or six of them offering what you liked and you could punch in any time. . . . We are entering the era of TV of plenty. . . the same thing that happened to radio. In TV, there has historically been a scarcity of channels. So if people might like to watch something other than soap operas during the daytime, they couldn't." He elaborated for *Videography* magazine: "Music is very popular in our society. The networks don't do much of it, basically, because it has a narrow appeal. . . . So our initial premise was there was a lack of programming here."

Thus Pittman, who in his pinstripe suits, button-down shirts and horn-rimmed glasses looks more like a banker than a rock video programmer, designed MTV as an alternative. The concept of radio as TV works like this: play a variety of videos from a wide array of bands—including many that have never been played on commercial radio before MTV, such as Duran Duran, Elvis Costello and Prince—while five video jocks (VJs) provide between-song patter.

When MTV first started, it lacked adequate commercial sponsors, but the number has more than doubled since then, to the point where the channel is playing as many ads as any successful TV or radio station. Pittman has geared these efforts to reach his hand-picked demographic, the 14-34 age spread, all of whom, he believes, have a taste for particular forms of music—a trend he called psychographics. "Music tends to be a predictor of behavior and of social values, rather than of entertainment," he explained to the *Washington Post*. "You tell me the music people like, and I'll tell you their views on abortion, whether we should increase our military arms, what their sense of humor is like, what their favorite TV programs are, their response to political candidates, even their taste in jokes."

For music-lovers, then, MTV became requisite. "You'd have to be a social outcast not to watch it," Pittman said. To insure that the station remain essential to music fans, Pittman engineered several controversial moves. The first was an exclusivity deal with major record labels, whereby MTV pays major record companies for the right to air videos by important artists—such as Madonna, Hall and Oates, and Prince—for a month before they are sent to other video programmers. The second came during October, 1984, when Pittman decided to buy the video channel started by rival cable mogul Ted Turner, thus insuring monopoly in the twenty-four-hour national video market.

Pittman and Warner-Amex also decided that the 25-54 age group was ripe for the video music market as well. They launched VH-1, a video version of adult-contemporary radio, on January 1, 1985, to play videos that wouldn't be appropriate on the youth-oriented MTV. "VH-1 gives us an outlet for more mature videos, directed at the older audience," Arista Record's Peter Baron told *Billboard*. "It'll also definitely make some of our artists [Barry Manilow, Air Supply, Aretha Franklin] try to understand the medium a little better and realize the impact effective video marketing can have for them. I think it will definitely translate into record sales for us."

Pittman admitted to *Billboard* that part of his goal with VH-1 was to boost the adult record-buying market: "The 25-plus group does buy a significant number of records; it's not the greatest number of record per capita for any age group, of course, but it is a good amount. Our task with VH-1 is to increase that number, to get these people to buy records from established artists as well as new ones." VH-1 certainly had little trouble attracting support. The demographic was attractive to upper-scale advertisers, like car companies, airlines and other retail manufacturers, who felt the $300-per-30-second-spot rate was a good gamble.

"I don't think I'm capable of guessing what 200 million people want, nor am I capable of copying the right things," Pittman told *Videography*. "I think it's best to try to find what people are really doing and what they really want. Time changes a lot of that. As we get into new industries like this one, there are no formulas, there are no precedents to look at. . . . The new technology serves me well because it allows us to find things without having a past, with only a future."

SOURCES:

PERIODICALS

Audio, May, 1982.
Billboard, October 10, 1981, January 12, 1985, January 26, 1985.
Cablevision, November 2, 1984.
Detroit Free Press, August 26, 1984, January 7, 1985, January 18, 1986.
Esquire, December, 1985.
Rolling Stone, September 22, 1983.
Time, January 7, 1985.
Variety, April 14, 1982.
Videography, September, 1981.
Washington Post, September 16, 1982.

—Sidelights by Gary Graff

Peter H. Pocklington

1941-

PERSONAL: Born November 18, 1941, in Regina, Saskatchewan, Canada; son of Basil B. (an insurance salesman) and Eileen (Dempsey) Pocklington; married Eva McAvoy, June 2, 1974; children: two sons, two daughters. *Education:* Attended schools in London, Ontario.

ADDRESSES: Office—2500 Sun Life Place, 10123 99 St., Edmonton, Alberta, Canada T5J 3H1.

OCCUPATION: Business executive.

CAREER: Management trainee, Robert Simpson Co. (department store), Toronto, Ontario; salesman and president of car dealerships in Tilbury, Ontario, 1967-69, Chatham, Ontario, 1969-71, and Edmonton, Alberta, 1971-82; chairman of Pocklington Financial Corp. Ltd. Acquired Edmonton Oilers hockey team, 1976, Gainers Ltd. meat packing, 1977, Fidelity Trust, 1979, Swift Canada, 1980, Capri Drilling, 1981, Edmonton Trappers Triple-A baseball team, 1981, and Oakland Stompers professional soccer team.

MEMBER: London (Ontario) Hunt and Country Club, Primrose Club (Toronto), Mayfair Golf and Country Club (Edmonton).

SIDELIGHTS: Tycoon Peter Pocklington has puzzled Canada's normally conservative business community for years. During the 1970s, he cut a high-rolling swath through the pin-striped financial world, quickly expanding a modest used car dealership into a business empire worth more than $1.4 billion. Then, just as quickly, his empire collapsed and he had to sell off many of his holdings. But no one is counting Peter Pocklington out. He is currently retrenching and claimed in a recent interview to still have a personal fortune of between $60 and $100 million.

At the height of his success, Pocklington was one of the richest men in Canada. Former U.S. president Gerald Ford sat on the board of one of his companies. He had a jet-setter's lifestyle and movie stars as friends. But Pocklington wasn't satisfied with his fortune in real estate, investments, meat-packing, and oil. Instead, living out the fantasies of a self-made man, he began turning his attention to the higher profile pursuits of sports and politics. In the process, he blew more than $1 million of his own money in a run for the leadership of the federal Progressive Conservative party and much more than that in questionable business decisions.

Ironically, his sports interests have served him well. He admits he bought the National Hockey League's Edmonton Oilers for an "ego trip" and not a financial investment. But the Oilers' high-flying on-ice performance has turned the franchise into a hot property. Led by superstar Wayne Gretzky, the Oilers have earned Pocklington two successive Stanley Cup victories.

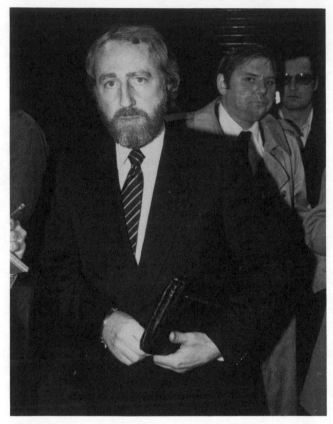

Pocklington, or Peter Puck as he is commonly known, is hardly a typical entrepreneur. Canadian author and broadcaster Peter Gzowski described him as the "man who would be king." In an infamous 1983 lawsuit, a clairvoyant he hired described him as "power-mad." But no matter what troubles have befallen him on his roller-coaster ride to success, Pocklington has remained completely confident. That is the hallmark of his career. As Gzowski wrote in *Saturday Night,* "Whatever he does, he does with gusto, chortling with pleasure, exclaiming on the excellence of the wine or his good fortune, and punctuating his conversation with cries of self-congratulation."

The son of a London, Ontario insurance salesman, Pocklington showed early signs of the *chutzpah* that was to mark his later business career. When he was a preschooler, he collected chestnuts from a neighbor's lawn and then tried to sell the nuts back to the owner. In his search for riches, he even sold his Christmas presents. And he convinced a group of friends to help him tear down a family barn and sell the wood for cash. The purchase and sale of cars would later become Pocklington's springboard to the business world. And, typically, he had an early education. One weekend while his parents were away, the young Pocklington unloaded the family car for $2,800 and a 1956 Plymouth. Although his parents were at first annoyed with the unauthorized trade, the subsequent sale of the Plymouth earned them an unexpected $800.

After quitting school at age 17, he tried a short stint as a management trainee with the Robert Simpson Co. department store in Toronto. He left the job with the characteristic declaration that he was worth ten times what Simpson would pay. After an early success with a couple of Eastern car dealerships, he pulled up stakes and moved to Alberta just as the oil boom was beginning. Pocklington would later say the lessons he had learned in the car business applied to every other enterprise. "It's all just selling cars, only with more zeroes," Pocklington told one interviewer.

By 1972, Pocklington began toying with real estate, making quick resales in both the American and Canadian markets. He continued to dabble until he crossed paths with one of Canada's fastest and slickest dealers—Nelson Skalbania. One realtor told *Alberta Report* magazine: "What Skalbania did was take a guy who was kind of ambitious, and that was Pocklington, and introduce him to the big game, rolling over this and rolling over that." And roll over he did. He purchased a jet boat company, a ski resort, a large Ford dealership in Toronto, and interests in Pop Shoppe International Ltd. In the fall of 1976, Pocklington purchased the Oilers from Skalbania, even though he had only seen one professional hockey game in his life. He got lost on his first trip to the Northlands Coliseum as owner of the team. In addition, he acquired a Triple-A baseball team, the Edmonton Trappers, and a professional soccer team, the Oakland Stompers.

Pocklington began to expand and diversify his portfolio with the purchase of the Edmonton-based meat packer Gainers Ltd. He confessed at the time that all he knew about food processing was "that cows went in one end and steaks came out the other." By October, 1980, he had acquired the Canadian holdings of Chicago-based Swift and Co. With the merger of Swift and Gainers, Pocklington formed Canada's third-largest packing business. In the fall of 1979, he purchased what would become the centerpiece of his financial empire—Fidelity Trust, an investment firm founded in 1909. He then formed Patrician Land Corp. as a subsidiary of Fidelity. Although he was expanding in various directions, all of his holdings had one common denominator—they had title to valuable real estate.

With his financial success came celebrity. He counted film stars like Paul Newman among his friends. He, his wife Eva, and their son lived in a Tudor-style mansion, complete with seven bathrooms and a collection of Renoir prints. He drove a vintage Rolls Royce convertible to work every morning. "He works harder at having fun than most men do at their jobs," Gzowski noted in *Saturday Night.* But with celebrity came notoriety. In the spring of 1981, Pocklington was wounded in a shoot-out between police and a man who had attempted to kidnap him and his wife. He recovered fully and, indeed, allowed television reporters to interview him from his hospital bed. And in 1983, a clairvoyant named Rita Burns sued Pocklington for $7 million, claiming he had promised her ten percent of the money he invested on her advice. She told a breathless public that he had taken LSD

and that he stood before a mirror every morning and told himself, "I am a god." A jury later dismissed her suit.

But even notoriety had its good points, according to this disciple of positive thinking. "We all have a few skeletons in the closet," the *Globe and Mail* quoted Pocklington as saying after his lawsuit victory. "If we got them all out we'd have quite a party." Pocklington is the embodiment of positive thinking. During his first year as owner of the Oilers, he insisted that all team members attend self-development seminars operated by a California institute. He often told friends and workers that they could do anything if they put their minds to it. But for Pocklington—the self-made man—positive thinking finally became wishful thinking when he decided to become Prime Minister of Canada.

Like many businessmen, he was convinced his skills could apply just as well to government as to the marketplace. Although he had earlier supported Prime Minister Pierre Trudeau, he believed the Liberal policies that had resulted in a high federal deficit and massive unemployment were inexcusable. He wanted to replace "the amateurs running the business of the country." So he submitted his name as a candidate in the June, 1983, leadership contest for the Progressive Conservative party.

For Pocklington, the political world was a simple place. The solutions to complex policy problems were made easy when business principles were applied. A good prime minister, he believed, would sell off Canada's crown corporations. He also proposed a flat twenty percent tax for all taxpayers earning more than $12,000. Many observers, however, found it difficult to take Pocklington's musings seriously. He had no background in public service. And he wasn't proposing a conventional route to political office; rather he aimed to take a direct stab at the top. Liberal senator and power broker Keith Davey said the world of politics was too sophisticated to offer itself up to Pocklington's ambitions. And Peter Lougheed, Alberta's Conservative premier and acquaintance of Pocklington, publicly dismissed him as a viable political alternative. The simple world of politics, however, was about to become complicated for Peter Pocklington. He launched his campaign by stating he would divorce himself from all business interests except his sports franchises. Yet financial troubles struck at precisely the same moment.

Public records showed that Pocklington's companies borrowed heavily during 1982 and early 1983 at high interest rates. A telling blow was struck when Fidelity Trust faltered. In early 1983, during the leadership campaign, it was revealed that Fidelity had exceeded a federally set 20-to-1 borrowing guideline because its asset base, largely real estate, had withered. A federal agency placed the company on a one-week operating license rather than the normal one-year permit. Pocklington had to inject $20.6 million of new capital into the company or find a new owner. When he couldn't come up with the money or a buyer, the government asked for management proposals from several companies to safeguard Fidelity's $840 million in public deposits. In late June, federal regulators appointed Vancouver-based First Trust as new manager of the trust company.

The man who would be prime minister suffered further embarrassment when his major car dealership was placed in receivership and his meat-packing company was reduced in size. It was clearly becoming difficult for Pocklington to base his leadership campaign on the strength of his business acumen. In addition, fellow right-wing Conservatives had trouble with many of his political ideas and dubbed his flat-tax proposal "a political nightmare." Pocklington was defeated on the first ballot of the leadership vote but showed some political savvy by crossing the floor to support the eventual winner and new prime minister, Brian Mulroney.

Observors began to write Pocklington off. He had, after all, seen $75 million of his own personal fortune slip through his fingers. But Pocklington continued to surprise the business community. Armed with his own sense of confidence, he began to rebuild. The road back wasn't easy. He had to give up the private Lear jet and the personal office chef. The Rolls Royce was traded in for a more modest Mercedes Benz. And he had to use his beloved Oilers as collateral for loans with a bank and later with the Alberta government.

In 1981 his companies had assets of $1.4 billion and sales of $900 million. In 1985 he reduced his portfolio to five companies with assets of $150 million and projected sales of $475 million. Pocklington has nevertheless maintained his old enthusiasm. In an interview with Robert Sheppard of the Toronto *Globe and Mail,* he said rumors of his demise were greatly exaggerated. "When you are worth between $60 and $100 million, you are not dead yet." He referred to his political debacle as "a great learning process. Truly, one of the highlights of my life." Pocklington still hopes Prime Minister Mulroney will recognize his talents and appoint him to head a royal commission to study tax laws. And he has steadfastly refused to part with the Oilers, despite several offers.

Pocklington once told *Maclean's* magazine: "This world seems to judge people on 'God, if you take a gamble and you lose, Holy Lord, you're a crook,' rather than 'Thank God, people take gambles and occasionally win and occasionally lose.'" Peter Pocklington clearly is a man who has lived by his philosophy.

AVOCATIONAL INTERESTS: Boat racing, skiing.

SOURCES:

BOOKS

Newman, Peter C., *The Acquisitors,* McClelland & Stewart, 1981.

PERIODICALS

Alberta Report, July 19, 1982, August 8, 1983, October 17, 1983, April 9, 1984.
Financial Post, April 2, 1983.
Maclean's, April 18, 1983, December 9, 1985.
Saturday Night, April, 1982.
Toronto Globe and Mail, May 16, 1983, September 29, 1983, October 19, 1983, January 28, 1985.
Toronto Life, January, 1984.
Winnipeg Free Press, October 6, 1982, October 20, 1982, October 22, 1982.
Winnipeg Sun, April 5, 1983.

—Sidelights by Ingeborg Boyens

Jean-Luc Ponty

1942-

PERSONAL: Born September 29, 1942, in Avranches, France; came to United States in 1973; son of a violin teacher and a piano teacher. *Education:* Left school at age thirteen to study violin privately; Conservatoire National Superieur de Musique, Paris, France, graduate, 1960.

ADDRESSES: Office—JLP Productions, Inc., P.O. Box 46425, Los Angeles, Calif. 90046.

OCCUPATION: Violinist; composer and producer.

CAREER: Classical violinist until 1964; member of Concerts Lamoureux Symphony Orchestra, Paris, France, 1960-63; jazz, rock, and fusion violinist, composer, and producer, 1964—. Head of JLP Productions, Inc. (music production company), Los Angeles, Calif.

Performed in Europe, 1964-69; appeared in nightclubs and at music festivals with George Duke Trio throughout the United States, 1969; formed group Experience and toured Europe, 1970-72; worked with Frank Zappa and the Mothers of Invention, 1969-74, Elton John, 1972, and the Mahavishnu Orchestra, 1974-75; since 1975, has toured and recorded with his own groups and with a number of other musicians. Appeared at numerous jazz festivals, including Antibes, 1964, Monterey, 1967 and 1969, Newport, 1970 and 1974, Berlin, 1971, and Montreux, 1972.

AWARDS, HONORS: Winner of *down beat* Readers' Poll and Critics' Poll in violin category, 1971-79.

DISCOGRAPHY:

RECORD ALBUMS

Sunday Walk, MPS, 1967.
Electric Connection, Pacific Jazz, 1968.
Jean-Luc Ponty: Experience, Pacific Jazz, 1969.
King Kong (with Frank Zappa), Pacific Jazz, 1970.
Astrorama, Far East, 1972.
Open Strings, MPS, 1972.
Live in Montreux, Inner City, 1972.
Ponty/Grappelli (with Stephane Grappelli), America, 1973.
Apocalypse (with Mahavishnu Orchestra), Columbia, 1974.
Upon the Wings of Music, Atlantic, 1975.
Visions of the Emerald Beyond (with Mahavishnu Orchestra), Columbia, 1975.
Violin Summit (with Grappelli, Stuff Smith, and Svend Asmussen), MPS, 1975.
Imaginary Voyage, Blue Note, 1976.
Aurora, Atlantic, 1976.
Sonata Erotica, Inner City, 1976.
Jean-Luc Ponty/Stephane Grappelli (with Grappelli), Inner City, 1976.
Jazz 60's, Volume II, Pacific Jazz, 1976.
Enigmatic Ocean, Atlantic, 1977.

Cantaloupe Island (with George Duke), Blue Note, 1977.
Cosmic Messenger, Atlantic, 1978.
Live, Atlantic, 1979.
A Taste for Passion, Atlantic, 1979.
Civilized Evil, Atlantic, 1980.
Mystical Adventures, Atlantic, 1982.
Individual Choice, Atlantic, 1983.
Open Mind, Atlantic, 1984.
Fables, Atlantic, 1985.

Also played on several albums by Frank Zappa and the Mothers of Invention, including *Hot Rats,* and on Elton John's *Honky Chateau,* 1972.

SIDELIGHTS: Jean-Luc Ponty has been compared to the legendary jazz saxophonist John Coltrane. According to Chris Albertson in *Stereo Review,* Ponty "did for the jazz violin what John Coltrane did for the saxophone: took it down a new path." Ponty certainly enjoys much of the credit for the increasing popularity of the jazz (particularly electric) violin, the instrument upon which he has built his substantial career. He has played to packed houses, recorded an average of more than an album per year, sold hundreds of thousands of records, and appeared on several television shows, including "Soundstage," "Rock Concert," and "The Tonight Show." Ponty is also the first jazz artist to record a video for a major record company. Fame, however, is not all there is in life for Ponty; even at the height of his success he gives priority to his musical values, which have evolved considerably since his years as a provincial schoolboy.

Ponty's parents may have been surprised at the direction in which their son's early music training eventually led him. His father, a music teacher in a small French town, taught violin and many other instruments, including the clarinet. At age three, Ponty was given a violin to play with; two years later he began serious violin and piano studies. He was trained in the classical repertoire on these instruments and by the time he was thirteen had decided to become a professional musician. He then quit school in order to devote his time and energy entirely to his violin and piano studies.

At age fifteen, Ponty entered the illustrious and highly competitive Conservatoire National Superieur de Musique in Paris. Although he excelled in his studies, and in 1960 won the Premier Prix for violin, his interest in jazz also originated during this time. Upon the invitation of his classmates, Ponty went to hear such notable jazz musicians as pianist Bud Powell, percussionist Kenny Clarke, and saxophonist Dexter Gordon, who were then playing in Parisian nightclubs. Ponty's friends also introduced him to popular jazz albums, some of which impressed him greatly. His initial attraction to jazz, however, owed a great deal to the activities that accompanied it. Much later in his career, he described this period to *Newsweek* writer Maureen Orth: "At first I didn't take jazz seriously. . . . I did it to get out of my environment of classical music studies, to chase girls and drive sports cars." Ponty admits that while his training as a classical musician had made him a musical snob, jazz changed his perception of classical works. In an interview with Howard Mandel of *down beat* Ponty stated: "When I was a classical musician, nothing but classical music was good to me. . . . Then I discovered jazz. . . , and there were musical works by very famous composers, sometimes favorite pieces, that didn't make it for me anymore, rhythmically or harmonically or melodically, because they sounded corny."

During his years at the Conservatoire National, Ponty learned to play the clarinet as a diversion from his intense violin studies. When he was seventeen years old, he discovered that a Parisian jazz band needed a clarinetist. He took advantage of the opportunity to learn the rudiments of jazz by playing with the band, though classical music was still his main interest. Occasionally Ponty jammed on the tenor saxophone and string bass, as well as the clarinet, but he eventually turned to the violin because he was most proficient at it and did not have the patience to learn other instruments that were more commonly played by jazz musicians. While Ponty did not initially value jazz, he told Orth, "I learned that in its own way jazz had a discipline as strong as the classics. I had been searching for years for a way to put my ideas about music together and be in balance with myself." Jazz, and later jazz-rock fusion allowed Ponty to find the vehicles of expression he desired.

Upon his graduation from the Conservatoire National, Ponty joined the Parisian Concerts Lamoureux Symphony

Orchestra. And when he was not performing with the symphony, he played with local jazz ensembles. Inspired by the work of many jazz artists, including trumpeter Miles Davis, saxophonist John Coltrane, and violinist Stephane Grappelli, Ponty quit the orchestra in 1963 to begin his full-time career as a jazz musician. He played regularly in clubs and very quickly received a recording contract, a success that he attributes to the novelty of the jazz violin at that time. Later he performed at the jazz festival in Antibes (in southern France), then the only major European jazz festival. The exposure skyrocketed Ponty's career: he was offered engagements throughout Europe.

Ponty's participation in the American jazz world began in 1967, when he was invited to attend a violin masterclass at the Monterey Jazz Festival in California. Like the Antibes festival, the Monterey festival, in which Ponty participated in both 1967 and 1969, brought his talent to the attention of the public and the music industry. He recorded three albums and played nightclub engagements with the George Duke Trio before returning to France.

Ponty moved quickly from freelance playing to forming his own band, Experience, in 1970. An avant-garde, free jazz group that emphasized improvisation, Experience disbanded two years after its inception. Ponty later told *down beat* writer Robert Palmer the reason for the breakup: "Experience was very free, and. . . I didn't feel comfortable at all. I didn't feel freer. On the contrary, I felt that I was going into cliches more and more, and that's why I decided to go back to more structure and more discipline."

After Ponty's producer sent a sample recording of the violinist's work to rock composer-arranger Frank Zappa, who was interested in working with some jazz musicians, Zappa asked Ponty to join his eclectic and notorious group, the Mothers of Invention. Ponty played four tours with the Mothers but indicated to Palmer that he still had not found his musical niche, "There was a lot of variety from show to show. But it was not enough freedom for me. There were still a lot of backgrounds and theatrical things that I didn't relate to." During this period in his career, Ponty also worked with other artists, including Elton John, on whose *Honky Chateau* album Ponty played the violin.

Dissatisfied with the European jazz scene, Ponty, in 1973, emigrated to Los Angeles, California, a musically progressive city and the one in which he found he was the most comfortable. Although Ponty was composing and arranging his own music, hoping to form a band, he joined John McLaughlin's Mahavishnu Orchestra. Ponty and McLaughlin had first met in 1969 during Ponty's first trip to the United States. The Mahavishnu Orchestra performed a brand of jazz fusion, combining elements of traditional jazz with Eastern (Indian) music. Ponty spent two years with this group and was featured as soloist on several albums, including *Apocalypse* and *Visions of the Emerald Beyond*. Personal and legal disputes, however, ended Ponty's fruitful association with McLaughlin and his orchestra.

Ponty then decided to resume his previous plans: he formed his own band, and frequently featured himself as soloist. Though the band's membership varied from album to album and year to year, the instrumentation was generally constant and included an electric guitarist, an electric bassist, a percussionist, and a keyboardist (acoustic piano and synthesizer) in addition to Ponty on the electric violin. The new group's instrumentation was similar to that of the Mahavishnu Orchestra, but unlike the previous group, its music was more emotionally appealing to Ponty. Attractive, scored or improvised melodies over hard rhythmic bass patterns, clean combinations of electronic timbres, and violin virtuosity soon became hallmarks of Ponty's work. Since he had begun playing jazz violin, Ponty had been experimenting with the available electronic technology, such as wah-wah pedals and phase shifters, and he eventually settled on the Barcus-Berry electric violin. He has also used a five-string electric violin and a violectra (a baritone violin with strings tuned one octave lower than those of the regular violin).

Working at home at a table with a piano nearby, Ponty composed and arranged all of the group's pieces. His music draws from a variety of sources, but Ponty did not have much time to listen to other artists' works. In composing, Ponty emphasizes inspiration. "The side of music I am most sensitive to is emotion, feelings," he told *down beat*. "If it comes by inspiration, it's more in that vein because it can be a reaction to some experience. That's the way I like to approach music. I don't like to say, 'Well, I have to write because I have an album to deliver on such and such a date.' Certain musicians are able to do that, which is nice, in a way. But sometimes the result is pretty mechanical, very technical. It becomes pretty sterile."

Although his composition style relies greatly on inspiration, the music itself is highly structured, and Ponty rehearses with his musicians as if he were a maestro. He described his rehearsal technique to Orth: "I give them structure and above that structure the soloist is free to use his imagination. . . . Then after we practice and practice and rehearse and rehearse, I write all the notes for the instruments like classical music. And then we rehearse again very tightly like a symphony orchestra." Ponty's desire to supervise every aspect of his compositions has led him to form his own production company, JLP Productions. He likes to mix his own tracks and is even involved in deciding on details of album cover art and copy.

Many of Ponty's records, such as *Imaginary Voyage*, *Enigmatic Ocean*, and *A Taste for Passion*, have been quite popular. The particularly successful *Imaginary Voyage* sold more than 200,000 copies and was for a long time high on the jazz charts. Ponty gained his following primarily by touring. While his early career was greatly advanced by his participation in jazz festivals, Ponty eventually turned to promotional tours instead. Because his music was diverging from traditional jazz idioms and gradually becoming a jazz-rock hybrid, he did not believe that it would appeal to the traditional-jazz-oriented festival audiences. But Ponty's fusion of jazz with elements of other musical styles has attracted an abundance of listeners; the band played to sell-out crowds throughout the United States. Later, the group performed in Europe and Japan as well, averaging six months per year on the road.

The tours were necessary because, with its mixture of jazz and rock, Ponty's work gets little radio airplay. Ponty expressed his views on creativity and radio versus tours as promotional media to Ed Harrison of *Billboard*: "If I wanted more airplay I'd take up vocals and go all the way. . . . I know the way I'm going about it is a much longer process, but I know it can work. I want to be myself and produce music that comes from inspiration. If it works and it's a commercial success, great. I just want to play for people or else I wouldn't go on the road and would stay in the studio and become a session musician or write arrangements."

Declaring that he needed a vacation from touring and composing, and time to ponder the future course of his work, Ponty surprised the music world in 1980 by disbanding his group. But he was not on vacation for very long. By 1982 he had organized another band and composed, arranged, and recorded *Mystical Adventures*. The new Ponty sound uses to greater advantage the capabilities of the electronic synthesizer and features a purer, less aggressive violin sound. Ponty's sources of inspiration and method of composition are also subtly different from those of his previous work.

But in Ponty's more recent work, as in everything he has done, the importance of emotion remains. "My inspiration nowadays comes from what I experience in my everyday life," he explained to Mandel; "from social events, the world's political scene, the search for the meaning of life. . . . I don't think so much about musical technique and forms and structures—it just kind of flows pretty naturally now. My music is very opposite to the events that are happening in the world, because it's kind of an ideal of another, purer world that I feel in myself and like to express in my music."

SOURCES:

BOOKS

Berendt, Joachim, *The Jazz Book: From New Orleans to Rock and Free Jazz*, translation by Dan Morgenstern, Barbara Bredigkeit, and Helmut Bredigkeit, Lawrence Hill & Co., 1975.
Coryell, Julie, and Laura Friedman, *Jazz-Rock Fusion: The People, the Music*, Dell, 1978.

PERIODICALS

Billboard, February 26, 1977, December 2, 1978, January 26, 1980.
down beat, December 4, 1975, December 1, 1977, January, 1984.
Melody Maker, August 30, 1975.
Newsweek, September 12, 1977.
New York Times, September 2, 1984.
Stereo Review, March, 1980.

—Sketch by Jeanne M. Lesinski

Anna Maximilian Potok
1907-

BRIEF ENTRY: Full name, Anna Maximilian Apfelbaum Potok; born June 4, 1907, in Warsaw, Poland. Polish-American fur designer. The president of Maximilian Furs, Inc. since 1953, Anna Maximilian Potok is considered the doyenne of international furriers. Over the years she has designed furs for numerous wealthy and prominent women from around the world, including Queen Elizabeth, the Duchess of Windsor, Nancy Reagan, Jacqueline Kennedy Onassis, Diana Ross, and Marilyn Monroe.

Potok's career began in Warsaw in 1922 when she joined her brother's thriving fur salon. Potok and her brother, Maximilian Apfelbaum, along with her husband and son, fled Poland in 1939, shortly before the Nazi invasion. The family settled in New York, where Potok and Apfelbaum opened a small shop on Fifth Avenue. In 1940 they moved their business to its present location on West 57th Street. Fashion mavens Diana Vreeland and Helena Rubinstein were early, enthusiastic customers; with their support, Maximilian Furs quickly became the preferred furrier among royalty, heads of state, and celebrities.

Potok assumed full control of the family operation upon her brother's death in 1961. Although she is nearing eighty, Potok has no plans to retire. "To the last minute of my life, I'll be in business," she told Harriet Shapiro of *People*. The *New York Times*'s Enid Nemy reports that age is of little consequence to the designer. "I think every day that today was good but tomorrow must be better, not only in business but for myself," Potok explains. "Every day has been a challenge from childhood on." *Address:* Maximilian Furs, Inc., 20 West 57th St., New York, N.Y. 10019.

Jack Manning/NYT Pictures

SOURCES:

PERIODICALS

New York Times, April 5, 1982.
People, February 1, 1982.

Christopher Pratt

1935-

PERSONAL: Born December 9, 1935 in St. John's, Newfoundland, Canada; son of John Kerr and Christine Emily (Daw) Pratt; married Mary West (an artist), September 12, 1957; children: John, Anne, Barbara, Edwyn. *Education:* Mount Allison University, Sackville, New Brunswick, B.F.A., 1961; also attended Glasgow School of Art, Glasgow, Scotland.

ADDRESSES: *Home*—P.O. Box 87, Mount Carmel, St. Mary's Bay, Newfoundland, Canada A0B 2M0.

OCCUPATION: Artist.

CAREER: Painter and printmaker. Art teacher at St. John's Memorial University, St. John's, Newfoundland, 1961-63; full-time artist, 1963—. Has exhibited work throughout Canada and the United Kingdom. Served on Canada Council, 1976-82.

MEMBER: Royal Canadian Academy of Arts, Canadian Society of Graphic Art, Royal Newfoundland Yacht Club (former commodore).

AWARDS, HONORS: D. Litt., Mount Allison University, 1972; D. Laws, St. John's Memorial University, 1972; Order of Canada, officer, 1973, companion, 1983.

SIDELIGHTS: St. Catherine's, Newfoundland, is a tiny, desolate village on Canada's eastern coast. The home of fishermen, it has no nightlife to speak of, let alone an art scene. Yet this is where one of Canada's foremost artists, Christopher Pratt, painted his most important canvasses. Pratt's work has reached far beyond the borders of St. Catherine's, the province of Newfoundland, or even Canada. His paintings now bring more than $70,000 each on the world market. His work may be dubbed "Maritime realism," but his style clearly has an appeal that defies regional labels.

Pratt's work is familiar even to those who don't follow art. His trademark colors are subtle and muted—cool greys and blues. His lines are often austere and architectural. And the steady light that falls on his paintings comes from no particular source. When he combines these colors, lines, and light with seemingly unending seas and skies, they have a haunting power that the viewer can't shake. There is a mystical interaction between the known and the unknown. In the familiar painting "Cottage," we are faced with the stark juxtaposition of a balcony barrier to the free, wide-open space of the horizon. In "Landing," the viewer must decide between mounting the stairs to the unknown or proceeding through an open door into a cell-like room.

The value of Pratt's work is enhanced by the painful process he goes through to finish a painting. He must rank among the least prolific of artists, completing little more than one painting a year. In an interview with *Maclean's*, Pratt said

Photograph by John Reeves. Courtesy of Arts & Communications

painting was a tortuous experience for him. But he admitted to "an intense flash, two or three seconds of satisfaction, of thinking maybe it isn't bad," when he finally finishes a piece. His wife, Mary, herself an accomplished painter, says Pratt suffers when he paints because his approach is as stark as his final product. "His is not a loving or embracing process. It's a philosophical, intellectual exercise," she told the interviewer.

The reference to philosophy is a common refrain when experts discuss Pratt's art. One critic called him a metaphysical painter who attempts to define the quality of experience. An *ArtsCanada* magazine writer said: "The resolution and harmony that Pratt finally achieves are won from a harsh existential conflict. His is the struggle of the eternal problems of necessity and existence."

His work defies easy classification. Along with painter Alex Colville, Pratt has been labelled a leader of Canada's "Maritime realists." Yet he is much more than a naturalist who hopes to duplicate life. While he does paint recognizable doors and windows and seas and skies, he pares them down to their essential elements so that the doors and windows become a way of looking inward, an examination of what we know and understand. And the seas and skies become a way of looking outward, towards the unknown. Pratt's recurring architectural forms are stripped down so they have more in common with geometric shapes than they do with their antecedents. They put Pratt closer to the abstract than the realist school. And by rejecting the human figure as a subject, Pratt has moved away from Colville's realistic style to his own, unique niche.

His work is the product of an obvious intellectual discipline. Yet he still has the candor of a small-town Newfoundlander. When a Canadian television reporter interviewed him recently, Pratt said he wouldn't talk about what art is "and all that old crap" on the grounds that he could "sound very pretentious about it." Regardless of the rigor he employs in his own work, he said art "is a very simple process in which making an art object or making a painting or whatever is no more nor less than adult play—simply doing what a child does with plasticine or with blocks, except you are doing it at a adult level."

Born in 1935, Pratt grew up in well-to-do surroundings in St. John's, the capital of the province of Newfoundland. St. John's in the 1940s and '50s was hardly an artistic centre, so it is not altogether surprising that Pratt had never heard of Picasso, Matisse or any other modern painters before he attended college. When he first went to Mount Allison University in New Brunswick, Pratt intended to fulfill his parents' expectations and take up medicine or engineering. An art class wasn't even on his course schedule. But then he met Mary West, whom he would eventually marry. She was enrolled in the art program and introduced him to her professors: Lawren Harris, Jr., son of the great "Group of Seven" painter, and Alex Colville, the well-known realist. Pratt told *Maclean's* his decision to become an artist was clinched when he watched Colville paint in an immaculate grey suit. Colville seemed to represent an inviting combination of artistic seriousness and middle-class respectability.

Despite Colville's influence, Pratt didn't apply his talents well. Instead of completing art class projects, Pratt would spend his time doing props for events like the junior prom. After a couple of years he dropped out altogether, returning to St. John's to try his hand at watercolors. But he soon decided he needed more training and enrolled in the Glasgow School of Art in Scotland. He didn't stay in Glasgow long enough to get beyond the drawing segments of the program, but the rigorous concentration on art fundamentals provided him with the confidence he needed to pursue painting as a career. Pratt returned to Mount Allison after two years in Glasgow. He graduated and then took a teaching job at St. John's Memorial University. But after completing only one picture during his two years in academia, he quit to paint full time.

Pratt and Mary retreated in 1963 to his father's summer house in St. Catherine's to raise a family and to paint. The seclusion of their new home ensured that Pratt was spared unnecessary visitors and disruptions. He finally did begin to paint seriously, drawing not from his lush surroundings but rather from his experiences. Pratt has never painted from real life or photographs. Unlike many artists, he likes to paint by artificial light, especially at night. His paintings are composites of things he remembers and things he sees. In the painting "Woman at a Dresser," Pratt took the design for the wallpaper pattern from an Eaton's mail order catalogue. He told Paul Duval, author of *High Realism in Canada:* "Art is not objectivity. The actual object can be far too

overwhelming. The last place I want to see when I am doing the painting is the place that inspired it."

Pratt has often found the source of his inspiration from the deck of a sailboat. He told *Saturday Night,* "The boat allows me to visit places I couldn't reach by land—to come and go and wander at will." Yachting became much more than a way of exploring for Pratt. He starting racing competitively in 1972 and has since won numerous Royal Newfoundland Yacht Club races.

Mary Pratt returned to painting when the four Pratt children were grown. For years she had sacrificed the development of her own career to raise children and promote Christopher's ambitions. From her vantage point in the kitchen she had seen a much different world. She painted familiar images of domestic life: eviscerated chicken on a Coca-Cola box, cod fillets on cardboard cartons, salmon on plastic wrap. She too was dubbed a realist, but her style was much different from that of her husband. That became apparent to Christopher when they both painted the same model. His work was removed and distant, while hers was richly sensual. Her photo-realist depictions of daily life found a critical and popular audience, and the Pratts became Canada's most famous painting couple. Christopher, however, confessed to *Maclean's* he had some problems adjusting to his wife's new-found prominence as an artist. "I'm less secure in the light of Mary's achievements than she is in mine," he said at the time.

The Pratts moved from St. Catherine's to St. John's in 1981. It is perhaps testimony to Christopher's new acceptance of his wife's success that Mary paints in a skylit studio while he has opted for the basement. Pratt has retained a refreshing small-town approach to his work. He lives and paints his native roots—those of maritime Newfoundland. His rare comments on art are unpretentious and straightforward. John Reeves wrote in *Saturday Night:* "Christopher Pratt leaves home infrequently and with reluctance, and believes that if Canadians are to achieve excellence in any field we must celebrate it with deeds as well as words." As Pratt's international success has proved, his deeds have resulted in a body of work that transcends the simple ocean cottages and seascapes of his native Newfoundland and makes him an artist understood around the world.

AVOCATIONAL INTERESTS: Yachting and yacht racing.

SOURCES:

BOOKS

Bringhurst, Robert, Geoffrey James, Russell Keziere, and Doris Shadbolt, editors, *Visions: Contemporary Art in Canada,* Douglas & McIntyre, 1983.
Duval, Paul, *High Realism in Canada,* Clarke, Irwin, 1974.

PERIODICALS

ArtsCanada, December, 1976-January, 1977.
Books in Canada, May, 1981.
Maclean's, September 21, 1981.
Saturday Night, April, 1977.
Vie des Arts, Summer, 1981.
Winnipeg Free Press, February 3, 1981.

—Sidelights by Ingeborg Boyens

Barbara Gardner Proctor

1933(?)-

PERSONAL: Born November 30, c. 1933, in Black Mountain N.C.; daughter of Bernice Gardner; married Carl Proctor (road manager for singer Sarah Vaughan), 1960 (divorced, 1962); children: Morgan. *Education:* Talladega College, Talladega, Ala., B.A. in psychology and sociology and B.A. in English education; also attended law school. *Politics:* Republican.

ADDRESSES: *Office*—Proctor & Gardner Advertising, Inc., 111 East Wacker Dr., Suite 321, Chicago, Ill. 60601.

OCCUPATION: Advertising agency executive.

CAREER: Jazz music critic and contributing editor, *Downbeat* magazine, beginning 1958; Vee-Jay Records International, Chicago, Ill., 1961-64, began writing descriptive comments for jazz record album covers, became international director; Post-Keyes-Gardner Advertising, Chicago, member of staff, 1965-68; Gene Taylor Associates (advertising agency), Chicago, member of staff, 1968-69; North Advertising Agency, Chicago, copy supervisor, 1969-70; Proctor & Gardner Advertising, Inc., Chicago, founder, creative director, and chief executive officer, 1971—.

Member of board of directors, Illinois Bell Telephone Co., Seaway National Bank, Mount Sinai Hospital, University of Illinois, Illinois State Chamber of Commerce, Cosmopolitan Chamber of Commerce, Chicago Better Business Bureau, Chicago Economic Development Corp., Chicago Urban League, Chicago Symphony, WTTW-TV Auction, and Smithsonian Institution.

MEMBER: National Academy of Radio Arts and Sciences, National Association for the Advancement of Colored People (member of board of directors), Chicago Advertising Club, Chicago Media Women, Chicago Women's Advertising Club.

AWARDS, HONORS: Chicago Advertising Woman of the Year Award, 1974-75; Fredrich Douglas Humanitarian Award, 1975; Blackbook Businesswoman of the Year Award; Small Businesswoman of the Year Award, 1978; Headline Award, 1978; Charles A. Stevens International Organization of Women Executive Achievers Award, 1978. Recipient of more than twenty advertising industry awards for excellence, including Clio Awards from the American Television Commercial Festival.

SIDELIGHTS: Advertising has its own form of natural selection. If you're not fit you don't survive. Fortunately Barbara Gardner Proctor's fitness training began long ago, and as a result she has been able to penetrate an industry which, until relatively recently, has been impregnable by women and minorities.

Proctor was born in Black Mountain, North Carolina. The product of a dirt-poor rural environment, she was raised by her grandmother and never knew her father. Her house had no electricity or running water. Her major source of inspiration, according to an *Ebony* article, was her grandmother, who told her as a child, "You're not cute, but you're smart, and one day you're going to amount to something." Amount to something she did; today Proctor is founder, creative director, and chief executive officer of Proctor & Gardner Advertising, Inc., in Chicago, the nation's second-largest black advertising agency, with billings in excess of $13 million annually.

She used her grandmother's words to her as a source for energy, encouragement, and strength. After working hard in school, she was awarded a scholarship to Talladega College in Alabama, where she earned two B.A. degrees, one in psychology-sociology, the other in English education. She spent several years after college moving from one job to another. Eventually her fondness for jazz led her to *Downbeat* magazine, where she was a music critic and contributing editor, and to Vee-Jay Records in Chicago, where she became an international director.

In 1960, she married Carl Proctor, who was then road manager for Sarah Vaughan. Their two-year union produced a son, Morgan, her only child. Later, after a divorce, she left the record industry and used her writing skills to get a position with a Chicago-based advertising agency as a copywriter. In five years she worked at three agencies and climbed the salary scale to an annual income of $40,000.

Proctor's early advertising work permitted her to hone her writing skills while cultivating creative talent as well. She evolved into a meticulous executive and developed a strong sense of the need for quality and equality advertising. In 1970, after being fired from an agency because she declared a television commercial concept tasteless and offensive, she set out to establish an agency of her own.

Having made the decision to go into business for herself, Proctor's first task was to acquire the necessary working capital. She applied for a small business loan, which was declined because she lacked the necessary collateral. Undaunted by this temporary setback, she convinced a loan officer to ask the heads of three advertising agencies the salary they would pay her as an employee. The responses were $65,000, $85,000 and $110,000 per year. Confident and determined, she convinced the loan officer to use her, personally, as collateral, and he granted her a loan for $80,000.

In 1971, Proctor opened her agency. Her advertising experience had made her privy to the industry's secrets and quirks, so she knew the maneuvering that would be required to achieve success. Rather than drop her maiden name, she retained it to give the impression that there was a man behind the scenes co-administrating her operation. To further the illusion of dual proprietorship, she named the agency Proctor & Gardner Advertising, Inc.

The climate was right for a minority agency; commercial awareness of the black consumer market was gradually mounting. Thus, Proctor & Gardner was able to tap into a virtually untouched market, totaling millions of dollars annually, and at the same time had the opportunity to improve the public's perception of blacks by creatively casting them in a positive and constructive manner.

Proctor's endeavor was quite monumental, because in the early 1970s the advertising industry wasn't exactly holding doors open for black women to set up their own agencies. But her years of experience prepared her well for such struggles, and she approached new challenges with her customary self-assurance and vigor. She viewed her gender and race not as handicaps but as assets. "I happen to be born female and Black," Proctor told Ebony, "but I am much more than that. To view one's self in terms of those two small biological characteristics is very self-limiting." And, she says, because there had never been a strong male figure in her life, she wasn't afraid of men and wouldn't be intimidated by them. So the self-reliant Proctor showcased her brains, skills and savvy, and before long the agency began to sign a number of sizeable accounts.

Chicago's Jewel Food Store chain, one of Proctor & Gardner's long-standing clients, credits the agency with helping to make its generic food campaign a success in 1978. Before Proctor & Gardner was commissioned to assist with their campaign, Jewel Food Stores had been receiving negative feedback from their shoppers, because they felt they were being sold inferior products in the generic packages. Proctor & Gardner rescued the campaign and gave it a stronger and more positive tone. As a Money article says, Proctor's "newspaper, radio, and TV ads typified her style—clear, direct messages that got right down to value for your money." As a result, the community's response became quite favorable. Such an understanding of the consumer market—particularly the black consumer market—has made Proctor's agency unique and has contributed significantly to its success. Today Proctor & Gardner's roster of accounts includes Kraft Foods, Sears & Roebuck, and Alberto-Culver.

Proctor's sexually and racially integrated staff consists of twenty-five people, including her son, Morgan, who says he some day would like to head the company. Proctor calls her employees "one of the best staffs in the world," according to an Ebony writer. But she's not sure she'd like to work for someone like herself, because "the kind of boss I am is a non-boss. I don't believe that it is necessary to tell professionals their job. If I have given you good directions and I have given you the opportunity to challenge them if you feel they are incorrect, and you bought the assignment, you damn well better deliver." As a reporter for Money magazine concludes, "Proctor has succeeded because she has a lot of determination and an absolute sense of what she wants to accomplish."

SOURCES:

PERIODICALS

Ebony, August, 1982.
Forbes, November 21, 1982, January 13, 1986.
Money, September, 1981.
New York Times, January 27, 1984.
Savvy, February, 1984.
Time, December 2, 1985.
Wall Street Journal, May 17, 1983.
Washington Post, January 27, 1984.

—Sidelights by Michelle Brown

Karen Ann Quinlan

1954-1985

OBITUARY NOTICE: Born March 29, 1954; died of respiratory failure due to acute pneumonia, June 11, 1985, in Morris Plains, N.J. Quinlan, who had been severely comatose since 1975, made legal and medical history in 1976 when a unanimous decision by the New Jersey Supreme Court allowed the removal of her life-support systems. The landmark "right-to-die" ruling made Quinlan "a symbol of the right of the terminally ill to decide their fates with their families," according to a *Chicago Tribune* report.

A former athlete and lifeguard who also liked to write poetry and play the piano, Quinlan lapsed into a coma on April 14, 1975, following a birthday celebration for her boyfriend. Doctors believe that her breathing was impaired by a combination of three alcoholic drinks, aspirin, and a "therapeutic" dose of the mild prescription tranquilizer Valium, plus a stringent diet, which consequently deprived her brain of oxygen. The exact cause of the coma, however, has not been conclusively determined. Several other factors may have contributed, Quinlan's adoptive parents said, including her low-blood-sugar condition, a fall on concrete two weeks prior to the birthday party, and possible lead poisoning from a factory job she had held.

Doctors determined after several months that Karen Ann would never return to a "cognitive state." Her parents were distressed, said a *Detroit Free Press* report, because she "was fighting the machine and it caused a great deal of discomfort." In addition, they stated, several years prior to becoming comatose, Karen Ann had expressed a wish never to be kept alive by elaborate life-sustaining means. The Quinlans, who had long given up hope that their daughter would recover, felt that she was suffering needlessly and decided to petition a New Jersey Superior Court judge to allow them to remove the respirator. The petition was denied, but the decision was reversed when the Quinlans appealed it to the New Jersey Supreme Court on March 31, 1976. The Supreme Court ruled that a person's right to privacy allowed the removal of life-supporting equipment and named Mr. Quinlan guardian, responsible for deciding Karen's fate. Death "would not be homicide, but rather expiration from natural causes," the judgment said, and therefore no one could be held criminally liable for disconnecting the respirator.

Unexpectedly, Karen Ann began breathing on her own after the respirator was removed. For ten years she remained

AP/Wide World Photos

alive, but in what was called a permanent vegetative state, never regaining consciousness. Her family continued their devotion to Karen Ann until her death at age thirty-one, and her father drove forty miles daily to visit her in a nursing home. Karen Ann's physical condition deteriorated sharply for several months prior to her death, and she suffered from severe lung infections. In her memory, the Quinlans founded the Karen Ann Quinlan Center for Hope, a hospice for terminally ill patients and their families.

SOURCES:

PERIODICALS

Chicago Tribune, June 13, 1985.
Detroit Free Press, June 12, 1985, June 13, 1985.

Patrick Redig

1948-

PERSONAL: Born July 31, 1948, in Hibbing, Minn.; son of Jack and Marian Redig; married, 1971; wife's name, Mary; children: Daniel, Jeffery, Amy. *Education:* St. Cloud State College (now University), B.S., 1970; University of Minnesota, D.V.M., 1974, Ph.D., 1980.

ADDRESSES: *Office*—Department of Veterinary Biology, College of Veterinary Medicine, University of Minnesota, St. Paul, Minn. 55108.

OCCUPATION: Veterinarian; university professor and researcher.

CAREER: University of Minnesota, College of Veterinary Medicine, St. Paul, member of staff, 1980—, currently associate professor of physiology in department of veterinary biology, co-founder and medical director of Raptor Research and Rehabilitation Program. Researcher on bird physiology and pathology. Lecturer on birds of prey throughout the United States and Europe.

WRITINGS: Contributor of numerous articles to professional journals and other publications.

SIDELIGHTS: Birds of prey are often misunderstood, blamed for the death of livestock and the spread of disease, and are popular subjects for science fiction or mystery movies. Veterinarian Patrick Redig, head of the Raptor Research and Rehabilitation Program at the University of Minnesota, is devoting his energies to preserving and treating birds of prey—or raptors—and to raising the level of public awareness concerning the problems facing these birds. He wants people to know that raptors are not as dangerous as they are often perceived to be and that they are a vital part of our delicate ecosystem.

Redig stepped into the national spotlight in 1980, when he presented an American bald eagle to the hostages returning from Iran. But most of his work is on a smaller, more personal scale—talking concerned callers through the process of handling wounded birds, treating injured raptors, and studying the animals' behavior and physiology. Although Redig is considered a pioneer in his field, he is modest when detailing his achievements, saying simply that programs like his are necessary if birds of prey, some of which are endangered species, are to endure. "Wildlife is not going to survive if left to itself," he told a *New York Times* reporter. "Economics and developers will continue to chop up the land and fields. So we need to provide the energy for wildlife to exist."

Redig says he has had a lifelong interest in birds of prey and has practiced falconry for many years. He has worked to protect birds from the jaws of steel traps, from lead poisoning, and from the widespread public attitude that

considers raptors to be vermin and killers of farm animals. He believes there is much that can be learned from birds of prey and hopes that his work will help clear the cloud of negative public opinion that hangs over them.

CN INTERVIEW

CN interviewed Patrick Redig by telephone on September 19, 1985.

CN: What originally prompted your interest in the preservation and rehabilitation of birds of prey?

REDIG: Well, I can't really cite any one particular factor. It's been a lifelong interest. For instance, as a child I used to be fascinated with basically anything that flies. But I always had a very keen interest in raptors, and as a youngster I used to spend a lot of time watching them. I raised several of them initially as pets and then later on practiced falconry for quite a few years. I still fly birds and hunt with them. And so it was kind of a natural gravitation towards this field of work as I developed my professional career, and went through college, and things like that.

CN: And that was all in Minnesota?

REDIG: Yes, I grew up in northern Minnesota.

CN: Do you consider yourself a pioneer in this field? Were you one of the first people to form a research facility and spend time on the rehabilitation of birds of prey?

REDIG: Yes.

CN: Are there any other veterinary schools in the country that are now doing research in this area?

REDIG: Not to the extent that we are. There's a long-standing program at [the University of California,] Davis, at the veterinary college there, and they probably preceeded us by a couple of years. But we've kind of risen to the top of the heap, if you will, in terms of the size of the program, and the organization, and the number of people that are maintained on a permanent basis.

CN: How many people do you have on your staff?

REDIG: I have about eight full-time people that are working on the raptor program.

CN: And raptors are birds of prey? Are the terms interchangeable?

REDIG: Yes. That includes eagles, owls, vultures, hawks, and falcons.

CN: What about other birds, like geese, or ducks, or swans? Do you work with those at all?

REDIG: Not to any extent. Over the years I've done a lot of work on them, but it's kind of peripheral to our main program here, and it's done on a case-load permitting basis. For instance, we've got a trumpeter swan restoration project here in the state of Minnesota, and I work with them when they have problems with diseases and things like that in their breeding flock. And the general public isn't often times very discriminating about what they bring. You know, they hear you work on raptors, and they kind of infer birds in general from that. Certainly, if somebody shows up on the back doorstep with a goose with a broken leg in their arms, we're going to do something for them.

CN: Have you also helped set up other programs or research facilities in any other places?

REDIG: Yes. I've been involved in consulting with a lot of people across the country, and actually over the whole world, in many aspects along those lines. I've developed a lot of original techniques that are involved in clinical management, both surgical and medical, for birds of prey. And I've written these up, published them, and generally made them available to anybody that wants them. I've lectured widely throughout the country and in Europe on basic techniques, organization of programs, goals and objectives, and things like that. I've provided an internship for students and graduated veterinarians and wildlife people too. They can come in and spend anywhere from a couple of weeks up to as long as six months. It's really at their own choosing how long they want to spend time here to learn what we do and then take that back home and apply it. We've had students

from France, Spain, Israel, and Denmark, along with Canada and all over the United States, here over the years.

CN: Why do you feel there is a need for programs like yours in this country?

REDIG: Well, we have a historical obligation here, I think. Ever since the invention of the firearm, and the settlement of this country, and the white man ethic—you know, that we're going to take over the land and make it subservient to our needs—raptors have been among a group of animals that has suffered tremendously throughout the duration of that time. And it's only since the 1970s that we've really gotten in there and taken a good look at what we're doing and started to make some restorative efforts to repair the damage that was done. The damage is physical, in terms of numbers and species of birds that have, if not outright lost, at least have been pushed perilously low in terms of numbers, habitats destroyed, environments poisoned, so that they can't survive. And then there's the attitudinal problem, which is still, to some extent, present in society: the belief that raptors, and predators in general, are vermin and that we should be destroying them. Well, we know that that's not the case now, but it takes a good generation for that attitude to be leached from the system.

CN: So the public image of such birds is still not high?

REDIG: It's on a regional basis. I think in our part of the country, here, it's improved dramatically over the last ten years, but I know other parts of the country where it's still not high, and they're shot on sight, you know, just regarded as targets. Of course a lot of the livestock people in the western states still regard the golden eagle as one of the big problems associated with sheep production, and they'd just as soon see the eagles and coyotes gone.

CN: What do they see as the problem with the eagle?

REDIG: They feel that the eagles are killing lambs.

CN: That they actually lift them up and carry them off?

REDIG: Well, not usually. The lamb weighs more than the eagle can carry, but what happens is that they're kind of a scapegoat, I think, because sheep are lambing in March out there in the western plains, and the weather is very bad, and a lot of lambs die shortly after they are born. Beyond that, sheep have one of the highest abortion rates of any domestic animal—they have spontaneous abortions. So you get eagles out there feeding on carcasses of dead lambs, and the assumption is made that they killed the lambs. Well, that's not to say they don't kill a lamb or two. They sure do. But, by and large, what's happened is that the western plains have been decimated of their native prey populations. For golden eagles, the natural prey is jackrabbits, and ground squirrels, and things of that sort. Well, they've pretty much eliminated those from the environment in many places, and that doesn't leave the eagles much to feed on. So, I think we owe them one, because we've treated them so badly in the past.

But, beyond that, we're looking to preserve an intact ecosystem. I believe very firmly in the concept of the web of life: We're all on this planet together, and we can't afford to have elements of this system being destroyed or otherwise removed. I heard a good analogy one time that I think speaks to this issue. Suppose you're sitting on an aircraft at an airport on the ramp getting ready to take off and some guy comes out with a drill and starts drilling out the rivets that are holding the wing skins on. At what point are you going to tell him that you don't want to be on that airplane anymore? You know, he can take out a rivet here and a rivet there and no big deal. But when do you say that's enough?

CN: What can be learned from projects like yours to further our understanding of birds of prey?

REDIG: Well, a couple of things, I guess. In addition to doing the rehabilitation work, we're doing a number of basic physiological studies on these birds—in other words, learning more about their internal workings, their internal systems—studies directed at learning how they determine how much food they need to eat, how efficient they are at digesting their food. We're looking at their immune systems and their ability to fend off infectious organisms. And this is important in birds of prey, because often times they are feeding on sick and dead prey, and the chances for disease transmission are much higher than they would be if they were feeding on a relatively clean diet, which humans commonly eat. So they've got immune mechanisms there that work differently than ours, really keyed into providing a

high level of protection. We may even learn something that could be useful for other domestic animals, or other wildlife, or people, too. We're gaining a more fundamental understanding of how immune systems work. In any case, the things we're looking at from a physiological and an immuniological point of view directly relate to how these animals adapt to their environment. In particular, where we're looking at an environment that is being changed as rapidly as ours currently is, we need this information about the operation of their adaptive mechanisms.

Beyond that, I think our program serves as somewhat of a barometer of the types of problems that birds are having for survival, which is reflected in the numbers, and the species, and the types of injuries admitted. I'll give you two examples of that. When I first started working on the birds back in the early 1970s, the problem of lead poisoning was recognized, by some people at least, as being a problem for waterfowl, but little or nothing had ever been said about it being a secondary poisoning problem in birds of prey. Over the years, we have witnessed the effect of lead on eagles, in particular, and actually established a pretty good data base which unequivocally demonstrates that a lot of bald eagles are suffering from lead poisoning. They get it because they feed on dead and crippled waterfowl, and in the course of doing that they ingest shotgun pellets, and they get lead

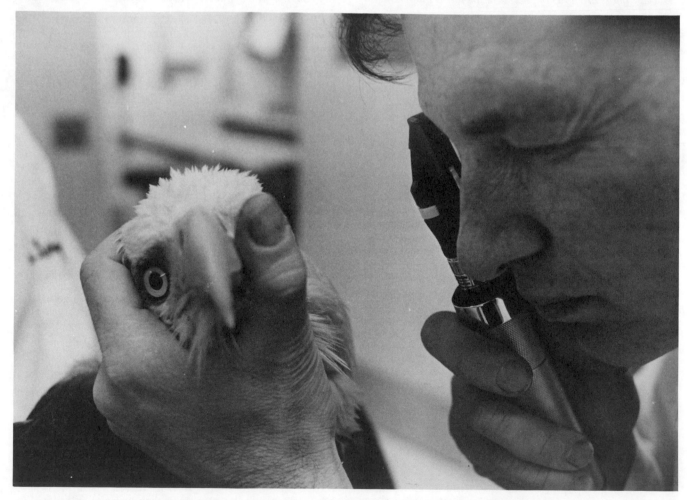

Patrick Redig examines the eye of an injured bald eagle. AP/Wide World Photos.

poisoning from that. Well, I think we did a lot of the work that established the fact that lead poisoning could indeed, and does, occur in eagles. Consequently we were involved as consultants to the National Wildlife Federation this summer, and a lawsuit against the federal government forced the establishment of broader use of steel shot in many areas where lead poisoning was a problem.

The other issue that we've been involved in is the effect of steel-jaw traps on eagles. This is not to take a stand on trapping or the use of steel-jaw traps, per se, but simply asking people to take a look at our data. We can show you that one of the major causes of death and injury in bald eagles is steel-jaw traps; not deliberate trapping, but inadvertent coincidental trapping that occurs when eagles go down and feed on open bait that is left for some fur-bearing mammal. In other cases, like in muskrat trapping, they'll set three, or four, or perhaps more traps around a muskrat house. A rat will come in and get caught in one trap, then an eagle may come down and feed on the carcass of that rat and step in another trap. Actually, despite what I said earlier about shooting and things like that, in point of fact, we lose more eagles to traps than we do to shooting, at least in this part of the country.

CN: It seems like that would be fairly hard to control.

REDIG: Absolutely. Hard to control and impossible to pass regulations, per se, that are going to do it. But what will work is an education program. Don't believe that trappers are themselves interested in killing off bald eagles. It is certainly not in their best interest, because it provides more ammunition to those folks that would like to see trapping outlawed directly. And certainly the attitudes that have been expressed by a lot of the trappers, that we've talked about with this issue, indicate that they are concerned about it. And so, among trappers themselves, there is a grass-roots educational program to illuminate it. It can't be controlled by regulation, but it can be controlled by good trapping technique. And, again, as a consequence of what we've shown with this, there are regulations, nonetheless, that have been passed in Minnesota, Wisconsin, the Dakotas, Wyoming, and a few other states that prohibit the use of exposed baits in the vicinity of a steel-jawed trap. Of course there is not going to be a game warden standing over every trap making sure that the bait is twenty-five feet away. Nevertheless, the regulation is on the books, and it does provide the basis for the awareness that is needed to deal with the situation.

CN: So a good part of your job, then, is to raise public awareness of these problems?

REDIG: I would say—if we had to say in so many words what we're trying to do—that's what we're trying to accomplish: to raise the level of public awareness. And the injured raptor provides an extremely effective and a very tangible means for a person to relate to the problems that we're seeing with the birds. In most instances, turning twenty-five or thirty previously injured gray-horned owls or red-tailed hawks loose to the wild again every year probably doesn't contribute substantively to the overall population dynamics. Although that argument probably takes on less significance when we're talking about bald eagles compared to falcons or some of the other species where the numbers are perilously low or if they are extremely long-lived birds.

Still, that aspect of it is somewhat secondary to our primary mission, and that's education and public awareness.

CN: How many birds do you treat a year?

REDIG: About three hundred and fifty, on average.

CN: And is that number growing over the years?

REDIG: Interestingly, no. We've been right around three hundred and twenty, three hundred and fifty, for the last eight years or so. And there are two reasons for that. I think one is that we've trained a lot of other people to do some of this work. We don't have all the cases coming in to us that we used to. So each year, even though the size of our program and the work exhibit become larger and we spread our share of influence further, thereby raising the potential of receiving more birds, by the same token we have more people out in the field that are shortstopping some of these birds and handling them in the local area rather than forwarding them to us. That's not all bad. I think we need to get a lot more people involved. The only birds that we still have sent directly to us, without question, are things like bald eagles, and peregrines, and things like that. So our numbers have stayed the same, but our focus has changed somewhat, and we see more eagles now than we used to.

CN: Of the birds that you treat each year, about how many would you say are returned to their natural habitats?

REDIG: On average, about forty-two percent. The remainder are split pretty evenly between those that are permanently crippled and are retained in captivity for display, education, and breeding (and also we use some birds here for research and teaching purposes) and those that, unfortunately, either die or have to be destroyed because of the severity of their injuries.

CN: You mentioned working to increase bird populations. Are there any endangered species that you can point to that have improved significantly because of your work to help their numbers grow?

REDIG: That's a good question, and one that it is going to be hard to answer, at least over the short term. Population dynamics move in slow and ponderous ways, and shifts are going to be pushed slowly over a period of fifteen to twenty years. I don't think that what we are doing is of, by itself, a magnitude where we're going to see an impact along those lines. I think we've helped a lot with the bald eagle in a couple of ways. We've turned a couple hundred eagles loose again, and we've turned a lot of adult birds loose and given them a second chance for survival. In fact, we have given some of them a third chance for survival. And we do have documentation for about a dozen cases of eagles that we have turned loose that have been seen again at nests in Wisconsin and Minnesota. We've color marked them so that we can identify them. In that sense, yes. The evidence points directly to that, that we have birds out there reproducing.

I think, though, that we've probably done more, again, in our area of public awareness. Let me give you an example. When we first started working on this in the early 1970s, the number of birds that were admitted to our program that had been shot was somewhere on the order of thirty-five percent. And if we just track those percentage figures over the course of time, we will see that in about 1975 the number was down around the mid-twenties, and then pretty soon it was sixteen percent, and it continued on down. And now, over the last five years, that number of projectile-injured birds has hovered right around four percent. I'll take credit for that. We've recently made a lot of racket about that. We've been on the news, and in the newspapers, and on TV, and we've let it be known that it is a very wrong and unpopular thing to go out and start shooting at hawks now.

CN: You have received considerable attention from the news media. What about attention in terms of governmental or private support or donations? Have you seen any increase or change in those at all?

REDIG: Yes, some very significant ones. The project has never received a large amount of governmental support, at least financially. They always thought we had a good idea and liked to see what we were doing, but we've had a relatively small amount of funding from the U.S. Fish and Wildlife Service; about $5,000 a year. That hasn't changed, and it doesn't appear that there is going to be any change. And that may be fine. I think the project has more regional appeal, and we do have a good base of private donations that does sustain the project. The state of Minnesota has their non-game wildlife checkoff fund, and for the last (I hate using numbers all the time because as soon as I use a number I'm sure I'm going to be wrong) four years, which is essentially the entire length of time that this program has been in effect, we have received about a third of our funding from them. Now there has been a little legislative maneuver here this last year that increased our level of funding from the state and took it out of the non-game project and made the general fund the source of that money. So that's very nice; that's a line item in the university budget, and it should stay there. Having said all that, I suspect that our annual budget is running around $120,000 a year right now, and we'll get about $45,000 of that from governmental sources. All the rest comes from private donations.

CN: And the University of Minnesota has been very supportive?

REDIG: The university has *not* been very supportive.

CN: It hasn't?

REDIG: They've provided us with space—which is significant, truly—but there's never been any financial support, no support in terms of personnel or anything like that. We've kind of come in through the back door on that one. We've succeeded in spite of them, and, of course, now that we've succeeded they point to us proudly as one of their programs.

CN: How do you receive your birds? Do they come in from all over the country? Do people hear about you and bring you injured birds?

REDIG: Yes. It's a very informal thing. Somebody is hiking, cross-country skiing, driving down the road; they've heard about us; they call us up and say: "I've got a bird. What do I do with it?" We try to convince them that they ought to bring it down. Alternatively, they get back home with this bird, and they start getting on the phone, and they call the police department, humane society, museum—somebody like that. Eventually, after about three or four phone calls,

somebody finally gives them our phone number, and they call us. Or they may take the bird directly over to a humane society or to a conservation officer, and they bring it down or see that it gets down to us. In the case of eagles or peregrine falcons, most of those birds do get funneled rather directly to conservation officers or special agents for the Fish and Wildlife Service, and they get them in to us. One of the things that works rather nicely there is that Republic Airlines has just been tremendous about helping us. For the last several years, they've provided free freight transportation for birds that are coming from outside our region. I can't even tell you the number right now, but literally dozens of eagles have been transported all over Minnesota, Wisconsin, and the Dakotas by Republic Airlines.

CN: It saves you a substantial amount of money?

REDIG: It saves us a substantial amount of money, and I think importantly, too, the folks in the air cargo business at Republic Airlines have become familiar with the program, and they do a first-class job of expediting the shipment of these birds. So there is no time lost there. And I think if there is any one thing that has helped us in our success rate, it may have been that, because without that service an eagle could be down, and it would be a week before, somehow or another, it could get transported down here. In this way we've heard about birds from California by a phone call in the morning, and we've got them here in the afternoon.

So that's kind of how birds get to us, I guess, by various means. Yesterday morning, for example, the phone rang, and a fellow from over here in St. Paul called me. He'd come back through St. Cloud in the morning and had passed through there about forty-five minutes earlier. He saw an owl sitting along the road on the freeway, and he went over and shooed it off into the median strip. I don't know why he didn't pick it up, but you'll never know why that is. At least he called me and told me that the owl was sitting out there on the strip. We have a cooperator who works with us up in St. Cloud, and I called her up and gave her this story, and I said, "I hope it's not a wild goose chase." By the middle of the afternoon, she'd been out there and recovered the owl and had it. And she's bringing it down here today.

CN: Are people afraid to pick up injured birds themselves?

REDIG: Well, some people are. They run the gamut. You know, we get the call from the person that's got this bird in their backyard, and they want us to come out and pick it up. Well, unfortunately, we can't run an ambulance service. Often times it's kind of fun to do. You kind of allay their fears and tell them: "That bird only weighs two pounds, and you weigh one hundred and twenty pounds. Now come on; let's get with it."

CN: You kind of talk them through it.

REDIG: We'll tell them to throw a blanket over it or something like that, so they can at least get it pinned down. Then if somebody does come out there, it hasn't wandered off into the next yard or something like that.

CN: One way that you seem to have gotten a lot of attention was when you presented the American bald eagle to the hostages returning from Iran. How were you selected to do that? How did that all come about?

REDIG: Well, it wasn't by any grand scheme. Fred Travalena, the singer and comedian, was in town performing. And Nancy Nelson—she's out in California now as a TV anchor, but she was working for one of the TV stations here in town, and she had given us a lot of publicity and was one of our long-time supporters—she brought Fred over to see the birds, because he liked eagles. Well, Fred had been asked to come to the return of the Iranian hostages out in Washington, D.C., at Constitution Hall. So they were sitting here looking at the eagles, and all of a sudden the light bulb came on, and the gears started turning and, "Hmmmm, how about if we could take an eagle to this little schtick?" And so the idea caught on, and that's how it came to pass.

CN: I see. Have you had other occasions like that where you've presented birds to people or to groups of people?

REDIG: Well, not like that. We do have a couple of birds that are trained here, and we use them for a lot of education and public programming work, and we have taken them to various places. In fact we've got two of them that are going down to Chicago for a big art show that is being held down there. We've taken them to Washington a couple of times when we were trying to make our case before Congress or something like that, to support legislation in favor of birds of prey or to help support our own program. We had an invite to come to the Republican convention, but we turned that one down.

SOURCES:

PERIODICALS

Esquire, December, 1984.
Minneapolis-St. Paul, January, 1983.
New York Times, November 18, 1976.

—Sidelights and interview by Amy C. Bodwin

Mary Lou Retton

1968-

PERSONAL: Born January 24, 1968, in Fairmont, W.Va.; daughter of Ronnie (owner of a coal transportation business) and Lois Retton. *Education:* Attended high school in Fairmont, W.Va. and took correspondence courses; studied gymnastics with Bela Karolyi in Houston, Tex.

ADDRESSES: Agent—John S. Traetta, National Media Group/High Bar Productions, Ltd., 250 West 57th St., New York, N.Y. 10107.

OCCUPATION: Gymnast.

CAREER: Gymnast since 1975, competing numerous national and international events, including the 1984 Summer Olympics in Los Angeles, Calif. Spokesperson for and endorser of a variety of commercial products and enterprises.

AWARDS, HONORS: Winner of one gold, two silver, and two bronze medals in gymnastics in 1984 Summer Olympics; named Sportswoman of the year by *Sports Illustrated*, 1984.

SIDELIGHTS: On August 3, 1984, gymnast Mary Lou Retton did far more than just win an Olympic gold medal. True, the flawless performance of the four-foot, nine-inch, sixteen-year-old won her a perfect 10 score in the all-around gymnastic category, but at the same time, the perpetual smile and enthusiasm displayed by the girl won her the hearts of all who watched.

Her victory was a many-faceted wonder. Mary Lou Retton's performance proved to the world that the United States was a gymnastic force to be reckoned with. She also proved to the gymnastic world that a gymnast need not be needle thin and wisp light. Many observers have been inclined to liken Retton's muscular, solid body more to that of a linebacker than the lithe creatures usually seen passing between the balance beam and uneven bars. Yet her delivery, while decisive, powerful, and daring is no less graceful than any the world has ever seen.

"I vault my best under pressure," she told the *New York Times* after her Olympic victory at UCLA's Pauley Pavilion before a crowd of 9,023. "It makes me fight harder. I knew if I stuck that vault I'd win it. I kept thinking 'stick, stick, stick,' I knew I had to get a 10." To "stick" in gymnastics means to descend from all the midair twisting and turning in perfect form and rock steady. And she did. "I can't describe how I felt," said the 92-pound Retton. "I had goosebumps going up and down me. I knew from the takeoff. I knew from the run—I just knew it."

Retton was born January 24, 1968, in Fairmont, West Virginia, a coal-mining town. She is the youngest of five

AP/Wide World Photos

children. Her father, Ronnie, owns a coal transportation equipment business and at one time was a New York Yankees farm-team shortstop. Her mother, Lois, started Mary Lou in acrobatic and ballet classes by the time she was four because, as the gymnast told the *New York Times,* "I was very hyper." She started serious gymnastic training when she was seven. At eight, she recalls watching the tiny Nadia Comaneci win three gold medals and countless hearts in the 1976 Olympics, just as thousands of aspiring young gymnasts must now remember watching her.

But perhaps the first tiny gymnast to have the world on a string was Olga Korbut who, at seventeen, reigned over the gymnastic events of the 1972 Munich Olympics. That year there were approximately 15,000 gymnasts practicing in private clubs in the United States, said *Harper's.* In 1982 there were 150,000, many inspired by Korbut. Today, there are over 500 private clubs in this country, and annual fees for gymnasts intent on Olympic competition can run more than $12,000 for tuition, room, gear and travel expenses.

Many of the most serious students leave home at tender, teen ages and move to the homes of teachers in the finer schools. That is what Retton did in early 1983. With her parents' permission she gave up regular high school classes (where she earned straight A's) for correspondence courses, and she left West Virginia to move in with a family who had another gymnast in the same school as the one Retton chose to attend—Karolyi's World Gymnastics. The Houston school is run by Bela Karolyi, the Romanian coach who, with his wife, Marta, instructed Comaneci on her road to fame before the couple defected to the United States in 1981.

Of her decision to leave home Retton told *Time:* "I knew that if I wanted to have a chance at a medal in the Olympics, I was not going to do it if I stayed home. And I had worked all of those long, hard years."

At the school she works out twice daily, except on her off-day, Monday, when the workout takes place only once. She and Karolyi met at a tournament in Reno in 1982. "I immediately recognized the tremendous physical potential of this little kid," Karolyi told *The New York Times*. In comparing his two star pupils, Karolyi told *Newsweek:* "Nadia was a great champion, but Mary Lou is bigger. She's got the psychological power to go through the most difficult moments without falling apart." And in the *New York Times* he said: "Nadia never lifted her eyes. Mary Lou communicates with her crowd."

The *New York Times* best describes Retton's personal best as "an affront to gravity called the Retton flip," in which she swings down from the high bar and slams her hips against the low bar, going into a front flip that ends when she lands in a seated position on the high bar.

Public recognition of Retton's talents first came in March, 1982, when she took top honors at the McDonald's American Cup competition. She was substituting, on a single day's notice, for schoolmate Dianne Durham who had been injured. But the road to fame was not clearly and simply Retton's from the start. After watching the February 5, 1983, Caesars Palace Invitational in Las Vegas, James Wolcott reported in *Harper's* that "it was Mary Lou Retton who looked the most aerodynamically self-propelled. No sylph she, Mary Lou has such a boxy, compact body that some coaches feel that she won't grow gracefully in the sport—that whatever pounds she adds in puberty will be maldistributed. For the time being, however, she's hitting everything with smacking emphasis, ending her routines with an exclamation mark. . . . For her exploits, Mary Lou was awarded first prize in the all-around and presented with an armful of flowers and a trophy nearly as tall as herself. . . . She said 'It feels *great*, and this is my first time, you know at beating the top seniors, and it feels absolutely excellent,' adding 'Name recognition is very important in gymnastics, and I hope this boosts my name right up there, somewhere.' "

Six weeks before the Olympics, Retton suffered an injury that a few years earlier might have sidelined her for the

Mary Lou Retton on the balance beam at the 1984 Summer Olympics. UPI/Bettmann Newsphotos.

competition and left her with a long, slow recuperation. After injuring her right knee during an exhibition match, the knee started locking on her. Examination showed that a cartilage fragment from her knee had broken off and lodged in the joint. She flew to St. Luke's Hospital in Richmond, Virginia for arthroscopy. She checked out the same day as her surgery and was back at practice in Houston the next day, according to *Time*.

At the Olympics, Retton's chief competitor was Ecaterina Szabo, seventeen, of Romania who was the world champion and pre-Olympic favorite. Szabo won gold medals in the floor exercise, the balance beam, and the vault, and she led her group to the team gymnastics title.

In the course of the competition for the all-around gold, Mary Lou took an early .15 lead, but the lead was erased when Szabo scored a 10 on the balance beam, while Retton's weakness on the uneven bars netted her only a 9.85. Retton was down .05 going into the last round of competition. Szabo had to go first on the uneven bars. "I saw her take a step on her dismount," Retton told *Sports Illustrated*," and I said to myself, 'You have a chance, Mary Lou.'" Szabo scored a 9.9 on the unevens, and it was time for Retton to take on the vault. If she scored 9.95 she would tie for the gold, but a perfect 10 would net her first place all alone.

That is exactly what Retton did; not just once, but twice. Gymnasts go through each routine twice, and the highest score of the two counts. Although Retton scored a perfect 10 on her first vault, she thrilled the partisan Los Angeles crowd by repeating her routine—and her perfect score—a second time.

"Mary Lou has two great qualities that put her where she is," Don Peters, U.S. women's team coach, told the *New York Times*. "First, physically, she is the most powerful gymnast who ever competed in the sport, and she takes great advantage of that in her tumbling and her vaulting. . . . Second, she's one hell of a competitor. As the pressure gets greater, Mary Lou gets greater."

But, as wonderful as the Olympics may have been, Mary Lou and her family are wise enough to know that the fickle public tends to have a short memory. Retton, with the advice of professionals, is taking on a number of lucrative endorsement contracts. Coordinating the campaign that *People* magazine refers to as the "Rettonization of America" is John Traetta, gymnastics coach for ten years at New York's DeWitt Clinton High School, who met Mary Lou three years ago while he was producing a gymnastics special for Caesars Palace. Traetta, president of National Media/Highbar Productions, is Retton's agent and has signed her to multi-year contracts with McDonald's, General Mills, Wheaties, and Vidal Sassoon. (She is the first woman, and only the third person, to be declared official spokesperson for the "breakfast of champions," although she owns up to preferring Cap'n Crunch cereal.) She has also agreed to endorse a line of girls' sportswear for the Dobie Originals division of Cluett, Peabody & Company and has signed with Hasbro Bradley to promote physical fitness toys for children.

In the four months immediately after the Olympics, Retton toured twenty-eight cities, appearing in parades, shows, and special events. And she was named Sportswoman of the Year for 1984 by *Sports Illustrated*. She is often escorted to functions by her older brother Ronnie, twenty-three, who shares a two-bedroom Houston condominium with her. She visits her family once each month and drives a red Corvette bearing the vanity license plate "Mary Lou" and the five-interlocked-ring Olympic symbol.

Retton continues to be captivating and remains captivated by her fame. "The people knew me!," she told *Sports Illustrated* "They said things like, 'Mary Lou, you've been in our home. You've been in our living room. We feel like we know you, Mary Lou!'. . . . I still think it's kind of neat, too. I mean, I'd understand people recognizing me if I had purple hair or something, but I'm just a normal teenager. I'm still Mary Lou."

And sometimes that can be a lonely person to be. She admits to having little contact with girls her own age, and while she keeps her eyes open for appealing boys, "I really don't have time," she told the *Chicago Tribune*. "You know, I'm still young, and here all of this stuff is happening to me and I have to take advantage of it. Gosh, this opportunity and period of my life may never come back again. There'll be time for boys and partying later."

Retton and other Olympic athletes with endorsement contracts keep their amateur standing by putting their earnings into a trust fund administered by the United States Gymnastics Federation. The organization pays for her training expenses from the fund, and when Retton is ready to give up her amateur status, a percentage of the trust is kept by the association, with the majority of it going to Retton.

From Christmas until March Retton will again be in serious training at Karolyi's school (where *People* says enrollment doubled after Retton's victory), and she is expected to start competing within a year of her last Olympic finale. She will have to decide for herself how long she wants to maintain the amateur status and rigorous schedule that led to the Olympic gold and fame.

SOURCES:

PERIODICALS

Chicago Tribune, March 10, 1985.
Christian Science Monitor, March 22, 1984, August 6, 1984, August 17, 1984, October 25, 1984, October 31, 1984.
Harper's, July 13, 1983.
Newsweek, July 30, 1984, August 13, 1984.
New York Times, March 4, 1984, May 14, 1984, July 31, 1984, August 1, 1984, August 4, 1984, August 5, 1984, September 24, 1984, April 28, 1985.
People, November 28, 1983, August 6, 1984, December 24, 1984.
Sports Illustrated, December 24, 1984.
Time, July 30, 1984, August 20, 1984.

—Sidelights by Mary Solomon Smyka

Charles Francis Richter

1900-1985

OBITUARY NOTICE: Born April 26, 1900, near Hamilton, Ohio; died of heart failure, September 30, 1985, in Pasadena, Calif. American seismologist and university professor. Richter studied earthquakes for more than fifty years, seeking to determine their origins, accurately estimate their energies, and understand the forces that cause them. Although he was originally interested in atomic physics, his career focus shifted after he was offered a position at the California Institute of Technology's Seismology Laboratory in 1927. In 1935, Richter helped develop the now-famous Richter scale with a colleague, Beno Gutenberg. The scale scientists had previously relied upon, the Mercalli scale, had measured quake intensity at the point of the seismometers, rather than at the quake's origin, and had concerned itself with ground shaking and damage done to structures, which varied depending upon whether the quake had occurred in populated or uninhabited areas. The Richter scale, on the other hand, determined the tremor's origin and measured the total energy the quake released, thus giving a more accurate measure of the quake no matter where it had occurred. Each increase of one on the Richter scale represents a tenfold increase in magnitude.

Richter himself regarded the development as routine work, something that had to be done, and never referred to the scale as the "Richter scale," in acknowledgment of Gutenberg's equal part in the project. Instead, he called it "the scale," "the magnitude scale," or "that confounded scale." The scientist also wrote two books during his career, a 1958 textbook, *Elementary Seismicity*, and a 1954 book he co-authored with Gutenberg, *Seismicity of the Earth and Associated Phenomenon*, revised from their earlier 1941 book, *Seismicity of the Earth*. Both are still well-regarded scientific references.

Richter believed that few people were actually killed by earthquakes, but rather that most were killed or injured in unsafe buildings or resulting fires. He recommended automatic utility shut-offs and long-term architectural changes in high-risk areas to minimize damage. To establish precautionary measures, he was active in the early 1960s in revising Los Angeles building codes, and he played a part in establishing state reforms. After retiring from California Institute of Technology in 1970 as a professor of seismology, he became a professor emeritus. He still returned to his office each day to assess seismographic data, however, and he also kept a working seismograph in the living room of his home. In later years, he continued to pursue his favorite avocational interests: reading, listening to classical music, hiking, and backpacking.

UPI/Bettmann Newsphotos

SOURCES:

BOOKS

Diehl, Digby, *Supertalk*, Doubleday, 1974.

PERIODICALS

Chicago Tribune, October 6, 1985.
Detroit Free Press, October 1, 1985.
Detroit News, October 1, 1985.
Field and Stream, February, 1973.
Los Angeles Times, December 3, 1958.
National Observer, February 15, 1971.
Newsweek, October 14, 1985.
New York Times, February 11, 1971, October 1, 1985.
NRTA Journal, May-June, 1971.
Time, October 14, 1985.
Washington Post, March 26, 1969.

Nelson Riddle

1921-1985

OBITUARY NOTICE: Full name, Nelson Smock Riddle; born June 1, 1921, in Oradell (some sources say Hackensack), N.J.; died of kidney failure and cardiac arrest, October 6, 1985. American composer, conductor, and arranger. During a career that spanned more than four decades Riddle supplied musical arrangements for a wide range of popular stars, among them Frank Sinatra, Judy Garland, and Linda Ronstadt. Riddle, who as a teenager joined a band touring near his home in New Jersey, played trombone during the big-band swing era of the 1940s with the Jerry Wald, Charlie Spivak, Les Elgart, and Tommy Dorsey dance bands. Following World War II, during which he played in the U.S. Army band, Riddle moved to California and joined NBC Radio as an arranger. In 1951 he began an eleven-year association with Capitol Records and in 1963 left Capitol for Reprise Records, serving as music director in both instances.

But it was only when Riddle struck out on his own as a composer and arranger in the 1950s that he became widely known. He provided orchestrations that were both swinging and sophisticated for artists as diverse as Ella Fitzgerald, Judy Garland, Nat King Cole, and especially Frank Sinatra. Praised by Sinatra as "the greatest arranger in the world," Riddle wrote the "charts"—as musicians call them—for songs like "I've Got You Under My Skin," "Chicago," "A Foggy Day," and "My Funny Valentine" that led to Sinatra's recording comeback in the mid-1950s. Noted for his ability to pace the tempo of his orchestrations to his vocalist's lead, Riddle employed rich combinations of string and brass instruments and a prominent rhythm section in his work.

However, due to the popularity of rock music during the 1960s and 1970s and a bout with illness, Riddle faded from the public eye until in 1982 a collaboration with rock star Linda Ronstadt thrust him back into the limelight. The collaboration resulted in *What's New,* an album of nine torch songs, mostly from the 1920s, 1930s, and 1940s, that surprised even the record industry with its commercial and critical success. The album quickly rose to top-ten status on the *Billboard* charts and sparked a two-week tour in the fall of 1983 for the unlikely duo and the forty-seven-piece Nelson Riddle Orchestra. A second collaboration of popular standards, *Lush Life,* also garnered favorable reviews, and a third album had been completed but not yet released at the time of Riddle's death.

In addition to his recordings, Riddle scored such movies as "Li'l Abner," "Paint Your Wagon," and "Can-Can" and such popular television series as "Route 66," "The Untouchables," and "Naked City." He received several Oscar and Emmy nominations and won an Academy Award in 1975 for his original score for the film "The Great Gatsby." Twice a recipient of Grammy awards—once in 1958 for his

"Cross-Country Suite" and again in 1983 for the Ronstadt *What's New* album—Riddle also served as music director for the inaugurations of President John F. Kennedy in 1961 and President Ronald Reagan in 1985.

SOURCES:

BOOKS

Biographical Dictionary of American Music, Parker Publishing, 1973.
The Complete Encyclopedia of Popular Music and Jazz, 1900-1950, Arlington House, 1974.
Contemporary American Composers: Biographical Dictionary, 2nd edition, G.K. Hall, 1982.
Who's Who in America, 43rd edition, Marquis, 1984.

PERIODICALS

Chicago Tribune, October 13, 1985.
Detroit Free Press, October 8, 1985.
Detroit News, October 7, 1985.
Los Angeles Times, October 13, 1985.
New York Times, October 8, 1985.
People, November 7, 1983.

Molly Ringwald

1968-

PERSONAL: Born March, 1968, in Sacramento, Calif.; daughter of Bob (a jazz musician) and Adele Ringwald. *Education:* High school student in Los Angeles, Calif.

ADDRESSES: Home—Los Angeles, Calif. *Agent*—International Creative Management, 8899 Beverly Blvd., Los Angeles, Calif. 90048.

OCCUPATION: Actress.

CAREER: Began acting and singing as a very young child; acted on stage in "The Glass Harp" and in West Coast production of "Annie"; regular cast member of television series "The Facts of Life," 1979-80; made guest appearances on a number of television programs, including "Diff'rent Strokes" and "The Merv Griffin Show"; has appeared in several made-for-television movies, including "Packin' It In," "P.K. and the Kid," and "Surviving"; feature films include "Tempest," 1982, "Spacehunter: Adventures in the Forbidden Zone," 1983, "Sixteen Candles," 1984, "The Breakfast Club," 1985, and "Pretty in Pink," 1986.

AWARDS, HONORS: Golden Globe Award nomination for best new actress, 1982, for "Tempest"; named one of the ten most beautiful women in America by *Harper's Bazaar*, 1985.

SIDELIGHTS: "I'm not a typical teenager," Molly Ringwald told *People.* "I'd be lying if I said I was. I'm not normal, but that's good because if I was normal I'd be bored to death." A brief review of some of Ringwald's many accomplishments supports the young actress's claim that she hasn't had time to be bored: she has five feature films and three television movies to her credit; she appeared for a season in a television situation comedy; and she's performed in a West Coast production of the Broadway musical "Annie." As for any claims to a "normal" teenage existence, she's accurate in saying she can't make them. She attends high school classes on movie sets, performs vocals in nightclubs with her father's jazz band, and socializes with famous movie stars like Warren Beatty and Jack Nicholson.

Adjectives like "fresh," "charming," "beguiling," and "unaffected" punctuate critical reviews of Ringwald's work. She seems quickly to have captured the hearts of critics, the movie-going public, and her fellow actors alike. One actress whose esteem Molly has earned, for example, is Ellen Burstyn, who appeared with her in a made-for-television movie entitled "Surviving." Interviewed by Hillary Johnson for *Rolling Stone*, Burstyn had these words of praise for her young co-star: "She has a huge talent. I was just amazed at her natural ability. She seems to understand intuitively what's needed in a scene, and she produces it. I haven't been so impressed by a young actor in a long time, if ever, and I think she's going to be an absolutely major actress—and a star."

Ringwald's acting career was underway by the time she was six years old. With her two older siblings, she performed in community theaters near her family's Sacramento, California, home. "I guess I really got involved in acting because my older brother and sister were into it," Ringwald told Bruce Cook of Knight-Ridder News Service. "I helped them memorize their lines, then I'd start doing all the parts myself." Her brother and sister ultimately lost interest in acting, but Molly continued to perform locally and eventually won a role in the West Coast road company production of "Annie." By that time her family had moved to Los Angeles, "in part to accommodate her blossoming career, in part to allow her father a wider range of club options," explained Johnson. At age thirteen she was selected to play Miranda in director Paul Mazursky's "Tempest." "I interviewed more than one hundred actresses for the role," Mazursky told *Seventeen.* "She's the only kid who wasn't afraid."

Ringwald's next feature film was "Spacehunter: Adventures in the Forbidden Zone," a 3-D movie that a *Rolling Stone* critic described as "an enjoyable comic-book adventure." While a *People* reviewer found Ringwald's performance in that film "atrocious," another declared in *Rolling Stone* that she "imbues the film with sparkling freshness."

"Sixteen Candles," released in 1984, earned Ringwald lavish praise for her performance. In that film, she plays Samantha, a teenager who awakens on her sixteenth birthday to discover that her entire family has forgotten the event, absorbed as they are in preparing for her older sister's wedding. Samantha considers her sixteenth birthday to be the most important one in her life, and she's chagrined to realize that her family has overlooked it. She proceeds through a day that seems to get worse at every turn: a handsome senior is oblivious to her romantic overtures, and she's the unwilling recipient of advances from a nerdy-looking freshman known among their classmates as "the Geek."

Ringwald "brings a great amount of charm to the role of Samantha," noted a writer for *Maclean's*. The *New Yorker's* Pauline Kael commented that Ringwald's "acting gives the picture a lyric quality. The tilt of Samantha's head suggests a guileless sort of yearning, and there's something lovely about the slight gaucheness of her restless, long arms." Gary Arnold, writing for the *Washington Post*, found Ringwald's performance delightful, but he complained about other aspects of the movie. For example, he felt that the actor who plays the Geek (Anthony Michael Hall) "gets so much screen time and makes such a likable impression that he seems to emerge inadvertently as the leading character. He's great fun, but the willowy, freckle-faced Ringwald is no slouch either; you regret seeing her supplanted."

"Sixteen Candles" was written and directed by John Hughes. According to Hillary Johnson, Hughes wrote the screenplay "with an eight-by-ten glossy of Molly taped above his word processor for inspiration, though he hadn't even met her." When he finally met Ringwald, Hughes liked her very much, he told Johnson. "A lot of kids who start out early as actors become affected. She was not."

After "Sixteen Candles," Ringwald went on to appear in Hughes's next effort, "The Breakfast Club," which was released in 1985. In that film, she and Anthony Michael Hall, her "Sixteen Candles" co-star, were joined by actors Ally Sheedy, Judd Nelson, and Emilio Estevez. "The Breakfast Club" is a portrayal of five high school students of diverse types (a jock, a brain, a wacky artist, a lowbrow troublemaker, and Ringwald's affluent popularity queen) who are imprisoned together in the school library to serve a day-long detention sentence. Strangers to one another at the beginning, the five come to know each other better as the day progresses. Several critics likened the film's plot structure to a marathon group-therapy session. "Sooner or later, everyone gets to play the Truth Game," observed David Denby in his review of the film for *New York*. By day's end, the characters "will have spent so much time attacking, defending, confessing, breaking down and breaking through that they will know all one another's secrets. New friendships will be formed, class barriers breached, old suspicions and hostilities swept away."

"The Breakfast Club," Louise Stanton wrote in *Films in Review*, "has an entertaining and thoughtful script . . . and a talented cast of young actors." Many other reviewers, while also impressed with the actors, were critical of the movie itself. The film has "a deadly self-importance," Janet Maslin wrote in the *New York Times*, but she added that Ringwald and Hall "are the movie's standout performers." Denby declared that "the form of *The Breakfast Club* is deplorable, yet much of the writing and acting is good." David Ansen found the film's premise "hokey" but concluded in his *Newsweek* review that the movie works because of its "five-terrific young actors." Like Ansen, *People's* Scot Haller felt that the film's premise was flawed, but he too was impressed with the talent its cast displayed. He was particularly pleased with Ringwald and Hall, of whom he wrote: "Both have the kind of gift that marks movie stars, the ability to create a communion with the camera that gives a freshness to their every move. *The Breakfast Club* overall deserves mediocre grades, but these two performers should go to the head of the class."

In 1985 Ringwald also appeared in "Surviving," a made-for-television movie in which she and actor Zach Galligan portray a troubled teenaged couple who commit suicide midway through the movie by locking themselves into her parents' garage with the car engine running. In addition to Ringwald and Galligan, the film also features Marsha Mason and Paul Sorvino as Ringwald's parents and Ellen Burstyn and Len Cariou as Galligan's parents. The second half of the film addresses the parents' reactions to their children's suicides. Charlotte Ross, co-chair of the National Committee for Youth Suicide Prevention, explained to *People* that "the idea of *Surviving* is to show that suicide is not a solution and to show how much pain it brings."

New York Times writer John Corry, who called "Surviving" "an enormously watchable production," noted that "three women [Burstyn, Mason, and Ringwald] carry the show." He was especially impressed with Ringwald, of whom he wrote: "She is a touching young actress. Her Lonnie is plaintive, a lost lamb looking for help. We mourn when she dies." In a review of "Surviving" for *People*, Jeff Jarvis wrote that Ringwald "proves herself to be young Hollywood's most naturally gifted actress. Playing her wonderfully expressive face like a soulful harmonica, Ringwald can give you love or hopelessness with a glance."

Like Corry and Jarvis, the *Washington Post's* Tom Shales generously praised Ringwald's "Surviving" performance. "In a way," he wrote, "the movie falls to pieces when the parents go to pieces, following the discovery of the bodies. For one thing, this marks the disappearance from the film of Molly Ringwald, . . . [who] is one of the most promising and casually scintillating young actresses around. Her freshness is a contrast here to the slightly stale professional slickness of Mason and Burstyn. . . . [Actor Zach Galligan is] an inhibited and self-conscious youngster who is completely outclassed by Ringwald."

"My days of playing the teen are coming to a close," Ringwald told *Harper's Bazaar* during the filming of "Pretty in Pink," her third feature movie for writer-director John Hughes. "This will be my goodbye to teenagedom." The film, which Hughes wrote expressly for Ringwald, is about "a sensitive girl from a poor, broken family fighting for identity in a rich kid's school," explained a writer for *Elle* magazine. Andrew McCarthy, one of Ringwald's co-stars in the film, described Ringwald as "a very smart, very savvy girl. . . . She's got good instincts," he told Bruce Cook. "She relies on them, and they haven't let her down yet."

"Molly has a sense about quality and the fact that quality endures," Hughes told *Rolling Stone* contributor Hillary Johnson. "She's extremely smart. She knows what schlock is. She can smell a sleazeball producer a mile away. . . . Her performances are flawless," Hughes continued. "Molly is a real, legitimate, world-class actress." Ringwald is more modest about her achievements: "I was lucky to be at the right place at the right time," she told Johnson, "and lucky my talent was recognized."

Despite her current success, Molly says she'd like to take a break from acting for a while. "I think I've said all I have to say about young people in these three movies for John," she explained to Bruce Cook during the filming of "Pretty in Pink." "I'm sort of planning to take a leave of absence for a while. I'm going to college in a while, maybe to the East Coast. I don't want to play 25-year-olds now, and I really don't want to play 18-year-olds when I'm 25. I like acting my age."

One future film role that she eagerly anticipates playing is the lead in "Edie." If made, that movie will be about sixties socialite-actress-model Edie Sedgwick, who died in 1971 of a barbiturate overdose. Ringwald's friend and career advisor Warren Beatty has reportedly purchased the film rights to the Sedgwick biography. When Ringwald first read the book, she became obsessed with its subject, she confessed to Johnson. "I don't know how to say it without sounding conceited," she said. "Just the way [Sedgwick] was—maybe it's something I want to be, or maybe it's something I am. It's the spirit and the style and . . . her energy. . . . It's some kind of similarity that I relate to." Her daughter's desire to play the lead in "Edie" disturbs Molly's mother, Adele Ringwald. "She was talking about that part for a year," Adele told Johnson. "And then I picked up the book and went, 'Oh!' I realized it would be impossible to do that role without nudity. I don't even want to think about it." In a discussion of the Sedgwick role with *Cosmopolitan,* Molly said: "I desperately want to do it, but not now—I'm too *young.*"

According to Ringwald, hers is a very close family, and despite her mother's misgivings about the Sedgwick role, her parents have been supportive and non-intrusive regarding their daughter's career decisions. "My parents have given me real strong morals and values," she told Johnson. "I went through a very rebellious stage, but it was short-lived. . . . I wouldn't be rebellious now, because I wouldn't hurt them for the world." Molly's father, Bob Ringwald, is a jazz pianist and banjo player, and Molly occasionally sings in his nightclub act. He's also blind, a factor that Molly says has made her sensitive to other people with physical shortcomings as well. Of her father's handicap, Ringwald says: "Only once in a while it hits me—'Wow, Dad's blind.' He's always bringing us into the room to read him stuff, or if he's typing something and loses his train of thought, I'll come into the room and read his last sentence to him. And it *still* doesn't hit me," she told Johnson. "He's amazing now, and if he wasn't blind, he would be ten times as amazing."

Molly has been singing with her father's bands since before she started kindergarten. She recorded an album with him when she was just six years old. It's not clear, however, whether or not Molly aspires to become famous for her musical abilities. For her, "singing is fun—something to do with her father," observed Johnson. After hearing Molly perform with her father's nightclub act, Johnson declared: "Her singing is a revelation. Her voice is penetrating—sassy and petulant, generous and warm, whatever the song requires—with a vibrato that reaches into every corner of the room. She does Fats Waller, Ella Fitzgerald, Billie Holiday, even Julie London." Another fan of Molly's singing is film director Paul Mazursky, who noted that "when people watch Molly, they see all this marvelous stuff on screen." Mazursky predicted that "if she ever sings in a movie, she'll blow them right out."

In addition to her accomplishments as a singer and actress, Ringwald has a number of fashion magazine photo spreads to her credit. In 1985 *Harper's Bazaar* named her one of the ten most beautiful women in America. But while some have declared her a glamorous beauty, others find her looks merely "cute." Noting that Ringwald's female teenage fans seem to identify strongly with her, Bruce Cook proposed that Ringwald's appealing but non-threatening appearance is responsible for that identification. "It's that face that gets them," Cook wrote. "I mean, she's nice looking and all, but she isn't inhumanly, unbelievably, absolutely gorgeous. . . . She's . . . cute—but not a threat. Molly Ringwald looks like the girl who sits across the aisle in third-period study, or maybe even a little like the one they see in the mirror."

Like many of her young fans, Molly Ringwald is a normal teenager "who hankers for McDonald's hamburgers and Doritos, who has crushes on Bruce Springsteen and Mel Gibson, [and] who worries about failing algebra," Johnson noted. Unlike them, however, she "is a movie star with something akin to adult standing in the industry." Ringwald enjoys acting, she told *Seventeen,* because "it gives you a chance to be what you aren't, do something really wild, play somebody crazy." She also likes to read (her favorite author is J. D. Salinger), and she hopes to be a writer someday. In the meantime, "while she takes the SATs and decides which colleges to apply to, Molly Ringwald also enjoys the simple pleasures—like bumping into Jack Nicholson at Warren's house," reported Todd Gold in *Cosmopolitan.* "Oh, it's okay," Ringwald told Gold. "Sometimes it's frustrating. But more often than not, being a movie star is really fun."

SOURCES:

PERIODICALS

Cosmopolitan, March, 1985.
Elle, October, 1985.
Films in Review, May, 1985.
Harper's Bazaar, September, 1985.
Maclean's, May 14, 1984, February 18, 1985.
Newsweek, February 25, 1985.
New York, February 18, 1985.
New Yorker, September 20, 1982, May 28, 1984, April 8, 1985.
New York Times, February 7, 1983, February 8, 1985, February 15, 1985.
People, June 6, 1983, June 4, 1984, February 11, 1985, February 18, 1985.
Rolling Stone, June 23, 1983, March 28, 1985, July 18, 1985.
Saturday Review, April, 1985.

Seventeen, November, 1982.
Springfield News-Sun (Springfield, Ohio), September 14, 1985.
Teen, March, 1985.
Time, March 3, 1986.
USA Today, March 6, 1986.
USA Weekend, February 21-23, 1986.
Washington Post, May 5, 1984, February 9, 1985, February 15, 1985.

—Sidelights by Mary Sullivan

Xavier Roberts

1955-

PERSONAL: Born October 31, 1955, in Cleveland, Ga.; son of Harold (an itinerant carpenter) and Eula (a textile worker and independent quilt maker) Roberts. *Education:* Attended Truett-McConnell Junior College for one and a half years.

ADDRESSES: Office—Babyland General Hospital, P.O. Box 714, 19 Underwood, Cleveland, Ga. 30528; and Babyland General Clinic, 402 East Howard Ave., Decatur, Ga. 30030.

OCCUPATION: Artist and entrepreneur.

CAREER: Worked at several jobs, including cook, bottle washer, potter, and state park employee; sold a variety of hand-crafted art objects, including pottery and "soft-sculpture" dolls at garage sales, flea markets, and arts shows; Original Appalachian Artworks, Inc. (manufacturers of, among other products, hand-made Cabbage Patch dolls), Cleveland, Ga., co-founder and chairman, 1978—.

SIDELIGHTS: Nigel Maynard, Cornela Lenora, Berton Pat, Clarissa Sadie, and Luna Trudy: This is a tiny sampling of names of Cabbage Patch Kids, creations of artist/entrepreneur Xavier Roberts. Cabbage Patch Kids are soft-sculpture dolls, all unique, "pathetic-looking prodigies," as Edward C. Baig describes them in *Fortune* magazine. But those big eyes, chubby cheeks, receding chins, and out-stretched arms appeal to the nurturing instincts of children and adults alike.

Roberts first became aware of this appeal in 1977. That's when he seriously began fashioning the cuddly dolls out of stretchy fabrics. His mother, a talented quilter and a textile mill employee, showed him how to "mold" the fabric. After stuffing each doll with soft filling, Roberts painted the eyes and sewed the mouths and other facial features. He then dressed the dolls in kids' garage-sale clothes. Originally dubbed "Little People" by Roberts, the dolls resemble one another, yet each is different.

Accompanied by the cloth dolls he and his mother had sewn, Roberts made the rounds at flea markets and craft fairs. He started out in his home town of Cleveland, Georgia, located in the foothills of the Appalachian mountain chain. There he established a rapport with passersby. Roberts told the *New York Times* that he would make comments about the dolls that potential customers were looking at, like "She's redhaired; she's short-tempered. Or she doesn't like cookies. They'd carry on with me and pretty soon they'd buy one. Then they'd send me letters afterwards about how the baby's doing."

The Little People sold for $30.00 at the beginning. Roberts concedes in the *Washington Post* that "that's a lot of money." Nevertheless, his creations became so popular in

the southeastern United States that prices quickly rose to $50.00, $60.00, then $125.00 per cloth doll. (Prices have since climbed to as much as $1,000.00 for a single Roberts original, with some collectors paying up to $5,000.00.) Soon Roberts's business grew to the point where he and several friends took over a former medical clinic and founded Original Appalachian Artworks, Inc. The clinic became Babyland General Hospital where the dolls were cared for by a staff that eventually grew to about 450. The staff helped perpetuate Roberts's original theme by dressing up as nurses and displaying the dolls in bassinets. Says Roberts in the *Washington Post:* "We bought a computer so we could mail out happy-birthday cards to people who'd bought Cabbage Patch dolls on the anniversary they adopted the dolls. We'd send them a Cabbage Patch Dispatch; it's like a fan club."

By the time that approximately 250,000 of Roberts's dolls had found homes, demand was quickly exceeding the supply. So, to help keep up with the rapidly expanding market, Roberts and his partners decided to license to Coleco Industries, the company that introduced the Adam computer. Unique in the industry, Roberts's contract with Coleco is actually a co-licensing agreement. He and his staff continue to manufacture and market the original Cabbage

Patch dolls, similar to the ones Roberts once sold at county fairs; the most identifiable feature of these dolls is the cloth face. The versions produced in Hong Kong by Coleco are slightly different; among other things, they have plastic faces. Needless to say, the dolls that are still handmade in Georgia sell for considerably more than the ones manufactured by Coleco in Hong Kong.

Roberts's marketing strategy, adopted by Coleco, is a "merchandising masterstroke," noted *Newsweek*. The babies are found in a cabbage patch, says Roberts, alluding to the old myth. So rather than *buy* the dolls, people *adopt* them, complete with adoption papers and birth certificate. And those adopting Cabbage Patch Kids are required to take an oath of adoption. Coleco's advertising campaign, which began in June of 1983, was precisely aimed at children, mostly during cartoon shows on Saturday morning, and proved highly successful. Coleco's $25.00, plastic-face versions of Cabbage Patch Kids (each one still unique, thanks to sophisticated computer programming) gave rise to the Cabbage Patch mania that soon swept the country. It didn't hurt sales any when a public relations representative for the firm sent the then-pregnant "Today Show" host, Jane Pauley, a Kid. Pauley devoted over five minutes to the dolls on network television. Myriad talk shows around the country took her lead. Sales were boosted further when Amy Carter was often televised carrying her Cabbage Patch Kid—one of the early ones—while her father was president of the United States.

Because Coleco was not ready for the huge success of its new, huggable product, there was a critical shortage of Cabbage Patch Kids. In contrast to the dolls' innocent appearances, the behavior of people determined to get their hands on a Cabbage Patch Kids sometimes became aggressive and even violent. For example, about 1,000 customers waited for eight hours to purchase the dolls at a Zayre department store in Wilkes-Barre, Pennsylvania. The crowd turned into a mob, and one woman's leg was broken in the skirmish. According to a *Newsweek* report, another customer in Texas had a contender's purse strap encircling her neck, almost strangling her, as she undauntedly clutched a Cabbage Patch Kid. A postman in Kansas City headed for London, England, to pick up a doll for his kindergarten-age daughter. And when two Milwaukee radio announcers joked that people holding up American Express cards could take home Cabbage Patch dolls dropped from a B-29 bomber at County Stadium, more than twenty hopeful parents showed up at the proposed time and waited in sub-zero weather, ready to catch the dolls.

How can a cloth doll cause such a stir? Experts observe that after several years of playing with high-tech toys, children are ready for what *Newsweek* writers call "the world's first post industrial toy." L.J. Davis writes in the *Washington*

Xavier Roberts's Babyland General Hospital in Cleveland, Georgia, where Cabbage Patch Kids are born. © 1984
Original Appalachian Artworks, Inc., Cleveland, GA. All rights reserved.

Post that Roberts "and his Kids arrived on the scene at what appears to have been the perfect psychological moment, when the nation was surfeited with beeping plastic that talked back to its owners and sometimes defeated them." These dolls seem to appeal to "a universal need that children have to hold something and cuddle it," comments Doris McNeely in *Newsweek.* Even great figures in history are known to have been delighted by dolls. Socrates and William Penn fall into this category, according to William Hoffman, author of *In Fantasy: The Incredible Cabbage Patch Phenomenon.* One particular allure of the Cabbage Patch Kid, notes Dr. Joyce Brothers in *Time* magazine, is that "[she] can be loved with all your might—even though she isn't pretty."

Regarding the use of the adoption angle as a marketing device, some adoption agencies expressed the view that so serious a subject should not be taken so lightly. Other agencies were positive about the idea, while "still others attempted to strike a solemn balance," commented Davis in the *Washington Post.* Dr. Bruce Axelrod, who directs Milwaukee's Comprehensive Mental Health Services, observes in the *New York Times* that "most children between the ages of six and twelve fantasize that they were really adopted. . . . Psychologically, this is a sign that the child is beginning to separate from the family, a necessary part of growing up." With a Cabbage Patch Kid, a child "can act out the fantasy of being adopted," adds Axelrod.

On the business side, the Cabbage Patch Kid fantasy has garnered $1.5 billion in sales through 1985. "Yearly sales of a million units makes for a bombshell product. Coleco is churning out a million Kids each month and still falling short of demand," writes Jeff Shear in *Esquire.*

The success of the Cabbage Patch Kids has attracted many counterfeit dolls, manufactured both in the United States and abroad. Original Appalachian Artworks counsel Stanley F. Birch, Jr., predicts in *Business Week* magazine that the bogus babies will be appearing by the hundreds of thousands. This is particularly a problem when the Cabbage Patch Kid supply becomes more ample. In addition, Roberts has added over fifty products to the market through licensing to numerous companies.

To protect himself and his interests, Roberts has hired detectives to be on the alert for Cabbage Patch Kid look-a-likes. While a number of cases had been taken to court or settled out of court before Roberts licensed to Coleco, not all judgments have been made in Roberts's favor. For instance, when the Hong Kong toy exporter Blue Box Factory Ltd. came out with the more economical Flower Kids, Roberts's lawyers charged the company with unfair competition and stepping over copyright lines. But Blue Box Factory spokesmen defended the Flower Kids by stating that, while the idea was indeed borrowed from the Cabbage Patch Kid concept, the dolls themselves were really not similar enough to cause any legal problems. In this case, the judge concurred. But Birch warns other imitators that they will definitely be prosecuted and may not be as lucky as Blue Box Factory was.

On the other hand, Martha Nelson Thomas of Louisville, Kentucky, had filed a similar suit against Roberts in 1980. She claimed that the original idea of soft dolls, like those

marketed by Roberts, was hers. Thomas recalled that in 1976 Roberts had been interested in having her supply the state park gift shop where he worked with her dolls. But then they couldn't agree on the price and so did not close the deal. "I started working on the design in 1971 and developed it over the years," Thomas told the *Christian Science Monitor.* "It's not completely honest to sell his dolls, and then, when asked where they originated, to omit my part." Citing that Thomas had not copyrighted her dolls, a Federal District Court judge ruled in Roberts's favor. Roberts's attorney, Birch, also noted in the *Christian Science Monitor* that his client's "expression of an idea is quite different from hers." And former Original Appalachian Artwork president, Paula Osborne, argued in the *New York Times* that "there have been soft dolls around for a long time."

Roberts's dolls have been compared to such megafads as the Hula Hoop of the 1950s. Roberts aims for the Cabbage Patch Kids to become classics like Barbie, Raggedy Ann, and "your ready friend the teddy bear, but with an identity," as Shear puts it in *Esquire.* Shear reports that Roberts is planning on providing the public with a "consistently reliable product," "the creation of a brand name," and an "animations and theme park." The product line includes not only the Cabbage Patch dolls, but also albums (the first one, by Tom and Steve Chapin, became gold within a month), books, lunch boxes, pencil sharpeners, seasonal doll outfits, a folding stroller, a baby carrier, and other paraphernalia related to Roberts's theme. With the help of Schlaifer Nance & Company, an Atlanta-based advertising agency, Roberts has licensed to additional major firms, including Milton Bradley, Parker Brothers, Thermos, Hasbro Toys, Elkay Industries, and Playtime Products. Riejel Textiles is even producing disposable Cabbage Patch Kid diapers. The creation of a brand name means that "I want to market my cowboy hats and my boots under my own name. I want to market my cowboy hats and my boots under my own name. I want to design houses, clothes and cars for people," Roberts told *Esquire.*

The animations and the theme park ideas are inspired by Walt Disney, one of Roberts's heroes. Like Disney, Roberts wants to "create a legend," he states. "I want to build fairy tales. Discover Cinderellas." And, like Disney, Roberts grew up on a farm, "an experience that became part and parcel of their products," writes Shear. "Disney saw himself as a 'rube' from Kansas City; Roberts sees himself as a 'mountain boy' from northeastern Georgia." Roberts has purchased more than 400 acres of land in Cleveland, Georgia. He envisions the park he will build there to be a Cabbage Patch Land with visitors acting as on-lookers and participants. The rides will be integrated into the main story of the park. From Georgia, Roberts wants to spread to Colorado, with a park there offering different adventures.

In addition, Roberts has come up with some new, huggable characters. They are the Furskins, a family of mountain bears. The family keeps a general store in Moody Hollow, Georgia (with the zip code 30528½). In *Rolling Stone* magazine, Roberts describes them as "not your normal lazy bears, but upscale ambitious" creatures. There's Hattie, Dudley, Boone, and Farrell, all of whom obviously come from the same genetic pool. They've got freckled noses, button eyes, and "tummies" featuring protruding navels. Roberts wryly observes in the *Wall Street Journal* that there's an uncanny resemblance to himself, "but I have a beard." Moreover, the Furskins and Roberts all wear boots. Roberts's signature appears on the Furskins' left feet, making each one an instant collectible. They carry a price tag of $60.00 each.

Roberts, who was named after bandleader Xavier Cugat, became a millionaire when he was twenty-five years old—two years *before* he licensed to Coleco. He attributes his phenomenal success to hard work and to the fact that he "believed in it so much," he told *Esquire.* "If you want something bad enough, you can will it into existence. You visualize it in your head in 3-D,. . . and it will materialize in front of you."

SOURCES:

BOOKS

Hoffman, William, *In Fantasy: The Incredible Cabbage Patch Phenomenon*, Taylor Publishing, 1984.

PERIODICALS

Business Week, January 16, 1984, March 3, 1986.
Christian Science Monitor, December 12, 1983.
Detroit News, October 3, 1985.
Esquire, November, 1984.
Fortune, December 26, 1983.
Newsweek, September 7, 1981, December 12, 1983.
New York Times, November 29, 1983, December 4, 1983, December 6, 1983.
People, January 2, 1984.
Rolling Stone, March 28, 1985.
Time, September 8, 1980, December 12, 1983.
Wall Street Journal, January 25, 1985.
Washington Post, November 30, 1983, October 16, 1984.

—*Sidelights by Victoria France Charabati*

Kevin Roche

1922-

PERSONAL: Full name, Eamonn Kevin Roche; born June 14, 1922, in Dublin, Ireland; came to United States, 1948, naturalized, 1964; son of Eamon and Alice (Harding) Roche; married Jane Tuohy, June 10, 1963; children: Eamon, Paud, Mary, Ann, Alice. *Education:* National University of Ireland, Dublin, B.Arch., 1945; Illinois Institute of Technology, Chicago, graduate study, 1948-49.

ADDRESSES: Office—Kevin Roche, John Dinkeloo & Associates, 20 Davis St., Hamden, Conn. 06517.

OCCUPATION: Architect.

CAREER: Michael Scott & Partners, Dublin, Ireland, designer, 1945-46, 1947-48; Maxwell Fry and Jane Drew, London, England, architect, 1946; United Nations Planning Office, New York City, architect, 1949; Eero Saarinen & Associates, Bloomfield Hills and Birmingham, Mich., and Hamden, Conn., associate, 1950-66; Kevin Roche, John Dinkeloo & Associates, Hamden, founding partner, 1966—. Member of board of trustees, American Academy in Rome, 1968-71, and Woodrow Wilson International Center for Scholars, Smithsonian Institution, 1969-71; member of Commission of Fine Arts, 1969—. Work has been exhibited at Museum of Modern Art, New York City, 1968 and 1971.

MEMBER: National Institute of Arts and Letters, National Academy of Design (academician), Royal Institute of Architects (Ireland; honorary fellow), Academie d'Architecture.

AWARDS, HONORS: Arnold Brunner Award, American Institute of Arts and Letters, 1965; Creative Arts Award in Architecture, Brandeis University, 1967; Medal of Honor, New York Chapter, American Institute of Architects, 1968; Bard Award, City Club of New York, 1968, 1977; California Governor's Award for Excellence in Design, 1968; New York State Award, 1968; Bard Citation, Citizens' Union of New York, 1968; Total Design Award, American Society of Industrial Design, 1976; D.Sc. National University of Ireland, 1977; Grand Gold Medal, Academie d'Architecture, 1977; Pritzker Prize, 1982.

SIDELIGHTS: In 1982 Kevin Roche won architecture's most prestigious and lucrative award, the Pritzker Prize. Given for outstanding work during an entire career, it acknowledges the recipient's valuable "contributions to humanity and the environment." In winning the prize, which brings a tax-free cash award of $100,000 and a Henry Moore bronze statuette, Roche joined the ranks of such winners as Philip Johnson, I. M. Pei, and Luis Barragan. The awarding Pritzker Committee specifically cited Roche's avoidance of the dictates of a rigid style in his large body of work. In a field of modernists, post-modernists, and romantic modernists, Roche defies classification and facile labels. The Pritzker jury, as quoted by the *New York Times*'s Paul

Goldberger, honored these qualities: "In this mercurial age, when our fashions swing overnight from the severe to the ornate, from contempt for the past to nostalgia for imagined times that never were, Kevin Roche's formidable body of work sometimes intersects fashion, sometimes lags fashion, and most often makes fashion."

Roche's refusal to be harnessed within the confines of any style is a product of his long association with the architect Eero Saarinen. Known for his widely varying and often flamboyant buildings, Saarinen eschewed the limits of a general architectural philosophy. He approached each of his projects as unique, with special problems and needs. Thus, each of his designs was unique and beyond categorization. Roche remarked to *Time* magazine that this was one of the most important things he learned from Saarinen: "What Saarinen taught us is not to find a new mold or formula for producing architecture like so many automobiles, but to design each building with a fresh enthusiasm for meeting its specific requirements."

Born in Dublin, Roche earned his bachelor's degree at the National University of Ireland and worked briefly as a designer with an Irish and then an English architectural firm. In 1948 he came to the United States to do postgraduate work at the Illinois Institute of Technology in Chicago under the great master of the "International Style" Ludwig Mies van der Rohe. After a year, however, Roche abandoned his studies and traveled around the United States. It was during this trek that Roche, according to art historian Vincent Scully in *Time*, "was bowled over by the bigness and power of American industrial architecture."

In 1950 Roche joined Saarinen's firm, Eero Saarinen and Associates. This association provided Roche with a creative atmosphere in which to work. Saarinen, while using some Miesian techniques, did not limit himself to the dictates of the all-pervasive "glass box" International Style. Roche's description of the architectural environment of the 1950's is telling. He explained in Paul Heyer's book *Architects on Architecture: New Directions in America* that "people had accepted Mies's as the ultimate solution—all you had to do was build it, and suddenly you were realizing the golden age—and there did not seem to be any reason to do anything different. To act contrary to that and still have ambitions of being a serious architect was an extremely difficult thing to do." But Saarinen was "very restless . . . he always wanted to move, change, try," and Roche was his willing companion.

Saarinen had just received the commission to design the $100,000,000 General Motors Technical Center in Warren, Michigan. He needed a key design staff to handle this huge project, and so in addition to hiring Roche he hired John Dinkeloo as his technical engineer and head of production. They designed the huge General Motors complex, which was completed in 1955. Generally regarded as a masterly summation of the International Style, the complex also reflects the purpose for which it was designed: It illustrates the precision of automotive technology.

In 1961, however, Saarinen died at the peak of his creative career. He left unfinished such major architectural projects as the Trans World Airlines Terminal at Kennedy International Airport, the Dulles International Airport Terminal near Washington, D.C., and the CBS Headquarters Building in New York City. Roche and Dinkeloo, by this time both partners in the firm, took over the company and saw these structures through to completion. The last Saarinen building was finished in 1965, and in 1966, according to Saarinen's wishes, the name of the firm was changed to Kevin Roche, John Dinkeloo & Associates.

During this time, Roche and Dinkeloo also earned commissions on their own. Their first major project, begun in 1961, was the Oakland Museum in Oakland, California. The city of Oakland wanted the museum complex to house an art museum, a natural history museum, and a cultural history museum. In order to devise a satisfactory design, Roche interviewed Oakland residents and studied the history of the area. He arrived at a plan whose central, integrating principle would be to illustrate the unique California environment in which nature and a rich cultural heritage blend harmoniously. The resulting regional museum encompasses four city blocks and looks more like a garden than a museum. The exhibit galleries are arranged in such a way that the roof of one gallery becomes the terrace of another. A walkway connects the different levels and functions of the museum, and all areas open to gardens, plazas, lawns,

courts, and wide stairways. Architectural historian Henry-Russell Hitchcock in 1977 hailed the Oakland building as "unique among the many museums and art centers built in the last fifteen years, for the urbanistic approach of Roche and Dinkeloo provided on top of the three branches of the museum complex a series of terraces which serve the city of Oakland as a focal public space of exceptional grace and amenity." The Oakland Museum design also moved the firm out of the shadow of Saarinen.

The next major project Roche embarked on was the design of the Ford Foundation headquarters in New York City. In his book *Kevin Roche, John Dinkeloo and Associates, 1962-1975*, Yukio Futagawa described the unusual office building as creating "an appropriate environment for its occupants, a space that allows members of the Foundation staff to be aware of each other—to share their common aims and purposes, and that assists them in fostering a sense of working family." To achieve this, Roche fashioned the offices in the twelve-story building around a central, vertical atrium running the entire height of the structure. All of the offices are glass-walled, and each opens out to this large garden court by means of sliding glass panels. This predominant use of glass prompted *New York Times* critic Ada Louise Huxtable to call the structure a "Crystal Palace." She asserted that "this luminous, transparent interior structure soars to the top in a complex counterpoint of the modular geometry of visible, stacked work floors bathed with golden light played against the huge open court with its illuminated greenery." The result of this design is "a horticultural spectacular and probably one of the most romantic environments ever devised by corporate man."

The Roche and Dinkeloo firm has had many corporate clients and, according to the needs and wants of each, the designs vary widely. Roche designed a 200,000-square-foot addition to the Deere & Company headquarters in Moline, Illinois, which was completed in 1978. The building was originally designed by Saarinen but the project was completed by Roche and Dinkeloo after Saarinen's death. On the new wing, Roche continued with Saarinen's choice of unpainted, rust-colored Corten steel, which had been the first major use of the material on a building. But Roche made changes inside the expansion that are strongly reminiscent of his design of the Ford Foundation headquarters. The three-story building is modeled around an atrium—this time a horizontal one—and none of the offices are private. Partitions delineate office space but do not reach the ceiling. Everything is part of a total "office landscape," as Goldberger described it in the *New York Times*.

Another major commission was the new Union Carbide corporate headquarters in Danbury, Connecticut. The huge building, which is situated in the midst of a 674-acre forest, encompasses so many offices that "if they were lined up on both sides of a hallway," disclosed Walter McQuade in *Fortune*, "it would be 2.6 miles long." But Roche arranged the offices into sixteen pod-like structures that branch out from a central four-story parking facility. Access to the structure is gained by a nineteen-lane road leading directly into the building. Parking is situated in such a way as to allow each employee to park within 150 feet of his office.

This unusual design prompted McQuade to predict that "the structure is likely to become a mecca for managers who need big new headquarters and for architects too." Unlike most corporate office buildings, Roche's design for Union Carbide provides an egalitarian and personalized environment. Roche made all the offices the same size, with the exception of the offices of the chairman, president, and fifteen other top managers, whose offices are simply multiples of the standard room size. Roche's design prevents the typical moving of partitions and furniture as the managers' fortunes in the company rise and fall. Thus, notes McQuade, "an executive can move up or down the corporate ladder without leaving his office."

Before arriving at this design, Roche interviewed hundreds of Union Carbide employees for almost an entire summer. He soon realized that each employee's needs were approximately the same, requiring the same amount of space. "Offices were a symbol of prestige, not of function," Roche asserted to McQuade. As furniture and desk accessories were also delegated according to this counterproductive and expensive system, Roche devised fifteen office arrangements designed in four different styles that were compatible with the overall design of the building. These styles were traditional, transitional, modern, and Scandinavian. Each employee could choose his own office's arrangement and the style of its furnishings. Goldberger, in the *New York Times*, called Roche's methods and design "a rather stunning experiment in democracy."

A dramatic change in approach from the Union Carbide building is Roche's design for the headquarters of the General Foods Corporation. Rather than evoking an egalitarian atmosphere, it strongly suggests one reminiscent of the feudal country estate. Goldberger reflected that "far more than any residence we build today, a corporate headquarters symbolizes both the financial power and control over land that huge country estates once possessed. This symbolism has rarely, if ever, been given literal expression architecturally." Looking like a classical country villa, the General Foods building is complete with portico and symmetrical side wings. It is built, however, with sleek, modern materials. The entire structure is blanketed in white aluminum siding, and the portico is capped by a glass dome. The lower levels of the building comprise a parking structure, which is reached by front and rear roads that lead directly into the building and under the portico. Only visitors use the grand front entrance; employees use the one in the back. Inside, the building's central, communal area is a nearly 100-foot-high atrium. It contains the employee cafeteria and is lighted by the glass dome. The offices of the company's president, chairman, and other high ranking executives are situated on the building's top floor in a semi-circle around the dome—a dramatic extension of the feudal theme. From this axis, the offices of other employees branch out into the two large wings. Goldberger observed that Roche's design "is perhaps the most curious mix of classicism and futurism ever produced."

The Roche and Dinkeloo firm has not limited itself to the design of corporate office buildings; one of its continuing, long-standing projects was the expansion and renovation of New York City's Metropolitan Museum of Art. These additions, noted Goldberger, are "so extensive that they constitute virtually a new museum." Roche designed the glass pavilion that houses the Metropolitan's spectacular acquisition, the Temple of Dendur. He also designed the

Andre Meyer Galleries of nineteenth-century European art and the American Wing. Although some critics, like Goldberger, have expressed the opinion that Roche's expansions, such as the Dendur pavilion and the Lehman Wing, have not been a total success, Roche's Meyer galleries and American Wing have earned high praise from critics Huxtable and Goldberger. Roche's design for the thirteen Meyer galleries "is among the most successful of the museum's changes to date," Huxtable declared in 1980. Roche's plan, which allows the paintings to be viewed in natural light when possible rather than in the constant glare of artificial light, gives the paintings a "near perfect" showcase. The paintings' "beauty and visibility have," declared Huxtable, "been dramatically reinforced by the . . . nature of their setting." Goldberger, similarly impressed with the American Wing, noted that it "is surely the best piece of the Metropolitan's new architecture."

Another Roche structure that has been greeted with acclaim is the United Nations Plaza building. A combination hotel and office building, it is the first of its kind in New York. Built to complement the Secretariat building, the United Nations Plaza provides much needed office space for United Nations personnel and hotel rooms for visiting dignitaries, diplomats, and heads of state. It is thirty-nine stories high and has an unusual shape for a skyscraper. Goldberger described it as "an abstract form, a tower that breaks out of the conventional box with diagonal cuts . . . and slices . . . which join to create a shape that is handsome . . . and responsive to the buildings around it." Bluish-green glass blankets the entire structure, making it seem, Goldberger observed, "almost weightless." Roche's plan for this building won him a Bard Award for urban design from the City Club of New York.

Throughout its existence, the firm of Roche and Dinkeloo has consistently been identified by its unique and unpredictable architectural solutions to design problems. The firm itself has gone through change. In 1981 John Dinkeloo died, and Roche now runs the firm. But the "look" of the buildings designed by the firm will probably not reflect the loss of Dinkeloo. Roche, always the head designer responsible for the unique vision of Roche and Dinkeloo buildings, will most likely continue to surprise.

SOURCES:

BOOKS

Futagawa, Yukio, *Kevin Roche, John Dinkeloo and Associates, 1962-1975,* Architectural Book Publishing, 1977.
Heyer, Paul, *Architects on Architecture: New Directions in America,* Walker & Co., 1966.

PERIODICALS

Architectural Forum, March, 1974
Fortune, December 13, 1982.
New York Times, November 26, 1967, November 21, 1975, June 8, 1976, July 24, 1978, September 19, 1978, June 18, 1979, March 23, 1980, May 19, 1980, October 17, 1980, April 15, 1982, July 3, 1983, February 20, 1984, July 8, 1984.
Time, April 26, 1982.

—*Sidelights by Anne M. G. Adamus*

John Rock
1890-1984

OBITUARY NOTICE: Born March 24, 1890, in Marlborough, Mass.; died of a heart attack, December 4, 1984, in Peterborough, N.H. American physician. Considered a pioneer in infertility testing and test-tube fertilization, Rock was best known for his contribution to the development and government approval of the oral contraceptive. After graduation from Harvard Medical School in 1918, he went into the practice of obstetrics and gynecology in Massachusetts, and in 1926 he began a thirty-year directorship at the Free Hospital for Women's Fertility and Endocrine Clinic. Experimenting with progesterone in the treatment of infertile patients, Rock discovered that the steroid would stop ovulation, allowing the reproductive system to "rest," and that after an average period of three to five months, 15 percent of the patients became pregnant. The effect later came to be called the "Rock rebound."

In 1944 Rock worked with Miria Menkin on the first successful fertilization of a human ovum in a test tube. Eight years later he met biochemist Gregory Pincus, who had been experimenting with the use of a synthetic progesterone for the purpose of oral contraception, and the two decided to collaborate. For their experimentation site, Rock and Pincus chose severely overpopulated Puerto Rico and began testing volunteers at the Rio Piedras housing project. Rock carefully studied the volunteers' medical records over a period of five years, and in 1959 he and Pincus determined that the synthetic progesterone was safe. In May of the following year the Food and Drug administration approved the oral contraceptive for public use.

A devout Roman Catholic throughout his lifetime, Rock next strove, unsuccessfully, to persuade the Catholic church to sanction the use of oral contraceptives for its members. In argument he wrote *The Time Has Come: A Catholic Doctor's Proposal to End the Battle for Birth Control.* In later years, Rock and his colleagues also experimented with a "morning after" birth control pill and a male contraceptive, nicknamed the "Rock strap."

AP/Wide World Photos

SOURCES:

PERIODICALS

Esquire, December, 1983.
Los Angeles Times, December 6, 1984, December 11, 1984.
Newsweek, December 17, 1984.
New York Times, December 5, 1984.
Washington Post, December 6, 1984, December 17, 1984.

Gabriela Sabatini

1970-

BRIEF ENTRY: Born May 16, 1970. Argentine professional tennis player. In the field of women's professional tennis, where prodigies are commonplace and anyone over the age of twenty is considered a veteran, young Gabriela Sabatini has made a name for herself as the player to watch in coming years. As an amateur, Sabatini won seven of the eight junior tournaments she entered in 1984. That same year, she became the youngest player ever to win a round at the U.S. Open. (In fact, she won *two* rounds, leading other players and the press to dub her The Great Sabatini.) Having turned professional, in April 1985 she defeated two of the top-ten ranked women in a single morning at the Family Circle Magazine Cup tournament. In June she reached the semi-finals of the French Open, becoming the youngest semi-finalist in that prestigious tournament's history and earning herself a number fifteen ranking. She competed in her first Wimbledon tournament in July of 1985 and in August reached the semi-finals of the United Jersey Bank Classic by beating the top seed, Pam Shriver, in the quarter-finals.

Although the recent history of women's tennis is full of astonishing prodigies—Chris Evert, Tracy Austin, Andrea Jaeger, Carling Bassett, Kathy Rinaldi—as *New York* magazine writer Michael Stone points out, "all of them have been baseliners, girls with dependable ground strokes and two-handed backhands. What makes Sabatini stand out is her complete game." She boasts a wide variety of shots, an impressive degree of intuition, and—at 5-foot-8, 125 pounds—the power of a much more mature player. According to a *Tennis* magazine reporter, Sabatini "hits out on her baseline drives and passing shots with go-for-broke swings that incorporate a full-torso turn. Her backhand is an outstanding shot. She can hit heavy topspin in rallies, speedy flat passing shots and sharp slices for changes of pace or approach shots." Chris Evert Lloyd told the *New York Times* that Sabatini "hits hard with topspin. . . . Baseliners mature faster, and me and Tracy Austin were tough at that age, but it is unusual for someone that young to have her court sense and variety of shots." Declared top-rated Martina Navratilova to another *New York Times* writer, "She has it all."

The daughter of Osvaldo (who works for General Motors in Argentina) and Beatriz Sabatini, Gabriela became interested in tennis as a very young child when she watched her father and older brother play at a Buenos Aires country club. At seven she began taking lessons herself and quickly exhibited a natural ability for the game. When she outgrew the local competition, like many tennis prodigies, she opted to sign on with a top coach and move to a location where a higher level of competition could be insured. For Sabatini, this meant moving to Florida under the wing of former Chilean Davis Cup star Patricio Apey. *Newsweek* reports that Apey and his wife, who shepherd eight young tennis players in their Key Biscayne home, employ a training system that is unique in

AP/Wide World Photos

the high-pressure world of professional tennis: "There is no set training schedule, and a girl who is tired can sleep late and skip some practice hours. Even star pupil Sabatini may work as little as an hour a day, although she has also been known to put in nine hours. And while good eating habits are encouraged, Gaby is free to indulge in her love for Big Macs." Ultimately, Apey feels that Sabatini's extreme love for the game combined with his loosely structured training program will help his protégée avoid the physical and mental burnout that has plagued many other tennis prodigies. As he told Stone: "We just try to have fun. . . . You can't play good tennis unless you're enjoying it, and right now Gaby is enjoying it."

SOURCES:

PERIODICALS

Newsweek, July 1, 1985.
New York, June 24, 1985.
New York Times, December 26, 1984, September 4, 1984, April 12, 1985, April 15, 1985, June 26, 1985, August 18, 1985.
Sporting News, July 15, 1985.
Tennis, April, 1985, June, 1985.
World Tennis, January, 1985.

Pat Sajak

1947(?)-

BRIEF ENTRY: Born c. 1947 in Chicago, Ill. American television game-show host. As host of television's daytime and nighttime versions of the game show "Wheel of Fortune," Sajak is seen by an estimated forty-two million viewers per day. Sajak's career began with a stint as an English-language announcer for a Chicago-area Spanish-language radio station. After fulfilling his military duty as a disc jockey in Saigon, South Vietnam (now Ho Chi Minh City, Vietnam), Sajak distinguished himself as a witty weatherman in Nashville and Los Angeles. In 1981 he was hired to replace the host on "Wheel of Fortune."

The show, which first aired in 1975, was described by *Detroit News* staff writer George Bulanda as "a glitzy version of the children's game called Hangman," with contestants trying to solve a word puzzle by choosing letters to fill in the puzzle's blanks. When the evening version of "Wheel of Fortune" began syndication in September, 1983, the show quickly attracted top viewer ratings and became the most successful show ever syndicated. By January, 1985, the show impressed experts by drawing five-day viewer ratings higher than the seven-day ratings' average culled by each of television's three major networks, and "Wheel of Fortune" profits for 1985 are estimated at $68 million.

"Wheel of Fortune" was created by talk-show host Merv Griffin, whose company produces the game show. Griffin, in a *People* article by Jane Hall, praised Sajak's "whimsical antics" and described Sajak as "a guy who looks like your favorite son-in-law." Sajak told Bulanda, "I'd like to think I fall somewhere between a gentle smarty-pants and a nice fellow." In an on-going comedy bit, "Saturday Night Live" comedian Martin Short characterizes Sajak as "a pretty decent guy." *Addresses: Home*—Glendale, Calif.

SOURCES:

PERIODICALS

Detroit News "Television," August 11, 1985.
People, April 1, 1985, July 15, 1985.

Elias Sarkis

1924-1985

OBITUARY NOTICE: Born July 20, 1924, in Shibaniyah, Lebanon; died June 27, 1985, in Paris, France. Lebanese government official. Sarkis was born in a small village outside Beirut, the son of a shopkeeper. He worked as a railroad office clerk in order to save enough money to attend St. Joseph University, from which he received a law degree in 1948. Lebanese President Camille Chamoun appointed him to the Court of Audits as a magistrate in 1953. Sarkis became presidential chief of staff to Lebanese army commander Faud Chehab when Chehab assumed the presidency in 1958 and retained that post when Chehab was succeeded by Charles Helou in 1964. Four years later Sarkis became governor of Lebanon's Central Bank, from which position he enhanced Lebanon's image as an important center for international finance.

Sarkis narrowly missed being elected president in 1970, but six years later, at the height of the bloody civil war between the Christian and Moslem factions, the Lebanese parliament elected him to the country's top spot, the first person of humble birth to ever hold that title. As president he encouraged the presence of the Syrian army as a peacekeeping force and sought a solution to the problems presented by the growing number of Palestinian refugees arriving in Lebanon. But Sarkis was unable to heal the wounds caused by centuries-old religious hatred and institutionalized social inequality, and the conflict ground on, destroying Beirut and Lebanon's economy in the process. The presence of the Syrian and Palestine Liberation Organization forces only added fuel to the situation and prompted an Israeli invasion in 1978. Conditions in Lebanon continued to deteriorate, prompting a second Israeli invasion in 1982. In August of that year, with Syria and Israel in virtual physical control of the country, the Lebanese parliament elected Bashir Gemayel to succeed Sarkis as president.

AP/Wide World Photos

SOURCES:

BOOKS

Current Biography, H. W. Wilson, 1979.
International Who's Who, 47th edition, Europa, 1983.
Who's Who in the World, 6th edition, Marquis, 1982.

PERIODICALS

Business Week, February 16, 1981.
Chicago Tribune, June 29, 1985.
Detroit News, June 29, 1985.
Newsweek, October 4, 1976, July 8, 1985.
New York Times, June 20, 1982, September 17, 1982, June 21, 1985, June 27, 1985.

David Schlessinger
1955-

BRIEF ENTRY: Born March 3, 1955, in Philadelphia, Pa. American entrepreneur. Schlessinger founded the discount bookstore chain Encore Books in 1973 when he was an 18-year-old college student. Using money he had borrowed from his younger brother and sister, plus his own life savings of $7000, Schlessinger purchased a small bookstore in downtown Philadelphia that specialized in used library books. Within six months of the store's opening Schlessinger transferred the operation to a new location with five times the floor space and better traffic flow. In 1975 a second store was opened in downtown Philadelphia and another on the campus of the University of Pennsylvania.

By the late 1970s Schlessinger had expanded his marketing policy to include some new titles at discount prices. Customer response to this move was overwhelming and began a trend that led to the discounting of best-sellers and trade books. Encore Books also began opening outlets in suburban locations, and in 1980 Schlessinger ordered a facelift for the chain, which by that time had grown to include ten locations. Within four years the chain had doubled in size with sales in excess of $10 million annually. In 1984 Schlessinger sold Encore Books to the Rite Aid Corp., the country's third-largest drugstore chain, for an estimated $5 million. Schlessinger, who was in 1984 named one of America's under-30 success stories by *Fortune* magazine, agreed to continue as president of Encore Books. *Address*: c/o Encore Books, 34 South 17th St., Philadelphia, Pa. 19102.

SOURCES:

PERIODICALS

Fortune, April 16, 1984.
Publishers Weekly, August 10, 1984, October 12, 1984.

Courtesy of Encore Books

Marge Schott

1928-

PERSONAL: Full name, Margaret Schott; born August 18, 1928, in Cincinnati, Ohio; daughter of Edward (in the lumber business) and Charlotte Unnewehr; married Charles J. Schott (a businessman), 1952 (died, 1968). *Education:* Attended University of Cincinnati, 1950-52.

ADDRESSES: Schottco Corp., 300 American Bldg., Cincinnati, Ohio 45202.

OCCUPATION: Business executive and baseball team owner.

CAREER: Schottco Corp. (holding company for a variety of enterprises), Cincinnati, Ohio, president, 1968—; part owner of Cincinnati Reds baseball team, 1981-84, sole owner, 1984—. Member of board of trustees, Cincinnati Chamber of Commerce.

SIDELIGHTS: She is the unlikeliest of all of major league baseball's owners: a feisty, plain-talking widow whose constant companion is a St. Bernard; a flamboyant socialite who once escorted a dancing bear to a New Year's ball; a hustling car dealer who prefers sitting among the fans to the exclusivity of the owner's box. Marge Schott bought full ownership of the Cincinnati Reds in December, 1984. "Baseball," New York Yankees owner George Steinbrenner told the *Cincinnati Enquirer* at the time, "may never be the same."

It is too early to judge Steinbrenner's prediction. But, clearly, Schott sees things differently than most baseball owners. She is a P.T. Barnum who, when she first became interested in the team, hired a plane to buzz the stadium trailing a banner suggesting that the former owners sell. She is the kind of person, she told the *Columbus Dispatch*, who "might take advice from a waitress in the coffee shop, but ignore it from my general manager." And, at a time when most baseball owners are fueling skyrocketing player salary inflation, Schott is a notorious penny pincher.

In 1985 Schott was one of three women (Jean Yawkey of Boston and Joan Kroc of San Diego are the others) who owned major league franchises. If it were up to her, she never would have joined the club. "My father-in-law once tried to buy the Reds," she told the *Cincinnati Enquirer*, "and my late husband also tried, I would have much preferred if they had gotten it so I could go sit anonymously in the stands."

Marge Schott was born in Cincinnati in 1928 and raised as a Reds fan. She was the second of five daughters born to Edward Unnewehr, who made a fortune in lumber and plywood. "My poor father," Schott told *Sports Illustrated*. "He kept trying to have a son and he kept getting girls." Marge was his favorite of the five. Unnewehr nicknamed his daughter "Butch," for her affinity with sports, and bought her a white Packard for promising to enroll at the University

of Cincinnati, rather than go away for college. Later, she was the only daughter he took into the family business. Marge's business career was brief. In 1952, at age twenty-four, she married Charles J. Schott, as her father cried through the wedding. Schott was a Cincinnatian who was heir to an industrial fortune. They moved to a seventy-acre estate in the posh section of town called Indian Hills, where Marge threw memorable society charity parties and Charles looked after business. "I was never so happy as when I stayed at home and my husband would go out and beat the bushes," she told the *New York Times*.

Early in their marriage, Marge found she could not bear children. "I wanted to have boys, all boys, a dozen of them," she told *Sports Illustrated*. The disappointment, she says, partly explains her affinity for her baseball players. It may also explain her penchant for animals. The Schotts adopted an elephant at the Cincinnati Zoo (they named him Schottzie) and turned their estate into a menagerie of cattle, bees, ducks, and St. Bernards.

Charles Schott died suddenly of a heart attack in 1968, at the age of forty-two, leaving everything to Marge, then thirty-nine. His Schottco Corporation, a large holding company, encompassed such businesses as a car dealership, a concrete products company, a shopping center, a brick manufacturing firm, and an insurance company. Most noteworthy among these various enterprises was Schott Buick, one of the largest automobile dealerships in Ohio. Upon her husband's death, Marge decided to assume control of the dealership, which had never made much money, and attempt to turn it around. But the General Motors executives in Detroit were reluctant to hand the franchise over to a woman with no business experience. "What I knew about the car business you could put in your left ear," Schott admitted to *Sports Illustrated*. "I never bluffed so much in my life. But I did it with such conviction that everybody thought I knew what I was doing."

At one point, she discovered that some of the management people at the dealership intended to try to force her out. In a surprising display of boldness, she fired all the department heads and moved everyone else up a notch. She took charge, on her own for the first time, and began to work to make the business a success. She tried outrageous promotions—including unveiling a new Opel model in the front hall of her house rather than in the showroom. In less than three years, sales jumped 40 percent at Schott Buick, and GM decided she could keep the franchise. Corporate executives told her to come to Detroit to sign the contracts. Instead, Schott made them come to Cincinnati. In 1980 she opened a second GM dealership, Marge's Chevrolet.

When American auto companies were slumping in the late seventies, Schott popularized the slogan "Buy American," which drew national attention as a rallying cry for domestic manufacturers and dealers. Schott was the first woman on the board of trustees of the Cincinnati Chamber of Commerce. She also serves as a board member on numerous charitable boards and as a trustee on several college panels. She gave seed money for a pilot program to house Cincinnati runaways.

Successful as she is in business, Schott makes it clear she is no feminist. "I can't stand Ms.," she told the *New York Times*. "Everytime somebody addresses me as Ms. on a letter, I throw it away. . . . The women I admire most are the women who are wives and mothers. They don't get enough credit. I think people have pooh-poohed wives and mothers, but it's a hell of a job to stay home. These women are raising the future of America."

In 1981, Schott became a limited partner in the Cincinnati Reds baseball team. She bought her small share, she told the *Cincinnati Enquirer*, "as a token of respect to my late husband." At the time, the once-proud "Big Red Machine" had fallen into disrepair. Conservative management had sold or traded most of the team's best players, and attendance had dipped more than 60 percent from the middle 1970s. There was even talk of moving the franchise to another city. Schott was resolved that her small share of the Reds would be more than a token. She tried to organize an "I Don't Like Dick Wagner Night," in honor of the team's general manager. When the Philadelphia Phillies—with ex-Reds Pete Rose, Joe Morgan, and Tony Perez on the roster—came to Cincinnati, Schott hired a plane to fly over Riverfront Stadium toting the message, "Tony, Pete, Joe, Help, Love, Marge."

"It was very frustrating sitting back and watching some of the stuff," Schott told *Cincinnati Magazine*. "It just kept getting so bad, it got to the point where finally you have to speak up. There's a time you reach in your life when you either do something important—step up to the plate and take a shot—or you'll never do it." Schott's turn at the plate came in late 1984. Reds majority owners William and James Williams bristled at Schott's stunts, but when they decided to sell the franchise—after losing $25 million in four years—Schott's offer was among the first they listened to. She bought the team for $13 million in December 1984, "as a Christmas present to the city," Schott told *People* magazine. Asked why she bought the sorry franchise, she told the *Cincinnati Enquirer*, "I couldn't stand the thought of someone taking the team my father and husband had rooted for and moving it to Denver or someplace like that."

She said at the time that she planned to use her business skills to help turn around the Reds, baseball's oldest franchise. She vowed to bring back Ladies' Day, keep a close watch on expenses, and get down into the stands to talk to the fans. "Being in the car business has helped me learn how to deal with the public," she told the *New York Times*. Schott showed up at the press conference announcing her purchase with her best friend—a 170-pound St. Bernard named Schottzie. She proclaimed the dog the team's new mascot ("There are too many chickens in baseball," she told *Sports Illustrated*), listed it in the team program ("eats from the left side of the plate"), and featured it on TV commercials with new Reds manager Pete Rose ("Can the dog hit?" Rose asks. "No, but she can sure eat," responds Schott).

"She's loaded with theater," Reds new general manager Bob Howsam told *Cincinnati Magazine*. "She does some wacky stuff. She's a fun person. It'll be great for us because she's a real goodwill ambassador. This town has an emotional equity in the Reds, and she understands that." Still, Schott cried at the press conference announcing her purchase, and later told *Cincinnati Magazine*, "It's a shame when something great happens in your life and there aren't some people living that you'd love to share it with. . . . I keep thinking, 'Why the hell aren't you Schotts alive?' Charlie, he's probably up there saying, 'This woman is an absolute nut.' "

Living with just her dogs in an enormous house, Schott says she is frequently lonely. "It's sort of the story of my life since Charlie died," she told *Sports Illustrated*, "When he was alive, I slept like a baby. But I sleep terrible now, I wake up every half hour and light a cigarette. I usually don't go to bed until three of four in the morning, and I'm exhausted. But, you know, your mind spins." Schott also has a tough side. Several days after she bought the Reds, she was introduced to baseball's other owners. She criticized them, particularly Steinbrenner, for spending too freely on players and "ruining the game." Steinbrenner responded by saying he would not buy a car from Marge Schott.

She vowed to cut costs by cancelling post-homer fireworks (which she did), and playing fewer night games to reduce lighting bills (which she hasn't done). "I'm sort of a nut about utility bills," she told *Cincinnati Magazine*. "If I spend more time at one [auto] dealership than another, you can always tell in the utility bills. I'm a light turner-outer."

Schott also vowed to bring back Cincinnati's baseball fans by improving the product. In 1985, her first year as majority owner, the Reds, with Pete Rose as manager, climbed from fifth to second place in the National League West. Attendance rose by 700,000. "I love Pete Rose," Schott told the *New York Times* of the man whose nickname is Charlie Hustle. "People call us Hustle and Bustle. Between our two big mouths, I don't think anyone else will get a word in edgewise." Rose returns the kind words. "If hustle, determination and hard work have anything to do with it, it won't take Marge long to make things work," he told *People* magazine. "Marge and I are pretty much alike, except she's got long hair and shaves her legs."

Schott, a chain-smoker given to pants suits, also has a keen sense of humor. Several years ago, when she couldn't get a date for a New Year's party, she took a dancing bear. "I had the bear wear a bow tie, because it was a formal affair," she told the *Cincinnati Enquirer*. "Anyway, it was one of the most enjoyable evenings I'd had in a long time." Asked if she would like to marry again, Schott told the *New York Times*: "My family says if I spent as much time husband-hunting as I do on my businesses, I would have found someone. My employees wanted to get me with Lee Iacocca, just to get rid of me." Without children, Schott is close to her twenty nieces and nephews, some of whom appear with her and her dogs on television commercials. And she has the Reds. "It's kind of fun, you know?" she told *Sports Illustrated*. "You feel like a mother. It's like getting 25 big sons. An expensive mothering job, right?"

SOURCES:

PERIODICALS

Cincinnati Enquirer, December 22, 1984, January 20, 1985, April 8, 1985, June 26, 1985.
Cincinnati Magazine, April, 1985.
Columbus Dispatch, January 13, 1985.
New York Times, December 22, 1984, March 8, 1985.
People, July 22, 1985.
Sports Illustrated, July 15, 1985.
Time, July 29, 1985.

—Sketch by Glen Macnow

Edward R. Schwinn, Jr.

1949(?)-

BRIEF ENTRY: Born c. 1949; American bicycle manufacturing company executive. Since 1979, Edward R. Schwinn, Jr. has been president and chief operating officer of the Chicago-based Schwinn Bicycle Company, founded by his great-grandfather, Ignaz Schwinn, in 1895. One of the largest bicycle manufacturers in the country, and the largest distributor of bicycle parts, the company has been dramatically restructured under the younger Schwinn's leadership.

Schwinn bicycles have long enjoyed a reputation for superior quality, based partly on their lifetime guarantee backed by a nationwide network of factory-trained mechanics. The company also sells a wide range of products, from bicycles under $100 to a top-of-the-line racing bicycle costing almost $3,000. Schwinn sells some one million bicycles each year and holds a market share of about 10 percent. Because of its ninety years in the business, the Schwinn Bicycle Company, Keith E. Leighty writes in the *Washington Post*, "is practically synonymous with American bicycles."

But at the time Edward R. Schwinn assumed control of the family business in 1979, the company was beset by several serious problems. Foreign made bicycles were crowding the American market; Schwinn's factories in the Chicago area were antiquated; and in 1980, the unionized workers went on a crippling three-month strike. Schwinn took drastic measures to overcome these problems. He closed the company's four factories in Chicago and moved production to a new, nonunion plant in Mississippi, while other production work was moved to the Far East. Some 65 percent of Schwinn's bicycles are now made overseas. As Leighty quotes Schwinn explaining, "customers do not care where the bikes are built, so long as they have the Schwinn quality." These changes, although angering some former company employees, markedly improved Schwinn's market position.

Financial details of the privately-held company are not available, but Schwinn's leadership has seen an increase in sales and a more aggressive advertising style. Because the company both imports bicycles and manufactures them in the United States, Schwinn tells Lee A. Daniels in the *New York Times*, "our competition is anybody who sells a bicycle." Schwinn sees the restructured Schwinn Bicycle

Company as well prepared for the competitive challenge. Speaking to Daniels, Schwinn explains: "People buy Schwinn because it's a recognizable name that represents high-quality." *Address:* Schwinn Sales, Inc., 1856 North Kostner Ave., Chicago, Ill. 60639.

SOURCES:

PERIODICALS

New York Times, February 14, 1985.
USA Weekend, December 20-22, 1985.
Washington Post, July 7, 1985.

Joe Sedelmaier

1933-

PERSONAL: Full name, John Josef Sedelmaier; born May 31, 1933, in Orrville, Ohio; son of Josef Heinrich and Anne Isabel (Baughman) Sedelmaier; married Barbara Jean Frank, June 6, 1965; children: John Josef, Nancy Rachel, Adam Frederich. *Education:* Art Institute of Chicago, B.F.A., 1955.

ADDRESSES: Office—Sedelmaier Film Productions, 2128 Sedgwick St., Chicago, Ill. 60614.

OCCUPATION: Director and cinematographer.

CAREER: Young & Rubicam (advertising agency), Chicago, Ill., art director, 1955-61; Clinton E. Frank Co. (advertising agency), Chicago, art director and associate creative director, 1961-64; J. Walter Thompson (advertising agency), Chicago, art director and producer, 1964-67; Sedelmaier Film Productions, Chicago, president, 1967—.

AWARDS, HONORS: Golden Ducat award, Mannheim Film Festival, 1968; Golden Gate award, San Francisco Film Festival, 1969; Gold Hugo award, Chicago Film Festival, 1976; Cannes Film Festival, Golden Lion award, 1972, 1979, 1981, Silver Lion award, 1979, 1981; second annual IDC award, Chicago, 1980; recipient of more than seventy Clio awards, including one for director of the year, 1981.

SIDELIGHTS: "Where's the beef?" It seemed as though everyone was asking this question in 1984. Even Ronald Reagan, in the middle of his heated campaign for a second term as U.S. president, plaintively asked voters where the beef was in his opponent's platform. The question was first asked by a little old lady in a television commercial proclaiming that Wendy's single hamburgers were meatier than Burger King's Whopper or MacDonald's Big Mac. The commercial first aired in January, 1984, and, as Barbara Lippert of the *Saturday Review* noted, "almost immediately the phrase became a national consumer warcry." Lippert felt that the star of the ad, Clara Peller, a grandmother in her eighties, was asking us in a comic, nonthreatening way "what happened to quality, honesty and consistency in this country and in our lives." The man behind the commercial, Peller, and the "Where's the beef?" slogan was award-winning director Joe Sedelmaier.

Sedelmaier is regarded by many in the advertising business as one of the best directors of television commercials working today. Amil Gargano of the New York advertising agency Ally & Gargano told *Esquire* that Sedelmaier is "the best comedic director in advertising," while Howard Rieger, senior vice-president of the N.W. Ayer agency, simply dubs him "the best." Confirming these glowing testaments is the fact that Sedelmaier has won more than seventy Clios, advertising's equivalent of the Emmy award, for his work in

Photograph by J. Verser Engelhard. Courtesy of Sedelmaier Film

commercials. He claims to have lost count of just how many awards he has collected.

Sedelmaier started working as an art director in the advertising field in 1955, when he landed a job with the firm Young & Rubicam shortly after graduating from the Art Institute of Chicago. He moved around, working at the Clinton E. Frank and J. Walter Thompson agencies. It was at Thompson that he began to shoot commercials, filming spots for his first account, the Alberto-Culver company. Although a neophyte—and an argumentative one at that—Sedelmaier was very successful. Rieger, a co-worker at Thompson at that time, disclosed to *Esquire* that "Joe worked on an extremely small budget, which [the agency's managers] liked. And he would feature people from the agencies in the ads, which they also liked. And he ended up winning a lot of awards. They liked that best of all."

Sedelmaier went on to do the Chun King Chinese food commercials for Thompson, but after about three years with the agency he decided to start his own production company. After setting up Sedelmaier Film Productions in 1967, though, he found ad agencies reluctant to hire him because

341

of his reputation of being difficult to work with; he was known for demanding complete artistic control on his projects, which is unheard of in the advertising business. Ad agencies work on campaigns for months and get full client approval before beginning to shoot commercials. When an agency hands storyboards (the shooting script) to a director, it expects to see the commercial shot exactly the way the storyboards specify. Sedelmaier, however, often discards the storyboards, retaining the central idea only. (According to Geoffrey Colvin in *Fortune*, Sedelmaier "won't touch a commercial if he doesn't like the idea.") Typically, after accepting a job, Sedelmaier will totally exclude the input of the sponsoring agency. He controls all aspects of a commercial: he produces, directs, designs the sets, selects the music, mixes the sound, supervises the editing, serves as his own lighting expert, and even directs the voice-over announcer. The amount of control Sedelmaier demanded scared off the large agencies.

At first Sedelmaier worked with smaller, regional agencies that were less afraid to take a risk. One very different commercial, one that prompted the national agencies to take another look at Sedelmaier, was the Southern Airways ad. Given the mandate to illustrate that all classes of travel on Southern Airways are first class, Sedelmaier came up with a very funny commercial. In it, a man enters one of the planes of a competing airline and walks through it to reach the coach section. Passing through first class on his way, he observes that the passengers revel in overstated luxury. Finally reaching the coach section, he pulls aside a curtain and is greeted by a scene resembling, according to *TV Guide*, "the lowest hold of a Palestine-bound refugee ship" in which "somber Slavic music played. . . [and] wretched passengers sat on the floor alongside their cardboard suitcases." The commercial was a hit and won Sedelmaier several awards.

Gradually, the larger ad agencies began to use Sedelmaier. He directed and produced commercials for Dunkin' Donuts, American Motors, Midas Muffler, Mr. Coffee (in which unhappy coffee drinkers rebel by throwing their cups and saucers out of windows), Jartran (its hauling abilities demonstrated by a slew of rapidly reproducing rabbits), and Aamco ("Ever wonder why things break down just as the warranty expires?"). He worked on the Federal Express account for six years, creating the ad featuring the fast-talking executive with sunken eyes and the slogan "When it absolutely, positively has to get there overnight." During the time Sedelmaier handled the Federal Express ads, the company grew, noted the *New York Times*'s Tamar Lewin, from "being one of the many small package delivery companies to No. 1."

Sedelmaier began to establish another reputation—that of a comic genius. He made commercials that made people laugh out loud and, most importantly, remember the products being advertised. He had developed a unique style; his commercials, instantly identifiable as "Sedelmaiers," are a peculiar blend of humor, fear, and paranoia. Susan Scherl of the Dancer Fitzgerald Sample agency told Lewin that "for a certain kind of ad, you don't even bid it out, because you know there's no one like Joe." Sedelmaier's ads exaggerate and lampoon the fears and headaches everyone experiences in daily living. *TV Guide* quoted one advertising professional, who described Sedelmaier's ads as "little 30-second nightmares." Jerry Della Femina, head of the New York

agency Della Femina Travisano & Partners, explained Sedelmaier's technique: "The fear that you're going to lose your job, that you'll be embarrassed in front of your peers, that you'll go to buy something and be taken advantage of. The humor makes it all palatable, and there's always some kind of hero at the end—Federal Express, Airborne, Kaypro, Wendy's—to save you."

Casting also sets Sedelmaier's commercials apart. Sedelmaier regards casting as one of his most important contributions to the look of a commercial. He often shuns professional actors, explaining that they acquire standard, stock expressions and do not look or act like real people. Sedelmaier told *Industry Week*'s James E. Braham that he does not "want to use well-known people, because you have so little time to build a character. It's not like a feature film. What I look for are 'interesting people.' Nine out of ten commercials. . . use faceless people, plastic people." Sedelmaier uses plumbers, architects, secretaries, and manicurists—like Clara Peller—who have an interesting look. To keep track of his funny characters, Sedelmaier maintains a file of snapshots of their faces. Some in the industry, however, think that by "interesting" Sedelmaier really means strange. One producer of commercials, quoted by Lynn Hirschberg in *Esquire*, said that Sedelmaier "uses freaks. . . . If a guy comes into a. . . casting session and he has a gimpy leg, Joe will cast him right away. Some people call that genius. I call it exploitation."

But the humor in Sedelmaier's commercials is not at the expense of his often peculiar characters. The humor comes from the situation, as Sedelmaier explained to *Theatre Crafts:* "What makes me laugh. . . is watching a person try to keep his dignity when everything around him is collapsing. Humor comes from the situation—not the punchline, which people will laugh at only once."

Many advertising people still question whether humor sells products. Sedelmaier obviously thinks it does. He told Braham that "I think you can be entertaining, and then you sell. But first, you have to get their attention. The best way to entertain is to make people laugh." The figures seem to affirm Sedelmaier's belief. The *New York Times* reported that Wendy's claims that a poll taken in January, 1984, indicated "a 27 percent increase from December in the number of consumers who thought Wendy's single hamburger was bigger than either the Big Mac or the Whopper."

With the success that has come from his commercials, Sedelmaier is thinking very seriously of following the footsteps of many of the top advertising directors and moving on to Hollywood to direct full-length motion pictures. Steven Spielberg, as quoted by Hirschberg, remarked that "Joe has coined a style of humor I can't wait to see in feature films. . . . He's a superb visual stylist, more closely resembling Jacques Tati than anyone else I can think of." Sedelmaier did sign on to direct Rodney Dangerfield in the film "Easy Money," but he bowed out three weeks before shooting was to begin. The reason he withdrew was that he could not have the complete artistic control he is now given in the advertising field. In Hollywood, where the star and box-office draw has a large role in artistic decisions, Sedelmaier ran into conflict. He disclosed to Hirschberg that he "would love to make a feature, but it has to be done on my terms."

SOURCES:

PERIODICALS

Esquire, August, 1983.
Fortune, June 13, 1983.
Industry Week, April 2, 1984.
New York Times, March 6, 1984.
Playboy, January, 1985.
Saturday Review, January-February, 1985.
TV Guide, March 10, 1984.
Theatre Crafts, January 1984.

—Sidelights by Anne M.G. Adamus

Susan Seidelman

1953(?)-

PERSONAL: Born c. 1953 in Philadelphia, Pa.; daughter of a hardware manufacturer and teacher. *Education:* Drexel University, bachelor's degree in film; New York University, master's degree in film.

ADDRESSES: Home—New York, N.Y. *Office*—c/o Orion Pictures Corp., 1875 Century Park E., Los Angeles, Calif. 90067.

OCCUPATION: Film director.

CAREER: After undergraduate study, worked for a short time as a production assistant at a television station; after receiving graduate degree, briefly worked as a freelance editor and assisted in production of television commercials; film director, 1982—. As a graduate student, directed award-winning shorts "And You Act Like One, Too," "Deficit," and "Yours Truly, Andrea G. Stern"; feature films include "Smithereens," 1982, and "Desperately Seeking Susan," 1985.

AWARDS, HONORS: Student Academy Award for "And You Act Like One, Too"; grant from American Film Institute to make "Deficit"; awards from Chicago Film Festival, American Film Festival, and Athens International Film Festival, for "Yours Truly, Andrea G. Stern"; "Smithereens" was the first independently produced film ever selected for the main competition at the Cannes Film Festival.

SIDELIGHTS: Although Susan Seidelman has been in the business of directing films only a few brief years, she has achieved a remarkable degree of success in her field. Every one of Seidelman's films has won acclaim for the Philadelphian cum New Yorker. The most prestigious accolade came when her "Smithereens" became the first independently produced film to be selected for the main competition in the Cannes Film Festival.

Seidelman is the oldest daughter of a hardware manufacturer and a teacher. She grew up a typical suburban kid on the outskirts of Philadelphia, with no real passion for the silver screen. She recalled for *Films in Review:* "I read about all the famous directors who spent their childhoods in the balconies of movie houses. I didn't go to the movies much. My idea of a great movie was 'The Parent Trap' with Hayley Mills." Her undergraduate degree is from Drexel University in Philadelphia, where she started out taking sewing and tailoring courses. She switched to film not for any love of the art, she told *Films in Review,* but "because it seemed like an easy way to earn a degree; just watch movies and bluff my way through college." Whether that choice was fate or just happy coincidence, Seidelman found she was hooked and happy about it.

After graduation she worked as an assistant television producer for a local UHF station and applied to film schools. She was turned down by Temple University but accepted by New York University, where the emphasis was on "hands-on" experience. Eleanor Hamerow, director of N.Y.U.'s graduate school, told the *New York Times* that every student must "direct, shoot, schlep, be a gaffer, be a unit manager. . . . They experience all the problems and difficulties of filmmaking and keep going through them on different levels." When she started at N.Y.U. in 1974, Seidelman recalls, her newfound love of film was insufficient. "I was intimidated," she told *People.* "Everybody else had seen fifty billion German Expressionist movies, so I started going to five or six movies a week to catch up."

Her first student film was the twenty-eight minute "And You Act Like One, Too," which was the story of a thirty-year-old housewife in a rut. The film won a Student Academy Award. Awarded a grant from the American Film Institute, the second Seidelman-directed film was called "Deficit." It was a revenge/mystery film about a "bad boy" character. Number three was "Yours Truly, Andrea G. Stern" and starred an eleven-year-old girl. It won awards at the Chicago Film Festival, the American Film Festival, and the Athens International Film Festival. That N.Y.U. hands-on education was probably key in helping Seidelman make the film that got her noticed at Cannes.

"Smithereens" is the story of a no-talent girl named Wren who tries to hitch a ride to the top on the coattails of punk rock musicians. She ends up being mistreated and cheated by people with the same lack of morals as she, eventually being thrown into the street and forced to turn to prostitution. Seidelman financed the film herself, first raising $25,000 from friends, relatives, and other interested or sympathetic parties. Shooting began in the summer of 1980, but two weeks later star Susan Berman broke her leg, and shooting was stopped for four months. With the portion of the film that was already complete, Seidelman used the time off to woo more investors—the film eventually cost $80,000—and to relearn some finer points of feature film-making. The budget was so tight that all of the actors performed on a deferred-payment basis.

She told *Film Comment:* "At N.Y.U., through my short films, I found a core group. A crew. Together we did 'Smithereens.' We had to do everything, which was hard, but I enjoyed the communal aspects of that kind of 'guerilla' filmmaking. . . . my apartment was a crash pad: Richard Hell [one of the performers] was living in the back room; the costume maker was on the floor, in a sleeping bag. Fun. . . . We sneaked around the subways, because we couldn't afford to pay for a permit. Chirine, the cinematographer had the camera in a flight bag. We'd sit there, take it out for a couple of shots, and put it back in. For two nights, we rode the subways from midnight to 6 a.m. Although it's a pain in the neck not being able to control your environment—we'd have to stop and get out every time a subway cop would enter—I liked the energy it all had."

The film caught the eye of not one, but two, 1982 Cannes judges. Pierre Henri Deleau at first selected it for the "Directors' Fortnight" at Cannes. But Cannes Festival director Gilles Jacob chose "Smithereens" to go into the main competition. Not only was it the first independently-produced film to win that honor, but it turned out that Seidelman was the only American and the only female in that competition. According to *People,* "An unofficial panel of French critics ranked it a respectable tenth in a field of twenty-three, just behind Jean-Luc Godard's 'Passion' and well ahead of Alan Parker's highly touted 'Shoot the Moon.'"

Seidelman told the *New York Times* that she sees the Cannes endorsement this way: "The French are very intrigued by pop culture. I think the Festival people saw in 'Smithereens' the quirky view of American youth." Not only on a professional level, but on a personal one, were the Cannes accolades important. About her family, Seidelman told the *New York Times:* "For a while, they were wondering 'Is it a phase she's going through? Hopefully, she'll get out of it and find a responsible job.' But they came to Cannes and for the first time they started taking me seriously." The night her film was shown at Cannes, Seidelman recalled for the *New York Times,* "I had to walk up this red-carpeted staircase. And the streets were roped off, and the guards kept saying to me 'Get over to the side, get over' and finally one woman pointed to me and said 'That's the director.'"

After Cannes, Seidelman was invited to California, got an agent, and met studio people. But she showed caution about making a major studio-backed film. The thought of haggling over complicated deals and having executives peering over her shoulder, telling her what to do, did not appeal to the free-spirited Seidelman. For a year she travelled with "Smithereens" on the Cannes Film Festival circuit, promoting her movie and "having lots of lunch" with studio executives.

After seeing "Smithereens," Midge Sanford and Sarah Pillsbury sent Seidelman the script for a film they were producing, written by Leora Barish, called "Desperately Seeking Susan." Sanford told *Films in Review:* "We were struck by the visual tones that Susan gave to 'Smithereens.' It was glamorous and seedy at the same time. We felt she was an enormous talent, and that she might like the script." Sanford told *New York* magazine, "We thought she would have a unique take on New York, not the New York that a lot of people see—the Plaza, or Bergdorf's."

Several things cause Seidelman's visual tones to be unique. Not only does she shoot scenes as she perceives them, filtered through her own personal life experiences, but she shows viewers a woman's-eye-view of things—something infrequently seen due to the scarcity of female directors. And she shows that view from her own vantage point—barely five feet from the floor. Said *American Film* of "Smithereens": "We're privy to a woman's perspective. We see it in the extreme low angles of 'Smithereens'—the diminutive Seidelman shoots from her own eye level and often concentrates on the subtle variegations of asphalt, concrete and cobble on the street." Seidelman told *Films in Review* she especially admires the works of directors Martin Scorsese, Roman Polanski, and Francis Ford Coppola. "They are very honest filmmakers. Also, they are relatively short men. I see things from low angles, and I'm fascinated by feet."

Before she could make a studio film—Orion sponsored "Desperately Seeking Susan"—Seidelman had to apply for membership in the Directors Guild of America. "Three members had to recommend me for membership," she told the *Los Angeles Time.* "The signatures on my application were from Marty Scorsese, Woody Allen and Mike Nichols, all directors I admire but had never met."

"Desperately Seeking Susan" is the story of a bored New Jersey housewife who tries to spice up her life by reading the ads in the personal columns of a tabloid. It was frequently described by critics as a mixture of a punk version of "Alice in Wonderland" and a "screwball comedy" a la "I Love Lucy." Roberta, the housewife, becomes particularly intrigued by the frequent ads headed "Desperately Seeking Susan," which two lovers ran when they wanted to arrange a rendezvous. Roberta, played by Rosanna Arquette, decides to spy on the pair during their next encounter. She gets bopped on the head and wakes up with amnesia, wearing the clothes of the desperately sought Susan, a trashy street-wise woman with the police and the mob looking for her. Through a series of strange twists, the real Susan, played by rock star Madonna, ends up in Roberta's comfortable suburban home. Eventually things are straightened out.

"Smithereens" was made in two years (due to delays caused by the star's broken leg and by weather) and cost $80,000. "Desperately Seeking Susan" was made in just four months with a budget of $5 million. When the film was first cast, it was Arquette who was the star. Madonna, at the time, was popular in New York but was not well known around the rest of the country, and she had never acted before except for musical videos. But by the time filming started, Madonna's second album, "Like a Virgin," had sold over three million copies. Suddenly Seidelman was handling the movie debut of one of the hottest rock stars of the year. Originally scheduled for October 1985, the release of "Desperately Seeking Susan" was moved up to March to take advantage of Madonna's popularity.

The film could have been a thin, senseless epic aimed at an audience of worshipful teen fans. But it ended up being far more. "Desperately Seeking Susan," while not a smash hit of monumental proportions, became a fun and appealing movie—it grossed $20 million and was seen by 400,000 viewers in its first three days—well directed and well received by audiences and critics. And Seidelman had herself a hit.

She is sensitive to the fact that she is a woman in a world still dominated by men. The *New York Times* declared about "Desperately Seeking Susan": "Industry observers have. . . noted that the commercial and artistic success of the film, which not only stars two women but was also produced, directed and written by women, should pry open doors traditionally shut to women in Hollywood." But Seidelman remains wary of Hollywood and the promises of the studios. She waited two years to make a movie after the success of "Smithereens." In the interim, she found herself inundated with offers to direct teenage films that she turned down. Seidelman told the *Los Angeles Times:* "I didn't want to get caught in the Hollywood trap that got other woman directors in the mid-'70s. Some of their movies were quite interesting, but they didn't do as well critically or at the box office. As a result those people never got another chance to make another movie. . . . I thought that was so unfair, given the fact that there are so many male directors who make mediocre or not-bad movies and then continue to

make not-bad movies for the rest of their lives. Not every movie has to be a hit for a director to keep working, but it seemed like with women, the executives said, 'Well, we gave her a shot; she can't direct—the movie wasn't a huge success.' "

Still avoiding the Hollywood scene, Seidelman lives in a loft in the SoHo area of New York City and enjoys frequenting the small clubs and bistros in her neighborhood. From all indications, it appears that she will continue to exercise a great deal of caution where her career is concerned. As demonstrated by the two-year gap between "Smithereens" and "Desperately Seeking Susan," she doesn't rush into new projects without careful consideration. As she told Deborah Caulfield of the *Los Angeles Times*, "If you're gonna get up at 5:30 a.m. every morning for two or three months and go to bed at 1 a.m., you better really believe in the thing."

SOURCES:

PERIODICALS

American Film, January-February, 1984.
Chicago Tribune, November 24, 1985.
Christian Science Monitor, December 9, 1982.
Film Comment, May-June, 1985.
Film Quarterly, winter, 1983-84.
Films in Review, June-July, 1985.
Los Angeles Times, January 9, 1983, January 13, 1983, March 28, 1985, April 2, 1985.
New Republic, December 6, 1982.
Newsweek, April 8, 1985.
New York, November 26, 1984.
New York Times, February 5, 1982, November 19, 1982, December 5, 1982, December 26, 1982, January 27, 1985, March 23, 1985, April 14, 1985.
People, February 21, 1983, April 8, 1985, April 29, 1985.
Rolling Stone, April 28, 1983.
Saturday Review, May-June, 1985.
Time, April 1, 1985.
Vogue, March, 1985.
Washington Post, March 29, 1985.

—Sidelights by Mary Solomon Smyka

Phil Silvers

1912-1985

OBITUARY NOTICE: Full name, Philip Silversmith; born May 11, 1912, in Brooklyn, N.Y.; died November 1, 1985, in Los Angeles, Calif. American actor and comedian. Phil Silvers is best remembered for his portrayal of Sergeant Ernie Bilko, the fast-talking con man of the popular television comedy series "The Phil Silvers Show." The series, which ran from 1955 to 1959, won Silvers three Emmy Awards and made him a national celebrity. He was also successful as a Broadway actor and film star.

Silvers began his career as a vaudeville singer at the age of thirteen. When his voice changed, he turned to comedy, working in vaudeville and burlesque and making his film debut in "Hit Parade of 1941." During the 1940s, Silvers appeared in some twenty feature films, specializing in the role of the hero's best friend in romantic comedies. In 1946, he moved to Broadway in "High Button Shoes," playing the part of Harrison Floy, a real estate swindler; the play ran for 727 performances. The hit play "Top Banana" followed in 1951, earning Silvers a Tony Award and the nickname "Top Banana," stage slang for the actor with top billing. Silvers's appearance in the film adaptation of the play led to a television contract and the role of Sergeant Bilko.

As Bilko, Silvers was one of the dominant figures of 1950s television. "His devilish grin and his way of barking commands at his ragtag platoon endeared him to a generation of television viewers," a *Chicago Tribune* writer remarked. Chronicling Bilko's outlandish moneymaking schemes at the imaginary Fort Baxter, an Army base in Kansas, "The Phil Silvers Show" quickly became the nation's most popular television program. It bested "The Milton Berle Show," which had held the honor for eight years. The program's 138 episodes are still in syndication in the United States and Europe.

Silvers's later films include the comedies "It's a Mad, Mad, Mad, Mad World," "A Funny Thing Happened on the Way to the Forum," and "The Boatniks." In 1972, Silvers starred in a Broadway revival of "Forum," for which he won his second Tony Award, but the show was closed when he suffered a stroke and was unable to perform. This stroke restricted Silvers's later work to the occasional guest appearance. In 1981, for example, he guest starred on the series "Happy Days" with his daughter, actress Cathy Silvers.

Despite the many successes of his career, Silvers was always best remembered for his role as Sergeant Bilko. Years after he had concluded the show, Martin Weil of the *Washington Post* reported, "New York cabdrivers would hail Mr. Silvers with a 'Hey Sarge!'" As Silvers himself once said, Jack Jones wrote in the *Los Angeles Times*, "I'll always be Bilko."

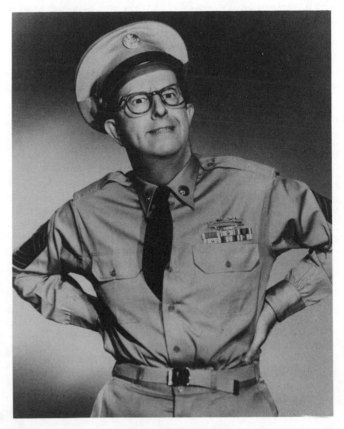

AP/Wide World Photos

SOURCES:

BOOKS

Allen, Steve, *Funny Men*, Simon & Schuster, 1956.
Saffron, Robert and Phil Silvers, *This Laugh Is on Me: The Phil Silvers Story*, Prentice-Hall, 1973.

PERIODICALS

Chicago Tribune, November 3, 1985.
Cosmopolitan, February, 1956.
Detroit Free Press, November 2, 1985.
Detroit News, November 2, 1985.
Holiday, November, 1956.
Los Angeles Times, November 2, 1985.
New Republic, November, 1951.
Newsweek, November 11, 1985.
New York Herald Tribune, September 26, 1955.
New York Times, November 2, 1985.
People, March 15, 1982.
Saturday Evening Post, March 15, 1952.
Time, November 11, 1985.
Washington Post, November 2, 1985.

Mary Sinclair

1918-

AP/Wide World Photos

PERSONAL: Born September 23, 1918, in Chisholm, Minn.; daughter of Joseph (manager of a school power plant) and Margaret Palcich; married William Sinclair (an attorney), September, 1945; children: John, Peter, Rosemary, Thomas, Ann. *Education*: College of St. Catherine, St. Paul, Minn., bachelor's degree in English and chemistry, 1940; University of Michigan, master's degree in environmental communications, 1973.

*ADDRESSES: Home—*5711 Summerset, Midland, Mich. 48640.

OCCUPATION: Social activist.

CAREER: Research librarian for Dow Chemical Co., Midland Mich., after graduation from college; associate editor of *Chemical Industries* magazine, New York, N.Y., during World War II; technical writer for Dow Chemical Co.; abstract writer, Library of Congress, Washington, D.C., during the 1950s; freelance writer in Midland; currently social activist, specializing in nuclear power and environmental issues. Lecturer.

SIDELIGHTS: When Mary Sinclair was working for the Library of Congress in Washington, D.C., in the 1950s, she never guessed that some of the documents she was reading on nuclear technology would lead her into battle with a powerful utility company. And she never anticipated the personal price she would pay for a victory.

Born in Chisholm, Minnesota, in 1918, Sinclair now lives in Midland, Michigan, where she and her husband raised five children in the shadow of a nuclear power plant that the local utility, Consumers Power Company, built just a few miles from her home. During her days at the Library of Congress, Sinclair had watched and learned about the emerging technology of nuclear power. And for many years, she supported nuclear power, even though she saw serious problems with the technology that was being promoted by the Atomic Energy Commission as safe, clean, and economical. Sinclair was confident that problems such as waste disposal and radiation leaks would be addressed and a solution would be found. But in 1967, when Consumers Power proposed plans to build a nuclear power plant in Midland, Sinclair realized the problems had not been solved. Her scientific interest in nuclear power quickly turned to personal concern, and in a drive to present facts that she felt were not reaching the public, she turned to activism.

Drawing upon years of science writing and editing, and on her accumulated knowledge of nuclear power, Sinclair began raising issues that she felt the citizens of Midland needed to know. The community's hostile reaction stunned her. Her children received pressure from peers at school, her husband's law practice began losing clients, and she became the target of harassment, including anonymous phone calls and letters. Her stance against the plant cost her the chance of any employment in Midland, she says. Yet she persisted with her campaign, writing letters to the editor of the Midland *Daily News*, forming the Saginaw Valley Nuclear Study Group, and attempting to persuade government officials and the Michigan Public Service Commission, which regulates utilities in Michigan, that her concerns were valid.

Sinclair fought against (and lost) the construction licensing of the plant, which Consumers Power originally projected to take seven years to complete and cost $350 million. As she lost battles in the courts and in her home town, Sinclair grew more determined to fight the plant. As it was being built, she uncovered evidence of construction problems, safety concerns, and design deficiencies. At the operating licensing hearings for the plant, she presented a list of eighteen reasons why the plant should not be permitted to operate. Her battle slowly gained strength, not only because of increasing concern in surrounding communities, but also because of serious doubts that one of the plant's key supporters was beginning to have. The Dow Chemical Company, which had contracted with Consumers Power to buy power from one of the two nuclear reactor units that were being built, began eyeing construction delays and cost overruns, and reevaluating its contract with Consumers.

Public opinion in Midland slowly began to change, and the *Daily News* praised Sinclair for standing up to ostracism and criticism with courage. The community was beginning to realize that Sinclair's objections might have merit, and she was given credit for prompting public discussion. The Nuclear Regulatory Commission announced it was fining Consumers Power $120,000 for plant construction violations. And when Consumers announced new cost estimates for the plant of more than $4 billion and a completion date in 1985, the utility's biggest customer decided to end its contract. Dow Chemical filed a lawsuit against Consumers to be freed of its contractual liabilities to buy power from the plant, and more than a year later, in July of 1984, Consumers Power abandoned the Midland plant because it was unable to obtain financing. It was scrapped amid intense public criticism, eighty-five percent completed, and at a cost to Consumers Power of $4.9 billion over 13 years.

The plant's towers stand silent over Midland, and Consumers Power is hoping to find a buyer for its costly project. Sinclair says she never expected the plant to be shut down and feels she has scored a victory of sorts over a technology she no longer supports. Her battle at Midland gained her national attention and has placed her on celebrity rolls. She has been interviewed by print media including the *Wall Street Journal*, *Ms.* magazine, and several Michigan newspapers. Sinclair also was the subject of a segment on the CBS news magazine "60 Minutes." She is modest about her achievements and about being cast into the spotlight; she laughs when asked if she feels like a celebrity. "I guess I'm a celebrity," she told *CN*. "But I don't feel like it."

Continuing to speak out against nuclear power, Sinclair is kept busy with speaking engagements and lectures. She says she would like to sit down some day and write a book but currently does not have the time. She has researched and written letters on alternative energy options but does not plan to abandon her stance on nuclear power and her campaign to change the "old-fashioned thinking" that she says still surrounds nuclear technology. "As long as there's somebody listening, something will happen," Sinclair says.

CN INTERVIEW

CN interviewed Mary Sinclair by telephone at her home in Midland, Mich., in June, 1985.

CN: You worked for the Library of Congress in Washington D. C., in the fifties. Was that when you first started becoming acquainted with atomic energy and with nuclear power plants?

SINCLAIR: I first got some knowledge of the technology, and of course I could tell there were certain problems but nothing too extraordinary. And we were getting reports from other industrial laboratories that had government funding, and university laboratories, and they were discussing problems. So I did learn something about the technology, and I figured they would be *solving* those problems.

CN: So you were supportive of that technology at that time, then?

SINCLAIR: Oh, yes. When I first raised questions, it wasn't with the idea of stopping it, just to make it as safe as possible.

CN: When did your ideas about nuclear technology begin to change?

SINCLAIR: Well, in the mid-sixties, I went back to free-lance writing for the Dow Chemical Company, and I started getting back into studying technical literature—kind of getting caught up. I had always retained a real interest in nuclear power, and at that point I began to read in the technical literature about some of the problems that hadn't been solved. And they were pretty serious. Also, they had identified problems that they certainly didn't know about in the early stages of the development of nuclear power, and there was no answer for those. I thought these were pretty serious issues and that they had better be raised early to make the technology safer.

Among the issues that I was looking at was that the Advisory Committee on Reactor Safeguard, which was the most prestigious group of scientists and engineers in the country that advised the Atomic Energy Commission, were writing to the chairman of the Commission telling him that there was an urgent need for more safety research in the large-sized plants that were then planned for construction—such as the Midland plant—and they spelled out the areas in which more work had to be done. And, furthermore, they were saying in this correspondence, which I had read in the *Congressional Quarterly*, that they had been seeing this for about three years, but nothing came of it. And they were concerned about it. So I thought that certainly if we started some discussion on this in the community it would require our elected representatives to prod the Atomic Energy Commission into *doing* something.

Also, I became aware of the fact that there was serious internal struggle within the Atomic Energy Commission about the adequacy of ratings and standards; and of course there was no solution to the nuclear waste problem. But none of these issues were being presented to the public at all. The promotional literature was saying that nuclear power was safe and economical. On top of that, Dow Chemical was buying the propaganda that the electricity from these plants would be cheaper, and so it was going to hook up the Dow-Midland Division to the nuclear plants. Of course this troubled me a lot, because I could see that the issues that I was looking at—that I thought ought to be handled some way—were coming from very good scientists whom I recognized and respected.

CN: In 1967, when Consumers Power announced the plans for the Midland Plant, what was your initial reaction?

SINCLAIR: I thought that it was a good move. That's before I began to find out the problems. I was quite enthusiastic about it. It was only later that I began to discover what was going on. My initial reaction was very positive.

CN: How was the plant promoted in the community around Midland?

SINCLAIR: They had huge ads in the paper, huge ads on TV, and on the radio; and of course, nationwide, there was a big advertising campaign for the nuclear plants that they were going to build all over the country. They were advertising very heavily throughout that period.

CN: Did you see things in the ads that differed from your knowledge of what would happen with the plants?

SINCLAIR: Well, at first I didn't. I just noticed that the ads were very positive and minimized any problems whatsoever with nuclear plants. There were ads like "Mom's apple pie is radioactive and so is mom. That doesn't make her a dangerous woman." And they were all over, like in the *Reader's Digest* and *Life* magazine. But after I began to learn something about the issues, then I realized how misleading—terribly misleading—the ads were. And yet that was about all the public was hearing in the mass media. The *problems* were only carried in the technical literature that nobody ever sees. So that's why I wanted to raise these issues, and I thought Midland might be the right community in which to raise them, because it is a highly technical community and people would recognize the scientists and the credibility of the sources that were saying these things. I thought that in doing that we could start to correct some of these problems in a pretty orderly way, just by having the community sort of gear into saying they want these problems solved.

CN: Did you anticipate that you would have any trouble convincing the community of the problems or getting the community to work with you?

SINCLAIR: I didn't anticipate—begin to anticipate—the kind of reaction I got. I just wandered into it to tell you the truth. I had no idea that there would be that much hostility or that Midland was so totally a company town. I suppose it isn't too much different from any other company town. Except I never realized just how much that was the mentality here, and I didn't realize just how intense it was. But that's what happened.

And of course after that started I was quite shaken up, but I decided that I knew what I was reading. I had done very difficult technical writing before, and it had always been accepted. And I had worked as an editor on a chemical magazine that was published nationally. By that time I had about ten or twelve years of science writing and editing experience. I knew what I was reading. I knew its significance, and I couldn't back away from it. I also thought my freedom of speech was very important to me, especially on this subject. I intended to discuss issues that could affect my family and my home. These plants were within *one mile* of my husband's office on Main Street and within about two miles of my home. All our lives—and our family's health and well-being—were all tied up right here. So certainly I was going to look into anything I thought could threaten that.

CN: How did you start your campaign or protest against the plants?

SINCLAIR: Well, as I say, the first thing I did was decide to write a letter to the editor of the local newspaper with the ideal that we might be able to get some community discussion going. But the hostile reaction was extraordinary.

I put the letters in the Saginaw/Bay City paper, too, and I had some responses from those places. People said that they were concerned and asked if I would send more information. Some of them sent me a little money—$5 or $10—for the information. As far as Midland was concerned, I tried putting a couple more letters into the paper, and then I also decided to get some more information, thinking, "Maybe there is something I'm missing here."

And it just so happened there was a seminar offered by the State University of New York, outside of Albany on—well, it was on environmental problems, but nuclear pollution was one of the things to be discussed. I think it was one of the earliest environmental seminars. I told my husband, "I've just got to go to that seminar because I'll have a chance to talk to people on the Atomic Energy Commission as well as people from some very good Eastern universities who were on the program. And I'll have a chance to see if there are some facts that I'm missing here." So I went, and I found out I was right. The people from the Atomic Energy Commission said they really didn't know, for example, what the long-term effects would be of low-level radiation that was routinely put into the air and water from the nuclear plants. But they did know that radiation caused cancer, was life-shortening, and, most important of all, caused genetic damage.

The engineers I met there said that they were concerned about what they called "scaling" from very small nuclear power plants—the small nuclear power plants that had been built up to that time—and jumping very quickly to very large-sized plants. What the engineers were saying was that when you scale up quickly like that you can't expect the computer codes designed for the smaller plants to give you accurate information over such a wide span or such an increase in size. You are just not going to get accurate information. I also got some very good papers from that seminar with good bibliographies, so it expanded my base of information, and I felt on very solid ground then for anything I wanted to say. When I got back I decided to start campaigning again, and that's how I got going.

CN: When you said that you had a hostile reaction in the community, what kind of things happened, was it just yourself or was your family affected as well?

SINCLAIR: My children were subjected to peer pressure. Because the other children's parents were upset with what I was saying, my children would be hassled at school. The truth is, I worried a lot about them. They told me later that when they were in high school they had made a pact among themselves not to worry me and tell me what was happening to them, because they knew I was so worried about so many things as it was.

CN: Were you ever able to find any support within the community?

SINCLAIR: Oh, yes. At first I had some people from the surrounding area take an interest. And then, for my first education effort, I sent out about twenty packets of papers I had collected on various issues to about twenty scientists that I knew. In my cover letter I said, "Don't you think you should discuss this now, before the plants are built?" I only got replies from about three of them—two of them were anonymous—and they said, "Well, we know you're right, but we're afraid it might cost us our jobs."

CN: *Were you working at the time?*

SINCLAIR: I had been free-lance writing for Dow Chemical. After I raised the issue in a very polite way in a letter to the editor I never got another job. It was like I was unemployable. So one of these scientists gave a packet of my information to Dorothy Dow who is the oldest daughter of Herbert Dow, and she came to my door one day and said I had done a good job and that she was very concerned about pollution, too, especially if she was going to be linked with the Midland Division of Dow Chemical, which her father founded. She said that she would pay the copying and mailing costs if I would write a letter to the board of directors and send them the information. She wanted the letter sent to both the board of directors of Dow and the board of directors of Consumers Power Company. I did that, and I got three letters from the board of directors of Dow and nothing at all from Consumers Power.

Since we couldn't get the issues addressed by the board of directors, the only other channel that was left was to enter the licensing hearing and put these questions in a petition. The licensing board is then required to deal with it. I started quite a campaign, and gradually there were citizens—Sierra Club members especially—who took an active interest. We put on a public forum and invited someone from Consumers. They flew in somebody. It was quite well attended. And after that we said that anyone who was interested could join us in what we called the Saginaw Valley Nuclear Safety Group.

CN: *You also took your campaign to the Michigan Public Service Commission, the governor, Congressional Representatives.*

SINCLAIR: Yes, I kept writing, and they finally told me that they were going to have a hearing and that I would be given fifteen minutes to discuss my views on nuclear power, and they wanted my paper two weeks in advance. At first I said to my husband, "I don't think I'm going to drive ninety miles to Lansing to discuss nuclear power for fifteen minutes. But he just looked at me and said: "You know, if they give you five minutes, go, because that's the process; that's all you've got. And just hope that there is at least one person in that hearing room that is listening and thinks that what you have got to say has some merit." I had never looked at it like that before. I wrote my paper and turned it in, and I found that you can get quite a bit in fifteen minutes if you put your mind to it. So I went to that hearing, and I talked to people there from other environmental groups. There were about twenty-five men in the room, and all of them worked for the utilities or the nuclear industry. They gave me fifteen minutes, and they had seen my paper, but I had not seen anything from them. What they had done was flown in experts from the East coast and the West coast. They had charts, and they had diagrams, and everything else. And they were given an hour to an hour and a half to expound their views. I could tell it was a rigged hearing. I was to be given a chance to speak, and they were to countermand with overwhelming amounts of information that was supposed to blow me out of the water. Towards the end I said, "I think that I should be given equal time." It

was sort of outrageous. Some of the men started looking a little sheepish; they knew what was going on.

CN: *It must've been very discouraging for you.*

SINCLAIR: Well, it was, because it was my first encounter with a hearing. But there were some people listening there, and this was my lesson in how the hearing process really operates. The things that you might suspect could happen, often don't, but other things do. There were two professors from the University of Michigan Nuclear Engineering Department at that meeting, and they were apparently impressed with what I said and the nature of my documentation. About a month later one of them called me and said that the University was going to put on the first Earth Day, and every department had to come up with a speaker or have some kind of a demonstration of how their particular discipline was affected by the environment. They asked me if I would present my environmental concerns. Well, that made me pretty nervous, I'll tell you, because that was going to be the toughest audience I had ever had. But I thought about it, and then I decided to go ahead and give it the best I could. So I presented it, and I had tough questions, but I felt very good about it. I felt we had a good exchange and that I had been able to hold my ground pretty well. I felt confident that I had presented them with information they might not have gotten from any other source.

Some time later I heard that one student, Richard Sandler, who had listened to me, had dropped out of his junior year in the Nuclear Engineering Department, because he decided he did not want to make a career out of a field that had so many life-threatening aspects to it. He went to Washington and became the first legislative aide on nuclear power issues. He worked for Phillip Hart, a senator from Michigan. By that time Senator Hart was getting questions on nuclear power. And so Rich Sandler handled those letters.

And some time after that I found in an obscure document the fact that all six safety tests on emergency cocoon test systems had failed. This is a very important emergency system, the ultimate backup system that the Atomic Energy Commission was depending on to prevent a meltdown, and it was their justification for putting large-sized plants near population centers. Well I knew it was very significant to the public to know that the tests had failed, but there had been nothing written about it. So I took this document along with other information I had got from a hearing that had been held on this, and I sent it to Richard Sandler. And I told him to give this information to a really good energy reporter in Washington, preferably on the *Washington Post*. He gave it to Thomas O'Toole, who is a very good energy writer on the *Post*, and O'Toole wrote an excellent story that was syndicated all over the country. After that this backup system problem appeared in every single licensing petition. The Atomic Energy Commission decided that they couldn't handle this issue in so many different places, and they decided to hold the National Safety Hearings in Washington. We were able to get sixty similar groups to join us and intervene in those hearings.

Once that National Safety Hearings started, then scientists from various laboratories on the Atomic Energy Commission, who felt that safety problems they knew about hadn't been addressed, realized that here was a national forum where these issues could be looked at. Of course, the newspapers really picked up on that, and in Washington, Congress began to be alerted to all of this. Then things began to happen. Congress passed a law that disbanded the Atomic Energy Commission because the Commission was both promoting and regulating. They established the Nuclear Regulatory Commission just to regulate nuclear power and not promote it, because Congress figured that was one of the reasons why the safety problems had not been solved. After that we got into the structure licensing hearings for Midland. One of the things that was so apparent was the quality-control breakdown they were experiencing even before the licensing started. Consumers Power had already spent $54 million on the Midland site before they even announced the public licensing hearing, and that in itself can prejudice the licensing board. When a licensing board knows that much money has been spent, they are all the more leery of finding anything wrong.

But the quality-control problems the Midland plant already had were the same kinds of things that were found previously at the Palisades plant [also in Michigan]. The Palisades plant had experienced so many quality-control problems that it hardly operated the first couple of years, and Consumers sued Bechtel, who was their builder there, and quite a few other contractors, for something like $350 million. What is strange—and I never will understand it—is how Consumers, who had this bad experience with quality-control problems with Bechtel at Palisades, turned right around and hired the same outfit to build Midland. By 1977 and '78 they discovered the full extent of the quality-control problems as far as soil compaction was concerned. That's when buildings began sinking and cracking abnormally. By August of 1978, they made their first report on the sinking and cracking of the last generator building. They reported that although the building was only twenty percent constructed, it had already sunk as much as it was expected to in forty years, and it was cracking.

Of course the NRC took great interest in that. And after a while, it became apparent that a number of other buildings were sinking and cracking. In fact, I think by November of 1978 the NRC had identified five safety-related buildings that were all affected by these problems. By December of 1979 the NRC issued an order which halted construction at the Midland plant pending their review of remedial measures to correct this soil problem. Consumers asked for a hearing on this. By asking for a hearing they were able to continue construction at Midland. And, of course, the Three Mile Island accident happened in March of 1979, and this impacted on all nuclear plants. Since the Midland plants were sister-plants to Three Mile Island, it became apparent that they had the same design deficiency.

Things were getting very intense. By this time the cost over-run and the delays were mounting terribly, but Consumers still kept insisting they were going to beat a deadline. The first time that they publicly admitted they couldn't was in April of 1983 at their annual meeting. By July of '83 Dow had cancelled their stream contract with Consumers and wanted out. Very shortly after that, Dow filed a lawsuit saying that Consumers had not disclosed to them the extent of the problems they had out there when they signed their contract. And that trial is still under way.

CN: And in July, 1984, the plant shut down.

SINCLAIR: Yes, that's right.

CN: Did you ever have any doubts throughout this fairly long process? Did you ever have any doubts about your stand? You expressed concern at one point that perhaps you had overlooked some pertinent information.

SINCLAIR: Well, that was very early, when I got this violent reaction locally. I began to say, well, I really want to be sure of my facts and study a little bit more to see if there is something I am missing; although I wouldn't have spoken out to begin with unless I had been pretty sure of my information. As a science writer and researcher, I had been trained to be very careful about these things. But I was willing to make another effort to be informed. For several years I just hoped we would be building a safer plant. But as I saw the quality control break down, not only here but elsewhere in the country, and the extent of the safety problems and how they were being dealt with or not dealt with—and also the covering-up in the industry was unbelievable—I decided nuclear power was not the way to go. I think by about the mid-1970s, I had decided it just was not right. Look at the large plants that are having serious problems and breakdowns all the time. I think that reflects the fact that nuclear power just hasn't been handled right in this country.

CN: A few hours away from Midland, the Detroit Edison Company has completed its Fermi II nuclear power plant, and that's having preliminary fuel-loading and is in the very early stages of startup. Have you had any interaction with that plant at all?

SINCLAIR: Yes, I have. I've joined the group down there in two press conferences now to try to bring issues about the Fermi plant to the public. Some of the people down there have done a pretty good job of researching the safety issues, but I was more interested in the economic issues, and these have not been publicized like they should have been. For instance, Detroit Edison today is selling more power out of the state from the excess capacity it has right now than it can expect from its share of Fermi II when the Fermi II plant goes on-line and it operates with any degree of reliability. They have so much excess capacity now that they are selling that excess capacity for about half of what they are charging their own customers.

One of their plants, the Greenwood plant, is only fully operational one percent of the time because it is oil fired and is one of the most expensive to operate. It costs six cents per kilowatt hour to operate the Greenwood plant. But when the Fermi II plant comes on line it is going to cost twenty-two cents per kilowatt hour. Twenty-two cents! And yet they are forging ahead and insisting on getting this plant on line. They don't need the power.

There have been whistle-blowers from that plant who have told about breakdowns in the computer system at Fermi II. There has been a revolution in computer technology since the Fermi plant was started in 1970, and as they have tried to update their computer design in the construction of that plant, some of the coding was not properly recorded or whatever from one system to another. These whistle-blowers claim that there is an extended period of time when you don't get the information you need from very important systems.

I think there is a separate story on the poor economics of the Fermi plant and how it's going to affect industry and business. The costs they are talking about so far don't even include the cost of waste disposal or decommissioning, which can be at least half of the construction cost of the plant. Then there's the huge volume of low-level waste these plants will generate. They don't have an answer for storing or disposing of it. I'm convinced enough that Fermi II is such an economic error that I am going to be doing what I can. It's very hard for me to do this, of course. I don't have documents all the time. I think the media should be digging into this more.

CN: What are your plans now for the future? What are you doing now?

SINCLAIR: I have been asked to give a lot of talks lately. I am going to speak in Philadelphia and in the state of Washington soon. And I've been urged to write a book. But I'd have to stop speaking in order to do the writing; they're not compatible, I find.

CN: You've been on "60 Minutes," and you've been interviewed by many major newspapers and magazines. Has that been a surprise? Has it been difficult to deal with?

SINCLAIR: It's a total surprise to me. I'm just overwhelmed. I just never expected anything like this to happen. Nor did I ever expect the Midland plant would actually shut down, to tell you the truth. I just hoped that by publicizing this they would start to do a better job. But, yes, it has been a total surprise. It was a total surprise to my family too.

CN: Do you feel like a celebrity?

SINCLAIR: I don't feel it, but people act like I am. I just feel like I'm still in the trenches, putting one foot in front of the other and trying to make something happen.

SOURCES:

PERIODICALS

Audubon, July, 1983.
Crain's Detroit Business, May 13, 1985.
Detroit Free Press, April 14, 1985.
Los Angeles Times, June 17, 1983.
Midland Daily News, December 8, 1983, July 17, 1984, May 20, 1985.
Ms., January, 1985.
Wall Street Journal, July 18, 1984.

—*Sidelights and interview by Amy C. Bodwin*

Frederick W. Smith

1944-

PERSONAL: Full name, Frederick Wallace Smith; born August 11, 1944, in Marks, Miss.; son of Frederick C. (a businessman) and Sally (Wallace) Smith; married Linda Black Grisham, 1969 (divorced, 1977); married Dianne Davis; children: eight. *Education:* Yale University, degree in economics and political science, 1966.

ADDRESSES: Home—Memphis, Tenn. *Office*—Federal Express Corp., P.O. Box 727, Memphis, Tenn. 38194.

OCCUPATION: Corporate executive; entrepreneur.

CAREER: Ardent Record Co., Memphis, Tenn., co-founder and operator, 1960-62; held controlling interest in Arkansas Aviation Sales, Little Rock, 1969-71; Federal Express Corp., Memphis, founder, president, chief executive officer, and chairman of board of directors, 1972—. Certified commercial pilot. *Military service:* U.S. Marine Corps, 1966-69; served two tours of duty in Vietnam, one in the Infantry and one as a pilot; became captain; received Silver Star, Bronze Star, and two Purple Hearts.

SIDELIGHTS: An undergraduate economics term paper that earned a C grade at Yale University in 1965 was eventually worth $2 billion to the Federal Express Corporation and its founder, Frederick W. Smith. In the paper Smith first proposed the idea of transporting small packages to cities throughout the United States with the promise of overnight delivery. And even though Smith's economics professor failed to be convinced that such a venture could be a success, in 1983 Federal Express became the first corporation in history to reach the $1 billion plateau within its first decade of operation. Employing innate entrepreneurial savvy, large influxes of venture capital, and a military-like strategy, Smith created a whole new industry—and set a standard for quality and service in that industry.

The idea behind Federal Express is a relatively simple one—that there is a market in American business for overnight door-to-door delivery of small, time-sensitive high-priority documents and packages. This delivery system, Smith reasoned, would work best if it was not dependent on commercial passenger airline scheduling, which does not conform to the time when most packages need to be transported: late at night when the airlanes are least active. Smith's operational innovation is based on a hub-and-spokes configuration in which all the packages are flown to one place—the Memphis International Airport with its ideal weather conditions and central location—sorted, and then rerouted to their intended destinations for next-day, morning delivery. Six nights a week at Federal Express's Super-Hub, as it is called, 2,700 well-paid part-time employees, many of them college students, working between the hours of 11 p.m and 3 a.m., organize close to one-half million pieces of freight, assisted by twenty-six miles of conveyor belts with electronic scanners, to be shipped on the compa-

AP/Wide World Photos

ny's own fleet of aircraft. *U.S. News & World Report* writer Cindy Skrzycki described the system this way: "A ZIP code is punched into a computer that produces a two-digit sticker. This triggers an electric eye that tells a mechanical arm when to punch the package down the next slide to a secondary sorting area. Someone types the code into a computer keyboard that sets off yet another electric eye to divert the package to the correct city container."

Smith's simple idea proved to be a complicated one to execute, because it entailed a large capital investment, a sophisticated operations procedure, political acumen, and advertising daring. Smith's emphasis on the importance of speed in moving packages—especially small replaceable parts and other products of the high technology economy as well as informational documents—was not fully understood when the company first started doing business. Smith saw something about the emerging American economy that others had not even thought about. "Steamboats and trains were the logistics arm of the Industrial Revolution's first stage," he told *Nation's Business*. "Trucks became a good logistics arm later—and still are because of their flexibility. But moving the parts and pieces to support the Electronics Age requires very fast transportation over long distances. I became convinced that a different type of system was going to be a major part of the national economy." The old industrial base of steel and automotive production was being replaced by a new one dominated by service industries and high-technology products in which a rapid transportation system would be imperative. Restricting Federal Express to a seventy-pound package limit (now 150 pounds), defined a clear market position for Smith, while changing economic and psychological factors contributed to the success of his idea. The public's perception of the unreliability of the U.S. Postal Service, and the fact that the decision on how a package is to be shipped is usually made by a secretary or middle manager, provided the psychological climate for success; and these factors were effectively exploited by Federal Express's ad campaign.

The innovative hub-and-spokes method gave Federal Express a strategic advantage over the conventional means of tying freight delivery to commercial passenger airline schedules. By separating small freight delivery from passenger systems, and by integrating air transport with ground transport via small trucks, Smith accomplished in one company what had never been done before. He realized the obvious: that packages, unlike people, do not have to be transported in a lineal pattern. Federal Express could service more cities with fewer airplanes and could guarantee service between smaller, usually poorly serviced areas—cities like Des Moines, Iowa, and Lubbock, Texas, and states like Nevada—as well as the major metropolitan markets. Smith realized there was little competition in the smaller markets, and this foresight greatly contributed to the success of his venture.

Frederick Wallace Smith was born in Marks, Mississippi, on August 11, 1944, while his parents, Frederick Smith and his fourth wife, Sally Wallace Smith, then 23, were inspecting one of their farm properties in northern Mississippi. Smith's father, a business success in his own right, founded the Dixie Greyhound Bus Lines and invested in the Toddle House, a quick-service restaurant chain, in 1934 during the heart of the Great Depression. The elder Smith turned the Toddle House into a national chain that he and his brother sold for a reported $22 million in stock in 1961. The bus company, when it was sold to the Greyhound Bus Lines, was one of the largest in the South. Robert A. Sigafoos, author of *Absolutely Positively Overnight!*, the biography of Frederick Smith, described the father as a man who enjoyed his hard won success, having made a fortune during the most difficult economic period in American history. "Smith became an active sportsman," wrote Sigafoos, "buying surplus U.S. naval vessels and renovating them into pleasure boats. He was an outgoing, flamboyant individual; he was a southern son of Horatio Alger. Failure in life was impossible for him; it simply was not one of the options he allowed himself."

Raised in Memphis, Tennessee, by his mother, who encouraged him not to be held back by a birth defect called Calve-Perthes (a bone socket hip disorder), Smith wore braces and used crutches as a child. Eventually, as he matured, he outgrew the disease and participated in a variety of sports and school activities. As a boy, he studied the battles of the Civil War and re-enacted them with his toy soldier collection. Smith attended a private preparatory school, Memphis University School, where he excelled in the classroom academically and as a leader. He loved sports—especially

basketball and football—and was voted "Best All-Around Student" his senior year. As a sophomore, in 1959, Smith learned to fly. His entrepreneurial spirit also manifested itself at this time when he and some classmates formed a business called the Ardent Record Company, a garage-studio operation that recorded local rock and roll bands. Although Smith ended his involvement with the company in 1962 when he entered Yale, Ardent Records is still in business today.

Smith majored in economics and political science at Yale, and by his senior year he had established enough of a campus identity to be elected into the Skull and Bones, a secret senior honor society. He helped revitalize the Yale Flying Club, first started after World War I by Juan Trippe, founder of Pan American World Airways. The infamous C grade on the economics paper outlining Smith's idea for Federal Express has made good headline copy, showing the bad judgment of Ivy League professors, but has probably garnered more attention than it deserves. By his own admission, Smith was not a good student. He told Altman: "to a ne'er-do-well student like myself, the grade was acceptable." And to Robert J. Flaherty in *Forbes* he stated, "I was a crummy student—like Winston Churchill."

After graduating from Yale in 1966 Smith was commissioned a second lieutenant in the U.S. Marine Corps Infantry and soon found himself in Vietnam. He started out as a platoon leader and ended up a company commander, having been involved in twenty-seven named operations during his first tour of duty. For his second tour, Smith enrolled in flight school, thinking the war was about to end and hoping he could serve in Hawaii or Japan. Instead, he ended up flying more than 200 ground-support missions in Quang Tri Province. He left the Marine Corps on July 21, 1969, with the rank of captain and with the Silver Star, Bronze Star, and two Purple Hearts among his medals. Smith credits his platoon sergeant, Jack Jackson, who lost his life in Vietnam, as a man who influenced him significantly on how to manage people. "Sgt. Jack was probably the wisest man I have ever met," Smith told Altman. "He had wisdom about what people who aren't officers think and want." The realities of war gave Smith the toughness to deal with business failure. It also motivated him to start a new business and fulfill his father's wish. "I got so sick of destruction and blowing things up—on people I had nothing against—that I came back determined to do something constructive," he told Flaherty.

Smith returned to civilian life and, in August 1969, bought controlling interest in Arkansas Aviation Sales, which was run by his stepfather. Smith turned the turbo-prop and corporate jet maintenance service into one that bought and sold used corporate jets. But the business left him unsatisfied, even though he was in a position to do well since he had the personal capital to put him at a competitive advantage.

Frederick Smith's life up to this point, at age twenty-seven, "was just a warmup for the brazenly bold adventure that [he] was about to pull off in the business world," wrote Flaherty. Smith incorporated the Federal Express Corporation in Delaware on June 18, 1971, with the name Federal chosen because his initial idea was to secure a contract with the Federal Reserve System for his company to transport, sort, and reroute checks for next day delivery; such a check clearing system, Smith estimated, would save the Federal Reserve System $3 million a day. But the contract fell through, because the individual district banks in the system could not reach an agreement on Smith's proposal.

The early history of Federal Express is the story of how Smith accomplished the impossible by pulling together complicated financial backing that almost broke down on a number of occasions. When Federal Express opened for business on a daily basis on April 17, 1973, with service to twenty-five cities, the first night's shipment included only 186 packages—an obvious disappointment to a company that now averages 477,409 pieces per night. In its first twenty-six months of business, Federal Express lost $29.3 million and owed its lenders $49 million. The 1973 Arab oil embargo also added to the young company's problems by contributing to increased fuel prices. It was not until July, 1975, that Federal Express had a profitable month, netting $55,000 and reaching a net income of $3.6 million for the 1975-76 fiscal year on revenues of $75 million.

While most start-up costs for new ventures are around $2 million to $3 million, Federal Express raised $91 million—about $40 million in equity capital and $50 million in loans, led by Chase Manhattan and First National of Chicago—and still came close to bankruptcy because of fiscal and management difficulties. The sources of support included New Court Securities (a Rothschild-backed company), General Dynamics, Heizer, Allstate Insurance, Prudential Insurance, and Citicorp Venture Capital Ltd. "To anyone who understands the venture-capital game, this is roughly equivalent to learning how to breathe under water," wrote Flaherty. At one point, on July 19, 1973, after a disappointing meeting with the General Dynamics board, Smith, waiting for a plane from Chicago to Memphis, decided on impulse to fly to Las Vegas where he parlayed a few hundred dollars into $27,000 playing blackjack; he sent back his winnings to company headquarters to make payroll. Such stories have contributed to Smith's larger-than-life reputation.

At the financial center of Federal Express was Smith's own personal wealth and that of his sisters. His father did not want Smith to waste the millions he would inherit, and before he died at the age of fifty-three in 1948, he wrote his son a letter to be opened on his twenty-first birthday requesting that the younger Smith put his funds to work. A family trust called Frederick Smith Enterprise Company, Inc., managed by the National Bank of Commerce in Memphis, was set up to be shared by Smith and his half sisters, Fredette and Laura. Smith's share was 38.5 percent.

The Enterprise Company and its principle assets of 164,800 shares of Squibb-Beechnut preferred convertible stock—valued at $13.3 million in 1971—proved to play a crucial role in the early stages of Federal Express. Smith, as the company's board president, was able to convince his half sisters to use their funds as seed capital in the new air transportation venture. The total investment ended up at $6.25 million for the Enterprise Company and $2.5 million of Smith's personal funds; Smith, as president and without prior board knowledge, signed a loan agreement for $2 million on behalf of the Enterprise Company with the Union Bank of Little Rock in February, 1973. Smith was indicted by a federal grand jury in Little Rock on January 31, 1975,

for forging loan documents on behalf of the Enterprise Company.

Smith took the position that as president he had the authority to commit the board and could secure board ratification if he needed it. "I felt at the time that I was the Enterprise Company. It's as simple as that. And I felt that both of the sisters felt the same way," he testified. Smith was acquitted on December 11, 1975. Previously, Smith's sisters had brought civil action against him and other parties for investing $6.25 million in Federal Express, requesting that the Enterprise Company be restored to a pre-Federal Express level of $17 million. In December, 1978, they reached an out-of-court settlement in which Smith agreed to buy out his sisters' stock in Enterprise Company and guarantee any loss.

In 1975 Federal Express found itself boxed in after it had outgrown its fleet of Dassault Falcon 20s and applied to the Civil Aeronautics Board for permission to use five Douglas DC-9s on larger routes, exempting them from the 7500-pound limit. The CAB answered the request on December 8, 1975, stating that the Federal Aviation Act of 1938 did not have broad enough authority to grant the request and that Federal Express needed legislative action. Smith assumed the leadership of the lobbying effort, effectively testifying before Congress during an eighteen-month campaign, charging that air cargo needs had been ignored by an outdated regulatory system. The resulting legislation was labelled the "Federal Express Bill" and was defeated by a counter effort lead by the Teamsters, the Air Transport Association, and Robert Prescott, founder and chairman of the Flying Tigers. But conditions changed with the Carter administration, which favored deregulation; on November 9, 1977, President Carter signed into law PL 95-163, which deregulated the cargo industry, making it the first industry decontrolled by Congress. Federal Express started purchasing Boeing 727s with a lift capacity of 42,000 pounds, and its future as a growth company was assured. Federal Express became a publicly-held company on April 12, 1978, and had a two-for-one stock split in September. It was listed on the New York Stock Exchange on December 28, 1978.

Federal Express's success is tied in part to its high visibility, created by humorous advertising campaigns; the slogan "absolutely, positively overnight" has become an easily recognizable phrase to most American television viewers. Federal Express introduced humor in its national advertising in 1977, with an ad conceived by Carl Ally and Amil Gargano, best known for their Volvo and Hertz campaigns. With fast-talking John Moschitta speaking nonstop nonsense in a one-minute commercial, Federal Express caught the imagination of the American public. Moschitta's "Dick-what's-the-deal-with-the-deal. Are-we-dealing? We're-dealing. Dave-its-a-deal-with-Don, Dave-and-Dick. Dick-its-a-Dork-with-Don-Deal-and-Dave. . . . " jarred the public into paying attention to Federal Express. Ally and Gargano's research showed that what people feared most was the possibility of a package not arriving on time; and the ad men exploited that fear. Another one of their commercials had a light-bulb shipper speaking into the phone: "I'm telling you, if I don't have that package on my desk here tomorrow, you understand, if I don't have that package on my desk by tomorrow, and Frank here will bear me out. . . . " These commercials, and others, told the Federal Express story with humor, which remains a primary technique in much of the company's advertising. The use of Federal Express has become such an accepted business practice that a 1984 *Newsweek* article called it "the middle-management equivalent of ordering up the corporate jet."

Rated one of the top ten companies in the United States in the 1985 edition of *The 100 Best Companies to Work for in America*, Federal Express is the quintessential contemporary company. The authors singled out Federal Express's personnel policies and wrote that management works at making Federal Express a "people company" with its Guaranteed Fair Treatment policy, a five-step grievance procedure involving top management. "Other policies include no layoffs; top wages; profit sharing; stock options to all managers; job posting; an open door to talk with managers at any time; paying up to $25,000 for productivity improvement suggestions; and offering unusual benefits such as the right to fly free on Federal Express planes and at reduced rates on other airlines." Federal Express obviously has worked hard at keeping its 31,000 nonunionized employees happy.

In its short history, Federal Express has evolved from a risk-taking adventuresome enterprise that experienced unprecedented growth after an initial period of heavy losses into a large, stable national company with a solid institutional identity. Smith, unlike Nolan Bushnell of Atari and Steven Jobs of Apple, has survived the various company transitions with his power and authority intact and with his focus on the future. Not ready to rest on past success, Federal Express introduced Zapmail, its electronic mail service in 1984, promising delivery of facsimile copies of documents anywhere in the United States within two hours. Although Zapmail lost over $100 million in its first year of operation, Smith feels confident that the investment in personnel, transmission machines, and a communications satellite will prove to be successful in the long run. Faith in such innovative ideas is one key element that has helped Frederick Smith guide Federal Express to the enviable position it now enjoys in the transportation and information field.

SOURCES:

BOOKS

Levering, Robert, Milton Moskowitz, and Michael Katz, *The 100 Best Companies to Work for in America*, New American Library, 1985.
Sigafoos, Robert A., *Absolutely Positively Overnight!*, St. Luke's Press, 1983.

PERIODICALS

Business Week, November 3, 1973, March 31, 1980, December 17, 1984.
Dun's Business Monthly, December, 1981.
Esquire, August 15, 1978.
Financial World, March 15, 1979, August 1, 1982.
Forbes, November 15, 1975, March 1, 1977, June 6, 1983, October 28, 1985, November 4, 1985.
Fortune, June 15, 1981.
Inc., June, 1984.
Management Today, July, 1983.
Nation's Business, November, 1981.
Newsweek, December 10, 1973, February 7, 1983, January 9, 1984.
New York, October 26, 1981.
New York Times, December 3, 1977, January 7, 1979.
Time, February 15, 1982, December 17, 1984.
U.S. News & World Report, December 24, 1979, October 6, 1980, December 20, 1982.
Washington Post, October 31, 1982.

—Sidelights by Jon Saari

Samantha Smith

1972-1985

OBITUARY NOTICE: Born June 29, 1972; died in an airplane crash, August 25, 1985, in Auburn, Me. American peace advocate and actress. In the fall of 1982, disturbed by network news reports and classroom discussions on the threat of nuclear war, Samantha Smith, then ten years old, wrote a letter to Soviet leader Yuri V. Andropov expressing her fears and asking him, "Why do you want to conquer the world, or at least our country?" In April of the following year the Soviet newspaper *Pravda* ran excerpts from Samantha's letter in an article calculated to convince the Soviet people of the worldwide respect for their leader. When Samantha learned of this use she wrote a second letter to Andropov, asking for a reply and an explanation.

The Soviet leader responded with a 500-word telegram in which he invited Samantha and her parents to visit the Soviet Union for two weeks as his guests. Samantha became an instant international celebrity, appearing on network news telecasts and talk shows, capturing the attention and the hearts of America. There were, however, those who feared Samantha was being used as a pawn in the ongoing propaganda war being waged by the two superpowers, but her trip to the Soviet Union failed to produce a meeting with Andropov, who was reportedly too burdened with matters of state to schedule a meeting with her. Instead, Samantha received a well-supervised, sanitized tour of the Soviet Union, with a special emphasis on Soviet schoolchildren.

The spotlight of public attention began to fade after Samantha's return from the Soviet Union; there were periodic news updates about the return to schoolgirl routine for "Andropov's pen pal," and gradually America turned its appetite for celebrity to new faces. But Samantha soon began to miss life in the public eye and, with the help of her father, who had assumed the role of manager for her, began to plan for a career in show business. During the 1984 election campaign she hosted a talk show on the cable television Disney Channel in which she interviewed many of the major candidates. In 1985 she was cast in a major role in the Robert Wagner television series "Lime Street," scheduled to air in the fall of that year.

While returning home to Maine on August 25, 1985, after completing filming for the first four episodes of the program in London, England, the airplane on which Samantha, her father, Arthur Smith, and six others were passengers crashed and exploded in a heavy rain in Auburn, Maine, killing all on board. After her death, a flower and a huge diamond were named after her in the Soviet Union. In addition, reported the *Detroit News*, she was the subject of a poem, published in *Pravda*, which stated, "The child has

AP/Wide World Photos

died, but she had time enough to shake the minds and souls of people."

SOURCES:

PERIODICALS

Chicago Tribune, August 27, 1985, August 30, 1985.
Christian Science Monitor, July 1, 1983, July 22, 1983, January 16, 1984.
Detroit News, October 8, 1985.
Newsweek, May 9, 1983.
New York Times, April 26, 1983, December 22, 1983, April 27, 1984, August 27, 1985.
People, May 16, 1983, January 2, 1984, June 3, 1985, September 9, 1985.
Time, March 11, 1985, September 9, 1985.
U.S. News and World Report, July 18, 1983.
Washington Post, August 27, 1985.

Peter W. Stroh

1927-

PERSONAL: Born December 18, 1927, in Detroit, Mich.; son of Gari Melchers (a brewery executive) Stroh; married 1963; wife's name, Nicole; children: two. *Education:* Princeton University, bachelor's degree, 1951; attended U.S. Brewer's Academy, 1953-54; also attended Wallerstein Brewing Seminar, 1955.

ADDRESSES: *Home*—Grosse Pointe Farms, Mich. *Office*—Stroh Brewery Co., 100 River Place, Detroit, Mich. 48207.

OCCUPATION: Brewery executive.

CAREER: While in school, worked summers in a boatyard and at family brewery; recruited by the Central Intelligence Agency (CIA), and worked in Washington, D.C., 1951-52, while awaiting security clearance, but a traffic accident prevented him from pursuing a career in intelligence; Stroh Brewery Co., Detroit, Mich., 1952—, member of board of directors, beginning 1965, vice-president 1965-68, director of operations, 1966-68, president, 1968-82, chief executive officer, 1980-82, chairman of board, 1982—. Member of board of directors, NBD Bancorp, Inc.; trustee, Detroit Medical Center Corp., McGregor Fund, New Detroit, Inc., and Brooks School. *Military service:* U.S. Navy, aviation training program, 1945-46.

MEMBER: United States Brewers Association (chairman, 1973-77), Economic Alliance for Michigan, Concerned Citizens for the Arts in Michigan (chairman), Economic Club of Detroit, Detroit Renaissance, Atlantic Salmon Federation.

AWARDS, HONORS: Named Humanitarian of the Year by March of Dimes, 1981; Business Statesman Award, Harvard Business School Alumni Club of Detroit, 1984.

SIDELIGHTS: With the name he carries, Peter W. Stroh bears the legacy of a 135-year-old tradition of brewing beer in Detroit, Michigan. As head of the Stroh Brewery Co., he has spearheaded the takeovers that transformed a family-owned, regional brewer into the third largest beermaker in America.

The Stroh Brewery began in 1850 with a few gallons of beer concocted in a copper kettle by Bernhard Stroh, who left Kirn, Germany, two years earlier. "He reportedly had only $150, but he invested in brewing one barrel of beer and, according to family legend, he put it on a wheelbarrow and went down the street to sell to his first customers himself," Bernhard's great-grandson Peter told Frank Angelo of the *Detroit Free Press.* From that humble beginning the company grew steadily and had the capacity—until the closing of its Detroit plant on May 31, 1985—to brew some thirty-

three million barrels, each barrel holding thirty-one gallons of beer, in seven plants across America.

In its 135-year-history, the company has withstood the challenge of fourteen years of Prohibition as well as the failures that have befallen the more than 120 American brewers that have closed in the last twenty years. In 1918, Prohibition halted Stroh Brewery's production of 300,000 barrels a year, but the company survived by branching out into soft drinks and ice cream. Stroh's continued making ice cream even after the end of Prohibition and will continue to do so in its Detroit plant. With Prohibition's repeal in 1933, the company resumed its proud fire-brewing of the traditional Bohemian Style Beer, while Peter Stroh was five years old and growing up in the elegant, monied Detroit suburb of Grosse Pointe.

Today, Stroh is considered one of Detroit's most powerful and compassionate community leaders. But he is a very private man, and he gives interviews rarely, preferring to spend his free time playing polo or hunting ducks and grouse. "He is the corporate giant who isn't listed in *Who's*

Who—a quiet, modest man who eschews awards for civic and charitable work," a *Detroit Free Press* reporter wrote.

In his own words, Stroh was "pampered" as a young man, encouraged to participate in mannered sports such as sailing, golfing and riding. He told reporter Steve Konicki of the *Detroit News*, "I think my family felt the more of those things I enjoyed doing, the more I would have in common with other people."

He went to Grosse Pointe Schools for a time and then spent several years at St. Paul's, a prep school in Concord, N.H. But Stroh's young mind was dreaming of adventure. His desire to set sail on worldwide adventure was fueled by a summertime stint at age sixteen working for a Maine sailboat owner, Jimmy Ducey. Stroh told the *Detroit News* that Ducey was scarred by polio, which had left him about "five feet tall and 80 or 90 pounds of nothing but guts and determination." "Looking back on it," Stroh continued, "of all the people I've worked for in my life, he was probably the best at what he did. He got 400 percent out of himself, so he felt that he had reason to expect 300 percent out of you."

The year after he graduated from St. Paul's, Stroh served in an aviation training program in the post-World War II Navy. The following year he spent on a waiting list trying to get into Princeton; in the meantime, he learned typing and shorthand at a Detroit business school. But he continued to dream of faraway adventure. "I wanted to unload relief supplies in Yugoslavia. I wanted to work on a tramp steamer bound for Argentina. Train polo ponies in Texas. . . seriously," Stroh told the *Detroit News*. "But I couldn't get my parents' permission."

At Princeton in 1947, he enrolled in the School of Public and International Affairs, hoping for a career with the foreign service. But the family business beckoned. The summer of 1950 saw him on the payroll of the Stroh Brewery as a plumber's helper in the maintenance department. His family figured it would give him a ground-floor view of the business. His first day of work at the brewery was the day his father, Gari Melchers Stroh, fifty-eight, then president of the company, died of lung cancer.

Upon graduation in 1951, Stroh's dream of international adventure and intrigue seemed comfortably close at hand. He was recruited by the Central Intelligence Agency (CIA), and it was with thoughts of becoming a secret agent that he worked in Washington, D.C., for a year while waiting for his security clearance. "One of my first jobs was to make photocopies of Polish agricultural journals from the war years," Stroh told the *Detroit News*. "I was described by some of my friends as becoming one of the world's ranking rutabaga experts." But just three days after he passed final security clearance, Stroh's fantasies of foreign service disappeared in the path of a runaway truck as he was crossing a Washington, D.C., intersection. The truck crushed his legs, and he was in the hospital for a year. Doctors said it was unlikely that he would ever walk again.

It was his "wonderful and wise uncle," company president John Stroh, who talked Peter Stroh out of entering the Harvard Business School after his recovery, Stroh said in November, 1984, when he received the Business Statesman

Award from the school's alumni club in Detroit. Instead of returning to the Ivy League, Stroh attended the U.S. Brewers Academy in Mt. Vernon, N.Y. in 1953-54. "It wasn't until perhaps 1954 or 1955 that I really had my legs screwed on properly," he told Konicki. "By then I had become deeply involved in the business."

By 1953, Stroh Brewery sales hit one million barrels a year for the first time and then doubled two years later. But it remained strictly a Detroit and Michigan beer. Stroh's growth began modestly in 1964, when it acquired the 91-year-old Goebel Brewing Co., which was once Michigan's leading beer producer. But by the early 1960s, the firm had fallen heavily into debt and was purchased by Stroh's for less than $2 million. In the next two years, Peter Stroh rose quickly through the corporate ranks; he was elected to the board of directors in February, 1965, became vice-president in June, 1965, and director of operations in May, 1966. He had also married his French-born wife, Nicole, in 1963. By 1968, he was the company's president, stepping into the position previously held by his uncle, John.

Through the 1970s, the appeal of Stroh's beer grew steadily in the Midwest. "From one beer lover to another. . . Stroh's" was the theme of a successful ad campaign designed to compete with the multi-million dollar media blitz of industry giants Anheuser-Busch and Miller Beer. Between 1970 and 1980, Stroh's sales more than doubled. By the end of the decade, Stroh's was among the top ten brewers in the country, a regional brewery holding its own with reported earnings of $350 million in a shrinking industry.

Hoping to expand its market beyond Michigan and neighboring states, the Stroh Brewery Company in 1981 expanded to the East Coast by acquiring the F & M Schaefer Company, the nation's twelfth-largest brewery. The purchase added Schaefer's modern Allentown, Pennsylvannia, brewery to Stroh's only existing plant, in Detroit.

Stroh's had become the nation's seventh-largest brewery and largest family-owned one when—in a takeover likened to the "minnow swallowing the whale" by some industry analysts—it bought out Milwaukee's Jos. Schlitz Brewing Company in 1982. It was one month after Peter Stroh was named chairman of the Stroh board. To buy Schlitz in 1982, Stroh borrowed more than half of the $494.7 million pricetag. It raised $170 million of that by mortgaging its Detroit brewing facilities and borrowing the money at a staggering 17.3 percent interest rate. The takeover transformed Stroh's into the nation's third-biggest brewery. From one brewery and two brands in 1978, the company went to fifteen brands and seven breweries by late 1983.

When analysts were critical of the debt the Detroit-based brewery acquired with the Schlitz purchase, Peter Stroh responded, according to a *Free Press* article, "We did not get five of the leading banks in the U.S. to lend us money in the anticipation that within two years [Stroh's] would be an entity that would not survive." But the move was also hailed because it gave Stroh's entry into the growing markets in the South and West without having to build breweries. Schlitz's plants in Winston-Salem, North Carolina, Van Nuys, California, St. Paul, Minnesota, Memphis, Tennessee, and Longview, Texas, provided the entry.

Yet the brewery's growth also came at a time when America's consumption of beer was on the downswing. Three years later, when Peter Stroh announced on February 8, 1985 that the firm's seventy-one-year-old Detroit brewery would shut down, it was because the firm found itself with too much production capacity for an American public increasingly shunning beer. In its seven breweries, Stroh's could produce more than thirty million barrels of beer, while sales in 1984 averaged about twenty-four million. By closing the Detroit plant, this margin would be erased.

"Unfortunately, our Detroit plant is our oldest and least efficient," said Stroh, according to the *Detroit Free Press*, in announcing the decision that stunned a city whose community self-esteem had been pilloried by a string of corporate pullouts. "No capital investment, concessions or any combination of these can transform it into a sufficiently viable brewery for the long term in the current industry environment. . . . I want to emphasize strongly that our need to close the plant is not a Detroit problem, a union problem, a power problem, a workers compensation problem or a utilities problem. It's just a problem of a plant that is very very old, geographically constricted and no longer competitive with the modern facilities which so dominate our industry today."

Robert Weinberg, a St. Louis-based consultant to the brewing industry, said the Stroh's decision was a good business move, although a personally agonizing one for the community-minded Peter Stroh. Said Weinberg to the *Detroit Free Press:* "To me, that is proof positive that the company is doing serious long-term planning—that the company is in the game for the long pull. They're going to do something that their senior manager must regard as personally repugnant, because it makes economic sense to do so."

But the company's fire-brewed tradition won't stop just because the block-long, red-brick Stroh complex on Detroit's near east side will be empty. Most beers are brewed with steam coils in stainless steel kettles, while Stroh's advertising boasts of a smoother flavor because it has been—and will continue to be—brewed in copper kettles over an open fire.

In addition, the Stroh Brewery and Stroh, himself, will continue a tradition of hometown civic-mindedness and community service, despite the demise of the production plant. This has been a long-standing commitment from Peter Stroh, evidenced by such efforts as the spearheading of a corporate drive to help feed the city's needy and enriching the city's riverfront. The Stroh Brewery is developing a twenty-one acre site along the Detroit River for office, retail, residential, and parking space and will maintain its headquarters at the site of this $150 million development called River Place.

Stroh was named March of Dimes Humanitarian of the Year in 1981, but it was an award he accepted reluctantly, as U.S. 6th Circuit Court of Appeals Judge Damon Keith recalled in a 1985 *Detroit Free Press* article: "I had to do a little arm-twisting to get him to accept the award. . . . He's one of the finest men I ever have met, and I can think of no one who is more committed and dedicated to the city than he is. He's so modest. He said he made a habit of not accepting any awards. He told me, 'I'm just an instrument, a little cog in the wheel.' But if you ever go to him for anything in terms of this community, any civic or charitable need, he's always willing to help."

But in Detroit—and across the nation—the name and the man will always be associated with Bohemian Style Beer. "Before we're through," Stroh told the *Wall Street Journal* in May, 1985, "we may come to the conclusion that beer is better for you than breakfast."

SOURCES:

PERIODICALS

Advertising Age, September 5, 1983.
Beverage World, October, 1983.
Business Week, December 3, 1979.
Detroit Free Press, November 4, 1975, September 14, 1983, November 21, 1984, February 9, 1985, February 10, 1985, May 3, 1985, May 10, 1985.
Detroit News, November 13, 1980, January 18, 1981, December 19, 1982.
Marketing and Media Decisions, May, 1985.
Newsweek, October 10, 1983, December 19, 1983.
New York Times, August 27, 1984.
People, December 6, 1982.
Time, April 26, 1982.
U.S.A. Today, February 24, 1983, September 6, 1983.
Wall Street Journal, May 5, 1982, June 16, 1982, September 8, 1983, February 6, 1985.

—Sidelights by Patricia Montemurri

Vic Tanny
1912(?)-1985

AP/Wide World Photos

OBITUARY NOTICE: Name originally, Victor A. Iannidinardo; born c. 1912; died of a heart attack (one source says a stroke), June 11, 1985, in Tampa, Fla. American physical fitness advocate and businessman. Tanny operated his first gym out of his mother's garage in Rochester, New York, in 1932, using broom handles with sandbags for weights. He later opened a professional gym in Rochester but moved to California and became a school teacher in the mid-1930s. In 1936 Tanny visited the Oakland, California, gym of Jack LaLanne and decided to re-enter the physical fitness business.

Tanny devised a new marketing concept that was to change the image America had of gyms from that of a stark, grimy setting peopled by sweaty men to one of family-oriented comfort and luxury. The gyms Tanny built featured gleaming chrome-plated equipment set in carpeted suites at complexes that also had spas, tennis courts, and swimming pools. He opened his first concept gym in California in 1939, and the enterprise began to grow rapidly after World War II. Tanny also innovated a time-payment plan for his customers, and within a few years he headed a nationwide chain of gyms that were to make him a millionaire. But Tanny's empire collapsed on him in 1961 when over-extended finances, back taxes, and union troubles forced him to sell most of his interest in the business. Until his death he continued to receive income from the gyms, which, under new management, are still using his name.

SOURCES:

PERIODICALS

Chicago Tribune, June 13, 1985.
Los Angeles Times, June 12, 1985.
Newsweek, June 24, 1985.
Time, June 24, 1985.
Washington Post, June 13, 1985.

Brandon Tartikoff

1949-

PERSONAL: Born 1949, in Freeport, Long Island, N.Y.; son of a clothing manufacturer; married Lilly Samuels (formerly a dancer with the New York City Ballet); children: Calla Lianne. *Education:* Received B.A. from Yale University.

ADDRESSES: Home—Coldwater Canyon, Calif. *Office*—NBC Television Network, 3000 West Alameda Ave., Burbank, Calif. 91523.

OCCUPATION: Television network executive.

CAREER: Worked in promotion department of American Broadcasting Co. (ABC) affiliate station in New Haven, Conn., 1971-73; WLS-TV (ABC affiliate), Chicago, Ill., director of advertising and promotion, 1973-76; ABC-TV, New York, N.Y., director of dramatic programs, 1976; National Broadcasting Co. (NBC) Entertainment, Burbank, Calif., director of comedy programs, 1977-78, vice-president of programs, 1978-80, president, 1980—. Played semiprofessional baseball with the New Haven Braves, 1971-73.

SIDELIGHTS: The youngest television executive ever to be appointed head of a network programming division, Brandon Tartikoff, president of National Broadcasting Company (NBC) Entertainment, puts NBC's ratings success—and his career—on the line every day with shows he hopes will entertain the public better than anything else in that time slot. With critical successes like "Cheers," "St. Elsewhere," and "The Cosby Show" to his credit, Tartikoff has raised NBC from its last-place ratings position, and has managed to have some fun at the same time. "I could make myself crazy worrying about how much a wrong decision will cost, so I just don't think about it," Tartikoff told the *New York Times* in 1980, shortly after being appointed to his prominent position. "My attitude is I'm going to have fun doing the job," he added, "and if it works out, fine."

Born in 1949, Tartikoff was a television baby, who claims he doesn't remember life without it. Shows like "Playhouse 90," "My Little Margie," "I Married Joan," and "Burns and Allen" filled many of his growing hours and planted ideas that would flower in the years to come. While attending Yale University, Tartikoff penned a soap opera parody that he tried unsuccessfully to persuade a local television station to broadcast. Although disappointed by the rejection, Tartikoff learned a valuable programming lesson from the director who turned him down: His own tastes should not dictate a programming choice. Tartikoff revealed the director's advice to *People* magazine: "He said, 'Take your camera to the New York bus terminal, photograph the first 100 people arriving, and whenever you make a decision think of those faces and say, "Now I like it, but will they like it?" ' "

AP/Wide World Photos

After graduating from Yale with honors, Tartikoff landed a job in the promotion department of the same station that turned down his soap opera idea. In 1973 he transferred to the American Broadcasting Company (ABC) affiliate in Chicago, WLS-TV, where he served as director of advertising and promotion. But he longed to work in network television, and spent all his vacation time for five years in Los Angeles seeking an entree into the network elite. "It was so clear to me that I had all this talent and that anybody who had a job I wanted should step aside and invite me to help them clean out their desks," Tartikoff told *People*. "I kept setting goals and was constantly frustrated that at 23 I was still stuck in local television."

The spark that ignited Tartikoff's creative flame and gained him the recognition of high-ranking network executives came in 1976 during his stint at the Chicago station. Trying his hand at boosting station ratings, he formulated the idea of a five-day festival of ape movies called "Gorilla My Dreams Week." Impressed with Tartikoff's creativity and programming passion, WLS general manager Lew Erlicht introduced him to Fred Silverman, then ABC's programming chief. Perceiving talent, Silverman brought Tartikoff to

ABC in 1976, where Tartikoff remained under Silverman's tutelage for a year as director of dramatic programs.

But Tartikoff's love of comedy lured him to NBC, where in 1977, he accepted an offer to become director of comedy programs. Within the year, Silverman also moved to NBC as president and promoted his protege to West Coast programming chief. Silverman reigned for three years as NBC's president and in 1980 named Tartikoff president of NBC Entertainment. Thus at 31 years old Tartikoff became the youngest television executive ever to be appointed head of a network programming division. Tartikoff's job revolved around the difficult task of bringing NBC out of its third-place ratings spot. When, in 1981, Silverman was replaced by Grant Tinker, Tartikoff's future seemed uncertain. Tartikoff later said that few in the industry would have been surprised if Tinker had formed his own team and dismissed Tartikoff. But Tinker did not blame Tartikoff for NBC's ratings woes. "I think he is the best guy to do the job—it's that simple," Tinker told *Time*.

Tinker's confidence in Tartikoff's hopes of creating ratings hits, however, was not enough to keep the network from losing additional viewers in Tinker's first year, with annual profits shrinking to about a quarter of those reported by first-place CBS. NBC then adopted a strategy committed to making quality the prime consideration in shows, seeking to become known as the network that would stick with new shows longer than the competition. Tartikoff supported this strategy of quality. "What an unconventional show needs is an incubation period," Tartikoff asserted in an interview with the *New York Times*. "The chance to develop an audience." Even when the early ratings of such critically-acclaimed series as the drama "St. Elsewhere," and the comedy "Cheers," both of which debuted in the fall of 1982, were disappointing, NBC stuck with them. "I don't give the public what they want," Tartikoff told *Time* "I'm more interested in giving them what they will want. I like to challenge the audience. That's not to say you don't do your share of pandering."

At least once, such so-called pandering paid off for the network. In 1983 NBC debuted "The A Team," a low-brow hit about outlaw Vietnam veterans that also earned the dubious top billing on the National Coalition on Television Violence's citing of the most violent shows on television; the series was a ratings success. But even Tartikoff acknowledged the show was not high-quality television. He claimed, however, that "The A Team" did serve a purpose by using its popular status to lead audiences into more substantive shows.

One of NBC's highest-quality shows, according to critical assessment, "St. Elsewhere" was called by *Newsweek* in 1983 the "season's most intelligent network effort as well as TV's most realistic medical series ever." Although the show initially suffered from low ratings, NBC chose to work on "St. Elsewhere" and, under Tartikoff's direction, transformed the show into one of national popularity. Tartikoff revised the scheduling and instructed writers to mix in some romance and reduce fragmented story lines to three or four per episode. Aware that "St. Elsewhere" lacked the life-and-death situation hooks that attract a viewer's attention, Tartikoff placed his convictions in the characters, telling *Newsweek* that "if the audience falls in love with the characters, the setting almost doesn't matter." He added, "This is one of the few shows I've ever taken home to run for friends before it airs."

With "Cheers," NBC's comedy series featuring regular patrons of a Boston saloon, popularity among the critics was easily won. The show premiered in a season when other network offerings were clearly inferior and was met from the outset with praise and glowing reviews from critics across the country. But critical acclaim did not initially influence the public, and "Cheers," which debuted at sixtieth out of sixty-three shows, soon fell to last place. But midway into the season, when the show was in trouble, one hopeful fact sustained its cast and crew: Tartikoff and Tinker like to watch "Cheers" because it made them laugh. Tartikoff revealed in *Esquire* that he might watch "The A Team" if he didn't have anything else to do in the hours he was home, but he was addicted to the characters of "Cheers." The series battled its way through the first season, and NBC picked it up for a second year. As Cameron Stauth of *Esquire* explained: "With all the publicity about 'Cheers' being the centerpiece of NBC's much-vaunted quality banquet of programming, Brandon Tartikoff would have had a tough time disowning this most beautiful baby of his." The show's producers relied on a combination of concern for quality, dismissal of the ratings, pressure on the press and critics to give the show free advertising, and the emergence of a cult following to turn "Cheers" into a hit. Their diligence was rewarded when "Cheers" garnered thirteen Emmy nominations.

Another of Tartikoff's ideas helped steer NBC into the number two position in the prime-time race among the three major networks by 1984: "The Cosby Show." A situation comedy created by comedian Bill Cosby about the trials of middle-aged parents, the show first aired in the fall of 1984 and proved to be a hit. It banks on the popularity of Cosby and features the kind of humor that Tartikoff has always loved. "It will remind people that all you need for a situation comedy to work and be popular is a star that they want to see and a show that is funny," Tartikoff told *Electronic Media*.

Staying one step ahead of a public demand for sensitive, though controversial, dramas has also contributed to NBC's advancement. The network's 1984 TV movie "The Burning Bed," starring Farrah Fawcett as a battered wife, even outdrew NBC's major league baseball World Series telecasts. NBC also produced "Adam," a movie about a missing child that, because of its socially provacative content, did not attract commercial sponsors. Although the viewer ratings and critical success of these movies served to reinforce what Tartikoff calls dedication to "shows we should be doing as responsible broadcasters," the reluctance of advertisers to endorse such programming may force networks to offer discounted rates. But networks cannot afford to back down from this programming, according to Tartikoff, regardless of the cost. "If we start walking away from opportunities to explore controversial subjects," he told *Electronic Media*, "those subjects are going to get explored by writers, directors and producers who will take their ideas to [cable or pay television outlets] or try to put them out as videocassettes or into theaters if need be."

As television audiences become increasingly fragmented, the networks have identified a need to diversify along with viewers by offering more than car chases, detective shows, domestic comedies and soap operas, Tartikoff asserted. But, he acknowledged, with diversification also comes the increased difficulty of convincing viewers that something innovative or unique is being shown. Even in prime time comedy, an area in which Tartikoff's career has flourished and on which NBC has built its fortune, appeal is fading. "I think the format of comedy is tired out, and so now it comes down to good writing, strong characterization and talent," Tartikoff informed *Electronic Media.*

Tartikoff points to his decision to cancel "Buffalo Bill," a short-lived serial, as one of his most difficult cancellation moves. While "Buffalo Bill" was a comedy, it differed enough from standard comedic fare that audiences were reluctant to accept it. Tartikoff explained that although the show was on the air for two different seasons, "a lot of people never even knew about it." By nature, television has discouraged producers from being adventurous with their shows, Tartikoff claimed. But NBC is committed to broadcasting comedy, even if that commitment means suffering short-term ratings setbacks. "It's just waiting for the best producers and writers to come over and do their work for NBC," Tartikoff told *Electronic Media.* "And I think that they're here because they know that we're a network that respects comedy, believes in it and is willing to sacrifice, in the short-run, the ratings and shares that we might be able to get with another type of show in order to build their shows for the long run."

In the early 1970s Tartikoff was diagnosed as having Hodgkin's disease, a cancer of the lymphatic system. At a stage in life when disease and death can seem foreign and unreal, Tartikoff was brought face-to-face with his own mortality, and with the realization that nothing in life is guaranteed. Through a regimen of chemotherapy and radiation treatments, the disease entered remission, but not without taking its toll on Tartikoff. "I used to think I was pretty hot stuff," Tartikoff told *Newsweek* when he had regained his health. "I'm still no poster child for humility, but I've got a better perspective on my priorities."

Called by *Newsweek* the "kid in TV's hot seat," Tartikoff has remained unpretentious when power and money have rewarded his achievements. With Tartikoff's prominence has also come public recognition and constant suggestions on how he should fill sixty-nine hours of programming each week. He has had ideas proposed to him in a dentist's chair, at a funeral, and in the aftermath of a car accident, while concepts have been offered by an NBC building guard as well as by U.S. President Ronald Reagan—all to feed what Tartikoff calls "the monster that never stops eating." Television, he told *People,* is that monster. "It chews things up and constantly needs replenishing," he said. Tartikoff's wife, Lilly Samuels, explained that Tartikoff does his job not for prestige but for television itself. "He loves it. At work he is so serious it's possible he frightens people. He doesn't politick, he just works," Samuels told *People* magazine. Echoed Tartikoff, "Everything I do is directed toward moving NBC into first place. It's the ideas that excite me the most."

SOURCES:

PERIODICALS

Electronic Media, September 6, 1984.
Esquire, February, 1984.
Los Angeles Times, December 22, 1982, January 13, 1984, May 23, 1984.
Newsweek, June 14, 1982, January 17, 1983, May 16, 1983.
New York Times, January 16, 1980, April 28, 1983, August 25, 1983.
People, November 12, 1984.
Playboy, June, 1982.
Time, December 3, 1984, September 16, 1985.
Washington Post, February 4, 1984.

—Sidelights by Amy C. Bodwin

Zehdi Labib Terzi

1924-

PERSONAL: Born February 20, 1924, in Jerusalem, Palestine (now Israel); father was a postal worker; married, 1960; wife's name Widad; children: Karimah (daughter), Kamel (son). *Education:* Attended law school but did not graduate.

ADDRESSES: Home and office—115 East 65th St., New York, N.Y. 10021.

OCCUPATION: Diplomat.

CAREER: Travel agent in Lebanon and Turkey; member of Palestine Liberation Organization (PLO), 1964—, has held posts in Brazil, Argentina, Lebanon, Turkey, Jordan, Egypt, and Spain, permanent United Nations observer, 1975—, member of executive council. *Military service:* British Army; served in civil service.

SIDELIGHTS: Few diplomats have mastered the tricky terrain of the United Nations as well as the man without a country, Zehdi Labib Terzi. The Palestine Liberation Organization's (PLO) representative to the UN has used his considerable diplomatic skills to develop an impressive network of support within that world body for the PLO's ultimate political goal: a separate Palestinian state.

Since 1975, he has adroitly worked the corridors and committee rooms of the UN to build the case for Palestinian statehood. A measure of his success is the complaint of Yehuda Blum, former Israeli delegate to the UN, who maintains that, thanks to Terzi, the significance of "the PLO has been inflated beyond what is warranted by its strength on the ground." Terzi's accomplishments are all the more remarkable when one considers that the PLO is not actually a member of the UN and he is not an official delegate, only an "observer."

Terzi's formula for success has been simple and consistent. He has nurtured cordial relations between the PLO and Soviet bloc countries to offset the United States' massive commitment to Israel, and he has built bridges to all of the important Third World blocs by supporting their causes. When the African bloc drafts a resolution condemning the apartheid system in South Africa, Terzi will help rally Arab support for the measure—drawing parallels between the South African government's treatment of blacks and Israel's treatment of Palestinians within its borders and on the occupied West Bank and Gaza Strip. When the United States denounces the Sandinista regime in Nicaragua, Terzi will jump to its defense. Three years ago, when Nicaragua was seeking a seat on the UN Security Council, Terzi worked behind the scenes to make sure his Sandinista friends got what they wanted. "It's my mission to see that we have friends on the council—at least nations that understand our cause and support it," Terzi told Jane

AP/Wide World Photos

Rosen, UN correspondent for the *Guardian* of London in an article that appeared in the *New York Times Magazine*.

According to Rosen, "Terzi is one of the most effective operators in the United Nations. He drafts or oversees most of the resolutions on Palestine that go to the General Assembly and Security Council. He can get his supporters to convene the Council almost any time the PLO wants. He has been largely responsible for a series of special Assembly sessions on Palestine and for a major international conference on Palestine held in Geneva [in 1983]. He was the dominant force behind the establishment of a General Assembly committee to push for a Palestinian cause, a division in the Secretariat to service the committee and a special information unit in the Secretariat to publicize the Palestinian case."

Small, dapper, and courtly in manner, Terzi is described by those who know him as a shrewd political strategist and a tireless worker driven by one thing: justice for the Palestinians. Terzi lives with his wife and two children in a Manhattan townhouse owned by the PLO, but his base of operations is most often the UN's delegates' lounge; he is said to spend more time there than any other representative. "It gives me easy access," he told Rosen. "I approach as many delegates as I can and I explain our cause to them. Sometimes I'll invite them to sit and have coffee and I come right out and say what we're here for. I tell them the Palestinian people need their help, so we can return to our homes."

Terzi was born in Jerusalem to an Eastern Orthodox Christian family. His father was a postal worker under the British mandate. His mother and three sisters still live in East Jerusalem. After the creation of Israel in 1948, East Jerusalem came under Jordanian control—a state of affairs that did not satisfy Terzi. "I was a Palestinian activist," he told Rosen, "and I didn't want anybody, including Jordan, to occupy Palestinian territory. The Jordanian security forces were constantly asking me about my movements. They made my life miserable, so I left."

In Lebanon, and later in Turkey, Terzi went into business as a travel agent but managed to stay close to the Palestinian resistance movement. When the PLO was formed in 1964, he joined. His first diplomatic assignment with the PLO was to serve as its representative in Brazil. Later, he was posted with the Arab League in Argentina and Spain. In 1974, when PLO Chairman Yasir Arafat came to the UN to deliver his famous "gun and olive branch" speech, Terzi was a member of the Palestinian delegation. The following year, he returned to the United States as the PLO's permanent UN observer.

Terzi's tenure has not been without controversy. An off-the-record meeting in 1979 with Andrew Young, then U.S. Ambassador to the UN, touched off a major furor. The problem was a promise made by former Secretary of State Henry Kissinger to Israel that prohibits any dialogue between the U.S. and the PLO until the PLO unequivocally recognizes Israel's right to exist. When word of the unauthorized meeting leaked out, supporters of Israel demanded—and got—Young's resignation.

Succeeding U.S. ambassadors to the UN have kept their distance from Terzi. When Terzi and former UN Ambassador Jeane Kirkpatrick would pass in the corridors, Terzi often said hello, but Kirkpatrick would only nod, cooly, in his direction. "I acknowledged his existence," she told the *New York Times*, "which is more than he does for Israel."

While the Andrew Young episode put a severe strain on relations between U.S. blacks and Jews, it helped strengthen black support for the PLO. Not long after the incident, several prominent black leaders traveled to the Middle East and met with Arafat. The PLO studied the possibility of moving its New York office to Harlem. Terzi considers civil rights leader Jesse Jackson a good friend and maintains close ties to several black congressmen. There was a minor flap in 1985 when Representative George Crockett, a black congressman from Detroit, invited Terzi to Washington, D.C., to address other members of Congress. The State Department, which restricts Terzi's travels to within a twenty-five-mile radius of New York, refused him permission to go to Washington.

Though he is considered a moderate within the PLO ranks, Terzi describes himself as a Marxist and jokes about his physical resemblance to Lenin. He has tried—without noticeable success—to persuade other Arab states to adopt a more conciliatory approach toward the Soviet Union, and he insists that the Soviets must be a party to any genuine resolution of the Middle East problem. "Any solution," he told *Newsweek*, "without the participation of the two superpowers is not a guaranteed solution."

He is also an outspoken advocate of the PLO's right to pursue armed resistance to Israel. "We have never given up the armed struggle," Terzi told *Newsweek*. "The armed struggle has been lessened, but I cannot connect that with our diplomatic initiatives." Terzi, who is a member of the PLO's executive council, believes it was "the gun that brought us to the attention of the world. You must remember that it's always time to carry the gun. Maybe now it's just not the right time to use it."

For all his success in mobilizing world opinion against Israel and its main backer, the United States, Terzi knows that ultimately the PLO must win U.S. support for his cause if there is ever to be a Palestinian homeland. Lacking direct access to any U.S. administration, Terzi can only hope that growing American isolation within the world body will cause the American public to reevaluate the price of U.S. relations with Israel.

After the 1982 Israeli invasion of Lebanon, which scattered the PLO to all corners of the Middle East and caused a major split within its ranks, many commentators began to write the PLO's obituary. Even within Arab ranks at the UN, some delegates seemed pleased by the prospect of seeing Terzi's influence reduced. Terzi, however, seems to have weathered the storm and has set about repairing the damage to the PLO's image. For the man without a country, it's business as usual in the delegate's lounge.

SOURCES:

BOOKS

Cobban, Helena, *The Palestine Liberation Organization: People, Power and Politics*, Cambridge University Press, 1984.
Hudson, Michael, *Arab Politics: The Search for Legitimacy*, Yale University Press, 1977.

PERIODICALS

Associated Press, September 29, 1979, February 12, 1985, March 4, 1985.
Maclean's, April 16, 1984.
Newsweek, September 3, 1979.
New York Times, January 19, 1976, March 23, 1976, March 25, 1976, March 26, 1976, June 19, 1976, July 23, 1977, November 19, 1977, August 14, 1979, August 15, 1979, August 17, 1979, August 19, 1979, August 20, 1979, August 21, 1979, August 22, 1979, August 27, 1979, September 8, 1979, November 8, 1979, March 5, 1982, October 21, 1983.
New York Times Magazine, September 16, 1984.

—Sidelights by Tom Hundley

Richard Thalheimer

1948(?)-

BRIEF ENTRY: Born c.1948. American marketing executive. Richard Thalheimer is founder and president of The Sharper Image, a San Francisco-based catalogue company that specializes in "toys for the executive." When Thalheimer introduced his service in the late 1970s, initial sales totaled $500,000. Today, The Sharper Image is a multi-million-dollar business catering to the whims and fantasies of young urban professionals.

Raised in Little Rock, Arkansas, in a retail-sales family, Thalheimer had always dreamed of owning a suit of armor. One item The Sharper Image offers—and its president owns—is a full-size, three-piece suit of armor that sells for close to $3,000. Thalheimer's marketing strategy is to sell articles that he himself would like to buy. His catalogue lists a variety of expensive security devices, electronic gadgets, and "fun" office furniture, including: a $250 bullet-proof vest; a $50 computerized wristwatch for joggers; a $35 light switch that is voice-activated; a $100 meter that tests the amount of salt in food; and a $900 Recaro racing car seat converted to an executive's chair.

Thalheimer credits a good deal of his success to a $129 course that he took on "How to Build a Great Fortune in Mail Order" and to the fact that direct-mail sales in general have more than doubled since 1975. Through computerized mailing lists, Thalheimer is able to pinpoint prospective customers, and he posts an average of twenty million catalogues per year. "What you have to appreciate," he explained to Wayne King of the *New York Times*, "is that a lot of our customers are really earning big money, so it's nothing to them to spend $300 on a toy."

Thalheimer, who described himself in the *Los Angeles Times Magazine* as "perhaps the ultimate yuppie," earned his seed money selling expensive watches to joggers. His catalogue first appeared in 1979, and business had grown each year through 1985, when the firm projected that 1986 sales would not increase. Realizing that his mail order market was saturated, Thalheimer began opening retail stores across the United States. Twelve Sharper Image stores opened in 1985, and plans called for an additional twenty outlets to open in 1986.

SOURCES:

PERIODICALS

Forbes, February 10, 1986.
Los Angeles Times Magazine, November 3, 1985.
Newsweek, November 16, 1981.
New York Times, May 1, 1982.

Eiji Toyoda

1913-

UPI/Bettmann Newsphotos

PERSONAL: Born September 12, 1913, in Kinjo, Nishi Kasugai, Aichi, Japan; son of Heikichi (in the family's automatic loom business) and Nao Toyoda; married Kazuko Takahashi, December 19, 1939; children: Kanshiro, Tetsuro, Shuhei, Sonoko. *Education:* University of Tokyo, B.M.E., 1936.

ADDRESSES: *Office*—Toyota Motor Corp., 1 Toyota-cho, Toyota-shi, Aichi 471, Japan.

OCCUPATION: Auto executive.

CAREER: Toyoda Automatic Loom Works, Aichi, Japan, trainee, 1936; Toyota Motor Co., Aichi, engineer, 1937, director, 1945, managing director, 1959-60, executive vice-president, 1960-67, president, 1967-82; Toyota Motor Corp., Aichi, chairman, 1982—. Chairman of Towa Real Estate Co. Ltd.; executive director of Toyota Central Research and Development Laboratories, Inc.; director of Aishin Seiki Co. Ltd., Toyoda Automatic Loom Works Ltd., Aichi Steel Works Ltd., and Toyoda Machine Works Ltd. Auditor, Toyoda Tsusho Kaisha Ltd.

MEMBER: Japan Automobile Manufacturers Association (president, 1972-80; supreme advisor, 1980—), Japan Motor Industrial Federation (advisor, 1980), Japan Federation Employers Association (executive director, 1967), Federation of Economic Organizations (executive director, 1967).

SIDELIGHTS: Eiji Toyoda, the man in the driver's seat of the Toyota Motor Company for nearly twenty years, is virtually unknown outside of Japan's Toyota City, headquarters of "the company that stopped Detroit," according to the *New York Times*. But like a latter-day Henry Ford, Toyoda has made his mark on the auto industry. He has not only presided over revolutionary changes in the way cars are built, he has seen his family-run business become a powerhouse in the world export market and has forged an unlikely alliance with an archrival, General Motors Corporation.

As chairman of one of the most powerful industrial clans in a nation of 120 million people, Toyoda has an almost Western flair as a go-getter and an empire builder that belies his reputation in Japan as a staunch political and economic conservative. The parallels between the Fords and the Toyodas extend from the assembly line to the board room. Today, the elder Toyoda shares power with his cousins: Shoichiro, who is president of Toyota Motor Corporation, and Shoichiro's younger brother Tatsuro, head of New United Motor Manufacturing Incorporated, the Toyota-GM joint venture headquartered in Fremont, Calif.

Toyoda's uncle, Sakichi, founded the original family business, Toyoda Automatic Loom Works, in 1926 in Nagoya, about 200 miles west of Tokyo. Sakichi's son, Kiichiro,

established Toyota Motor Company in 1937 as an affiliate of the loom works. The family was so involved in the business that Eiji's father Heikichi (younger brother of Sakichi) even made his home inside the spinning factory. "From childhood, machines and business were always there right in front of me," Eiji Toyoda said in an interview in *The Wheel Extended*, a quarterly review published by his company. "By seeing the two together, I probably developed an understanding of both, from a child's point of view." Toyoda describes himself as a combination engineer-administrator: "I don't really think of myself as an engineer, but rather as a manager. Or maybe a management engineer. Actually, I graduated from engineering school, but more important is the work a person accomplishes in the 10 or 15 years after school."

What Toyoda accomplished for Toyota Motor was dazzling success at a time when Detroit automakers were struggling to stay profitable. Toyota, Japan's number one automaker, spearheaded the tidal wave of small, low-priced cars that swept the United States after successive energy crises in the mid- and late-1970s. Enraged by the invasion of Japanese imports, Toyoda's counterpart at the Ford Motor Company, then-Chairman Henry Ford II, vowed, "We'll push them back to the shores." It never happened. Instead, Ford and his lieutenants turned to Toyota to negotiate a possible cooperative venture in the United States—an unsuccessful effort that preceeded GM's historic agreement in 1983 to jointly produce Toyota-designed subcompacts at an idle GM plant in Fremont.

In addition to running the largest corporation in Japan—and the world's third largest automaker, behind GM and Ford—Toyoda has overseen the development of a highly efficient manufacturing system that is being copied worldwide. It "represents a revolutionary change from certain tenets of mass production and assembly-line work originally applied by Henry Ford," wrote *New York Times* Tokyo correspondent Steve Lohr. In short, Toyoda's career could be said to echo the company's U.S. advertising slogan: "Oh, what a feeling!"

After graduating in 1936 with a mechanical engineering degree from the University of Tokyo—training ground for most of Japan's future top executives—the twenty-three-year-old Toyoda joined the family spinning business as an engineering trainee and transferred a year later to the newly formed Toyota Motor Company. The company was a relative newcomer to the auto business in Japan. The country's first car, a steam-powered vehicle, was produced just after the turn of the century, followed in 1911 by the introduction of the DAT model, forerunner of Datsun/Nissan, Toyota's nearest rival today.

The Toyoda family patriarch, Sakichi, the son of a poor carpenter, had invented the first Japanese-designed power loom in 1897 and perfected an advanced automatic loom in 1926, when he founded Toyoda Automatic Loom Works. He ultimately sold the patents for his design to an English firm for $250,000, at a time when textiles was Japan's top industry and used the money to bankroll his eldest son Kiichiro's venture into automaking in the early 1930s.

Numerous stories have sprung up over the years concerning why auto company was named Toyota rather than Toyoda. A *Business Week* article claims the family consulted a numerologist in 1937 before establishing its first auto factory: "Eight was their lucky number, he advised. Accordingly, they modified their company's name to Toyota, which required eight calligraphic strokes instead of ten. Sure enough, what is now Toyota Motor Corp. soon became not only the biggest and most successful of Japan's automakers, but also one of the most phenomenally profitable companies in the world." But a *New York Times* story notes the family changed the spelling in the 1930s because "it believed the sound [of the new name] resonated better in Japanese ears."

After Eiji joined the family business in 1936, he worked on the A1 prototype, the forerunner of the company's first production model, a six-cylinder sedan that borrowed heavily from Detroit automotive technology and resembled the radically styled Chrysler Airflow model of that period. During those early years, Toyoda gained lots of hands-on experience. "I tried in the past to see how much I could really tell by touch," he said in *The Wheel Extended*. "It was hard for me to recognize a difference of one hundredth of a millimeter. I must have had a lot of free time. Still, I think it is important to know how much of a difference one can sense." It was a philosophy he shared with his cousin

Kiichiro, who often told his employes: "How can you expect to do your job without getting your hands dirty?"

In his spare time, Eiji Toyoda studied rockets and jet engines and, on the advice of his cousin, even researched helicopters. "We gathered materials in an attempt to make a helicopter and made prototype rotary wings," he said in *The Wheel Extended*. "By attaching the wings on one end of a beam, with a car engine on the other, we built a contraption that could float in the air. . . . We weren't doing it just for fun. However, the war intensified, and it became hard to experiment because of a shortage of materials."

The war left Japan's industry in a shambles, and the automaker began rebuilding its production facilities from scratch. Recalled Toyoda: "Everything was completely new to us. Design and production, for example, all had to be started from zero. And the competitive situation allowed for not even a single mistake. We had our backs to the wall, and we knew it."

But while Kiichiro Toyoda was rebuilding the manufacturing operations, Japan's shattered economy left the company with a growing bank of unsold cars. By 1949, the firm was unable to meet its payroll, and employes began a devastating fifteen-month strike—the first and only walkout in the company's history—which pushed Toyota to the brink of bankruptcy. In 1950, the Japanese government ended the labor strife by forcing Toyota to reorganize and split its sales and manufacturing operations into separate companies, each headed by a non-family member. Kiichiro Toyoda and his executive staff resigned en masse; Kiichiro died less than two years later.

Eiji Toyoda meanwhile had been named managing director of the manufacturing arm, Toyota Motor Company. In what some automakers must view as a supreme irony, he was sent to the United States in 1950 to study the auto industry and return to Toyota with a report on American manufacturing methods. After touring Ford Motor's U.S. facilities, Toyoda turned to the task of redesigning Toyota's plants to incorporate advanced techniques and machinery. Returning from another trip to the United States in 1961, only four years after the establishment of Toyota Motor Sales USA, a prophetic Toyoda told employees in a speech recorded in a company brochure: "The United States already considers us a challenger. . . . But we must not just learn from others and copy them. That would merely result in being overwhelmed by the competition. We must produce superior automobiles, and we can do it with creativity, resourcefulness and wisdom—plus hard work. Without this . . . and the willingness to face adversity, we will crumple and fall under the new pressures."

In 1967, Toyoda was named president of Toyota Motor Company—the first family member to assume that post since Kiichiro resigned in 1950. The family power wasn't consolidated until 1981, when Sadazo Yamamoto was replaced as president of Toyota Motor Sales by Shoichiro Toyoda, son of Kiichiro and nicknamed the "Crown Prince" by the Japanese press. A year later, the two branches of the company were unified in the new Toyota Motor Corporation, with Eiji Toyoda as chairman and Shoichiro Toyoda as president and chief executive officer. A *Business Week* article at the time quoted a Japanese economist as saying the return of the Toyoda family to power was a "restoration of the bluest of blue blood."

At this stage of the company's history, there may be a strong family presence (after a stretch of non-family leadership for most of the postwar period), but not "control" in the Western sense. The top three family members own just over one percent of Toyota Motor stock, according to Britain's *Financial Times*. In contrast, the Ford family in the United States controls 40 percent of the voting power in the Ford Motor Company.

The Toyodas led their company to a record year in 1984. Toyota sold an all-time high 1.7 million vehicles in Japan and the same number overseas. Profits peaked at $2.1 billion for the fiscal year ending March 31, 1985. While that performance would certainly earn Toyota a mention in automotive history books, Eiji Toyoda and his company may be better remembered for a distinctive management style that's been copied by hundreds of Japanese companies and is gaining growing acceptance in this country. The Toyota approach, adopted at its ten Japanese factories and twenty-four plants in seventeen countries, has three main objectives: Keeping inventory to an absolute minimum through a system called *kanban*, or "just in time," insuring that each step of the assembly process is performed correctly the first time, and cutting the amount of human labor that goes into each car.

Despite the predominance of robots and automation at Toyota, the company firmly believes in the principle of lifetime employment; displaced workers are not laid off, but frequently transferred to other jobs. Toyoda believes the day when robots totally replace humans is a long way off. He told *The Wheel Extended*: "At the current stage, there is a greater difference between humans and robots than between cars and magic clouds. Robots can't even walk yet. They sit in one place and do exactly as programmed. But that's all. There is no way that robots can replace all the work of humans."

Due in part to that sort of philosophy, it's not surprising that company loyalty is so high. Toyota's 60,000 employes in Japan, for instance, are encouraged to make cost-cutting suggestions, an idea that Eiji Toyoda borrowed from Ford after his first visit to the United States. Since the system began in 1951, more than ten million suggestions have flooded the executive offices—nearly 1.7 million in 1983 alone. "The Japanese," asserts Toyoda, "excel in improving things."

SOURCES:

PERIODICALS

Automotive News, May 11, 1981.
Business Week, August 2, 1982, December 24, 1984, November, 4, 1985.
Detroit Free Press, September 15, 1982, December 19, 1984, February 24, 1985, April 15, 1985.
Financial Times, August 24, 1981.
Forbes, July 6, 1981.
Fortune, July 9, 1984.
Japan Economic Journal, February 2, 1982, January 11, 1983, May 17, 1983, June 11, 1985.
Motor Trend, January, 1978.
Nation's Business, January, 1985.
New York Times, May 27, 1974, September 14, 1980, March 21, 1982, November 24, 1982.
The Wheel Extended (Toyota Motor Corp. quarterly), spring, 1984.
U.S. News and World Report, December 17, 1984.
Wall Street Journal, February 18, 1981, April 15, 1981.

—Sketch by Anita Lienert and Paul Lienert

Kathleen Turner

1954(?)-

PERSONAL: Born c. 1954, in Springfield, Mo.; daughter of a U.S. foreign service officer; married Jay Weiss (a real estate developer), 1984. *Education:* Attended Central School of Speech and Drama, London, England, and Southwest Missouri State University; University of Maryland, M.F.A.

ADDRESSES: *Agent*—Susan Geller, Guttman & Pam Ltd., 120 El Camino, Suite 104, Beverly Hills, Calif. 90212.

OCCUPATION: Actress.

CAREER: After performing in a number of college stage productions, began working in television commercials; member of cast of daytime drama "The Doctors," beginning 1977; appeared in a number of stage plays, including "Gemini" on Broadway; actress in feature films, including "Body Heat," 1981, "The Man With Two Brains," 1983, "A Breed Apart" (unreleased), 1983, "Romancing the Stone," 1984, "Crimes of Passion," 1984, "Prizzi's Honor," 1985, "Jewel of the Nile," 1985, and "Peggy Sue Got Married," 1986.

AWARDS, HONORS: Golden Globe Award for best actress in a comedy film, 1985, for "Prizzi's Honor"; named Star of the Year by National Association of Theater Owners, 1985.

SIDELIGHTS: Kathleen Turner has been hailed as a director's dream, a versatile and thoroughly professional performer with classic all-American looks. Her beauty, coupled with her husky, languorous voice, got her noticed in the 1981 hit "Body Heat," her first movie, in which she gave a sizzling performance as the scheming seductress Matty Walker. But it has been her subsequent roles, in which her looks have been, to some extent, downplayed, that have elicited the most critical acclaim for her acting ability: the whiney-voiced tease in the spoof "The Man With Two Brains," the flinty, base, and bawdy prostitute in "Crimes of Passion," the plain-Jane author of romance novels in "Romancing the Stone," and the mob hit-woman in "Prizzi's Honor."

"In the age of high-definition imagery, when the wise star sells one quality and one quality only (and then, of course, complains about type-casting), Turner is the changeling's changeling," observed critic Richard Schickel in *Film Comment* magazine. Turner, he wrote, is "perhaps the movies' first authentically mysterious female presence since Garbo was hiding in plain sight." Turner told United Press International's Hollywood reporter Vernon Scott that she sees "aspects of myself" in the characters she has portrayed. "It's a matter of exaggerating yourself," she said.

If she seems adept at adapting to new film roles, it may be a mental and emotional nimbleness she acquired while growing up abroad. Born in Springfield, Missouri, one of four

AP/Wide World Photos

children of an American foreign service officer, Turner lived in Canada, Cuba, Washington, D.C., Venezuela, and London. "Unstable?" she asked in an interview with Michael Musto of *Saturday Review.* "No, my mother would kill me if I ever said that. I loved it." Her parents encouraged their children to study hard and work hard, a dictum that remained constant during the various address changes, which Turner sees as a positive influence on her development as an actress. "The parts of myself I hated in Caracas I didn't have to be in London," she told Brad Darrach of *People* magazine. "Our parents told us we could become whatever we wanted because we were smart, well educated and willing to work. And we swallowed it."

In London, she studied acting at the Central School of Speech and Drama. But when her father died in 1973, Turner returned to Missouri, where her mother's family lived, and enrolled at Southwest Missouri State University. "The cultural shock was the worst imaginable," she told Christian Williams in the *Washington Post.* "My hair was quite short, but the other girls' was long. All of my skirts were midis, but they were all in minis. That cast doubts on my sexuality, I think. I didn't help the adjustment much. On my first date, the boy asked me how I liked school. I remember saying, with full English accent, 'Oh, the school's all right, but the people are so bloody stupid.' I was quite affected, I'm sure. But I was just drawing on a different pool of experience, from living abroad. When the kids talked about 'Leave It to Beaver,' I didn't even know what it was."

She soon transferred to the University of Maryland, where she earned a Master of Fine Arts degree. Her first professional role, according to Williams, was as an ingenue in the Maryland Bicentennial Pageant. Turner says her college education in Missouri and Maryland gave her the chance to work constantly at becoming an actress. In an article by Hollywood columnist Shirley Eder in the *Detroit Free Press*, Turner said college acting "gave me a chance to do 20 shows a year. I remember having just two weeks in the whole school year when I wasn't performing or rehearsing. In college, your reputation isn't on the line, and it's safe. You can make a total ass of yourself and nobody cares."

In New York, the head of the first agency she signed with said he had doubts about taking her on, "because my voice would present so many problems," Turner told Eder. "I told him, my voice was exactly why I'd be hired, because it was different." Williams described Turner's voice as a purr that would "make Lauren Bacall turn her head—and whisk Humphrey Bogart out of the room. It is a voice so chesty and remarkable that each word, forming within, seems to linger a moment in fond farewell before its reluctant emigration from the mouth."

In New York, she was cast as bad girl Nora Aldrich on the soap opera "The Doctors" and appeared in the Broadway Show "Gemini" for nine months. It was in the soap opera, portraying what she called an "incompetent villainess," that Turner says she honed her screen presence and "learned to handle a camera," she told Williams. "Oh, I loved it. I found out that you could do things just with the rate at which you open and close your eyes. Things that in a theater would be lost except to the first 10 rows. And things with your voice, that you could never do on stage."

It was in Canada, in a production of Chekhov's "The Seagull," that she got the chance to read for "Body Heat." Turner impressed Lawrence Kasdan, who wrote and directed the film, with a dazzling audition. She described the audition, in Kasdan's office, to Williams: "Larry handed me the scene where Matty talks about her past. I just stretched out on the couch and did it, and when I finished, he said, I didn't think I'd ever hear the part read exactly as I wrote it.' "

Her allure was enhanced, according to David Chute in *Film Comment* magazine, with lines that teased and tempted her co-star, William Hurt, and the audience: "My body temperature runs a couple of degrees higher than normal, around a hundred," Matty tells Hurt's character, Ned Racine. "I don't mind. I guess it's the engine or something. Runs a little fast." UPI's Scott feels that "It was Kathleen's raw, animal sensuality in the role of Matty that helped make 'Body Heat' a box-office sensation. She came on as low-down and sultry, a woman of unbridled passion who took her sex where she found it. The sweatier the better."

After "Body Heat," Turner told Scott, producers wanted to typecast and duplicate the siren image. "Any role with impact is associated with the actress who plays it," she said. "I've met a lot of men who confuse me with Matty. I don't think of myself in terms of sensuality. I didn't have an image of Matty before I started work. The question was finding the right physical attitude, walking in tight skirts, for instance. Once I found the body, the rest of the character came along. . . . Matty always watched herself. She was aware of her body at all times. I don't think I would be comfortable with those characteristics. . . . Matty absolutely knew she had the power to excite and seduce men. I certainly don't feel that way. I'm sure women like her exist and some live off that appeal. And I was afraid she would be despised by other women."

Turner's next film was a drastic departure from "Body Heat." As comedian Steve Martin's wife, Dolores, in "The Man With Two Brains" in 1983, Turner showed a funny lady flair. Wrote critic Pauline Kael in the *New Yorker:* "Kathleen Turner, who was so laboriously steamy in 'Body Heat,' comes alive in comedy; she coos with pleasure as she frustrates this fool." Musto, in the *Saturday Review*, said Turner was "an outrageously funny villainess—a parody of Matty—who got her comeuppance when Steve Martin yelled 'Into the mud, scum queen!' and pushed."

In 1984, Turner married Manhattan real estate developer Jay Weiss and continued her work on the big screen in two polar-opposite starring performances. In the comedy "Romancing the Stone," she played frustrated, repressed romance novel author Joan Wilder, who is transformed in a Colombian jungle adventure into one of the heroines she writes about. Wrote Schickel in *Film Comment:* "One had the feeling [Turner] wasn't working a little literary conceit, either. Somehow, somewhere, she had observed the manners of ladies who work the edges of the writing game—doing soaps, maybe, or ghosting diet books. She had their shy willfulness down perfectly. And their look. These women exchange shopping hints with their friends, but are too absorbed in their work to try them out."

Actor-producer-director Michael Douglas said that when he auditioned Turner for the part, "All I knew at the time was that sultry, vamp quality," he told writer Michael Gross in *Rolling Stone* magazine. Turner, in the same article, recalls her casting as "your typical kind of meeting in the producer's office. I think I had on a short skirt. I figure my legs are my best asset, so I try to use them. Michael had talked to all the people I'd worked with, because one of the major considerations was living with a supposedly temperamental actress-type female in the jungles of Mexico for three months." Douglas said a screen test "showed us she was a consummate actress." Turner added that she was glad the script had a capable heroine. "They let her save herself, thank God! I'm tired of supposedly capable women who always end up getting rescued by the man."

In sharp contrast to the romp that was "Romancing the Stone," Turner played a character living on the edge in director Ken Russell's "Crimes of Passion." Jack Kroll, writing in *Newsweek*, said Turner "gives a gutsy and gallant performance as a woman why by day is Joanna, a cool and careful business person, and by night is China Blue, a street hooker who hurls herself into the foulest and most degrading acts." Schickel called it "a dangerous performance, but she never falls off the high wire—even when the rest of the movie hits the tanbark." Musto, in *Saturday Review,* wrote that Turner "manages to make her sleazy character not just sympathetic, tortured and pathetic, but kind of delightful. . . . You have to admire her just for having the guts to accept it." Turner told Musto many people counseled her against taking the part: "Let's just say the world didn't tell me to do it. Some people certainly said 'Don't go near it,' and I angered a lot of people who couldn't understand why I did. But on the other hand, when my husband saw it, even though he didn't care for [much of the movie,] he said he could see the acting challenge that was there, which is what attracted me in the first place."

In 1985, the chance to work with director John Huston, actor Jack Nicholson and a plum role as an upwardly mobile, unorthodox hit-woman for the Mafia put her into "Prizzi's Honor." In the satirical comedy, she plays Irene Walker, who marries a hit-man of the old school, Charley Partanna, played by Nicholson. "Irene Walker, the handsome woman in the designer suit whom [Nicholson] loves at first double take, is played by that estimable chameleon, Kathleen Turner, as a sort of yuppie princess," wrote Richard Schickel in a *Time* review. With this role, said *New York Times* critic Janet Maslin, "Turner blends the steaminess of her performance in 'Body Heat' with the comedy of 'The Man With Two Brains' to create a kind of meta-enchantress Hollywood doesn't often produce anymore."

Turner takes all the praise with characteristically cool style. "It's great," she told Musto. "At the same time, there lurks the fear that you have got to fall on your face sometime. I thought it might be "Crimes." I was happy with my work, but I wasn't sure other people would see what I wanted to put into it. . . . If I can read a scene and already I have seen myself playing it, then why spend the time and effort on it?" Her co-star in "Romancing the Stone," Michael Doug-

las, told *People* magazine that "Kathleen can do it all. She's funny, sexy, vulnerable and endlessly intriguing because you never know which side she's going to show you next. It's obvious she's going to be a big star."

Turner says she also has other things in mind. "I want to be a great person and look back on a lot of good things. I'd like to influence a lot of people very nicely to the end of my life," said Turner in *Saturday Review.* "My husband asked me if I had always meant to be a star and I said no, I didn't think about that. Except that when I think about it now, I always wanted this level of work, I wanted access to the best roles and the best directors and scripts. What the heck did I think I was going to be if not a star?"

SOURCES:

PERIODICALS

American Film, November, 1984.
Detroit Free Press, March 31, 1984.
Film Comment, September-October, 1981, April, 1985.
Maclean's, April 2, 1984.
Newsweek, October 29, 1984, June 17, 1985.
New Yorker, November 9, 1981, June 27, 1983, April 30, 1984, June 24, 1985.
New York Times, March 30, 1984, June 9, 1985, June 14, 1985.
Penthouse, November, 1981.
People, December 24, 1984.
Playboy, November, 1981.
Rolling Stone, May 24, 1984, December 20, 1984.
Saturday Review, January-February, 1985.
Time, April 2, 1984, October 29, 1984, June 10, 1985.
United Press International, April 11, 1984.
Us, July 29, 1985.
Washington Post, August 28, 1981.

—Sidelights by Patricia Montemurri

Benita Valente

1934(?)-

PERSONAL: Born c. 1934 in Delano, Calif.; daughter of Lawrence Guiseppe and Severina Antonia (Masdonati) Valente; married Anthony Phillip Checchia (director of the Marlboro Music Festival and coordinator of the opera program at the Curtis Institute of Music), November 21, 1959; children: Peter. *Education:* Curtis Institute of Music, graduate, 1960; studied voice with Chester Hayden, Martial Singher, Lotte Lehmann, and Margaret Harshaw.

ADDRESSES: *Office*—c/o Anthony Checchia, 135 South 18th St., Philadelphia, Pa. 19103.

OCCUPATION: Opera singer.

CAREER: Lyric soprano; made Freiburg Opera debut in 1962 and Metropolitan Opera debut in 1973; has appeared throughout North America and Europe in numerous operas, including *Rigoletto, La Traviata, The Marriage of Figaro, Faust, The Magic Flute,* and *Rinaldo.* Soloist; has performed in concert with many orchestras in the United States and abroad.

AWARDS, HONORS: Winner of Metropolitan Opera National Council Audition, 1960.

SIDELIGHTS: Benita Valente is not the stereotypical diva. Instead of basking in her fame and being temperamentally difficult, Valente is a reserved artist, whose rise to prominence as an operatic soprano has only come at midcareer, after years of performing in choral concerts and oratorios. Valente's masterful vocal technique and musicality have made her consistently in demand. She has appeared throughout the United States and Europe, performing such roles as Pamina in Mozart's *The Magic Flute,* Euridice in Gluck's *Orfeo and Euridice,* and Almirena in Handel's *Rinaldo.* She is also renowned for her interpretations of the German lied, an intimate solo song in which she particularly excels. Commenting on Valente's success, Harvey E. Phillips of the *New York Times* states, "Singers of her vocal quality, musicianship, sense of style and feeling for textual values are rare."

The youngest of four daughters, Valente was raised on a farm near Delano, California. Music played an important role in her childhood: her parents, opera enthusiasts and good singers, taught her to sing at an early age. Valente received her first structured musical training at the local elementary school and later Delano High School, where she was singled out by the music teacher, Chester Hayden. Under Hayden's influence, Valente learned the piano, the rudiments of music, and foreign languages. "I've always been aware of my voice and its effect on people," she told Phillips. "By the time I was 13 I knew what I wanted to do with my life."

While in her teens, Valente began to study with the famous German-American soprano Lotte Lehmann at the Music Academy of the West in Santa Barbara, California. According to *High Fidelity* writer Herbert Kupferberg, the five years Valente spent under Lehmann's tutelage were fruitful and strongly influenced her proficiency in the lieder repertoire; she attributes in particular her view of the lyrics' importance to Lehmann. A scholarship later allowed Valente to attend the prestigious Curtis Institute of Music in Philadelphia, Pennsylvania, where she studied under the renowned French baritone Martial Singher.

At Curtis, Valente met her future husband, Anthony Checchia, a bassoonist and later director of the Vermont-based Marlboro Music Festival, an eight-week class in chamber music for professional and amateur musicians. Checchia is not Valente's only connection to this festival; while completing her studies, she attended a session at Marlboro and worked directly with the famed Austrian-American pianist, Rudolf Serkin, then the festival's artistic director. Linda Blandford of the *New York Times Magazine* stresses the importance of Valente's contact with Serkin, whose tireless devotion to music as an art rather than a career had a great impact on his pupil. Valente, in turn, demonstrates a similar respect for the music she performs.

In 1960, the year she graduated from Curtis, Valente won the Metropolitan Opera National Council Audition, an annual vocal competition. Although the winner receives a cash prize and frequently a contract with the Metropolitan Opera in New York City, Valente was not engaged and would not make her Met debut until more than ten years later. Like many aspiring singers, she went to Europe, where for two years she performed with opera companies in small cities, particularly Freiburg and Nuremburg, Germany. Valente reminisced to Kupferberg, "In my first year at Freiburg I did eight roles, from Gilda to Margiana in Cornelius' *The Barber of Bagdad*. I was able to develop gradually, normally."

From the beginning of her professional career, Valente established a dual reputation—that of a concert soloist and that of an operatic soprano. Although she has sung in oratories, masses, requiems, and choral symphonies, as well as given recitals of arias, Valente is most recognized outside of opera for her performances of lieder. Included in her repertoire are the works of Mozart, Schubert, and Wolf, all of which she sings masterfully. For her pure-toned voice, clear diction, and subtle inflections, Valente is considered one of the best lieder interpreters in the United States. When asked by Phillips why she does not make nationwide tours, Valente replied, "I could do marvelous recitals. . . . But touring lieder sounds like death. You're always by yourself and the program is always pre-set for you. Also it is the most exacting work—the strain is terrific. For me to do lieder concerts is just asking for trouble." Instead, Valente prefers to share her programs with other soloists and to sing modern works, such as Villa-Lobos's "Bachianas brasileiras no. 5." and Earl Kim's "Exercises en Route," a piece composed with her voice in mind.

In her operatic career, Valente has performed with many companies in this country and abroad, and she has had leading roles in nearly a dozen operas, including Verdi's *La Traviata* and *Rigoletto* and Mozart's *Idomeneo* and *The Marriage of Figaro*. In 1973, she finally made her debut with the Met, singing the part of Pamina in *The Magic Flute*, and since then she has been regularly cast in Met roles. At one point in her career, however, Valente had to make special efforts to obtain operatic parts. She told Bernard Holland of the *New York Times*: "About 12 or 13 years ago, I saw my schedule heavy with everything but opera, and I started to campaign—with opera houses and with my management. I said that I wanted to do certain opera roles, and I didn't care where I did them just so they were done." Valente's

perseverance was rewarded. Now many of her fifty to sixty engagements per year are for operatic parts. Yet, she said in an *Opera News* interview, she enjoys the diversity of her schedule: "I never wanted opera alone. . . . I love opera—it's certainly less lonely!—but I started out with lieder *and* opera, hand in hand. The two have always been together, and they always will be."

A retiring person, Valente has not persued fame; it has come to her as a result of her impeccable performances. "I'm a shy person who doesn't fit into the star pattern of glamour and personality," she confided to Phillips. "I think that the old-fashioned, larger-than-life image of a singer prevails. . . . But I can't be that kind of person, no matter what the public wants." This modesty is in part responsible for the many years it has taken for Valente to gain her present stature and for the disappointing lack of recordings of her work. "For years I was under the mistaken impression that if I really sang well, that's all I had to do," she told Linda Blandford of the *New York Times Magazine*. "I was not the kind who went in and sat in front of the manager's desk and said, 'I want, this, that and the other thing.' Finally I started feeling that I had to go and get it."

Though Valente has now achieved many of her artistic goals, she continually strives to improve her performances. She told Blandford: "I work hard, all the time. I never stop working, never stop trying to improve, never stop thinking about what I'm doing." Occasionally she even takes a lesson from former Met soprano Margaret Harshaw. When Nan Robertson of *The New York Times* asked Valente about her professional outlook, she replied, "I'm still crescendo-ing. . . . I tell myself, be patient. Work hard. Sing well."

SOURCES:

PERIODICALS

Christian Science Monitor, May 18, 1983, February 1, 1984, April 25, 1984.
High Fidelity, April, 1978, November, 1983, April, 1985, June, 1985.
New York, March 7, 1983.
New Yorker, July 26, 1982.
New York Times, August 17, 1973, September 16, 1973, August 26, 1975, August 6, 1982, February 13, 1983.
New York Times Magazine, February 3, 1985.
Opera News, February 21, 1976, February 18, 1984, March 17, 1984, April 14, 1984.
Time, January 30, 1984.

—*Sidelights by Jeanne Lesinski*

Edward Van Halen

1957-

PERSONAL: Born January 26, 1957, in Nijmegen, Netherlands; came to United States in 1967; son of Jan (a musician) and Eugenia Van Halen; married Valerie Bertinelli (an actress), April, 1981. *Education:* Attended Pasadena City College.

ADDRESSES: Home —Hollywood Hills, Calif. *Office* —c/o Warner Brothers Records, Inc., 3300 Warner Blvd., Burbank, Calif. 91505.

OCCUPATION: Rock and roll guitarist.

CAREER: Guitarist with bands Broken Combs and Mammoth in California in the early 1970s; with band Van Halen, 1974—.

DISCOGRAPHY:

ALL WITH BAND Van HALEN; ALL PRODUCED BY WARNER BROTHERS

Van Halen (includes "You Really Got Me," "Jamie's Cryin,'" "On Fire," "Runnin' With the Devil," "I'm the One," "Ain't Talkin' 'Bout Love," "Little Dreamer," "Feel Your Love Tonight," "Atomic Punk," "Eruption," and "Ice Cream Man"), 1978.
Van Halen II (includes "Dance the Night Away," "Outta Love Again," "Somebody Get Me a Doctor," "You're No Good," "Bottoms Up!," "Women In Love. . .," "Beautiful Girls," "D.O.A.," and "Spanish Fly"), 1979.
Women and Children First (includes "Tora! Tora!," "And the Cradle Will Rock. . .," "Romeo Delight," "Fools," "In a Simple Rhyme," "Could This Be Magic?," "Loss of Control," "Take Your Whiskey Home," and "Everybody Wants Some!"), 1980.
Fair Warning (includes "Mean Street," "So This Is Love?," "Push Comes to Shove," "Sinner's Swing," "Unchained," "Dirty Movies," "Hear About It Later," "Sunday Afternoon in the Park," and "One Foot Out the Door"), 1981.
Diver Down (includes "Where Have All the Good Times Gone!," "Little Guitars," "Hang 'Em High," "Secrets," "Intruder," "Pretty Woman," "Big Bad Bill," "Dancing in the Street," "Cathedral," "Happy Trails," and "The Full Bug"), 1982.
1984 (includes "1984," "Jump," "Panama," "Top Jimmy," "Drop Dead Legs," "Hot for Teacher," "I'll Wait," "Girl Gone Bad," and "House of Pain"), 1984.
5150 (includes "Why Can't This Be Love"), 1986.

WITH OTHERS

Nicolette (with Nicolette Larson), Warner Brothers, 1978.
Thriller (with Michael Jackson), Epic, 1982.
Star Fleet Project (with Brian May and others), EMI.

SIDELIGHTS: In an era when a great deal of popular music is made by synthesized keyboards, synthesized drums, and

AP/Wide World Photos

even synthesized voices, it is the guitar that, nevertheless, remains the backbone of rock and roll. From the very beginning of the genre, it has been the raspy, raunchy wail of the electric guitar that has most eloquently characterized the rock sound.

And it is the guitar players who have invariably become the heroes of rock and roll: Scotty Moore, James Burton, John McLaughlin, Jimmy Page, Jeff Beck, Jimi Hendrix. The status of the rock guitarist was firmly established by the 1960s, when rabid fans of British guitar virtuoso Eric Clapton began scrawling "Clapton is God" in subways and on walls all over England, leaving no doubt as to who ruled the music scene.

Such hero-worship inspired countless youths to try their own hands at playing the guitar. Among them was a young Dutch immigrant, Edward Van Halen, who now ranks among the top players in the world and who, according to many accounts, may be the most inventive guitar stylist of his generation. As *Playboy* writer Charles M. Young says: "Eric Clapton used to be God. Jeff Beck and Jimmy Page were God for a while. Eddie Van Halen seems to be God right now."

Born in the Netherlands, the son of a professional clarinet and saxophone player, Van Halen was introduced to music early in life. He and his brother Alex began taking classical piano lessons at age six and continued for many years. "We had an old Russian teacher who was a very fine concert pianist; in fact, our parents wanted us to be concert pianists," Van Halen told Jas Obrecht of *Guitar Player* magazine. "I wasn't into rock in Holland at all," he explained, "because there really wasn't much of a scene going on there." But when the family moved to Southern California in 1967, "I heard Jimi Hendrix and Cream [Clapton's band at the time], and I said, 'Forget the piano, I don't want to sit down—I want to stand up and be crazy.' "

But it was Alex who was first to buy a guitar. Following his older brother's lead, Edward decided he would learn to play drums and provide accompaniment. He got a paper route and bought a drum set. Then, he told Obrecht, "while I was out doing my paper route, so I could keep up on the drum payments, Alex would play my drums. Eventually he got better than me—he could play 'Wipe Out' and I couldn't. So I said, 'You keep the drums and I'll play guitar.' From then on we have always played together."

Van Halen bought his first electric guitar, "a $70 model with four pickups," and began to copy solos—especially those of Eric Clapton—by slowing thirty-three r.p.m. records down to sixteen r.p.m. Clapton remains his biggest influence even today. In a *Rolling Stone* article, Debby Miller notes that Van Halen "asks you to name any old Cream song, and then he recreates the Eric Clapton solo, note for note. . . . Clapton is his only hero in the world,"

Miller goes on to say that "Eddie's been screwing up ever since he was a kid." He was often in trouble in school and felt that he never really fit in with the other kids. *Rolling Stone* describes him as "a geek," and Van Halen admitted to Miller that he still feels he is "much geekier" than the fans who idolize him. "Everybody," he said, "goes through teenage growing up; getting f——ed around by a chick or not fitting in with the jocks at school. I just basically locked myself up in a room for four or five years and said to myself, 'Hey, this guitar's never gonna f—— me. . . .' What I put into it, it gives me back."

While still in high school, Edward and Alex formed their first bands, Broken Combs and then Mammoth. "I used to sing and play lead [guitar] in Mammoth," Van Halen related to Obrecht, "and I couldn't stand it—I'd rather just play." They had been renting a PA system, for vocal amplification, from another Los Angeles area group, the Red Ball Jets, whose lead singer was David Lee Roth. "I figured it would be much cheaper if we just got him in the band," Van Halen says, "so he joined."

They soon added bass player Mike Anthony, who had been working in yet another local group. Anthony recalled his first encounter with Roth and the Van Halens to *Rolling Stone*'s Miller. His former band was opening for Mammoth, and "I remember standing on the side of the stage watching Edward and Alex play, and thinking, 'Wow, these guys are

good.' Then Dave came up the side of the stage, and I forget what he was dressed in, some kind of a tux vest. . . with a cane and a hat. He had long hair. I don't know if he had it colored, but I know he'd done something weird to it. And he said, 'How do you like my boys?' And I just went, 'Jesus Christ, get this guy away from me.' "

Still, Anthony was persuaded to join the group in 1974. When the subject of a new name came up, Edward and Alex voted for Rat Salade, but, according to Miller, Roth "thought it would be classier to call themselves Van Halen," and in the end he prevailed. The quartet, Edward told Obrecht, "played everywhere and anywhere, from backyard parties to places the size of your bathroom. And we did it all without a manager, agent, or record company. We used to print up flyers announcing where we were going to play and stuff them into high school lockers." They played at numerous Southern California clubs and auditoriums, performing a mixture of original material and cover tunes. Eventually they became the opening act for a number of well-known performers, including Nils Lofgren, Santana, and UFO.

During a four-month engagement at the Starwood club in Los Angeles, Van Halen came to the attention of Gene Simmons, bass player for Kiss, who financed the group's first demo tape. They were also spotted there by Marshall Berle, their future manager, who arranged for Warner Brothers vice-president Ted Templeman to come and hear them at the Starwood. "I saw their set," Templeman told Miller, "and there were like eleven people in the audience, and they were playing like they were at the Forum." Edward recalled to Obrecht that it was a "rainy Monday night in May 1977, and Berle told us that there were some people coming to see us, so play good. It ended up that we played a good set in front of an empty house." At the end of the evening, "Templeman said, 'It's great,' and within a week we were signed up. It was right out of the movies."

They began recording immediately and within three weeks had forty songs on tape. They initially picked nine of these, wrote a new one in the studio, added a couple more, and released their first LP, *Van Halen*, in 1978. Edward told *Guitar Player*: "Because we were jumping around, drinking beer, and getting crazy, I think there's a vibe on the record. A lot of bands keep hacking it out and doing so many overdubs and double-tracking that their music doesn't sound real. . . . We kept it really live." The album sold over two million copies and was followed by five others that sold well over one million copies each.

The members of Van Halen became millionaire rock stars. They were able to insist that all brown M&Ms be removed from candy bowls backstage at their concerts. And Edward, says Miller, "who used to drive to rehearsals with the doors to his car wired shut with guitar strings," bought two Lamborghinis. Their offstage antics became notorious in a business that is not easily shocked. Alex, "the band's handsomest member," according to Miller, had "the worst reputation for munching on backstage visitors." And David Lee Roth—described by *People* writer David Gritten as "a publicist's dream and a parent's nightmare"—took out insurance with Lloyd's of London against paternity suits.

But, "Eddie's idea of making an appearance at backstage parties," wrote Miller, "is to dart through them slumped over, in a Groucho kind of walk, making a beeline for a closet or anywhere there's privacy." He told Gritten, "I've always been the quiet one in the band —the rest of the guys make up for me." Edward has been known to seek shelter in arena kitchens, and when Julian Lennon came to visit after a show in New Jersey, Van Halen dragged him into a bathroom for a quiet talk."

"All in all," reported Miller, "the backstage scene is calmer than it was a few years ago, when girls routinely danced nude on the tables." This is due, in part, to Mike's marriage and to Edward's well-publicized marriage to actress Valerie Bertinelli. "I don't like one-night stands," Van Halen told the *Rolling Stone* interviewer. "I don't like getting the clap. I wanna have kids. I wanna go through life with somebody."

The pairing of Van Halen and Bertinelli has puzzled many observers of the entertainment industry. She is, as Gritten puts it, "the milk-fresh sweetheart" who played the virginal Barbara Cooper on the CBS sitcom "One Day at a Time"; and he is the driving force behind a band that is often placed at the heavy-metal end of the rock and roll spectrum—not exactly the gentlest sub-category of the genre. The question on many people's minds, says Gritten, is, "What's a nice girl like that doing with a guy who plays guitar with his teeth?" The answer, replies Bertinelli, is simple: "He's not the typical rock star. It shocked *me* that he was so normal."

They met when Bertinelli's brother took her backstage at a Van Halen concert. The two entertainers were fans of each other's work, and they both admit to being very nervous. "After the concert," Bertinelli told Gritten, "we sat and talked for hours and hours. We realized we had a lot in common. We talked about our parents, Holland, how strict our upbringings had been, what it's like to be sensitive and scared of people. He has the same kind of scared feelings I have about the business." She was surprised to learn that Van Halen still lived at home with his parents. "As soon as I met them I could see why he was so normal," she recalled. "I mean, does Mick Jagger live with his mother?"

Both Catholics, Bertinelli and Van Halen go to church when they have time. They lead as quiet a life as possible in their Hollywood Hills home, and they "hardly ever go out" she says. Gritten notes that exceptions include "small dinners with friends or expeditions to watch Edward's lederhosen-clad father play sax and clarinet with a polka band in San Fernando." (The senior Van Halen has also made guest appearances on his sons' albums.)

Edward is still very close to his parents. Obrecht of *Guitar Player* asked if they ever attend Van Halen concerts, and Edward replied: "Yeah. My dad cries when he sees us play because he loves it. You know, he's so happy. It really is like his dream come true: The family music tradition is continuing, and it's also his name. . . . When I was in school, everybody said, 'Forget my parents. They're assholes.' Not me. I was always the weirdo. I'd say, 'Hey, I love my parents. I'll do anything for them. They've always busted their ass for me.' On my dad's birthday last year we retired him and bought him a boat. I want to make my people happy."

The stable family life and espousing of old-fashioned values may be atypical for a rock star, but the fact remains that Van Halen has built a reputation as the quintessential rock guitarist—wild, faster than most, and as loud as any in the business. And he is widely recognized as one of the most influential stylists working today. As Obrecht writes, "very few guitarists have had as intense an impact in as short a time as Eddie Van Halen," who wrestles "devastating feedback, kamikaze vibrato moans, sustained harmonics, white-hot leads, and liquid screams out of a cranked-to-the-max homemade guitar."

He is often cited by rock critics and by his peers for his innovation, his creativity, and his unwillingness to rest on past accomplishments. Writes Obrecht: "In the August '79 *Guitar Player*, Ted Nugent proclaimed him 'a fantastic guitarist.' Three months later Cheap Trick's Rick Nielsen discussed Van Halen's deft use of the vibrato bar. Then in the first cover story of the '80s, Pat Travers declared Van Halen the state-of-the-art rock guitarist, adding 'I don't think there's anybody better for saying more, getting a better sound.' "

And Van Halen constantly seeks to expand the limits of his ability in order to maintain a freshness in his music. He has done flamenco-style solos on a nylon-string guitar ("Spanish Fly"), he has played with a slide on a steel-string acoustic guitar ("Could This Be Magic"), he has elicited an incredible variety of unusual sounds and noises from his homemade electric guitar, and he has perfected a unique right-hand tapping technique. The latter had become something of a trademark until a number of other guitarists began using it. Van Halen described the technique to Obrecht, saying that he hits 'a note with my left-hand finger while I tap my right index finger on the fingerboard exactly one octave up. When it's an exact octave, you bring out the harmonic plus the lower note. . . . Now this is my latest: I hammer-on and pull-off with my left hand and reach behind my left hand with my right and use my right index finger below my left hand, so that it acts as a sixth finger. In other words, my right-hand finger changes the lowest note."

Van Halen works so hard to discover new sounds, in part, because he hates to be copied. He told Obrecht: "I guess they always say that imitation is the highest form of flattery. I think this is a crock. . . . I don't like people doing things exactly like me. Some of the things I do I know no one has done. . . . What I don't like is when someone takes what I've done, and instead of innovating on what I came up with, they do my trip! They do my melody. Like I learned from Clapton, Page, Hendrix, Beck—but I don't play like them. I innovated; I learned from them and did my own thing out of it. Some of those guys out there are doing my thing, which I think is a lot different."

Van Halen's innovation carries over into live performances. He doesn't necessarily try to recreate, note-for-note, solos as he recorded them on albums, believing instead that the "feel" of rock and roll—with a measure of spontaneity—is more important than technical perfection.

In concert, Van Halen is a group that delivers everything its fans expect. Referring to a recent tour, Miller of *Rolling Stone* says, "You get a ring of fire, a phenomenal light show, loud but pristine sound and a solo in which Michael tosses his bass off a twenty-foot drop, then rolls around, wrestling it to the floor." She calls Alex "a brilliantly musical drummer, almost as responsible as his brother for the heart-stopping power of 'Jump.'" (One time, when the band was opening for the Rolling Stones in Florida, Alex had broken his hand in four places. He tied a drumstick to his wrist with a shoelace and performed as usual.)

"Whenever Eddie steps up to play a solo," continues Miller, "the kids go mad." The guitar is at the core of the group's distinctive sound, and many fans come to concerts mainly to watch Edward at work. By most accounts, they're rarely disappointed. Van Halen's philosophy, he told Obrecht, is that a rock performance must "move you in any way. Depress you, make you happy, make you horny, make you rowdy. Anything." He says that during live performances he likes to play loud, "but there is a difference between being just loud and having what I call a warm, brown sound—which is a rich, toney sound. I guess a lot of people are tone deaf and can't figure it out because they just crank it up with a lot of treble just for the sake of being loud. Anyone can do that. I can actually play so loud onstage that you won't hear anything else, but I don't really like to do that."

He achieves his characteristic sound with guitars that he assembles himself using primarily components made by Charvel and, more recently, Kramer. The most unusual—at least for a rock guitarist—feature of Eddie's instruments is that they usually have only one electrical pickup and only one control, a volume knob. Compared to the more common Gibson Les Paul (with two pickups, four knobs, and a switch) and Fender Stratocaster (with three pickups, three knobs, and a switch), Van Halen's guitars are stripped to the bare essentials.

He explained to Obrecht the impetus behind his desire to construct his own instruments: "A Les Paul to me was just the clichéd guitar, the rock and roll guitar. I liked the sound, but it didn't fit my body." He also wanted a guitar with a tremolo arm attachment, so he tried switching to a Stratocaster, "and Dave and Al just turned and started throwing sticks at me! They said, 'Don't use that guitar. It sounds too thin.'" It was then that he put together his own guitar with a lighter, Stratocaster-shaped body that had a sound similar to the Les Paul. Through the years, Van Halen has become quite proficient at guitar-making, and he has experimented with a great many variations and construction techniques. (One interesting technique involved removing a chunk from a guitar body with a chainsaw. It didn't work very well, he reports). But, although he now owns a fair-sized collection of instruments, including a few rare models, the guitars he uses today are basically similar to the one he put together when the group was playing high school dances.

In 1985, to the surprise of no one, David Lee Roth and Van Halen parted company. Through the years, tension between Roth and Edward Van Halen was widely reported, but, as *Musician* interviewer J.D. Considine said, "the bickering that had long been a part of the band's creative process was becoming increasingly obvious. [At one time] Roth put it

this way: 'What Eddie and I do is, we *argue*. . . . Somehow we reach a compromise. No one is ever happy except the public.'" But as Roth's solo EP (extended play record), *Crazy from the Heat*, and its attendant videos began to receive more and more air play, rumors of a breakup increased, and it appeared that the two would have even more difficulty than usual in reaching future compromises. Roth was enjoying the solo success, and it began to look as though a movie career was in the offing. Wrote Considine: "Say what you will about Roth's singing, his video work was almost universally acclaimed, leaving him eager to expand his horizons. Sensing that the moment was right, Roth began shopping a cinematic treatment based on *Crazy from the Heat.*"

And the band began to wonder about where they fit into his future plans. Edward Van Halen told Considine: "We were basically in the twilight zone, not knowing whether Dave wanted to do a record or not. . . . He left us hanging there for quite a while—like six to eight months." Finally, it became obvious that Roth had other plans. "Dave is not a rock 'n' roller," concluded Van Halen. "He wants to be a movie star." And so, according to Considine, the group "decided to hand Roth his walking papers and went shopping for a new singer."

They found their man in singer-guitarist Sammy Hagar, a solo performer with a number of albums to his credit. Some observers expressed doubts about the new lineup, believing that Hagar had been around too long and had established such a strong individual presence that he would have trouble fitting into a group. Media wags began to refer to them as Van Hagar. But the band tried hard to project a positive attitude. "I personally don't think Van Halen, the way it used to be, was as good as it is now with Sammy," Edward Van Halen told Considine, "and I don't think Sammy was as good on his own before he joined our forces. It's incredible. . . . As Al says, you have to drive a Volkswagen to appreciate a Porsche. This definitely be the Porsche."

The new Van Halen immediately set to work on a premier album and in February of 1986 released *5150* (the title is a police code for "criminally insane"). As usual, Edward originated the majority of the musical ideas, with Hagar writing most of the lyrics in place of Roth, and the rest of the band being credited with various contributions to the creative process. And, as Considine pointed out, "Where once an important part of the band's edge was the creative tension between the Ed-Al-Mike-Dave relationship, now the band works in harmony. . . . Sammy's singing fits perfectly with the sound of the band. . . . [He] has plenty of range and can scream like a banshee, but his sound is always under control. To a certain extent, it's the vocal equivalent of Eddie's guitar sound, combining a cutting edge with an underlying warmth. Best of all, Sammy's melodic instincts are so in sync with Edward's that the songs move forward like a sonic juggernaut, a seemingly unstoppable force."

So, while other bands might have had difficulty surviving the loss of a lead singer, Van Halen goes on, the group's members maintaining that they expect to get even better in the future. And Edward Van Halen, in particular, continues to thrive on the individuality that has made him one of the top musicians in the business. He doesn't care what other bands do, what kind of guitars other players use, or how other rock musicians act. "I'm not into the star bullshit at all," he told *Guitar Player*. "A lot of people get off on it—let their hair grow long, buy a Les Paul and a Marshall [amplifier], and be a rock and roll star. I don't even consider myself a rock star. I enjoy playing guitar. Period. I had an English class where I had to do an essay on what my future plans were—what I wanted to do in life. I said I wanted to be a professional rock guitarist—not a rock star."

SOURCES:

BOOKS

Guitar Player Legends of Guitar: Hendrix/Van Halen, GPI Publications, 1984.

Pareles, John, and Patricia Romanowski, editors, *The Rolling Stone Encyclopedia of Rock & Roll*, Summit Books, 1983.

PERIODICALS

Audio, August, 1982.

Guitar Player, December, 1980, July, 1981, August, 1981, December, 1982, January, 1984, March, 1984, July, 1984.

Los Angeles Times, January 15, 1984, February 4, 1984, May 15, 1984, October 30, 1984.

Musician, February, 1986.

New York Times, November 28, 1982.

People, July 6, 1981, November 9, 1981, February 20, 1984.

Playboy, July, 1985.

Rolling Stone, September 4, 1980, June 10, 1982, March 1, 1984, June 21, 1984, December 20, 1984.

Stereo Review, May, 1984.

TV Guide, March 5, 1983.

Variety, May 12, 1982.

Washington Post, October 12, 1982, March 4, 1984, March 28, 1984.

—Sketch by Peter M. Gareffa

Jim Varney

1949-

BRIEF ENTRY: Born June 15, 1949, in Lexington, Ky. American actor and comedian. Popularly known as the fictional character Ernest P. Worrell that was created by the Carden & Cherry Advertising Agency for its series of television commercials, Jim Varney portrays a humorous know-it-all who relentlessly interrupts his neighbor Vern with exuberant, fast-talking advice. He's "a good ol' boy with a cornpone spiel," wrote George Bullard in the *Detroit News*; "part Soupy Sales and part Oral Roberts," assessed an article in the *Detroit Free Press*. Wearing his alias's garb of faded blue jeans, a T-shirt, a denim vest, and a baseball cap, Varney delivers his shtick as Ernest while gaping wide-eyed into the camera and punctuating his vernacular with the catchy run-together phrase "KnowhutImean?" Meanwhile the commercial's other character, Vern, remains silent and unseen—except for a hand or foot that sometimes responds by slamming a window or pushing away a ladder. Varney (as Ernest) has developed into a "phenomenal merchandiser," remarked an associate of one of the commercial's sponsors—which range from dairy products and natural gas to car dealerships and TV stations. Summing up the heat pump spot that Ernest does for MichCon, a spokesman for the utility explained, "We try to find a way to . . . have it be memorable . . . so it will mean something. . . . "

What all this means for Varney is success. Since first having signed to play Ernest for Carden & Cherry in 1981, the actor has appeared in an excess of 1500 commercials aired in more than 100 cities around the country. The result has afforded Varney widespread notoriety and numerous other acting opportunities, such as the co-starring role opposite Chad Everett in the 1983 network television series "The Rousters" and starring roles in both the February 1985 Abitron number-one-rated television special "Hey, Vern! It's My Family Album" and the 1985 science fiction movie spoof "Dr. Otto and the Riddle of the Gloom Beam." In addition, Varney's endorsements have increased and diversified to include public service spots for local and national organizations like the Girl Scout Cookie Sale, Boy Scouts Scout-O-Rama, Dental Health Week, United Way, Buddies of Nashville, Clean Up Dallas, and the Special Olympics.

Prior to becoming popular as Ernest, Varney had already begun establishing his career as an actor. Having attained numerous stage roles in high school and won some local competitions, the young performer subsequently studied acting at Barter Theatre in Virginia. At eighteen Varney headed for New York, where he landed feature roles in several dinner theatre productions, including "Death of a Salesman," "Camelot," "The Homecoming," and "Guys and Dolls." Later he went to Hollywood and appeared in the

Courtesy of Carden & Cherry Advertising Agency

network television shows "Operation Petticoat," "America 2Nite," "Pink Lady and Jeff," "Fernwood Tonight," "Pop Goes the Country," and "Alice," and a number of television specials starring Johnny Carson, Susan Anton, Johnny Cash, and Alan King. Varney also performed stand-up comedy at clubs in various cities, did his first commercial series for Carden & Cherry, and worked intermittently at laying tile and driving a truck while waiting for his "big break." As Varney confided in a *Detroit Free Press* article, he's adaptable.

SOURCES:

PERIODICALS

Detroit Free Press, July 7, 1985, March 7, 1986.
Detroit News, May 2, 1985.
People, December 2, 1985.
Time, January 20, 1986.
Variety, October 5, 1983.

Arlene Violet

1943-

PERSONAL: Born August 19, 1943, in Providence, R.I.; daughter of Henry A. (an alderman) and Alice Violet. *Education:* Salve Regina College, B.A., 1966; Boston College, J.D., 1974. *Politics:* Republican.

ADDRESSES: Office—Attorney General's Office, 72 Pine St., Providence, R.I. 02903.

OCCUPATION: Attorney general of Rhode Island.

CAREER: Roman Catholic nun, member of Sisters of Mercy, 1961-84; teacher at an inner-city Catholic junior high school in Providence, R.I., beginning 1966; did work with inner-city poor people and senior citizens in Providence; summer intern for Rhode Island Legal Services, Providence, 1971-73; attorney; admitted to Bar of State of Rhode Island, 1974; judicial assistant to Justice Thomas Paolino, Rhode Island Supreme Court, 1974-75; head of Consumer Affairs Division, Rhode Island Attorney General's Office, 1975-76; attorney in private practice in Providence, specializing in civil rights, juvenile justice, environmental, and poverty cases, 1976-84; attorney general of Rhode Island, 1985—.

SIDELIGHTS: Arlene Violet is the first elected female attorney general in the United States. A former nun who quit her religious post to run for public office, she thrust herself into the limelight in January of 1985, within five days of assuming the job of attorney general, with her decision to retry Claus von Bulow, the socialite, on charges that he murdered his wife. At that time, Alan Dershowitz, the noted Harvard Law School professor and one of von Bulow's lawyers, called the decision a political one. Violet retorted that "people who know me, Arlene Violet, know that I do not make political decisions. I try to call a shot exactly the way it is." (On June 19, 1985, a jury found von Bulow not guilty of two counts of attempted murder.) Two months later, she made headlines again by persuading a Rhode Island judge to disqualify himself from supervising an agency in which he was involved. Once, she called child molesters "scum of the earth." She joked with a *New York Times* writer that she was known as "Atilla the Nun" in some quarters. Said the reporter: "She has taken on her new job with the zeal of a field marshall."

Arlene Violet is the daughter of the late Henry A. "Mickey" Violet, a well-known Providence political figure who served as alderman and member of the state Board of Elections. He was known as a "Republican with a heart." "One of my great recollections was around Christmas time," Violet told the *Providence Sunday Journal.* "I was seven years old, and he joked with me that he hoped Santa Claus was going to do better by us than he was, because all he had left was a $20 bill. . . . And when we were getting the groceries out of the car, this old woman came up. In the neighborhood, the kids used to call her Dirty Neck, always used to tease her. She

asked my father for a dollar. And he just handed her the $20 bill. And not only did he give her all he had, but he said he was really grateful she asked."

According to newspaper accounts, Arlene Violet always wanted to be a nun—though there was no pressure from her father or her mother, Alice, to do so. The teachers at Tyler school, from which she graduated in 1958, were Sisters of Mercy. The order, which is known for its social activism, also taught at St. Xavier Academy, from which she graduated in 1961. What impressed her was the sisters' service to the poor. "These nuns would go into a neighborhood and shake down all the merchants to donate food and bread and meat, and they would then distribute it in the neighborhood," she recalled in a newspaper interview. In 1961, she entered the order's Salve Regina College, taking her final vows eight years later.

From 1969 until 1971, she was heavily involved in inner-city work in South Providence, where she taught junior high school. Her ministry consisted of poor people, senior citizens, or anybody else who might need help. But within a short time, she began to feel somewhat constrained in her role. She began to view law as a logical extension of her ministry, and enrolled at Boston College Law School. Her education was financed by money she earned working summers as an intern at Rhode Island Legal Services, and through scholarships. She received her law degree from Boston College Law School in 1974, took a job as a legal assistant to Senior Justice Thomas Paolino of the Rhode Island Supreme Court, and subsequently ran the Rhode Island Attorney General's Consumer Affair Division in 1975 and 1976. She left the attorney general's office in 1976 to open her own private law practice.

During Arlene Violet's eight years in private law practice, she did not stray far from her mission of helping the poor. She took on cases for Rhode Island's handicapped adults, children, senior citizens, indigents, low income workers, the unemployed, and environmentalists. Violet was active in a campaign to stop an extension of I-84, which resulted in the abandonment of the project. She served as a consultant attorney to the Rhode Island Protection and Advocacy System, a non-profit agency that represents handicapped persons. She also served as co-counsel for the Rape Crisis Center on a case involving confidentiality of records.

In 1982, Violet made her first attempt for public office, running as a Republican against incumbent Attorney General Dennis Roberts II, a Democrat. There were a number of things that worked against her in that election, which she lost badly. She ran as a Republican in a heavily Democratic state. And her opponent was a two-term incumbent who is a member of a well-established Rhode Island dynasty. (Roberts is the nephew of a longtime Democratic chieftain and former governor of the same name.) Besides the obvious political problems, there was "the nun issue." The Most Reverend Louis Gelineau, bishop of the Diocese of Providence, was not happy with Violet's candidacy. In a state where sixty-five percent of the 950,000 residents adhere to the Catholic faith, religion is a serious matter. The "nun issue" crippled her badly, according to political observers. One voter summed it up to a *Providence Evening Bulletin* reporter in this way: "I think she is a very intelligent person, but I have reservations, to tell you the truth. . . . I was brought up in Catholic schools, and I was shocked to see a nun go out in the political field. . . . I might be old fashioned, but that's the way I feel." Violet lost the race to Roberts fifty-seven percent to forty-three percent.

But "the nun issue" was to go away by early 1984. She decided to run against Roberts one more time. Bishop Gelineau told her that she couldn't be a nun and a candidate for public office at the same time. There was talk that she might temporarily leave the Sisters of Mercy and return at the end of her political career. But Gelineau said, "The church does not consider it appropriate that priests and religious hold public office, and it is also incorrect for a religious to think that one consecrated can abandon that life 'temporarily' to serve in a public office." Arlene Violet decided on December 23, 1983, two days before Christmas, to offer her resignation to her order. She called the decision "very personal and painful." As she told the *New York Times*, "What the decision came down to was being a Sister of Mercy in name only, or being a Sister of Mercy in reality."

The 1984 campaign against Roberts was among the most hard-fought on the east coast. The campaign advertising became a symbol of that visciousness. "Imagine this for a minute," said an announcer in a radio ad for Arlene Violet. "You're sitting at home watching television with your family. A gang breaks down the front door, grabs the television set, and walks out of your house. Well, the police caught them. All fifteen. It had been going on for a while. But the present attorney general thought it was easier to make deals than to send them to jail." A thirty-second television spot depicted her going into court. The ad said simply, "It's hard to be proud, and when it's hard to be proud, it's time to get mad."

Roberts's ads weren't nice, either. One said: "In the six years Dennis Roberts has been attorney general, twice as many violent criminals are behind bars. . . . That's the job Dennis Roberts has been doing. And Arlene Violet? She has experience, too. Compassionate experience. Helping people in need. The kind of experience that would be good background for director of social services. But attorney general?" Roberts also enlisted the aid of a local politician for a television advertisement. "I saw her ad on television the other night talking about her handling criminal cases and her arguing before juries," said Rep. Keven A. McKenna of Providence. "She didn't handle criminal cases, nor did she argue before juries. Now is the time for a little truth in advertising. She's never prosecuted a criminal." Roberts even brought in Pennsylvania's Republican attorney general to promote him for re-election. And one of Roberts's aides even called Violet a liar during the campaign.

Still, Arlene Violet prevailed and became the state's new attorney general—but just barely. There were 400,608 votes cast. Her margin of victory was 5,102 ballots—50.6 percent to Roberts's 49.4 percent.

Since being sworn in as attorney general, she has become something of a whirling dervish—meeting with judges, giving speeches, and so on. Besides the von Bulow case, she made headlines in July, 1985, by asking Superior Court Judge Thomas Caldarone, Jr., to step down from supervising a grand jury. Caldarone was a former board member of the Rhode Island Housing and Mortgage Finance Corporation, which was being investigated by the grand jury. Caldarone stepped aside to avoid any appearance of conflict of interest.

New York Times reporter Carol Lawson notes that Violet "is very conscious of being in the spotlight as the first woman to hold the job of attorney general." Violet told Lawson: "I don't want to do a poor job because I don't want to foreclose other talented women from having this position. I just want to make sure I keep the position open for them." And when asked by a *Providence Sunday Journal* interviewer how she wanted to be remembered, Violet replied, "I want to be remembered as somebody who tried hard and gave 100 percent."

SOURCES:

PERIODICALS

America, December 8, 1984.
Commonweal, January 27, 1984.
Ms., December, 1984.

National Catholic Reporter, August 27, 1982, January 27, 1984.

New York Times, September 16, 1975, January 7, 1984, January 8, 1984, January 20, 1984, January 28, 1984, May 6, 1984, November 8, 1984, January 6, 1985, January 14, 1985, March 8, 1985.

People, June 18, 1979.

Providence Evening Bulletin, October 29, 1982.

Providence Journal, October 4, 1984, July 23, 1985.

Providence Sunday Journal, January 1, 1984, November 4, 1984, April 14, 1985.

Washington Post, January 28, 1984.

—Sidelights by Tim Kiska

Andreas Vollenweider

1953-

PERSONAL: Surname is pronounced "Fole-en-veye-der"; born 1953, in Zurich, Switzerland; son of Hans Vollenweider (an organist, pianist, and composer); married c. 1971; wife's name, Beata (a kindergarten teacher).

ADDRESSES: Office—c/o CBS Records, 51 West 52nd St., New York, N.Y. 10019.

OCCUPATION: Harpist.

CAREER: Played and toured Europe for a short time with group Poetry and Music; solo performer. Composer of several film scores.

DISCOGRAPHY:

ALL RECORD ALBUMS

. . . Behind the Gardens—Behind the Wall—Under the Tree. . ., (includes "Behind the Gardens—Behind the Wall—Under the Tree [including; Red—Dark Blue—Yellow]," "Pyramid—In the Wood—In the Bright Light," "Micro-Macro," "Skin and Skin," "Moonlight, Wrapped Around Us," "Lion and Sheep," "Sunday," "Afternoon," and "Hands and Clouds"), CBS, 1981.
Caverna Magica, vocals by Corinna Curschllas, CBS, 1982.
White Winds, (includes "Wall of the Stairs/Hall of the Mosaics," "The Phases of the Three Moons," "Sister-seed," "The Stone," and "Trilogy"), vocals by Elena Ledda, CBS, 1985.

Also recorded three albums with group Poetry and Music.

SIDELIGHTS: He tried saxophone, and he played at the guitar, but it wasn't until Andreas Vollenweider discovered the harp that he found his musical direction. Since then, he's become one of the strongest cult acts in the music world, playing a formless combination of jazz and classical styles that is often lumped in with the improvisational "new music" approach of artists like George Winston and Keith Jarrett.

And because it's on the harp—an instrument seldom used outside of classical or baroque orchestras—Vollenweider is exploring musical territory many of his peers never imagined. "It has something to do with the way I learned the instrument," he told the *Detroit Free Press.* "I was kind of a wild animal, hard to put in school and things like that. I never had enough discipline to actually learn an instrument in school."

It seemed that Vollenweider was destined for a career in music, however. He was born in Zurich, Switzerland, in 1953, to a musical family; his father, in fact, was a prominent organist and composer. "I grew up in a family of musicians and painters and designers," Vollenweider said.

"There was always creativity around me, I was never forced to do anything I didn't want to, but I'm sure that's where my interest comes from." It took a while for that interest to find a focus. His curly reddish-brown hair, lively eyes, and whimsical grin are the physical hallmarks of someone not always willing to follow prescribed rules. He described himself as a Bohemian "enfant sauvage" who rarely attended school and drove his music teachers crazy because he wouldn't follow the sheet music they gave him.

Instead, he learned to improvise on brass, string, and keyboard instruments, gaining proficiency through almost aimless trial and error. Then he found the harp, and it was a musical love affair. "I feel at home with this instrument," he told the *Detroit Free Press.* "I can express what I feel and my thoughts. . . . For centuries, in many different cultures, the harp had a very important place. It was more or less the bridge between spiritual things and the earthy. In the last 50 or 100 years, that's changed—it's more and more becoming the music of Walt Disney. . . . For me, the harp is incapable of a certain range of expression, the range of violence and darkness. It is an instrument of brightness and light, and therefore fits my need to counteract some of the world's negative forces. . . . The harp is [also] a very erotic instrument. I can be very erotic. When you touch it, there is no possibility of hurting it, because it sounds so perfectly beautiful when you just touch it in the first instant. It shimmers when you just touch it."

Shimmer, however, doesn't always translate into good music, and it took Vollenweider a while to pluck out the right direction for his harp-oriented creation. In the process, he played through Poetry and Music, a group that mixed mood pieces with recited poetry, recorded three albums and toured throughout Europe. Vollenweider also composed a few movie scores, but his determination not to write in dark tones to convey fear, violence and danger scared away many film producers. What he eventually settled into was "music that leaves space for the one who is listening to it, space for the creativity of the listener." It is soft, spectral, and, often, formless. Accompanied by all manners of percussion, guitar, and woodwinds, Vollenweider bends and shapes his notes by plucking the strings, lightly hammering them or caressing them up and down.

To aid his technique, he grew long fingernails, which he protects with an additional layer of false nails. He also developed a system which amplifies the harp by putting a small electronic pickup on each string. "The harp has a natural character," he explained to the *Detroit Free Press*. "To this character I've added mechanical alterations and electronics which enable me to achieve the full range of an orchestra, from the lowest notes to the highest. . . . Also, I make my own strings. The bass strings are made of silver-wound steel. They're very thick and sound very deep; I modified them electronically so they sound deeper still. Sometimes they are deeper than an electric guitar, and you can only pluck strings like that, but I wrap my thumb and middle finger with tape to protect me from the heavier gauge metal. . . . All this I've done invisibly, I hope. I don't think the sound should show how it's made. The electronics shouldn't have a life of its own."

During the early 1980s, Vollenweider was signed by CBS Records. His first two records—*Caverna Magica* and *Behind the Gardens*—sold about a million copies, mostly in Europe. In Germany, *Caverna Magica* was named 1982's best pop album by the influential *Audio* magazine, beating out Billy Joel's *An Innocent Man* and Michael Jackson's *Thriller*. America, however, wasn't deaf to Vollenweider's music. His albums became the first in history to climb *Billboard*

magazine's pop, jazz, *and* classical charts. And in New York's prestigious Rizzoli bookstore, 15,000 customers bought Vollenweider records when the owners began playing it over the store's speakers.

Musicians as diverse as rock star Peter Wolf and avant-garde artist George Winston publicly admired the music. "He's just wonderful at creating textures and composing incredibly beautiful music," Winston told the *Detroit News*. "I instantly loved it." One Vollenweider fan—pop star Carly Simon—did more than pay lip service to his work. She produced his New York debut concert in October, 1984. "When I first heard Andreas' music in a store in SoHo a year ago, I knew I had discovered something that was going to change me in a wonderful way," Simon told the *New York Times*. "I became so obsessed with his music that anyone who came to my house was introduced to it within the first 10 or 15 minutes."

CBS started to realize what it had when statements like that began to appear in print. For Vollenweider's first American tour in late 1984, the company hired a high-powered California publicity firm that usually handles rock acts to pump the press. And in early 1985, CBC prepared a full-scale campaign for his new album, *White Winds*.

The efforts helped sell more records, though it's unlikely Vollenweider will ever reach the sales ranks of Jackson or Joel. Not that it matters to him; he's happy with a marginal degree of popularity and surprised at the size of his following. "I am, of course, excited," he said in a *Detroit Free Press* interview. "I didn't expect it all, what happened [in America]. It's getting to be like it was in Europe—and I didn't expect what happened there, either."

SOURCES:

PERIODICALS

Detroit Free Press, October 24, 1984.
Detroit News, May 23, 1985.
Digital Audio, August, 1985.
Newsweek, May 13, 1985.
New York Times, October 19, 1984.
People, August 5, 1985.
Wall Street Journal, October 24, 1984.

—Sidelights by Gary Graff

Faye Wattleton

1943-

BRIEF ENTRY: Full name, Alyce Faye Wattleton; born July 8, 1943, in St. Louis, Mo. Registered nurse and association executive. In 1978, at the age of thirty-four, Wattleton became the first woman, first black, and youngest president of the Planned Parenthood Federation of America. The largest private health agency in the United States, Planned Parenthood was founded in 1916 and now provides medical, educational, and counseling services to three million people per year from its 190 affiliates across the country. With the appointment of Wattleton, Planned Parenthood transformed its image from what she described as "a conservative, middle-of-the-road organization," with a traditionally low-keyed approach, to a more active and aggressive proponent of reproductive rights. Under her direction, the federation has successfully lobbied to keep family planning funds in the federal budget, halted a proposal that would require parental notification for minors receiving birth-control prescriptions, and defended abortion rights for women. In addition, Wattleton recently launched an aggressive direct mail campaign to increase private contributions to Planned Parenthood, and she has devised a million-dollar defense strategy against the activities of pro-life groups such as Right to Life. The funds will be designated for litigation costs and for establishing community education programs, among others.

Wattleton, who holds a bachelor's degree in nursing from Ohio State University and a master's degree in maternal and infant health care from Columbia University, became interested in family planning and abortion rights while doing her student nursing at Harlem Hospital. Among her patients there were teenage mothers with drug-dependent babies, mothers who could not afford to properly feed and clothe their many children, and even some mothers who had no homes for their newborn infants. Wattleton recalls that one case in particular affected her deeply—that of a seventeen-year-old girl who died from a self-induced abortion.

After graduating from Columbia, Wattleton worked for two years as a public-health nurse in Dayton, Ohio, and again she was treating victims of badly administered, illegal abortions. Because of her accomplishments in bringing pre-natal health care into the neighborhoods, Wattleton was appointed executive director of the local Planned Parenthood agency in Ohio in 1970. In 1977, the U.S. Congress passed the Hyde Amendment, prohibiting the federal funding of abortions, except for situations where the mother's life is threatened. Shortly afterwards, several Planned Parenthood clinics providing abortion services were firebombed by pro-life groups. Incensed by these events, Wattleton seized

AP/Wide World Photos

the opportunity to become national president of Planned Parenthood in 1978. She said, "I felt it was doing something to prevent needless suffering—young women facing unwanted pregnancies, the tragedies of illegal and unsafe abortions."

SOURCES:

PERIODICALS

Ebony, September, 1978.
New York Times, February 3, 1978, April 15, 1982, April 5, 1983.
New York Times Magazine, March 30, 1980.
People, May 22, 1978, May 24, 1982.
Savvy, February, 1985.
Time, February 7, 1983.
Vogue, January, 1982.

Bruce Weitz

1943-

PERSONAL: Full name, Bruce Peter Weitz; born May 27, 1943, in Norwalk, Conn.; son of Alvin Weitz (a liquor store owner) and Sybil Weitz Rubel; married second wife, Cecilia Hart (an actress), 1973 (divorced, 1980). *Education:* Carnegie Institute of Technology (now Carnegie-Mellon University), B.A., 1964, M.F.A., 1966.

ADDRESSES: Home—Hollywood Hills, Calif. *Office*—c/o National Broadcasting Company, Inc., 30 Rockefeller Plaza, New York, N.Y. 10112.

OCCUPATION: Actor.

CAREER: Restaurant manager on Formentera (a Spanish island), 1966; actor at Long Wharf Repertory Theater, New Haven, Conn., 1967; actor and student at Guthrie Theater, Minneapolis, Minn., 1967-69; cast actor at Arena Stage, Washington, D.C., 1970-76; appeared in thirteen Shakespeare-in-the-Park productions, New York, N.Y., 1976-80; performed in a number of Broadway productions, including "Death of a Salesman," "Norman, Is That You?" and "The Basic Training of Pavlo Hummel," 1978-80; appeared on numerous television series and made-for-television movies, beginning 1977; member of cast of "Hill Street Blues" television series, 1981—.

AWARDS, HONORS: Nominated for four Emmy Awards, National Academy of Television Arts and Sciences, for work on "Hill Street Blues"; winner of Emmy Award for best supporting actor in a drama series, 1984, for "Hill Street Blues."

SIDELIGHTS: He began by performing Shakespeare in the Park and the plays of Arthur Miller. But when actor Bruce Weitz gained fame, it was for portraying a grubby, growling detective whose kindest salutation was calling someone "Dog Breath." Weitz is best known as Mick Belker, the fang-baring undercover detective from NBC's "Hill Street Blues." As "Hill Street" became one of television's most popular shows, Weitz's Belker became one of the show's most popular characters. He is a lovable, albeit feral cop who was usually talking on the phone to his overbearing mother or biting the suspects he was trying to arrest. "People think Mick and I are one and the same, that he's my alter ego," Weitz told the Newhouse News Service. "We may share emotions, but we're quite different. Our way of expressing ourselves is different, our backgrounds are different. He's a street person, and I'm from the Connecticut country."

Weitz was born in 1943 in Norwalk, Connecticut, the son of a liquor store owner and a housewife. Because of Weitz's father's poor health, the family moved to Miami when Bruce was eleven. Eight years later, Weitz's father died. Young Bruce's energies were pumped into athletics and working as

AP/Wide World Photos

a delivery boy for his father. He recalls his childhood as an unhappy one. He was short, overweight, and unpopular with classmates. "I ate a lot because I was unhappy," Weitz told *TV Guide.* "Misery was the prevailing emotion, I never felt open enough with my parents to talk about it." In high school, Weitz met English teacher Dan Bowden, who became his mentor and surrogate father. The teacher recognized the teenager's potential as well as his rebellion, and steered him into acting. "I decided to become an actor," Weitz told *TV Guide.* "I had all the misconceptions; that it was glamorous and easy."

Weitz, who played baseball and football in high school, turned down several athletic scholarships in order to attend the Carnegie Institute of Technology drama department in Pittsburgh, Pennsylvania. While there, he met Steven Bochco, who would later become executive producer of the "Hill Street" series. "Bruce was a 1,100 pound bull when I met him," Bochco told *People* magazine. During Weitz's freshman year, a drama instructor warned him to lose forty pounds from his 190-pound frame or risk being dropped from the program. The advice hurt, but the aspiring actor took it to heart. When he graduated from Carnegie in 1966, he was one of eleven students left from the original class roster of ninety-one. Weitz now carries 150 pounds on his five-foot-eight frame.

After graduation, Weitz was drafted into the Army. He served just three weeks before receiving a Section 8 discharge for being "unable to adjust." He then went to Spain to visit a friend for two weeks and ended up staying a year, running a restaurant on Formentera, the smallest of the Balearic Islands, where there was no electricity or tap water. "I baked chocolate cakes on a wood-burning stove," he told *TV Guide*. "I found it romantic running my own restaurant on an island off the coast of Spain. It was right out of an old Bogart movie."

Weitz came back to the United States in 1967 to resume his acting career. He performed in repertory around the country, at such places as the Guthrie Theater in Minneapolis, Minnesota, the Long Wharf Theater in New Haven, Connecticut, and the Arena Stage in Washington, D.C. In New York, he appeared in Arthur Miller's "Death of a Salesman," and in thirteen Shakespeare-in-the-Park productions for Joseph Papp. "Sometimes I worked and sometimes I didn't," he told the *Chicago Tribune*. "I was certainly not successful, at least not financially."

In 1977, Weitz moved to Los Angeles "to make money. I was tired of putting in an enormous amount of energy, working a lot and not making a good living," he told the *Chicago Tribune*. Weitz looked up his old friend Bochco, by then a successful television producer, who introduced Weitz to people at Universal Studios. Weitz garnered small television guest appearances on such shows as "Quincy," "Lou Grant," "The Rockford Files," "Happy Days," and "The White Shadow." In 1981, he got his first significant television role, playing the jealous, murderous boyfriend in the NBC movie, "Death of a Centerfold—the Dorothy Stratten Story."

He also acted in five pilots for NBC. The first four bombed; the fifth was Bochco's "Hill Street Blues." Bochco says he wrote the character of Belker with Weitz in mind. But prior to auditions, Grant Tinker—then the head of MTM Productions—had other ideas, regarding Weitz as too clean cut for the role. Knowing of Tinker's reservations, Belker showed up for the audition with three days worth of stubble, his now-famous watchman's cap, and a wardrobe bought from a second-hand store. "I jumped up on Grant Tinker's desk and growled—and I bit him," Weitz told the *New York Daily News*. "He took it with a fair amount of humor." As Bochco told *TV Guide*, Weitz "was growling and carrying on, he rolled on the floor. When he was finished, there was a dead silence in the room. Tinker said, 'I'm not going to be the one to tell him he doesn't have a job.' I immediately hired Bruce." Mick Belker developed from a single idea given Weitz during early rehearsals. He was told he was playing the shortest vice officer in the country. "It was enough," Weitz told United Press International. "Can you imagine the hostility that comes to a man his size in that job? On the basis of that description I did an actor's homework. I constructed his bad story."

At its debut in 1981, "Hill Street" was an unusual show in its depth and reality. It featured an ensemble of more than a dozen characters, each of whom had his or her flaws and passions revealed in every sixty-minute episode. Mick Belker began as the comic relief, a quick-tempered animal who would chomp the bad guys and befriend the loons, such as a would-be vampire and a costumed maniac who called himself "Captain Freedom." Weitz fought to expand the character, introducing his mother and later his girlfriend, both of whom helped reveal Belker's sentimental side. "I want him to have kind of a soft underbelly," Weitz told the Newhouse News Service. "They want to make him a caricature instead of a character. . . . The guy's not a cannibal. He's really a very gentle man." And, Weitz told *People*, "Mick has values he won't compromise. That's very appealing." Others recognized that appeal. Over "Hill Street's" first five years, Weitz was nominated for four Emmys as best supporting actor. He won the award in 1984. *Orlando Sentinel* television critic Noel Holston called Weitz "the keeper of the show's pathos. . . . They could no more drop Mick Belker from the roster than Ringling Bros. and Barnum and Bailey Circus could have fired Emmett Kelly . . . . He also has TV's best growl since Rin Tin Tin."

Some of those growls became part of America's vernacular during the mid-1980s. Belker gave new meaning to the phrase "dog breath," and popularized insults such as "dirt bag" and "hair ball." As Weitz told Newhouse News Service, "You can't go wrong with lines like that. . . . If our writers ever leave, then I'm out the door myself."

Still, he stayed with "Hill Street" following the show's 1985 shakeup, which ended with Bochco and a half-dozen cast members leaving. "Once every eight or 10 years a show like this comes along—'Gunsmoke,' or 'The Defenders' or 'The Naked City'—and you stay with it," Weitz told United Press International. "I've had a number of parts that were infinitely more challenging and a few that have been more fun. But none that made me more money or attracted nearly this much attention."

Off-camera, Weitz shies away from attention. He does not discuss his two marriages, both of which ended in divorce. His second marriage, to actress Cecilia Hart, ended in 1980 after seven years. "I think I did a disservice to the two women I married," he told *People*. "I don't enjoy giving up time to be with someone, and I'm not looking to marry again." Weitz is active in the PTA, promoting a campaign against drug and alcohol abuse. He admits to an alcohol problem himself and chain smokes menthol cigarettes. "I have a guarded trust," he told *TV Guide*. "I don't let a lot of people get close to me—it takes a long time." Actor Ed Marinaro, who plays Sergeant Joe Coffey in "Hill Street," described his friend for *TV Guide* as "a very sensitive, compassionate guy. [But] I see him as private."

The success of "Hill Street Blues" has changed Weitz's life. He describes the salary as "fantastic" and recently bought a house in an exclusive neighborhood in Hollywood Hills. "The series is an actor's dream and I have a sense now of who I am in the business," he told *People*. But success hasn't brought Weitz everything he'd like: "I still haven't gotten one inch taller."

AVOCATIONAL INTERESTS: Golf, racquetball, weaving, cooking, reading (his favorite author is John Fowles).

SOURCES:

PERIODICALS

Chicago Tribune, March 1, 1985.
Detroit Free Press, May 7, 1983, September 24, 1984, August 6, 1985.
Newhouse News Service, June 7, 1982.
New York Daily News, April 23, 1983.
Orlando Sentinel, April 3, 1985.
People, September 26, 1983.
TV Guide, March 12, 1983.
United Press International, March 8, 1984.
Washington Post, January 7, 1985, August 8, 1985.

—Sketch by Glen Macnow

Sharlene Wells

1965(?)-

BRIEF ENTRY: Born c. 1965. American beauty queen. Miss America 1985, Sharlene Wells, has a squeaky clean image that stands out in sharp contrast to that of the winner of the 1984 pageant, Vanessa Williams. Williams was compelled to declare, "I am not a slut," according to a *People* interviewer, after *Penthouse* magazine published nude photos of her, and she was forced to resign her crown. Wells's statements to the press have been quite different.

The Utah beauty noted, for example, that the judges were probably looking for someone like her to rebuild the pageant's tarnished image. Her credentials seem ideally suited to the task. A Mormon Sunday-school teacher, she neither drinks, smokes, nor gambles. She has also said that she opposes premarital sex, abortion, and the Equal Rights Amendment. Wells told the *New York Times* that she has always lived a life "above reproach—I live my values seven days a week."

SOURCES:

PERIODICALS

New York Times, September 17, 1984.
People, September 10, 1984, November 26, 1984.

Michael Wigler

1948(?)-

BRIEF ENTRY: Born c. 1948. American molecular biologist and cancer researcher. From the Cold Spring Harbor Laboratory in New York, scientist Michael Wigler has succeeded in isolating a human gene within normal cells that can cause them to turn cancerous. The genes, called oncogenes, in their normal state trigger rapid growth during embryonic development. But later in life the genes can be re-activated—by radiation or carcinogens—to grow at an unnatural rate, causing life-threatening cancer. These so-called "Jekyll and Hyde" genes may be the key to the cause of all cancer.

Wigler, who received a $600,000 grant from the American Business Cancer Foundation, has now isolated the oncogenes responsible for cancers of the bladder, colon, lung, breast, and nerve tissue. And while the isolation of these genes may not lead to eradication of cancer, early detection will be made easier and treatment more effective. "We may be coming," Wigler commented in *Newsweek,* "to the end of the road."

SOURCES:

PERIODICALS

Newsweek, May 3, 1982.
New York Times, April 20, 1982, November 6, 1984.
Time, September 28, 1981.

AP/Wide World Photos

Peter C. Wilson

1913-1984

OBITUARY NOTICE: Born March 8, 1913, in Yorkshire, England; died June 3, 1984, in Paris, France. Art auctioneer and business executive. As chairman of Sotheby & Co. from 1958 until his retirement in 1980, Peter C. Wilson transformed the auction house from a small, centuries-old fine arts concern to an international, $575-million-per-year firm that widely influences the world art market. Educated at Eton and Oxford University, Wilson once considered a career in journalism. He briefly worked for the Reuters news agency and for *Connoiseur,* an art magazine. He joined Sotheby's in 1936 and two years later became a partner and director. During World War II Wilson served with British Intelligence in London and New York, returning to Sotheby's shortly after the war.

Wilson's first successful attempt to expand his company's operations took place in 1954, when he arranged the sale of deposed King Farouk's art collection. Four years later Wilson was named Sotheby's chairman. Within weeks of his appointment he had acquired a collection of Impressionist and Post-Impressionist paintings from the estate of New York financier Jakob Goldschmidt. The collection, which included works by Cezanne, Van Gogh, and Renoir, sold for an unprecedented $2,186,800. The Goldschmidt sale ushered in the era of multimillion-dollar art auctions and firmly established Wilson's name in the art world.

In 1964 Wilson engineered the purchase of New York's Parke-Bernet & Co., the largest art auction house in the United States. Under his direction Sotheby's opened offices and galleries in thirty-six cities around the world. Due to Wilson's vast knowledge of art and shrewd commercial instinct, Sotheby's enjoys a reputation as a thriving, innovative enterprise. It became the first auction establishment to open sale outlets outside its own country and the first to employ computers and closed-circuit and satellite television. Wilson was made Commander, Order of the British Empire in 1970.

AP/Wide World Photos

SOURCES:

BOOKS

Current Biography, Wilson, 1968.

PERIODICALS

London Times, June 5, 1985.
New York Times, November 10, 1979, August 30, 1980.

Robert Winship Woodruff

1889-1985

OBITUARY NOTICE: Born December 6, 1889, in Columbus, Ga.; died March 7, 1985, in Atlanta, Ga. American business executive and philanthropist. Known as the patriarch of Coca-Cola, Woodruff served with that company for more than sixty years and was credited with building it into an international financial empire. When he took over as president of Coca-Cola in 1923, the company was heavily in debt, but within the first seven years net profits increased by $8 million. Under Woodruff's direction, the business expanded from its one-product focus to producing 250 different items, and it saw such innovations as the soft-drink vending machine, the six-pack carton, and the king-sized bottle. During World War II, Woodruff made Coca-Cola available to all servicemen for five cents, and the United States government responded by financing transportation of the product and of the necessary parts for building bottling plants. And, despite the fact that sugar was being rationed because of the war, the government agreed to allot Coca-Cola the sugar it required to keep up G.I. morale. As a result, sixty-four bottling plants were built overseas, and, at the end of the war, millions of Coca-Cola fans returned home.

In 1939 Woodruff became chairman of the board and chairman of the executive committee of Coca-Cola. After retiring in 1955, he continued to serve as director and chairman of the board's finance committee until becoming director emeritus in 1981. He retired completely from Coke's board of directors in 1984, when a change in the company's bylaws prohibited the election of directors over the age of seventy-one.

Woodruff was also known for his generous charitable contributions. Beginning in 1937, for instance, Woodruff donated approximately $215 million to Emory University, which had been his alma mater from 1908 until 1909. Among his other numerous contributions were $10 million for the Atlanta University Center Library and more than $28 million for cultural programs in Atlanta. In appreciation of his support, the Atlanta Arts Alliance renamed its complex the Robert W. Woodruff Arts Center in 1982.

SOURCES:

PERIODICALS

New York Times, March 21, 1984.
Time, August 18, 1980.
Town & Country, December, 1983.
U.S. News and World Report, March 28, 1983.
Wall Street Journal, March 21, 1984, April 20, 1984.

Courtesy of the Coca-Cola Company

"Weird Al" Yankovic

1959-

PERSONAL: Full name, Alfred Matthew Yankovic; born October 23, 1959. *Education:* California Polytechnic State University, B.S. in architecture, 1979.

ADDRESSES: *Home*—Hollywood, Calif. *Office*—c/o Rock 'n' Roll Records, CBS Records, 51 West 52nd St., New York, N.Y. 10019.

OCCUPATION: Singer; satirist.

CAREER: During high school and college, began writing parodies of popular rock and roll songs, recording them, and sending them to radio stations; worked in the mailroom of a syndication company in Los Angeles; singer and satirist.

AWARDS, HONORS: Grammy Award nomination for best comedy recording, 1986, for *Dare to Be Stupid*.

DISCOGRAPHY:

RECORD ALBUMS; ALL PRODUCED BY ROCK 'N' ROLL RECORDS/CBS RECORDS

"Weird Al" Yankovic, (includes "My Bologna," "I Love Rocky Road," "Stop Draggin' My Car Around," "Another One Rides the Bus," "Ricky"), 1983.

"Weird Al" Yankovic in 3-D (includes "Eat It, " "I Lost on Jeopardy," "King of Suede," "Polkas on 45," "Nature Trail to Hell," "Buy Me a Condo," "Mr. Popeil," "Theme from Rocky XIII," "Midnight Star"), 1984.

Dare to Be Stupid (includes "Dare to Be Stupid, " "Like a Surgeon," "I Want a New Duck," "Girls Just Want to Have Lunch," "Yoda," "Slime Creatures from Outer Space," "One More Minute," "Cable TV"), 1985.

SIDELIGHTS: It's not every rock star who cuts his first record in the bathroom across the hall from the college radio station, but "Weird Al" Yankovic is not like other rock stars. How many rock stars have a degree in architecture? How many rock stars play the electric accordion? How many rock stars ride to fame on such songs as "My Bologna"?

"It sounded pretty nice in there," Yankovic told *Mix* magazine, explaining his rest room recording debut. "The tiled walls gave it a nice warm reverb. I didn't have the time or money to use a recording studio, so we ran lines from the 2-track in the radio station down the hall to the bathroom at 3 o'clock in the morning." Unconventional, perhaps, but millions of fans have come to expect that from "Weird Al," the rock iconoclast who reminds us that, in the end, it's only rock and roll.

Yankovic's hits include, "Eat It," to the tune of Michael Jackson's "Beat It," "I Love Rocky Road," to Joan Jett's "I Love Rock 'n' Roll," and "Like a Surgeon," to Madonna's

"Like a Virgin." He told the *Detroit Free Press:* "Just doing the kind of material I do, people tag me as a one-hit wonder, a novelty artist. . . . Each time I come out with a hit, they call me a one-hit wonder. This has been going on for five or six years now."

Satirizing rock hits is probably not the type of job Yankovic's parents had in mind when they were raising their only child in Lynwood, California. "I was pretty boring and studious all through my childhood," Yankovic told the *San Diego Union*. "I was a real nerd type, not a class clown type. I got offered several scholarships, and it was only after I went away to college that I cut loose and got a little bit weird." When he was seven, Yankovic's parents decided he should learn to play the accordion, partly because two aunts already had the instrument and partly because he shares the name of—although he is no relation to—Frank "Polka King" Yankovic. "I like to think it wasn't to torture me but more because of the relationship with the name," the satirist told *People* magazine. "They had a pile of his records in the garage and thought, 'Wouldn't this be cute?' or something." Yankovic mastered the instrument but found it somewhat professionally confining. "It was very difficult to call up booking agents and say, 'Hey, 'I play the accordion. Got any rock bands I can play with?' "

As a young man, Yankovic buried himself in his music. His influences include such American humorists as Tom Lehrer, Allan Sherman, and Spike Jones, as well as musicians Frank Zappa, Flo and Eddie, and England's now defunct Bonzo Dog Band. "These were great people that I didn't get to hear in their prime," Yankovic told a *Mix* interviewer. "All of a sudden I was hearing great things that were recorded 30 and 40 years ago. I thought it was wonderful because there wasn't anything like it on the radio at the time. I felt that it would be great if there were more things like this. Radio was really getting homogenized for a while."

Writing parody upon parody and recording them onto cassettes, Yankovic sent them to Dr. Demento, the California radio disc jockey who is known for airing offbeat material. "He started playing the tapes and I thought it was great," Yankovic told *People*. "I was just a high school kid and getting all this airplay. I guess you could call him my De-mentor. I really owe it all to him."

Although he majored in architecture at Cal Poly, Yankovic maintained his interest in parodies. The song that finally brought him widespread recognition was his send up of the Knack tune "My Sharona" ("My Bologna"). He recorded it in 1979 in the college bathroom, the only place on campus that provided him with enough echo. That hit won airplay on the nationally syndicated "Dr. Demento Radio Show," where Yankovic's accordion adaptation of Queen's "Another One Bites The Dust" ("Another One Rides the Bus") one year later became the most requested tune in the program's ten-year history.

Since then, Yankovic's parodies have included "I Lost On Jeopardy" (a remake of Greg Kihn's "Jeopardy"), "Stop Draggin' My Car Around" (to Tom Petty's "Stop Draggin' My Heart Around"), "Girls Just Want to Have Lunch" (to Cyndi Lauper's "Girls Just Want to Have Fun"), and original tunes like "I'll Be Mellow When I'm Dead" and "Mr. Popeil," a swipe at the late-night master of Veg-O-Matic and other household esoterica. He has even starred in his own Showtime cable television special in 1985 called "The Complete Al," a spoof of himself and such rock anthologies as "The Complete Beatles" and "This is Elvis."

"Weird Al" Yankovic (foreground) and backup singers filming a video for Yankovic's fifties-style parody "One More Minute," August 1985. AP/Wide World Photos.

"I've kind of given up trying to account for people's tastes," Yankovic told the *San Diego Union*. "I write what I think is funny and play it for some friends. If they think it's funny, I assume a couple of other million people will also. If I think of an idea or concept that I think is funny, I have no trouble making a song. Getting the idea is the hard part." Most—but not all—rock stars readily give Yankovic permission to parody their work. Legal permission is needed, so Yankovic usually sends them a couple verses, "to see if they have a sense of humor about themselves," he told *People*. Ray Davies of the Kinks and ex-Beatle George Harrison have balked, but most agree, especially since Michael Jackson gave Weird Al the nod. "Eat It," sung to the tune of Jackson's highly successful "Beat It," was Yankovic's breakthrough hit. "For a parody, a song's got to be very popular, instantly recognizable," Yankovic told *People*. "When Michael Jackson gave us permission to do 'Eat It' I was completely knocked out because of who he is—the single most popular person in the universe today."

Yankovic accompanied the recording with a music video, bitingly similar to Jackson's, that used actual scenes and some dancers from the rock star's own video. "My goal is to help Michael Jackson make some more money," Yankovic quipped to the *Detroit Free Press*. "If we can get him enough so he'll buy the other glove, I'll be happy." The "Eat It" video quickly went into heavy rotation on cable television's MTV and marked the second time Yankovic had produced a successful music video. A year earlier he had filmed his top-100 hit "Ricky," a send up of television's Ricardo family from the "I Love Lucy" series, that was sung to the tune of Toni Basil's "Mickey." When "Ricky" made it onto *Billboard* magazine's charts, Yankovic quit his mailroom job at a Los Angeles syndication company and decided to become Weird Al fulltime. "Ricky Ricardo has always been one of my major role models," Yankovic told the *Detroit Free Press*. "I always wanted to grow up to be a Puerto Rican bandleader."

"Generally, we have good reaction from the people we parody," he said. "Michael Jackson likes 'Eat It' quite a bit. I heard from Lucille Ball; she thought 'Ricky' was great. I haven't heard anything bad from the people I parody."

To anyone who has ever cracked a joke about a rock song, parodying popular music might seem easy. But Yankovic says that's deceiving. "Anybody who thinks that anybody can do this type of stuff should read the thousands of letters I get from people each year saying, 'I've got the next big thing for you, and it's this,' " he told the *San Diego Union*. "The ideas are generally horrible and I return them. I got an amazing number of ideas for a parody of [Michael Jackson's] 'Thriller.' Think of anything that rhymes with 'Thriller'—griller, chiller, Phyllis Diller—anything at all, and I got it."

Yankovic has written several original tunes in an effort to break away from his stereotype of strictly a satirical musician. Still, that is clearly what his audience looks to him for. And he recognizes it. "I want people to take music a little less seriously," Yankovic told *USA Today*. "I want to meet Slim Whitman because I like his mustache. My real dream is to have a meal with Jodie Foster and write a song about it entitled, 'My Dinner with Jodie.' " "Actually, I think there would be a big public backlash if I did write [more] original songs," he told the *Detroit Free Press*. "The public is used to me doing parodies. When we do an original, they come up and say, 'That's great, Al. But what's it a parody of?'. . . . There's enough straight rock 'n' roll musicians around, anyway. I'd like to think I'm filling some sort of void."

SOURCES:

PERIODICALS

Detroit Free Press, March 31, 1984, April 16, 1984, August 7, 1985.
Hollywood Reporter, November 2, 1984.
Home Viewer, October, 1985.
Life, July, 1985
Los Angeles Herald Examiner, July 29, 1985.
Los Angeles Times, June 16, 1985.
Mix, June, 1985.
People, April 9, 1984, April 16, 1984, August 5, 1985.
Rolling Stone, October 10, 1985.
San Diego Union, July 19, 1985.
Spin, August, 1985.
Toronto Star, August 16, 1985.
TV Guide, September 7, 1985.
Variety, March 27, 1985.
Washington Post, May 19, 1983.

—Sidelights by Stephen Advokat

Cumulative Nationality Index

This index lists all newsmakers alphabetically under their respective nationalities.

Index citations allow access to *CN* quarterly issues as well as the annual cumulation. For example, "Allred, Gloria **1985**:2" indicates that an entry on Allred appears in both *CN* 1985, Issue 2, and the *CN* 1985 cumulation.

Sajak, Pat
  Brief Entry **1985**:4
Schlessinger, David
  Brief Entry **1985**:1
Schott, Marge **1985**:4
Schwinn, Edward R., Jr.
  Brief Entry **1985**:4
Sedelmaier, Joe **1985**:3
Seidelman, Susan **1985**:4
Silvers, Phil
  Obituary **1985**:4
Sinclair, Mary **1985**:2
Smith, Frederick W. **1985**:4
Smith, Samantha
  Obituary **1985**:3
Stroh, Peter W. **1985**:2
Tanny, Vic
  Obituary **1985**:3
Tartikoff, Brandon **1985**:2
Thalheimer, Richard
  Brief Entry **1985**:2
Turner, Kathleen **1985**:3
Valente, Benita **1985**:3
Van Halen, Edward **1985**:2
Varney, Jim
  Brief Entry **1985**:4
Violet, Arlene **1985**:3
Wattleton, Faye
  Brief Entry **1985**:3
Weitz, Bruce **1985**:4
Wells, Sharlene
  Brief Entry **1985**:1
Wigler, Michael
  Brief Entry **1985**:1
Woodruff, Robert Winship
  Obituary **1985**:1
Yankovic, "Weird Al" **1985**:4

ARGENTINE
Sabatini, Gabriela
  Brief Entry **1985**:4

BRITISH
Leach, Robin
  Brief Entry **1985**:4
Lennox, Annie **1985**:4
Wilson, Peter C.
  Obituary **1985**:2

BRUNEI
Bolkiah, Sultan Muda Hassanal **1985**:4

CANADIAN
Coffey, Paul **1985**:4
Fonyo, Steve
  Brief Entry **1985**:4
Garneau, Marc **1985**:1
Haney, Chris
  Brief Entry **1985**:1
Johnson, Pierre Marc **1985**:4
Lalonde, Marc **1985**:1
Pocklington, Peter H. **1985**:2
Pratt, Christopher **1985**:3

DANISH
Lander, Toni
  Obituary **1985**:4

FRENCH
Chagall, Marc
  Obituary **1985**:2
Dubuffet, Jean
  Obituary **1985**:4
Petrossian, Christian
  Brief Entry **1985**:3
Ponty, Jean-Luc **1985**:4

GERMAN
Becker, Boris
  Brief Entry **1985**:3
Mengele, Josef
  Obituary **1985**:3

INDIAN
Gandhi, Indira
  Obituary **1985**:1

IRISH
Geldof, Bob **1985**:3
McGuinness, Martin **1985**:4

ISRAELI
Arens, Moshe **1985**:1

ITALIAN
Gucci, Maurizio
  Brief Entry **1985**:4

JAPANESE
Miyake, Issey **1985**:2
Toyoda, Eiji **1985**:2

LEBANESE
Berri, Nabih **1985**:2
Sarkis, Elias
  Obituary **1985**:3

NICARAGUAN
Cruz, Arturo **1985**:1

NIGERIAN
Olajuwon, Akeem **1985**:1

PALESTINIAN
Terzi, Zehdi Labib **1985**:3

SOUTH AFRICAN
Blackburn, Molly
  Obituary **1985**:4

SPANISH
Miro, Joan
  Obituary **1985**:1

SOVIET
Chernenko, Konstantin
  Obituary **1985**:1
Gorbachev, Mikhail **1985**:2
  Brief Entry **1985**:1

SWEDISH
Lindbergh, Pelle
  Obituary **1985**:4

SWISS
Vollenweider, Andreas **1985**:2

Cumulative Occupation Index

This index lists all newsmakers by their occupations or fields of primary activity.

Index citations allow access to *CN* quarterly issues as well as the annual cumulation. For example, "Boone, Mary **1985**:1" indicates that an entry on Boone appears in both *CN* 1985, Issue 1, and the *CN* 1985 cumulation.

Cumulative Subject Index

This index lists key subjects, company names, products, organizations, issues, awards, and professional specialties.

Index citations allow access to *CN* quarterly issues as well as the annual cumulation. For example, "Pierce, Frederick S.   **1985**:3" indicates that an entry on Pierce appears in both *CN* 1985, Issue 3, and the *CN* 1985 cumulation.

Cumulative Subject Index